# Accounting 1

A Pearson Custom Publication

# Accounting 1

Compiled from:

*Financial and Management Accounting:*
*An Introduction* Fourth Edition
by Pauline Weetman

*Managerial Accounting for Business Decisions*
Third Edition
by Ray Proctor

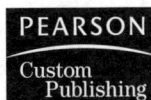

PEARSON
Custom
Publishing

Pearson Education Limited
Edinburgh Gate
Harlow
Essex CM20 2JE

And associated companies throughout the world

*Visit us on the World Wide Web at:*
www.pearsoned.co.uk

First published 2011

This Custom Book Edition © 2011 Published by Pearson Education Limited

Compiled from:

*Financial and Management Accounting: An Introduction* Fourth Edition
by Pauline Weetman
ISBN 978 0 273 70369 3
Copyright © Pearson Education Limited 1996, 1999, 2003, 2006

*Managerial Accounting for Business Decisions* Third Edition
by Ray Proctor
ISBN 978 0 273 71755 3
Copyright © Pearson Education Limited 2002, 2006, 2009

ISBN 978 0 85776 023 4

Printed and bound in Great Britain by Henry Ling Limited at the Dorset Press,
Dorchester DT1 1HD

# Contents

The following chapters are from:

*Financial and Management Accounting:*
*An Introduction*
Fourth Edition
by Pauline Weetman

The following chapters are from:

*Managerial accounting for Business Decisions*
Third Edition
by Ray Proctor

The following chapters are from:
*Financial and Management Accounting:*
*An Introduction*

Fourth Edition
by Pauline Weetman

# Chapter 1

# Who needs accounting?

## Summary financial highlights

| Summary | 2005 | 2004 | % change |
|---|---|---|---|
| Retail Sales (£m) | 708.7 | 672.5 | +5% |
| Turnover (£m) | 419.0 | 381.1 | +10% |
| Operating Profit (£m) | 36.2 | 30.3 | +19% |
| Earnings per share (pence) | 13.1 | 10.7 | +22% |
| Dividend per share (pence) | 5.7 | 5.7 | 0% |
| Net debt (£m) | 4.7 | 9.4 | −50% |

### Delivering value to stakeholders

The Body Shop has an established reputation as a socially and environmentally responsible company. We believe that our values are consistent with strong and sustained financial performance, and that profits with principles must be achieved in order to sustain the long-term future of the Group. The Body Shop is committed to maintaining high standards of social and environmental performance.

We believe in doing business with integrity and transparency. This means using our ethical principles to inform the way we do business, setting ourselves and our business partners clear standards of practice. It also involves engaging stakeholders with our business aims and publicly reporting on our performance within the overall context of our business strategy.

The overall strategic direction of the Group's values is reviewed periodically by the Board in consultation with the Director of Values. The Director of Values reports into the Chief Executive Officer and has overall responsibility for directing the Group's social and environmental programme. Strategic values objectives are aligned with the business objectives as well as stakeholder perceptions and expectations. These objectives are fully embraced by the senior management team, who have responsibility for balancing the interests of all key stakeholder groups.

Sub-committees help direct the social and environmental approach of the business. These include an Issues Management Group, which reports into the Risk Committee; a Corporate Health and Safety Strategy Group; an Environmental Steering Group; and an Animal Protection Steering Group.

Source: The Body Shop International PLC, *Annual Report and Accounts 2005*, p. 1 (Table) and p. 20 (Text).

### Discussion points

1 Who might be included in the 'key stakeholder groups' mentioned the extract?

2 To what extent does the 'Summary' meet the needs of users of financial statements?

**Contents**

**Learning outcomes**

After studying this chapter you should be able to:

- Define, and explain the definition of, accounting.
- Explain what is meant by a *conceptual framework*.
- Explain the distinguishing features of a sole trader, a partnership and a limited company.
- List the main users of financial information and their particular needs.
- Discuss the usefulness of financial statements to the main users.

Additionally, for those who choose to study the Supplement:

- Define the basic terminology of business transactions.

## 1.1  Introduction

**Activity 1.1**

*Before starting to read this section, write down one paragraph stating what you think the word 'accounting' means. Then read this section and compare it with your paragraph.*

There is no single 'official' definition of accounting but for the purposes of this text the following wording will be used:

| Definition | **Accounting** is the process of identifying, measuring and communicating financial information about an entity to permit informed judgements and decisions by users of the information.[1] |
| --- | --- |

This definition may appear short but it has been widely quoted over a number of years and is sufficient to specify the entire contents of this introductory textbook.

Taking the definition word by word, it leads to the following questions:

1  What is the process?
2  How is financial information identified?
3  How is financial information measured?
4  How is financial information communicated?
5  What is an entity?
6  Who are the users of financial information about an entity?
7  What types of judgements and decisions do these users make?

Writing the questions in this order is slightly dangerous because it starts by emphasising the process and waits until the final question to ask about the use of the information. The danger is that accountants may design the process first and then hope to show that it is suitable to allow judgements and decisions by users. This is what has often happened over many years of developing the process by accountants.

In order to learn about, and understand, accounting by taking a critical approach to the usefulness of the current processes and seeing its limitations and the potential for improvement, it is preferable to reverse the order of the questions and start by specifying the users of financial information and the judgements and decisions they make. Once the users and their needs have been identified, the most effective forms of communication may be determined and only then may the technical details of measurement and identification be dealt with in a satisfactory manner.

Reversing the order of the questions arising from the definition of accounting is the approach to be used in this book because it is the approach which has been taken by those seeking to develop a **conceptual framework** of accounting.

This chapter outlines the meaning of the words conceptual framework and in particular the *Framework for the Preparation and Presentation of Financial Statements* which has been developed for international use in accounting practice. The chapter explains the nature of three common types of business **entity** and concludes by drawing on various views relating to the users of accounting information and their information needs.

Because the understanding of users' needs is essential throughout the entire text, the chapter introduces David Wilson, a **fund manager** working for a large insurance company. In order to balance the demands of users with the restrictions and constraints on preparers of financial information, the chapter also introduces Leona Rees who works as an **audit manager** with an **accountancy firm**. Both of them will offer comments and explanations as you progress through the text.

| Activity 1.2 | *How does this section compare with your initial notions of what accounting means? If they are similar, then it is likely that the rest of this book will meet your expectations. If they are different, then it may be that you are hoping for more than this book can achieve. If that is the case, this may be a useful point at which to consult your lecturer, tutor or some other expert in the subject to be sure that you are satisfied that this book will meet your personal learning outcomes.* |
| --- | --- |

## 1.2 The development of a conceptual framework

A **conceptual framework** for accounting is a statement of principles which provides generally accepted guidance for the development of new reporting practices and for challenging and evaluating the existing practices. Conceptual frameworks have been developed in several countries around the world, with the UK arriving a little late on the scene. However, arriving late does give the advantage of learning from what has gone before. It is possible to see a pattern emerging in the various approaches to developing a conceptual framework.

The conceptual frameworks developed for practical use by the **accountancy profession** in various countries all start with the common assumption that **financial statements** must be useful. The structure of most conceptual frameworks is along the following lines:

- Who are the users of financial statements?
- What are the information needs of users?
- What types of financial statements will best satisfy their needs?
- What are the characteristics of financial statements which meet these needs?
- What are the principles for defining and recognising items in financial statements?
- What are the principles for measuring items in financial statements?

The most widely applicable conceptual framework is the *Framework for the Preparation and Presentation of Financial Statements* produced by the International Accounting Standards Board (IASB). This *Framework* was issued in 1989 and either reflects, or is reflected in, national conceptual frameworks of the USA, Canada, Australia and the UK. The thinking in all those documents can be traced to two discussion papers of the 1970s in the UK and the USA. In the UK, *The Corporate Report*[2] was a slim but highly influential document setting out the needs of users and how these might be met. Two years earlier the *Trueblood Report*[3] in the USA had taken a similar approach of identifying the needs of users, although perhaps coming out more strongly in support of the needs of shareholders and creditors than of other user groups. In the UK, various documents on the needs of users have been prepared by individuals invited to help the process[4] or those who took it on themselves to propose radical new ideas.[5]

Since January 2005, all **listed** companies in member states of the European Union (EU) have been required by an accounting regulation called the IAS regulation[6] to use a system of international financial reporting standards set by the International Accounting Standards Board. The UK ASB has been influential in the development of these international reporting standards and, over a period of years, has been moving UK accounting practice closely into line with the international standards. For **unlisted** companies and other organisations not covered by the IAS regulation of the EU, the UK ASB has a conceptual framework of its own, called the *Statement of Principles*.[7] This document has many similarities to the IASB's *Framework*.

| Activity 1.3 | *Most conceptual frameworks start with the question: Who are the users of financial statements? Write down a list of the persons or organisations you think would be interested in making use of financial statements, and their possible reasons for being interested. Have you included yourself in that list? Keep your list available for comparing with a later section of this chapter.* |
| --- | --- |

## 1.3  Framework for the preparation and presentation of financial statements

The IASB's *Framework* has seven main sections.

1 Introduction – purpose of the *Framework*, users and their information needs.
2 The objective of financial statements.
3 Underlying assumptions.
4 Qualitative characteristics of financial statements.
5 The elements of financial statements.
6 Recognition of the elements of financial statements.
7 Measurement of the elements of financial statements.

Sections 1 and 2 of the *Framework* are written at a general level and a reader would find no difficulty in reviewing these at an early stage of study, to gain a flavour of what is expected of financial statements. The remaining sections are a mixture of general principles, which are appropriate to first-level study of the subject, and some quite specific principles which deal with more advanced problems. Some of those problems need an understanding of accounting which is beyond a first level of study. This book will refer to aspects of the various sections of the *Framework*, as appropriate, when particular issues are dealt with. You should be aware, however, that this book concentrates on the basic aspects of the *Framework* and does not explore every complexity.

A conceptual framework is particularly important when practices are being developed for reporting to those who are not part of the day-to-day running of the business. This is called **external reporting** or **financial accounting** and is the focus of the *Financial Accounting* half of this book. For those who are managing the business on a day-to-day basis, special techniques have been developed and are referred to generally as **internal reporting** or **management accounting**. That is the focus of the *Management Accounting* half of this book.

Before continuing with the theme of the conceptual framework, it is useful to pause and consider the types of business for which accounting information may be required.

**Activity 1.4**

*Visit the website of the International Accounting Standards Board at **www.iasb.org.uk** and find the link to the IASB Framework. (You may have to follow the link to 'standards' although the Framework is not a formal standard.) What does the IASB say about the purpose of the Framework? How was it developed? What are the similarities and differences between the ASB and IASB in the way each describes its conceptual framework?*

*Visit the website of the Accounting Standards Board at **www.asb.org.uk** and find the link to the Statement of Principles. What does the ASB say about the purpose of the Statement of Principles? How was it developed?*

web activity

## 1.4  Types of business entity

The word **entity** means 'something that exists independently'. A business entity is a business that exists independently of those who own the business. There are three main categories of business which will be found in all countries, although with different titles in different ones. This chapter uses the terminology common to the UK. The three main categories are: **sole trader**, **partnership** and **limited liability company**. This list is by no means exhaustive but provides sufficient variety to allow explanation of the usefulness of most accounting practices and their application.

**Activity 1.5**    *Before reading the next sections, take out a newspaper with business advertisements or a business telephone directory, or else take a walk down your local high street or drive round the trading estate. Write down the names of five businesses, shops or other organisations. Then read the sections and attempt to match your list against the information provided in each.*

### 1.4.1    Sole trader

An individual may enter into business alone, either selling goods or providing a service. Such a person is described as a **sole trader**. The business may be started because the sole trader has a good idea which appears likely to make a profit, and has some cash to buy the equipment and other resources to start the business. If cash is not available, the sole trader may borrow from a bank to enable the business to start up. Although this is the form in which many businesses have started, it is one which is difficult to expand because the sole trader will find it difficult to arrange additional finance for expansion. If the business is not successful and the sole trader is unable to meet obligations to pay money to others, then those persons may ask a court of law to authorise the sale of the personal possessions, and even the family home, of the sole trader. Being a sole trader can be a risky matter and the cost of bank borrowing may be at a relatively unfavourable rate of interest because the bank fears losing its money.

From this description it will be seen that the sole trader's business is very much intertwined with the sole trader's personal life. However, for accounting purposes, the business is regarded as a separate economic entity, of which the sole trader is the owner who takes the risk of the bad times and the benefit of the good times. Take as an example the person who decides to start working as an electrician and advertises his or her services in a newspaper. The electrician travels to jobs from home and has no business premises. Tools are stored in the loft at home and the business records are in a cupboard in the kitchen. Telephone calls from customers are received on the domestic phone and there are no clearly defined working hours. The work is inextricably intertwined with family life.

For accounting purposes that person is seen as the owner of a business which provides electrical services and the business is seen as being separate from the person's other interests and private life. The owner may hardly feel any great need for accounting information because he or she knows the business very closely, but accounting information will be needed by other persons or entities, mainly the government (in the form of **HM Revenue and Customs**) for tax collecting purposes. It may also be required by a bank for the purposes of lending money to the business or by another sole trader who is intending to buy the business when the existing owner retires.

### 1.4.2    Partnership

One method by which the business of a sole trader may expand is to enter into **partnership** with one or more people. This may permit a pooling of skills to allow more efficient working, or may allow one person with ideas to work with another who has the money to provide the resources needed to turn the ideas into a profit. There is thus more potential for being successful. If the business is unsuccessful, then the consequences are similar to those for the sole trader. Persons to whom money is owed by the business may ask a court of law to authorise the sale of the personal property of the partners in order to meet the obligation. Even more seriously, one partner may be required to meet all the obligations of the partnership if the other partner does not have sufficient personal property, possessions and cash. This is described in law as **joint and several liability** and the risks have to be considered very carefully by those entering into partnership.

Partnership may be established as a matter of fact by two persons starting to work together with the intention of making a profit and sharing it between them. More often there is a legal agreement, called a **partnership deed**, which sets out the rights and duties of each partner and specifies how they will share the profits. There is also **partnership law**, which governs the basic relationships between partners and which they may use to resolve their disputes in a court of law if there is no partnership deed, or if the partnership deed has not covered some aspect of the partnership.

For accounting purposes the partnership is seen as a separate economic entity, owned by the partners. The owners may have the same intimate knowledge of the business as does the sole trader and may therefore feel that accounting information is not very important for them. On the other hand, each partner may wish to be sure that he or she is receiving a fair share of the partnership profits. There will also be other persons requesting accounting information, such as HM Revenue and Customs, banks who provide finance, and individuals who may be invited to join the partnership so that it may expand even further.

### 1.4.3   Limited liability company

The main risk attached to either a sole trader or a partnership is that of losing personal property and possessions, including the family home, if the business fails. That risk would inhibit many persons from starting or expanding a business. Historically, as the UK changed from a predominantly agricultural to a predominantly industrial economy in the nineteenth century, it became apparent that owners needed the protection of **limited liability**. This meant that if the business failed, then the owners might lose all the money they had put into the business but their personal wealth would be safe.

There are two forms of limited liability company. The **private limited company** has the word 'Limited' (abbreviated to 'Ltd') in its title. The **public limited company** has the abbreviation 'plc' in its title. The private limited company is prohibited by law from offering its **shares** to the public, so it is a form of limited liability appropriate to a family-controlled business. The public limited company is permitted to offer its shares to the public. In return it has to satisfy more onerous regulations. Where the shares of a public limited company are bought and sold on a **stock exchange**, the public limited company is called a **listed company** because the shares of the company are on a list of share prices.

In either type of company, the owners are called **shareholders** because they share the ownership and share the profits of the good times and the losses of the bad times (to the defined limit of liability). Once they have paid in full for their shares, the owners face no further risk of being asked to contribute to meeting any obligations of the business. Hopefully, the business will prosper and the owners may be able to receive a share of that prosperity in the form of a cash **dividend**. A cash dividend returns to the owners, on a regular basis and in the form of cash, a part of the profit created by the business.

If the company is very small, the owners may run the business themselves. If it is larger, then they may prefer to pay someone else to run the business. In either case, the persons running the business on a day-to-day basis are called the **directors**.

Because limited liability is a great privilege for the owners, the company must meet regulations set out by Parliament in the form of a **Companies Act**. At present the relevant law is the Companies Act 1985.

For accounting purposes the company is an **entity** with an existence separate from the owners. In the very smallest companies the owners may not feel a great need for accounting information, but in medium or large size companies, accounting information will be very important for the shareholders as it forms a report on how well the directors have run the company. As with other forms of business there will be a need to provide accounting information to HM Revenue and Customs for tax-collecting purposes. The list of other users will expand considerably because there will be a greater variety of sources of finance, the company may be seeking to attract more **investors**, employees will be concerned about the well-being of the business, and even the customers and suppliers may want to know more about the financial strength of the company.

Although the law provides the protection of limited liability, this has little practical meaning for many small family-controlled companies because a bank lending money to the business will ask for personal guarantees from the shareholder directors. Those personal guarantees could involve a mortgage over the family home, or an interest in life assurance policies. The potential consequences of such personal guarantees, when a company fails, are such that the owners may suffer as much as the sole trader whose business fails.

Exhibit 1.1 summarises the differences between a partnership and a limited liability company that are relevant for accounting purposes.

**Exhibit 1.1**
**Differences between a partnership and a limited liability company**

|  | Partnership | Limited liability company |
|---|---|---|
| *Formation* | Formed by two or more persons, usually with written agreement but not necessarily in writing. | Formed by a number of persons registering the company under the Companies Act, following legal formalities. In particular there must be a written **memorandum** and **articles of association** setting out the powers allowed to the company. |
| *Running the business* | All partners are entitled to share in the running of the business. | Shareholders must appoint **directors** to run the business (although shareholders may appoint themselves as directors). |
| *Accounting information* | Partnerships are not obliged to make accounting information available to the wider public. | Companies must make accounting information available to the public through the **Registrar of Companies**. |
| *Meeting obligations* | All members of a general partnership are jointly and severally liable for money owed by the firm. | The personal liability of the owners is limited to the amount they have agreed to pay for shares. |
| *Powers to carry out activities* | Partnerships may carry out any legal business activities agreed by the partners. | The company may only carry out the activities set out in its **memorandum** and **articles of association**. |
| *Status in law* | The partnership is not a separate legal entity (under English law), the partnership property being owned by the partners. (Under Scots law the partnership is a separate legal entity.) | The company is seen in law as a separate person, distinct from its members. This means that the company can own property, make contracts and take legal action or be the subject of legal action. |

Exhibit 1.2 identifies the differences between the public limited company and the private limited company that are relevant for accounting purposes.

**Exhibit 1.2**
**Brief comparison of private and public companies**

| | Public company | Private company |
|---|---|---|
| *Running the business* | Minimum of two directors. | Minimum of one director. |
| | Must have a company secretary who holds a relevant qualification (responsible for ensuring the company complies with the requirements of company law). | The sole director may also act as the company secretary and is not required to have a formal qualification. |
| *Ownership* | Shares may be offered to the public, inviting subscription. | Shares must not be offered to the public. May only be sold by private arrangements. |
| | Minimum share capital £50,000. | No minimum share capital. |
| *Accounting information* | Extensive information required on transactions between directors and the company. | Less need for disclosure of transactions between directors and the company. |
| | Information must be made public through the Registrar of Companies. Provision of financial information to the public is determined by size of company, more information being required of medium and large companies. | |
| | Accounting information must be sent to all shareholders. | |

**Activity 1.6**

*Look at the list of five organisations which you prepared before reading this section. Did the list match what you have just read? If not, there are several possible explanations. One is that you have written down organisations which are not covered by this book. That would apply if you have written down 'museum', 'town hall' or 'college'. These are examples of public sector bodies that require specialised financial statements not covered by this text. Another is that you did not discover the name of the business enterprise. Perhaps you wrote down 'Northern Hotel' but did not find the name of the company owning the hotel. If your list does not match the section, ask for help from your lecturer, tutor or other expert in the subject so that you are satisfied that this book will continue to meet your personal learning outcomes.*

## 1.5 Users and their information needs

Who are the users of the information provided by these reporting entities? This section shows that there is one group, namely the **management** of an organisation, whose information needs are so specialised that a separate type of accounting has evolved called **management accounting**. However, there are other groups, each of which may believe it has a reasonable right to obtain information about an organisation, that do not enjoy unrestricted access to the business and so have to rely on management to supply suitable information. These groups include the owners, where the owners are not also the managers, but extend further to employees, lenders, suppliers, customers, government and its branches, and the public interest. Those in the wider interest groups are sometimes referred to as **stakeholders**.

## 1.5.1  Management

Many would argue that the foremost users of accounting information about an organisation must be those who manage the business on a day-to-day basis. This group is referred to in broad terms as **management**, which is a collective term for all those persons who have responsibilities for making judgements and decisions within an organisation. Because they have close involvement with the business, they have access to a wide range of information (much of which may be confidential within the organisation) and will seek those aspects of the information which are most relevant to their particular judgements and decisions. Because this group of users is so broad, and because of the vast amount of information potentially available, a specialist branch of accounting has developed, called management accounting, to serve the particular needs of management.

It is management's responsibility to employ the resources of the business in an efficient way and to meet the objectives of the business. The information needed by management to carry out this responsibility ought to be of high quality and in an understandable form so far as the management is concerned. If that is the case, it would not be unreasonable to think that a similar quality (although not necessarily quantity) of information should be made available more widely to those stakeholders who do not have the access available to management.[8] Such an idea would be regarded as somewhat revolutionary in nature by some of those who manage companies, but more and more are beginning to realise that sharing information with investors and other stakeholders adds to the general atmosphere of confidence in the enterprise.

## 1.5.2  Owners as investors

Where the owners are the managers, as is the case for a sole trader or a partnership, they have no problem in gaining access to information and will select information appropriate to their own needs. They may be asked to provide information for other users, such as HM Revenue and Customs or a bank which has been approached to provide finance, but that information will be designed to meet the needs of those particular users rather than the owners.

Where the ownership is separate from the management of the business, as is the case with a limited liability company, the owners are more appropriately viewed as investors who entrust their money to the company and expect something in return, usually a **dividend** and a growth in the value of their investment as the company prospers. Providing money to fund a business is a risky act and investors are concerned with the **risk** inherent in, and **return** provided by, their investments. They need information to help them decide whether they should buy, hold or sell.[9] They are also interested in information on the entity's financial performance and financial position that helps them to assess both its cash-generation abilities and the stewardship of management.[10]

Much of the investment in shares through the Stock Exchange in the UK is carried out by **institutional investors**, such as pension funds, insurance companies, unit trusts and investment trusts. The day-to-day business of buying and selling shares is carried out by a **fund manager** employed by the institutional investor. Private investors are in the minority as a group of investors in the UK. They will often take the advice of an **equities analyst** who investigates and reports on share investment. The fund managers and the equities analysts are also regarded as users of accounting information.

The kinds of judgements and decisions made by investors could include any or all of the following:

(a) Evaluating the performance of the entity.
(b) Assessing the effectiveness of the entity in achieving objectives (including compliance with **stewardship** obligations) established previously by its management, its members or owners.
(c) Evaluating managerial performance, efficiency and objectives, including investment and dividend distribution plans.
(d) Ascertaining the experience and background of company directors and officials including details of other directorships or official positions held.
(e) Ascertaining the economic stability and vulnerability of the reporting entity.
(f) Assessing the **liquidity** of the entity, its present or future requirements for additional **working capital**, and its ability to raise long-term and short-term finance.
(g) Assessing the capacity of the entity to make future reallocations of its resources for economic purposes.
(h) Estimating the future prospects of the entity, including its capacity to pay **dividends**, and predicting future levels of investment.
(i) Making economic comparisons, either for the given entity over a period of time or with other entities at one point in time.
(j) Estimating the value of present or prospective interests in or claims on the entity.
(k) Ascertaining the ownership and control of the entity.[11]

That list was prepared in 1975 and, while it is a valid representation of the needs of investors, carries an undertone which implies that the investors have to do quite a lot of the work themselves in making estimates of the prospects of the entity. Today there is a stronger view that the management of a business should share more of its thinking and planning with the investors. The list may therefore be expanded by suggesting that it would be helpful for investors (and all external users) to know:

(a) the entity's actual performance for the most recent accounting period and how this compares with its previous plan for that period;
(b) management's explanations of any significant variances between the two; and
(c) management's financial plan for the current and forward accounting periods, and explanations of the major assumptions used in preparing it.[12]

If you look through some annual reports of major listed companies you will see that this is more a 'wish list' than a statement of current practice, but it is indicative of the need for a more progressive approach. In the annual reports of large companies you will find a section called the *Operating and Financial Review* (or similar title). This is where the more progressive companies will include forward-looking statements which stop short of making a **forecast** but give help in understanding which of the trends observed in the past are likely to continue into the future.

### 1.5.3    Employees

Employees and their representatives are interested in information about the stability and profitability of their employers. They are also interested in information that helps them to assess the ability of the entity to provide remuneration, retirement benefits and employment opportunities.[13] Employees continue to be interested in their employer after they have retired from work because in many cases the employer provides a pension fund.

The matters which are likely to be of interest to past, present and prospective employees include: the ability of the employer to meet wage agreements; management's intentions regarding employment levels, locations and working conditions; the pay, conditions and terms of employment of various groups of employees; job security; and the contribution made by employees in other divisions of the organisation. Much of this is quite specialised and detailed information. It may be preferable to supply this to employees by means of special purpose reports on a frequent basis rather than waiting for the annual report, which is slow to arrive and more general in nature. However, employees may look to financial statements to confirm information provided previously in other forms.

### 1.5.4  Lenders

Lenders are interested in information that enables them to determine whether their loans, and the related interest, will be paid when due.[14]

Loan **creditors** provide finance on a longer-term basis. They will wish to assess the economic stability and vulnerability of the borrower. They are particularly concerned with the risk of **default** and its consequences. They may impose conditions (called **loan covenants**) which require the business to keep its overall borrowing within acceptable limits. The financial statements may provide evidence that the loan covenant conditions are being met.

Some lenders will ask for special reports as well as the general financial statements. Banks in particular will ask for **cash flow projections** showing how the business plans to repay, with interest, the money borrowed.

### 1.5.5  Suppliers and other trade creditors

Suppliers of goods and services (also called **trade creditors**) are interested in information that enables them to decide whether to sell to the entity and to determine whether amounts owing to them will be paid when due. Suppliers (trade creditors) are likely to be interested in an entity over a shorter period than lenders unless they are dependent upon the continuation of the entity as a major customer.[15] The amount due to be paid to the supplier is called a **trade payable** or an **account payable**.

Trade creditors supply goods and services to an entity and have very little protection if the entity fails because there are insufficient assets to meet all **liabilities**. They are usually classed as **unsecured creditors**, which means they are a long way down the queue for payment. So they have to exercise caution in finding out whether the business is able to pay and how much risk of non-payment exists. This information need not necessarily come from accounting statements; it could be obtained by reading the local press and trade journals, joining the Chamber of Trade, and generally listening in to the stories and gossip circulating in the geographic area or the industry. However, the financial statements of an entity may confirm the stories gained from other sources.

In recent years there has been a move for companies to work more closely with their suppliers and to establish 'partnership' arrangements where the operational and financial plans of both may be dovetailed by specifying the amount and the timing of goods and services required. Such arrangements depend heavily on confidence, which in turn may be derived partly from the strength of financial statements.

### 1.5.6  Customers

Customers have an interest in information about the continuance of an entity, especially when they have a long-term involvement with, or are dependent upon, its prosperity.[16] In particular, customers need information concerning the current and future supply of goods and services offered, price and other product details, and conditions of sale. Much of this information may be obtained from sales literature or from sales staff of the enterprise, or from trade and consumer journals.[17]

The financial statements provide useful confirmation of the reliability of the enterprise itself as a continuing source of supply, especially when the customer is making payments in advance. They also confirm the capacity of the entity in terms of **non-current assets** (also called **fixed assets)** and working capital and give some indication of the strength of the entity to meet any obligations under guarantees or warranties.[18]

### 1.5.7  Governments and their agencies

Governments and their agencies are interested in the allocation of resources and, therefore, in the activities of entities. They also require information in order to regulate the activities of entities, assess taxation and provide a basis for national income and economic statistics.[19]

Acting on behalf of the UK government's Treasury Department, HM Revenue and Customs collects taxes from businesses based on profit calculated according to commercial accounting practices (although there are some specific rules in the taxation legislation which modify the normal accounting practices). HM Revenue and Customs has the power to demand more information than appears in published financial statements, but will take these as a starting point.

Other agencies include the regulators of the various utility companies. Examples are Ofcom[20] (the Office of Communications) and Ofgem[21] (the Office of Gas and Electricity Markets). They use accounting information as part of the package by which they monitor the prices charged by these organisations to consumers of their services. They also demand additional information designed especially to meet their needs.

### 1.5.8  Public interest

Enterprises affect members of the public in a variety of ways. For example, enterprises may make a substantial contribution to the local economy by providing employment and using local suppliers. Financial statements may assist the public by providing information about the trends and recent developments in the prosperity of the entity and the range of its activities.[22]

A strong element of public interest has been aroused in recent years by environmental issues and the impact of companies on the environment. There are costs imposed on others when a company pollutes a river or discharges harmful gases into the air. It may be perceived that a company is cutting corners to prune its own reported costs at the expense of other people. Furthermore, there are activities of companies today which will impose costs in the future. Where an oil company has installed a drilling rig in the North Sea, it will be expected one day to remove and destroy the rig safely. There is a question as to whether the company will be able to meet that cost. These costs and future liabilities may be difficult to identify and quantify, but that does not mean that companies should not attempt to do so. More companies are now including descriptions of environmental policy in their annual reports, but regular accounting procedures for including environmental costs and obligations in the financial statements have not yet been developed.

**Activity 1.7**

*Look back to the list of users of financial statements which you prepared earlier in this chapter. How closely does your list compare with the users described in this section? Did you have any in your list which are not included here? Have you used names which differ from those used in the chapter? Are there users in the chapter which are not in your list? If your list does not match the section, ask for help from your lecturer, tutor or other expert in the subject so that you are satisfied that this book will continue to meet your personal learning outcomes.*

## 1.6 General purpose or specific purpose financial statements?

Some experts who have analysed the needs of users in the manner set out in the previous section have come to the conclusion that no single set of general purpose financial statements could meet all these needs. It has been explained in the previous section that some users already turn to special reports to meet specific needs. Other experts hold that there could be a form of general purpose financial statements which would meet all the needs of some user groups and some of the needs of others.

This book is written on the assumption that it *is* possible to prepare a set of general purpose financial statements which will have some interest for all users. The existence of such reports is particularly important for those who cannot prescribe the information they would like to receive from an organisation. That is perhaps because they have no bargaining power, or because they are many in number but not significant in economic influence.

Preparers of general purpose financial statements tend to regard the owners and long-term lenders as the primary users of the information provided. There is an expectation or hope that the interests of these groups will overlap to some extent with the interests of a wider user group and that any improvements in financial statements will be sufficient that fewer needs will be left unmet.[23]

The primary focus of the *Framework* is on general purpose financial statements.[24] It takes the view that many users have to rely on the financial statements as their major source of financial information. Financial statements should be prepared with their needs in mind. The *Framework* assumes that if financial statements meet the needs of investors, they will also meet the needs of most other users.[25]

## 1.7 Stewards and agents

In an earlier section, the needs of investors as users were listed and the word 'stewardship' appeared. In the days before an industrial society existed, 'stewards' were the people who looked after the manor house and lands while the lord of the manor enjoyed the profits earned. Traditionally, accounting has been regarded as having a particular role to play in confirming that those who manage a business on behalf of the owner take good care of the resources entrusted to them and earn a satisfactory profit for the owner by using those resources.

As the idea of a wider range of users emerged, this idea of the 'stewardship' objective of accounting was mentioned less often (although its influence remains strong in legislation governing accounting practice). In the academic literature it has been reborn under a new heading – that of **agency**. Theories have been developed about the relationship between the owner, as 'principal', and the manager, as 'agent'. A conscientious manager, acting as an agent, will carry out his or her duties in the best interest of the owners, and is required by the law of agency to do so. However, not all agents will be perfect in carrying out this role and some principals will not trust the agent entirely. The principal will incur costs in monitoring (enquiring into) the activities of the agent and may lose some wealth if the interests of the agent and the interests of the principal diverge. The view taken in **agency theory** is that there is an inherent conflict between the two parties and so they spend time agreeing contracts which will minimise that conflict. The contracts will include arrangements for the agent to supply information on a regular basis to the principal.

While the study of agency theory in all its aspects could occupy a book in itself, the idea of conflicts and the need for compromise in dealing with pressures of demand for, and supply of, accounting information may be helpful in later chapters in understanding why it takes so long to find answers to some accounting issues.

## 1.8 Who needs financial statements?

In order to keep the flavour of debate on accounting issues running through this text, two people will give their comments from time to time. The first of these is David Wilson, a fund manager of seven years' experience working for an insurance company. He manages a UK **equity portfolio** (a collection of company shares) and part of his work requires him to be an equities analyst. At university he took a degree in history and has subsequently passed examinations to qualify as a chartered financial analyst (CFA).[26]

The second is Leona Rees, an audit manager with a major accountancy firm. She has five years' experience as a qualified accountant and had previously spent three years in training with the same firm. Her university degree is in accounting and economics and she has passed the examinations to qualify for membership of one of the major accountancy bodies.

David and Leona had been at school together but then went to different universities. More recently they have met again at workout sessions at a health club, relaxing afterwards at a nearby bar. David is very enthusiastic about his work, which demands long hours and a flexible attitude. He has absorbed a little of the general scepticism of audit which is expressed by some of his fund manager colleagues.

Leona's main role at present is in company audit and she is now sufficiently experienced to be working on the audit of one listed company as well as several private companies of varying size. For two years she worked in the corporate recovery department of the accountancy firm, preparing information to help companies find sources of finance to overcome difficult times. She feels that a great deal of accounting work is carried out behind the scenes and the careful procedures are not always appreciated by those who concentrate only on the relatively few well-publicised problems.

We join them in the bar at the end of a hectic working week.

DAVID: *This week I've made three visits to companies, attended four presentations of preliminary announcements of results, received copies of the projector slides used for five others that I couldn't attend, and collected around 20 annual reports. I have a small mound of brokers' reports, all of which say much the same thing but in different ways. I've had to read all those while preparing my monthly report to the head of Equities Section on the performance of my fund and setting out my strategy for three months ahead consistent with in-house policy. I think I'm suffering from information overload and I have reservations about the reliability of any single item of information I receive about a company.*

LEONA: *If I had to give scores for reliability to the information crossing your desk, I would give top marks to the 20 annual reports. They have been through a very rigorous process and they have been audited by reputable audit firms using established standards of auditing practice.*

DAVID: *That's all very well, but it takes so long for annual reports to arrive after the balance sheet date that they don't contain any new information. I need to get information at the first available opportunity if I'm to keep up the value of the share portfolio I manage. The meetings that present the preliminary announcements are held less than two months after the accounting year-end. It can take another six weeks before the printed annual report appears. If I don't manage to get to the meeting I take a careful look at what the company sends me in the way of copies of projector slides used.*

LEONA: *Where does accounting information fit in with the picture you want of a company?*

DAVID: *It has some importance, but accounting information is backward-looking and I invest in the future. We visit every company in the portfolio once a year and I'm looking for a confident management team, a cheerful-looking workforce and a general feeling that things are moving ahead. I'll also ask questions about prospects: how is the order book; which overseas markets are expanding; have prices been increased to match the increase in raw materials?*

LEONA: *Isn't that close to gaining insider information?*

DAVID: *No – I see it as clarification of information which is already published. Companies are very careful not to give an advantage to one investor over another – they would be in trouble with the Stock Exchange and perhaps with the Financial Services Authority if they did give price-sensitive information. There are times of the year (running up to the year-end and to the half-yearly results) when they declare a 'close season' and won't even speak to an investor.*

LEONA: *So are you telling me that I spend vast amounts of time auditing financial statements which no one bothers to read?*

DAVID: *Some people would say that, but I wouldn't. It's fairly clear that share prices are unmoved by the issue of the annual report, probably because investors already have that information from the preliminary announcement. Nevertheless, we like to know that there is a regulated document behind the information we receive – it allows us to check that we're not being led astray. Also I find the annual report very useful when I want to find out about a company I don't know. For the companies I understand well, the annual report tells me little that I don't already know.*

LEONA: *I'll take that as a very small vote of confidence for now. If your offer to help me redecorate the flat still stands, I might try to persuade you over a few cans of emulsion that you rely on audited accounts more than you realise.*

---

**Activity 1.8**

*As a final activity for this chapter, go back to the start of the chapter and make a note of every word you have encountered for the first time. Look at the Glossary at the end of the book for the definition of each technical word. If the word is not in the Glossary it is probably in sufficiently general use to be found in a standard dictionary.*

---

## 1.9 Summary

This chapter has explained that accounting is intended to provide information that is useful to a wide range of interested parties (stakeholders).

Key points are:

- **Accounting** is the process of identifying, measuring and communicating financial information about an entity to permit informed judgements and decisions by users of the information.

- A **conceptual framework** for accounting is a statement of principles which provides generally accepted guidance for the development of new reporting practices and for challenging and evaluating the existing practices.

- The *Framework* of the IASB provides broad principles that guide accounting practice in many countries.

- The *Statement of Principles* of the UK ASB has many similarities to the IASB's *Framework*.
- Since January 2005, all **listed companies** in member states of the EU have been required by an accounting regulation to use a system of international financial reporting standards (IFRS) set by the IASB.
- Business **entities** in the UK are either **sole traders**, **partnerships** or **limited liability** companies.
- **Users** of accounting information include management, owners, employees, lenders, suppliers, customers, governments and their agencies, and the public interest.
- **Stakeholders** are all those who might have a legitimate interest in receiving financial information about a business because they have a 'stake' in it.
- General purpose **financial statements** aim to meet the needs of a wide range of users.
- The relationship between the owner, as 'principal', and the manager, as 'agent' is described in the theory of **agency** relationships. Accounting information helps to reduce the potential conflicts of interest between principal and agent.

## Further reading

IASB (1989) *Framework for the Preparation and Presentation of Financial Statements*, International Accounting Standards Board.

ASSC (1975) *The Corporate Report*, Accounting Standards Steering Committee.

Beattie, V. (ed.) (1999) *Business Reporting: The Inevitable Change?*, Research Committee of The Institute of Chartered Accountants of Scotland.

ICAS (1988) *Making Corporate Reports Valuable*, discussion paper of the Research Committee of The Institute of Chartered Accountants of Scotland.

Marston, C. (1999) *Investor Relations Meetings: Views of Companies, Institutional Investors and Analysts*, Research Committee of The Institute of Chartered Accountants of Scotland.

Weetman, P. and Beattie, A. (eds) (1999) *Corporate Communication: Views of Institutional Investors and Lenders*, Research Committee of The Institute of Chartered Accountants of Scotland.

# QUESTIONS

The Questions section of each chapter has three types of question. 'Test your understanding' questions to help you review your reading are in the 'A' series of questions. You will find the answers to these by reading and thinking about the material in the book. 'Application' questions to test your ability to apply technical skills are in the 'B' series of questions. Questions requiring you to show skills in problem solving and evaluation are in the 'C' series of questions. A letter [S] indicates that there is a solution at the end of the book.

## A    Test your understanding

**A1.1**    Define 'accounting' and identify the separate questions raised by the definition. (Section 1.1)

**A1.2**    The following technical terms appear for the first time in this chapter. Check that you know the meaning of each. (If you can't find them again in the text, there is a Glossary at the end of the book.)

- accounting standards
- agency
- annual report
- broker
- business entity
- capital
- cash flow projections
- conceptual framework
- directors
- entity
- equities analyst
- external reporting
- financial accounting
- financial information
- financial statements
- fund manager
- general purpose financial statements
- HM Revenue and Customs
- limited liability company
- liquidity
- loan covenants
- management accounting
- partnership
- portfolio [of investment]
- portfolio of shares
- Registrar of Companies
- share capital
- shareholders
- sole trader
- specific purpose financial statements
- stakeholders
- stewardship
- unsecured creditors

## B    Application

### B1.1
Brian and Jane are planning to work in partnership as software consultants. Write a note (100–200 words) to explain their responsibilities for running the business and producing accounting information about the financial position and performance of the business.

### B1.2
Jennifer has inherited some shares in a public company which has a share listing on the Stock Exchange. She has asked you to explain how she can find out more about the financial position and performance of the company. Write a note (100–200 words) answering her question.

### B1.3
Martin is planning to buy shares in the company that employs him. He knows that the directors of the company are his employers but he wonders what relationship exists between the directors and the shareholders of the company. Write a note (100–200 words) answering his question.

## C    Problem solving and evaluation

### C1.1
The following extracts are typical of the annual reports of large listed companies. Which of these extracts satisfy the definition of 'accounting'? What are the user needs that are most closely met by each extract?

(a) Suggestions for improvements were made by many employees, alone or in teams. Annual savings which have been achieved total £15m. The best suggestion for improvement will save around £0.3m per year for the next five years.

(b) As of 31 December, 3,000 young people were learning a trade or profession with the company. This represents a studentship rate of 3.9%. During the reporting period we hired 1,300 young people into training places. This is more than we need to satisfy our employment needs in the longer term and so we are contributing to improvement of the quality of labour supplied to the market generally.

(c) During the year to 31 December our turnover (sales) grew to £4,000 million compared to £2,800 million last year. Our new subsidiary contributed £1,000 million to this increase.

(d) It is our target to pay our suppliers within 30 days. During the year we achieved an average payment period of 33 days.

# Supplement to Chapter 1

# Introduction to the terminology of business transactions

*The following description explains the business terminology which will be encountered frequently in describing transactions in this textbook. The relevant words are highlighted in bold lettering. These technical accounting terms are defined in the* Financial Accounting Terms Defined *section at the end of the book.*

Most businesses are established with the intention of earning a **profit**. Some do so by selling goods at a price greater than that paid to buy or manufacture the goods. Others make a profit by providing a service and charging a price greater than the cost to them of providing the service. By selling the goods or services the business is said to earn *sales revenue*.

Profit arising from transactions relating to the operation of the business is measured by deducting from sales revenue the expenses of earning that revenue.

**Revenue** from sales (often abbreviated to 'sales' and sometimes referred to as 'turnover') means the value of all goods or services provided to customers, whether for *cash* or for *credit*. In a *cash sale* the customer pays immediately on receipt of goods or services. In a *credit sale* the customer takes the goods or service and agrees to pay at a future date. By agreeing to pay in the future the customer becomes a **debtor** of the business. The amount due to be collected from the debtor is called a **trade receivable** or an **account receivable**. The business will send a document called a **sales invoice** to the credit customer, stating the goods or services provided by the business, the price charged for these and the amount owing to the business.

Eventually the credit customer will pay cash to settle the amount shown on the invoice. If (s)he pays promptly the business may allow a deduction of discount for prompt payment. This deduction is called *discount allowed* by the business. As an example, if the customer owes £100 but is allowed a 5% discount by the business, he will pay £95. The business will record cash received of £95 and discount allowed of £5.

The business itself must buy goods in order to manufacture a product or provide a service. When the business buys goods it *purchases* them and holds them as an **inventory** of goods (also described as a 'stock' of goods) until they are used or sold. The goods will be purchased from a supplier, either for **cash** or for **credit**. In a **credit purchase** the business takes the goods and agrees to pay at a future date. By allowing the business time to pay, the supplier becomes a **creditor** of the business. The name creditor is given to anyone who is owed money by the business. The business will receive a purchase invoice from the supplier describing the goods supplied, stating the price of the goods and showing the amount owed by the business.

Eventually the business will pay cash to settle the amount shown on the purchase invoice. If the business pays promptly the supplier may permit the business to deduct a discount for prompt payment. This is called **discount received** by the business. As an example, if the business owes an amount of £200 as a **trade payable** but is permitted a 10% discount by the supplier, the business will pay £180 and record the remaining £20 as **discount received** from the supplier.

The purchase price of goods sold is one of the **expenses** of the business, to be deducted from sales revenue in calculating profit. Other expenses might include wages, salaries, rent, rates, insurance and cleaning. In each case there will be a document providing evidence of the expense, such as a wages or salaries slip, a landlord's bill for rent, a local authority's demand for rates, an insurance renewal note or a cleaner's time sheet. There will also be a record of the cash paid in each case.

Sometimes an expense is incurred but is not paid for until some time later. For example, electricity is consumed during a quarter but the electricity bill does not arrive until after the end of the quarter. An employee may have worked for a week but not yet have received a cash payment for that work. The unpaid expense of the business is called an *accrued expense* and must be recorded as part of the accounting information relevant to the period of time in which the expense was incurred.

On other occasions an expense may be paid for in advance of being used by the business. For example, a fire insurance premium covering the business premises is paid annually in advance. Such expenditure of cash will benefit a future time period and must be excluded from any profit calculation until that time. In the meantime it is recorded as a **prepaid expense** or a **prepayment**.

Dissatisfaction may be expressed by a customer with the quantity or quality of goods or service provided. If the business accepts that the complaint is justified it may replace goods or give a cash refund. If the customer is a credit customer who has not yet paid, then a cash refund is clearly inappropriate. Instead the customer would be sent a **credit note** for sales returned, cancelling the customer's debt to the business for the amount in dispute. The credit note would record the quantity of goods or type of service and the amount of the cancelled debt.

In a similar way the business would expect to receive a credit note from a supplier for *purchases returned* where goods have been bought on credit terms and later returned to the supplier because of some defect.

## S   Test your understanding

**S1.1**   The following technical terms appear for the first time in this Supplement. Check that you know the meaning of each.

- Profit
- Sales revenue
- Cash sale
- Credit sale
- Debtor
- Trade receivable
- Discount allowed
- Purchases
- Cash purchase
- Credit purchase
- Creditor
- Trade payable
- Discount received
- Expense
- Accrued expense
- Prepaid expense
- Credit note for sales returned
- Credit note for purchases returned

# Chapter 2

# A systematic approach to financial reporting: the accounting equation

## REAL WORLD CASE

### Balance sheet

Shareholders' funds decreased by £644 million to £4,374 million and net debt improved by £640 million to £1,397 million in the year, decreasing gearing to 32% (2004: 41%). Return on Group capital employed decreased from 10.1% to 4.9% in the year reflecting lower operating profit performance and the disposal of Shaw's.

### Summary balance sheet

|  | 2005 £m | Restated[1,2] 2004 £m |
|---|---|---|
| Fixed assets | 7,299 | 8,452 |
| Current assets | 4,319 | 4,055 |
| Creditors: amounts falling due within one year | (5,097) | (4,906) |
| Net current liabilities | (778) | (851) |
| Total assets less current liabilities | 6,521 | 7,601 |
| Creditors: amounts falling due after more than one year | (1,730) | (2,194) |
| Provisions for liabilities and charges | (332) | (308) |
| **Total net assets** | 4,459 | 5,099 |
| Total shareholders' funds (including non-equity interests) | 4,374 | 5,018 |
| Equity minority interests | 85 | 81 |
| **Capital employed** | 4,459 | 5,099 |

1 Restated for change in accounting policy in accordance with UITF Abstract 38 – Accounting for ESOP Trusts.
2 Restated for change in classification of Sainsbury's Bank's assets, liabilities and cash.

Source: Sainsbury Annual Review and Summary Financial Statement 2005, pp. 30–1.

### Discussion points

1 How does this balance sheet reflect the accounting equation?

2 How does the group explain the main changes?

## Contents

## Learning outcomes

After studying this chapter you should be able to:

- Define and explain the accounting equation.
- Define assets.
- Apply the definition to examples of assets.
- Explain and apply the rules for recognition of assets.
- Define liabilities.
- Apply the definition to examples of liabilities.
- Explain and apply the rules for recognition of liabilities.
- Define ownership interest.
- Explain how the recognition of ownership interest depends on the recognition of assets and liabilities.
- Use the accounting equation to show the effect of changes in the ownership interest.
- Explain how users of financial statements can gain assurance about assets and liabilities.

Additionally, for those who choose to study the Supplement:

- Explain how the rules of debit and credit recording are derived from the accounting equation.

## 2.1  Introduction

Chapter 1 considered the needs of a range of users of financial information and summarised by suggesting that they would all have an interest in the resources available to the business and the obligations of the business to those outside it. Many of these users will also want to be reassured that the business has an adequate flow of cash to support its continuation. The owners of the business have a claim to the resources of the business after all other obligations have been satisfied. This is called the **ownership interest** or the **equity interest**. They will be particularly interested in how that ownership interest grows from one year to the next and whether the resources of the business are being applied to the best advantage.

Accounting has traditionally applied the term **assets** to the resources available to the business and has applied the term **liabilities** to the obligations of the business to persons other than the owner. Assets and liabilities are reported in a financial statement called a **balance sheet**. The balance sheet is a statement of the financial position of the entity at a particular point in time. It may be described by a very simple equation.

## 2.2  The accounting equation

The **accounting equation** as a statement of financial position may be expressed as:

| Assets | minus | Liabilities | equals | Ownership interest |
|--------|-------|-------------|--------|--------------------|

The ownership interest is the residual claim after liabilities to third parties have been satisfied. The equation expressed in this form emphasises that residual aspect.

Another way of thinking about an equation is to imagine a balance with a bucket on each end. In one bucket are the assets (A) minus liabilities (L). In the other is the ownership interest (OI).

If anything happens to disturb the assets then the balance will tip unevenly unless some matching disturbance is applied to the ownership interest. If anything happens to disturb the liabilities then the balance will tip unevenly unless some matching disturbance is applied to the ownership interest. If a disturbance applied to an asset is applied equally to a liability, then the balance will remain level.

### 2.2.1  Form of the equation: national preferences

If you have studied simple equations in a maths course you will be aware that there are other ways of expressing this equation. Those other ways cannot change the magnitudes of each item in the equation but can reflect a different emphasis being placed on the various constituents. The form of the equation used in this chapter is the sequence which has, for many years, been applied in most balance sheets reported to external users of accounting information in the UK. The balance sheets that have been reported to external users in some Continental European countries are better represented by another form of the equation:

| Assets | equals | Ownership interest | plus | Liabilities |
|---|---|---|---|---|

The balance analogy remains applicable here but the contents of the buckets have been rearranged.

A disturbance on one side of the balance will require a corresponding disturbance on the other side if the balance is to be maintained.

### 2.2.2　International variation

The International Accounting Standards Board (IASB) has developed a set of accounting standards which together create an accounting system which in this book is described as the **IASB system**. The IASB offers no indication as to which of the above forms of the accounting equation is preferred. That is because of the different traditions in different countries. Consequently, for companies reporting under the IASB system, the form of the equation used in any particular situation is a matter of preference related to the choice of presentation of the balance sheet. That is a communication issue which will be discussed later. This chapter will concentrate on the nature of the various elements of the equation, namely assets, liabilities and ownership interest.

**Activity 2.1**

*Make a simple balance from a ruler balanced on a pencil and put coins on each side. Satisfy yourself that the ruler only remains in balance if any action on one side of the balance is matched by an equivalent action on the other side of the balance. Note also that rearranging the coins on one side will not disturb the balance. Some aspects of accounting are concerned with taking actions on each side of the balance. Other aspects are concerned with rearranging one side of the balance.*

## 2.3　Defining assets

An **asset** is defined as:

*a resource controlled by the entity as a result of past events and from which future economic benefits are expected to flow to the entity.*[1]

To understand this definition fully, each phrase must be considered separately.

### 2.3.1　Controlled by the entity

**Control** means the ability to obtain the economic benefits and to restrict the access of others. The items which everyone enjoys, such as the benefit of a good motorway giving access to the business or the presence of a highly skilled workforce in a nearby town, provide benefits to the business which are not reported in financial statements because there would be considerable problems in identifying the entity's share of the benefits. If there is no control, the item is omitted.

The condition of control is also included to prevent businesses from leaving out of the balance sheet some items which ought to be in there. In past years, practices emerged of omitting an asset and a corresponding liability from a balance sheet on the grounds that there was no effective obligation remaining in respect of the liability. At the same time, the business carefully retained effective control of the asset by suitable legal agreements. This practice of omitting items from the balance sheet was felt to be unhelpful to users because it was concealing some of the resources used by the business and concealing the related obligations.

The strongest form of control over an asset is the right of ownership. Sometimes, however, the entity does not have ownership but does have the right to use an item. This right may be very similar to the right of ownership. So far as the user of accounting information is concerned, what really matters is the availability of the item to the entity and how well the item is being used to earn profits for the business. Forms of **control** may include an agreement to lease or rent a resource, and a licence allowing exclusive use of a resource.

### 2.3.2    Past events

Accounting depends on finding some reasonably objective way of confirming that the entity has gained control of the resource. The evidence provided by a past transaction is an objective starting point. A transaction is an agreement between two parties which usually involves exchanging goods or services for cash or a promise to pay cash. (The supplement to Chapter 1 explains basic business transactions in more detail.) Sometimes there is no transaction but there is an event which is sufficient to give this objective evidence. The event could be the performance of a service which, once completed, gives the right to demand payment.

### 2.3.3    Future economic benefits

Most businesses use resources in the expectation that they will eventually generate cash. Some resources generate cash more quickly than others. If the business manufactures goods in order to sell them to customers, those goods carry a future economic benefit in terms of the expectation of sale. That benefit comes to the entity relatively quickly. The business may own a warehouse in which it stores the goods before they are sold. There is a future economic benefit associated with the warehouse because it helps create the cash flow from sale of the goods (by keeping them safe from damage and theft) and also because at some time in the future the warehouse could itself be sold for cash.

The example of the warehouse is relatively easy to understand, but in other cases there may be some uncertainty about the amount of the future economic benefit. When goods are sold to a customer who is allowed time to pay, the customer becomes a **debtor** of the business (a person who owes money to the business) and the amount of the **trade receivable** is regarded as an asset. There may be some uncertainty as to whether the customer will eventually pay for the goods. That uncertainty does not prevent the trade receivable being regarded as an asset but may require some caution as to how the asset is measured in money terms.

| Activity 2.2 | *Write down five items in your personal possession which you regard as assets. Use the definition given in this section to explain why each item is an asset from your point of view. Then read the next section and compare your list with the examples of business assets. If you are having difficulty in understanding why any item is, or is not, an asset you should consult your lecturer, tutor or other expert in the subject area for a discussion on how to apply the definition in identifying assets.* |

## 2.4  Examples of assets

The following items are commonly found in the assets section of the balance sheet of a company:

- land and buildings owned by the company
- buildings leased by the company on a 50-year lease
- plant and machinery owned by the company
- equipment leased (rented) by the company under a finance lease
- vehicles
- raw materials
- goods for resale
- finished goods
- work-in-progress
- trade receivables (amounts due from customers who have promised to pay for goods sold on credit)
- prepaid insurance and rentals
- investments in shares of other companies
- cash held in a bank account.

Do all these items meet the definition of an asset? Exhibits 2.1 and 2.2 test each item against the aspects of the definition which have already been discussed. Two tables have been used because it is conventional practice to separate assets into current assets and non-current assets. **Current assets** are held with the intention of converting

### Exhibit 2.1
### Analysis of some frequently occurring non-current assets (fixed assets)

|  | Controlled by the entity by means of | Past event | Future economic benefits |
|---|---|---|---|
| *Land and buildings owned by the company* | Ownership. | Signing the contract as evidence of purchase of land and buildings. | Used in continuing operations of the business; potential for sale of the item. |
| *Buildings leased (rented) by the company on a 50-year lease* | Contract for exclusive use as a tenant. | Signing a lease agreeing the rental terms. | Used in continuing operations of the business. |
| *Plant and machinery owned by the company* | Ownership. | Purchase of plant and equipment, evidenced by receiving the goods and a supplier's invoice. | Used in continuing operations of the business. |
| *Equipment used under a finance lease* | Contract for exclusive use. | Signing lease agreeing rental terms. | Used in continuing operations of the business. |
| *Vehicles owned by the company* | Ownership. | Purchase of vehicles, evidenced by taking delivery and receiving a supplier's invoice. | Used in continuing operations of the business. |

**Exhibit 2.2**
**Analysis of some frequently occurring current assets**

|  | Controlled by the entity by means of | Past event | Future economic benefits |
|---|---|---|---|
| *Raw materials* | Ownership. | Receiving raw materials into the company's store, evidenced by goods received note. | Used to manufacture goods for sale. |
| *Goods purchased from supplier for resale* | Ownership. | Receiving goods from supplier into the company's store, evidenced by the goods received note. | Expectation of sale. |
| *Finished goods (manufactured by the entity)* | Ownership. | Transfer from production line to finished goods store, evidenced by internal transfer form. | Expectation of sale. |
| *Work-in-progress (partly finished goods)* | Ownership. | Evaluation of the state of completion of the work, evidenced by work records. | Expectation of completion and sale. |
| *Trade receivables (amounts due from customers)* | Contract for payment. | Delivery of goods to the customer, obliging customer to pay for goods at a future date. | Expectation that the customer will pay cash. |
| *Prepaid insurance premiums* | Contract for continuing benefit of insurance cover. | Paying insurance premiums in advance, evidenced by cheque payment. | Expectation of continuing insurance cover. |
| *Investments in shares of other companies* | Ownership. | Buying the shares, evidenced by broker's contract note. | Expectation of dividend income and growth in value of investment, for future sale. |
| *Cash held in a bank account* | Ownership. | Depositing cash with the bank, evidenced by bank statement or certificate. | Expectation of using the cash to buy resources which will create further cash. |

them into cash within the business cycle. **Non-current assets**, also called **fixed assets**, are held for continuing use in the business. The business cycle is the period (usually 12 months) during which the peaks and troughs of activity of a business form a pattern which is repeated on a regular basis. For a business selling swimwear, production will take place all winter in preparation for a rush of sales in the summer. Painters and decorators work indoors in the winter and carry out exterior work in the summer. Because many businesses are affected by the seasons of the year, the business cycle is normally 12 months. Some of the answers are fairly obvious but a few require a little further comment here.

First, there are the items of buildings and equipment which are rented under a lease agreement. The benefits of such leases are felt to be so similar to the benefits of ownership that the items are included in the balance sheet as assets. Suitable wording is used to describe the different nature of these items so that users, particularly **creditors**, are not misled into believing that the items belong to the business.

Second, it is useful to note at this stage that partly finished items of output may be recorded as assets. The term 'work-in-progress' is used to describe work of the business which is not yet completed. Examples of such work-in-progress might be: partly finished items in a manufacturing company; a partly completed motorway being built by a construction company; or a continuing legal case being undertaken by a firm of lawyers. Such items are included as assets because there has been an event in the partial completion of the work and there is an expectation of completion and eventual payment by a customer for the finished item.

Finally, it is clear that the relative future economic benefits of these assets have a wide variation in potential risk. This risk is a matter of great interest to those who use accounting information, but there are generally no accounting techniques for reporting this risk in financial statements. Consequently, it is very important to have adequate descriptions of assets. Accounting information is concerned with the words used to describe items in financial statements, as well as the numbers attributed to them.

**Definitions**

> An **asset** is a resource controlled by the entity as a result of past events and from which future economic benefits are expected to flow.[2]
>
> A **current asset** is an asset that satisfies any of the following criteria:
>
> (a) it is expected to be realised in, or is intended for sale or consumption in, the entity's normal operating cycle;
> (b) it is held primarily for the purpose of being traded;
> (c) it is expected to be realised within 12 months after the balance sheet date;
> (d) it is cash or a cash equivalent.[3]
>
> A **non-current asset** is any asset that does not meet the definition of a current asset.[4] Non-current assets include tangible, intangible and financial assets of a long-term nature. These are also described as **fixed assets**.[5]

## 2.5 Recognition of assets

When an item has passed the tests of definition of an asset, it has still not acquired the right to a place in the balance sheet. To do so it must meet further tests of recognition. **Recognition** means reporting an item by means of words and amounts within the main financial statements in such a way that the item is included in the arithmetic totals. An item which is reported in the notes to the accounts is said to be **disclosed** but *not* **recognised**.

The conditions for recognition have been expressed in the following words:

> An **asset** is **recognised** in the balance sheet when:
>
> it is probable that the future economic benefits will flow to the entity and the asset has a cost or value that can be measured reliably.[6]

### 2.5.1 Probable that economic benefits will flow

To establish probability needs evidence. What evidence is sufficient? Usually more than one item of evidence is looked for. In the case of non-current assets (fixed assets) which have a physical existence, looking at them to make sure they do exist is a useful precaution which some auditors have in the past regretted not taking. Checking on physical existence is not sufficient, however, because the enterprise may have no control over the future economic benefit associated with the item. Evidence of the benefit from non-current assets may lie in: title deeds of property; registration documents for vehicles plus the purchase invoice from the supplier; invoices from suppliers of plant and equipment or office furniture; a written lease agreement for a computer or other type of equipment; and also the enterprise's internal forecasts of the profits it will make by using these non-current assets. This is the kind of evidence which the auditor seeks in forming an opinion on the financial statements.

For current assets the evidence of future benefit comes when the assets are used within the trading cycle. A satisfactory sales record will suggest that the present **inventory (stock)** of finished goods is also likely to sell. Analysis of the time that credit customers have taken to pay will give some indication of whether the **trade receivables** should be recognised as an asset. Cash can be counted, while amounts deposited in banks may be confirmed by a bank statement or bank letter. Internal projections of profit and cash flow provide supporting evidence of the expected benefit from using current assets in trading activities.

### 2.5.2 Reliability of measurement

Reliable measurement of assets can be quite a problem. For the most part, this book will accept the well-tried practice of measuring an asset at the cost of acquiring it, allowing for any reduction in value through use of the asset (depreciation) or through it falling out of fashion (obsolescence). The suitability of this approach to measurement will be discussed in Chapter 14 as one of the main unresolved problems of accounting.

### 2.5.3 Non-recognition

Consider some items which pass the definition test but do not appear in a balance sheet:

- the workforce of a business (a human resource)
- the strength of the management team (another human resource)
- the reputation established for the quality of the product
- the quality of the regular customers
- a tax refund which will be claimable against profits in two years' time.

These items all meet the conditions of rights or other access, future economic benefits, control and a past transaction or event. But they all have associated with them a high level of uncertainty and it could be embarrassing to include them in a balance sheet of one year, only to remove them the following year because something unexpected had happened.

All these items fail one of the recognition tests and some fail both. The workforce as a whole may be reliable and predictable, but unexpected circumstances can come to all and the illness or death of a member of the management team in particular can have a serious impact on the perceived value of the business. A crucial member of the workforce might give notice and leave. In relation to the product, a reputation for quality may become well established and those who would like to include brand names in the balance sheet argue for the permanence of the reputation. Others illustrate the relative transience of such a reputation by bringing out a list of well-known biscuits or sweets of 30 years ago and asking who has heard of them today. Reliable customers of good quality are valuable to a business, but they are also fickle and may change their allegiance at a moment's notice. The tax refund may be measurable in amount, but will there be taxable profits in two years' time against which the refund may be claimed?

It could be argued that the assets which are not recognised in the financial statements should be reported by way of a general description in a note to the accounts. In practice, this rarely happens because accounting tries to avoid raising hopes which might subsequently be dashed. This cautious approach is part of what is referred to more generally as **prudence** in accounting practice.

## 2.6  Defining liabilities

A **liability** is defined as: 'a present obligation of the entity arising from past events, the settlement of which is expected to result in an outflow from the entity of resources embodying economic benefits'.[7] This wording reads somewhat tortuously but has been designed to mirror the definition of an asset.

The most familiar types of liabilities arise in those situations where specific amounts of money are owed by an entity to specific persons called creditors. There is usually no doubt about the amount of money owed and the date on which payment is due. Such persons may be **trade creditors**, the general name for those suppliers who have provided goods or services in return for a promise of payment later. Amounts due to **trade creditors** are described as **trade payables**. Other types of creditors include bankers or other lenders who have lent money to the entity.

There are also situations where an obligation is known to exist but the amount due is uncertain. That might be the case where a court of law has found an entity negligent in failing to meet some duty of care to a customer. The company will have to pay compensation to the customer but the amount has yet to be determined.

Even more difficult is the case where an obligation might exist if some future event happens. Neither the existence nor the amount of the obligation is known with certainty at the balance sheet date. An example would arise where one company has guaranteed the overdraft borrowing of another in the event of that other company defaulting on repayment. At the present time there is no reason to suppose a default will occur, but it remains a possibility for the future.

The definition of a liability tries to encompass all these degrees of variation and uncertainty. It has to be analysed for each separate word or phrase in order to understand the full implications.

### 2.6.1  Present obligation

A legal obligation is evidence that a liability exists because there is another person or entity having a legal claim to payment. Most liabilities arise because a legal obligation exists, either by contract or by statute law.

However, a legal obligation is not a necessary condition. There may be a commercial penalty faced by the business if it takes a certain action. For example, a decision to close a line of business will lead to the knowledge of likely redundancy costs long before the employees are actually made redundant and the legal obligation becomes due. There may be an obligation imposed by custom and practice, such as a condition of the trade that a penalty operates for those who pay bills late. There may be a future obligation caused by actions and events of the current period where, for example, a profit taken by a company now may lead to a taxation liability at a later date which does not arise at this time because of the wording of the tax laws.

### 2.6.2    Past events

A decision to buy supplies or to acquire a new non-current asset is not sufficient to create a liability. It could be argued that the decision is an event creating an obligation, but it is such a difficult type of event to verify that accounting prefers not to rely too much on the point at which a decision is made.

Most liabilities are related to a transaction. Normally the transaction involves receiving goods or services, receiving delivery of new non-current assets such as vehicles and equipment, or borrowing money from a lender. In all these cases there is documentary evidence that the transaction has taken place.

Where the existence of a liability is somewhat in doubt, subsequent events may help to confirm its existence at the balance sheet date. For example, when a company offers to repair goods under a warranty arrangement, the liability exists from the moment the warranty is offered. It may, however, be unclear as to the extent of the liability until a pattern of customer complaints is established. Until that time there will have to be an estimate of the liability. In accounting this estimate is called a **provision**. Amounts referred to as **provisions** are included under the general heading of liabilities.

### 2.6.3    Outflow of economic benefits

The resource of cash is the economic benefit transferable in respect of most obligations. The transfer of property in settlement of an obligation would also constitute a transfer of economic benefits. More rarely, economic benefits could be transferred by offering a resource such as labour in settlement of an obligation.

**Activity 2.3**

*Write down five items in your personal experience which you regard as liabilities. Use the definition given in this section to explain why each item is a liability from your point of view. Then read the next section and compare your list with the examples of business liabilities. If you are having difficulty in understanding why any item is, or is not, a liability you should consult your lecturer, tutor or other expert in the subject area for a discussion on how to apply the definition in identifying liabilities.*

## 2.7    Examples of liabilities

Here is a list of items commonly found in the liabilities section of the balance sheets of companies:

- bank loans and overdrafts
- trade payables (amounts due to suppliers of goods and services on credit terms)
- taxation payable
- accruals (amounts owing, such as unpaid expenses)
- provision for deferred taxation
- long-term loans.

The first five items in this list would be classified as **current liabilities** because they will become due for payment within one year of the balance sheet date. The last item would be classified as **non-current liabilities** because they will remain due by the business for longer than one year.

**Definitions**

> A **liability** is a present obligation of the entity arising from past events, the settlement of which is expected to result in an outflow from the entity of resources embodying economic benefits.[8]
>
> A **current liability** is a liability which satisfies any of the following criteria:
>
> (a) it is expected to be settled in the entity's normal operating cycle;
> (b) it is held primarily for the purpose of being traded;
> (c) it is due to be settled within 12 months after the balance sheet date.[9]
>
> A **non-current liability** is any liability that does not meet the definition of a current liability.[10] Non-current liabilities are also described as **long-term liabilities.**

## 2.8 Recognition of liabilities

As with an asset, when an item has passed the tests of definition of a liability it may still fail the test of recognition. In practice, because of the concern for prudence, it is much more difficult for a liability to escape the balance sheet.

The condition for recognition of a liability uses wording which mirrors that used for recognition of the asset. The only difference is that the economic benefits are now expected to flow *from* the enterprise. The conditions for recognition have been expressed in the following words:

> A **liability** is **recognised** in the balance sheet when:
>
> ● it is probable that an outflow of resources embodying economic benefits will result from the settlement of a present obligation and
> ● the amount at which the settlement will take place can be measured reliably.[11]

What kind of evidence is acceptable? For current liabilities there will be a payment soon after the balance sheet date and a past record of making such payments on time. For non-current liabilities (long-term liabilities) there will be a written agreement stating the terms and dates of repayment required. The enterprise will produce internal forecasts of cash flows which will indicate whether the cash resources will be adequate to allow that future benefit to flow from the enterprise.

Reliable measurement will normally be based on the amount owing to the claimant. If goods or services have been supplied there will be an invoice from the supplier stating the amount due. If money has been borrowed there will be a bank statement or some other document of a similar type, showing the lender's record of how much the enterprise owes.

In cases which fail the recognition test, the documentary evidence is likely to be lacking, probably because there is not sufficient evidence of the existence or the measurable amount. Examples of liabilities which are not recognised in the balance sheet are:

● a commitment to purchase new machinery next year (but not a firm contract)
● a remote, but potential, liability for a defective product, where no court action has yet commenced
● a guarantee given to support the bank overdraft of another company, where there is very little likelihood of being called upon to meet the guarantee.

Because of the prudent nature of accounting, the liabilities which are not recognised in the balance sheet may well be reported in note form under the heading **contingent liabilities**. This is referred to as **disclosure** by way of a note to the accounts.

Looking more closely at the list of liabilities which are not recognised, we see that the commitment to purchase is not legally binding and therefore the outflow of resources may not occur. The claim based on a product defect appears to be uncertain as to occurrence and as to amount. If there has been a court case or a settlement out of court then there should be a provision for further claims of a similar nature. In the case of the guarantee the facts as presented make it appear that an outflow of resources is unlikely. However, such appearances have in the past been deceiving to all concerned and there is often interesting reading in the note to the financial statements which describes the contingent liabilities.

An analysis of some common types of liability is given in Exhibit 2.3.

**Exhibit 2.3**
**Analysis of some common types of liability**

| Type of liability | Obligation | Transfer of economic benefits | Past transaction or event |
|---|---|---|---|
| *Bank loans and overdrafts (repayable on demand or in the very short term)* | The entity must repay the loans on the due date or on demand. | Cash, potentially within a short space of time. | Receiving the borrowed funds. |
| *Trade payables (amounts due to suppliers of goods and services)* | Suppliers must be paid for the goods and services supplied, usually about one month after the supplier's invoice is received. | Cash within a short space of time. | Taking delivery of the goods or service and receiving the supplier's invoice. |
| *Taxation payable (tax due on company profits after the balance sheet date)* | Cash payable to the Inland Revenue. Penalties are charged if tax is not paid on the due date. | Cash. | Making profits in the accounting year and submitting an assessment of tax payable. |
| *Accruals (a term meaning 'other amounts owing', such as unpaid bills)* | Any expense incurred must be reported as an accrued liability (e.g. electricity used, gas used, unpaid wages), if it has not been paid at the balance sheet date. | Cash. | Consuming electricity or gas, using employees' services, receiving bills from suppliers (note that it is not necessary to receive a gas bill in order to know that you owe money for gas used). |
| *Provision for deferred taxation (tax due in respect of present profits but having a delayed payment date allowed by tax law)* | Legislation allows companies to defer payment of tax in some cases. The date of future payment may not be known as yet. | Cash eventually, but could be in the longer term. | Making profits or incurring expenditure now which meets conditions of legislation allowing deferral. |
| *Long-term loans (sometimes called debenture loans)* | Balance sheet will show repayment dates of long-term loans and any repayment conditions attached. | Cash. | Received borrowed funds. |

## 2.9  Defining the ownership interest

The ownership interest is defined in the Framework as equity. **Equity** is the residual interest in the assets of the entity after deducting all its liabilities.[12]

The term **net assets** is used as a shorter way of saying 'total assets less total liabilities'. Because the ownership interest is the residual item, it will be the owners of the business who benefit from any increase in assets after liabilities have been met. Conversely it will be the owners who bear the loss of any decrease in assets after liabilities have been met. The ownership interest applies to the entire net assets. It is sometimes described as the owners' wealth, although economists would take a view that the owners' wealth extends beyond the items recorded in a balance sheet.

If there is only one owner, as in the sole trader's business, then there is no problem as to how the ownership interest is shared. In a partnership, the partnership agreement will usually state the profit-sharing ratio, which may also be applied to the net assets shown in the balance sheet. If nothing is said in the partnership agreement, the profit sharing must be based on equal shares for each partner.

In a company the arrangements for sharing the net assets depend on the type of ownership chosen. The owners may hold **ordinary shares** in the company, which entitle them to a share of any dividend declared and a share in net assets on closing down the business. The ownership interest is in direct proportion to the number of shares held.

Some investors like to hold **preference shares**, which give them a preference (although not an automatic right) to receive a dividend before any ordinary share dividend is declared. The rights of preference shareholders are set out in the articles of association of the company. Some will have the right to share in a surplus of net assets on winding up, but others will only be entitled to the amount of capital originally contributed.

**Definitions**

> The **ownership interest** is called **equity** in the IASB *Framework*.
>
> **Equity** is the residual interest in the assets of the entity after deducting all its liabilities.
>
> **Net assets** means the difference between the total assets and the total liabilities of the business: it represents the amount of the ownership interest in the entity.

## 2.10  Recognition

There can be no separate recognition criteria for the ownership interest because it is the result of recognising assets and recognising liabilities. Having made those decisions on assets and liabilities the enterprise has used up its freedom of choice.

## 2.11  Changes in the ownership interest

It has already been explained that the owner will become better off where the net assets are increasing. The owner will become worse off where the net assets are decreasing. To measure the increase or decrease in net assets, two accounting equations are needed:

| | | | |
|---|---|---|---|
| At time t = 0 | **Assets$_{(t0)}$ – Liabilities$_{(t0)}$** | equals | **Ownership interest$_{(t0)}$** |
| At time t = 1 | **Assets$_{(t1)}$ – Liabilities$_{(t1)}$** | equals | **Ownership interest$_{(t1)}$** |

Taking one equation away from the other may be expressed in words as:

| Change in (assets – liabilities) | equals | Change in ownership interest |
|---|---|---|

or, using the term 'net assets' instead of 'assets – liabilities':

| Change in net assets | equals | Change in ownership interest |
|---|---|---|

The change in the ownership interest between these two points in time is a measure of how much better off or worse off the owner has become, through the activities of the business. The owner is better off when the ownership interest at time $t = 1$ is higher than that at time $t = 0$. To calculate the ownership interest at each point in time requires knowledge of all assets and all liabilities at each point in time. It is particularly interesting to know about the changes in assets and liabilities which have arisen from the day-to-day operations of the business.

The term **revenue** is given to any increase in the ownership interest arising from the operations of the business and caused by an increase in an asset which is greater than any decrease in another asset (or increase in a liability). The term **expense** is given to any reduction in the ownership interest arising from the operations of the business and caused by a reduction in an asset to the extent that it is not replaced by a corresponding increase in another asset (or reduction in a liability).

The owner or owners of the business may also change the amount of the ownership interest by deciding to contribute more cash or other resources in order to finance the business, or deciding to withdraw some of the cash and other resources previously contributed or accumulated. The amount contributed to the business by the owner is usually referred to as **capital**. Decisions about the level of capital to invest in the business are financing decisions. These financing decisions are normally distinguished separately from the results of operations.

So another equation may now be derived as a subdivision of the basic accounting equation, showing analysis of the changes in the ownership interest.

| Change in ownership interest | equals | Capital contributed/withdrawn by the ownership plus **Revenue** minus **Expenses** |
|---|---|---|

The difference between revenue and expenses is more familiarly known as profit. So a further subdivision of the basic equation is:

| Profit | equals | **Revenue** minus **Expenses** |
|---|---|---|

### 2.11.1    Revenue and expense

**Revenue** is created by a transaction or event arising during the operations of the business which causes an increase in the ownership interest. It could be due to an increase in cash or trade receivables, received in exchange for goods or services. Depending on the nature of the business, revenue may be described as sales, turnover, fees, commission, royalties or rent.

An **expense** is caused by a transaction or event arising during the operations of the business which causes a decrease in the ownership interest. It could be due to an outflow or depletion of assets such as cash, inventory (stock) or non-current assets (fixed assets). It could be due to a liability being incurred without a matching asset being acquired.

**Definitions**

> **Revenue** is created by a transaction or event arising during the ordinary activities of the entity which causes an increase in the ownership interest. It is referred to by a variety of different names includiing sales, fees, interest, dividends, royalties and rent.[13]
>
> An **expense** is caused by a transaction or event arising during the ordinary activities of the business which causes a decrease in the ownership interest.[14]

## 2.11.2   Position after a change has occurred

At the end of the accounting period there will be a new level of assets and liabilities recorded. These assets and liabilities will have resulted from the activities of the business during the period, creating revenue and incurring expenses. The owner may also have made voluntary contributions or withdrawals of capital as a financing decision. The equation in the following form reflects that story:

| **Assets** minus **Liabilities** at the end of the period | equals | **Ownership interest at the start of the period** plus **Capital contributed/ withdrawn in the period** plus **Revenue of the period** minus **Expenses of the period** |
|---|---|---|

## 2.12   Assurance for users of financial statements

The definitions of assets and liabilities refer to expected flows into or out of the business. The recognition conditions refer to the evidence that the expected flows in or out will occur. The directors of a company are responsible for ensuring that the financial statements presented by them are a faithful representation of the assets and liabilities of the business and of the transactions and events relating to those assets and liabilities. Shareholders need reassurance that the directors, as their agents, have carried out this responsibility with sufficient care. To give themselves this reassurance, the shareholders appoint a firm of auditors to examine the records of the business and give an opinion as to whether the financial statements correspond to the accounting records and present a true and fair view. (Chapter 1 explained the position of directors as agents of the shareholders. Chapter 4 explains the regulations relating to company financial statements and the appointment of auditors.)

Meet again David and Leona as they continue their conversation on the work of the auditor and its value to the shareholder as a user of accounting information provided by a company.

**DAVID:** *I've now coated your ceiling with apple green emulsion. In return you promised to convince me that I rely on audited accounting information more than I realise. Here is your chance to do that. I was looking today at the annual report of a company which is a manufacturing business. There is a production centre in the UK but most of the production work is carried out in Spain where the operating costs are lower. The distribution operation is carried out from Swindon, selling to retail stores all over the UK. There is an export market, mainly in France, but the company has only scratched the surface of that market. Let's start with something easy – the inventories (stocks) of finished goods which are held at the factory in Spain and the distribution depot in Swindon.*

**LEONA:** *You've shown right away how limited your understanding is, by choosing the asset where you need the auditor's help the most. Everything can go wrong with inventories (stocks)! Think of the accounting equation:*

**Assets – Liabilities = Ownership interest**

*If an asset is overstated, the ownership interest will be overstated. That means the profit for the period, as reported, is higher than it should be. But you won't know that because everything will appear to be in order from the accounts. You have told me repeatedly that you buy the future, not the past, but I know you look to the current profit and loss account as an indicator of future trends of profit. And so do all your friends.*

DAVID: *How can the asset of finished goods inventories be overstated? It's quite a solid item.*

LEONA: *There are two types of potential error – the physical counting of the inventory and the valuation placed on it. There are two main causes of error, one being carelessness and the other an intention to deceive. I've seen situations where the stocktakers count the same stack of goods twice because they don't have a marker pen to put a cross on the items counted. I've also heard of situations where items are counted twice deliberately. We always attend the end-of-year counting of the inventory and observe the process carefully. I wish there weren't so many companies with December year-ends. Counting inventory on 2 January is never a good start to the new year.*

DAVID: *I suppose I can believe that people lose count but how does the valuation go wrong? All companies say that they value inventories at cost as the usual rule. How can the cost of an item be open to doubt?*

LEONA: *Answering that question needs a textbook in itself. The subject comes under the heading of 'management accounting'. Take the goods that you know are manufactured in Spain. There are costs of materials to make the goods, and labour to convert raw materials into finished goods. There are also the running costs of the production unit, which are called the overheads. There is an unbelievable variety of ways of bringing those costs together into one item of product. How much does the company tell you about all that? I know the answer – nothing.*

DAVID: *Well, I could always ask them at a briefing meeting. I usually ask about the profit margin on the goods sold, rather than the value of the goods unsold. But I can see that if the inventories figure is wrong then so is the profit margin. Do you have a systematic procedure for checking each kind of asset?*

LEONA: *Our magic word is* **CEAVOP**. *That stands for:*

*Completeness of information presented.*
*Existence of the asset or liability at a given date.*
*Amount of the transaction is correctly recorded.*
*Valuation reported for assets and liabilities is appropriate.*
*Occurrence of the transaction or event took place in the period.*
*Presentation and disclosure is in accordance with regulations and accounting standards or other comparable regulations.*

*Every aspect of that list has to be checked for each of the assets and liabilities you see in the balance sheet. We need good-quality evidence of each aspect before we sign off the audit report.*

DAVID: *I probably believe that you do a great deal of work with your CEAVOP. But next time I come round to paint your kitchen I'll bring a list of the situations where the auditors don't appear to have asked all the questions in that list.*

## 2.13 Summary

This chapter has set out the accounting equation for a situation at any one point in time:

| Assets | minus | Liabilities | equals | Ownership interest |
|---|---|---|---|---|

Key points are:

- An **asset** is a resource controlled by the entity as a result of past events and from which future economic benefits are expected to flow.
- A **current asset** is an asset that satisfies any of the following criteria:
  (a) it is expected to be realised in, or is intended for sale or consumption in, the entity's normal operating cycle;
  (b) it is held primarily for the purpose of being traded;
  (c) it is expected to be realised within twelve months after the balance sheet date;
  (d) it is cash or a cash equivalent.[15]
- A **non-current asset** is any asset that does not meet the definition of a current asset. Non-current assets include tangible, intangible and financial assets of a long-term nature. These are also described as **fixed assets**.
- A **liability** is a present obligation of the entity arising from past events, the settlement of which is expected to result in an outflow from the entity of resources embodying economic benefits.
- A **current liability** is a liability which satisfies any of the following criteria:
  (a) it is expected to be settled in the entity's normal operating cycle;
  (b) it is held primarily for the purpose of being traded;
  (c) it is due to be settled within 12 months after the balance sheet date.
- A **non-current liability** is any liability that does not meet the definition of a current liability. Non-current liabilities are also described as **long term liabilities.**
- The **ownership interest** is called **equity** in the IASB *Framework*.
- **Equity** is the residual interest in the assets of the entity after deducting all its liabilities.
- **Net assets** means the difference between the total assets and the total liabilities of the business: it represents the amount of the ownership interest in the entity.
- **Recognition** means reporting an item in the financial statements, in words and in amounts, so that the amounts are included in the arithmetic totals of the financial statements. Any other form of reporting by way of note is called 'disclosure'. The conditions for recognition of assets and liabilities are similar in wording.
- At the end of an accounting period the assets and liabilities are reported in a balance sheet. Changes in the assets and liabilities during the period have caused changes in the ownership interest through revenue and expenses of operations. The owner may also have voluntarily added or withdrawn capital. The final position is explained on the left-hand side of the equation and the movement to that position is explained on the right-hand side:

| **Assets** minus **Liabilities** at the end of the period | equals | **Ownership interest at the start of the period** plus **Capital contributed/ withdrawn in the period** plus **Revenue of the period** minus **Expenses of the period** |
|---|---|---|
|  |  |  |

- As with any equation, it is possible to make this version more complex by adding further details. That is not necessary for the purpose of explaining the basic processes, but the equation will be revisited later in the book when some of the problems of accounting are opened up. The helpful aspect of the accounting equation is that it can always be used as a basis for arguing a feasible answer. The limitation is that it cannot give an opinion on the most appropriate answer when more than one option is feasible.

In Chapter 3 there is an explanation of how the information represented by the accounting equation is displayed in a form which is useful to the user groups identified in Chapter 1.

### Further reading

IASB (1989) *Framework for the Preparation and Presentation of Financial Statements*, section 5 'The Elements of Financial Statements' and section 6 'Recognition of the Elements of Financial Statements', International Accounting Standards Board.

# QUESTIONS

The Questions section of each chapter has three types of question. 'Test your understanding' questions to help you review your reading are in the 'A' series of questions. You will find the answers to these by reading and thinking about the material in the book. 'Application' questions to test your ability to apply technical skills are in the 'B' series of questions. Questions requiring you to show skills in problem solving and evaluation are in the 'C' series of questions. A letter [S] indicates that there is a solution at the end of the book.

## A    Test your understanding

**A2.1**    Write out the basic form of the accounting equation. (Section 2.2)

**A2.2**    Define an asset and explain each part of the definition. (Section 2.3)

**A2.3**    Give five examples of items which are assets. (Section 2.4)

**A2.4**    Use the definition to explain why each of the items in your answer to **A.2.3** is an asset. (Section 2.4)

**A2.5**    Explain what 'recognition' means in accounting. (Section 2.5)

**A2.6**    State the conditions for recognition of an asset. (Section 2.5)

**A2.7**    Explain why an item may pass the definition test but fail the recognition test for an asset. (Section 2.5)

**A2.8**    Give three examples of items which pass the definition test for an asset but fail the recognition test. (Section 2.5)

**A2.9**    Some football clubs include the players in the balance sheet as an asset. Others do not. Give the arguments to support each approach. (Section 2.5)

**A2.10**  Define a liability and explain each part of the definition. (Section 2.6)

**A2.11**  Give five examples of items which are liabilities. (Section 2.7)

**A2.12**  Use the definition to explain why each of the items in your answer to **A2.11** is a liability. (Section 2.7)

**A2.13**  State the conditions for recognition of a liability. (Section 2.8)

**A2.14**  Explain why an item may pass the definition test but fail the recognition test for a liability. (Section 2.8)

**A2.15**  Define the term 'equity'. (Section 2.9)

**A2.16**  Explain what is meant by 'net assets'. (Section 2.9)

**A2.17**  Set out the accounting equation for a change in the ownership interest. (Section 2.11)

**A2.18**  Define 'revenue' and 'expenses'. (Section 2.11.1)

**A2.19**  Set out the accounting equation which represents the position after a change has occurred. (Section 2.11.2)

**A2.20**  Explain the auditor's approach to giving assurance about assets and liabilities. (Section 2.12)

## B    Application

**B2.1** [S]
Classify each of the items in the following list as: asset; liability; neither an asset nor a liability.

(a)  cash at bank
(b)  loan from the bank
(c)  letter from the bank promising an overdraft facility at any time in the next three months
(d)  trade receivable (an amount due from a customer who has promised to pay later)
(e)  trade receivable (an amount due from a customer who has promised to pay later but has apparently disappeared without leaving a forwarding address)
(f)  trade payable (an amount due to a supplier of goods who has not yet received payment from the business)
(g)  inventory of finished goods (fashion clothing stored ahead of the spring sales)
(h)  inventory of finished goods (fashion clothing left over after the spring sales)
(i)  investment in shares of another company where the share price is rising
(j)  investment in shares of another company where the share price is falling
(k)  lender of five-year loan to the business
(l)  customer to whom the business has offered a 12-month warranty to repair goods free of charge
(m) a motor vehicle owned by the business
(n)  a motor vehicle rented by the business for one year
(o)  an office building owned by the business
(p)  an office building rented by the business on a 99-year lease, with 60 years' lease period remaining.

**B2.2** [S]
Explain whether each of the items from question **B.2.1** above which you have identified as assets and liabilities would also meet the conditions for recognition of the item in the balance sheet.

**B2.3** [S]
Explain why each of the following items would not meet *either* the definition *or* the recognition conditions of an asset of the business:

(a)  a letter from the owner of the business, addressed to the bank manager, promising to guarantee the bank overdraft of the business
(b)  a list of the customers of the business
(c)  an order received from a customer
(d)  the benefit of employing a development engineer with a high level of 'know-how' specifically relevant to the business
(e)  money spent on an advertising campaign to boost sales
(f)  structural repairs to a building.

## C    Problem solving and evaluation

**C2.1**
The following information has been gathered from the accounting records of Pets Parlour:

**Assets and liabilities at 31 December Year 4**

| | £ |
|---|---:|
| Cash at bank | 500 |
| Borrowings | 6,000 |
| Trade receivables (debtors) | 5,000 |
| Property, plant and equipment | 29,000 |

**Revenue and expenses for the year ended 31 December Year 4**

| | £ |
|---|---:|
| Fees charged for work done | 20,000 |
| Interest paid on borrowings | 1,000 |
| Administration costs incurred | 1,500 |
| Salaries paid to employees | 14,000 |

**Required**

Using the accounting equation, calculate:

(a)  The amount of ownership interest at 31 December Year 4.
(b)  The amount of net profit for the year.
(c)  The amount of the ownership interest at 1 January Year 4.

## Activities for study groups

Obtain the annual report of a listed company. From the balance sheet list the items shown as assets and liabilities. (This will require you to look in detail at the notes to the accounts using the references on the face of the balance sheet.) Share out the list of assets and liabilities so that each person has four or five assets and four or five liability items.

**1**  Separately, using the definitions and recognition criteria, prepare a short statement explaining why each item on your list passes the tests of definition and recognition. State the evidence you would expect to see, as auditor, to confirm the expected future inflow of economic benefit from any asset and the expected future outflow of benefit from any liability.

**2**  Present your explanations to the group and together prepare a list of assets and a separate list of liabilities in order of the uncertainty which attaches to the expected future benefit.

**3**  Read the 'contingent liability' note, if there is one, to find examples of liabilities which have not been recognised but have been disclosed. Why will you not find a 'contingent asset' note?

## Notes and references

1.  IASB (1989), *Framework for the Preparation and Presentation of Financial Statements*, para. 49(a).
2.  IASB (1989), *Framework for the Preparation and Presentation of Financial Statements*, para. 49(a).
3.  IAS 1 (2004), para. 57.
4.  IAS 1 (2004), para. 57.
5.  IAS 1 para. 58 permits the use of alternative descriptions for non-current assets provided the meaning is clear.
6.  IASB (1989), *Framework*, para. 89.
7.  IASB (1989), *Framework*, para. 49(b).
8.  IASB (1989), *Framework*, para. 49(b).
9.  IAS 1 (2004), para. 60.
10.  *Ibid.*
11.  IASB (1989), *Framework*, para. 91.
12.  IASB (1989), *Framework*, para. 49(c).
13.  IASB (1989), *Framework*, para. 74.
14.  IASB (1989), *Framework*, para. 78.
15.  IAS 1 (2004), para. 57.

## Supplement to Chapter 2

# Debit and credit bookkeeping

*You do not have to read this supplement to be able to progress through the rest of the textbook. In the main body of each chapter the explanations are all given in terms of changes in elements of the accounting equation. However, for those who would like to know how debits and credits work, each chapter will have a supplement putting into debit and credit form the material contained in the chapter.*

## Recording in ledger accounts

The double entry system of bookkeeping records business transactions in ledger accounts. It makes use of the fact that there are two aspects to every transaction when analysed in terms of the accounting equation.

A ledger account accumulates the increases and reductions either in a category of business activities such as sales or in dealings with individual customers and suppliers.

Ledger accounts may be subdivided. Sales could be subdivided into home sales and export sales. Separate ledger accounts might be kept for each type of non-current asset, e.g. buildings and machinery. The ledger account for machinery might be subdivided as office machinery and production machinery.

Ledger accounts for rent, business rates and property insurance might be kept separately or the business might instead choose to keep one ledger account to record transactions in all of these items, giving them the collective name administrative expenses. The decision would depend on the number of transactions in an accounting period and on whether it was useful to have separate records.

The managers of the business have discretion to combine or subdivide ledger accounts to suit the information requirements of the business concerned.

## Using the accounting equation

Before entries are made in ledger accounts, the double entry system of bookkeeping assigns to each aspect of a business transaction a **debit** or a **credit** notation, based on the analysis of the transaction using the accounting equation.

In its simplest form the accounting equation is stated as:

| **Assets** | minus | **Liabilities** | equals | **Ownership interest** |
|---|---|---|---|---|

To derive the debit and credit rules it is preferable to rearrange the equation so that there is no minus sign.

| **Assets** | equals | **Liabilities** | plus | **Ownership interest** |
|---|---|---|---|---|

There are three elements to the equation and each one of these elements may either *increase* or *decrease* as a result of a transaction or event. The six possibilities are set out in Exhibit 2.4.

**Exhibit 2.4**
**Combinations of increases and decreases of the main elements of transactions**

*Left-hand side of the equation*

| Assets | Increase | Decrease |
|---|---|---|

*Right-hand side of the equation*

| Liabilities | Decrease | Increase |
|---|---|---|
| Ownership interest | Decrease | Increase |

The double entry bookkeeping system uses this classification (which preserves the symmetry of the equation) to distinguish debit and credit entries as shown in Exhibit 2.5.

**Exhibit 2.5**
**Rules of debit and credit for ledger entries, basic accounting equation**

| | *Debit entries in a ledger account* | *Credit entries in a ledger account* |
|---|---|---|
| *Left-hand side of the equation* | | |
| Asset | Increase | Decrease |
| *Right-hand side of the equation* | | |
| Liability | Decrease | Increase |
| Ownership interest | Decrease | Increase |

It was shown in the main body of the chapter that the ownership interest may be increased by:

● earning revenue; and
● new capital contributed by the owner;

and that the ownership interest may be decreased by:

● incurring expenses; and
● capital withdrawn by the owner.

So the 'ownership interest' section of Exhibit 2.5 may be expanded as shown in Exhibit 2.6.

That is all you ever have to know about the rules of bookkeeping. All the rest can be reasoned from this table. For any transaction there will be two aspects. (If you find there are more than two, the transaction needs breaking down into simpler steps.) For each aspect there will be a ledger account. Taking each aspect in turn you ask yourself: *Is this an asset, a liability, or an aspect of the ownership interest?* Then you ask yourself: *Is it an increase or a decrease?* From Exhibit 2.6 you then know immediately whether to make a debit or a credit entry.

Examples of the application of the rules of debit and credit recording are given in the supplement to Chapter 5 for a service business and in the supplement to Chapter 6 for a manufacturing business. They will also be used in later chapters to explain how particular transactions are reported.

Exhibit 2.6

**Rules of debit and credit for ledger entries, distinguishing different aspects of ownership interest**

|  | Debit entries in a ledger account | Credit entries in a ledger account |
| --- | --- | --- |
| *Left-hand side of the equation* |  |  |
| Asset | Increase | Decrease |
| *Right-hand side of the equation* |  |  |
| Liability | Decrease | Increase |
| Ownership interest | Expense | Revenue |
|  | Capital withdrawn | Capital contributed |

## S  Test your understanding

(The answer to each of the following questions is either **debit** or **credit**)

**S2.1**  What is the bookkeeping entry for an increase in an asset?

**S2.2**  What is the bookkeeping entry for a decrease in a liability?

**S2.3**  What is the bookkeeping entry for an increase in an expense?

**S2.4**  What is the bookkeeping entry for a withdrawal of owner's capital?

**S2.5**  What is the bookkeeping entry for an increase in revenue?

# Chapter 3

# Financial statements from the accounting equation

## Cash flow

After deducting interest, tax and dividend payments, £467 million of operating cash flow was available to fund our capital investment programme, demonstrating BAA's continued strong conversion of operating profit to cash. The APP joint venture and the other investment property sales generated a further cash inflow of £625 million. The balance of the £1,403 million capital investment during the year was funded by increased net debt. The table below summarises the Group's cash flow movements during the year.

### Summary cash flow (£ million)

|  | 2005 | 2004 |
| --- | --- | --- |
| Cash flow from operating activities | 957 | 853 |
| Interest, tax and dividends | (490) | (447) |
| Net cash flow from operations | 467 | 406 |
| Capital expenditure and investment | (1,433) | (1,266) |
| Cash impact of property transactions | 625 | (7) |
| Other | 31 | 15 |
| Increase in net debt (net of issue costs) | (310) | (825) |

Source: BAA Annual Report 2004/5, p. 34.

## Discussion points

1 What do we learn about cash flow from the information in the table?

2 How does the description in words help the user to understand the information in the table?

**Learning outcomes**

After studying this chapter you should be able to:

- Explain the benefits and problems of producing annual financial statements.
- Explain the purpose and structure of the balance sheet.
- Explain the purpose and structure of the income statement (profit and loss account).
- Explain the purpose and structure of the cash flow statement.
- Comment on the usefulness to users of the financial statements prepared.

Additionally for those who choose to study the Supplement:

- Apply the debit and credit form of analysis to the transactions of a short period of time, summarising them in a list which may be used for preparation of simple financial statements.

## 3.1   Introduction

In the previous chapter the accounting equation was developed as a representation of the relationships among key items of accounting information: assets, liabilities and the ownership interest. An understanding of the accounting equation and the various elements of the equation provides a systematic approach to analysing transactions and events, but it gives no guidance as to how the results should be communicated in a manner which will be helpful and meaningful to users. The accounting equation is used in this chapter as a basis for explaining the structure of financial statements. Ideas beyond the accounting equation are required as to what qualities are expected of financial statements.

The various financial statements produced by enterprises for the owners and other external users are derived from the accounting equation. The *Framework* identifies the purposes of financial reporting as producing information about the financial position, performance and financial adaptability of the enterprise. The three most familiar **primary financial statements**, and their respective purposes, are:

| *Primary financial statement* | *Purpose is to report* |
|---|---|
| Balance sheet | Financial position |
| Income statement (Profit and loss account) | Performance |
| Cash flow statement | Financial adaptability |

This chapter explains the general shape and content of each of these financial statements.

## 3.2  Who is in charge of the accounting system?

Since 2005 two different accounting systems have existed for companies in the UK, depending on the type of company. When you look at the name of a company listed on the Stock Exchange, such as Vodaphone, BskyB, Cadbury Schweppes and Dixons, you are really looking at a family group of companies all owned by one parent company. One set of financial statements representing all the companies in the group. Under the law of the European Union (EU), these group financial statements for listed companies must apply the accounting system set out by the International Accounting Standards Board (**IASB system**). Other companies in the UK may choose to follow the IASB system of standards but there is no requirement to do so. All companies in the UK that do not apply the IASB system must apply the accounting system set out by the UK Accounting Standards Board (ASB). The ASB's system is also used by many bodies in the UK public sector such as town and city councils, hospital trusts and universities.

Fortunately for those studying the subject, the ASB and the IASB have been working closely together for many years and there are relatively few differences between the two systems. However there is a potential difference in the appearance and the wording of financial statements. Companies applying the UK ASB's accounting system must use specifications of the sequence and content of items (called **formats** of financial statements) set out in UK company law which is based on EU directives. Companies applying the IASB's system to their listed group reporting have a choice in how they present their financial statements. As a consequence we are now seeing variety in the content and sequence of financial statements published in the annual reports of groups listed on the Stock Exchange. This chapter gives you a flavour of the formats that you might see in financial statements. Where there are differences in words used, this chapter gives the wording of the IASB system first, followed by the wording of UK company law and ASB standards in brackets. As an example, the description:

income statement (profit and loss account)

means that the IASB system uses **income statement** in its illustrations of a profit statement, while UK law and ASB standards use **profit and loss account** in their illustrations of a profit statement.

## 3.3  The accounting period

In the far-away days of traders sailing out of Italian ports on three-year voyages, the **accounting period** was determined by the date of return of the ship, when the accounts could be prepared for the whole voyage. That rather leisurely view of the scale of time would not be tolerated in an industrial and commercial society where there is always someone demanding information. The convention is that businesses should prepare financial statements at least once in every calendar year. That convention is a requirement of law expressed in the Companies Act 1985 in the case of limited liability companies. Where companies have a Stock Exchange listing they are required to produce an interim report six months into the accounting year. Some companies voluntarily produce quarterly reports to shareholders, reflecting the practice of listed companies in the USA. For internal management accounting purposes, a business may produce reports more frequently (e.g. on a monthly or a weekly basis).

Businesses may choose their accounting date as a time convenient to their activities. Many companies choose 31 December for the year-end, but others (including many of the utility companies which were formerly owned by the government) use 31 March. Some prefer a September or October date after the peak of the summer sales has passed. Whatever the choice, companies are expected to keep the same date from one year to the next unless there is a strong reason for changing.

The use of a 12-month accounting period should not be too much of a problem where the trading cycle fits neatly into a year. If the business is seasonal, there will be a peak of production to match the seasonal peak of sales and the pattern will be repeated every year. There could be a few technical problems of deciding exactly how to close the door on 31 December and whether transactions towards the end of the year are to be included in that year or carried to the next period. These problems can be dealt with by having systematic 'cut-off' rules. There is a bigger problem for those companies whose trading cycle is much longer. It could take two years to build a section of a motorway or three years to build a bridge over a wide river estuary. Such a company will have to subdivide the work on the main contract so that some can be reported each year.

The use of the 12-month accounting period also causes problems for recognition of assets and liabilities. Waiting for the ship to arrive was much safer evidence for the Venetian traders than hoping it was still afloat or relying on reported sightings. For today's business the equivalent situation would be waiting for a property to be sold or for a large customer to pay the amount due as a debt. However, in practice the balance sheet cannot wait. Notes to the accounts give additional explanations to help users of financial statements evaluate the risk, but it is all quite tentative.

## 3.4  The balance sheet

The **balance sheet** reflects the accounting equation. You saw in Chapter 2 that there is more than one way to write the accounting equation. That means there is more than one way to present a balance sheet. You will find throughout your study of accounting that there is often more than one approach to dealing with an activity or solving a problem. This is the first time but there will be more. It means that you need to be flexible in your approach to reading and using financial statements.

### 3.4.1  Focus on the ownership interest

One form of the accounting equation focuses on the ownership interest as the result of subtracting liabilities from assets. The equation is as follows:

| **Assets** | minus | **Liabilities** | equals | **Ownership interest** |
|---|---|---|---|---|

UK companies who apply this form of the equation will present the balance sheet in a narrative form, reading down the page, as follows:

| |
|:---:|
| **Assets** |
| minus |
| **Liabilities** |
| equals |
| **Ownership interest** |

The assets are subdivided into current assets and non-current assets (defined in Chapter 2), while the liabilities are subdivided into current liabilities and non-current liabilities (also defined in Chapter 2). The ownership interest may also be subdivided to show separately the capital contributed or withdrawn and the profit of the period. Because current assets and current liabilities are closely intertwined in the day-to-day operations of the business, they are grouped close to each other in the balance sheet (Exhibit 3.1).

Exhibit 3.1
**Structure of a balance sheet**

| |
|:---:|
| **Non-current assets** |
| plus |
| **Current assets** |
| minus |
| **Current liabilities** |
| minus |
| **Non-current liabilities** |
| equals |
| **Capital at start of year** <br> plus/minus <br> **Capital contributed or withdrawn** <br> plus <br> **Profit of the period** |

Exhibit 3.1 represents a **format** set out in the Companies Act 1985 (although with more detail) as one of the permitted formats. For many years it has been the format most commonly used by UK companies and continues to be used by some UK companies that have moved to the IASB system of accounting. Most companies will try to confine the balance sheet to a single side of A4 paper but there is not much space on one sheet of A4 paper to fit in all the assets and liabilities of a company. Consequently a great deal of use is made of notes to the accounts which explain the detail. The balance sheet shows only the main categories of assets and liabilities.

### 3.4.2 Balancing assets and claims on assets

Another form of the accounting equation focuses on balancing the assets against the claims on assets. The claims on assets come from the ownership interest and from liabilities of all types. The equation is as follows:

| Assets | equals | Ownership interest | plus | Liabilities |
|---|---|---|---|---|

UK companies who apply this form of the equation will present the balance sheet vertically on one sheet of paper but the sequence will be different:

| Assets |
|---|
| equals |
| Ownership interest |
| plus |
| Liabilities |

In some countries there is a preference for lining up the balance sheet horizontally to match the accounting equation even more closely.

| Assets | Ownership interest |
|---|---|
| | plus |
| | Liabilities |

**Activity 3.1** *Before reading further, make sure that you can explain why each item in the accounting records is an asset or a liability, as shown in the foregoing list. If you have any doubts, read Chapter 2 again before proceeding with this chapter.*

### 3.4.3 Example of balance sheet presentation

The following list of assets and liabilities of P. Mason's legal practice was prepared from the accounting records of transactions summarised at 30 September Year 5:

| | £ |
|---|---|
| Land and buildings | 250,000 |
| Office furniture | 30,000 |
| Receivables (debtors) for fees | 1,200 |
| Prepayment of insurance premium | 540 |
| Cash at bank | 15,280 |
| **Total assets (A)** | **297,020** |
| Trade payables (creditors) | 2,800 |
| Long-term loan | 150,000 |
| **Total liabilities (L)** | **152,800** |
| **Ownership interest (A – L)** | **144,220** |

Exhibit 3.2 shows how this would appear in a balance sheet based on the 'ownership interest' form of the equation. Exhibit 3.3 shows how the same information would appear in a balance sheet based on the 'claims on assets' form of the equation.

Exhibit 3.2

**Balance sheet: Assets minus liabilities equals ownership interest**

| P. Mason's legal practice Balance sheet at 30 September Year 5 | £ | £ |
|---|---|---|
| **Non-current assets** | | |
| Land and buildings | | 250,000 |
| Office furniture | | 30,000 |
| *Total non-current assets* | | 280,000 |
| **Current assets** | | |
| Receivables (debtors) for fees | 1,200 | |
| Prepayment of insurance premium | 540 | |
| Cash at bank | 15,280 | |
| *Total current assets* | 17,020 | |
| **Current liabilities** | | |
| Trade payables (creditors) | (2,800) | |
| *Current assets less current liabilities* | | 14,220 |
| | | 294,220 |
| **Non-current liabilities** | | |
| Long-term loan | | (150,000) |
| Net assets | | 144,220 |
| **Ownership interest** | | 144,220 |

The balance sheet in Exhibit 3.2 is more informative than the list of assets and liabilities from which it was prepared because it has been arranged in a helpful format. The first helpful feature is the use of headings (shown in Exhibit 3.2 in bold) for similar items grouped together, such as non-current assets, current assets, current liabilities and non-current liabilities. The second helpful feature is the use of **subtotals** (identified in Exhibit 3.2 by descriptions in italics and shaded) for similar items grouped together. The subtotals used in this example are those for: total non-current assets; total current assets; and current assets less current liabilities. There are no standard rules on use of subtotals. They should be chosen in a manner most appropriate to the situation.

A person using this balance sheet can see at a glance that there is no problem for the business in meeting its current liabilities from its resources of current assets. The financing of the business is split almost equally between the non-current liabilities and the ownership interest, a split which would not be regarded as excessively risky by those who lend to businesses. The non-current assets used as a basis for generating profits from one year to the next are collected together as a group, although the balance sheet alone cannot show how effectively those assets are being used. For that, an income statement (profit and loss account) is needed.

The balance sheet in Exhibit 3.3 is again more informative than the list of assets and liabilities from which it was prepared because it has been arranged in a helpful format. It offers a helpful feature in the use of headings (in bold) for similar items grouped together. It is also helpful in providing subtotals (identified by descriptions in italics and shaded) for similar items grouped together. The subtotals used in this example are those for: total non-current assets and total current assets. There could also be subtotals for the current assets less current liabilities. There are no standard rules on use of subtotals. They should be chosen in a manner most appropriate to the situation.

Exhibit 3.3
**Balance sheet: Assets equal ownership interest plus liabilities**

| P. Mason's legal practice Balance sheet at 30 September Year 5 | £ | £ |
|---|---|---|
| **Non-current assets** | | |
| Land and buildings | | 250,000 |
| Office furniture | | 30,000 |
| *Total non-current assets* | | 280,000 |
| **Current assets** | | |
| Receivables for fees | | 1,200 |
| Prepayment of insurance premium | | 540 |
| Cash at bank | | 15,280 |
| *Total current assets* | | 17,020 |
| **Total assets** | | 297,020 |
| **Ownership interest** | | 144,220 |
| **Non-current liabilities** | | |
| Long-term loan | | 150,000 |
| **Current liabilities** | | |
| Trade payables | | 2,800 |
| **Total ownership interest plus liabilities** | | 297,020 |

A person using this balance sheet can again see at a glance that there is no problem for the business in meeting its current liabilities from its resources of current assets. The financing of the business is split almost equally between the non-current liabilities and the ownership interest, a split which would not be regarded as excessively risky by those who lend to businesses. The non-current assets used as a basis for generating profits from one year to the next are collected together as a group, although the balance sheet alone cannot show how effectively those assets are being used.

## 3.5 The income statement (profit and loss account)

For many years in the UK, **profit and loss account** was the only title used for the financial statement reporting profit of the period. From 2005 many of those listed groups following the IASB's system have chosen to follow an example given by the IASB which uses the heading **income statement**, found more commonly in US company reports. It is not compulsory for listed group companies to use 'income statement' and some retain the 'profit and loss account' heading. The income statement (profit and loss account) reflects that part of the accounting equation which defines profit:

| **Profit** | equals | **Revenue** minus **Expenses** |
|---|---|---|

The expenses of a period are matched against the revenue earned in that period. This is described as the application of the **matching concept** in accounting.

As with the balance sheet, it is presented in a vertical form so that it can be read down the page as a narrative (Exhibit 3.4).

**Exhibit 3.4**
**Structure of an income statement (profit and loss account)**

| |
|---|
| **Revenue** |
| minus |
| **Expenses** |
| equals |
| **Profit** |

## 3.5.1 Example of presentation

The accounting records of P. Mason's legal practice at 30 September Year 5 showed that the ownership interest could be explained as follows (using brackets to show negative items):

| | £ |
|---|---|
| *Increases in ownership interest* | |
| Capital contributed at start of month | 140,000 |
| Fees | 8,820 |
| *Decreases in ownership interest* | |
| Computer rental and on-line searches | (1,500) |
| Gas | (100) |
| Electricity | (200) |
| Telephone/fax | (1,000) |
| Salary of assistant | (1,800) |
| Ownership interest at end of month | 144,220 |

The statement of profit is quite simple, as shown in Exhibit 3.5.

**Exhibit 3.5**
**Financial statement of profit, in a useful format**

**P. Mason's legal practice**
**Income statement (profit and loss account) for the month of September**

| | £ | £ |
|---|---|---|
| **Revenues** | | |
| Fees | | 8,820 |
| **Expenses** | | |
| Computer rental and on-line searches | (1,500) | |
| Gas | (100) | |
| Electricity | (200) | |
| Telephone/fax | (1,000) | |
| Salary of assistant | (1,800) | |
| *Total expenses* | | (4,600) |
| Net profit of the month | | 4,220 |

## 3.5.2 Comment

The income statement (profit and loss account) improves on the mere list of constituent items by providing headings (shown in bold) for each main category. As this is a very simple example, only two headings and one subtotal are required. Headings and subtotals are most useful where there are groups of items of a similar nature. The resulting net profit shows how the revenues and expenses have contributed overall to increasing the ownership interest during the month.

**Activity 3.2**

*Taking each item of the income statement (profit and loss account) in turn, explain to an imaginary friend why each item of revenue and expense is regarded as increasing or decreasing the ownership interest. If necessary, look back to the definitions of revenue and expense in Chapter 2. Make sure that you feel confident about the income statement (profit and loss account) before you move on.*

## 3.6 The cash flow statement

It was shown in Chapter 1 that liquidity is of interest to more than one user group, but of particular interest to creditors of the business.

**Liquidity** is measured by the cash and near-cash assets and the change in those assets, so a financial statement which explains cash flows should be of general interest to user groups:

| **Cash flow** | equals | **Cash inflows to the enterprise** minus **Cash outflows from the enterprise** |
|---|---|---|

The **cash flow statement** will appear in a vertical form:

| **Cash inflows** |
|---|
| minus |
| **Cash outflows** |
| equals |
| **Change in cash assets** |

In a business there will be different factors causing the inflows and outflows of cash. The enterprise will try to make clear what the different causes are. Subdivisions are commonly used for operating activities, investing activities and financing activities:

- *Operating activities* are the actions of buying and selling goods, or manufacturing goods for resale, or providing a service to customers.
- *Investing activities* are the actions of buying and selling non-current assets for long-term purposes.
- *Financing activities* are the actions of raising and repaying the long-term finance of the business.

Exhibit 3.6 sets out the basic structure of a basic cash flow statement.

Exhibit 3.6
**Structure of a cash flow statement**

| |
|---|
| ***Operating activities*** **Cash inflows** minus |
| **Cash outflows** |
| plus |
| ***Investing activities*** **Cash inflows** minus **Cash outflows** |
| plus |
| ***Financing activities*** **Cash inflows** minus **Cash outflows** |
| equals |
| **Change in cash assets** |

## 3.6.1  Example of cash flow presentation

The cash transactions of P. Mason's legal practice for the month of September were recorded as follows:

**Accounting records**

| Year 5 | | £ |
|---|---|---|
| *Cash received* | | |
| Sept. 1 | Capital contributed by P. Mason | 140,000 |
| Sept. 1 | Loan from bank | 150,000 |
| Sept. 19 | Fees received from clients | 7,620 |
| | Total cash received | 297,620 |
| *Cash paid* | | |
| Sept. 1 | Land and buildings | 250,000 |
| Sept. 5 | Prepayment of insurance premium | 540 |
| Sept. 26 | Supplier for office furniture | 30,000 |
| Sept. 30 | Salaries | 1,800 |
| | Total cash paid | 282,340 |
| | Cash remaining at 30 September | 15,280 |

The cash flow statement would be presented as shown in Exhibit 3.7.

## 3.6.2  Comment

The cash flows, listed at the start of section 3.5.1 in the accounting records for the legal practice, relate to three different types of activity which are brought out more clearly in the cash flow statement by the use of headings and subtotals. The headings are shown in bold and the subtotals are highlighted by italics and shading. The story emerging from the cash flow statement is that the owner put in £140,000 and the bank lent £150,000, providing a total of £290,000 in start-up finance. Of this amount, £280,000 was used during the month to pay for non-current assets. That left £10,000 which, when added to the positive cash flow from operations, explains why the cash resources increased by £15,280 over the month.

**Exhibit 3.7**
**Financial statement showing cash flows of an enterprise**

| **P. Mason's legal practice** | |
|---|---|
| **Cash flow statement for the month of September Year 5** | |
| | £ |
| **Operating activities** | |
| Inflow from fees | 7,620 |
| Outflow to insurance premium | (540) |
| Outflows to salaries | (1,800) |
| *Net inflow from operations* | 5,280 |
| **Investing activities** | |
| Payment for land and building | (250,000) |
| Payment for office furniture | (30,000) |
| *Net outflow for investing activities* | (280,000) |
| **Financing activities** | |
| Capital contributed by owner | 140,000 |
| Five-year loan from bank | 150,000 |
| *Net inflow from financing activities* | 290,000 |
| Increase in cash at bank over period | 15,280 |

It is quite common to compare the increase in ownership claim caused by making a profit with the increase in the cash resources of a business caused by operations. In this case the profit is £4,220 (Exhibit 3.5) but the operations have added £15,280 to the cash assets of the business.

To make the comparison, Exhibit 3.8 takes the income statement (profit and loss account) of Exhibit 3.5 and sets alongside it the cash flows relating to operations.

Exhibit 3.8 shows that the cash flow from fees was £1,200 less than the fee revenue earned because some customers had not paid at the month end. This is the amount shown in the balance sheet (Exhibit 3.2) as receivables for fees. Exhibit 3.8 also shows that expenses of rental, gas, electricity and telephone amounting to £2,800 in total had not been paid at the month end. These are shown as **trade payables** in the balance sheet. The cash flow from operations is reduced by the payment for the insurance premium which does not affect the income statement (profit and loss account) for the month.

**Exhibit 3.8**
**Comparison of profit and cash flow for the month of September**

| **P. Mason's legal practice** | | |
|---|---|---|
| | *Profit* | *Cash flow* |
| | £ | £ |
| **Revenues** | | |
| Fees/cash received | 8,820 | 7,620 |
| **Expenses** | | |
| Computer rental and on-line searches | (1,500) | nil |
| Gas | (100) | nil |
| Electricity | (200) | nil |
| Telephone/fax | (1,000) | nil |
| Salary of assistant | (1,800) | (1,800) |
| Payment for insurance premium | nil | (540) |
| *Total expenses/total cash paid* | 4,600 | (2,340) |
| Net profit of the month | 4,220 | |
| Increase in cash in the month | | 5,280 |

Users of financial statements regard both the profit and the cash flow as interesting items of information. The profit shows the overall increase in ownership claim which contributes to the overall wealth of the business. The cash flow shows the ability of the business to survive financially through planning the timing and amount of inflows and outflows of cash.

## 3.7 Usefulness of financial statements

Here are Leona and David, still working on Leona's flat, discussing the usefulness of financial statements.

**LEONA:** *Which financial statement is the most important for you?*

**DAVID:** *It has to be the income statement (profit and loss account). Profit creates wealth. Future profit creates future wealth. I have to make a forecast of each company's profit as part of my planning to meet our overall investment strategy. Maybe I should qualify that by adding that cash flow is also important, especially where there is high uncertainty about future prospects. We talk about 'quality of profits' and regard some types of profit as of higher quality than others. Cash flow support is one aspect of that quality. We have doubts about some accounting amounts which don't have a close relationship to cash. A business cannot survive if it can't pay its way.*

**LEONA:** *Where does that leave the balance sheet?*

**DAVID:** *I'm not sure. It is a list of resources and claims on those resources. We are share-holders and so we have a claim on those resources but we don't think about it to any great extent because we are concentrating on the going concern aspects of the business, rather than closing down and selling the assets. The balance sheet numbers don't mean very much because they are out of date.*

**LEONA:** *We studied research at university which suggested that cash flow is the answer and income statements (profit and loss accounts) are too difficult to understand. It was suggested that the balance sheet should show what the assets could be sold for. I don't think the ideas had caught on in practice, but they seemed to have some merits.*

**DAVID:** *I like to know the dynamics of the business. I like to see the movements of different aspects and the interactions. I think I would feel that cash flow alone is concentrating on only one aspect of the wealth of the business. I suppose the balance sheet is a useful check on the position which has been reached as a result of making profits for the period. One thing we do look at in the balance sheet is how much has been borrowed for use in the business. We don't like to see that become too high in comparison with the ownership interest.*

**LEONA:** *At least you are admitting to seeing something in the financial statements. I still have to persuade you that the auditors are important in giving you the reassurance you obviously obtain.*

**Activity 3.3**

*Analyse your own view of wealth and changes in wealth. Which items would you include in your personal balance sheet today? Which items would you include in your personal 'profit and loss' account for the past year? Which items would you include in your personal cash flow statement? Has your view of 'wealth' been modified as a result of reading these first three chapters? If so, how have your views changed?*

## 3.8  Summary

This chapter has explained the structure of the main financial statements produced by business and non-business entities.

Key points are:

- An **accounting period** of 12 months is common for financial reporting.
- The **primary financial statements** produced by a wide range of entities are the balance sheet, the income statement (profit and loss account) and the cash flow statement.
- A **balance sheet** presents financial position at a point in time. The **format** of the balance sheet will vary depending on which version of the accounting equation is preferred by the entity preparing the balance sheet.
- An **income statement** (profit and loss account) presents the performance over a period of time. The income statement (profit and loss account) presents financial performance by **matching** revenue and expenses to arrive at a profit of the period.
- A **cash flow statement** presents the financial adaptability over a period of time. It explains changes in the cash position over a period caused by operating cash flows, investing cash flows and financing cash flows.
- Since 2005 two different accounting systems (consisting of **accounting standards** and legislation) have existed for companies in the UK, depending on the type of company. The **IASB system** applies to the group financial statements of listed companies. Other companies may choose voluntarily to follow the IASB system. The **UK system**, based on UK law and the standards of the UK ASB, applies to all companies that do not follow the IASB system.
- The **accounting standards** of the UK ASB are very similar to those of the IASB.

# QUESTIONS

The Questions section of each chapter has three types of question. 'Test your understanding' questions to help you review your reading are in the 'A' series of questions. You will find the answers to these by reading and thinking about the material in the book. 'Application' questions to test your ability to apply technical skills are in the 'B' series of questions. Questions requiring you to show skills in problem solving and evaluation are in the 'C' series of questions. A letter [S] indicates that there is a solution at the end of the book.

## A  Test your understanding

**A3.1**  Explain why an accounting period of 12 months is used as the basis for reporting to external users of financial statements. (Section 3.3)

**A3.2**  Explain how the structure of the balance sheet corresponds to the accounting equation. (Section 3.4)

**A3.3**  Explain how the structure of the income statement (profit and loss account) represents a subsection of the accounting equation. (Section 3.5)

**A3.4**  Explain how the structure of the cash flow statement represents another subsection of the accounting equation. (Section 3.6)

**A3.5** List three features of a balance sheet format which are particularly useful in making the format helpful to readers. (Section 3.4.3)

**A3.6** List three features of an income statement (profit and loss account) format which are particularly useful in making the format helpful to readers. (Section 3.5.1)

**A3.7** List three features of a cash flow statement format which are particularly useful in making the format helpful to readers. (Section 3.6.1)

# B    Application

**B3.1** [S]

John Timms is the sole owner of Sunshine Wholesale Traders, a company which buys fruit from farmers and sells it to supermarkets. All goods are collected from farms and delivered to supermarkets on the same day, so no inventories (stocks) of fruit are held. The accounting records of Sunshine Traders at 30 June Year 2, relating to the year then ended, have been summarised by John Timms as follows:

|  | £ |
|---|---|
| Fleet of delivery vehicles, after deducting depreciation | 35,880 |
| Furniture and fittings, after deducting depreciation | 18,800 |
| Trade receivables | 34,000 |
| Bank deposit | 19,000 |
| Trade payables (creditors) | 8,300 |
| Sales | 294,500 |
| Cost of goods sold | 188,520 |
| Wages and salaries | 46,000 |
| Transport costs | 14,200 |
| Administration costs | 1,300 |
| Depreciation of vehicles, furniture and fittings | 1,100 |

**Required**

(a)  Identify each item in the accounting records as either an asset, a liability, or ownership interest (identifying separately the expenses and revenues which contribute to the change in the ownership interest).

(b)  Prepare a balance sheet at 30 June Year 2.

(c)  Prepare a profit and loss statement for the year ended 30 June Year 2.

**B3.2** [S]

Prepare a balance sheet from the following list of assets and liabilities, regarding the ownership interest as the missing item.

|  | £ |
|---|---|
| Trade payables (creditors) | 43,000 |
| Cash at bank | 9,000 |
| Inventories (stocks) of goods for resale | 35,000 |
| Land and buildings | 95,000 |
| Wages due to employees but not paid | 2,000 |
| Vehicles | 8,000 |
| Five-year loan from a bank | 20,000 |

Explain how the balance sheet will change for each of the following transactions:

(a)  The wages due to the employees are paid at £2,000.

(b)  One-quarter of the inventory (stock) of goods held for resale is destroyed by fire and there is no insurance to cover the loss.

(c)  Goods for resale are bought on credit at a cost of £5,000.

**There are no questions in the C series for this chapter.**

## Activities for study groups

Return to the annual reports your group obtained for the exercise in Chapter 1. Find the balance sheet, income statement (profit and loss account) and cash flow statement. Use the outline formats contained in this chapter to identify the main areas of each of the published statements. Work together in preparing a list of features which make the formats useful to the reader. Note also any aspects of the presentation which you find unhelpful at this stage. (It may be useful to look back on this note at the end of the course as a collective check on whether your understanding and awareness of annual report items has improved.)

## Supplement to Chapter 3

# Using the accounting equation to analyse transactions

*In the main body of the chapter the transactions of P. Mason's legal practice are set out in summary form and are then presented in financial statements. This supplement goes back one stage and looks at the transactions and events for the month of September which resulted in the summary and financial statements shown in the chapter.*

The list of transactions and events is as follows:

| | |
|---|---|
| Sept. 1 | P. Mason deposits £140,000 in a bank account to commence the business under the name *P. Mason's legal practice*. |
| Sept. 1 | P. Mason's legal practice borrows £150,000 from a finance business to help with the intended purchase of a property for use as an office. The loan is to be repaid in five years' time. |
| Sept. 1 | A property is purchased at a cost of £75,000 for the land and £175,000 for the buildings. The full price is paid from the bank account. |
| Sept. 3 | Office furniture is purchased from Stylecraft at a cost of £30,000. The full price is to be paid within 90 days. |
| Sept. 5 | An insurance premium of £540 is paid in advance. The insurance cover will commence on 1 October. |
| Sept. 8 | An applicant is interviewed for a post of legal assistant. She agrees to start work on 10 September for a salary of £24,000 per annum. |
| Sept. 11 | Invoices are sent to some clients for work done in preparing contracts for them. The total of the invoiced amounts is £8,820. Clients are allowed up to 30 days to pay. |
| Sept. 19 | Cheques received from clients in payment of invoices amount to £7,620. |
| Sept. 26 | Payment is made to Stylecraft for the amount due for office furniture, £30,000. |
| Sept. 28 | Bills are received as follows: for computer rental and on-line searches, £1,500; gas, £100; electricity, £200; and telephone/fax, £1,000. |
| Sept. 30 | Legal assistant is paid salary of £1,800 for period to end of month. |

In the Supplement to Chapter 2 a table was prepared, based on the accounting equation, showing the classification used for debit and credit bookkeeping entries. As a reminder, the form of the equation used to derive the debit and credit rules is:

| **Assets** | equals | **Liabilities** | plus | **Ownership interest** |
|---|---|---|---|---|

As a further reminder, the rules are set out again in Exhibit 3.9. Each of the transactions of P. Mason's legal practice for the month of September is now analysed in terms of the effect on the accounting equation and the resulting debit and credit entries which would be made in the accounting records.

Exhibit 3.9
**Rules for debit and credit recording**

|  | Debit entries in a ledger account | Credit entries in a ledger account |
|---|---|---|
| *Left-hand side of the equation* |  |  |
| Asset | Increase | Decrease |
| *Right-hand side of the equation* |  |  |
| Liability | Decrease | Increase |
| Ownership interest | Expense | Revenue |
|  | Capital withdrawn | Capital contributed |

## Analysis of each transaction

Sept. 1    P. Mason deposits £140,000 in a bank account to commence the business under the name *P. Mason's legal practice.*

The business acquires an asset (cash in the bank) and an ownership interest is created through contribution of capital.

| *Transaction number: 1* | Debit | Credit |
|---|---|---|
| Asset | Bank £140,000 |  |
| Ownership interest |  | Capital contributed £140,000 |

Sept. 1    P. Mason's legal practice borrows £150,000 from a finance business to help with the intended purchase of a property for use as an office. The loan is to be repaid in five years' time.

The business acquires an asset of cash and a long-term liability is created.

| *Transaction number: 2* | Debit | Credit |
|---|---|---|
| Asset | Bank £150,000 |  |
| Liability |  | Long-term loan £150,000 |

Sept. 1    A property is purchased at a cost of £75,000 for the land and £175,000 for the buildings. The full price is paid from the bank account.

The business acquires an asset of land and buildings (£250,000 in total) and the asset of cash in the bank is reduced.

| *Transaction number: 3* | Debit | Credit |
|---|---|---|
| Asset | Land and buildings £250,000 | Bank £250,000 |

Sept. 3    Office furniture is purchased from Stylecraft at a cost of £30,000. The full price is to be paid within 90 days.

The business acquires an asset of furniture and also acquires a liability to pay the supplier, Stylecraft. The liability is called a trade payable (creditor).

| Transaction number: 4 | Debit | Credit |
|---|---|---|
| Asset | Furniture £30,000 | |
| Liability | | Trade payable (Stylecraft) £30,000 |

Sept. 5    An insurance premium of £540 is paid in advance. The insurance cover will commence on 1 October.

The business acquires an asset of prepaid insurance (the benefit of cover exists in the future) and the asset of cash at bank is reduced.

| Transaction number: 5 | Debit | Credit |
|---|---|---|
| Asset | Prepayment £540 | Bank £540 |

Sept. 8    An applicant is interviewed for a post of legal assistant. She agrees to start work on 10 September for a salary of £24,000 per annum.

The successful outcome of the interview is an *event* and there is an expected future benefit from employing the new legal assistant. The employee will be controlled by the organisation through a contract of employment. The organisation has a commitment to pay her the agreed salary. It could be argued that the offer of employment, and acceptance of that offer, create an asset of the human resource and a liability equal to the future salary. That does not happen because the *recognition* conditions are applied and it is felt too risky to recognise an asset when there is insufficient evidence of the future benefit. Commercial prudence dictates that it is preferable to wait until the employee has done some work and pay her at the end of the month for work done during the month. The accounting process is similarly prudent and no accounting recognition takes place until the payment has occurred. Even then it is the expense of the past which is recognised, rather than the asset of benefit for the future.

Sept. 11    Invoices are sent to some clients showing fees due for work done in preparing contracts for them. The total of the invoiced amounts is £8,820. Clients are allowed up to 30 days to pay.

Earning fees is the main activity of the legal practice. Earning fees makes the owner better off and is an example of the more general activity *of increasing the ownership interest* by creating revenue. The clients have not yet paid and therefore the business has an asset called a **trade receivable (debtor)**.

| Transaction number: 6 | Debit | Credit |
|---|---|---|
| Asset | Trade receivables £8,820 | |
| Ownership interest (revenue) | | Fees for work done £8,820 |

Sept. 19    Cheques received from clients in payment of invoices amount to £7,620.

When the customers pay, the amount due to the business from debtors will be decreased. So the asset of trade receivables decreases and the asset of cash in the bank increases.

| Transaction number: 7 | Debit | Credit |
|---|---|---|
| Asset | Bank £7,620 | Trade receivables £7,620 |

Sept. 26    Payment is made to Stylecraft for the amount due for office furniture, £30,000.

The asset of cash in the bank decreases and the liability to Stylecraft decreases to nil.

| Transaction number: 8 | Debit | Credit |
|---|---|---|
| Asset | | Bank £30,000 |
| Liability | Trade payable (Stylecraft) £30,000 | |

Sept. 28    Bills are received as follows: for computer rental and on-line searches, £1,500; gas, £100; electricity, £200; and telephone/fax £1,000 (total £2,800).

The computer rental, on-line searches, gas, electricity and telephone have been used up during the period and are all expenses which reduce the ownership interest. They are unpaid and, therefore, a liability is recorded.

| Transaction number: 9 | Debit | Credit |
|---|---|---|
| Liability | | Trade payables £2,800 |
| Ownership interest | Expenses £2,800 | |

Sept. 30    Legal assistant is paid salary of £1,800 for period to end of month.

The asset of cash at bank decreases and the salary paid to the legal assistant is an expense of the month.

| Transaction number: 10 | Debit | Credit |
|---|---|---|
| Asset | | Bank £1,800 |
| Ownership interest | Expense £1,800 | |

## Summarising the debit and credit entries

The formal system of bringing together debit and credit entries is based on ledger accounts. These are explained in the supplement to Chapter 5. For the present it will be sufficient to use a spreadsheet (Exhibit 3.10) to show how the separate debit and credit entries analysed in this Supplement lead to the list of items used in the main part of the chapter as the basis for the financial statements presented there.

Exhibit 3.10
**Spreadsheet of transactions for P. Mason's legal practice, during the month of September**

| Date | Assets | | | | | Liabilities | | Ownership interest | | |
|---|---|---|---|---|---|---|---|---|---|---|
| | Land and buildings £ | Office furniture £ | Trade receivables £ | Pre-payments £ | Cash at bank £ | Trade payables £ | Bank loan £ | Revenue £ | Expenses £ | Owner's capital contributed £ |
| 1 Sept. | | | | | 140,000 Dr | | | | | 140,000 Cr |
| 1 Sept. | | | | | 150,000 Dr | | 150,000 Cr | | | |
| 1 Sept. | 250,000 Dr | | | | 250,000 Cr | | | | | |
| 3 Sept. | | 30,000 Dr | | | | 30,000 Cr | | | | |
| 5 Sept. | | | | 540 Dr | 540 Cr | | | | | |
| 11 Sept. | | | 8,820 Dr | | | | | 8,820 Cr | | |
| 19 Sept. | | | 7,620 Cr | | 7,620 Dr | | | | | |
| 26 Sept. | | | | | 30,000 Cr | 30,000 Dr | | | | |
| 28 Sept. | | | | | | 2,800 Cr | | | 2,800 Dr | |
| 30 Sept. | | | | | 1,800 Cr | | | | 1,800 Dr | |
| *Total debit entries in each column* | | | | | | | | | | |
| | 250,000 Dr | 30,000 Dr | 8,820 Dr | 540 Dr | 297,620 Dr | 30,000 Dr | nil | nil | 4,600 Dr | nil |
| *Total credit entries in each column* | | | | | | | | | | |
| | nil | nil | 7,620 Cr | nil | 282,340 Cr | 32,800 Cr | 150,000 Cr | 8,820 Cr | nil | 140,000 Cr |
| *Surplus of debits over credits (or credits over debits)* | | | | | | | | | | |
| | 250,000 Dr | 30,000 Dr | 1,200 Dr | 540 Dr | 15,280 Dr | 2,800 Cr | 150,000 Cr | 8,820 Cr | 4,600 Dr | 140,000 Cr |

In the spreadsheet there are dates which correspond to the dates of the foregoing ten separate analyses of transactions. The debit and credit entries are shown with Dr or Cr alongside to distinguish them. For each column all the debit entries are totalled and all the credit entries are totalled separately. The surplus of debits over credits (or credits over debits) is calculated and shown in the final line. This allows a summarised list to be prepared as shown in Exhibit 3.11.

A spreadsheet is useful where there are not too many entries, but ledger accounts become essential when the volume of information increases.

**Exhibit 3.11**
**Summary of debit and credit entries for each category of asset, liability and ownership interest**

|  | Debit | Credit |
|---|---|---|
|  | £ | £ |
| Assets |  |  |
| Land and buildings | 250,000 |  |
| Office furniture | 30,000 |  |
| Trade receivables (debtors) | 1,200 |  |
| Prepayment | 540 |  |
| Cash at bank | 15,280 |  |
| Liabilities |  |  |
| Trade payables (creditors) |  | 2,800 |
| Long-term loan |  | 150,000 |
| Ownership interest |  |  |
| Revenue |  | 8,820 |
| Expenses | 4,600 |  |
| Capital contributed |  | 140,000 |
| Totals | 301,620 | 301,620 |

*Note*: The totals of each column have no particular meaning, but they should always be equal because of the symmetry of the debit and credit records, and so are useful as an arithmetic check that no item has been omitted or recorded incorrectly.

Turning the spreadsheet back to a vertical listing, using the debit column for items where the debits exceed the credits, and using the credit column for items where the credits exceed the debits, the list becomes as in Exhibit 3.11. You will see that this list is the basis of the information provided about P. Mason's legal practice in the main body of the chapter, except that the debit and credit notation was not used there.

**Activity 3.4**

*The most serious problem faced by most students, once they have understood the basic approach, is that of making errors. Look back through this Supplement and think about the errors which might have been made. What type of error would be detected by finding totals in Exhibit 3.11 which were not in agreement? What type of error would not be detected in this way because the totals would be in agreement despite the error? Types of error will be dealt with in the supplement to Chapter 5.*

## S    Test your understanding

**S3.1**    [S] Analyse the debit and credit aspect of each transaction listed at (a), (b) and (c) of question **B3.2**.

**S3.2**    Prepare a spreadsheet similar to that presented in Exhibit 3.10, setting out on the first line the items contained in the list of assets and liabilities of question **B3.2** and then on lines 2, 3 and 4 adding in the transactions (a), (b) and (c). Calculate the totals of each column of the spreadsheet and show that the accounting equation remains equal on both sides.

# Chapter 4

# Ensuring the quality of financial statements

## 2004/05 Group highlights

|  |  | Reported basis | At constant exchange rates[1][2] |
|---|---|---|---|
| Like for like sales |  | up 5.0% |  |
| Sales | £1,614.4m | up 0.6%[2] | up 7.8% |
| Operating profit | £218.9m | up 4.1%[2] | up 11.3% |
| Profit before tax | £210.3m | up 5.3%[2] | up 12.1% |
| Earnings per share[3] | 8.2p | up 9.3%[2] | up 15.5% |
| Dividend per share | 3.0p | up 20.0% |  |
| Return on capital employed[3] | 26.5% | up from 25.9%[2] |  |
| Gearing[3] | 11.3% | down from 11.8%[2] |  |

(1) See page 29 for reconciliation to Generally Accepted Accounting Principles ('GAAP') figures.
(2) 2000/01 to 2003/04 restated for the implementation in 2004/05 of the amendment to FRS 5, 'Application Note G – Revenue Recognition'.
(3) Earnings per share, return on capital employed and gearing are defined on page 130.
(4) 53 week year.

## Introduction

The key drivers of operating profitability are the:

● rate of sales growth,
● balance between like for like sales growth and sales from new store space,
● achieved gross margin,
● level of cost increases experienced by the Group,
● level of net bad debt charge relating to the in-house credit card in the US, and
● movements in the US dollar to pound sterling exchange rate, since the majority of the Group's profits are generated in the US and the Group reports in pounds sterling.

Source: Signet Group plc Annual Report and Accounts 2005, inside cover and p. 24.

## Discussion points

1 How does the company present the information it regards as most relevant to the needs of readers?

2 The group provides information 'at constant exchange rates' to eliminate the effects of exchange rate fluctuations. How relevant is this information to the needs of users?

## Contents

## Learning outcomes

After studying this chapter you should be able to:

- List and explain the qualitative characteristics desirable in financial statements.
- Explain the approach to measurement used in financial statements.
- Explain why there is more than one view on the role of prudence in accounting.
- Understand and explain how and why financial reporting is regulated or influenced by external authorities.
- Be aware of the process by which financial statements are reviewed by an investor.

## 4.1  Introduction

The previous chapter used the accounting equation as a basis for explaining the structure of financial statements. It showed that design of formats for financial statements is an important first step in creating an understandable story from a list of accounting data.

The objective of financial statements is to provide information about the financial position, performance and changes in financial position of an entity that is useful to a wide range of users in making economic decisions.[1]

Information about financial position is provided in a **balance sheet**. Information about performance is provided in an **income statement** (profit and loss account).[2] Information about changes in the cash position is provided in a **cash flow statement**. These three statements were explained in outline in Chapter 3. Information about changes in financial position is also provided in a separate statement, described in Chapter 12. Notes to the financial statements provide additional information relevant to the needs of users. These notes may include information about risks and uncertainties relating to assets, liabilities, revenue and expenses.[3]

## 4.2  Qualitative characteristics of financial statements

The IASB *Framework* sets out qualitative characteristics that make the information provided in financial statements useful to users. The four principal qualitative characteristics are:

- understandability
- relevance
- reliability
- comparability.[4]

The principal qualitative characteristics of relevance and reliability have further subheadings, as follows:

- relevance
  - materiality
- reliability
  - faithful representation
  - substance over form
  - neutrality
  - prudence
  - completeness.

Each of these characteristics is now described.

### 4.2.1  Understandability

It is essential that the information provided in financial statements is readily **understandable** by users.[5] Users are assumed to have a reasonable knowledge of business and economic activities and accounting, and a willingness to study the information with reasonable diligence. Information on complex matters should not be omitted from financial statements merely on the grounds that some users may find it difficult to understand.

## Relevance

Information has the quality of **relevance** when it influences the economic decisions of users by helping them evaluate past, present or future events or confirming, or correcting, their past evaluations.[6]

Information has a predictive role in helping users to look to the future. Predictive value does not necessarily require a forecast. Explaining unusual aspects of current performance helps users to understand future potential. Information also has a confirmatory role in showing users how the entity has, or has not, met their expectations.[7]

### Materiality

Information is **material** if its omission or misstatement could influence the economic decisions of users taken on the basis of the financial statements. Materiality depends on the size of the item or error judged in the particular circumstances of its omission or misstatement.[8]

The IASB *Framework* takes the view that materiality is a cut-off point in deciding whether information is important to users. The description of an item may make it material. The amount of an item may make it material.

For example, the balance sheet of a business shows inventories of raw materials and inventories of finished goods as two separate items. That is because the users of financial statements are interested in the types of inventory held as well as the amount of each. The risks of holding raw materials are different from the risks of holding finished goods. However the inventory of finished goods is not separated into the different types of finished goods because that would give too much detail when the risks of holding finished goods are relatively similar for all items.

## Reliability

Information has the quality of **reliability** when it is free from material error and bias and can be depended upon by users to represent faithfully what it either purports to represent or could reasonably be expected to represent.[9]

Information may be relevant but so unreliable that it could be misleading (e.g. where a director has given a highly personal view of the value of an investment). On the other hand, it could be reliable but quite non-relevant (e.g. the information that a building standing in the centre of a major shopping street was bought for 50 guineas some 300 years ago).

### Faithful representation

**Faithful representation** is important if accounting information is to be reliable. Faithful representation involves the words as well as the numbers in the financial statements. Sometimes it may be difficult for the managers of an entity to find the right words to describe a transaction and convey the problems of making reliable measurement. In such cases it will be important to disclose the risk of error surrounding recognition and measurement.[10]

### Substance over form

If information is to meet the test of faithful representation, then the method of accounting must reflect the **substance** of the economic reality of the transaction and not merely its **legal form**.

For example, a company has sold its buildings to a bank to raise cash and then pays rent for the same buildings for the purpose of continued occupation. The company carries all the risks and problems (such as repairs and insurance) that an owner would carry. One view is that the commercial substance of that sequence of transactions is comparable to ownership. Another view is that the legal form of the transaction is a sale. The characteristic of substance over form requires that the information in the financial statements should show the commercial substance of the situation.[11]

### Neutrality

The information contained in financial statements must be **neutral**. This is also described as being 'free from bias'. Financial statements are not neutral if, by the selection and presentation of information, they influence the making of a decision or judgement in order to achieve a predetermined result or outcome.[12]

This condition is quite difficult to enforce because it has to be shown that the entity producing the financial statements is trying to influence the decisions or judgements of all members of a class of users of the information. It would be impractical to know the decision-making process of every individual user.

### Prudence

The preparers of financial statements have to contend with uncertainty surrounding many events and circumstances. The existence of uncertainties is recognised by the disclosure of their nature and extent and by the exercise of **prudence** in the preparation of the financial statements. Prudence is the inclusion of a degree of caution in the exercise of the judgements needed in making the estimates required under conditions of uncertainty, such that gains and assets are not overstated and losses and liabilities are not understated.[13]

### Completeness

It almost goes without saying that information cannot be reliable if it is not **complete**. The information in financial statements must be complete, within the bounds of materiality and cost. An omission can cause information to be false or misleading and thus to lack reliability and relevance.[14]

### 4.2.4   Comparability

**Comparability** means that users must be able to compare the financial statements of an enterprise over time to identify trends in its financial position and performance. Users must also be able to compare the financial statements of different enterprises to evaluate their relative financial position, performance and changes in financial position.[15] Financial statements should show corresponding information for the previous period.[16]

### Consistency

This concerns the measurement and display of the financial effect of like transactions and other events being carried out in a consistent way throughout an entity within each accounting period and from one period to the next, and also in a consistent way by different entities.[17]

However, the need for **consistency** should not be allowed to become an impediment to the introduction of improved accounting practices. Consistency does not require absolute uniformity.[18]

### Disclosure of accounting policies

This is another important aspect of **comparability**. **Disclosure** means that users of financial statements must be informed of the accounting policies employed in the preparation of financial statements. Managers must also disclose changes in accounting policies and the effect of those changes.[19]

**Exhibit 4.1**
**UK ASB: Relationships of the qualitative characteristics of financial information**

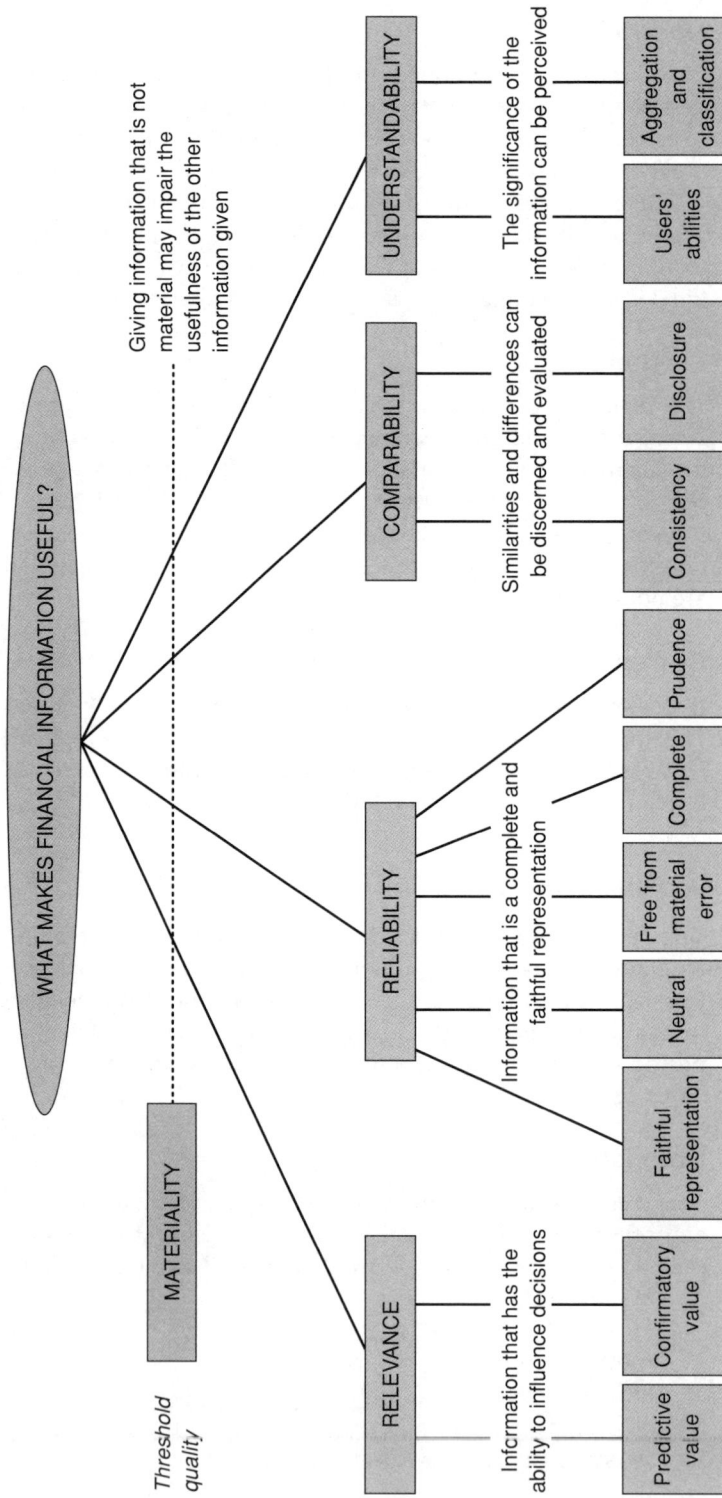

*Source:* ASB (1999), *Statement of Principles for Financial Reporting*, p. 34. Reproduced with the permission of the Accounting Standards Board.

The annual report of a company will usually have a separate section headed 'Accounting policies'. It will be located immediately after the primary financial statements, leading into the detailed notes to the accounts. The statement of accounting policies is essential reading for any user of the annual report.

### 4.2.5    Constraints on relevant and reliable information

**Relevance** and **reliability** are twin targets which may cause some tension in deciding the most appropriate way to report accounting information. There is a trade-off between relevance and reliability when it comes to ensuring that information is delivered in a timely manner so that it is still relevant, and when it comes to deciding whether the costs of producing further information exceed the benefits.

#### Timeliness

If information is provided in a timely way, the reliability may be less than 100% because some aspects of a transaction are not yet complete. If reporting is delayed until all aspects of a transaction are known then the relevance may be less than 100% because investors have become tired of waiting. The balance of **timeliness** is achieved by considering how best to serve the needs of users in making economic decisions.[20]

#### Benefit and cost

The benefits derived from information should be greater than the costs of providing it. The analysis is complicated because the benefits fall mainly on the users, while the costs fall mainly on the provider. It is important for standard-setters to consider the benefits and costs as a whole.[21]

### 4.2.6    UK ASB

The UK ASB's representation of the relationships between the various qualitative characteristics is set out in Exhibit 4.1.[22]

In many ways the ideas of the UK ASB reflect those of the IASB which were written ten years earlier. However during that ten-year period the ASB had time to benefit by thinking about ways of clarifying some aspects of the IASB's ideas. One difference in presentation is that the ASB suggests that materiality is a test to be applied at the threshold of considering an item. If any information is not material, it does not need to be considered further.

**Activity 4.1**    *Look back to Exhibit 4.1. Is there any aspect of that diagram which came as no surprise to you? Is there any aspect of that diagram which was a surprise to you? Having read the explanations in this section, do you hold the same surprise that you did at the outset? With the benefit of hindsight, can you explain why you were surprised or not surprised? Has this analysis caused you to modify your own objectives for what you hope to learn from this book?*

## 4.3    Measurement in financial statements

You have seen in Chapter 2, sections 2.5 and 2.8, that the recognition of assets and liability requires reliability of measurement. You have seen in Chapter 3 the methods of presentation of accounting information containing numbers that represent measurement. We now need to know more about the accounting measurement principles that establish reliability and about the disclosure of information that allows users of financial statements to understand the measurement process.

The accounting measurement principles that are most widely known in the UK are found within the Companies Act 1985:[23]

- going concern
- accruals
- consistency
- prudence.

The IASB *Framework* describes the accrual basis and going concern as 'underlying assumptions' in the preparation of financial statements. It describes **prudence** as a 'constraint' on relevance and reliability. Consistency is an aspect of comparability.

### 4.3.1    Going concern

**Definition**

> The financial statements are normally prepared on the assumption that an entity is a **going concern** and will continue in operation for the foreseeable future. Hence, it is assumed that the entity has neither the intention nor the need to liquidate or curtail materially the scale of its operations; if such an intention or need exists the financial statements may have to be prepared on a different basis and, if so, the basis used is disclosed.[24]

The UK Companies Act statement on **going concern** is rather like a crossword clue, in being short and enigmatic. It states: 'The company shall be presumed to be carrying on business as a going concern.' More guidance is needed on measurement.

For companies applying UK accounting standards there is guidance in FRS 18. It requires an entity to prepare its financial statements on a going concern basis unless the entity is being liquidated or has ceased trading, when a 'break-up' valuation may be more appropriate. On a forced sale, very little is obtained for the assets of a business. If the company is still operating but the directors are aware of conditions that cast doubts on the company's ability to continue as a going concern, they should disclose those uncertainties. They must take into account all available information about the 'foreseeable future'.

If the company is staying in business then the directors are allowed to use valuations that reflect continuity. They do not have to report 'break-up' values, which are values for immediate sale of assets. Investors are probably quite happy when the company is continuing as a going concern. They will be more concerned about the risk that it will not continue. For that reason, the directors are required to make a statement in their report to confirm that the business remains a 'going concern' for the foreseeable future. There is no readily available definition of 'foreseeable future' but the guidance given in the UK to directors and auditors points towards considering a period of 12 months from the balance sheet date.

### 4.3.2    Accruals (also called 'matching')

**Definition**

> Under the **accruals** basis, the effects of transactions and other events are recognised when they occur (and not as cash or its equivalent is received or paid) and they are recorded in the accounting records and reported in the financial statements of the periods to which they relate.[25]

The IASB explains that financial statements prepared on the accruals basis are useful for stewardship purposes because they report past transactions and events but are also helpful to users for forward-looking information because they show obligations to pay cash in the future and resources that represent cash to be received in the future.

The UK Companies Act explains the accruals concept as a requirement that all income and charges (i.e. expenses) relating to the financial year shall be taken into account, without regard to the date of receipt or payment.

The word 'accrue' means 'to fall due' or 'to come as a natural result'. If, during a year, a company sells £100m of goods but collects only £80m from customers, it records sales as £100m in the profit and loss account. The cash yet to be collected from customers is reported as an asset called 'debtor' in the balance sheet. If, during the year, it uses electricity costing £50m but has only paid £40m so far, it records the expense of £50m in the profit and loss account. The unpaid electricity bill is reported as a liability called 'accruals' in the balance sheet.

The idea of matching is also used in applying the idea of accruals. Matching has two forms, matching losses or gains against time and matching expenses against revenue. Time matching occurs when a gain or loss is spread over the relevant period of time, such as receiving interest on a loan or paying rent on a property. Matching of revenues and expenses occurs when costs such as labour are matched against the revenue earned from providing goods or services.

### 4.3.3     Consistency

Consistency is described in the IASB *Framework* as an aspect of comparability (see section 4.2.4). The UK Companies Act requires that accounting policies shall be applied consistently within the same accounts and from one period to the next.

### 4.3.4     Prudence

The Companies Act does not define prudence but uses the word prudent in relation to measurement. It requires that the amount of any item shall be determined on a prudent basis, and in particular:

(a) only profits realised at the balance sheet date shall be included in the profit and loss account; and
(b) all liabilities and losses which have arisen or are likely to arise in respect of the financial year shall be taken into account, including those which only become apparent between the balance sheet date and the date on which it is signed by the board of directors.

The UK ASB has said that decisions about recognition of income or assets and of expenses or liabilities require evidence of existence and reliability of measurement. Stronger evidence and greater reliability of measurement are required for assets and gains than for liabilities and losses.[26]

### 4.3.5     Realisation

There is no clear statement of the conditions that will make a profit **realised**. It is not specifically defined in the IASB system. It is an example of an idea that is so widely used that it appears to be almost impossible to explain. If you turn to a dictionary you will find 'realise' equated to 'convert into cash'. The accounting standard FRS 18[27] confirms that it is the general view that profits shall be treated as realised when evidenced in the form of cash or other assets whose cash **realisation** is reasonably certain. However, the standard avoids linking realisation to 'prudence', explaining that a focus on cash does not reflect more recent developments in financial markets. Evidence of 'reasonable certainty' in such markets does not necessarily require cash. It is based on confidence in the reliable operation of the market.

*Take a piece of paper having two wide columns. Head the left-hand column 'My thoughts on measurement in accounting' and head the right-hand column 'What the book tells me about measurement'. Fill in both columns and then exchange your paper with a fellow student. Discuss with each other any similarities and differences in the left-hand column and relate these to your personal views and prior experience. Discuss with each other any similarities and differences in the right-hand column and evaluate the extent to which different people see books differently. Finally, discuss with each other the extent to which reading this section has changed your views on measurement as a subject in accounting.*

## 4.4 Views on prudence

The Companies Act makes an explicit link between prudence and realisation that reflects UK accounting practice when the Companies Act was written. The IASB's *Framework* avoids mentioning realisation and describes prudence in terms of 'a degree of caution'.[28] From the UK ASB, the standard FRS 18 acknowledges the meaning of realisation but breaks the link between realisation and prudence.[29] Because FRS 18 is relatively new, it is not possible to say whether it will change the entrenched conservatism of accounting practice which tends towards understatement on grounds of caution. Where does that leave the student of accounting who wants to understand the meaning of prudence?

The most important message for students of accounting (and for many practitioners) is contained in the IASB's *Framework*:[30]

> *. . . the exercise of prudence does not allow . . . the deliberate understatement of assets or income, or the deliberate overstatement of liabilities or expenses, because the financial statements would not be neutral and, therefore, not have the quality of reliability.*

Why are there different views on understatement and overstatement, depending on the item being reported? Here is your first chance to use the accounting equation to solve a problem:

| **Assets** | minus | **Liabilities** | equals | **Capital contributed/withdrawn** plus **Profit** |
|---|---|---|---|---|

| **Profit** | equals | **Revenue** minus **Expenses** |
|---|---|---|

*Ask yourself what will happen to profit in the accounting equation if the amount of an asset is increased while the liabilities and the capital contributed remain the same. Then ask yourself what will happen to profit in the accounting equation if the amount of a liability is decreased while the assets and the capital contributed remain the same. Next ask yourself what will happen to profit if revenue is overstated. Finally ask yourself what will happen to profit if expenses are understated.*

Assuming that capital contributed/withdrawn remains constant, overstating assets will overstate profit. Understating liabilities will overstate profit. Overstating revenue will overstate profit. Understating expenses will overstate profit.

### Examples

A market trader buys £100 of stock on credit, promising to pay the supplier at the end of the day. The trader sells three-quarters of the stock at a price of £90 and takes the rest home to keep for next week's market. At the end of the day the trader has £90 in cash, one-quarter of the stock which cost £25, and owes £100 to the supplier. How much profit has the trader made? The answer is that the profit is £15 (£90 received for the sale of stock less the cost of the items sold, £75, being three-quarters of the stock purchased). The accounting equation is:

| Assets minus Liabilities at the end of the period | equals | Ownership interest at the start of the period plus Capital contributed/ withdrawn plus Revenue of the period minus Expenses of the period |
|---|---|---|
| stock £25 + cash £90 – liability £100 | equals | nil + nil + revenue £90 – expenses £75 |
| £15 | equals | £15 |

1   Supposing the trader 'forgets' part of the liability and thinks it is only £84 owing, rather than £100. The assets remain at stock £25 + cash £90, which equals £115. The liability is now thought to be £84 and therefore the equation becomes:

| £25 + £90 – £84 | equals | nil + nil + revenue £90 – expenses £75 + [?] £16 [?] |
|---|---|---|
| £31 | equals | £31 |

For the equation to be satisfied there must be a total of £31 on both sides. The total of £31 is therefore written in. The recorded profit is still only £15, calculated as revenue £90 minus expenses £75, so there is a 'hole' amounting to £16 on the right-hand side of the equation. The accounting equation has to balance so the extra £16 is written in, surrounded by question marks, on the right-hand side. It is assumed on the right-hand side that the trader has either forgotten to record revenue of £16 or has recorded too much expense, so that the amount appears to represent an unexplained profit. Thus *understating a liability will overstate profit*. That favourable news might mislead a competitor or investor. It might be bad news when the Inland Revenue demands tax on profit of £31. Also there is the unpaid supplier who may not be entirely patient when offered £84 rather than £100.

2   Supposing instead that the trader 'forgets' there is some unsold stock left. The only recorded asset would be the cash at £90 and there would be a liability of £100. This gives negative net assets of (£10) and, because the accounting equation has to balance, suggests that there is a 'forgotten' expense of £25 on the right-hand side. The equation then becomes:

| £90 – £100 | equals | nil + nil + £90 – £75 – [?] £25 [?] |
|---|---|---|
| (£10) | equals | (£10) |

This would cause the Inland Revenue to ask a lot of questions as to why there was no record of stock remaining, because they know that omitting stock from the record is a well-tried means of fraudulently reducing profits and therefore reducing tax bills. *Understating an asset will understate profit*.

These two examples have illustrated the meaning of the warning that deliberate understatement or overstatement is not acceptable. The general message of prudence is: *avoid overstating profit*. In down-to-earth terms, don't raise the readers' hopes too high, only to have to tell them later that it was all in the imagination.

## 4.5 Regulation of financial reporting

Because the external users of accounting information do not have day-to-day access to the records of the business, they rely on the integrity and judgement of management to provide suitable information of a high quality. But will the management be honest, conscientious and careful in providing information? In an ideal world there should be no problem for investors in a company because, as shareholders, they appoint the directors and may dismiss them if dissatisfied with the service provided. However, the world is not ideal. Some companies are very large and they have many shareholders whose identity changes as shares are bought and sold. Over the years it has been found that regulation is needed particularly for financial reporting by companies. The general regulation of companies in the UK is provided by parliamentary legislation, through the Companies Act 1985.

However since 2005 the regulation of financial reporting by UK companies has taken two separate routes depending on the type of company.

The group financial statements of listed companies must comply with the IAS Regulation set by the European Commission. The IAS Regulation takes precedence over the relevant sections of the Companies Act. The IAS Regulation was issued in 2002, requiring listed group financial statements from 2005 to apply approved International Financial Reporting Standards, IFRS (previously called International Accounting Standards, IAS). The UK government subsequently permitted individual companies and non-listed groups to choose to apply IFRS. Any companies not taking up this choice must continue to apply the relevant sections of the Companies Act and follow the accounting standards set by the UK Accounting Standards Board (ASB). Other organisations that are not companies (such as sole traders, partnership, public sector bodies) have to look to the regulations that govern their operations to decide which accounting guidance to follow.

So how can we tell which accounting system has been applied in any situation? Look first for the audit report, if there is one. That will include a paragraph starting 'In our opinion'. In that paragraph the auditors will specify the accounting system on which their opinion is based. If there is no auditors' report, look for the Note on Accounting Policies. There will usually be a paragraph stating the accounting system that has been applied.

### 4.5.1 The IAS Regulation

In 2002 the European Commission issued the *IAS Regulation* which took effect from 1 January 2005. Its purpose is to harmonise the financial information presented by public listed companies in order to ensure a high degree of transparency and comparability of financial statements. The Regulation is relatively short but has been extended and clarified by a trail of subsequent documents. The European Commission publishes all documents on its website[31] in the languages of all Member States but that is more detail than is necessary for a first year course.

A Regulation is directly applicable in Member States. It has a higher status than a Directive, which is an instruction to Member States on the content of their national laws. Before the Regulation was issued, the company law of Member States was harmonised by following the Fourth and Seventh Directives on company law. Companies in Member States did not need to know the Directives because the national company law applied the Directives. Now that the IAS Regulation is directly applicable, Member States must ensure that they do not seek to apply to a company any additional elements of national law that are contrary to, conflict with or restrict a company's compliance with IASs.

The Commission decides on the applicability of IFRS within the Community. It is assisted by an Accounting Regulatory Committee and is advised by a technical group called the European Financial Reporting and Accounting Group EFRAG.[32] The tests for adoption of IFRS are that the standards:

(a)  do not contradict specific principles of the Fourth and Seventh Directive,
(b)  are conducive to the European public good, and
(c)  meet the criteria of understandability, relevance, reliability and comparability required of financial information needed for making economic decisions and assessing the stewardship of management.

A standard that is adopted is said to be **endorsed**. If a standard is awaiting endorsement, or is rejected, it may be used as guidance if it is not inconsistent with endorsed standards. If a rejected standard is in conflict with adopted standards, it may not be used. When the European Commission first announced the endorsement process there were fears expressed that this would be used to create 'European IFRS' by selecting some IFRS and rejecting others. The Commission's reply was that the EU cannot give its powers to a body (the IASB) that is not subject to EU jurisdiction, and it is necessary for the EU to endorse standards as part of its duty in setting laws for Member States.

## 4.5.2    UK company law

### Companies Act 1985

The Companies Act 1985 sets many rules for investing in and operating companies. Parts of the Act cover the information presented in financial statements. For companies and other organisations that do not follow the IAS Regulation, the Companies Act 1985 prescribes formats of presentation of the balance sheet and profit and loss account. Companies must select one of the permitted formats. It also prescribes methods of valuation of the assets and liabilities contained in the balance sheet, broadly expecting that normally these items will be recorded at their cost at the date of acquisition, subject to diminutions in value since that date. Some other approaches to valuation are permitted, but these are carefully regulated and are subject to requirements for prudence, consistency and an expectation that the business is a going concern (i.e. will continue for some time into the future). The UK legislation places strong emphasis on the requirement to present a **true and fair** view in financial statements.

Since the early 1980s company law on financial reporting has been harmonised with that of other Member States in the EU through the Fourth and Seventh Directives of the EU (*see* Chapter 7).

The directors are responsible for the preparation of company accounts. Exhibit 4.2 sets out the statement made by directors of one major public company regarding their responsibilities in these matters. This type of statement will be found in the annual reports of most of the large listed companies. It is regarded as an important aspect of giving reassurance to investors and others that there is a strong system of corporate governance within the company. It is also intended to clarify any misunderstandings the shareholders may have about the work of directors as distinct from the work of the auditors (*see* below).

The Companies (Audit, Investigations and Community Enterprise) Act, 2004 made changes intended to improve the reliability of financial reporting, the independence of auditors and disclosure to auditors. In particular it required a statement to be inserted in the directors' report confirming that there is no relevant information that has not been disclosed to the auditors. The role of the Financial Reporting Review Panel was strengthened by giving it new powers to require documents. HM Revenue and Customs was authorised to pass information about companies to the FRRP.

**Exhibit 4.2**
**Statement of directors' responsibilities as expressed in the annual report of a public limited company**

> **Statement of directors' responsibilities**
>
> Company law requires the directors to prepare accounts for each financial year which give a true and fair view of the state of affairs of the company and of the group and of the profit or loss and cash flows of the group for that period. In preparing these accounts, the directors have adopted suitable accounting policies and then applied them consistently, made judgements and estimates that are reasonable and prudent, followed applicable accounting standards and adopted the going concern basis.
>
> The directors are responsible for ensuring that the company keeps proper accounting records which disclose with reasonable accuracy at any time the financial position of the company and enable them to ensure that the accounts comply with the IAS Regulation/Companies Act 1985. They are also responsible for safeguarding the assets of the company and taking reasonable steps for the prevention and detection of fraud and other irregularities.

### Company Law Reform

A major inquiry into proposals for modernising company law, starting in the late 1990s,[33] led to a final report in 2001 which made recommendations to government. The government then issued a series of consultation documents leading in March 2005 to a White Paper[34] and draft legislation for further consultation. Changes in company law are usually slow, so it takes time for recommended changes to be put into action. Some changes are implemented ahead of others.

At the heart of the Company Law Review was the idea 'think small first'. This reflected a concern that company law has grown by being written for the larger company and then 'slimmed down' for the smaller company. This has tended to leave too great a burden on small companies. Focusing first on the small company should reduce the risk of excessive burden. Disclosure by small companies is described in outline in Chapter 7.

The government indicated that its law reform would also deal with a new EU Directive on audit. Audit is described further in section 4.5.11.

### 4.5.3   The Financial Reporting Council

The Financial Reporting Council (FRC)[35] describes itself as the UK's independent regulator for corporate reporting and governance. It is recognised in its regulatory role by the Department of Trade and Industry. The government effectively delegates responsibility to an independent body but maintains close interest in the strategy and operations of the FRC.

The FRC's aim is to promote confidence in corporate reporting and governance. To achieve this aim it sets itself five key objectives, in promoting:

● high quality corporate reporting
● high quality auditing
● high standards of corporate governance
● the integrity, competence and transparency of the accountancy profession
● its effectiveness as a unified independent regulator.

The FRC is one regulator but it has a wide range of functions:

- setting, monitoring and enforcing accounting and auditing standards
- statutory oversight and regulation of auditors
- operating an independent investigation and discipline scheme for public interest cases
- overseeing the regulatory activities of the professional accountancy bodies
- promoting high standards of corporate governance.

There are five operating bodies (subsidiaries of the FRC) to carry out these functions.

- Accounting Standards Board
- Auditing Practices Board
- Professional Oversight Board For Accountancy
- Financial Reporting Review Panel
- Accountancy Investigation & Discipline Board.

Each one of these is now described.

## 4.5.4 UK Accounting Standards Board

Traditionally, professions in the UK have been expected to regulate their own affairs and control their members. The accounting profession satisfied this expectation between 1970 and 1990 by forming the Accounting Standards Committee (ASC) and requiring members of each professional body to apply accounting standards or face disciplinary action. Over a period of years there was growing dissatisfaction with this pure self-regulatory model because the disciplinary aspects appeared to be applied only rarely and the existence of potential conflicts of self-interest was pointed to by some critics as weakening the standard-setting process. Consequently, in 1990 the purely self-regulatory approach was abandoned in favour of an independent regime having statutory backing, but retaining some self-regulatory features. The independent standard setting body was created as the Accounting Standards Board (ASB).

Since 1990 the ASB has published Financial Reporting Standards (FRSs) setting standards of practice which go beyond the requirements of company law in particular problem areas. In the period from 1970 to 1990 the standards set by the ASC were called Statements of Standard Accounting Practice (SSAPs). Those SSAPs which remained valid were adopted by the ASB and are gradually being replaced. SSAPs and FRSs collectively are referred to as 'accounting standards'. The Accounting Standards Board (ASB) is recognised as a standard-setting body under the Companies Act 1985.

The UK ASB is gradually harmonising its standards with those of the IASB so that eventually all companies will apply the same accounting standards, irrespective of whether they present financial statements under the IAS Regulation or the Companies Act. Until that happens there will continue to be some differences between ASB standards and IASB standards but in general this need not be of concern in a first year of study.

The ASB collaborates with accounting standard-setters from other countries and the IASB both in order to influence the development of international standards and in order to ensure that its standards are developed with due regard to international developments.

The ASB has up to ten Board members, of whom two (the Chairman and the Technical Director) are full-time, and the remainder, who represent a variety of interests, are part-time. ASB meetings are also attended by three observers. Under the ASB's constitution, votes of seven Board members (six when there are fewer than ten members) are required for any decision to adopt, revise or withdraw an accounting standard. Board members are appointed by a Nominations Committee comprising the chairman and fellow directors of the Financial Reporting Council (FRC).

The Accounting Standards Board is independent in its decisions on issuing standards. Before doing so the Board consults widely on all its proposals.

### 4.5.5 Auditing Practices Board

The Auditing Practices Board (APB) was established in April 2002, and replaces a previous APB which had been in place since 1991. APB is a part of the Financial Reporting Council. The APB is committed to leading the development of auditing practice in the UK and the Republic of Ireland so as to establish high standards of auditing, meet the developing needs of users of financial information and ensure public confidence in the auditing process.

### 4.5.6 Professional Oversight Board for Accountancy

The Professional Oversight Board for Accountancy (POBA) contributes to the achievement of the Financial Reporting Council's own fundamental aim of supporting investor, market and public confidence in the financial and governance stewardship of listed and other entities by:

- independent oversight of the regulation of the auditing profession by the recognised supervisory and qualifying bodies;
- monitoring the quality of the auditing function in relation to economically significant entities;
- independent oversight of the regulation of the accountancy profession by the professional accountancy bodies.

### 4.5.7 Financial Reporting Review Panel

When the Accounting Standards Board was established in 1990 it was felt to be important that there was a mechanism for enforcing accounting standards. An effective mechanism had been lacking in the previous process of setting standards. Accordingly the Financial Reporting Council established a Financial Reporting Review Panel (FRRP) which enquires into annual accounts where it appears that the requirements of the Companies Act, including the requirement that annual accounts shall show a true and fair view, might have been breached. The FRRP has the power to ask companies to revise their accounts where these are found to be defective. If companies do not voluntarily make such a revision, the FRRP may take proceedings in a court of law to require the company to revise its accounts. These powers are contained in the Companies Act 1985 and delegated to the FRRP by the Secretary of State for Trade and Industry. So far the FRRP has not found it necessary to resort to legal action, having found its powers of persuasion were sufficient.

The Financial Reporting Review Panel (FRRP), (referred to as 'the Panel') considers whether the annual accounts of public companies and large private companies comply with the requirements of the Companies Act 1985, including applicable accounting standards. The Panel does not offer advice on the application of accounting standards or the accounting requirements of the Companies Act 1985.

The Panel can ask directors to explain apparent departures from the requirements. If it is not satisfied by the directors' explanations it aims to persuade them to adopt a more appropriate accounting treatment. The directors may then voluntarily withdraw their accounts and replace them with revised accounts that correct the matters in error. Depending on the circumstances, the FRRP may accept another form of remedial action – for example, correction of the comparative figures in the next set of annual financial statements. Failing voluntary correction, the Panel can exercise its powers to secure the necessary revision of the original accounts through a court order. The FRRP has enjoyed a long and successful record in resolving all cases brought to its attention without having to apply for a court order. The Panel maintains a legal costs fund of £2m for this purpose. Also, if the case concerns accounts issued under listing rules, the Panel may report to the Financial Services Authority.

### 4.5.8 Accountancy Investigation and Discipline Board

The Accountancy Investigation and Discipline Board (AIDB) is the independent, investigative and disciplinary body for accountants in the UK. It has up to eight members. The AIDB is responsible for operating and administering an independent disciplinary scheme ('the Scheme') covering members of the major professional bodies.

The AIDB will deal with cases which raise or appear to raise important issues affecting the public interest in the UK and which need to be investigated to determine whether or not there has been any misconduct by an accountant or accountancy firm.

### 4.5.9 Committee on Corporate Governance

The Committee on Corporate Governance works to satisfy the FRC's responsibility for promoting high standards of corporate governance. It aims to do so by:

- maintaining an effective Combined Code on Corporate Governance and promoting its widespread application;
- ensuring that related guidance, such as that on internal control, is current and relevant;
- influencing EU and global corporate governance developments;
- helping to promote boardroom professionalism and diversity; and
- encouraging constructive interaction between company boards and institutional shareholders.

### 4.5.10 The Financial Services Authority

Under the Financial Services and Markets Act 2000, the Financial Services Authority (FSA) is a single regulator with responsibility across a wide range of financial market activity. It is required to maintain confidence in the UK financial system, to promote public understanding of the financial system, to secure protection for consumers and to reduce the scope for financial crime. The FSA is an independent, non-governmental body and receives no funds from government. It reports annually to Parliament through the Treasury.

The FSA regulates listing of companies' shares on the UK stock exchange. The work is carried out by a division called the UK Listing Authority (UKLA). When a company first has its shares listed, it must produce a prospectus, which is normally much more detailed than the annual report. The regulations covering the content of a prospectus are set by the UKLA. Once a company has achieved a listing, it must keep up with ongoing obligations under the Listing Rules, which includes providing accounting information to the market in the annual report and press releases. Details of the Listing Rules are not necessary for first-year study but if you are interested you can read them on the FSA's website: www.fsa.gov.uk.

### 4.5.11 Auditors

The shareholders of companies do not have a right of access to the records of the day-to-day running of the business, and so they need someone to act on their behalf to ensure that the directors are presenting a true and fair view of the company's position at a point in time and of the profits generated during a period of time. To achieve this reassurance, the shareholders appoint a firm of auditors to investigate

**Exhibit 4.3**
**Sample audit report**

---

**INDEPENDENT AUDITOR'S REPORT TO THE SHAREHOLDERS OF XYZ PLC**

We have audited the group financial statements of (name of entity) for the year ended . . . which comprise the Group Income Statement, the Group Balance Sheet, the Group Cash Flow Statement, the Group Statement of Change in Shareholders' Equity and the related notes. These group financial statements have been prepared under the accounting policies set out therein.

We have reported separately on the parent company financial statements of (name of entity) for the year ended and on the information in the Directors' Remuneration Report that is described as having been audited.

**Respective responsibilities of directors and auditors**
The directors' responsibilities for preparing the Annual Report and the group financial statements in accordance with applicable law and International Financial Reporting Standards (IFRSs) as adopted for use in the European Union are set out in the Statement of Directors' Responsibilities.

Our responsibility is to audit the group financial statements in accordance with relevant legal and regulatory requirements and International Standards on Auditing (UK and Ireland). We report to you our opinion as to whether the group financial statements give a true and fair view and whether the group financial statements have been properly prepared in accordance with the Companies Act 1985 and Article 4 of the IAS Regulation. We also report to you if, in our opinion, the Directors' Report is not consistent with the group financial statements, if we have not received all the information and explanations we require for our audit, or if information specified by law regarding director's remuneration and other transactions is not disclosed. We review whether the Corporate Governance Statement reflects the company's compliance with the nine provisions of the 2003 FRC Combined Code specified for our review by the Listing Rules of the Financial Services Authority, and we report if it does not. We are not required to consider whether the board's statements on internal control cover all risks and controls, or form an opinion on the effectiveness of the group's corporate governance procedures or its risk and control procedures.

We read other information contained in the Annual Report and consider whether it is consistent with the audited group financial statements. The other information comprises only [the Directors' Report, the Chairman's Statement, the Operating and Financial Review and the Corporate Governance Statement]. We consider the implications for our report if we become aware of any apparent misstatements or material inconsistencies with the group financial statements. Our responsibilities do not extend to any other information.

**Basis of audit opinion**
We conducted our audit in accordance with International Standards on Auditing (UK and Ireland) issued by the Auditing Practices Board. An audit includes examination, on a test basis, of evidence relevant to the amounts and disclosures in the group financial statements. It also includes an assessment of the significant estimates and judgments made by the directors in the preparation of the group financial statements, and of whether the accounting policies are appropriate to the group's circumstances, consistently applied and adequately disclosed.

We planned and performed our audit so as to obtain all the information and explanations which we considered necessary in order to provide us with sufficient evidence to give reasonable assurance that the group financial statements are free from material misstatement, whether caused by fraud or other irregularity or error. In forming our opinion we also evaluated the overall adequacy of the presentation of information in the group financial statements.

**Opinion**
In our opinion:
the group financial statements give a true and fair view, in accordance with IFRSs as adopted for use in the European Union, of the state of the group's affairs as at . . . and of its profit[loss] for the year then ended; and the group financial statements have been properly prepared in accordance with the Companies Act 1985 and Article 4 of the IAS Regulation.

Registered auditors' Address
Date

the company's financial records and give an opinion on the truth and fairness of the financial information presented. Exhibit 4.3 sets out the wording of a typical audit report to the shareholders of a public company. There are some words and phrases in this report which will become more familiar as you progress through the text. These include 'historical cost convention' (Chapter 14), 'revaluation of certain fixed assets' (Chapter 12) and 'accounting policies' (introduced in Chapter 3 but mentioned again at various points).

You will note that the auditors do not look at all the pages of the annual report. The earlier part of the annual report is important to the companies in setting the scene and explaining their businesses. These earlier pages are reviewed by the auditors to ensure that anything said there is consistent with the information presented in the audited financial statements. You will also note that the auditors have their own code of practice, referred to as International Standards for Auditing (ISAs). The ISAs are prepared by the International Auditing and Assurance Standards Board (IAASB) which operates under a body called the International Financial Accounting Committee (IFAC). The standards are then adopted by national standard setters. In the UK the national standard setter is the Auditing Practices Board (APB) which is one of the arms of the Financial Reporting Council.

What surprises some readers is the phrase 'reasonable assurance that the accounts are free from material misstatement'. The auditors are not expected to be totally certain in their opinion and they are only looking for errors or fraud which is material. The meaning of the word 'material' has proved difficult to define and it tends to be a matter left to the judgement of the auditor. The best guidance available is that an item is material if its misstatement or omission would cause the reader of the annual report (shareholder or creditor) to take a different decision or view based on the financial statements.

## 4.5.12 The tax system

Businesses pay tax to HM Revenue and Customs (as the tax collecting agent of the government) based on the profits they make. Sole traders and partnerships pay income tax on their profits while companies pay corporation tax. There are differences in detail of the law governing these two types of taxes but broadly they both require as a starting point a calculation of profit using commercial accounting practices. The law governing taxation is quite separate from the law and regulations governing financial reporting, so in principle the preparation of financial statements is not affected by tax matters. That is very different from some other countries in the EU where the tax law stipulates that an item must be in the financial accounting statements if it is to be considered for tax purposes. Those countries have an approach to financial reporting which is more closely driven by taxation matters.

In the UK the distinction may be blurred in practice in the case of sole traders because HM Revenue and Customs is the main user of the financial statements of the sole trader. Similarly, tax factors may influence partnership accounts, although here the fairness of sharing among the partners is also important. The very smallest companies, where the owners also run the business, may in practice have the same attitude to tax matters as does the sole trader or partnership. For larger companies with a wider spread of ownership, the needs of shareholders will take priority.

## 4.5.13 Is regulation necessary?

There are those who would argue that all this regulatory mechanism is unnecessary. They take the view that in a market-based economy, competitive forces will ensure that those providing information will meet the needs of users. It is argued that investors will not entrust their funds to a business which provides inadequate information. Banks will not lend money unless they are provided with sufficient information to answer their questions about the likelihood of receiving interest and eventual repayment of the loan. Employee morale may be lowered if a business appears non-communicative regarding its present position and past record of performance. Suppliers may not wish to give credit to a business which appears secretive or has a reputation for producing poor-quality information. Customers may be similarly doubtful.

Against that quite attractive argument for the abolition of all regulations stand some well-documented financial scandals where businesses have failed. Employees have lost their jobs, with little prospect of finding comparable employment elsewhere; suppliers have not been paid and have found themselves in financial difficulties as a result. Customers have lost a source of supply and have been unable to meet the requirements of their own customers until a new source is found. Those who have provided long-term finance for the business, as lenders and investors, have lost their investment. Investigation shows that the signs and warnings had existed for those who were sufficiently experienced to see them, but these signs and warnings did not emerge in the published accounting information for external use.

Such financial scandals may be few in number but the large-scale examples cause widespread misery and lead to calls for action. Governments experience pressure from the electorate and lobby groups; professional bodies and business interest groups decide they ought to be seen to react; and new regulations are developed which ensure that the particular problem cannot recur. All parties are then reasonably satisfied that they have done their best to protect those who need protection against the imbalance of business life, and the new practices are used until the next scandal occurs and the process starts over again.

There is no clear answer to the question 'Is regulation necessary?' Researchers have not found any strong evidence that the forces of supply and demand in the market fail to work and have suggested that the need for regulation must be justified by showing that the benefits exceed the costs. That is quite a difficult challenge but is worth keeping in mind as you explore some of the more intricate aspects of accounting regulation.

**Activity 4.4**

*Look back through this section and, for each subheading, make a note of whether you were previously aware that such regulation existed. In each case, irrespective of your previous state of knowledge, do you now feel a greater or a lesser sense of confidence in accounting information? How strong is your confidence in published accounting information? If not 100%, what further reassurance would you require?*

## 4.6 Reviewing published financial statements

If you look at the annual report of any large listed company you will find that it has two main sections. The first part contains a variety of diagrams and photographs, a statement by the chairman, a report by the chief executive and, in many cases, an Operating and Financial Review which may extend to a considerable number of pages. Other aspects of the business, such as its corporate governance and environmental policy, may also be explained. This first part is a mixture of unregulated and broadly regulated material. There are many sources of influence on its contents, some of which will be explained in later chapters of this book.

The second part contains the financial statements, which are heavily regulated. As if to emphasise this change of status, the second part of the annual report will often have a different appearance, perhaps being printed on a different colour or grade of paper, or possibly having a smaller print size. Appendix I to this book contains extracts from the financial statements of a fictitious company, Safe and Sure plc, which will be used for illustration in this and subsequent chapters.

Relaxing after a hard workout at the health club, David Wilson took the opportunity to buy Leona a drink and tell her something about Safe and Sure prior to a visit to the company's headquarters to meet the finance director.

DAVID: *This is a major listed company, registered in the UK but operating around the world selling its services in disposal and recycling, cleaning and security. Its name is well known and its services command high prices because of the company's reputation gained over many years. Basically it is a very simple business to understand. It sells services by making contracts with customers and collects cash when the service is performed.*

*In preparation for my visit I looked first at the performance of the period. This company promises to deliver growth of at least 20% in revenue and in profit before tax so first of all I checked that the promise had been delivered. Sure enough, at the front of the annual report under 'Highlights of the year' there was a table showing revenue had increased by 22.4% and profit before tax had increased by 20.4%. I knew I would need to look through the profit and loss account in more detail to find out how the increases had come about, but first of all I read the operating review (written by the chief executive) and the financial review (written by the finance director). The chief executive gave more details on which areas had the greatest increase in revenue and operating profit and which areas had been disappointing. That all helps me in making my forecast of profit for next year.*

*The chief executive made reference to acquisitions during the year, so I knew I would also need to think whether the increase in revenue and profits was due to an improvement in sales and marketing as compared with last year or whether it reflected the inclusion of new business for the first time.*

*In the financial review, the finance director explained that the business tries to use as little working capital as possible (that means they try to keep down the current assets and match them as far as possible with current liabilities). I guessed I would need to look at the balance sheet to confirm that, so I headed next for the financial statements at the back of the annual report, pausing to glance at the auditors' report to make sure there was nothing highlighted by them as being amiss.*

*The financial statements are quite detailed and I wanted a broad picture so I noted down the main items from each in a summary format which leaves out some of the detail but which I find quite useful.*

## 4.6.1    Income statement (profit and loss account)

**Safe and Sure plc**
**Summary income statement (profit and loss account) with comparative figures**

|  | Notes | Year 7 £m | Year 6 £m |
|---|---|---|---|
| **Continuing operations** | | | |
| Revenue | | 714.6 | 589.3 |
| Cost of sales | | (491.0) | (406.3) |
| Gross profit | | 223.6 | 183.0 |
| Expenses and interest | | (26.1) | (26.0) |
| Profit before tax | | 197.5 | 157.0 |
| Tax on profit | | (62.2) | (52.4) |
| Profit for the period from continuing operations | | 135.3 | 104.6 |
| **Discontinued operations** | | | |
| Loss for the period from discontinued operations | | (20.5) | (10.0) |
| **Profit for the period** attributable to ordinary shareholders | | 114.8 | 94.6 |

**DAVID:** *It is part of my job to make forecasts of what the next reported profit of the company is likely to be (i.e. the profit of Year 8). This is March Year 8 now so there are plenty of current signs I can pick up, but I also want to think about how far Year 7 will be repeated or improve during Year 8. A few years ago I would have made a rough guess and then phoned the finance director for some guidance on whether I was in the right area. That's no longer allowed because the Financial Services Authority tightened up the rules on companies giving information to some investors which is not available to others, especially where that information could affect the share price.*

*One easy way out is for me to collect the reports which come in from our stockbrokers. Their analysts have specialist knowledge of the industry and can sometimes work out what is happening in a business faster than some of the management. However, I like to form my own opinion using other sources, such as trade journals, and I read the annual report to give me the background structure for my forecast. The company has helpfully separated out the effect of continuing and discontinued operations, which helps me in making a forecast.*

*When I meet the finance director next week I'll have with me a spreadsheet analysing revenue and profit before tax – so far as I can find the data – by product line and for each of the countries in which the company trades. I'll also ask the following questions:*

1 *Although the revenue has increased, the ratio of gross profit to revenue on continuing operations has increased only very slightly, from 31.1% in Year 6 to 31.3% in Year 7. That suggests that the company has increased revenue by holding price rises at a level matching the increase in operating costs. I would like to see the company pushing ahead with price rises but does the company expect to see a fall in demand when its prices eventually rise?*

2 *The tax charge on continuing operations has decreased from approximately 33% to 31.5%, slightly higher than the rate which would be expected of UK companies. I know that this company is trading overseas. You say in your financial review that the tax charge is 30% in the UK and rates on overseas profits will reduce, so am I safe in assuming that 30% is a good working guide for the future in respect of this company?*

3 *With all this overseas business there must be an element of foreign exchange risk. You say in your financial review that all material foreign currency transactions are matched back into the currency of the group company undertaking the transaction. You don't hedge the translation of overseas profits back into sterling. You also say that using Year 6 exchange rates the Year 7 profit, including the effect of the discontinued operations, would have been £180.5m rather than the £177.0m reported. That seems a fairly minimal effect but are these amounts hiding any swings in major currencies where large downward movements are offset by correspondingly large upward movements?*

4 *Your increase in revenue, comparing £714.6m to £589.9m, is 21.1% which is meeting the 20% target you set yourself. However, elsewhere in the financial statements I see that the acquisitions in Year 7 contributed £13.5m to revenue. If I strip that amount out of the total revenue I'm left with an increase in respect of activities continuing from Year 6 which is only 19%. When the scope for acquisitions is exhausted, will you be able to sustain the 20% target by organic growth alone?*

## 4.6.2 Balance sheet

**DAVID:** *Looking at the balance sheet, this is a fairly simple type of business. It is financed almost entirely by equity capital (shareholders' funds), so there are none of the risks associated with high levels of borrowings which might be found in other companies.*

*Again, I have summarised and left out some of the details which aren't significant in financial terms.*

**Safe and Sure plc**
**Summarised balance sheet (with comparative amounts)**

| | Notes | Year 7 £m | Year 6 £m |
|---|---|---|---|
| **Non-current assets** | | | |
| Intangible assets | | 260.3 | 237.6 |
| Tangible assets | | 137.5 | 121.9 |
| Investments | | 2.8 | 2.0 |
| Taxation recoverable | | 5.9 | 4.9 |
| | | 406.5 | 366.4 |
| **Current assets** | | | |
| Inventories (stocks) | | 26.6 | 24.3 |
| Amounts receivable (debtors) | | 146.9 | 134.7 |
| Six-month deposits | | 2.0 | – |
| Cash and cash equivalents | | 105.3 | 90.5 |
| | | 280.8 | 249.5 |
| **Current liabilities** | | | |
| Amounts payable (creditors) | | (159.8) | (157.5) |
| Bank overdraft | | (40.1) | (62.6) |
| | | (199.9) | (220.1) |
| *Net current assets* | | 80.9 | 29.4 |
| *Total assets less current liabilities* | | 487.4 | 395.8 |
| **Non-current liabilities** | | | |
| Amounts payable (creditors) | 9 | (2.7) | (2.6) |
| Bank and other borrowings | 10 | (0.2) | (0.6) |
| Provisions | 11 | (20.2) | (22.2) |
| *Net assets* | | 464.3 | 370.4 |
| **Capital and reserves** | | | |
| *Shareholders' funds* | | 464.3 | 370.4 |

**DAVID:** *By far the largest non-current (fixed) asset is the intangible asset of goodwill arising on acquisition. It reflects the fact that the group has had to pay a price for the future prospects of companies it has acquired. Although the company reports this in the group's balance sheet, and I like to see whether the asset is holding its value from the group's point of view, I have some reservations about the quality of the asset because I know it would vanish overnight if the group found itself in difficulties.*

*The other non-current assets are mainly equipment for carrying out the cleaning operations and vehicles in which to transport the equipment. I've checked in the notes to the accounts that vehicles are being depreciated over four to five years and plant and equipment over five to ten years, all of which sounds about right. Also, they haven't changed the depreciation period, or the method of calculation, since last year so the amounts are comparable. Estimated useful lives for depreciation are something I watch closely. There is a great temptation for companies which have underperformed to cut back on the depreciation by deciding the useful life has extended. (Depreciation is explained more fully in Chapter 8.)*

*I think I might ask a few questions about working capital (the current assets minus the current liabilities of the business). Normally I like to see current assets somewhat greater than current liabilities – a ratio of 1.5 to 1 could be about right – as a cushion to ensure the liabilities are met as they fall due. However, in this company the finance director makes a point of saying that they like to utilise as little working capital as possible, so I'm wondering why it increased from £29.4m in Year 6 to more than £80m in Year 7. There appear to be two effects working together: current assets went up and current liabilities went down. Amounts receivable (trade debtors) increased in Year 7 in absolute terms but that isn't as bad as it looks when allowance is made for the increase in revenue.*

*Amounts receivable in Year 7 are 20.6% of continuing revenue, which shows some control has been achieved when it is compared with the Year 6 amount at 22.8% of revenue. My questions will be:*

1 *Mostly, the increase in the working capital (net current assets) appears to be due to the decrease in bank borrowing. Was this a voluntary action by the company or did the bank insist?*
2 *The second major cause of the increase in the working capital is the increase in the balance held in the bank account. Is that being held for a planned purpose and, if so, what?*
3 *The ratio of current assets to current liabilities has increased from last year. What target ratio are you aiming for?*

*I always shudder when I see 'provisions' in a balance sheet. The notes to the financial statements show that these are broadly:*

| | £m |
|---|---|
| For treating a contaminated site | 12.0 |
| For restructuring part of the business | 4.2 |
| For tax payable some way into the future | 4.0 |
| Total | 20.2 |

*I shall want to ask whether the estimated liability in relation to the contaminated site is adequate in the light of any changes in legislation. I know the auditors will have asked this question in relation to existing legislation but I want to think also about forthcoming legislation.*

*I am always wary of provisions for restructuring. I shall be asking more about why the restructuring is necessary and when it will take place. I want to know that the provision is sufficient to cover the problem, but not excessive.*

*The provision for tax payable some way into the future is an aspect of prudence in accounting. I don't pay much attention unless the amount is very large or suddenly changes dramatically. (An explanation of deferred taxation is contained in Chapter 10.)*

### 4.6.3    Cash flow statement

DAVID: *Cash is an important factor for any business. It is only one of the resources available but it is the key to survival. I've summarised the totals of the various main sections of the cash flow statement. 'Net cash' means the cash less the bank borrowings.*

**Safe and Sure plc**
**Summary cash flow statement (with comparative amounts)**
**Consolidated cash flow statement for the years ended 31 December**

| | Notes | Year 7 £m | Year 6 £m |
|---|---|---|---|
| Net cash from operating activities | | 143.0 | 116.3 |
| Net cash used in investing activities | | (98.3) | (85.3) |
| Net cash used in financing activities | | (10.2) | (46.4) |
| Net increase/(decrease) in cash and cash equivalents* | | 34.5 | (15.4) |

*What I'm basically looking for in the cash flow statement is how well the company is balancing various sources of finance. It generated £143m from operating activities and that was more than sufficient to cover its investing activities in new fixed assets and acquisitions. There was also enough to cover the dividend of £29.5m, which is a financing activity but that was partly covered by raising new loan finance. This is why the cash used in financing activities is only £10.2m. I come back to my earlier question of why they are holding so much cash.*

**Activity 4.5**

*Read David's explanation again and compare it carefully with the financial statements. It is quite likely that you will not understand everything immediately because the purpose of this book as a whole is to help you understand published financial statements and we are, as yet, only at the end of Chapter 4. Make a note of the items you don't fully understand and keep that note safe in a file. As you progress through the rest of the book, look back to that note and tick off the points which subsequently become clear. The aim is to have a page full of ticks by the end of the book.*

## 4.7 Summary

The objective of financial statements is to provide information about the financial position, performance and changes in financial position of an entity that is useful to a wide range of users in making economic decisions.

The four principal qualitative characteristics, as described by the IASB *Framework*, are:

- understandability
- relevance
- reliability
- comparability.

**Relevance** and **reliability** are twin targets which may cause some tension in deciding the most appropriate way to report accounting information.

The accounting measurement principles that are most widely known in the UK are found within the Companies Act 1985:

- going concern
- accruals
- consistency
- prudence.

Prudence in accounting means exercising a degree of caution when reporting assets, liabilities and profits. Overstatement of assets causes the overstatement of profit. Understatement of liabilities causes the overstatement of profit. Prudence requires avoiding overstating profit but also avoiding deliberate understatement of profit.

Regulation of financial reporting in the UK comes from several sources.

- The IAS Regulation requires all listed groups of companies to prepare financial statements using the system of the International Accounting Standards Board (IASB system). Other companies may choose to follow the IASB system.
- Companies that do not follow the IASB system must comply with UK company law.
- The Financial Reporting Council regulates accounting and auditing matters under the authority of UK company law.
- The Financial Reporting Council oversees the UK Accounting Standards Board which sets accounting standards for companies that are complying with UK company law.
- The Financial Reporting Review Panel takes action against companies whose annual reports do not comply with the relevant accounting system (IASB or UK company law).
- The Financial Services Authority regulates a wide range of financial service activities including the London Stock Exchange. It sets Listing Rules for companies listed on the Stock Exchange.
- Auditors give an opinion on whether financial statements present a true and fair view of the profit or loss of the period and the state of affairs at the end of the period. They are professionally qualified accountants with auditing experience who are members of a recognised professional body.

- The UK tax system charges corporation tax on company profits. Her Majesty's Revenue and Customs (HMRC) start with the accounting profit in calculating the amount of tax payable but there are some special rules of accounting for tax purposes.

## Further reading

IASB (1989), *Framework for the Preparation and Presentation of Financial Statements*, International Accounting Standards Board.

Paterson, R. (2002), 'Whatever happened to Prudence?', *Accountancy*, January, p. 105.

The website of the Financial Reporting Council explains the methods and nature of regulation of financial reporting and the accountancy profession: www.frc.org.uk

# QUESTIONS

The Questions section of each chapter has three types of question. 'Test your understanding' questions to help you review your reading are in the 'A' series of questions. You will find the answers to these by reading and thinking about the material in the book. 'Application' questions to test your ability to apply technical skills are in the 'B' series of questions. Questions requiring you to show skills in problem solving and evaluation are in the 'C' series of questions. A letter [S] indicates that there is a solution at the end of the book.

## A    Test your understanding

**A4.1**    Explain what is meant by each of the following: (section 4.2)

(a) relevance;
(b) reliability;
(c) faithful representation;
(d) neutrality;
(e) prudence;
(f) completeness;
(g) comparability;
(h) understandability; and
(i) materiality.

**A4.2**    Explain the accounting measurement principles of each of the following: (section 4.3)

(a) going concern;
(b) accruals;
(c) consistency;
(d) the concept of prudence.

**A4.3**    Explain why companies should avoid overstatement of assets or understatement of liabilities. (section 4.4)

**A4.4**    Explain the responsibilities of directors of a company towards shareholders in relation to the financial statements of a company. (section 4.5.2)

**A4.5**    Explain the impact on financial statements of each of the following: (section 4.5)

(a) company law;
(b) the International Accounting Standards Board; and
(c) the UK tax law.

**A4.6**    Explain how the monitoring of financial statements is carried out by each of the following: (section 4.5)

(a) the auditors; and
(b) the Financial Reporting Review Panel.

## B    Application

**B4.1** [S]

Explain each of the following:

(a)  The IAS Regulation
(b)  The Financial Reporting Council
(c)  The Auditing Practices Board

**B4.2** [S]

Explain any two accounting measurement principles, explaining how each affects current accounting practice.

**B4.3** [S]

Discuss the extent to which the regulatory bodies explained in this chapter have, or ought to have, a particular concern for the needs of the following groups of users of financial statements:

(a)  shareholders;
(b)  employees;
(c)  customers; and
(d)  suppliers.

## C    Problem solving and evaluation

**C4.1**

Choose one or more characteristics from the following box that you could use to discuss the accounting aspects of each of the statements 1 to 5 and explain your ideas:

- relevance
- understandability
- completeness
- reliability
- materiality
- prudence
- comparability
- neutrality
- faithful representation

1  Director: 'We do not need to tell shareholders about a loss of £2,000 on damaged stock when our operating profit for the year is £60m.'
2  Shareholder: 'I would prefer the balance sheet to tell me the current market value of land is £20m than to tell me that the historical cost is £5m, although I know that market values fluctuate.'
3  Analyst: 'If the company changes its stock valuation from average cost to FIFO, I want to hear a good reason and I want to know what last year's profit would have been on the same basis.'
4  Regulator: 'If the company reports that it has paid "*commission on overseas sales*", I don't expect to discover later that it really meant bribes to local officials.'
5  Director: 'We have made a profit on our drinks sales but a loss on food sales. In the Notes to the Accounts on segmental results I suggest we combine them as "food and drink". It will mean the annual report is less detailed for our shareholders but it will keep competitors in the dark for a while.'

**C4.2**

Choose one or more accounting measurement principles from the following box that you could use to discuss the accounting aspects of each of the problems 1–5 and explain your ideas.

- going concern
- accruals
- consistency
- prudence.

1  Director: 'The fixed assets of the business are reported at depreciated historical cost because we expect the company to continue in existence for the foreseeable future. The market value is much higher but that is not relevant because we don't intend to sell them.'
2  Auditor: 'We are insisting that the company raises the provision for doubtful debts from 2% to 2.5% of debtor amount. There has been recession among the customer base and the financial statements should reflect that.'

**3** Analyst: 'I have great problems in tracking the depreciation policy of this company. It owns several airports. Over the past three years the expected useful life of runways has risen from 30 years to 50 years and now it is 100 years. I find it hard to believe that the technology of tarmacadam has improved so much in three years.'

**4** Auditor: 'We have serious doubts about the ability of this company to renew its bank overdraft at next month's review meeting with the bank. The company ought to put shareholders on warning about the implications for the financial statements.'

**5** Shareholder: 'I don't understand why the company gives a profit and loss account and a cash flow statement in the annual report. Is there any difference between profit and cash flow?'

## Activities for study groups

Continuing to use the annual reports of a company that you obtained for Chapter 1, look for the evidence in each report of the existence of the directors, the auditors and the various regulatory bodies.

In your group, draw up a list of the evidence presented by companies to show that the annual report has been the subject of regulation. Discuss whether the annual report gives sufficient reassurance of its relevance and reliability to the non-expert reader.

### Notes and references

1. IASB (1989), *Framework*, para. 12.
2. *Ibid.*, para. 20.
3. *Ibid.*, para. 21.
4. *Ibid.*, para. 24.
5. *Ibid.*, para. 25.
6. *Ibid.*, para. 26.
7. *Ibid.*, paras. 27–8.
8. *Ibid.*, paras. 29–30.
9. *Ibid.*, para. 31.
10. *Ibid.*, paras. 33–4.
11. *Ibid.*, para. 35.
12. *Ibid.*, para. 36.
13. *Ibid.*, para. 37.
14. *Ibid.*, para. 38.
15. *Ibid.*, para. 39.
16. *Ibid.*, para. 42.
17. *Ibid.*, para. 39.
18. *Ibid.*, para. 41.
19. *Ibid.*, para. 40.
20. *Ibid.*, para. 43.
21. *Ibid.*, para. 44.
22. ASB (1999), *Statement of Principles*, p. 34.
23. Companies Act 1985, sch. 4, paras. 10–14.
24. IASB (1989), *Framework*, para. 23.
25. IASB (1989), *Framework*, para. 23.
26. ASB (1999), Appendix III, paras. 21–3.
27. ASB (2000), Financial Reporting Standard 18 (FRS 18) *Accounting Policies*, Accounting Standards Board, para. 28.
28. IASB (1989), *Framework*, para. 37.
29. ASB (2000), Appendix IV, paras. 12 to 20.
30. IASB (1989), *Framework*, para. 27.
31. http://europa.eu.int/comm/internal_market/accounting/index_en.htm
32. www.efrag.org/
33. Details can be found on the website of the Department of Trade and Industry, www.dti.gov.uk/cld/review.htm
34. Company Law Reform, March 2005, Cm. 6456, DTI.
35. www.frc.org.uk/

# Chapter 7

# Published financial statements

## Group overview

GUS is a retail and business services group. Its activities comprise general merchandise retailing through Argos Retail Group, information and customer relationship management services through Experian, and luxury goods through a majority shareholding in Burberry Group plc.

## Five year summary

| Profit by division | 2001 £m | 2002 £m | 2003 £m | 2004 £m | 2005 £m |
|---|---|---|---|---|---|
| Continuing operations: | | | | | |
| Argos Retail Group | | | | | |
| Argos | 169 | 212 | 241 | 298 | 309 |
| Homebase | – | – | 2 | 102 | 92 |
| Financial Services | (6) | (18) | (13) | (5) | – |
| Wehkamp | 18 | 19 | 20 | 21 | 20 |
| | 181 | 213 | 250 | 416 | 421 |
| Experian | | | | | |
| Experian North America | 156 | 155 | 171 | 180 | 188 |
| Experian International | 61 | 69 | 85 | 102 | 130 |
| | 217 | 224 | 256 | 282 | 318 |
| Burberry | 69 | 90 | 117 | 141 | 166 |
| Central activities (including GGF and gusco.com) | (3) | (7) | (16) | (20) | (24) |
| | 464 | 520 | 607 | 819 | 881 |
| Discontinued operations: | | | | | |
| Argos Retail Group | 36 | 42 | 35 | – | – |
| Lewis | 31 | 31 | 32 | 44 | 55 |
| Property | 30 | 25 | 26 | 18 | – |
| | 97 | 98 | 93 | 62 | 55 |
| | 561 | 618 | 700 | 881 | 936 |
| Net interest | (74) | (67) | (58) | (54) | (26) |
| **Profit before amortisation of goodwill, exceptional items and taxation** | 487 | 552 | 642 | 827 | 910 |
| Amortisation of goodwill | (92) | (99) | (143) | (193) | (207) |
| Exceptional items | (85) | (72) | (90) | 58 | (10) |
| Profit before taxation | 310 | 380 | 409 | 692 | 693 |
| Tax on profit on ordinary activities | (106) | (122) | (141) | (192) | (221) |
| Profit after taxation | 204 | 258 | 268 | 500 | 472 |
| Equity minority interests | – | (1) | (17) | (27) | (49) |
| Profit for the financial year | 204 | 257 | 251 | 473 | 423 |

Source: GUS Annual Report and Financial Statements 2005, p. 1 and p. 90 (Table).

## Discussion points

1  Which activities are the main contributors to the profit of the GUS group?

2  What does the five-year summary tell us about GUS as a group?

# Contents

<table>
<tr><td>

**Learning outcomes**

</td><td>

After reading this chapter you should be able to:

● Explain the key international influences that affect accounting practice in the UK.

● Explain the structure of company reporting as set out in the *Framework* and in UK guidance.

● Explain the main contents of (a) the balance sheet, (b) the income statement (profit and loss account) and (c) the cash flow statement as presented by larger companies.

● Define 'parent company' and 'subsidiary company' and explain how a group is structured.

● Explain the main features of group financial statements.

● Explain the nature of, and reason for, other forms of communication beyond the annual report.

</td></tr>
</table>

## 7.1 Introduction

It is explained in Chapters 1 and 4 that in the case of sole traders and partnerships the groups of persons who have an interest in the financial statements are limited to the owners themselves, HM Revenue and Customs and organisations such as banks which are asked to provide finance for the company. For limited liability companies the list of potential users widens and the access to internal information becomes restricted. Even the owners of a limited liability company, called the equity holders (shareholders) are not permitted access to the day-to-day records of the company and are treated as being outsiders of (external to) the company they own. The quality and amount of information communicated to these users who are external to the company becomes a matter which is too important to be left entirely to the discretion of the directors running the company.

Chapter 4 outlined the various regulatory authorities which exist to establish the quality and quantity of information to be published by limited liability companies. There are over one million limited liability companies in the UK, although only a few thousand are listed on the Stock Exchange and of these only around 500 have their shares bought and sold regularly. The number of major listed companies, and their importance to the economy in terms of the funds invested in them, means it is appropriate to take them as the benchmark for current practice in external reporting. The practices applied by larger limited liability companies set a good example as a starting point for smaller ones and for organisations that are not limited liability companies, such as charitable trusts or public sector bodies.

In this chapter, and in Chapters 8 to 12, there is mention only of **limited liability companies** because the aim of this book is to provide an understanding of the accounting information published by companies. The more general word **enterprise** (meaning a business activity or commercial project) could be substituted throughout for limited liability company most of what is said in these chapters because the principles and practice described here have a wider application beyond companies, although modifications may be necessary when the needs of the users and the purposes of the enterprise are different from those relevant to a limited liability company.

## 7.2 International influences

Chapter 3 explained that, since January 2005, two different accounting systems have existed for companies in the UK, depending on the type of company. For the group financial statements of a listed company the accounting system set out by the International Accounting Standards Board (IASB) must be applied. All other companies, and the separate companies in the group, may choose to follow IASB standards but there is no requirement to do so. Companies that do not choose to follow the international accounting standards must continue to follow the rules of UK company law and the UK ASB's accounting standards.

For many years there has been a strong international influence on and from UK accounting practice so the change to international accounting standards in 2005 did not bring many surprises. The UK accounting standard setting body was a founder member of the International Accounting Standards Committee (IASC), set up in 1973, and has been closely involved in its work since that date. In 2001, with an organisational change, the IASC became the IASB but the close similarity between international accounting standards and UK accounting standards continued. The UK ASB has worked continuously towards matching UK standards to IFRS.

Since 1980 the law regulating financial reporting in the UK (now contained in the Companies Act 1985 and related legislation) has reflected its membership of the European Union (EU) and the work of regulators across the EU to harmonise aspects of financial reporting. From 2005 the law governing financial reporting in the UK has been split into two routes. One route is the rule of UK company law influenced by the EU. The other route is the IASB system of accounting as endorsed by the EU.

### 7.2.1 The European Union

The UK is a member state of the EU and is required to develop its laws so as to harmonise with those of other Member States of the EU. There are two procedures by which the EU influences the accounting practices of UK-based companies.

1 The European Commission, which is the permanent secretariat and staff of the EU, issues a Regulation which overrides national laws and applies to all companies specified in the Regulation.
2 The European Commission issues Directives which are incorporated in national laws of Member States.

### The IAS Regulation

In 2002 the European Commission issued the first IAS Regulation. The IAS Regulation is a direct instruction to companies in all Member States. It required that, by 2005, all **listed** companies in the European Union would use IASB standards in preparing their **group** financial statements. This was intended to cause convergence ('bringing together') of accounting practices, and so improve the movement of capital across the stock markets of the EU. The Commission, which prepares and implements the legislation of the European Parliament, has established procedures for giving European approval to each of the IASB Standards. It takes advice from the European Financial Reporting Advisory Group (EFRAG), a team of experts that includes a UK member. The final recommendation to the Commission is made by the Accounting Regulatory Committee, which includes representatives of all Member States. The process of approving IASB standards for use in the EU is called **endorsement**.

### Harmonisation through Directives

For many aspects of regulation within the EU, the process of harmonisation starts when a **Directive** is issued by the European Commission, setting out the basic rules which should be followed in each Member State's national laws. For limited liability companies in the UK, two such Directives have been particularly important. These are the Fourth Directive and the Seventh Directive. Together they specify the content of the Companies Act 1985, which was issued in 1985 and amended by a further Act in 1989. One important aspect of Directives is that they specify **formats** for the financial statements (see section 7.3.2) which ensure that all companies produce documents that are similar in appearance and present items in a systematic order. The idea of having standard formats was not a familiar concept in the UK before the Directives became effective in the 1980s, but became accepted during the 1980s and 1990. Having standard formats makes it easier for the reader to find the starting point in reading the financial statements. In later chapters we will see that having standard formats does not solve all the problems of comparability and understandability. For companies that do not apply IFRS these formats continue to apply. For companies using the IFRS there is potentially more flexibility of presentation.

| Activity 7.1 | *From your general interest reading, or perhaps from your study of law, make a list of other areas of activity in which the UK law is harmonised with that of other countries in the EU.* |
|---|---|

### 7.2.2 IASB

The International Accounting Standards Board (IASB) is an independent body that sets International Financial Reporting Standards (IFRS). It was formed in 2000 as the successor to the International Accounting Standard Committee (IASC) which had been setting International Accounting Standards (IAS) since 1973. These IAS have been adopted by the IASB and will gradually be revised as IFRS. In the meantime the description 'IFRS' is used as a collective name for all forms of international accounting standard, whatever the precise title of the standard.

The IASB's objective is to bring about convergence of national accounting standards and international accounting standards to high-quality solutions. This will help participants in the world's capital markets and other users to make economic decisions.

There are many similarities between the UK accounting standards and the IASB Standards. There are also some differences where the UK standard setter believes a particular approach is justified, or where historical developments have a strong influence. The UK Accounting Standards Board works on projects with the IASB, as do other countries' standard setting bodies, all seeking to develop international convergence.

## 7.3 Accounting framework

Chapter 1, section 1.3 has explained that the IASB has developed a *Framework* of principles and definitions that are used in setting accounting standards. The UK ASB has also issued a *Statement of Principles*. There are many similarities between these documents because the UK ASB benefited from the earlier work of the IASB. The explanations in this chapter draw mainly on the IASB *Framework*, adding more information where this is needed to understand the separate ideas of the UK ASB.

## The primary financial statements

The IASB requires a complete set of financial statements to comprise:[1]

- a balance sheet
- an income statement (showing the profit or loss for the period)
- a statement of changes in equity
- a cash flow statement, and
- notes that summarise the accounting policies and give other explanations.

The IASB also gives general guidance on how to prepare and present the financial statements but stops short of giving precise rules on presentation. There is discretion for companies to present information in a way that best suits the company and those who are likely to use the information.

The UK ASB requires the same four primary statements but with some differences of names. The income statement is called a profit and loss account. The statement of changes in equity is replaced by two items: a statement of total recognised gains and losses and a note of changes in share capital and reserves (explained in Chapter 12 of this book). The Companies Act 1985 sets out formats of financial statements (see section 7.3.2) which give detailed rules on the sequence of information. These formats apply to companies that do *not* follow the IFRS.

A comparison of the primary statements in the IASB and UK ASB systems is shown in Exhibit 7.1.

**Exhibit 7.1**
**Primary statements – IASB and UK ASB compared**

| **IASB system** | **UK ASB and company law** |
|---|---|
| Balance sheet | Balance sheet |
| Income statement | Profit and loss account |
| Cash flow statement | Cash flow statement |
| Statement of changes in equity | |
| • Statement of recognised income and expense<br>*plus* | • Statement of total recognised gains and losses<br>*plus* |
| • *Transactions with equity holders (e.g. dividends paid)<br>*plus* | • Reconciliation of movements in shareholders' funds[†] |
| • *Changes in the retained earnings (accumulated profit or loss)<br>*plus* | |
| • *Changes in each class of equity and each reserve | |

Key: * may be shown on the face of the statement of changes in equity or in notes.
[†] Shown with primary statements or in notes

The IASB's Framework explains that the objective of financial statements is to provide information about the financial position, performance and changes in financial position of an entity that is useful to a wide range of users in making economic decisions.[2]

### Financial position

Information about financial position is reported primarily in a balance sheet. It reports economic resources controlled by the company, its financial structure, its liquidity and its solvency. Information about economic resources held by the entity allows users of the information to estimate future cash flows from those resources. Information about financial structure is useful in predicting future needs for borrowing or for raising new equity finance. Liquidity refers to the availability of cash in the near future after taking account of commitments in the same period. Solvency refers to the availability of cash to meet financial commitments as they fall due. The balance sheet is not a statement of the value of the company because there are limitations in the measurement process and also because not all items which are of value to the company are included in the balance sheet.

### Performance

Information about the performance of an entity is primarily provided in an income statement (profit and loss account). Performance is indicated by profitability and changes in profitability. Information about performance is useful in evaluating how well the resources of the entity have been used to generate profit. Statements of financial performance are seen as providing an account of the stewardship of management and also as helping readers to check the accuracy of previous estimates they may have made about the expected outcome of the period.

### Changes in financial position

Information about changes in financial position of an entity is useful to help assess the operating, investing and financing activities of the period. It is usually found in a statement of cash flows.

### 7.3.2 Formats for financial statements

The word **format** means 'shape'. A format for a financial statement sets out the shape of the document. It sets out the items to be reported and the sequence in which they are reported. Section 7.2.1 explains that EU Directives have guided the formats used by UK companies for many years, as set out in company law and UK accounting standards. Since 2005 the group financial statements of listed companies have followed the IASB system of reporting. The IASB system does not specify formats. It does provide some lists of items to be included in financial statements but there is no requirement to present these items in any particular sequence. This means that companies have choices in the shape of their financial statements. This book describes the shapes of financial statements that you are likely to see in company reports but you will need to be flexible in understanding that companies do have choices.

### 7.3.3 Categories of financial information

The primary financial statements are the core of a much wider range of sources of financial information which users may obtain about a company. The relative position of the primary financial statements is shown in Exhibit 7.2

### Activity 7.2

*Write down three items of accompanying information about a company which you feel would be useful in the annual report of a company. Exchange lists with other members of the group and establish the similarities and differences across the group. To what extent would one general set of financial statements with notes and accompanying information meet your collective expectations?*

### 7.3.4 Notes and accompanying information

The annual report contains the primary financial statements, notes to the financial statements and accompanying information.

Exhibit 7.2
**Categories of financial information**

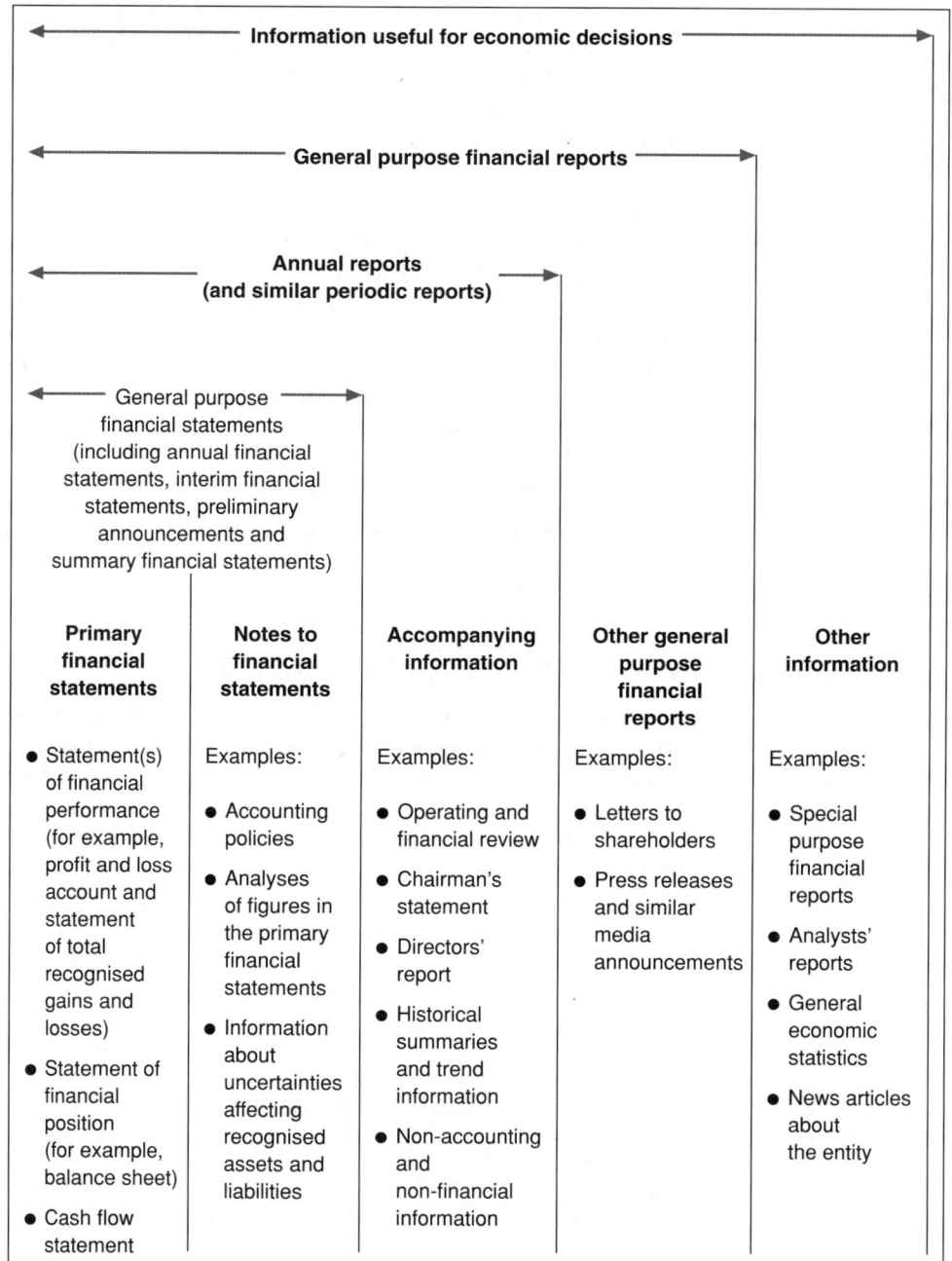

| Primary financial statements | Notes to financial statements | Accompanying information | Other general purpose financial reports | Other information |
|---|---|---|---|---|
| • Statement(s) of financial performance (for example, profit and loss account and statement of total recognised gains and losses)<br><br>• Statement of financial position (for example, balance sheet)<br><br>• Cash flow statement | Examples:<br><br>• Accounting policies<br><br>• Analyses of figures in the primary financial statements<br><br>• Information about uncertainties affecting recognised assets and liabilities | Examples:<br><br>• Operating and financial review<br><br>• Chairman's statement<br><br>• Directors' report<br><br>• Historical summaries and trend information<br><br>• Non-accounting and non-financial information | Examples:<br><br>• Letters to shareholders<br><br>• Press releases and similar media announcements | Examples:<br><br>• Special purpose financial reports<br><br>• Analysts' reports<br><br>• General economic statistics<br><br>• News articles about the entity |

*Source*: ASB (1999) *Statement of Principles for Financial Reporting*, Accounting Standards Board, Introduction. Reproduced with the permission of the Accounting Standards Board.

## Notes to the financial statements

Notes to the financial statements are essential in amplifying and explaining the primary financial statements. They may contain additional information that is relevant to the needs of users about the items in the balance sheet, income statement and cash flow statement. The notes and the primary financial statements form an integrated whole. The wording of the notes is as important as the numbers if ambiguity is to be avoided.

For companies that do not follow the IFRS, many of these notes are required by regulations such as the Companies Act 1985 or relevant UK accounting standards. The ASB also warns that notes to the accounts are not the place to correct or justify a misrepresentation in the primary financial statements. That potential misrepresentation should be dealt with by amending the financial statement to eliminate the problem.

### Accompanying information

Accompanying information is any other information additional to the primary financial statements and notes. It could be information which is highly relevant but of lower reliability than the financial statements and notes. It could be information which will only interest a particular group of users. Such accompanying information may not be subject to the audit process which is compulsory for the primary financial statements and notes. The IASB does not give a view on the accompanying information beyond the notes to the financial statements. The view of the UK ASB is that such accompanying information may be very important, one example being the Operating and Financial Review now presented by large companies as management's explanation of the information given in the financial statements (see Chapter 14). Accompanying information may include disclosures of a voluntary or evolutionary nature.

Many annual reports include highlights pages showing amounts, ratios and other calculations that distil a great deal of information into a few key items. The UK ASB agrees that highlights can be useful but warns against focusing attention exclusively on one or two measures. You cannot read about financial statements for long without meeting the phrase 'the bottom line'. That refers to the line in the income statement (profit and loss account) which reports the profit attributable to the equity holders (ordinary shareholders). It may be described as **earnings** for equity holders (ordinary shareholders). When this amount is divided by the number of shares which have been issued by the company it becomes the **earnings per share**. Investors, financial journalists and brokers' analysts have traditionally paid great attention to the earnings per share. The standard setters (both the IASB and the UK ASB) would prefer to discourage this narrow focus and encourage instead a 'building block' approach where the company produces information in such a way that the user of the annual statement can create useful arrangements and combinations of information.

Companies also produce accompanying information for specialised needs. Regulated industries (such as gas, electricity, telecommunications and water) provide supplementary information about their regulated activities. Some companies give non-financial performance indicators (such as speed of answering customer enquiries, or level of customer satisfaction). Graphs, charts, diagrams and even photographs are all ways of providing accompanying information which adds to users' understanding of a document.

## 7.4 Balance sheet

### 7.4.1 What items must be reported?

Companies that follow the IASB system of accounting in presenting a balance sheet have choices in the way they present their balance sheet. There is no particular **format** required[3] but some items are listed in the relevant standard as a minimum set of disclosures (see Supplement 7.1 to this chapter). Companies choose the form of layout for items in the balance sheet.

Companies that do not follow the IASB system of accounting must comply with the Companies Act 1985 and the UK accounting standards. The Companies Act 1985 contains more detail of the format that must be used. The details are set out in Supplement 7.2 to this chapter.

### 7.4.2    What formats are used?

Companies applying the IASB system do not have to follow any particular format but it is likely that any balance sheet you see will resemble one of the three formats described in this section because they will retain some of the traditions of the UK system that has existed for more than 20 years.

Companies that do not apply the IASB system of accounting must follow the requirements of the Companies Act 1985 and the standards of the UK ASB. The Companies Act 1985 permits two different formats of balance sheet, each conforming to the accounting equation but permitting different layouts on the page. The word format means 'shape' so it covers the items to be reported and the sequence in which they are reported. The most commonly used format in the UK is Format 1, which uses the accounting equation to create a vertical format as shown in Exhibit 7.3.

**Exhibit 7.3**
**Vertical format of balance sheet**

| Assets |
| --- |
| minus |
| Liabilities |
| equals |
| Ownership interest |

Format 2 uses the accounting equation to create a horizontal format as shown in Exhibit 7.4.

**Exhibit 7.4**
**Horizontal form of balance sheet**

| Assets | equal | Ownership interest |
| --- | --- | --- |
| | | plus |
| | | Liabilities |

Format 2 is observed more commonly in the financial statements of Continental European countries where the horizontal format is preferred.

Some companies use a variation on Format 2 which stacks the assets on top and the ownership interest and liabilities underneath (see Exhibit 7.5).

**Exhibit 7.5**
**Assets above, ownership interest plus liabilities below**

| Assets |
| --- |
| equals |
| Ownership interest |
| plus |
| Liabilities |

When you read a balance sheet you should first of all look at the overall structure to see where the main sections of **assets**, **liabilities** and **ownership interest** are placed. Then you can begin to look at each section in more detail. The process is something like seeing a landscape painting for the first time. You stand back to look at the overall impression of the landscape and the main features first. Then you step forward to look at some of the details in different parts of the painting. Finally if you are very enthusiastic you move in closer and start to examine the details of the texture, brush strokes and shading.

### 7.4.3    Descriptions in the balance sheet

You will see from the Supplement that the balance sheet formats contain some words you will recognise but also many new words. Non-current assets (fixed assets) are separated from current assets. Current liabilities (due in less than one year) are separated from non-current liabilities (due in more than one year). Some of the items under the Companies Act headings A to J may look rather strange at this stage (particularly A, D, I and J). Do not worry about that at present. If they are appropriate to first-level study they will be explained at some point in this text. If they are not explained, then they are relatively rare in occurrence and the time taken to explain them will outweigh the benefits you would gain from understanding.

The ownership interest is shown at heading K as **capital** and **reserves**. The word **capital** here means the claim which owners have because of the number of shares they own and the word **reserves** means the claim which owners have because the company has created new wealth for them over the years. Various labels are used to describe the nature of that new wealth and how it is created. Some of the new wealth is created because new investors pay more than a specified amount for the shares. Paying more is referred to as paying a **premium**, so this kind of ownership interest is labelled the **share premium**. Some of the new wealth is created because the fixed assets held by the company increase in value and that new valuation is recorded. This kind of owner-ship interest is labelled the **revaluation reserve**. Some of the new wealth is created by making profits through operating activities. This kind of ownership interest is labelled the **retained earnings** reserve.

### 7.4.4    Subtotals

Subtotals in financial statements help to group information within financial statements into useful sections. There are no rules about the placing of subtotals in either the IASB lists or the Companies Acts formats. Companies have to decide for themselves where to place subtotals and totals in presentation of the list of items in the format. You will need to be flexible in reading balance sheets and using the subtotals provided.

**Activity 7.3**    *Read again the format for the balance sheet. How many of the items there came as no surprise to you? How many looked unfamiliar? Make a note of these and check that you find out about them in later chapters.*

### 7.4.5    Illustration

The remainder of this chapter explores the published financial statements of a hypo-thetical listed company, Safe and Sure plc, which operates in a service industry. There is a parent company called Safe and Sure plc and it owns some subsidiary companies that together make up a 'group'. Buildings and vehicles are the main fixed assets. The Safe and Sure Group sells recycling and cleaning services to customers based on the high reputation of the company's products and name. The Safe and Sure Group follows the IASB system of accounting and has chosen a format that is similar to Format 1 (see Exhibit 7.3).

The following illustration sets out the balance sheet of the Safe and Sure Group plc for Year 7 with comparative amounts alongside for the previous year. The balance sheet is followed by a comment on matters of particular interest.

**Safe and Sure Group plc**
**Consolidated balance sheet at 31 December**

| | Notes | Year 7 £m | Year 6 £m |
|---|---|---|---|
| **Non-current assets** | | | |
| Intangible assets | 1 | 260.3 | 237.6 |
| Tangible assets | 2 | 137.5 | 121.9 |
| Investments | 3 | 2.8 | 2.0 |
| Taxation recoverable | 4 | 5.9 | 4.9 |
| | | 406.5 | 366.4 |
| **Current assets** | | | |
| Inventories (stocks) | 5 | 26.6 | 24.3 |
| Amounts receivable (debtors) | 6 | 146.9 | 134.7 |
| Six-month deposits | | 2.0 | – |
| Cash and cash equivalents | | 105.3 | 90.5 |
| | | 280.8 | 249.5 |
| **Current liabilities** | | | |
| Amounts payable (creditors) | 7 | (159.8) | (157.5) |
| Bank overdraft | 8 | (40.1) | (62.6) |
| | | (199.9) | (220.1) |
| *Net current assets* | | 80.9 | 29.4 |
| *Total assets less current liabilities* | | 487.4 | 395.8 |
| **Non-current liabilities** | | | |
| Amounts payable (creditors) | 9 | (2.7) | (2.6) |
| Bank and other borrowings | 10 | (0.2) | (0.6) |
| Provisions | 11 | (20.2) | (22.2) |
| *Net assets* | | 464.3 | 370.4 |
| **Capital and reserves (ownership interest)** | | | |
| Called-up share capital | 12 | 19.6 | 19.5 |
| Share premium account | 13 | 8.5 | 5.5 |
| Revaluation reserve | 14 | 4.6 | 4.6 |
| Retained earnings | 15 | 431.6 | 340.8 |
| *Equity holders' funds* | | 464.3 | 370.4 |

## 7.4.6 Discussion

The first feature to note is the title, *Consolidated balance sheet*. Companies listed on the Stock Exchange are generally using one name as an umbrella for a group of several companies linked together under one parent. It is thought to be more useful to the shareholders of the parent company to see all the assets controlled by that company within the single financial statement. The word **control** is important here. The parent company owns the other companies. They each own their separate assets. The parent company controls the use of those assets indirectly by controlling the companies it owns. The balance sheet as presented here represents a group where the parent company owns 100% of all the other companies in the group (called its subsidiary undertakings). A similar consolidated balance sheet would be produced if the parent owned less than 100%, provided it had the same element of control. The only additional item would be a **minority interest** in the ownership claim to indicate the proportion of the equity interest in subsidiaries held by shareholders outside the group. The minority interest is also called a **non-controlling interest**.

The second feature to note in the balance sheet as presented is that there are two columns of figures. Companies are required to present the figures for the previous year, in order to provide a basis for comparison.

The balance sheet follows the accounting equation and this company has helpfully set out in the left-hand margin the main elements of the equation. There are some phrases in the balance sheet which you are meeting for the first time but you should not feel intimated by new titles when you can work out what they mean if you think about the ordinary meanings of words.

*Intangible assets* means assets which may not be touched – they have no physical existence. Examples are the goodwill of a business or the reputation of a branded product.

*Tangible non-current (fixed) assets* is another phrase which you are seeing here for the first time, but again you can work out the meaning. You know from Chapter 2 what **non-current assets** are and you know that tangible means 'something that may be touched'. So you would not be surprised to find that note 2 to the accounts gives more detail on land and buildings, plant, equipment, vehicles and office equipment.

*Investments* here means shares in other companies which are not subsidiary undertakings within the group.

The *taxation recoverable* is an amount of tax which has been paid already but may be reclaimed in 18 months' time because of events that have occurred to reduce the tax due, after the tax was paid.

*Current assets* comprise inventories (stocks), receivables (debtors) and cash. They are set out in order of increasing liquidity. Inventories (stocks) are the least readily convertible into cash while amounts receivable (debtors) are closer to collection of cash. Cash itself is the most liquid asset. The notes to the accounts contain more detailed information. Take as an example note 4, relating to inventories (stocks). It appears as follows:

| Note 4 | Year 7 | Year 6 |
|---|---|---|
| **Inventories (stocks)** | £m | £m |
| Raw materials | 6.2 | 5.4 |
| Work-in-progress | 1.9 | 1.0 |
| Finished products | 18.5 | 17.9 |
| | 26.6 | 24.3 |

The notes are shown in full in Appendix I at the end of this book. There is a note relating to amounts receivable (debtors), mainly relating to trade receivables (trade debtors). Amounts payable (creditors) has a similar type of note to the balance sheet.

The *non-current liabilities* include long-term borrowings, which are quite low in amount compared with those of many other companies of this size. The provisions relate to future obligations caused by: treating a contaminated site; reorganisation of part of the business; and future tax payable.

That stage of the balance sheet concludes with the net assets, defined as all assets minus all liabilities. Drawing a total at this point is not a requirement of any format, but is used by many companies as the point which creates a pause in the balance sheet before moving on to the ownership interest.

For a company the *ownership interest* is described as *capital and reserves*. The ownership interest in a company is specified in company law as comprising the claim created through the shares owned by the various equity holders (shareholders) and the claim representing additional reserves of wealth accumulated since the company began. That wealth is accumulated by making profits year after year. The claim is reduced when the owners take dividends from the company. (Further information on the reporting of share capital, reserves and dividends is contained in Chapter 12.)

The ownership interest is the part of the balance sheet which causes greatest confusion to most readers. It is purely a statement of a legal claim on the assets after all liabilities have been satisfied. The word *reserves* has no other significance. There is nothing to see, touch, count or hold. To add to the potential confusion, company law delights in finding names for various different kinds of ownership interest. If you are the kind of person who takes a broad-brush view of life you will not worry too much about share premium account, revaluation reserve and retained earnings.

They are all part of accounting terminology which becomes important to a company lawyer when there is a dispute over how much dividend may be declared, but are less important to the investor who says 'How much is my total claim?'

## 7.5 Income statement (profit and loss account)

### 7.5.1 What items must be reported?

Companies that follow the IASB system of accounting in presenting an income statement must report the profit or loss for the period. There is no particular format required[4] but some items are listed in the relevant standard as a minimum set of disclosures (see Supplement 7.4 to this chapter). Companies choose the form of layout of the items in the income statement.

Companies that do not follow the IASB system of accounting must comply with the Companies Act 1985 and the UK accounting standards. The Companies Act 1985 contains more detail of the items to be reported and the format that must be used. The details are set out in Supplement 7.3 to this chapter.

### 7.5.2 What formats are used?

Companies applying the IASB system do not have to follow any particular format but it is likely that any income statement (profit and loss account) you see will resemble one of the formats described in this section because they will retain some of the traditions of the UK system that has existed for more than 20 years.

Companies that do not apply the IASB system of accounting must follow the requirements of the Companies Act 1985 and the standards of the UK ASB. The Companies Act 1985 permits four different formats of profit and loss account but the version most frequently observed in the UK is format 1 (see Supplement 7.4).

### 7.5.3 Illustration

The published income statements (profit and loss accounts) of most major companies are very similar to the illustration set out here for Safe and Sure plc.

**Safe and Sure Group plc**
**Consolidated income statement (profit and loss account)**
**for the years ended 31 December**

|  | Notes | Year 7 £m | Year 6 £m |
|---|---|---|---|
| **Continuing operations** |  |  |  |
| Revenue | 16 | 714.6 | 589.3 |
| Cost of sales | 16 | (491.0) | (406.3) |
| Gross profit |  | 223.6 | 183.0 |
| Distribution costs |  | (2.2) | (2.5) |
| Administrative expenses | 17 | (26.2) | (26.5) |
| Profit from operations |  | 195.2 | 154.0 |
| Interest receivable (net) | 18 | 2.3 | 3.0 |
| Profit before tax | 19 | 197.5 | 157.0 |
| Tax | 20 | (62.2) | (52.4) |
| Profit for the period from continuing operations |  | 135.3 | 104.6 |
| **Discontinued operations** |  |  |  |
| Loss for the period from discontinued operations | 21 | (20.5) | (10.0) |
| **Profit for the period** attributable to equity holders |  | 114.8 | 94.6 |
| Earnings per share | 22 | 11.74 | 9.71 |

## 7.5.4 Discussion

The first point to note is the heading. This is a consolidated income statement (profit and loss account) bringing together the results of the activities of all the companies in the group during the year. The individual companies will also produce their own separate profit and loss accounts and these are added together to produce the consolidated picture. Where one company in the group sells items to another in the group, the sale and purchase are matched against each other on consolidation so that the results reported reflect only sales to persons outside the group.

The second point to note is that the income statement (profit and loss account) as presented by the company is more informative than the lists contained in Supplements 7.3 or 7.4 might suggest. That is partly because the company has used subtotals to break up the flow and make it digestible for the reader. One very common subtotal is the **gross profit** calculated as revenue minus the cost of the goods or services sold as revenue.

Starting at the top of the income statement we see that the word *revenue* is used to describe the sales of goods or services. **Revenue** is sometimes described as **turnover** or **sales**. Revenue (turnover) represents sales to third parties outside the group of companies. The **cost of sales** is the total of the costs of materials, labour and overheads which relate closely to earning the sales. The gross profit is sometimes referred to as the **gross margin** and is monitored closely by those who use the financial statements to make a judgement on the operations of the company. Within any industry the gross profit as a percentage of revenue (or turnover, or sales) is expected to be within known limits. If that percentage is low then the company is either underpricing its goods or else taking the market price but failing to control costs. If the percentage is high, then the company is perhaps a market leader which can command higher prices for its output because of its high reputation. However, it might also be seen by customers and competitors as charging too much for its goods or services.

The next item in the profit and loss account is *distribution costs*, which would include the costs of delivering goods to customers. For this company the distribution costs are low because it provides services by contract and does not carry out much distribution work. For many users the trends in an amount are more interesting than the actual amount. They might ask why the amount has decreased. On the other hand, it is not a particularly significant component of the overall picture and the users might show little interest. They would pay more attention to the *administrative expenses*, a collective term for all those costs which have to be incurred in order to keep the business running but which are less closely related to the direct activity of creating revenue (making sales). The directors' salaries, head office costs and general maintenance of buildings and facilities are the kinds of details brought together under this heading. Directors' salaries are always a matter of some fascination and companies are expected to give considerable detail in the notes to the accounts about how much each director is paid and what other benefits are provided.

The *profit from operations* is the end of the first stage of the profit and loss account, where the story of the business operations is complete. The rest of the profit and loss account is concerned with the cost of financing the company.

*Interest* is paid on loans and received on investments, usually brought together in one net amount which shows, in this case, an excess of interest receivable over interest payable. That suggests a fairly cash-rich company with relatively low levels of borrowing. Next comes the *corporation tax*, which all companies must pay as a percentage of the profit before tax. The percentage is a standard percentage applied to the profit calculated according to the tax rules. Because the tax rules are not identical to the accounting rules, the percentage appears to vary when the reader looks at the profit and loss account. Helpful companies will explain the tax charge in the Operating and Financial Review, as well as providing more detailed notes to the accounts on the tax charge.

That information ends with the profit for the period from continuing operations. Investors or analysts who want to make a forecast of future profits may decide to use this figure as a starting point because the activities will continue. Separately below this line the group shows the results in this period of operations that have been discontinued. Usually operations are discontinued because they are performing poorly so it is no great surprise to see a loss here. The loss is part of the performance of the period but investors can see that the bad news of this operation will not continue in future. Finally the equity holders (ordinary shareholders) see the profit for the period attributable to them.

They do not see here any mention of a reward in the form of a dividend which returns to them some of the wealth created by the company during the period. That information will appear in a statement of changes in equity which is explained in Chapter 12.

## 7.6 Cash flow statement

The presentation of cash flow statements by companies is guided by IAS 7, *Cash Flow Statements*. (There is a UK standard, FRS 1, which sets out a different form of cash flow statement[5] but in this chapter the version required by IAS 7 is used because it is more likely that you will find this one in published financial statements.)

The benefits of cash flow information are explained in IAS 7.[6] A cash flow statement, when used in conjunction with the rest of the financial statements, provides users with information on solvency and liquidity. It shows how cash is generated in the business and helps users to understand how much flexibility is available to adapt to changing circumstances and opportunities.

### 7.6.1 What items must be reported?

The cash flow statement presents three classifications of cash flows.[7] These are:

- operating activities
- investing activities
- financing activities.

**Definitions**

**Operating activities** are the principal revenue-producing activities of the entity and other activities that are not investing or financing activities.

**Investing activities** are the acquisition and disposal of long-term assets and other investments not included in cash equivalents.

**Financing activities** are activities that result in changes in the size and composition of the contributed equity and borrowings of the entity.

Safe and Sure uses these classifications, as shown in the next section. We need two more definitions of terms in the cash flow statement. These are **cash** and **cash equivalents**.

**Definitions**

**Cash** comprises cash on hand and demand deposits.

**Cash equivalents** are short-term, highly liquid investments that are readily convertible to known amounts of cash and which are subject to an insignificant risk of changes in value.[8]

## 7.6.2    Illustration

**Safe and Sure Group plc**
**Consolidated cash flow statement for the years ended 31 December**

| | Notes | Year 7 £m | Year 6 £m |
|---|---|---|---|
| **Cash flows from operating activities** | | | |
| Cash generated from operations | 23 | 196.7 | 163.5 |
| Interest paid | | (3.1) | (2.4) |
| UK corporation tax paid | | (20.1) | (18.3) |
| Overseas tax paid | | (30.5) | (26.5) |
| **Net cash from operating activities** | | **143.0** | **116.3** |
| **Cash flows from investing activities** | | | |
| Purchase of tangible non-current assets | | (60.0) | (47.5) |
| Sale of tangible non-current assets | | 12.0 | 10.1 |
| Purchase of companies and businesses | 25 | (27.7) | (90.1) |
| Sale of a company | | 3.1 | – |
| Movement in short-term deposits | | (30.7) | 36.3 |
| Interest received | | 5.0 | 5.9 |
| **Net cash used in investing activities** | | **(98.3)** | **(85.3)** |
| **Cash flows from financing activities** | | | |
| Issue of ordinary share capital | 27 | 3.1 | 2.0 |
| Dividends paid to equity holders | | (29.5) | (24.4) |
| Net loan movement (excluding overdraft) | 26 | 16.2 | (24.0) |
| **Net cash used in financing activities** | | **(10.2)** | **(46.4)** |
| **Net increase/(decrease) in cash and cash equivalents*** | | **34.5** | **(15.4)** |
| Cash and cash equivalents at the beginning of the year | | 27.9 | 45.3 |
| Exchange adjustments | | 2.8 | (2.0) |
| Cash and cash equivalents at the end of the year | 29 | 65.2 | 27.9 |

* Cash on demand and deposits of maturity less than three months, net of overdrafts.

**Note 23 Cash flow from operating activities**
**Reconciliation of operating profit to net cash flow from operating activities**

| | Year 7 £m | Year 6 £m |
|---|---|---|
| Profit before tax from continuing operations | 195.2 | 154.0 |
| Loss from discontinued operations | (20.5) | (10.0) |
| Profit from operations | 174.7 | 144.0 |
| Depreciation charge | 33.2 | 30.1 |
| Increase in inventories (stocks)* | (1.9) | (1.1) |
| Increase in trade receivables (debtors)* | (7.4) | (5.3) |
| Decrease in trade payables (creditors)* | (0.4) | (3.6) |
| Net cash inflow from continuing activities | 198.2 | 164.1 |
| Cash outflow in respect of discontinued item | (1.5) | (0.6) |
| Net cash inflow from operating activities | 196.7 | 163.5 |

* *Note*: It is not possible to reconcile these figures with the balance sheet information because of the effect of acquisitions during the year.

## 7.6.3    Discussion

The first line of the cash flow statement is *cash flows from operating activities*, highlighted by the company as an important feature. Note 23 to the accounts explains why this is not the same as operating profit. When a company makes a profit it earns revenue which is greater than the expenses. Some of the revenue is collected as cash but some will be collected later when the credit customers pay. When expenses are incurred, some are paid for immediately but others relate to goods and services taken from suppliers. Note 23 to the accounts is set out above and shows that cash is generated by profits but is used when inventory (stock) levels increase and when trade receivables (debtors) increase. Allowing inventories (stocks) to increase will use up cash because more has to be paid for them. Allowing trade receivables (debtors) to increase means that credit customers are not paying the cash so fast and therefore the cash is not coming in. That will diminish cash flow. Allowing trade payables (creditors) to decrease is a further way of diminishing cash flow because it means that suppliers are being paid faster.

There is one other line in note 23 which gives pause for thought. That is the fourth line *depreciation charge*. **Depreciation** is a measure of how much a fixed asset has been used up. It is an amount which is deducted from profits as a measure of using up the cost of the fixed asset in the accounting period. It does not of itself generate cash, but it stops the owners removing so much cash from the company that they are unable to replace a fixed asset at the end of its useful life. Since it is not a cash item it has to be added back to the reported profit. By way of illustration, suppose a company pays £100 for goods and sells them for £150. It has generated £50 cash. In the profit and loss account £10 is deducted for depreciation, so the reported profit becomes £40. The reconciliation of profit to cash flow from operations will be written as:

|  | £ |
|---|---|
| Operating profit | 40 |
| *add* Depreciation | 10 |
| Cash inflow from operating activities | 50 |

There is more about depreciation in Chapter 8 and more about cash flow in Chapter 14.

The cash generated from operations is used first of all to pay interest on loans, as a reward to lenders, and to pay taxation to the government. Deducting these items leaves the net cash from operating activities. This is the amount left over for long-term investment.

In the next section we find the cash flows from investing activities. The purchase of tangible non-current (fixed) assets is also called **capital expenditure**. Cash is paid to purchase new businesses and cash is received from selling companies or businesses no longer required. Safe and Sure has put some of its cash into short-term deposits to earn interest. In Year 6, Safe and Sure reduced the amount on short-term deposit, converting it back to cash that was available for spending, but in Year 7 it increased the amount on deposit, reducing the amount of cash available to spend in other ways. The final item in this investment section is interest received which is the reward for investment.

The third section shows the cash flows from financing activities. For some companies the cash inflow from operating activities may be insufficient to cover all the investment requirements for capital expenditure and acquisitions, so more finance has to be raised from external sources. Safe and Sure is not in such a difficult position because the cash generated from operations is greater than the cash paid out for investing activities. However there is one further important outflow in the dividends paid to equity holders (shareholders). Dividend is the reward to equity holders (shareholders) for investing in the company. For the particular cash flow statement presented here, the broad story is that the company generated sufficient cash from its operations to cover loan interest, to pay the tax due, meet its investment needs and pay dividends. Despite that positive amount, the company has increased its loans by £16.2m and marginally increased its share capital by £3.1m, so that a total of £34.5m has been added to cash and deposits repayable on demand.

The company explained its cash flow management as follows in the Operating and Financial Review: 'The group's businesses are structured to use as little fixed and working capital as is consistent with the profit and earnings growth objective in order to produce a high cash flow.'

**DAVID WILSON** comments on cash flow in the company: *Cash is an important factor for any business. It is only one of the resources available but it is the key to survival.*

*What I'm basically looking for in the cash flow statement is how well the company is balancing various sources of finance. It generated £196.7m from operating activities. The servicing of investment cost £3.1m in loan interest and the company paid taxes of £50.6m. That left net cash from operations amounting to £143.0m. That was used to cover its investing activities in new fixed assets costing £48m (£60m less £12m) and acquisitions costing £24.6m after allowing for the sale of a company. Cash was used to increase short-term deposits by £30.7m. Interest received was £5m. The net cash used for investing activities amounted to £98.3m. If I deduct this from the £143m cash flow generated there is an increase in cash of £44.7m. The company had to pay a dividend of £29.5m, leaving £15.2m surplus cash. There was no immediate need for any long-term financing flows with a healthy cash flow like that. Nevertheless the company raised £3.1m in cash cash through an issue of shares to the employees' share option scheme and, perhaps surprisingly, there was an increase of £16.2m in short-term loans. Add the £15.2m to the £3.1m and £16.2m and you arrive at £34.5m which is the increase in cash and cash equivalents of the period. That brings me back to my earlier question of why they are holding so much cash and short-term deposits.*

*The company in this example has told me that it carries out its financial management by recognising that the tax bill has to be paid first of all. Then it plans its investment in fixed assets and its programme of disposals. Once the investment has been decided the company aims to pay a dividend which will satisfy the expectations of investors. Surplus cash after that is available for acquisition of other companies and, because this company is always looking for good opportunities to expand, it will borrow ahead of time so that it is in a position to move quickly when a target presents itself. The company does not agree with IAS 7's requirement to separate out the bank deposits which had more than three months to run when they were made. The deposits are placed largely for six months, so that many have less than six months to run at the balance sheet date. It is all very accessible cash and the company sees it all as one pool.*

*In the Operating and Financial Review the finance director explains the company's view of cash flow as follows:*

---

The Group's businesses are structured to utilise as little fixed and working capital as is consistent with the profit and earnings growth objective in order to produce a high cash flow. The impact of working capital on cash flow was held to an increase in Year 7 of £9.7m (Year 6: £10.0m).

A net cash flow of £196.7m was generated from operating activities. That was boosted by other amounts of cash from interest received. After paying interest and tax, the Group had £143.0m remaining. Fixed assets required £48.0m after allowing for the proceeds of selling some of our vehicle fleet in the routine replacement programme. That left £95m from which £24.6m was required to pay for acquisitions. The remaining £70.4m covered dividends of £29.5m leaving £40.9m. We received £5m interest on investments and raised £3.1m in ordinary share capital to give a net inflow of liquid funds in the year of £49.0m. Out of that amount, short-term deposits have increased by £14.5m, leaving an increase in cash of £34.5m.

---

*You can see there are lots of different ways of interpreting the information in the cash flow statement. What is important is that the information is available.*

## 7.7 Group structure of companies

Most major companies in the UK operate using a group structure. Within a group there is a **parent** company which controls **subsidiary** companies undertaking various different aspects of the operations of the business. It would in theory be possible to have all the operations located within one company but in practice, because company law draws very tight boundaries around a single company, there is some safety for the organisation in having different parts of the business packaged separately. If something goes seriously wrong with one subsidiary company, that company may be allowed to fail without irreparable damage to the total group. This approach has not always worked out in practice because very often the banks which lend money to a subsidiary will request guarantees from other companies in the group. So if one subsidiary fails in a spectacular way, it may drag the rest of the group with it.

Other reasons for retaining separate subsidiaries include: employee loyalty, product reputation, taxation legislation and overseas operations. When a new company is taken into the group, a sense of pride in the formerly independent company may be retained by continuing to use the traditional company name. The company name may be linked to a reputation for a high-quality product so that it is desirable to perpetuate the benefit of that reputation. Tax legislation applies to individual companies and not to the group as a whole. Efficient use of the tax laws may require different types of business to operate in different companies. Operations located in other countries will come under the legal systems of those countries and may be required to have a separate legal identity.

For accounting purposes the group as a whole is the economic entity for which financial statements are prepared. An entity should prepare and publish financial statements if there is a legitimate demand for the information that its financial statements would provide and it is a cohesive economic unit.[9] The process of combining all the financial statements of the companies within a group is called **consolidation**. This chapter will explain sufficient aspects of the preparation of consolidated financial statements to allow an understanding of annual reports of groups of companies. The full complexities of consolidation and the wider aspects of group accounting may be found in advanced textbooks.

**Definition**

> **Consolidated** financial statements are the financial statements of a group presented as those of a single economic entity.[10]

**Consolidated financial statements** recognise the parent's control of its subsidiaries. Consolidation is a process that aggregates the total assets, liabilities and results of all companies in the group. The consolidated balance sheet brings together all the assets controlled by the parent and shows all the liabilities to be satisfied from those assets. The consolidated income statement (profit and loss account) brings together all the revenues and costs of the companies in the group.

### 7.7.1 Defining a group

The smallest group consists of two companies. A group is created when one company (the **parent**) has **control** of another company (the **subsidiary**). There is no upper limit to the number of companies which may form a group.

The International Accounting Standards Board has defined a group as a parent and all its subsidiaries.[11] A parent is an entity that has one or more subsidiaries.[12] A subsidiary is an entity, including an unincorporated entity such as a partnership, that is controlled by another entity (known as the **parent**).[13] **Consolidated** financial statements must include all **subsidiaries** of the parent.[14]

**Control** is the power to govern the financial and operating policies of an entity so as to obtain benefits from its activities.[15] Control is presumed to exist when the parent owns, directly or indirectly, more than half of the voting power of an entity. Control also exists where the parent owns half or less than half of the voting power of an entity where there is:[16]

(a) power over more than half of the voting rights by virtue of an agreement with other investors;

(b) power to govern the financial and operating policies of the entity under a statute or an agreement;

(c) power to appoint or remove the majority of the members of the board of directors or equivalent governing body;

(d) power to cast the majority of votes at a meeting of the board of directors or equivalent governing body.

### 7.7.2    The importance of control

Control describes the highest degree of influence that an investor can have over its investee. If an investor (the parent) controls its investee (the subsidiary), it has the ability to direct the investee's operating and financial policies with a view to gaining economic benefit from its activities. The parent becomes fully accountable for the risks and rewards arising from its subsidiary's activities and obtains access to any benefits generated by the subsidiary's activities.

Whatever the percentage holding, the concept of control is the guiding principle which allows the consolidated balance sheet to report *all* the assets and *all* the liabilities of the combined companies. The consolidated profit and loss account reports *all* the profit generated by those assets and liabilities.

### 7.7.3    The parent company's balance sheet

In some annual reports the parent company may choose continue to produce its own balance sheet, showing as an asset the cost of the investment in the subsidiary, but this information is not regarded as being particularly useful. The investment in the subsidiary is reported by the parent company as a single-line item but the consolidated balance sheet shows all the assets and all the liabilities of the group under each separate heading. The group balance sheet is more useful to readers. In previous chapters, where the financial statements of Safe and Sure plc have been discussed, the group accounts have been used.

### 7.7.4    Acquisition

The general term **business combination** may be applied to any transaction whereby one company becomes a subsidiary of another. The most common form of business combination is an **acquisition** where one party (the **acquirer**) is clearly the dominant entity and the other (the **acquiree**) is seen to be under new control. The method of accounting used to produce consolidated financial statements in an acquisition is called the **acquisition method** (also described as the **purchase method**).[17] In this introductory text you do not need to worry about the details of the method of producing consolidated financial statements. All you need to do is recognise the descriptions used and be aware that when you see these words you are reading information about a group of companies combined.

**Activity 7.4**    *Check your understanding of the terms: parent, subsidiary, control, acquisition. Write down a definition of each and then look back through this section to test your definition against that in the text.*

## 7.8  Group financial statements

This section explains how the acquisition of a subsidiary affects the balance sheet of the parent company. It shows how the group's balance sheet and income statement (profit and loss account) are created. It also explains the nature of goodwill arising on acquisition and it outlines the nature and treatment of associated companies.

### 7.8.1  The parent company's balance sheet

When an acquisition takes place, the parent company acquires shares in the subsidiary in exchange for cash or for shares in the parent. The parent company will offer cash if it has adequate cash resources to make the offer and it appears that those selling the shares would prefer to take cash for investment elsewhere. The parent company will offer its own shares in exchange where it may not have sufficient cash resources available or where it thinks it can persuade those selling their shares in the target company of the desirability of acquiring shares in the new parent. Many deals offer a mixture of shares and cash.

For a cash purchase the effect on the parent company's balance sheet, in terms of the accounting equation, is:

| **Assets ↑↓** | − | Liabilities | = | Ownership interest |
|---|---|---|---|---|
| Decrease in asset of cash Increase in asset of investment in subsidiary | | | | |

For a share exchange, the effect on the parent company's balance sheet is to increase the assets and increase the ownership interest. In terms of the accounting equation:

| **Assets ↑** | − | Liabilities | = | **Ownership interest ↑** |
|---|---|---|---|---|
| Increase in asset of investment in subsidiary | | | | Increase by new shares issued |

### 7.8.2  The group's consolidated balance sheet

In the group's consolidated balance sheet the parent company's assets and liabilities are added to the assets and liabilities of the subsidiary companies. The assets and liabilities of the subsidiary take the place of the parent company's investment in the subsidiary. Exhibit 7.6 shows the net assets of P and S separately. The arrows indicate the net assets of S moving in to take the place of P's investment in S. Removing the investment in S from the balance sheet of P and replacing it with the net assets of S leads to the group's consolidated balance sheet. Exhibit 7.7(a) shows the resulting amalgamation. The assets and liabilities in Exhibit 7.7(a) are then rearranged under each asset and liability category to result in Exhibit 7.7(b).

### 7.8.3  The group income statement (profit and loss account)

Investors and their advisers may wish to use the income statement (profit and loss account) of the group to make predictions of the future profitability of the group. To be able to do this, they must know how much of the current year's profit relates to continuing operations and how much relates to changes during the year. The illustration of the income statement of Safe and Sure plc in section 7.5.3 shows how the consolidated profit and loss is subdivided into continuing activities and discontinued activities.

Exhibit 7.6
**Separate net assets of parent and subsidiary**

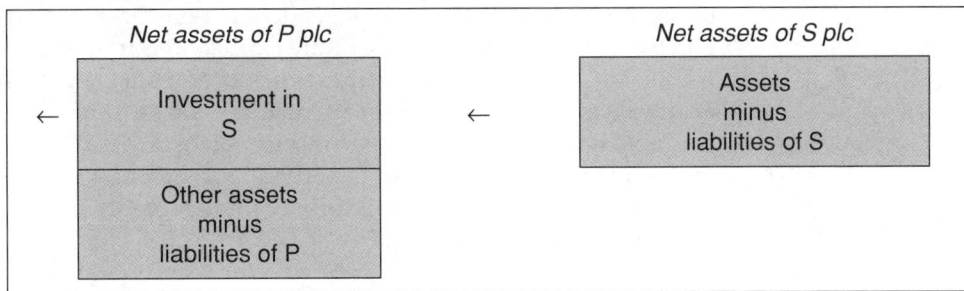

Exhibit 7.7
**Completing the process of consolidation**

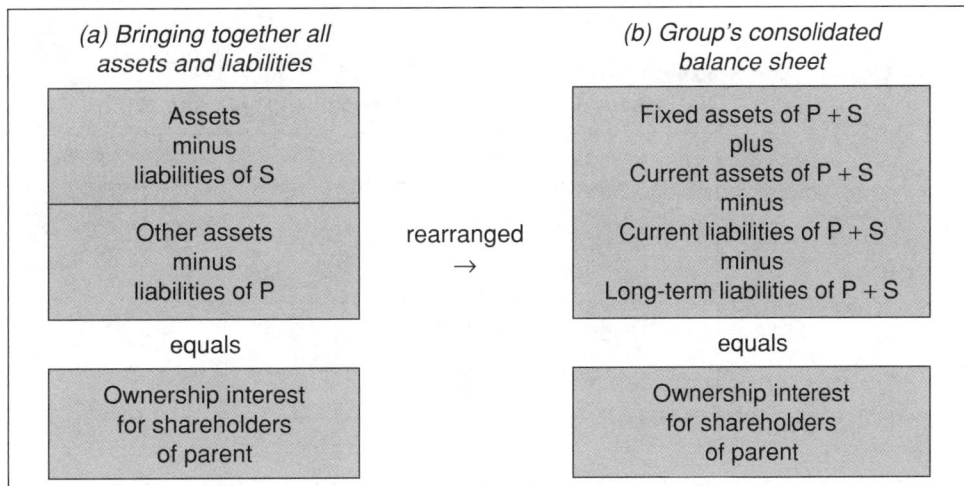

One rule of acquisition accounting is that, where a subsidiary is acquired part-way through the year, only the profits earned after the date of acquisition may be included in the group profit and loss account. The analyst seeking to make a forecast for the year ahead will be helped by a note to the accounts showing what the profit would have been from a full 12-month contribution.

Groups are not required to present separately the parent company's income statement (profit and loss account). It is not felt to be particularly interesting to users as, generally, the parent company's main income comprises the dividends received from its investments in subsidiaries. Usually it is the subsidiaries which carry out the operations generating profit. It is far more interesting to know about the underlying operating profits which allow those dividends to be paid to the parent.

**Activity 7.5**

*P plc pays cash of £6m for an investment in net assets of S Ltd having a net book value (equal to fair value) of £6m. Explain how this transaction will affect the balance sheet of P plc as the parent company and explain how it will affect the group balance sheet of P Group plc, whose only subsidiary is S Ltd.*

### 7.8.4    Goodwill on acquisition

In the illustration presented in Exhibit 7.6 and Exhibit 7.7 the net assets of the subsidiary were shown as being of the same magnitude as the amount of the investment in the subsidiary so that the substitution of the former for the latter was a neat replacement process. That situation is unlikely to apply in real life because the price paid for an investment will rarely depend solely on the net assets being acquired. The purchaser will be looking to the future expectations from the investment and the seller will be seeking a reward for all that has been built into the business which cannot readily be quantified in terms of tangible assets. The future expectations will rest upon the reputation of the product or service, the quality of the customers, the skills of the workforce and the state of the order book, amongst many other things. The price negotiated for the business will include some recognition of all these qualities under the global heading of **goodwill**.

In these circumstances the price paid for the investment in the subsidiary will be greater than the amount of the net assets of the subsidiary. When the consolidation into the group balance sheet is attempted, a space will appear. Exhibit 7.8 shows the separate net assets of P plc and S plc. The amount of the cost of the investment in S is greater than the net assets of S plc.

**Exhibit 7.8**
**Net assets of the separate companies P plc and S plc**

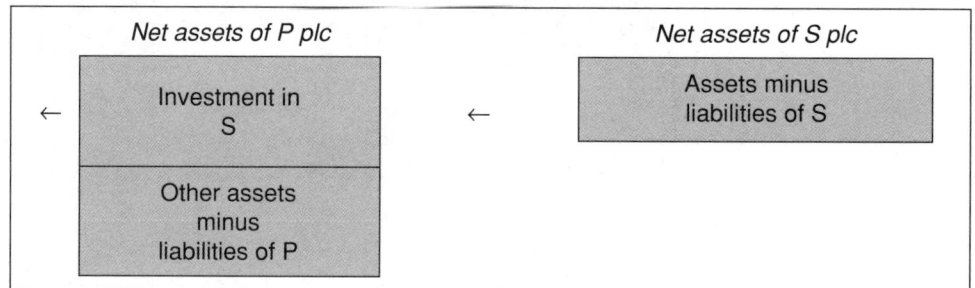

Exhibit 7.9 shows the resulting consolidation. The space shaded is equal to the difference between the amount of the investment in S and the net assets of S. This space is, in arithmetic terms, nothing more than a **difference on consolidation** but has traditionally been called **goodwill** because it is explained in terms of paying for something more than the underlying net assets.

**Exhibit 7.9**
**Group net assets of the P group**

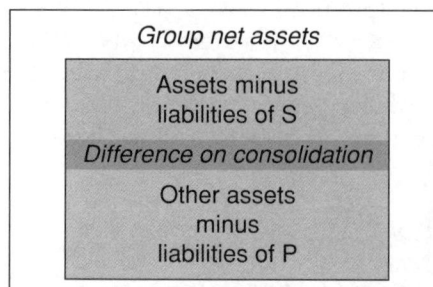

**Definition**

**Goodwill** is defined as future economic benefits arising from assets that are not capable of being individually identified and separately recognised.[18]

Goodwill is recognised in the balance sheet as an asset and is measured as the excess of the cost of the business combination over the fair value of the net assets acquired.[19]

The existence of a difference on consolidation is an inescapable consequence of the process of combining the balance sheets of parent and subsidiary. For many years it caused one of the most difficult problems facing the accounting standard setters. The questions asked were: 'How should this consolidation difference be reported in the balance sheets of succeeding years?' and 'Is it an asset?'

After a great deal of international debate and disagreement, the IASB has taken the view that acquisition goodwill is an asset that should be tested regularly by means of an **impairment test** which asks, 'Can the business expect to recover the carrying value of the intangible asset, through either using it or selling it?' If the answer is 'no' then the asset is impaired and its value must be reduced. An expense of impairment will appear in the income statement (profit and loss account). If the answer is 'yes' then the asset value should remain in the balance sheet.

**Definition**

> **Impairment** means 'damaged' or 'spoiled'. Where the carrying value of goodwill cannot be recovered through sale or use, it is said to be 'impaired'. The asset value in the balance sheet must be reduced.

**Activity 7.6**

> *P pays cash of £8m for an investment in net assets of S Ltd having a net book value (equal to fair value) of £6m. Explain how this transaction will affect the balance sheet of P plc as the parent company and explain how it will affect the group balance sheet of P Group plc, whose only subsidiary is S Ltd.*

## 7.8.5 Associated companies

Where company P holds less than a controlling interest in company A, it may nevertheless have a significant influence over company A. Such significant influence would involve the power to participate in the financial and operating policy decisions of company A. Significant influence is presumed to exist when one company or a group of companies holds 20% or more of the ordinary shareholders' voting rights of another company, unless the facts indicate that significant influence is not possible.[20]

Where significant influence over a company exists, that company is called an **associated company**. The group must show in its balance sheet the group's share of the net assets of the associated company as a single line item, and must show in the income statement (profit and loss account) the group's share of the profits or losses of the associated company.

This treatment of an investment in an associated company is called **equity accounting** because it reports the parent's and the group's share of the investment in the ownership interest (also referred to as the equity).

For investments which do not meet the conditions of being reported as associated companies, the accounting treatment is to record the investment at cost in the balance sheet and to record in the profit and loss account of the group only the dividend income received from the associate.

## 7.9 Beyond the annual report

The annual report is a regulated base of information on which a reporting cycle is built. The cycle begins when the company makes its first announcement of the results of the financial year. This announcement is made in a manner dictated by Stock Exchange rules and is called a 'preliminary announcement' because it is a preliminary to the issue of the full annual report. It is also called a 'press release' because it forms the basis of the information which first appears in the financial press.

The cycle continues with reports being issued in the period between annual reports. These are called 'interim reports'. The London Stock Exchange requires half-yearly reports. The regulators of the US stock exchanges require quarterly reports. All UK listed companies provide half-yearly reports and some voluntarily provide quarterly reports.

Other questions arising beyond the annual report are:

- What help exists for small and medium-sized companies to reduce the burden of communication for regulatory purposes?
- How do larger companies avoid information overload for their shareholders?
- Can users have confidence in additional information provided beyond the annual report?
- What developments is the UK government currently implementing or planning?

This section outlines developments on these issues.

### 7.9.1   Preliminary announcements

The **preliminary announcement** is the first external communication of the financial performance and position of a company in relation to the financial year most recently completed. When the year-end results and half-yearly results are ready for publication, a preliminary announcement of key information is made in a manner set out by the Stock Exchange which aims at fair and equal access for all investors. The preliminary announcement is usually accompanied by a press release, giving the information to the media, and by meetings with professional investors and brokers' analysts at which key personnel in the company (usually the chairman, chief executive and finance director) will make speeches and answer questions.

The institutional shareholders and their advisers will form expectations about the position and performance in advance of the announcement. They look carefully at the preliminary announcement in comparison with their expectations.

Company law does not prescribe the content of the preliminary announcement or the interim report. The Company Law Review report of 2001 recommended that regulation of the preliminary announcement was best carried out by the market regulator rather than by parliamentary legislation. The report did suggest that company law should require that the preliminary announcement be published on the company's website, with electronic notification to shareholders. However, that recommendation was not taken up in the Company Law Reform Bill of 2005. Instead the Bill included a general provision that companies may use electronic communication of documents providing the recipient agrees.

The content of the preliminary statement is influenced by guidance to listed companies, formerly provided by the Stock Exchange but transferred to the Financial Services Authority in 2000. The guidance leaves scope for flexibility in disclosure and measurement. That has caused the UK ASB to write non-mandatory guidance on good practice.

There is no obligation on companies to send these preliminary announcements to shareholders so that in practice only the institutional shareholders and their advisers see them. The ASB suggests that it would be fairer if all shareholders were entitled to request a copy of the announcement. Companies are also encouraged to use ways of publicising the preliminary announcements which will make them more readily available to the private investor.

Reliability is a key requirement of the preliminary announcement. The Stock Exchange requires the company's auditors to agree to the release of the preliminary announcement. There is an expectation that the information in the preliminary announcement will be consistent with the annual report when it eventually appears.

The rules of the Financial Services Authority and the Stock Exchange do not regulate the content of the preliminary announcement other than the requirement for profit and loss information and any significant information necessary for the purpose of assessing the results being announced. In practice many of these announcements include more information than the profit and loss account. The ASB recommends a narrative commentary, a summarised profit and loss account, a summarised balance sheet and a summarised cash flow statement. Increasingly it is found that companies are using the text of the Operating and Financial Review as the basis for the narrative comment in the preliminary announcement.

In general the ASB wishes to improve the timeliness, quality, relevance and consistency of preliminary announcements within the constraints of reliability. It could be that in the longer term the preliminary announcement would increasingly take over the role of the annual report. The delay in publishing the annual report is related to the need to publish a paper-based document. The Company Law Review report recommends that electronic means of communication could speed up the process considerably.

### 7.9.2 Interim reports

**Interim reports** are issued by companies as updating bulletins in between annual reports. They are mainly used by listed companies in response to the requirements of market regulators. Some market regulators ask for half-yearly reports. Others ask for quarterly reports. The international accounting standard IAS 34[21] provides guidance on interim reporting.

One interesting accounting question is how to measure the results of half a year. One view is that the results of half a year should represent the actual events of that half-year. This is called the 'discrete' method. A different view is that the result for six months should represent half of the results of the full year. This is called the 'integral' method. Why does this make a difference? Imagine a company which manufactures and sells fireworks. The costs will fall evenly through the year but most of the sales will arise in the months leading to 5 November. Using the discrete method, the first six months of the calendar year will show low profits or perhaps losses. The second six months will show relatively high profits. Using the integral method each half-year will show the same profit at 50% of the total figure of the year.

IAS 34 requires the discrete method to be used as far as possible. Some expense items, such as taxation, may have to be spread evenly over the year.

In matters of disclosure the IASB recommends that the interim report should include a balance sheet, income statement, statement of changes in equity and cash flow, together with explanatory notes and comments.

**Activity 7.7**

*Obtain the interim report and the annual report of a major listed company. Compare the interim report with the annual report. What are the information items in the interim report? How do they compare with the full year in the annual report? What statements of accounting policy are made in the interim report?*

### 7.9.3 Prospectus

When a major company wants to raise significant amounts of finance through selling shares on the Stock Market, it issues a **prospectus**. The contents of the prospectus are regulated by the UK Listing Authority, backed up on some items by the Companies Act 1985. The document is often several hundred pages in length and quite formidable in appearance. It contains more detail than the annual report. The prospectus is a public document but there is no central archive of prospectuses so it is useful in research projects to retain copies as they appear. Some business libraries retain copies.

### 7.9.4   Small and medium-sized companies

The amount of detail in the information presented by companies depends on their size. The Companies Act 1985 defines small and medium-sized companies. The definitions are based on turnover, balance sheet totals and average number of employees. The amounts for turnover and balance sheet totals are altered from time to time by Statutory Instrument to keep pace with inflation, so it is perhaps easiest to take as a 'rule of thumb' the employee limits of 50 for a small company and 250 for a medium-sized company. For these companies there are substantial exemptions from requirements to publish information (although they must still provide details to shareholders if asked to do so). Generally they are not listed companies and so are not required to meet the obligations placed on listed companies. Most of these small and medium sized companies are likely to continue to present financial statements based on UK ASB standards and company law.

During the 1980s, concerns were expressed about the 'burden' of regulation for small companies. This burden was seen as falling from all directions, including tax laws, employment laws, product protection laws, health and safety laws and accounting regulation. The government of the time committed itself to reducing this burden. One consequence was that the UK Accounting Standards Board introduced a Financial Reporting Standard for Smaller Entities (FRSSE). This condenses into one standard the essential aspects of all the separate accounting standards for larger companies. It reduces disclosure requirements but maintains standards for measurement. Small companies may choose either to apply the FRSSE in full or to comply with the full range of separate standards.

The Companies Act 1985 permits small and medium-sized companies to file 'abbreviated' financial statements with the Registrar of Companies. The word 'abbreviated' can be explained as 'cutting down the detail' but views have been expressed that this has gone too far and that abbreviated financial statements do not provide useful information about small companies. It allows them, for example, to maintain confidentiality of profit margins. The White Paper of 2005[22] acknowledged this concern but noted that the option was popular with many companies. It said that the Government intended to retain the option for abbreviated financial statements but would require small and medium sized companies to disclose revenue (turnover).

The 2005 White Paper contained a separate section covering small companies. These were defined as meeting two or more of the conditions: turnover not more than £5.6m, balance sheet total not more than £2.8m, employees not more than 50. Separate schedules were provided setting out items to be reported in the balance sheet and profit and loss account.

### 7.9.5   Avoiding information overload

Even the very largest companies may take advantage of the rule which allows them to publish summary financial statements. These are usually very much shorter than the full annual report and are offered to shareholders as an alternative to the full report. There is a short form of the balance sheet, profit and loss account and cash flow statement, no notes to the accounts but usually an accompanying commentary by the company directors. Shareholders are reminded of the existence of the full report and invited to ask for a copy if desired.

### 7.9.6   'Pro forma' financial statements

'Pro forma' financial statements represent a recent development in company reporting that is causing some confusion among users of accounting information, and some concern among the regulators. When companies first announce their profits of the financial year, or the results of an interim period, they do so through an 'earnings announcement' at the Stock Exchange. This is accompanied by a press release which may draw investors' attention to a particular component of the financial statements. According to the dictionary, the phrase 'pro forma' means 'as a matter of form'. The underlying accounting meaning is 'outside the normal reporting regulations'. It usually involves selective editing from a larger body of information that has been prepared under accounting rules. The risk is that the selective information may not, by itself, represent a true and fair view. This does not necessarily mean that the information is bad or misleading, but it does mean that the investor is deprived of the full protection of regulation.

### 7.9.7 Electronic publication of documents

Chapter 4 (Section 4.5.2) explains the progress of a major review of company law in the UK. One conclusion of the Review was that the law allows financial reporting to be a slow process. The White Paper of March 2005 confirmed that a document supplied in electronic form would be validly delivered if that form had been agreed by the intended recipient (or the intended recipient had not replied when asked for a preference). However shareholders and others having a right to receive information would be able to ask for a paper copy of a document.

## 7.10 Summary

- Company law in the UK includes sections that implement EU Directives. This means that UK company accounting has for many years been harmonised with company accounting in other Member States of the EU, but mainly in matters of disclosure. Member states have continued to require or permit different measurement practices.

- From 2005 listed groups of companies in EU Member States have been required to follow the IASB system of reporting. Individual companies and unlisted groups have the choice of the IASB system or UK company law and UK ASB standards.

- The primary financial statements under both systems include a balance sheet, income statement (profit and loss account) and cash flow statement. Under the IASB system a statement of changes in equity is required. Under the UK ASB standards a statement of recognised gains and losses is required and a note of movements on reserves.

- Formats set out the content and layout of financial statements. Under UK company law there are detailed formats required for the balance sheet and profit and loss account. The IASB system is more flexible on layout but provides lists of essential items.

- A group of companies consists of a parent and subsidiaries. All must be included. A subsidiary is defined by the control exercised by the parent. Control is commonly evidenced by the parent holding more than half of the voting power in the subsidiary. Control may be evidenced in other kinds of agreements relating to shareholdings or to the board of directors.

- A consolidated balance sheet contains the total assets and liabilities of the group of companies, after eliminating any amounts receivable and payable between group companies.

- A consolidated income statement (profit and loss account) contains the total revenues and expenses of the group of companies, after eliminating any transactions and profits made between group companies.

- A consolidated cash flow statement contains the total cash flows of the group of companies, after eliminating any cash flows between group companies.

- Goodwill arising on acquisition is calculated by comparing the fair value of the payment for the subsidiary with the fair value of net assets acquired. It represents future economic benefits arising from assets that are not capable of being individually identified and separately recognised.

- Goodwill is recognised as an asset in the balance sheet and is tested annually for impairment.

- Beyond the annual report there is a range of corporate communications – often found most readily by visiting a company's website.

- For small companies special disclosure rules apply to reduce the burden of providing information.

## Further reading

IAS 1 (2004) *Presentation of financial statements*. International Accounting Standards Board. This is a detailed standard, some of which is beyond a first level course, but the examples of financial statements given in the Appendix show the types of presentation that companies might use or adapt.

IFRS 3 (2004) *Business combinations*. International Accounting Standards Board. (This is a very detailed standard which is beyond a first level course but the definitions in the Appendix may be useful in explaining terms encountered in financial statements.)

## Useful websites

International Accounting Standards Board: *www.iasb.org*

UK Accounting Standards Board: *www.asb.org.uk*

London Stock Exchange: *www.londonstockex.co.uk*

Financial Services Authority: *www.fsa.gov.uk*

UK Company Law Review: *www.dti.gov.uk*

# QUESTIONS

The Questions section of each chapter has three types of question. 'Test your understanding' questions to help you review your reading are in the 'A' series of questions. You will find the answers to these by reading and thinking about the material in the book. 'Application' questions to test your ability to apply technical skills are in the 'B' series of questions. Questions requiring you to show skills in problem solving and evaluation are in the 'C' series of questions. A letter [S] indicates that there is a solution at the end of the book.

## A    Test your understanding

**A7.1**    What is a Directive? (Section 7.2.1)

**A7.2**    What is the IAS Regulation? (Section 7.2.1)

**A7.3**    What is the role of the IASB? (Section 7.2.2)

**A7.4**    Name the primary financial statements and explain the purpose of each. (Section 7.3.1)

**A7.5**  The following technical terms appear in this chapter. Check that you know the meaning of each. (If you cannot find them again in the text, they are defined at the end of the book.)

(a)  revenue
(b)  capital
(c)  non-current asset
(d)  depreciation
(e)  directors
(f)  earnings for equity holders (ordinary shareholders)
(g)  earnings per share
(h)  external users (of financial statements)
(i)  financial position
(j)  gross
(k)  gross margin
(l)  gross profit
(m)  net
(n)  net assets
(o)  primary financial statements
(p)  reserves
(q)  revaluation reserve
(r)  share premium
(s)  tangible fixed assets
(t)  turnover.

**A7.6**  How do companies report: (Section 7.3.1)

(a)  financial position;
(b)  performance; and
(c)  changes in financial position?

**A7.7**  What are the main headings to be found in most company balance sheets? (Section 7.4)

**A7.8**  In the Companies Act formats, what is the reason for the order of items under heading C: current assets? (Section 7.4)

**A7.9**  What are the main headings to be found in most company income statements (profit and loss accounts)? (Section 7.5)

**A7.10**  What are the main sections of a cash flow statement prepared according to IAS 7? (Section 7.6)

**A7.11**  Why does depreciation appear as a line item in the reconciliation of operating profit with cash flow? (Section 7.6.3)

**A7.12**  Explain why groups of companies are formed. (Section 7.7)

**A7.13**  Explain the purpose of consolidated financial statements. (Section 7.7)

**A7.14**  Define the terms: (Section 7.7.1)

(a)  group;
(b)  parent company; and
(c)  subsidiary.

**A7.15**  Explain, using the accounting equation, the effect on the parent company's balance sheet of a cash payment for an investment in a subsidiary company. (Section 7.8.1)

**A7.16**  Explain, using the accounting equation, the effect on the parent company's balance sheet of a share issue in exchange for shares in the subsidiary company. (Section 7.8.1)

**A7.17**  Explain what is meant by goodwill on acquisition. (Section 7.8.4)

**A7.18**  What is an associated company? (Section 7.8.5)

**A7.19** Apart from the annual report, what other documents do companies use to communicate financial statement information to investors, creditors and other users of financial statements? (Section 7.9)

## B   Application

**B7.1** [S]
Write a letter to the financial controller of a company advising on the factors which a company should take into consideration when deciding how to arrange information in financial statements.

**B7.2** [S]
Write a note for financial analysts explaining how the published income statement (profit and loss account) provides a useful indication of the financial performance of a company.

**B7.3** [S]
What features are likely to make a balance sheet helpful to users?

**B7.4** [S]
Could a cash flow statement be presented as the only financial statement reported by a company? Explain your view.

## C   Problem solving and evaluation

**C7.1** [S]
A listed company is of the view that shareholders might welcome a statement of highlights and supplementary information as a leaflet to be inserted in the annual report. Give advice on the principles to be followed in making such information useful to users.

## Activities for study groups

Continuing to use the annual reports of companies which you obtained for Chapters 1 and 4, find the financial statements (balance sheet, profit and loss account and cash flow statement) and the notes to the accounts.

1   Compare the financial statements with the formats and presentations shown in this chapter, and note any differences which you observe. Look at the notes to the accounts for items which are required by the regulations but are included in the notes rather than the main financial statements.

2   Find the Operating and Financial Review (sometimes named the finance director's review) and compare the cash flow discussion there with the FRS 1 presentation. Form a view on how readily the discussion may be related to the financial statement.

3   In your group, take the list of qualitative characteristics listed at section 4.2 and use the financial statements as a means of illustrating how the company has met those characteristics. If you have a set of different annual reports, each member of the group should take the role of a finance director pointing out the qualitative characteristics of their own company's financial statements. The group together should then decide on a ranking with a view to nominating one of the annual reports for an award of 'Communicator of the Year'.

## Notes and references

1. IAS 1 (2003), *Presentation of Financial Statements*, para. 8.
2. IASB *Framework*, para. 12.
3. The Appendix to IAS 1 (2003) gives an illustration which is not compulsory.
4. The Appendix to IAS 1 (2003) gives an illustration which is not compulsory.
5. ASB (1996), Financial Reporting Standard (FRS 1), *Cash Flow Statements*, Accounting Standards Board (revised from 1991 version).
6. IASB (2004), IAS 7 *Cash flow statements*, para. 4.
7. IAS 7 (2004), para. 6.
8. IAS 7 (2004), para. 6.
9. ASB (1999), ch. 2, 'The reporting entity', Principles section.
10. IAS 27 (2004) *Consolidated and separate financial statements*, para. 4.
11. IAS 27 (2004), para. 4.
12. IAS 27 (2004), para. 4.
13. IAS 27 (2004), para. 4.
14. IAS 27 (2004), para. 12. A scope exclusion for temporary control, retained in the first 2003 version was removed by IFRS 5 issued in March 2004, see BC 14.
15. IAS 27 (2004), para. 4.
16. IAS 27 (2004), para. 13.
17. IFRS 3 (2004), para. 1 uses the description 'purchase method' but the exposure draft modifying IFRS 3, issued in 2005, uses the description 'acquisition method'.
18. IFRS 3 (2004), Appendix A.
19. IFRS 3 (2004), para. 51. In this section it is assumed in the explanations that fair value equals book value of net assets of subsidiary.
20. IAS 28 (2004), paras. 2 and 6.
21. IASB (2004), IAS 34 *Interim financial reporting*.
22. Company Law Reform, March 2005, Cm. 6456, DTI.

## Supplement to Chapter 7.1

# Information to be presented on the face of the Balance sheet, as required by IAS 1

*Note that this is a list of items, not a format, so a company could choose to present the items in a different sequence.*

There must be separate headings for current and non-current assets, and current and non-current liabilities.[1]

As a minimum the face of the balance sheet must include the following line items:[2]

(a) Property, plant and equipment
(b) Investment property
(c) Intangible assets
(d) Financial assets
(e) Investments accounted for using the equity method
(f) Biological assets
(g) Inventories
(h) Trade and other receivables
(i) Cash and cash equivalents
(j) Trade and other payables
(k) Provisions
(l) Financial liabilities (excluding items shown under (j) and (k))
(m) Liabilities and assets for current tax
(n) Deferred tax assets and deferred tax liabilities
(o) Minority interests within equity (ownership interest)
(p) Issued capital and reserves attributable to equity holders of the parent.

An entity must disclose further sub-classifications of these line items, classified in a manner appropriate to the entity's operations. These further sub-classifications may be presented either on the face of the balance sheet or in notes.[3]

1. IAS 1 (2003), para. 51.
2. IAS 1 (2003), para. 68.
3. IAS 1 (2003), para. 74.

## Supplement to Chapter 7.2

# Balance sheet format 1, as prescribed by the Companies Act 1985

*The Companies Act sets out the format as a list of items. The list attaches letters A to K to the main headings and uses roman numerals for subheadings of items which are important but slightly less important than the main headings. The headings labelled by letters A to K and the subheadings labelled by roman numerals must be shown in the main body of the balance sheet. There are further lists of detailed items which must be reported but which may be contained in additional pages of notes to the balance sheet. These lists are given arabic numerals to identify them. There is a general rule that where an item under any heading is not relevant to the company, or is of zero amount, it need not be disclosed. So if a company does not mention one of the items in the format, it has to be presumed that the particular item is not relevant to that company.*

A  **Called-up share capital not paid**

B  **Fixed assets**
- I  *Intangible assets*
  1 Development costs
  2 Concessions, patents, licences, trade marks and similar rights and assets
  3 Goodwill
  4 Payments on account
- II  *Tangible assets*
  1 Land and buildings
  2 Plant and machinery
  3 Fixtures, fittings, tools and equipment
  4 Payments on account and assets in course of construction
- III  *Investments*
  1 Shares in group undertakings
  2 Loans to group undertakings
  3 Participating interests (excluding group undertakings)
  4 Loans to undertakings in which the company has a participating interest
  5 Other investments other than loans
  6 Other loans
  7 Own shares

C  **Current assets**
- I  *Stocks*
  1 Raw materials and consumables
  2 Work-in-progress
  3 Finished goods and goods for resale
  4 Payments on account
- II  *Debtors*
  1 Trade debtors
  2 Amounts owed by group undertakings
  3 Amounts owed by undertakings in which the company has a participating interest
  4 Other debtors
  5 Called-up share capital not paid
  6 Prepayments and accrued income

III *Investments*
  1 Shares in group undertakings
  2 Own shares
  3 Other investments
IV *Cash at bank and in hand*

**D  Prepayments and accrued income**

**E  Creditors: amounts falling due within one year**
  1 Debenture loans
  2 Bank loans and overdrafts
  3 Payments received on account
  4 Trade creditors
  5 Bills of exchange payable
  6 Amounts owed to group undertakings
  7 Amounts owed to undertakings in which the company has a participating interest
  8 Other creditors including taxation and social security
  9 Accruals and deferred income

**F  Net current assets (liabilities)**

**G  Total assets less current liabilities**

**H  Creditors: amounts falling due after more than one year**
  1 Debenture loans
  2 Bank loans and overdrafts
  3 Payments received on account
  4 Trade creditors
  5 Bills of exchange payable
  6 Amounts owed to group undertakings
  7 Amounts owed to undertakings in which the company has a participating interest
  8 Other creditors including taxation and social security
  9 Accruals and deferred income

**I  Provisions for liabilities and charges**
  1 Pensions and similar obligations
  2 Taxation, including deferred taxation
  3 Other provisions

**J  Accruals and deferred income**

**Minority interests***

**K  Capital and reserves**
  I    *Called-up share capital*
  II   *Share premium account*
  III  *Revaluation reserve*
  IV   *Other reserves*
     1 Capital redemption reserve
     2 Reserve for own shares
     3 Reserves provided by the articles of association
     4 Other reserves
  V    *Profit and loss account*

**Minority interests***

*Note*: Where minority interests are relevant, they are to be treated as having a letter attached. Companies may choose one of the two permitted locations.

## Supplement to Chapter 7.3

# Information to be presented on the face of the Income Statement as required by IAS 1

As a minimum, the face of the income statement must include line items that present the following amounts for the period:[4]

(a) revenue
(b) finance costs
(c) share of the profit or loss of associates and joint ventures accounted for using the equity method
(d) tax expense
(e) a single amount comprising the total of (i) the after-tax profit or loss of discontinued operations and (ii) the after-tax gain or loss recognised on disposal of the discontinued operation
(f) profit or loss.

If there is a minority interest in a subsidiary (where the parent holds less than 100% of the share capital of the subsidiary) then the profit or loss attributable to the minority interest must be disclosed separately from the profit or loss attributable to equity shareholder in the parent.[5]

An entity must disclose additional line items, headings and subtotals on the face of the income statement when such presentation is relevant to an understanding of the entity's financial performance.[6]

4. IAS 1 (2003), para. 81.
5. IAS 1 (2003), para. 82.
6. IAS 1 (2003), para. 83.

## Supplement to Chapter 7.4

# UK Companies Act
# Profit and loss account format 1 – list of contents

1  Turnover
2  Cost of sales
3  Gross profit
4  Distribution costs
5  Administrative expenses
6  Other operating income
7  Income from shares in group undertakings
8  Income from participating interests (excluding group undertakings)
9  Income from other fixed asset investments
10  Other interest received and similar income
11  Amounts written off investments
12  Interest payable and similar charges
13  Tax on profit or loss of ordinary activities
14  Profit or loss on ordinary activities after taxation
15  Extraordinary income
16  Extraordinary charges
17  Extraordinary profit or loss
18  Tax on extraordinary profit or loss
19  Other taxes not shown under the above items
20  Profit or loss for the financial year

# Chapter 8

# Non-current (fixed) assets

## New stores

During the period we opened ten stores adding 37,000 square feet of net retail space. Two stores were relocated. At the period end, total selling space was 562,000 square feet (2004: 525,000 square feet), of which 33,750 square feet opened in the 26 weeks to 29 January 2005. Ottakar's traded from 131 stores at the period end. Of these, 38 stores covering 280,000 square feet are in our Lifestyle format which includes a coffee shop, and comprises some 50% of our total selling space – a net increase of three stores (2004: 35 stores covering 260,700 square feet).

## Former Hammicks stores

In April 2003 we acquired 24 stores from Hammicks Bookshops Limited. We have now traded for a full year from these stores and we are pleased with their progress. Sales and gross margins are growing to an expected level as buying practices and product sales mix become integrated with the rest of the business.

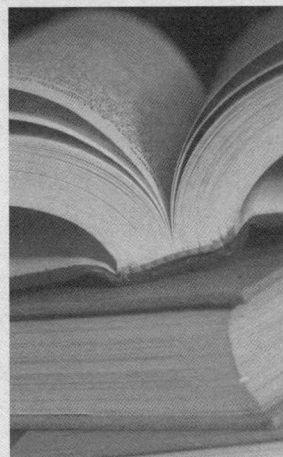

## Current strategy

At the period end, Ottakar's traded from 131 branches nationwide and is the UK's second largest specialist chain behind Waterstone's. The book market is undergoing considerable change with the expansion of specialist chains such as Ottakar's and established penetration by the supermarkets and the Internet. The market is valued at some £2.5bn (source: Book Marketing Limited) and Ottakar's believes it has an 8% share of this market. The market is growing at an annualised rate of 3 to 5% (source: Book Marketing Limited) spurred on by a new level of consumer interest in books galvanised by film and other media. Over the years Ottakar's will continue to pursue its PRISM strategy comprising physical expansion, range development, innovation, staff welfare and margin growth.

### Consolidated balance sheet

| | Note | 29 January 2005 £000 | 31 January 2004 Restated £000 |
|---|---|---|---|
| **Fixed assets** | | | |
| Intangible assets | 10 | 674 | 722 |
| Tangible assets | 11 | 33,882 | 30,552 |

### Notes to the financial statements

| | Freehold Land and Buildings £000 | Short Leasehold Land and Buildings £000 | Fixtures and Fittings £000 | Office Equipment £000 | Motor Vehicles £000 | Total £000 |
|---|---|---|---|---|---|---|
| **Net book value** | | | | | | |
| At 29 January 2005 | – | 4,832 | 23,310 | 5,733 | 7 | 33,882 |
| At 31 January 2004 | 367 | 5,178 | 19,741 | 5,262 | 4 | 30,552 |

Source: Ottakar's Annual Report 2005, pp. 5, 8, 25, 34.

## Discussion point

1 Why is it important for the company to give descriptive information about the investment in fixed assets?

2 What is the largest fixed asset category by net book value?

## Contents

## Learning outcomes

After studying this chapter you should be able to:

- Define a non-current (fixed) asset and apply the definition.
- Explain the recognition conditions that are applied to tangible non-current (fixed) assets, intangible non-current (fixed) assets and non-current (fixed) asset investments.
- Explain users' needs for information about non-current (fixed) assets.
- Describe and explain the non-current (fixed) asset information provided in annual reports of companies.
- Evaluate the usefulness of published information about non-current (fixed) assets.
- Explain the nature of depreciation.
- Calculate depreciation, record the effect on the accounting equation and report the result in financial statements.

Additionally, for those who choose to study the Supplement:

- Record non-current (fixed) assets and depreciation in ledger accounts.

## 8.1  Introduction

If you have progressed through Chapters 1 to 7 you are now familiar with the accounting equation and the analysis of transactions or events using that equation. You know what is meant by the terms asset, liability, revenue, expense and ownership interest. You are aware of the structure of the primary financial statements and the way in which they seek to provide information which is relevant and reliable.

This chapter starts a new phase of the text which will help you to develop a critical awareness of some of the component items in the financial statements. Chapters 8 to 12 progress through the main sections of the balance sheet. Inevitably, they also cover relevant aspects of the income statement (profit and loss account) and the cash flow statement because transactions involving the balance sheet will sometimes have an effect in the other financial statements.

It is important at this stage not to become so enthusiastic for the intricacies of accounting procedures as to lose sight of the importance of user needs, which were set out in Chapter 1. That chapter set out, in section 1.2, the structure of most conceptual frameworks, which provides a sequence for each of Chapters 8 to 12, as follows:

- What are the principles for defining and recognising these items?
- What are the information needs of users in respect of the particular items?
- What information is currently provided by companies to meet these needs?
- Does the information show the desirable qualitative characteristics of financial statements?
- What are the principles for measuring, and processes for recording, these items?

That analysis is applied to non-current (fixed) assets in this chapter.

## 8.2  Definitions

The following definition of an asset was provided in Chapter 2.

**Definition**

> An **asset** is a resource controlled by the entity as a result of past events and from which future economic benefits are expected to flow.[1]

The following definitions explain the nature of tangible and non-tangible non-current assets. The word 'tangible' means 'able to be touched'. So 'intangible' means 'not able to be touched'.

**Definitions**

> A **non-current asset** is any asset that does not meet the definition of a current asset.[2] Non-current assets include tangible, intangible and financial assets of a long-term nature. These are also described as **fixed assets**.[3]
>
> **Tangible non-current (fixed) assets** are assets that have physical substance and are held for use in the production or supply of goods or services, for rental to others, or for administrative purposes on a continuing basis in the reporting entity's activities.[4]
>
> An **intangible asset** is an identifiable non-monetary asset without physical substance.[5]

These definitions are taken from different sources because the definitions have been developed and discussed at different times for different purposes. The IASB and the UK ASB have both spent many years in discussion over the subjects of accounting for tangible and intangible non-current assets because these are complex matters.

### 8.2.1 Examples of non-current (fixed) assets

The following is a sample of the non-current (fixed) assets found in company balance sheets.

*Tangible non-current (fixed) assets*

- Land and buildings owned by the entity
- Buildings leased by the entity
- Plant and equipment (owned or leased)
- Vehicles (owned or leased)
- Office equipment
- Assets under construction
- Telecommunications network
- Airport runways
- Water pipes and sewers
- Oil and mineral reserves.

*Intangible non-current (fixed) assets*

- Newspaper titles and publishing rights
- Patents
- Trade marks
- Goodwill purchased
- Brand names purchased.

*Investments*

- Long-term investments in subsidiary companies
- Long-term investments in other companies.

That sample was taken from only 10 annual reports of leading companies. Looking at more companies would soon extend the list considerably. The potential variety and the likelihood of encountering something new is one reason why definitions are essential.

### 8.2.2 Cost of a non-current (fixed) asset

There is one issue which is not as straightforward as it seems. That is the question of measuring the cost of a non-current (fixed) asset. When a toffee manufacturer buys a new toffee-shaping machine, the purchase price will be known from the supplier's invoice and the manufacturer's catalogue, but should the costs of delivery and installation be added to the amount recorded as the asset cost? When an insurance company buys a new head office, the purchase price will be shown in the contract, but should the legal costs be added to the amount recorded as the asset cost? When a new head office building is under development and interest is being paid on the funds borrowed to finance the development, should the interest paid on the borrowed funds be added to the cost of the development as part of the asset value?

The answer in all three cases is 'yes', although the third example causes greatest discussion and debate. The general principle is that the cost of a non-current (fixed) asset is the purchase price or the amount spent on its production together with any other expenditure incurred in bringing the non-current (fixed) asset to working condition for its intended use at its intended location.

**Definition** | The **cost** of a non-current (fixed) asset is the purchase price or the amount spent on its production together with any costs directly attributable to bringing the non-current (fixed) asset to working condition for its intended use at its intended location.

### 8.2.3 Repairs and improvements

There are sometimes problems in deciding whether a payment for a repair to a non-current (fixed) asset should be treated as an expense of the business or an asset. The key lies in the words of the definition of an asset and the phrase *future economic benefits*. If the payment relates to some act which merely preserves the existing life of the asset and the existing expectations of benefit from the asset, then the payment is treated as a repair and reported as an **expense**. The asset of cash decreases and there is a decrease in the ownership interest caused by the expense.

If the payment relates to some act which significantly extends the useful life of the asset, or increases the future economic benefit expected from the asset, then the payment is treated as an **improvement** and reported as an asset. It may be reported as a separate asset but, more usually, the amount will be added to the cost or value recorded for the asset which has been improved. The asset of cash decreases and is replaced by an asset of improvements. There is no effect on the ownership interest.

The following are examples of improvements and repairs.

#### Improvements

- Extensions to a building which increase the operating capacity of the business.
- A new roof which gives a building an extra ten years of life.
- A new engine for a delivery van which is more powerful than the existing engine and allows faster delivery in hilly districts.
- Renewing the fittings and interior decoration of a hotel to attract international visitors instead of the traditional local customers.

#### Repairs

- A new roof, required because of storm damage, which will keep the building weatherproof for the remainder of its estimated life.
- A new engine for a delivery van which replaces an existing damaged engine.
- Redecorating inside a building to preserve the existing standards of cleanliness and appearance.

**Activity 8.1**

*Imagine you are the owner of a big hotel in the centre of town. Make a list of the items you would expect to include in your business balance sheet as non-current (fixed) assets. Make a list of the types of repair which would be classed as 'improvements'. Use the definition of a non-current (fixed) asset to show that your list includes items which are correctly classified.*

## 8.3 Recognition

This section outlines the recognition issues faced in reporting non-current assets in the separate categories of tangible assets, intangible assets, and investment assets.

### 8.3.1 Tangible non-current (fixed) assets

Tangible non-current (fixed) assets are those items which can be touched, seen or heard and meet the conditions set out in the definition of a non-current (fixed) asset. **Recognition** by reporting in the balance sheet presents no problem where the future benefit can be identified and the cost of the asset can be measured. (Look back to section 2.5 for an explanation of recognition.) The evidence of cost is usually a purchase invoice. Some tangible non-current (fixed) assets are recorded at a valuation made subsequent to the purchase. Revaluations are discussed in Chapter 12.

As the list in the previous section indicates, there is considerable variety in tangible non-current (fixed) assets. The common feature is that they all have a limited life expectancy. They may wear out, be used up, go out of fashion, break down or be sold for scrap. Whatever the reason, the effect is the same and is called **depreciation**. Users have many questions to ask about tangible non-current (fixed) assets, such as:

- What kinds of tangible fixed assets are in use?
- How old are they?
- How has the company measured the depreciation?
- Where is the depreciation recorded?

Answering those questions will take up most of the remainder of this chapter.

## 8.3.2 Intangible non-current (fixed) assets

An intangible non-current (fixed) asset is an item which meets the definition of a non-current (fixed) asset but has no physical substance. It cannot be touched, seen or heard. The evidence of its existence is the benefit flowing from it. For many years, items such as patents, trade marks and licences to manufacture products have been bought and sold between companies. The purchase has been recorded as a non-current (fixed) asset and depreciated over the estimated life of the patent, trade mark or licence. The estimated life is decided by law (for patents and trade marks) or by legal contract (for licences). The depreciation of intangible non-current (fixed) assets is usually referred to as **amortisation** (in which you may recognise the French word *mort* meaning *death*).

The intangible non-current (fixed) asset which has attracted most accounting-related comment in recent years has been the brand name of a company's product. When a company works over many years to develop the reputation of its product, that reputation creates an expected future benefit for the company and meets the definition of an **asset** as set out in Chapter 2. However, the generally held view is that it should not be recognised in the balance sheet because it fails the **recognition** test of Chapter 2. The conventional argument is that there is no measurable **cost** of the reputation gained by the brand name and the value cannot be measured with reliability.

That is the generally held view which was challenged in the mid-1980s by a number of leading companies. Some had bought other companies which had developed brand names. The new owners argued that they were buying the other company purely because of the quality of the brand name and they wanted to show that brand name in the new balance sheet. They had a reasonable argument because they had paid a price in the market and could show the cost of the brand name acquired. Other companies who had developed their own brand names did not want to be left behind and so paid expert valuers to calculate a value for their home-grown brands. A new professional specialism of brand valuation gained prominence and the experts claimed they could measure the value of a home-grown brand with reliability.

The companies which reported brand names in the balance sheet argued that the brand had a long life and did not require amortisation. This argument gave them the advantage of expanding the balance sheet without the disadvantage of amortisation appearing in the income statement (profit and loss account).

The IASB has issued a standard, IAS 38, covering accounting for intangible assets. Internally generated brand names must *not* be recognised as intangible assets. This rule applies to similar assets such as publishing titles, customer lists, or newspaper titles. Purchased brand names or trade marks or patents may be reported in a balance sheet if they meet the conditions for recognition. Recognition requires that it is probable that the expected economic benefit will flow to the entity, and the cost of the asset can be measured reliably.

If the intangible asset has a finite life it must be amortised over its useful life. The method of amortisation must reflect the pattern of use of the asset.

**Activity 8.2**

*A company which has manufactured a well-known brand of brown bread for many years has decided that the brand name is so well known that it should appear in the balance sheet. Write down two arguments in favour of this, to be made by the company's finance director, and two arguments against, which will appear in a newspaper article.*

### 8.3.3    Investments

Investments exist in many different forms but the essential feature is an ability to generate future economic benefits so that the wealth of the owner increases. This increase in wealth may arise because the value of the investment increases, or may arise because the investment creates income for the owner in the form of a distribution such as interest paid or dividends. Companies may hold investments for a variety of reasons. A non-current (fixed asset) investment is one which is held for long-term purposes, such as shares in another company which has close trading links with the investing company.

The number of shares held may be such as to give direct control of the investment or may be of a lesser amount which indicates a long-term relationship, without direct control, in a similar line of business.

Non-current (fixed) asset investments may be held so that resources are available to meet a long-term obligation, such as the payment of pensions. Such non-current (fixed) assets are normally found in the balance sheets of insurance companies or pension funds, rather than in the balance sheet of the company employing staff.

The features which make investments different as non-current (fixed) assets are the importance of the increase in value of the investment itself and the fact that they are not used in the production or service process. Both features require a different kind of accounting treatment from that given to other non-current (fixed) assets. Those special treatments are advanced accounting matters and will not be dealt with in any detail in this text. What you should look for in accounts is the existence of non-current (fixed) asset investments and the information provided about them. The questions users will ask are: 'How well is this investment keeping up its value?' and 'How important is the income from this investment to the overall profit of the company?'

## 8.4  Users' needs for information

**Activity 8.3**

*Before you read this section, make a list of the information about non-current (fixed) assets which would be useful to you if you wished to learn more about a specific company. Then read the section and compare it with your list. How far-thinking are you in respect of accounting information?*

Analysts who write reports for professional and private investors have a particular interest in the non-current (fixed) assets because these are the base from which profits are generated. They want to know what types of assets are held, how old they are and what plans the company has for future investment in non-current (fixed) assets.

The analysts also want to know about the impact of the depreciation charge on the profit of the year. They are aware that detailed aspects of calculations of depreciation may vary from one year to the next and this may affect the comparability of the profit amounts.

To estimate the remaining life of the assets, analysts compare the accumulated depreciation with the total cost (or value) of the non-current (fixed) assets. If the accumulated depreciation is relatively low, then the non-current (fixed) assets are relatively new. Other companies in the industry will be used for comparison. The analysts also compare the depreciation charge for the year with the total cost (or value) of the assets and expect to see a similar relationship from one year to the next. A sudden change will cause them to ask more questions about a change in the basis of calculation.

## 8.5 Information provided in the financial statements

In Chapter 7 the balance sheet of Safe and Sure plc was presented. The balance sheet showed a single line of information on tangible non-current (fixed) assets. This section shows how that single line becomes understandable when read in conjunction with the notes to the accounts, the statement of accounting policy and the finance director's review.

### 8.5.1 Balance sheet

|  | Notes | Year 7 £m | Year 6 £m |
|---|---|---|---|
| **Non-current assets** |  |  |  |
| Tangible assets | 2 | 137.5 | 121.9 |

### 8.5.2 Notes to the balance sheet

In the notes to the balance sheet there is considerably more information:

**Note 2 Tangible non-current assets**

|  | Land and buildings £m | Plant and equipment £m | Vehicles £m | Total £m |
|---|---|---|---|---|
| Cost or valuation |  |  |  |  |
| At 1 January Year 7 | 28.3 | 96.4 | 104.8 | 229.5 |
| Additions at cost | 3.9 | 18.5 | 37.8 | 60.2 |
| On acquisitions | 0.3 | 1.0 | 0.7 | 2.0 |
| Disposals | (0.6) | (3.1) | (24.7) | (28.4) |
| At 31 December Year 7 | 31.9 | 112.8 | 118.6 | 263.3 |
| Aggregate depreciation |  |  |  |  |
| At 1 January Year 7 | 2.2 | 58.8 | 46.6 | 107.6 |
| Depreciation for the year | 0.5 | 13.5 | 19.2 | 33.2 |
| On acquisitions | 0.1 | 0.7 | 0.6 | 1.4 |
| Disposals | (0.2) | (2.8) | (13.4) | (16.4) |
| At 31 December Year 7 | 2.6 | 70.2 | 53.0 | 125.8 |
| Net book value at 31 December Year 7 | 29.3 | 42.6 | 65.6 | 137.5 |
| Net book value at 31 December Year 6 | 26.1 | 37.6 | 58.2 | 121.9 |

**Analysis of land and buildings at cost or valuation**

|  | Year 7 £m | Year 6 £m |
|---|---|---|
| At cost | 10.4 | 7.1 |
| At valuation | 21.5 | 21.2 |
|  | 31.9 | 28.3 |

The majority of the group's freehold and long-term leasehold properties were revalued during Year 5 by independent valuers. Valuations were made on the basis of the market value for existing use. The book values of the properties were adjusted to the revaluations and the resultant net surplus was credited to the revaluation reserve.

**Analysis of net book value of land and buildings**

|                              | Year 7 | Year 6 |
|------------------------------|-------:|-------:|
|                              | £m     | £m     |
| Freehold                     | 24.5   | 21.0   |
| Leasehold:                   |        |        |
| Over 50 years unexpired      | 2.1    | 2.4    |
| Under 50 years unexpired     | 2.7    | 2.7    |
|                              | 29.3   | 26.1   |

If the revalued assets were stated on the historical cost basis the amounts would be:

|                              | Year 7 | Year 6 |
|------------------------------|-------:|-------:|
|                              | £m     | £m     |
| Land and buildings at cost   | 15.7   | 14.5   |
| Aggregate depreciation       | (2.2)  | (1.9)  |
|                              | 13.5   | 12.6   |

It is clear from the extensive nature of note 2 to the balance sheet that tangible non-current (fixed) assets are regarded as important by those who regulate the information. All companies present a detailed note of this kind because the information is required by IAS 16, *Property, Plant and Equipment*.

### 8.5.3    Statement of accounting policy

In addition the company is required, by the accounting standard IAS 1, *Presentation of Financial Statements*, to disclose its significant accounting policies. For this company the wording of the accounting policy statement is as follows:

**Freehold and leasehold property**
*Freehold and leasehold land and buildings are stated either at cost or at their revalued amounts less depreciation. Full revaluations are made at five-year intervals with interim valuations in the intervening years, the most recent being in Year 0.*

*Provision for depreciation of freehold land and buildings is made at the annual rate of 1% of cost or the revalued amounts. Leasehold land and buildings are amortised in equal annual instalments over the periods of the leases subject to a minimum annual provision of 1% of cost or the revalued amounts. When properties are sold the difference between sales proceeds and net book value is dealt with in the income statement (profit and loss account).*

**Other tangible non-current (fixed) assets**
*Other tangible non-current assets are stated at cost less depreciation. Provision for depreciation is made mainly in equal annual instalments over the estimated useful lives of the assets as follows:*

*4 to 5 years     vehicles*
*5 to 10 years    plant, machinery and equipment*

### 8.5.4    Operating and financial review

There is also a comment in the finance director's report, as a contribution to the operating and financial review:

*Capital expenditure*
*The major items of capital expenditure are vehicles, equipment used on customers' premises and office equipment, particularly computers. Disposals during the year were mainly of vehicles being replaced on a rolling programme.*

*Find the annual report of a company of your choice. This may be through access to the website, or by requesting a printed copy of the annual report through the website **www.ft.com**, or by using the free annual reports offer on the London Stock Exchange page of the Financial Times.*

*In the annual report find the information that corresponds to the extracts from Safe & Sure given in section 8.5. What are the similarities and differences? What do you learn about the non-current (fixed) asset base of your chosen company?*

## 8.6 Usefulness of published information

Here is David Wilson to explain how useful he sees the information provided by companies about their tangible non-current (fixed) assets. If you look back to Chapter 4 you will see that he was about to visit the company and had made a preliminary list of questions. He has now made the visit and has a better understanding of what is reported in the balance sheet. He talks to Leona in a break at a workout session.

DAVID: *I told you that in making my review before visiting the company I looked closely at the type of tangible non-current (fixed) assets held and the estimated useful life. I also checked that the depreciation period and method of calculation had not changed from previous years.*

*As I was making a site visit I took the opportunity to look at the various non-current (fixed) assets. This is a group of companies, expanding by acquisition of other companies, and each acquisition brings in more land and buildings. Some of these assets are recorded at valuation rather than original cost. The company has to review the valuation on a regular That is quite a common practice and I have confidence in the firm of valuers used.*

*Plant and equipment has an aggregate depreciation of £70.2m which is 62% of the cost of the assets at £112.8m. It seems to me that must be saying that the plant and equipment is more than half-way through its estimated life. The finance director wasn't too enthusiastic about this interpretation. He pointed out that when another company is acquired the non-current (fixed) assets may be quite old and have to be brought into the group balance sheet, but once they are in group control there is a strict policy of evaluation and replacement. He views the depreciation policy as being at the prudent end of the spectrum, so the realistic life remaining might be marginally over half, but discretion and the fast-moving nature of the industry requires an element of caution. He called in the plant manager who showed me the replacement schedules for plant and equipment for the next three years. It certainly reassured me that risk of obsolescence is probably not a serious worry. I also met the vehicle fleet supervisor who showed me similar replacement schedules for the vehicles.*

*I saw how the vehicle fleet is managed so that every vehicle is idle for the minimum time. Each vehicle is assigned to a group of cleaning operatives, whose shifts are scheduled so that the vehicle's use is maximised. Plant and equipment are the responsibility of area managers who have to look after security, maintenance and efficiency of usage. I thought it was all really quite impressive.*

*The depreciation charge for the plant and equipment in Year 7 is £13.5m which is 12% of the cost of £112.8m and suggests an estimated life of just over eight years is being applied. That is within the range of five to ten years stated as the company's accounting policy. I think the wording 'five to ten years' is too vague. Using five years would double the depreciation charge compared with ten. I tried to pin down the finance director so that I can get a good figure for my forecast but all he would say was that there is no reason to suppose there are any unusual features in the amount in the accounts. The depreciation charge for vehicles is £19.2m which is 16% of the cost of £118.6m. That suggests an estimated life of just over six years is being applied. I asked the finance director how that squared with the accounting policy statement of estimated useful lives of four to five years for vehicles. He did seem to sigh a little at that point but was quite patient in explaining that there are some fully depreciated vehicles still in use (because they are quite prudent in their estimates of depreciation) and so the depreciation charge is not the 20% to 25% I was looking for. I'll need to think about that one but I might move my estimate for next year closer to 20%.*

*You asked me how this company's information measures up to the qualitative characteristics (set out in Chapter 4). Relevance I would rate highly, because there is plenty of information in the notes which I can use to ask questions about the effective use of non-current (fixed) assets and the impact on income statement (profit and loss account) through the depreciation charge. Reliability, faithful representation and neutrality are qualities I leave to the auditors. Prudence is something which seems to come out strongly in conversation with the finance director. The detailed schedule of assets which I saw suggests that completeness is not a problem. Comparability is fine because there are amounts for the previous year and the standard format allows me to make comparison with other companies in the industry. Understandability is perhaps more of a problem than I thought. Those fully depreciated assets caught me out.*

**LEONA:** *Well, I have now heard you admit that there is some value in having auditors. Shall I tell you how much you have missed? You could have asked more searching questions about the way in which they measure the cost of plant and equipment. Does it include delivery charges and installation costs? You could have asked whether a technical expert inside the company estimates and reviews the asset lives used, or whether the finance director makes a guess. Did you ask whether they are perhaps verging on being over-prudent so that surprises come later when the depreciation charge is less than expected? You could have asked how the interim valuations are carried out. These are all questions we ask as auditors so that you may treat the information as being reliable and a faithful representation.*

Hopefully you now have a feeling for the information provided by companies on tangible non-current (fixed) assets and how it is used by the professional investor. The nature and recording of depreciation is now explained.

## 8.7 Depreciation: an explanation of its nature

**Activity 8.5**

*Before you read this section, write down what you think 'depreciation' means. Then read the section and compare it with your initial views. Depreciation is a very subjective matter and there are different views of its purpose, so your answer may be interesting even if it does not match the text. You should consult your lecturer, tutor or other expert in the area to understand why your perceptions may be different.*

**Definitions**[6]

**Depreciation** is the systematic allocation of the depreciable amount of an asset over its useful life.

The **depreciable amount** is the cost of an asset, or other amount substituted for cost, less its residual value.

**Residual value** is the estimated amount that an entity would currently obtain from disposal of the asset, after deducting the estimated cost of disposal, if the asset were already of the age and in the condition expected at the end of its useful life.

The asset may be an item of plant or equipment which is wearing out through being used. It may be a payment made by a company for the right to become a tenant of a property. That payment purchases a lease which reduces in value through the passage of time. The asset may be a computer system which becomes out of date in a very short space of time because of obsolescence. It may be a machine which produces goods for which demand falls because of changing market conditions.

The definition shows that depreciation is a device used in accounting to allocate (spread) the cost of a non-current (fixed) asset over its useful life. The process of spreading cost over more than one accounting period is called **allocation**.

In terms of the accounting equation, the useful life of the non-current (fixed) asset is being reduced and this will reduce the ownership interest.

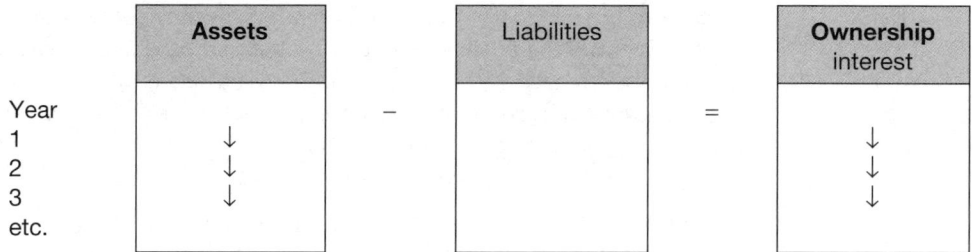

| | Assets | | Liabilities | | Ownership interest |
|---|---|---|---|---|---|
| Year | | – | | = | |
| 1 | ↓ | | | | ↓ |
| 2 | ↓ | | | | ↓ |
| 3 | ↓ | | | | ↓ |
| etc. | | | | | |

As the asset becomes older, the depreciation of one year is added to the depreciation of previous years. This is called the **accumulated depreciation** or **aggregate depreciation**. The accumulated depreciation at the end of any year is equal to the accumulated depreciation at the start of the year plus the depreciation charge for that year.

Deducting the accumulated depreciation from the original cost leaves the **net book value**. The net book value could also be described as the cost remaining as a benefit for future years.

Showing the effect of depreciation by use of arrows and the accounting equation is relatively easy. Deciding on the amount of depreciation each year is much more difficult because there are so many different views of how to calculate the amount of asset used up in each period.

## 8.7.1 Calculation of depreciation

Calculation of depreciation requires three pieces of information:

1 the cost of the asset;
2 the estimated useful life; and
3 the estimated residual value.

The total depreciation of the non-current (fixed) asset is equal to the cost of the non-current (fixed) asset minus the estimated residual value. The purpose of the depreciation calculation is to spread the total depreciation over the estimated useful life.

The first point at which differences of opinion arise is in the estimation of the useful life and residual value. These are matters of judgement which vary from one person to the next.

Unfortunately the differences do not stop at those estimates. There is also no agreement on the arithmetical approach to spreading the total depreciation over the useful life. Some people are of the opinion that a non-current (fixed) asset is used evenly over time and that the depreciation should reflect the benefit gained from its use. Others argue that the non-current (fixed) asset declines in value most in the early years and so the depreciation charge should be greater in earlier years.

## 8.7.2    Straight-line method

Those who are of the opinion that a non-current (fixed) asset is used evenly over time apply a method of calculation called straight-line depreciation. The formula is:

$$\frac{\text{Cost} - \text{Expected residual value}}{\text{Expected life}}$$

To illustrate the use of the formula, take a non-current (fixed) asset which has a cost of £1,000 and an estimated life of five years. The estimated residual value is nil. The calculation of the annual depreciation charge is:

$$\frac{£1,000 - \text{nil}}{5} = £200 \text{ per annum}$$

The depreciation rate is sometimes expressed as a percentage of the original cost. In this case the company would state its depreciation policy as follows:

*Accounting policy:*
*Depreciation is charged on a straight-line basis at a rate of 20% of cost per annum.*

**Exhibit 8.1**
**Pattern of depreciation and net book value over the life of an asset**

| End of year | Depreciation of the year (a) £ | Total depreciation (b) £ | Net book value of the asset (£1,000 – b) £ |
|---|---|---|---|
| 1 | 200 | 200 | 800 |
| 2 | 200 | 400 | 600 |
| 3 | 200 | 600 | 400 |
| 4 | 200 | 800 | 200 |
| 5 | 200 | 1,000 | nil |

**Exhibit 8.2**
**Graph of net book value over Years 1 to 5, for the straight-line method of depreciation**

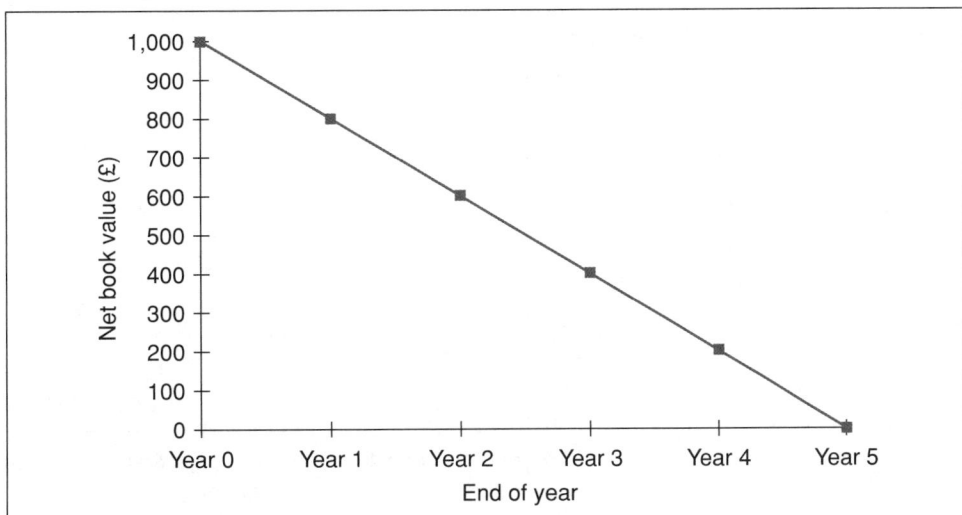

The phrase 'straight-line' is used because a graph of the net book value of the asset at the end of each year produces a straight line. Exhibit 8.1 sets out the five-year pattern of depreciation and net book value for the example used above.

Exhibit 8.2 shows a graph of the net book value at the end of each year. The graph starts at the cost figure of £1,000 when the asset is new (Year 0) and reduces by £200 each year until it is zero at the end of Year 5.

### 8.7.3   Reducing-balance method

Those who believe that the asset depreciates most in earlier years would calculate the depreciation using the formula:

*Fixed percentage × Net book value at the start of the year*

Take the example of the asset costing £1,000. The fixed percentage applied for the reducing-balance method might be as high as 50%. The calculations would be as shown in the table in Exhibit 8.3.

You will see from the table in Exhibit 8.3 that under the reducing-balance method there is always a small balance remaining. In this example, the rate of 50% is used to

**Exhibit 8.3**
**Calculation of reducing-balance depreciation**

| Year | Net book value at start of year (a) £ | Annual depreciation (b) = 50% of (a) £ | Net book value at end of year (a − b) £ |
|------|------|------|------|
| 1 | 1,000 | 500 | 500 |
| 2 | 500 | 250 | 250 |
| 3 | 250 | 125 | 125 |
| 4 | 125 | 63 | 62 |
| 5 | 62 | 31 | 31 |

**Exhibit 8.4**
**Graph of net book value over Years 1 to 5, for the reducing-balance method of depreciation**

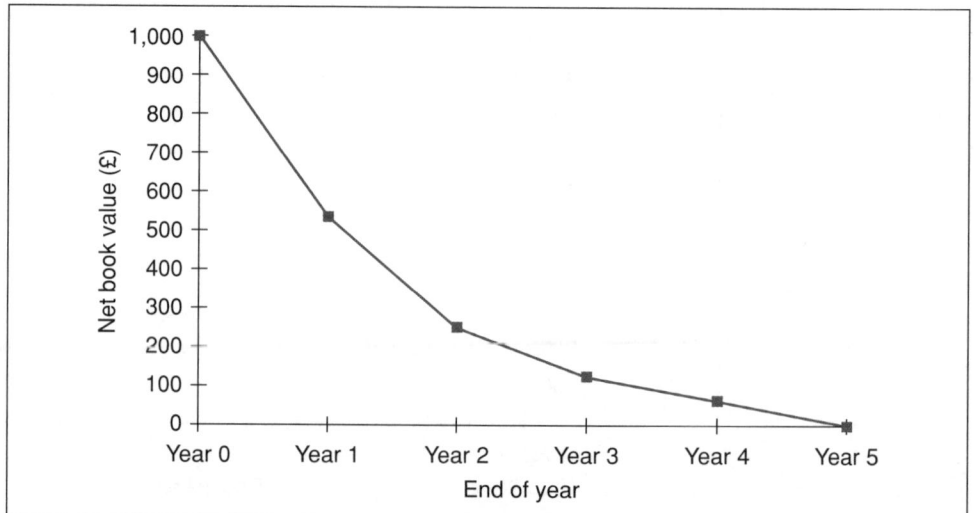

bring the net book value to a relatively small amount. The formula for calculating the exact rate requires a knowledge of compound interest and may be found at the end of the Supplement to this chapter. For those whose main interest is in understanding and interpreting accounts it is not necessary to know the formula, but it is useful to be aware that a very much higher percentage rate is required on the reducing-balance method as compared with the straight-line method. As a useful guide, the reducing-balance rate must be at least twice the rate of the straight-line calculation if the major part of the asset is to be depreciated over its useful life.

A graph of the net book value at the end of each year under the reducing-balance method is shown in Exhibit 8.4. The steep slope at the start shows that the net book value declines rapidly in the early part of the asset's life and then less steeply towards the end when most of the benefit of the asset has been used up.

## 8.7.4  Which method to choose?

The separate recording of asset at cost and accumulated depreciation is accounting information provided in many countries. The UK practice at a general level is consistent with the IASB standard. Country-specific factors may lead to differences in matters of detail such as the choice of depreciation method or the estimated life of non-current (fixed) assets. In some countries, the depreciation expense in the accounting income statement (profit and loss account) must match that used for the purposes of calculating taxable profit. This may encourage the use of the reducing-balance method, giving a higher expense (and so a lower profit) in the early years of the asset's life. In the UK there are separate rules in tax law for calculating depreciation, and so this has no effect on accounting profit.

The choice of depreciation method should be based on the expected pattern of usage of the asset. If the usage is evenly spread then the straight-line method is appropriate. If the usage is heaviest in early years then the reducing-balance method is the best representation of the economic activity. In practice, it is found that most UK companies use straight-line depreciation. In some other countries, particularly those where tax rules and accounting laws are closely linked, the reducing-balance method is commonly observed. So it appears that there are different international practices that may reflect different conditions in the respective countries. David and Leona discuss the problem.

DAVID: *The choice of depreciation method may have a significant impact on reported profit. Companies that are actively investing in non-current (fixed) assets will do so in the expectation of increased profits. However it may take some time for such profits to emerge. If, in the meantime, there is a relatively high charge to income statement (profit and loss account) through reducing-balance depreciation, profits may fall in the short term. In contrast the use of straight-line depreciation will have a less dramatic impact on reported profit immediately following the new investment, so the company avoids a dip in profits.*

LEONA: *I can't accept that as a valid argument to give to the auditor. I ask the company what the pattern of usage is. If the company tells me that the asset produces benefit evenly over its useful life, I can accept straight-line depreciation. If, on the other hand, I hear that the asset is more productive in its early years of life, I expect to see reducing-balance depreciation.*

DAVID: *Well let me try your social conscience. I came across a case of a UK company that had been taken over by a German parent company. The UK company had always used straight-line depreciation and was making small profits each year. The parent company had always used reducing-balance depreciation and so changed the accounting method of the UK subsidiary. Small profits turned into large losses and the parent company said that there would have to be a reduction in the workforce to cut costs. The employee representatives said that nothing had changed except that the accountants had redefined the game. They blamed the accountants for the resulting job losses and increased unemployment.*

**LEONA:** *My role is confined to giving an opinion on the accounting information. If a particular accounting process is detrimental to the public interest then it is the job of government to legislate.*

**Activity 8.6**    *Consider the discussion between David and Leona. Do you share the concern of the employee representatives as described by David? Do you agree with Leona that the economic impact of accounting information is not a problem for the auditor? What is your view on the social responsibility attached to financial reporting?*

### 8.7.5    Retaining cash in the business

Suppose that the policy of the owner is to take all the available profits as drawings for personal use. Take a company that has fee income of £120,000 and pays wages and other costs of £58,000. If the company did not recognise the expense of depreciation the owner's drawings could be as high as £62,000. Suppose now that depreciation of non-current (fixed) assets is calculated as £10,000. The net profit after depreciation becomes £52,000. The owner can still see £62,000 in the bank account but knows £10,000 of that amount represents using up non-current (fixed) assets. Leaving the £10,000 in the bank will allow the business to save cash for asset replacement. The owner should withdraw no more than £52,000.

It is often said that depreciation limits the amount of profits available for cash drawings by the owner and encourages saving for asset replacement. However there is nothing to stop the business spending the £10,000 on some purpose other than replacement of non-current (fixed) assets. We can only say that cash withheld from shareholders *may* be used to replace assets at the end of the asset life.

## 8.8    Reporting non-current (fixed) assets and depreciation in financial statements

This section moves step by step through the recording process. First, it looks at a situation of straight-line depreciation with no residual value for the asset. Then it takes in the additional complication of an estimated residual value.

### 8.8.1    Straight-line depreciation, no residual value

When a retail company wants new premises, it must either buy a shop or rent one. Renting is referred to as **leasing**. When the rent agreement is signed, the tenant may pay an agreed price for the privilege of having the lease. This is called the initial payment for the lease. It is paid in addition to the annual rental payment. The initial payment to acquire the lease provides a benefit of occupation for the entire period of the lease and so is a non-current (fixed) asset. Because the lease has a known life, it must be depreciated.

On 1 January Year 2 Electrical Instruments purchased a three-year lease of a shop for a payment of £60,000. Using the straight-line method of depreciation the amount of depreciation each year will be calculated on a straight-line basis as £20,000 (one-third of the cost of the lease). The income statement (profit and loss account) will report this amount as an expense in each of the three years of the lease. The balance sheet will show on one line the original cost of £60,000 and, on a second line, the accumulated depreciation to be subtracted at the end of each year.

The financial statements over the period of three years will show the following information relating to this lease:

| Income statement (profit and loss account) (extract) | | | |
|---|---|---|---|
| Year ended 31 December | Year 2 | Year 3 | Year 4 |
| | £000s | £000s | £000s |
| Depreciation expense | (20) | (20) | (20) |

| Balance sheet (extract) | | | |
|---|---|---|---|
| At 31 December | Year 2 | Year 3 | Year 4 |
| | £000s | £000s | £000s |
| Lease at cost | 60 | 60 | 60 |
| Less accumulated depreciation | 20 | 40 | 60 |
| Net book value | 40 | 20 | nil |

## 8.8.2  Straight-line depreciation with a residual value

In the case of Electrical Instruments the lease had no residual value. Take now the example of The Removals Company which commences business on 1 January Year 2 by paying cash for a van costing £60,000. It is estimated to have a useful life of three years and is estimated to have a residual value of £6,000. On 31 December Year 2 the owner calculates annual depreciation of the van as £18,000, using the formula:

$$\frac{Cost - Estimated\ residual\ value}{Estimated\ life}$$

During each year of operating the van, the company collected £120,000 in cash from customers and paid £58,000 in cash for drivers' wages, fuel and other running costs.

These transactions and events may be summarised using the accounting equation and a spreadsheet similar to that used in Chapter 5 (Exhibit 5.3). In Exhibit 8.5 there is a spreadsheet for the first year of the use of the van by the company. The assets section of the spreadsheet has three columns, one of which is for cash but two of which are for the van. The two columns for the van keep a separate record of the original cost and the accumulated depreciation. The original cost is the positive part of the asset but the accumulated depreciation is the negative part of the asset. Taking the accumulated depreciation from the original cost leaves the net book value. That is the amount of cost not yet amortised which acts as a measure of the benefit remaining in the asset for the future. In Exhibit 8.6 the information collected together by Exhibit 8.5 is presented in the form of a balance sheet and an income statement (profit and loss account).

**Exhibit 8.5**

**Spreadsheet analysing transactions and events of The Removals Company into the elements of the accounting equation**

| | Transaction or event | Assets | | | Ownership interest | |
|---|---|---|---|---|---|---|
| | | Van at cost | Accumulated depreciation of van | Cash | Capital contributed or withdrawn | Profit = revenue minus (expenses) |
| Year 2 | | £ | £ | £ | £ | £ |
| 1 Jan. | Owner contributes cash | | | 60,000 | 60,000 | |
| 1 Jan. | Purchase furniture van | 60,000 | | (60,000) | | |
| All year | Collected cash from customers | | | 120,000 | | 120,000 |
| All year | Paid for wages, fuel, etc. | | | (58,000) | | (58,000) |
| 31 Dec. | Calculate annual depreciation | | (18,000) | | | (18,000) |
| | Totals | 60,000 | (18,000) | 62,000 | 60,000 | 44,000 |

⌐————— 104,000 —————⌐  ⌐—— 104,000 ——⌐

**Exhibit 8.6**

**The Removals Company: Balance sheet at end of Year 2 and Income statement (profit and loss account) for Year 2**

**The Removals Company**
**Balance sheet at 31 December Year 2**

| | £ |
|---|---|
| **Non-current (fixed) assets** | |
| Furniture van at cost | 60,000 |
| Accumulated depreciation | (18,000) |
| Net book value | 42,000 |
| **Current assets** | |
| Cash | 62,000 |
| Total assets | 104,000 |
| **Ownership interest** | |
| Ownership interest at the start of the year | nil |
| Capital contributed during the year | 60,000 |
| Profit of the year | 44,000 |
| | 104,000 |

**The Removals Company**
**Income statement (profit and loss account)**
**for the year ended 31 December Year 2**

| | £ | £ |
|---|---|---|
| **Revenue** | | |
| Fees for removal work | | 120,000 |
| **Expenses** | | |
| Wages, fuel and other running costs | (58,000) | |
| Depreciation | (18,000) | |
| | | (76,000) |
| Net profit | | 44,000 |

**Exhibit 8.7**
**Spreadsheet analysis of transactions of The Removals Company, Year 3**

| | Transaction or event | Assets | | | Ownership interest | | |
|---|---|---|---|---|---|---|---|
| | | Van at cost | Accumulated depreciation of van | Cash | Ownership interest at start of year | Capital contributed or withdrawn | Profit = revenue minus (expenses) |
| Year 3 | | £ | £ | £ | £ | £ | £ |
| 1 Jan. | Amounts brought forward at start of year | 60,000 | (18,000) | 62,000 | 104,000 | | |
| All year | Collected cash from customers | | | 120,000 | | | 120,000 |
| All year | Paid for wages, fuel, etc. | | | (58,000) | | | (58,000) |
| 31 Dec. | Calculate annual depreciation | | (18,000) | | | | (18,000) |
| | Totals | 60,000 | (36,000) | 124,000 | 104,000 | | 44,000 |

⌞———— 148,000 ————⌟     ⌞———— 148,000 ————⌟

**Exhibit 8.8**
**The Removals Company: Balance sheet at end of Year 3 and Income statement (profit and loss account) for Year 3**

**The Removals Company**
**Balance sheet at 31 December Year 3**

| | £ |
|---|---|
| **Non-current (fixed) assets** | |
| Furniture van at cost | 60,000 |
| Accumulated depreciation | (36,000) |
| Net book value | 24,000 |
| **Current assets** | |
| Cash | 124,000 |
| Total assets | 148,000 |
| **Ownership interest** | |
| Ownership interest at the start of the year | 104,000 |
| Profit of the year | 44,000 |
| | 148,000 |

**The Removals Company**
**Income statement (profit and loss account)**
**for the year ended 31 December Year 3**

| | £ | £ |
|---|---|---|
| **Revenue** | | |
| Fees for removal work | | 120,000 |
| **Expenses** | | |
| Wages, fuel and other running costs | (58,000) | |
| Depreciation | (18,000) | |
| | | (76,000) |
| Net profit | | 44,000 |

### 8.8.3 Continuing to use the non-current (fixed) asset

So far, the accounting entries have related to the first year of the business so that there was no need to ask any questions about the position at the start of the period. To show the full impact of the progressive depreciation of the asset, the spreadsheet and financial statements are now presented for Year 3. Exhibit 8.7 sets out the spreadsheet and Exhibit 8.8 sets out the financial statements. It is assumed that for Year 3 the amounts of cash collected from customers and the amounts paid in cash for running costs are the same as for Year 2. No further capital is contributed by the owner and no new vans are acquired.

The first line of the spreadsheet in Exhibit 8.7 shows the position at the start of the year. The asset columns show the amounts as they were at the end of the previous year. The ownership interest shows the amount resulting at the end of the previous year, as seen in the Year 2 balance sheet. The columns for revenue and expenses are empty at the start of the year, awaiting the transactions and events of Year 3.

### 8.8.4 Disposing of the non-current (fixed) asset

During Year 4 the amounts of cash received from customers and cash paid for running costs are the same as they were in Year 3. Exhibit 8.9 sets out the spreadsheet for the transactions and events.

**Exhibit 8.9**
**Spreadsheet analysis of transactions of The Removals Company, Year 4**

| | Transaction or event | Assets | | | Ownership interest | | |
|---|---|---|---|---|---|---|---|
| | | Van at cost | Accumulated depreciation of van | Cash | Ownership interest at start of year | Capital contributed or withdrawn | Profit = revenue minus (expenses) |
| Year 4 | | £ | £ | £ | £ | £ | £ |
| 1 Jan. | Amounts brought forward at start of year | 60,000 | (36,000) | 124,000 | 148,000 | | |
| All year | Collected cash from customers | | | 120,000 | | | 120,000 |
| All year | Paid for wages, fuel, etc. | | | (58,000) | | | (58,000) |
| 31 Dec. | Calculate annual depreciation | | (18,000) | | | | (18,000) |
| | Totals | 60,000 | (54,000) | 186,000 | 148,000 | | 44,000 |

        192,000               192,000

Now suppose that the van is sold for £6,000 in cash on the final day of December Year 4. The spreadsheet contained in Exhibit 8.9 requires further attention, the additional accounting impact of the sale being seen in Exhibit 8.10.

**Exhibit 8.10**

**Spreadsheet analysis of transactions of The Removals Company, Year 4, including sale of non-current (fixed) asset**

| | Transaction or event | Assets | | | Ownership interest | | |
|---|---|---|---|---|---|---|---|
| | | Van at cost | Accumulated depreciation of van | Cash | Ownership interest at start of year | Capital contributed or withdrawn | Profit = revenue minus (expenses) |
| Year 4 | | £ | £ | £ | £ | £ | £ |
| 1 Jan. | Amounts brought forward at start of year | 60,000 | (36,000) | 124,000 | 148,000 | | |
| All year | Collected cash from customers | | | 120,000 | | | 120,000 |
| All year | Paid for wages, fuel, etc. | | | (58,000) | | | (58,000) |
| 31 Dec. | Calculate annual depreciation | | (18,000) | | | | (18,000) |
| 31 Dec. | Van disposal | (60,000) | 54,000 | 6,000 | | | |
| | Totals | nil | nil | 192,000 | 148,000 | | 44,000 |

⌐———— 192,000 ————⌐        ⌐———— 192,000 ————⌐

The disposal of the van must be analysed in stages:

1 collecting cash;
2 transferring ownership of the vehicle;
3 removing the vehicle from the accounting records.

When the vehicle is removed from the record, two columns must be reduced to zero. These are the *van at cost* column and the *accumulated depreciation* column. The van at cost column shows the original cost of £60,000 and the accumulated depreciation shows the amount of £54,000 which has to be deducted to show the amount of the net book value. The asset of cash increases by £6,000. In terms of the accounting equation:

| **Assets** | | – | Liabilities | = | Ownership interest |
|---|---|---|---|---|---|
| | £ | | no change | | no change |
| **Increase in cash** | **6,000** | | | | |
| **Decrease van:** | | | | | |
| **At cost** | **60,000** | | | | |
| **Accumulated depreciation** | **(54,000)** | | | | |
| | **6,000** | | | | |

The resulting balance sheet and income statement (profit and loss account) are shown in Exhibit 8.11.

Exhibit 8.11

**The Removals Company: Balance sheet at end of Year 4 and Income statement (profit and loss account) for Year 4**

**The Removals Company**
**Balance sheet at 31 December Year 4**

|  | £ |
|---|---|
| *Non-current (fixed) assets* | nil |
| *Current assets* | |
| Cash | 192,000 |
| Total assets | 192,000 |
| *Ownership interest* | |
| Ownership interest at the start of the year | 148,000 |
| Profit of the year | 44,000 |
|  | 192,000 |

**The Removals Company**
**Income statement (profit and loss account)**
**for the year ended 31 December Year 4**

|  | £ | £ |
|---|---|---|
| *Revenue* | | |
| Fees for removal work | | 120,000 |
| *Expenses* | | |
| Wages, fuel and other running costs | (58,000) | |
| Depreciation | (18,000) | |
|  | | (76,000) |
| Net profit | | 44,000 |

## 8.8.5 Selling for a price which is not equal to the net book value

The previous illustration was based on selling the van for £6,000, an amount equal to the net book value. Suppose instead it was sold for £9,000. There is a gain on disposal of £3,000. This gain is reported in the income statement (profit and loss account).

| Assets | | − | Liabilities | = | Ownership interest |
|---|---|---|---|---|---|
|  | £ | | | | |
| Increase cash | 9,000 | | | | |
| Decrease van: | | | no change | | Increase by £3,000 |
| At cost | 60,000 | | | | |
| Accumulated depreciation | (54,000) | | | | |
|  | 6,000 | | | | |

If the amount of the gain or loss on disposal is relatively small, it may be deducted from the depreciation charge. In that situation the income statement (profit and loss account) would appear as shown in Exhibit 8.12 where bold printing highlights the difference when compared with the income statement (profit and loss account) in Exhibit 8.11. If the gain or loss is **material** it will be reported separately.

Exhibit 8.12
**Income statement (profit and loss account) for Year 4 when proceeds of sale exceed net book value of non-current (fixed) asset**

| | | |
|---|---|---|
| **The Removals Company** | | |
| **Income statement (profit and loss account)** | | |
| **for the year ended 31 December Year 4** | | |
| | £ | £ |
| *Revenue* | | |
| Fees for removal work | | 120,000 |
| *Expenses* | | |
| Wages, fuel and other running costs | (58,000) | |
| **Depreciation (18,000 – 3,000)** | **(15,000)** | |
| | | (73,000) |
| Net profit | | 47,000 |

| 8.8.6 | **A table of depreciation expense** |
|---|---|

To test your understanding of the impact of depreciation you may wish to use a table of the type shown in Exhibit 8.13. It shows that, whatever the proceeds of sale of the asset, the total expense in the income statement (profit and loss account) will always be the same but the amount of expense each year will vary.

Exhibit 8.13
**Table of depreciation charge**

**(a)** A van cost £60,000, was estimated to have a useful life of three years and a residual value of £6,000. It was sold for £9,000 on the last day of Year 3. Net profit before depreciation is £62,000.

| Year | Net profit before depreciation | Depreciation expense of the year | Net profit after depreciation | Cost less accumulated depreciation | Net book value |
|---|---|---|---|---|---|
| | £ | £ | £ | £ | £ |
| 1 | 62,000 | 18,000 | 44,000 | 60,000 – 18,000 | 42,000 |
| 2 | 62,000 | 18,000 | 44,000 | 60,000 – 36,000 | 24,000 |
| 3 | 62,000 | 15,000 | 47,000 | 60,000 – 54,000 | 6,000 |
| Total depreciation charge | | 51,000 | | | |
| Total reported net profit | | | 135,000 | | |

Proceeds of sale exceed net book value by £3,000. This gain is deducted from the depreciation expense of £18,000 leaving £15,000 as the expense of the year.

**(b)** A van cost £60,000, was estimated to have a useful life of three years and a residual value of £9,000. The annual depreciation was calculated as £17,000. The van was sold for £9,000 on the last day of Year 3. Net profit before depreciation is £62,000.

| Year | Net profit before depreciation | Depreciation expense of the year | Net profit after depreciation | Cost less accumulated depreciation | Net book value |
|---|---|---|---|---|---|
| | £ | £ | £ | £ | £ |
| 1 | 62,000 | 17,000 | 45,000 | 60,000 – 17,000 | 43,000 |
| 2 | 62,000 | 17,000 | 45,000 | 60,000 – 34,000 | 26,000 |
| 3 | 62,000 | 17,000 | 45,000 | 60,000 – 51,000 | 9,000 |
| Total depreciation | | 51,000 | | | |
| Total reported net profit | | | 135,000 | | |

Net book value equals proceeds of sale so the depreciation charge of Year 3 is the same as that of previous years.

If you compare the two tables (a) and (b) you will see that:

- total depreciation over the three years is the same in both cases;
- total net profit after depreciation over the three years is the same in both cases;
- annual depreciation in Years 1 and 2 is lower in table (b);
- net profit after depreciation in Years 1 and 2 is higher in table (b);
- net book value of the asset at the end of Years 1 and 2 is higher in table (b);
- the depreciation charge in Year 3 is higher in table (b);
- the net profit after depreciation in Year 3 is lower in table (b).

This is an example of what is referred to in accounting as an **allocation** problem (a 'sharing' problem). The expense is the same in total but is allocated (shared) differently across the years of the asset's life. As a result, there are different amounts in the income statement (profit and loss account) for each year but the total profit over the longer period is the same.

### 8.8.7    Impairment

An asset is impaired when the business will not be able to recover the amount shown in the balance sheet, either through use or through sale. If the enterprise believes that impairment may have taken place, it must carry out an **impairment review**. This requires comparison of the net book value with the cash-generating ability of the asset. If the comparison indicates that the recorded net book value is too high, the value of the asset is reduced and there is an expense in the income statement (profit and loss account).[7]

The impairment test may be applied to intangible non-current (fixed) assets such as goodwill, in order to justify non-amortisation. If no impairment is detected it may be argued that the asset has maintained its value and so amortisation is not necessary. If there has been impairment of the historical cost net book value, then the loss in asset value becomes an expense for the income statement (profit and loss account).

## 8.9  Summary

- A **non-current asset** is any asset that does not meet the definition of a current asset.[8] Non-current assets include tangible, intangible and financial assets of a long-term nature. These are also described as **fixed assets**.
- **Tangible non-current (fixed) assets** are assets that have physical substance and are held for use in the production or supply of goods or services, for rental to others, or for administrative purposes on a continuing basis in the reporting entity's activities.
- **An intangible asset** is an identifiable non-monetary asset without physical substance.
- Users need information about the cost of an asset and the aggregate (accumulated) depreciation as the separate components of net book value. Having this detail allows users to estimate the proportion of asset life remaining to be used. This information will be reported in the notes to the balance sheet.
- Users also need information about the accounting policy on depreciation and its impact on the reported asset values. This information will be found in the notes to the accounts on accounting policies and the notes. There may also be a description and discussion in the Operating and Financial Review, including a forward-looking description of intended capital expenditure.

● **Depreciation** is estimated for the total life of the asset and then allocated to the reporting periods involved, usually annual reporting. No particular method of depreciation is required by law. Preparers of financial statements have to exercise choices. Companies in the UK commonly use straight-line depreciation. An alternative is reducing-balance depreciation. This is found more commonly in some other countries. Choice of depreciation method affects the comparability of profit.

## Further reading

The following standards are too detailed for a first level course but the definitions sections may be helpful.

IASB (2004) IAS 38, *Intangible Assets*, International Accounting Standards Board.

IASB (2004) IAS 16, *Property, Plant and Equipment*, International Accounting Standards Board.

# QUESTIONS

The Questions section of each chapter has three types of question. 'Test your understanding' questions to help you review your reading are in the 'A' series of questions. You will find the answers to these by reading and thinking about the material in the book. 'Application' questions to test your ability to apply technical skills are in the 'B' series of questions. Questions requiring you to show skills in problem solving and evaluation are in the 'C' series of questions. A letter [S] indicates that there is a solution at the end of the book.

## A    Test your understanding

**A8.1**    State the definition of a non-current (fixed) asset and explain why each condition is required. (Section 8.2)

**A8.2**    Explain the categories: (Section 8.2.1)

(a)  tangible non-current (fixed) assets;
(b)  intangible non-current (fixed) assets; and
(c)  non-current (fixed) asset investments;

and give an example of each.

**A8.3**    What do users of financial statements particularly want to know about non-current (fixed) assets? (Section 8.4)

**A8.4**    What type of information would you expect to find about non-current (fixed) assets in the financial statements and notes of a major UK listed company? (Section 8.4)

**A8.5**    State the definition of depreciation. (Section 8.7)

**A8.6**    What is meant by **accumulated depreciation** (also called **aggregate depreciation**)? (Section 8.7)

**A8.7**    What information is needed to calculate annual depreciation? (Section 8.7.1)

**A8.8**    What is the formula for calculating straight-line depreciation? (Section 8.7.2)

**A8.9**    How is reducing-balance depreciation calculated? (Section 8.7.3)

**A8.10**   How does depreciation help to retain cash in a business for asset replacement? (Section 8.7.5)

**A8.11**   Why does the net book value of a non-current (fixed) asset not always equal the proceeds of sale? (Section 8.8.5)

**A8.12**   Why is depreciation said to cause an **allocation** problem in accounting? (Section 8.8.6)

**A8.13**  How should the cost of a non-current (fixed) asset be decided? (Section 8.2.2)

**A8.14**  [S] What are the matters of judgement relating to non-current (fixed) assets which users of financial statements should think about carefully when evaluating financial statements?

**A8.15**  What is meant by **impairment**? (Section 8.8.7)

## B    Application

**B8.1** [S]
On reviewing the financial statements of a company, the company's accountant discovers that expenditure of £8,000 on repair to factory equipment has been incorrectly recorded as a part of the cost of the machinery. What will be the effect on the income statement (profit and loss account) and balance sheet when the error is corrected?

**B8.2**
On 1 January Year 1, Angela's Employment Agency was formed. The owner contributed £300,000 in cash which was immediately used to purchase a building. It is estimated to have a 20-year life and a residual value of £200,000. During Year 1 the agency collects £80,000 in fee income and pays £60,000 in wages and other costs. Record the transactions and events of Year 1 in an accounting equation spreadsheet. (See Exhibit 8.5 for an illustration.) Prepare the balance sheet at the end of Year 1 and the income statement (profit and loss account) for Year 1.

**B8.3**
Assume that fee income and costs are the same in Year 2 as in Year 1. Record the transactions and events of Year 2 in an accounting equation spreadsheet. Prepare the balance sheet at the end of Year 2 and the income statement (profit and loss account) for Year 2.

**B8.4**
Angela's Employment Agency sells the building for £285,000 on the final day of December Year 3. Record the transactions and events of Year 3 in an accounting equation spreadsheet. (See Exhibit 8.9 for an illustration.) Assume depreciation is calculated in full for Year 3.

**B8.5**
Explain how the accounting equation spreadsheet of your answer to question **B8.4** would alter if the building had been sold for £250,000.

**B8.6**
On 1 January Year 1, Company A purchased a bus costing £70,000. It was estimated to have a useful life of three years and a residual value of £4,000. It was sold for £8,000 on the last day of Year 3.

On 1 January Year 1, Company B purchased a bus also costing £70,000. It was estimated to have a useful life of three years and a residual value of £7,000. It was sold for £8,000 on the last day of Year 3.

Both companies have a net profit of £50,000 before depreciation. Calculate the depreciation charge and net profit of each company for each of the three years. Show that over the three years the total depreciation charge for each company is the same. (See Exhibit 8.13 for an example.)

## C    Problem solving and evaluation

**C8.1** [S]
The Biscuit Manufacturing Company commenced business on 1 January Year 1 with capital of £22,000 contributed by the owner. It immediately paid cash for a biscuit machine costing £22,000. It was estimated to have a useful life of four years and at the end of that time was

estimated to have a residual value of £2,000. During each year of operation of the machine, the company collected £40,000 in cash from sale of biscuits and paid £17,000 in cash for wages, ingredients and running costs.

**Required**

(a) Prepare spreadsheets for each of the four years analysing the transactions and events of the company.
(b) Prepare a balance sheet at the end of Year 3 and an income statement (profit and loss account) for that year.
(c) Explain to a non-accountant how to read and understand the balance sheet and income statement (profit and loss account) you have prepared.

**C8.2** [S]

The biscuit machine in question **C8.1** was sold at the end of Year 4 for a price of £3,000.

**Required**

(a) Prepare the spreadsheet for Year 4 analysing the transactions and events of the year.
(b) Prepare the balance sheet at the end of Year 4 and the income statement (profit and loss account) for Year 4.
(c) Explain to a non-accountant the accounting problems of finding that the asset was sold for £3,000 when the original expectation was £2,000.

**C8.3** [S]

The Souvenir Company purchased, on 1 January Year 1, a machine producing embossed souvenir badges. The machine cost £16,000 and was estimated to have a five-year life with a residual value of £1,000.

**Required**

(a) Prepare a table of depreciation charges and net book value over the five-year life using straight-line depreciation.
(b) Make a guess at the percentage rate to be used in the reducing-balance calculation, and prepare a table of depreciation charges and net book value over the five years using reducing-balance depreciation.
(c) Using the straight-line method of depreciation, demonstrate the effect on the accounting equation of selling the asset at the end of Year 5 for a price of £2,500.
(d) Using the straight-line method of depreciation, demonstrate the effect on the accounting equation of disposing of the asset at the end of Year 5 for a zero scrap value.

## Activities for study groups

Turn to the annual report of a listed company which you have used for activities in previous chapters. Find every item of information about non-current (fixed) assets. (Start with the financial statements and notes but look also at the operating and financial review, chief executive's review and other non-regulated information about the company.)

As a group, imagine you are the team of fund managers in a fund management company. You are holding a briefing meeting at which each person explains to the others some feature of the companies in which your fund invests. Today's subject is *non-current (fixed) assets*. Each person should make a short presentation to the rest of the team covering:

1  the nature and significance of non-current (fixed) assets in the company;
2  the asset lives stated in the accounting policies for depreciation purposes;
3  the asset lives estimated by you from calculations of annual depreciation as a percentage of asset cost;
4  the remaining useful life of assets as indicated by comparing accumulated depreciation with asset cost;
5  the company's plans for future investment in non-current (fixed) assets.

## Notes and references

1. IASB (1989) *Framework for the Preparation and Presentation of Financial Statements, para 49(a)* 6.
2. IASB (2004) IAS 1 para. 57.
3. IASB (2004) IAS 1 para. 58 permits the use of alternative descriptions for non-current assets provided the meaning is clear.
4. ASB (1999) FRS 15, *Measurement of Tangible Fixed Assets*, para. 2.
5. IASB (2004) IAS 38 *Intangible Assets*, para. 8.
6. IASB (2004) IAS 16, *Property, Plant and Equipment*, para. 6.
7. There remain international differences on the precise method of estimating cash-generating ability. There are detailed rules in IAS 38 but these are beyond a first-level text.
8. IASB (2004) IAS 1 para. 57.

## Supplement to Chapter 8

# Recording non-current (fixed) assets and depreciation

*The rules for debit and credit entries in a ledger account should by now be familiar but are set out again in Exhibit 8.14 for convenience. If you still feel unsure about any aspect of Exhibit 8.14 you should revisit the supplements of earlier chapters before attempting this one.*

In this supplement you will concentrate primarily on the ledger accounts for the non-current (fixed) assets. It takes The Removals Company of the main chapter as the example for illustration.

**Exhibit 8.14**
**Rules for debit and credit entries in ledger accounts**

|  | Debit entries in a ledger account | Credit entries in a ledger account |
|---|---|---|
| *Left-hand side of the equation* |  |  |
| Asset | Increase | Decrease |
| *Right-hand side of the equation* |  |  |
| Liability | Decrease | Increase |
| Ownership interest | Expense | Revenue |
|  | Capital withdrawn | Capital contributed |

## Information to be recorded

The Removals Company commences business on 1 January Year 2 by paying cash for a van costing £60,000. The cash was contributed by the owner. The van is estimated to have a useful life of three years and is estimated to have a residual value of £6,000. On 31 December Year 2 the owner calculates annual depreciation of the van as £18,000, using the formula:

$$\frac{\text{Cost} - \text{Estimated residual value}}{\text{Estimated life}}$$

During each year of operating the van, the company collected £120,000 in cash from customers and paid £58,000 in cash for drivers' wages, fuel and other running costs.

The transactions of Year 2 have been analysed in Exhibit 8.5 for their impact on the accounting equation. That same list may be used to set out the debit and credit bookkeeping entries, as shown in Exhibit 8.15.

**Exhibit 8.15**
**Analysis of transactions for The Removals Company, Year 2**

| Date | Transaction or event | Amount | Dr | Cr |
|---|---|---|---|---|
| Year 2 | | £ | | |
| 1 Jan. | Owner contributes cash | 60,000 | Cash | Ownership interest |
| 1 Jan. | Purchase furniture van | 60,000 | Van at cost | Cash |
| All year | Collected cash from customers | 120,000 | Cash | Sales |
| All year | Paid for running costs | 58,000 | Running costs | Cash |
| 31 Dec. | Calculate annual depreciation | 18,000 | Depreciation expense | Accumulated depreciation |

Ledger accounts required to record transactions of Year 2 are as follows:

| | | | |
|---|---|---|---|
| L1 | Ownership interest | L4 | Accumulated depreciation of van |
| L2 | Cash | L5 | Sales |
| L3 | Van at cost | L6 | Running costs |
| | | L7 | Depreciation of the year |

**L1 Ownership interest**

| Date | Particulars | Page | Debit | Credit | Balance |
|---|---|---|---|---|---|
| Year 2 | | | £ | £ | £ |
| Jan. 1 | Cash | L2 | | 60,000 | (60,000) |

**LEONA's comment:** *This ledger account shows the opening contribution to the start of the business which establishes the ownership interest.*

**L2 Cash**

| Date | Particulars | Page | Debit | Credit | Balance |
|---|---|---|---|---|---|
| Year 2 | | | £ | £ | £ |
| Jan. 1 | Ownership interest | L1 | 60,000 | | 60,000 |
| Jan. 1 | Van | L3 | | 60,000 | nil |
| Jan.–Dec. | Sales | L5 | 120,000 | | 120,000 |
| Jan.–Dec. | Running costs | L6 | | 58,000 | 62,000 |

**LEONA's comment:** *For convenience in this illustration all the sales and running costs have been brought together in one amount for the year. In reality there would be a large number of separate transactions recorded throughout the year. The balance at the end of the year shows that there is £62,000 remaining in the bank account.*

**L3 Van at cost**

| Date | Particulars | Page | Debit | Credit | Balance |
|---|---|---|---|---|---|
| Year 2 | | | £ | £ | £ |
| Jan. 1 | Cash | L2 | 60,000 | | 60,000 |

LEONA's comment: *The van is recorded by a debit entry and this entry remains in the ledger account for as long as the van is in use by the company. A separate ledger account is maintained for the cost of the asset because it is regarded as a useful piece of information for purposes of financial statements.*

**L4 Accumulated depreciation of van**

| Date | Particulars | Page | Debit | Credit | Balance |
|---|---|---|---|---|---|
| Year 2 | | | £ | £ | £ |
| Dec. 31 | Depreciation for the year | L7 | | 18,000 | (18,000) |

LEONA's comment: *The accumulated depreciation account completes the story about the van. It has an original cost of £60,000 and an accumulated depreciation at the end of Year 2 equal to £18,000. The accumulated depreciation account will always show a credit balance because it is the negative part of the asset. Deducting accumulated depreciation from cost gives a net book value of £42,000.*

**L5 Sales**

| Date | Particulars | Page | Debit | Credit | Balance |
|---|---|---|---|---|---|
| Year 2 | | | £ | £ | £ |
| Jan.–Dec. | Cash | L2 | | 120,000 | (120,000) |

LEONA's comment: *For convenience all the sales transactions of the year have been brought together in one single amount, but in reality there would be many pages of separate transactions.*

**L6 Running costs**

| Date | Particulars | Page | Debit | Credit | Balance |
|---|---|---|---|---|---|
| Year 2 | | | £ | £ | £ |
| Jan.–Dec. | Cash | L2 | 58,000 | | 58,000 |

LEONA's comment: *As with the sales transactions of the year, all running costs have been brought together in one single amount, but in reality there will be several pages of separate transactions recorded over the year.*

**L7 Depreciation of the year**

| Date | Particulars | Page | Debit | Credit | Balance |
|------|------------|------|-------|--------|---------|
| Year 2 | | | £ | £ | £ |
| Dec. 31 | Accumulated depreciation | L4 | 18,000 | | 18,000 |

LEONA's comment: *The depreciation of the year is a debit entry because it is an expense. The process of depreciation is continuous but that is not convenient for ledger account recording, so companies prefer a single calculation at the end of the year.*

At this point a trial balance may be prepared, as explained in the Supplement to Chapter 5, and shown in Exhibit 8.16.

**Exhibit 8.16**
**Trial balance at the end of Year 2 for The Removals Company**

| Ledger account title | £ | £ |
|---------------------|---|---|
| L1   Ownership interest | | 60,000 |
| L2   Cash | 62,000 | |
| L3   Van at cost | 60,000 | |
| L4   Accumulated depreciation of van | | 18,000 |
| L5   Sales | | 120,000 |
| L6   Running costs | 58,000 | |
| L7   Depreciation | 18,000 | |
| Totals | 198,000 | 198,000 |

## Closing at the end of Year 2 and starting the ledger accounts for Year 3

At the end of the year the balances on asset and liability accounts are *carried forward* to the next year. The phrase 'carried forward' means that they are allowed to remain in the ledger account at the start of the new year. The balances on revenue and expense accounts are treated differently. After the trial balance has been prepared and checked, the amounts on each revenue account and expense account are *transferred to an income statement (profit and loss account)*. Transferring a balance requires an entry of the opposite type to the balance being transferred. A debit entry is made to transfer a credit balance. A credit entry is made to transfer a debit balance. Matching but opposite entries are made in the income statement (profit and loss account). This is called 'closing' the expense or revenue account.

**L5 Sales**

| Date | Particulars | Page | Debit | Credit | Balance |
|------|------------|------|-------|--------|---------|
| Year 2 | | | £ | £ | £ |
| Jan.–Dec. | Cash | L2 | | 120,000 | (120,000) |
| Dec. 31 | Transfer to profit and loss account | L8 | 120,000 | | nil |

LEONA's comment: *The ledger account for sales shows a credit balance of £120,000 for the total transactions of the year. This is transferred to the income statement (profit and loss account) by making a debit entry of similar amount, so that the balance of the sales account is reduced to nil.*

### L6 Running costs

| Date | Particulars | Page | Debit | Credit | Balance |
|------|-------------|------|-------|--------|---------|
| Year 2 | | | £ | £ | £ |
| Jan.–Dec. | Cash | L2 | 58,000 | | 58,000 |
| Dec. 31 | Transfer to income statement (profit and loss account) | L8 | | 58,000 | nil |

LEONA's comment: *The ledger account for running costs shows a debit balance of £58,000 for the total transactions of the year. This is transferred to the income statement (profit and loss account) by making a credit entry of similar amount, so that the balance of the running costs account is reduced to nil.*

### L7 Depreciation of the year

| Date | Particulars | Page | Debit | Credit | Balance |
|------|-------------|------|-------|--------|---------|
| Year 2 | | | £ | £ | £ |
| Dec. 31 | Accumulated depreciation | L4 | 18,000 | | 18,000 |
| Dec. 31 | Transfer to income statement (profit and loss account) | L8 | | 18,000 | nil |

LEONA's comment: *The ledger account for depreciation expense shows a debit balance of £18,000 for the depreciation charge of the year. This is transferred to the income statement (profit and loss account) by making a credit entry of similar amount, so that the balance of the depreciation expense account of the year is reduced to nil.*

### L8 Income statement (profit and loss account)

| Date | Particulars | Page | Debit | Credit | Balance |
|------|-------------|------|-------|--------|---------|
| Year 2 | | | £ | £ | £ |
| Dec. 31 | Sales | L5 | | 120,000 | (120,000) |
| Dec. 31 | Running costs | L6 | 58,000 | | (62,000) |
| Dec. 31 | Depreciation of the year | L7 | 18,000 | | (44,000) |

LEONA's comment: *The income statement (profit and loss account) in ledger form shows all items of revenue in the credit column and all items of expense in the debit column. The balance in the third column shows, at the end of the ledger account, the profit of £44,000 for the year. There is one final entry to be made, and that is to transfer the £44,000 balance of the income statement (profit and loss account) to the ownership interest account. That requires a debit entry in the income statement (profit and loss account) to remove the credit balance.*

**L8 Income statement (profit and loss account)**

| Date | Particulars | Page | Debit | Credit | Balance |
|------|-------------|------|-------|--------|---------|
| Year 2 | | | £ | £ | £ |
| Dec. 31 | Sales | L5 | | 120,000 | (120,000) |
| Dec. 31 | Running costs | L6 | 58,000 | | (62,000) |
| Dec. 31 | Depreciation | L7 | 18,000 | | (44,000) |
| Dec. 31 | Transfer to ownership interest | L1 | 44,000 | | nil |

**L1 Ownership interest**

| Date | Particulars | Page | Debit | Credit | Balance |
|------|-------------|------|-------|--------|---------|
| Year 2 | | | £ | £ | £ |
| Jan. 1 | Cash | L2 | | 60,000 | (60,000) |
| Dec. 31 | Transfer from income statement (profit and loss account) | L8 | | 44,000 | (104,000) |

LEONA's comment: *The transfer from the income statement (profit and loss account) is shown as a credit entry in the ledger account for the ownership interest. That credit entry matches the debit entry, removing the balance from the ledger account. As a check on the common sense of the credit entry, go back to the table at the start of this Supplement (Exhibit 8.14), which shows that a credit entry records an increase in the ownership interest. In the ledger account the credit entry of £44,000 increases the ownership interest from £60,000 to £104,000.*

## Subsequent years

The income statement (profit and loss account)s for Year 3 and Year 4 are identical to that for Year 2. The cash account flows on in a pattern similar to that of Year 2. These ledger accounts are therefore not repeated here for Years 3 and 4. Attention is concentrated on the asset at cost and the accumulated depreciation.

**L3 Van at cost**

| Date | Particulars | Page | Debit | Credit | Balance |
|------|-------------|------|-------|--------|---------|
| Year 2 | | | £ | £ | £ |
| Jan. 1 | Cash | L2 | 60,000 | | 60,000 |
| Year 3 | Balance | b/fwd | | | 60,000 |
| Year 4 | Balance | b/fwd | | | 60,000 |

LEONA's comment: *The asset continues in use from one year to the next and so the ledger account remains open with the balance of £60,000 remaining. At the start of each new year the balance on each asset account is brought forward (repeated) from the previous line to show clearly that this is the amount for the start of the new accounting year. Because this is merely a matter of convenience in tidying up at the start of the year, the abbreviation 'b/fwd' (for 'brought forward') is entered in the 'page' column to show that there are no debit or credit entries for transactions on this line.*

**L4 Accumulated depreciation**

| Date | Particulars | Page | Debit | Credit | Balance |
|------|-------------|------|-------|--------|---------|
| Year 2 | | | £ | £ | £ |
| Dec. 31 | Depreciation charge for the year | L7 | | 18,000 | (18,000) |
| Year 3 | | | | | |
| Dec. 31 | Depreciation charge for the year | L7 | | 18,000 | (36,000) |
| Year 4 | | | | | |
| Dec. 31 | Depreciation charge for the year | L7 | | 18,000 | (54,000) |

**LEONA**'s comment: *The accumulated depreciation account is now showing more clearly what the word 'accumulated' means. Each year it is building in a further amount of £18,000 annual depreciation to build up the total shown in the 'balance' column. After three years the accumulated depreciation has built up to £54,000.*

**L7 Depreciation of the year: Year 3**

| Date | Particulars | Page | Debit | Credit | Balance |
|------|-------------|------|-------|--------|---------|
| Year 2 | | | £ | £ | £ |
| Dec. 31 | Accumulated depreciation | L4 | 18,000 | | 18,000 |
| Dec. 31 | Transfer to income statement (profit and loss account) | L8 | | 18,000 | nil |

**L7 Depreciation of the year: Year 4**

| Date | Particulars | Page | Debit | Credit | Balance |
|------|-------------|------|-------|--------|---------|
| Year 2 | | | £ | £ | £ |
| Dec. 31 | Accumulated depreciation | L4 | 18,000 | | 18,000 |
| Dec. 31 | Transfer to income statement (profit and loss account) | L8 | | 18,000 | nil |

**LEONA**'s comment: *The depreciation of the year is an income statement (profit and loss account) item and so is transferred to the income statement (profit and loss account) each year in Years 3 and 4 in the manner explained earlier for Year 2.*

## Disposal of the asset

At the end of Year 4 the asset is sold for a cash price of £6,000. To remove the asset requires entries in the 'Van at cost' account (L3), the 'Accumulated depreciation' account (L4) and the 'Cash' account (L2). The corresponding debit and credit entries are recorded in a 'Non-current (fixed) asset disposal' account (L9).

Exhibit 8.17 shows the breakdown of the sale transaction into the removal of the asset at cost, the removal of the accumulated depreciation, and the collection of cash. The entry required to remove a balance on a ledger account is the opposite to the amount of the balance. So in the 'Van at cost' account (L3) a credit entry of £60,000 is required to remove a debit balance of £60,000. In the 'Accumulated depreciation' account (L4) a debit entry is required to remove a credit balance of £54,000. In the 'Cash' account (L2) there is a debit entry of £60,000 to show that the asset of cash has increased. In each case the 'Disposal' account (L9) collects the matching debit or credit.

LEONA's comment: *The disposal account is a very convenient way of bringing together all the information about the disposal of the van. The first two lines show the full cost and accumulated depreciation. The balance column, on the second line, shows that the difference between these two items is the net book value of £6,000. Collecting cash of £6,000 is seen to match exactly the net book value, which means that there is no depreciation adjustment on disposal.*

## Sale for an amount greater than the net book value

In the main text of this chapter there is a discussion of the consequences of selling the van for £9,000 cash. There would be no problem in recording that in the book-keeping system. Everything explained in the previous section would be unchanged except for the amount of the cash received. The Disposal account would now be recorded as:

| L9 Non-current (fixed) asset disposal account | | | | | |
|---|---|---|---|---|---|
| Date | Particulars | Page | Debit | Credit | Balance |
| Year 2 | | | £ | £ | £ |
| Dec. 31 | Van at cost | L3 | 60,000 | | 60,000 |
| Dec. 31 | Accumulated depreciation | L4 | | 54,000 | 6,000 |
| Dec. 31 | Cash | L2 | | 9,000 | (3,000) |
| Dec. 31 | Transfer to income statement (profit and loss account) | L8 | 3,000 | | nil |

**Exhibit 8.17**
**Analysis of debit and credit aspects of sale of a fixed asset**

| Date | Transaction or event | Amount | Dr | Cr |
|---|---|---|---|---|
| Year 4 | | £ | | |
| Dec. 31 | Removal of asset at cost | 60,000 | Disposal | Van at cost |
| Dec. 31 | Accumulated depreciation | 54,000 | Accumulated depn | Disposal |
| Dec. 31 | Cash | 6,000 | Cash | Disposal |

**L3 Van at cost**

| Date | Particulars | Page | Debit | Credit | Balance |
|---|---|---|---|---|---|
| Year 2 | | | £ | £ | £ |
| Jan. 1 | Cash | L2 | 60,000 | | 60,000 |
| Year 3 | Balance | b/fwd | | | 60,000 |
| Year 4 | Balance | b/fwd | | | 60,000 |
| Dec. 31 | Disposal | L9 | | 60,000 | nil |

**L4 Accumulated depreciation**

| Date | Particulars | Page | Debit | Credit | Balance |
|---|---|---|---|---|---|
| Year 2 | | | £ | £ | £ |
| Dec. 31 | Depreciation charge for the year | L7 | | 18,000 | (18,000) |
| Year 3 | | | | | |
| Dec. 31 | Depreciation charge for the year | L7 | | 18,000 | (36,000) |
| Year 4 | | | | | |
| Dec. 31 | Depreciation charge for the year | L7 | | 18,000 | (54,000) |
| Dec. 31 | Disposal | L9 | 54,000 | | nil |

**L9 Non-current (fixed) asset disposal account**

| Date | Particulars | Page | Debit | Credit | Balance |
|---|---|---|---|---|---|
| Year 2 | | | £ | £ | £ |
| Dec. 31 | Van at cost | L3 | 60,000 | | 60,000 |
| Dec. 31 | Accumulated depreciation | L4 | | 54,000 | 6,000 |
| Dec. 31 | Cash | L2 | | 6,000 | nil |

The income statement (profit and loss account) for Year 4 would be recorded as:

| | L8 Income statement (profit and loss account) | | | | |
|---|---|---|---|---|---|
| Date | Particulars | Page | Debit | Credit | Balance |
| Year 2 | | | £ | £ | £ |
| Dec. 31 | Sales | L5 | | 120,000 | (120,000) |
| Dec. 31 | Running costs | L6 | 58,000 | | (62,000) |
| Dec. 31 | Depreciation of the year | L7 | 18,000 | | (44,000) |
| Dec. 31 | Gain on disposal | L9 | | 3,000 | (47,000) |

**LEONA**'s comment: *This income statement (profit and loss account) in ledger form matches the income statement (profit and loss account) presented at Exhibit 8.12 in the main text as a financial statement, although you will see that the latter is much more informative.*

## Formula for calculating percentage rate for reducing-balance depreciation

The rate of depreciation to be applied under the reducing-balance method of depreciation may be calculated by the formula:

$$\text{rate} = (1 - {}^n|(R/C)) \times 100\%$$

where:  $n$ = the number of years of useful life
$R$ = the estimated residual value
$C$ = the cost of the asset.

For the example given in the main chapter:

$n$ = 5 years
$C$ = £1,000
$R$ = £30 (The residual value must be of reasonable magnitude. To use an amount of nil for the residual value would result in a rate of 100%.)

$$\text{rate} = (1 - \sqrt[5]{(30/1,000)}) \times 100\%$$

To prove that the rate is 50% you will need a scientific calculator or a suitable computer package. You may know how to calculate a fifth root using logarithms. Otherwise, if you have a very basic calculator it may be easier to use trial-and-error methods.

## S Test your understanding

**S8.1** Prepare ledger accounts to report the transactions and events of questions **C8.1** and **C8.2**.

**S8.2** Write a short commentary on each ledger account prepared in S1, to enable a non-accountant to understand their purpose and content.

# Chapter 9

# Current assets

## Balance sheets at 2 January 2005 (Note 1)

| Notes | | Group 2004 £m | Group 2003 (restated) £m | Company 2004 £m | Company 2003 (restated) £m |
|---|---|---|---|---|---|
| | **Current assets** | | | | |
| 13 | Stocks | 708 | 672 | – | – |
| 14 | Debtors | | | | |
| | – Due within one year | 1,182 | 1,221 | 141 | 161 |
| | – Due after one year | 67 | 81 | 22 | 44 |
| 19a | Investments | 145 | 242 | – | – |
| 19a | Cash at bank and in hand | 201 | 191 | – | – |

## 13 Stocks

| | Group 2004 £m | Group 2003 £m |
|---|---|---|
| Raw materials and consumables | 227 | 202 |
| Work in progress | 60 | 45 |
| Finished goods and goods for resale | 421 | 425 |
| | 708 | 672 |

### (I) Stocks

Stocks are valued at the lower of average cost and estimated net realisable value. Cost comprises direct material and labour costs together with the relevant factory overheads (including depreciation) on the basis of normal activity levels. Amounts are removed from stock based on the average value of the items of stock removed.

### Raw Materials and Suppliers

The Group uses a wide range of raw materials in the production of its confectionery and beverage products. The main raw materials are: cocoa beans, sugar and other sweeteners (including polyols and artificial sweeteners such as aspartame), dairy products including milk, fruit and nuts. Cadbury Schweppes buys its raw materials from about 40,000 suppliers around the world. No single supplier accounts for more than 10% of the Group's raw material purchases. The Group developed a Human Rights and Ethical Trading (HRET) policy in 2000.

The Group seeks to minimise the impact of price fluctuations and ensure security of supply by entering into forward agreements and long-term contracts where such agreements and contracts are available.

Cocoa beans are imported from West Africa and the Far East. West Africa accounts for over 60% of world production. The Group buys cocoa beans and cocoa butter from a range of suppliers. The Group attempts to minimise the effect of cocoa price movements and secure its future cocoa requirements by entering into forward and future contracts for cocoa beans and cocoa butter.

The Group purchases most of its sugar at prices essentially set by the European Union or maintained by various national governments through quotas and duties. Only a relatively small proportion of the Group's sugar requirements are purchased at fluctuating world prices. The Group has not experienced and does not anticipate difficulty in obtaining adequate supplies of sugar for its operations, with sources available from numerous supplies.

**Risk factors**

*Raw Materials*
The Group's profitability depends to some extent upon the cost of raw materials from around the world, which exposes the Group to price and supply fluctuation. Key items such as cocoa, milk, sugar and packaging materials are subject to potentially significant fluctuations in price and availability. While the Group takes measures to protect itself against the short-term impact of these fluctuations, there is no assurance that in the long-term any increase in costs can be recovered from customers. A failure to recover these costs from customers could decrease the Group's profitability.

Source: Cadbury Schweppes plc, Report and Accounts and Form 20–F 2004, pp. 12, 17, 93, 101, 116.

**Discussion points**

1  What are the proportions of raw materials, work-in-progress and finished goods inventories?

2  How does the company deal with the volatile prices of cocoa and sugar?

## Contents

**Learning outcomes**

After studying this chapter you should be able to:

- Define a current asset and apply the definition.
- Explain the operation of the working capital cycle.
- Explain the factors affecting recognition of inventories (stocks), receivables (debtors) and investments.
- Explain how the information presented in a company's balance sheet and notes, in relation to current assets, meets the needs of users.
- Explain the different approaches to measurement of inventories (stocks) and cost of goods sold.
- Analyse provisions for doubtful debts using a spreadsheet.
- Analyse prepayments using a spreadsheet.
- Explain the term 'revenue' and the application of principles of revenue recognition.

Additionally, for those who choose to study the Supplement:

- Record receivables (debtors) and prepayments in ledger accounts.

## 9.1 Introduction

This chapter will continue the progress through the balance sheet which we began in Chapter 8. As in that chapter, the approach will be:

- What are the principles for defining and recognising these items?
- What are the information needs of users in respect of the particular items?
- What information is currently provided by companies to meet these needs?
- Does the information show the desirable qualitative characteristics of financial statements?
- What are the principles for measuring, and processes for recording, these items?

## 9.2 Definitions

Definitions were provided in Chapter 2. They are repeated here for convenience.

**Definition**

An **asset** is a resource controlled by the entity as a result of past events and from which future economic benefits are expected to flow.[1]

A **current asset** is an asset that satisfies any of the following criteria:

(a) it is expected to be realised in, or is intended for sale or consumption in, the entity's normal operating cycle;
(b) it is held primarily for the purpose of being traded;
(c) it is expected to be realised within twelve months after the balance sheet date;
(d) it is cash or a cash equivalent.[2]

The following list is a sample of the current assets found in most company balance sheets:

- raw materials
- work-in-progress
- finished goods
- trade receivables (debtors)
- amounts owed by other companies in a group
- prepayments and accrued income
- investments held as current assets
- short-term bank deposits
- bank current account (also called 'cash at bank')
- cash in hand.

| Activity 9.1 | *Using the definition provided, explain why each item in the foregoing list may be classed as a current asset. Could a plot of land ever be treated as a current asset?* |
|---|---|

The definition of a current asset refers to 'the entity's normal operating cycle'. The operating cycle experienced by many businesses lasts for 12 months, covering all the seasons of one year. One year is the reporting period most commonly used by most enterprises for reporting to external users of financial statements.

## 9.3 The working capital cycle

**Working capital** is the amount of long-term finance the business has to provide in order to keep **current assets** working for the business. Some short-term finance for current assets is provided by the suppliers who give credit by allowing time to pay, but that is not usually sufficient. Some short-term finance for current assets is provided by short-term bank loans but, in most cases, there still remains an excess of **current assets** over **current liabilities**.

The working capital cycle of a business is the sequence of transactions and events, involving current assets and current liabilities, through which the business makes a profit.

Exhibit 9.1 shows how the working capital cycle begins when suppliers allow the business to obtain goods on credit terms, but do not insist on immediate payment. While they are waiting for payment they are called **trade creditors**. The amounts owing to suppliers as creditors are called **trade payables** in the balance sheet. The goods obtained by the business are used in production, held for resale or used in providing a service. While the goods acquired are held by the business they are called the **inventories (stocks)** of the business. Any products manufactured from these goods and held for resale are also part of the inventories (stocks) of the business. The resulting product or service is sold to customers who may pay immediately in cash, or may be allowed time to pay. If they are allowed time to pay they become **debtors** of the business. Debtors eventually pay and the business obtains cash. In the balance sheet the amount due from **trade debtors** is described as **trade receivables**. **Cash** is a general term used to cover money held in the bank, and money held in notes and coins on the business premises. Cash held in the bank will be in an account such as a current account which allows immediate access. Finally the cash may be used to pay the suppliers who, as creditors, have been waiting patiently for payment.

Inventories (stocks), receivables (debtors) and cash are all current assets of the business and will be dealt with in this chapter. Creditors who have supplied goods to the business are current liabilities and will be dealt with in the next chapter.

**Exhibit 9.1**
**The working capital cycle for a manufacturing or service business**

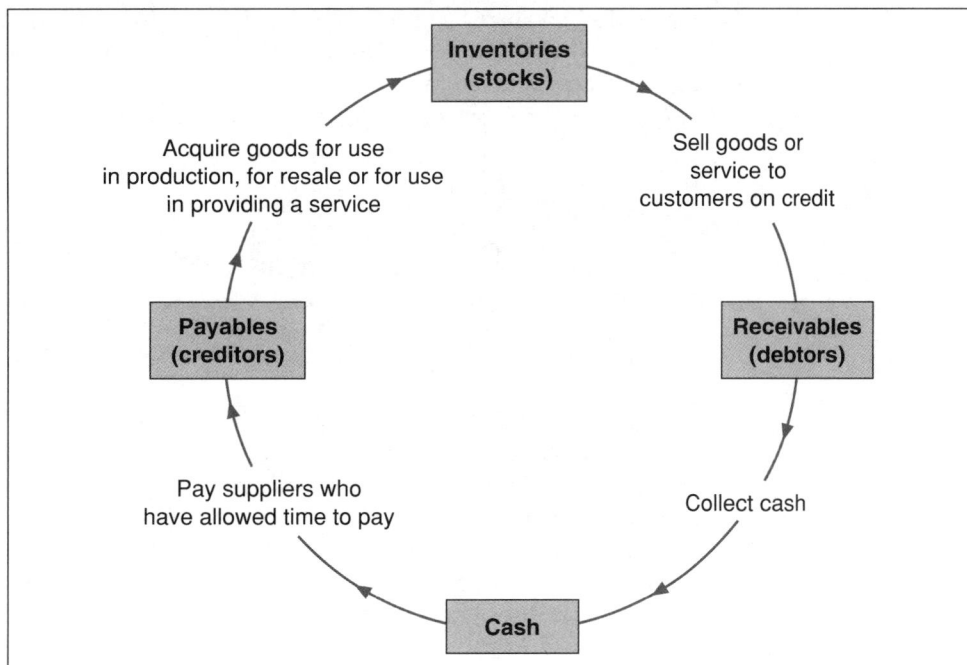

**Working capital** is calculated as **current assets** minus **current liabilities**. If the working capital is low, then the business has a close match between current assets and current liabilities but may risk not being able to pay its liabilities as they fall due. Not all the current assets are instantly available in cash. There may be some delay in selling the inventories (stocks) of unsold goods. An impatient supplier or bank manager may cause difficulties if cash is not available when payment of a liability is due. On the other hand, if current assets are very much greater than current liabilities, then the business has a large amount of finance tied up in the current assets when perhaps that finance would be better employed in the acquisition of more fixed assets to expand the profit-making capacity of the operations.

Definition

> **Working capital** is the amount which a business must provide to finance the current assets of a business, to the extent that these are not covered by current liabilities. It is calculated by deducting current liabilities from current assets.

## 9.4 Recognition

The general conditions for recognition were set out in Chapter 2. An item that meets the definition of an asset should be recognised if there is sufficient evidence that the new asset has been created and the item can be measured at a monetary amount with sufficient reliability. There is no doubt that inventories (stocks), receivables (debtors), investments and cash are commonly recognised in a balance sheet but it is useful to be aware of the element of doubt which may be attached to the expectation of economic benefit which creates the asset and to the reliability of measurement. That awareness is essential to understanding the level of uncertainty which surrounds reported financial statements.

### 9.4.1 Inventories (stocks)

'Inventories' means lists of items. You might come across an inventory if you rent a flat and the owner has a list of the contents that is checked at the start and end of your tenancy. The pronunciation is *IN-ven-t'rees*, with stress on the first syllable 'IN' and not *INVENTOR-ees*, which sounds like a collection of inventors.

**Definition**

> **Inventories** are assets:
>
> (a) held for sale in the ordinary course of business;
> (b) in the process of production for sale; or
> (c) in the form of materials or supplies to be consumed in the production process or in the rendering of services.[3]

If a company is presenting its financial statements using the IASB's accounting system you will probably see the description 'inventories'. If the company is following UK company law and UK ASB standards then you will probably see the description 'stocks'. The remainder of this chapter explains the IASB's system for reporting inventories. The rules of UK law and standards are very similar. In business entities there are three main categories of inventories: raw materials, work-in-progress and finished goods. Consider these in reverse order.

### Finished goods

The future economic benefit expected from finished goods is that they will be sold to customers for a price which exceeds the cost of purchase or manufacture. That makes a profit which increases the ownership interest. However, until the sale is agreed with the customer, this expected benefit is uncertain and the qualitative characteristic of **prudence** (explained in Chapter 4) dictates that it is safer not to anticipate that the profit will arise. The value of the inventories of finished goods is therefore measured at the **cost** of purchase or manufacture. In most cases that is a reliable measure because it is based on recorded costs and is not anticipating an uncertain selling price. Sometimes there may be a disappointment where goods are manufactured and then it is found there is a lack of demand. Where there is strong doubt about the expected selling price, such that it might be less than the cost of purchase or manufacture, the inventories (stock) of finished goods are valued at the net realisable value. This is defined as the estimated proceeds from sale of the items in question, less all costs to be incurred in marketing, selling and distributing these items.

The accounting policy note of most companies confirms this prudent approach. You will see in a later section of this chapter that Safe and Sure plc recognises inventories in its balance sheet at the lower of cost and net realisable value.

### Work-in-progress

During the course of production the asset of finished goods is gradually being created. The expected future benefit of that activity is gradually building up as the work moves towards completion. A business could wait until the asset is totally finished, before recognising the asset in the balance sheet. That would satisfy the qualitative characteristic of **prudence**, supported by the characteristic of **reliability**, but would run into problems with the characteristic of **relevance**. Where work-in-progress is a substantial aspect of the operations of the business, users need to know how much work-in-progress there is, whether it is increasing or decreasing, and what risks are attached. The risks attached to work-in-progress are often greater than those attached to finished goods because there is the risk of non-completion to add to all the risks faced when the goods are completed and awaiting sale. There is a reliable measurement, in the cost of work completed at the date of the balance sheet, but careful checking is required by the managers of the business to ensure that this is a reliable measure.

A particularly important type of **work-in-progress** is the construction contract (long-term contract) such as may be found in the engineering and building industries. A company building a bridge over three years will want to tell the shareholders about the progress being made in creating profit. Each year a portion of the total contract price will be reported as turnover and costs of the period will be matched against that turnover to calculate profit. The value of the work completed will be recognised as an asset in the balance sheet, sometimes called work-in-progress. The reporting of profit on construction contracts (long-term contracts) is reviewed later in this chapter, in section 9.11.

### Raw materials

The approach to recognition is the same as that for finished goods. Raw materials are expected to create a benefit by being used in the manufacture of goods for sale. On grounds of prudence the profit is not anticipated and the raw materials are measured at the lower of cost and net realisable value.

### 9.4.2    Receivables (debtors) and prepayments

**Debtors** are those persons who owe money to a business. Usually the largest amount shown under this heading relates to customers buying goods on credit. These are the **trade receivables (trade debtors)**. Additionally, the business may have lent money to another enterprise to help that enterprise in its activities. There may be loans to employees to cover removal and relocation expenses or advances on salaries. The business may be due to receive a refund of overpaid tax.

Trade receivables (debtors) meet the recognition conditions because there is an expectation of benefit when the customer pays. The profit on the sale of the goods is known because the customer has taken the goods or service and agreed the price. Trade receivables (debtors) are therefore measured at the selling price of the goods and the profit is recognised in the income statement (profit and loss account). There is a risk that the customer will not pay, but the view taken is that the risk of non-payment should be seen quite separately from the risk of not making a profit on a sale. The risk of non-payment is dealt with by reducing the reported value of the asset using an estimate for doubtful debts. That process is explained later in the chapter.

**Prepayments** are amounts of expenses paid in advance. Insurance premiums, rent of buildings, lease charges on a vehicle, road fund licences for the delivery vans and lorries, are all examples of items which have to be paid for in advance. At the balance sheet date some part of the future benefit may remain. This is recognised as the prepayment. Take the example of an insurance premium of £240 paid on 1 October to cover a 12-month period. At the company's year-end of 31 December, three months' benefit has expired but nine months' benefit remains. The balance sheet therefore reports a prepayment of £180.

**Definition** | **Prepayment** An amount paid for in advance for an benefit to the business, such as insurance premiums or rent in advance. Initially recognised as an asset, then transferred to expense in the period when the benefit is enjoyed.

### 9.4.3    Investments

Investments held as current assets are usually highly marketable and readily convertible into cash. The expectation of future economic benefit is therefore usually sufficient to meet the conditions of recognition. Measurement is more of a problem.

There are two possible measures. One is the cost of the investment and the other is the market value. Recognising the investment at cost is prudent and reliable, but not as relevant as the current market value which is the amount of cash that could be released by sale of the investment. There is no agreed answer to this problem at the present time, although the issue has been debated in the standard-setting context. Most businesses report current asset investments at cost but a smaller number use the market value. Using the market value is called **marking to market**. It is a departure from the normal practice of recording assets at original cost but is justified in terms of the requirement of company law that financial statements should show a **true and fair view** (see Chapter 4). It is seen in companies whose business involves dealing in investments.

### 9.4.4   Cash

Recognising cash is no problem either in the expectation of benefit or in the measurement of the asset. The amount is known either by counting cash in hand or by looking at a statement from the bank which is holding the business bank account. The expectation of benefit lies in making use of the cash in future to buy fixed assets or to contribute to the working capital cycle so that the business earns a profit. In the meantime, cash which is surplus to immediate requirements should be deposited in such a way that it is earning interest. Where a company has substantial cash balances there should be indications in the income statement (profit and loss account) that investment income has been earned, to provide a benefit to the business.

**Activity 9.2**

*This section has covered in some detail the characteristics of various groups of current assets. Before reading the next section, write down what information you would expect to see, in respect of these groups of assets, in the balance sheet and notes to the accounts. Then read the section and consider similarities to, or differences from, the views given there.*

## 9.5  Users' needs for information

Investors have an interest in knowing that current assets are not overstated. If the assets are overstated the profit of the business will be overstated (see the explanation in Chapter 4, using the accounting equation). They will want to know particularly whether there has been allowance for inventories of goods which may not lead to sales and whether there has been allowance for customers who may not be able to pay the debts shown as due to the business. They may also want the reassurance that the auditors have established the existence of all the current assets, particularly ensuring that a very portable asset such as cash is where it ought to be in the ownership of the company.

The needs of users do not stop with the investors. The trade creditors who supply goods and services to the business are strongly reliant on the working capital cycle for their eventual payment. Employees look for their salaries and wages from the cash generated during the working capital cycle. They want to know that the cash will be there on the day it is required, rather than being tied up in inventories or receivables (debtors) awaiting release as cash. Tax collecting authorities, such as the Inland Revenue and the Customs and Revenue, have definite dates on which payments are required. All these persons have an interest in the working capital of the business and how it is managed. The concern of creditors and employees is primarily with the flow of cash and its availability on the day required. That information will not appear in the balance sheet but there will be some indications of flow in the cash flow statement (outlined in Chapter 3).

## 9.6   Information provided in the financial statements

In Chapter 7 the balance sheet of Safe and Sure plc contained three lines relating to current assets:

|  | Notes | Year 2 £m | Year 1 £m |
|---|---|---|---|
| **Current assets** | | | |
| Inventories (stocks) | 5 | 26.6 | 24.3 |
| Amounts receivable (debtors) | 6 | 146.9 | 134.7 |
| Six-month deposits | | 2.0 | – |
| Cash and cash equivalents | | 105.3 | 90.5 |
| | | 280.8 | 249.5 |

There is more information provided in the notes to the balance sheet.

### 9.6.1   Details in notes

There are two relevant notes, of which note 5 deals with inventories and note 6 with receivables (debtors):

| Note 5 | Year 2 £m | Year 1 £m |
|---|---|---|
| **Inventories (stocks)** | | |
| Raw materials | 6.2 | 5.4 |
| Work-in-progress | 1.9 | 1.0 |
| Finished products | 18.5 | 17.9 |
| | 26.6 | 24.3 |

This company is a service company so it is not surprising that stocks do not figure prominently in the overall collection of current assets. It is perhaps more surprising that there are inventories of finished products, but reading the description of the business shows that there is a Products Division which manufactures special cleaning chemicals under the company name.

The note on receivables (debtors) shows that the main category is trade receivables (debtors):

| Note 6 **Amounts receivable (debtors)** | Year 2 £m | Year 1 £m |
|---|---|---|
| Trade receivables (trade debtors) | 128.1 | 117.0 |
| Other receivables (debtors) | 10.9 | 9.8 |
| Prepayments and accrued income | 7.9 | 7.9 |
| | 146.9 | 134.7 |

There is no indication of the nature of 'other receivables (debtors)'. It could indicate employees who have received loans or advances of salaries. It could indicate a loan to a company which has trading links with the group but is not a full subsidiary. Prepayments are expenses paid in advance of gaining the benefit, as explained in the previous section of this chapter.

### 9.6.2   Accounting policy

It will be shown later in this chapter that the valuation of inventories is a matter of potential variation from one person to the next, so it is important to know that the company has followed an acceptable policy in its valuation of inventories. The accounting policy note of Safe and Sure provides that confirmation (see Exhibit 9.2). For the moment you will have to accept that this form of wording represents standard practice, but each phrase will be explained later in the chapter.

**Exhibit 9.2**
**Accounting policy note**

---

**SAFE and SURE plc Accounting policy**

Inventories (stocks and work-in-progress) are stated at the lower of cost and net realisable value, using the first-in-first-out principle. Cost includes all direct expenditure and related overheads incurred in bringing the inventories to their present condition and location.

---

### 9.6.3 Operating and financial review

The finance director of Safe and Sure commented as follows in his review:

> *The group's businesses are structured to utilise as little fixed and working capital as is consistent with the profit and earnings growth objective in order to produce a high cash flow.*

The focus on **working capital** is perhaps an indication of the importance seen in explaining how the company manages its current assets and current liabilities. It also shows that for this business the high cash flow is planned and is not an accident of events.

### 9.6.4 Analyst's view

DAVID WILSON comments: *This is a service business and so holds inventories of goods to be used in the service process. The note to the balance sheet does not actually say what the inventories are, so I asked when I made my visit. They tell me the raw materials are inventories of cleaning materials and chemicals for processes such as disinfecting. My main concern is to be assured that there is nothing in the inventories which could carry a risk of losing value through obsolescence or deterioration. There is not much problem of that with cleaning materials. The finished goods took me by surprise until I found out that there is a Products Division. It was actually the cleaning products that I knew best from years ago but I thought they had moved entirely into service contracts.*

*In any event, inventories are not all that important for this company. The receivables (debtors) amount is much larger. I know they have a relatively low risk of bad debts because most customers pay in advance for their contracts.*

*When I started as an analyst I worked alongside someone who had twenty years' experience. He told me that he had always used what he called 'the 10% test' when looking at inventories (stocks) and receivables (debtors) in a balance sheet. He worked out what effect a 10% error in the inventories or receivables would have on the profit before tax. In this case a 10% error in inventories would be £2.7m. The profit from operations is £195.2m. A difference of £2.7m on £195.2m is 1.4%. An error of 1.4% in profit would not have a significant impact on the view of most investors. So in this company inventories is not a matter which needs time taken for questions. On the other hand, a 10% error in receivables (debtors) would be £14.7m. That is 7.5% of profit from operations. So receivables (debtors) are worth more attention. If this were a company I didn't know, I would ask about the quality of the asset and the type of customer who is given credit. In fact I do know the answer here. The finance director told me that when I met him. The receivables (debtors) are largely public sector bodies such as local authorities and hospitals who insist on paying after the work has been done to their satisfaction. There could be a risk of non-payment because of shoddy work but there is little risk of non-payment through default.*

*The final point to note in relation to current assets is that this company is a cash-generating business. I looked at the cash flow statement for the past five years which shows that the group builds up cash balances, buys another company, and then generates even more cash. I suppose that can't go on for ever but there are no signs of problems at present.*

**LEONA:** *I told you I would be looking for admissions of how much you rely on the auditor without knowing it. Your '10% test' is a very rough-and-ready example of the ratio analysis we carry out on a systematic basis as part of our analytical review of the financial statements. Maybe one day I'll tell you more about that. We have quite a long list of ratios which we calculate. We also look at interrelationships between ratios and relative changes in one compared with another.*

*It is also an application of what we call 'materiality'. When we see an asset – in this case it is receivables (debtors) – where an error in estimation of the asset value could cause a serious impact on profit, we identify that as a matter for special attention. We would probably spend more time on receivables (debtors) than on inventories in our audit of this company but we would target the risk-related aspects of what is reported about each asset. For receivables (debtors) it is the risk of non-payment through either disputed debts or lack of funds. For inventories it is the risk of obsolescence or similar loss which is not covered by insurance.*

*Have you decided on how the company's information on current assets meets the list of desirable qualitative characteristics?*

**DAVID:** *You're trying to get me to admit that I need the auditors. Reliability is in the auditors' hands as far as the numbers go, but I place a lot of reliance on my assessment of the qualities of senior management when I meet them. You can't audit that kind of feeling. It's all a matter of chemistry. Also, the main current asset is receivables (debtors) and I know they are reliable because the finance director told me what class of customer was involved. I didn't need the auditors for that. Relevance probably scores about eight out of ten because there aren't any complications here with unusual types of inventories. Faithful representation and neutrality are something I leave to the auditors for now but I'll be asking questions next year if the information in the financial statements turns out not to be neutral. Prudence, I know, is built into all aspects of accounting which uses historical cost measures. That sometimes works against relevance. Completeness is not a problem for current assets. The company is unlikely to leave anything out. They are more likely to include too much. I do expect the auditor to check that the assets are there. Comparability is a matter of presentation. This company has a five-year summary elsewhere in the annual report and gives the previous year's amounts in the financial statements. As for understandability, I like to think that I can see my way around figures for inventories, receivables (debtors) and cash. I usually get the answers I want when I phone the financial controller.*

**LEONA:** *But don't you see that by admitting that you have to ask more questions to help you understand the amounts, there must be some further explanations which the company could give in the annual report so that your understanding may be shared by others?*

**DAVID:** *My fund manager colleagues would say that only the professional investors have the expertise. Even if more information were reported by companies, only the professionals would know how to use it.*

## 9.7  Measurement and recording

The basic measurement rule applying to all current assets is that they should be measured at the *lower* of **cost** and **net realisable value**.[4] The exception is receivables (debtors) which are measured at selling price because the related profit is earned when the sale is made and not when the credit customer chooses to pay.

The next three sections look at issues of measurement and recording, in relation to inventories, receivables (debtors) and current asset investments, which are essential to an understanding of how much variability and uncertainty lies behind the apparent confidence of the numbers reported in financial statements.

## 9.8 Inventories (stocks) of raw materials and finished goods

The analysis of transactions involving inventories of raw materials, work-in-progress and finished goods has been explained in detail in Chapter 6 and will not be repeated here. This section examines the problems created by the general rule that inventories must be valued at the lower of cost and net realisable value. This rule is a consequence of the **prudence** concept, based on not anticipating a sale until the goods are delivered to the customer.

**Net realisable value** means the estimated selling price in the ordinary course of business less the estimated costs of completion and the estimated costs necessary to make the sale. For example, damaged inventories are sold at auction for £10,000. The auctioneer charges selling commission of 20% which is £2,000. The amount received by the seller is £8,000, called the net realisable value.

**Definition**

> **Net realisable value** is the estimated selling price in the ordinary course of business less the estimated costs of completion and the estimated costs necessary to make the sale.[5]

This section covers first of all the accounting equation in relation to the rule. It then looks at the meaning of cost and the allocation of overhead costs. Various specific models to deal with changing input prices are then discussed and the section concludes with the rules to be applied in financial reporting.

### 9.8.1 Lower of cost and net realisable value

Consider the example of a container of coffee beans purchased by a coffee manufacturer at a cost of £1,000. The beans are held for three months up to the balance sheet date. During that time there is a fall in the world price of coffee beans and the container of coffee beans would sell for only £800 in the market.

When the asset is acquired, the impact on the accounting equation is an increase of £1,000 in the asset of inventories and a decrease of £1,000 in the asset of cash.

| Assets ↑↓ | – | Liabilities | = | Ownership interest |
|---|---|---|---|---|
| + **£1,000** inventories − **£1,000 cash** | | | | |

At the end of the year the asset is found to be worth £800 and the ownership interest is reduced because the asset has fallen in value. The asset is reduced by £200 and an expense of loss of value in inventories value is reported in the income statement (profit and loss account).

| Assets ↓ | – | Liabilities | = | Ownership interest ↓ |
|---|---|---|---|---|
| − **£200** inventories | | | | − **£200 expense** |

If a business fails to report a fall in the value of the asset of inventories, the profit of the period will be overstated.

Where there are separate categories of inventories the rule of 'lower of cost and net realisable value' must be applied to each category separately. Suppose, for example, there is an inventory (stock) of paper at a cost of £2,000 with a net realisable value of £2,300 and an inventory (stock) of pens with a cost of £1,800 and a net realisable value of £1,400. The lower amount must be taken in each case, giving a value of £3,400 for inventories (calculated as £2,000 plus £1,400).

## 9.8.2     Meaning of cost

The **cost** of inventories comprises all costs of purchase, costs of conversion and other costs incurred in bringing the inventories to their present location and condition.[6] This expenditure will include not only the cost of purchase but also costs of converting raw materials into finished goods or services.

Costs of purchase include the price charged by the supplier, plus transport and handling costs, plus import duties, and less discounts and subsidies.[7] Costs of conversion include items readily identifiable with the product, such as labour, expenses and subcontractors' costs directly related to the product. They also include production overheads and any other overheads directly related to bringing the product or service to its present condition and location. **Production overheads** are items such as depreciation of machines, service costs, rental paid for a factory, wages paid to supervisory and support staff, costs of stores control and insurance of production facilities.

### Example

Take the example of a business which purchases 10 wooden furniture units for conversion to a customer's specification for installation in a hotel. The units cost £200 each and the labour cost of converting them is £100 each. Production overheads for the period are fixed at £3,500. Two units remain unsold at the end of the period. These two units will be recorded in the balance sheet at £1,300, calculated as £650 each (materials cost of £200 plus labour cost of £100 plus a share of the production overheads at £350 per item).

That was easy because there were 10 identical units to take equal shares of the production overheads. But suppose they had all been different and required different amounts of labour? Would it have been fair to share the overheads equally? Probably not. The problems of sharing out production overhead costs create a chapter in themselves and are studied further as part of management accounting. You need to be aware, in reading published accounting information, that there is considerable scope for discretion to be exercised by management in the allocation of overheads between completed goods and goods held in inventories. The general risk of overstatement of assets applies here. If the asset is overstated by having too much production overhead allocated, the profit of the period is also overstated because it is not bearing the share of production overheads which it should.

## 9.8.3     Costs when input prices are changing

One very tiresome problem faced by the accounts department in its record keeping is that suppliers change their prices from time to time. Goods held in store may have arrived at different times and at different unit prices. How does the accounts department decide on the unit price to be charged to each job when all the materials look the same once they are taken into store?

In some cases it may be possible to label the materials as they arrive so that they can be identified with the appropriate unit price. That is a very time-consuming process and would only be used for high-value low-volume items of materials. In other cases a convenient method is needed which gives an answer that is useful and approximately close to the true price of the units used. Some possibilities are shown in Exhibit 9.3 using three options – first-in-first-out (FIFO), last-in-first-out (LIFO) and average cost. In each case, Exhibit 9.3 takes a very simple approach, not complicated by having inventory at the start of the period. In real life the calculations can be even more tricky.

**Exhibit 9.3**
**Pricing the issue of goods to production**

There are three parts to this illustration. Part (a) contains a table setting out the data to be used in the calculation. Part (b) defines the three bases of calculation. Part (c) uses the data from part (a) to illustrate each of the three bases.

**(a) Data**

| Date | Received | Unit price | Price paid | Issued to production |
|---|---|---|---|---|
| | Units | £ | £ | Units |
| 1 June | 100 | 20 | 2,000 | – |
| 20 June | 50 | 22 | 1,100 | – |
| 24 June | – | – | – | 60 |
| 28 June | – | – | – | 70 |
| Total | 150 | | 3,100 | 130 |

**(b) Bases of calculation**
*First-in-first-out (FIFO)*
Assume that the goods which arrived first are issued first.

*Last-in-first-out (LIFO)*
Assume that the goods which arrived last are issued first.

*Average cost*
Assume that all goods are issued at the average price of the inventories held.

**(c) Calculations**

| Basis | Date | Quantity and unit price | Issued to production | Held in inventories | Total |
|---|---|---|---|---|---|
| | | | £ | £ | £ |
| **FIFO** | | | | | |
| | 24 June | 60 units at £20 | 1,200 | | |
| | 28 June | 40 units at £20 | | | |
| | | 30 units at £22 | 1,460 | | |
| | 30 June | 20 units at £22 | | 440 | |
| Total | | | 2,660 | 440 | 3,100 |

▶

**Exhibit 9.3 continued**

| LIFO | | | | | |
|---|---|---|---|---|---|
| | 24 June | 50 units at £22 | | | |
| | | 10 units at £20 | 1,300 | | |
| | 28 June | 70 units at £20 | 1,400 | | |
| | 30 June | 20 units at £20 | | 400 | |
| *Total* | | | *2,700* | *400* | *3,100* |

| *Average* | | | | | |
|---|---|---|---|---|---|
| | 24 June | 60 units at *£20.67 | 1,240 | | |
| | 28 June | 70 units at *£20.67 | 1,447 | | |
| | 30 June | 20 units at *£20.67 | | 413 | |
| *Total* | | | *2,687* | *413* | *3,100* |

*Note*: *Weighted average [(100 × 20) + (50 × 22)]/150 = £20.67.

### 9.8.4 Approximation when dates are not recorded

In business there may not be time to keep the detailed records shown in the calculations in Exhibit 9.3. In such cases the sales volume is known in total but the dates of sales are not recorded. The calculation then uses the best approximation available, which usually means working through the costs from the oldest date, for FIFO, or the most recent date, for LIFO, without attempting to match the various batches bought and sold during the year.

### 9.8.5 Choice of FIFO, LIFO or average cost

Look at table (c) of Exhibit 9.3 and compare it with table (a) of that exhibit. You will see from table (a) that the total amount spent on materials during the month was £3,100. You will see from table (c) that the total of the cost of goods issued to production, plus the cost of unsold goods, is always £3,100 irrespective of which approach is taken. All that differs is the allocation between goods used in production and goods remaining unsold. Cost can never be gained or lost in total because of a particular allocation process, provided the process is used consistently over time. The FIFO approach suffers the disadvantage of matching outdated costs against current revenue. The LIFO approach improves on FIFO by matching the most recent costs against revenue, but at the expense of an inventory value which becomes increasingly out of date. The average cost lies between the two and becomes more intricate to recalculate as more items come into inventory. In practice, the choice for internal reporting in management accounting is a matter of finding the best method for the purpose.

There is an effect on profit of the year which may influence management choice. When prices are rising and inventories volumes are steady or increasing, FIFO gives a lower cost of sales and so a higher profit than LIFO. If there were no regulations, companies that wished to show high profits (perhaps to impress investors buying shares in the company) might prefer FIFO. Companies that wished to show lower profits (perhaps to reduce tax bills) might prefer LIFO.

The IASB standard IAS 2 prohibits the use of LIFO. In the UK the tax authorities will not accept LIFO valuation. In the USA the LIFO method of valuation is permitted. Investors need to read the accounting policy note in the financial statements to find which approach a company has used.

| Activity 9.3 | Look back to Exhibit 9.3 and write your own table of data for goods received, unit price, price paid and goods issued to production. Create calculations of cost of goods sold, using the various models in Exhibit 9.3 (FIFO, LIFO and average price). Check that the value of goods issued to production, plus the value of goods held in stock, will always add up to the same answer in total. |
|---|---|

## 9.9  Receivables (debtors)

The measurement of receivables (debtors) requires attention to bad and doubtful debts. A debt is described as a **bad debt** when there is no further hope of the customer paying the amount owed. This might be due to the customer being declared bankrupt or else disappearing without trace. If the customer is known to be in difficulties or there is some dispute over the amount owed, the debt is described as a **doubtful debt**. The company still hopes to recover the cash owed but realistically has some doubt. Evidence of doubtful debts may be seen in slow payment, partial payments, the need for several reminders or even rumours in the business community. A company will usually analyse the age of its debts to help identify those which may be doubtful.

### Example

At the end of Year 1 the Garden Pond Company has a balance sheet comprising £2,000 receivables (debtors), £7,000 other assets and £9,000 ownership interest that consists of £1,800 ownership interest at the start of the period and £7,200 profit of the period. On the balance sheet date the manager of the company reviews the receivables (debtors) list and decides that debts amounting to £200 are doubtful because there are rumours of a customer not paying other suppliers in the trade. The balance sheet at the end of Year 1 is amended to show that the asset is of lower value than was thought and the ownership interest has consequently diminished.

Exhibit 9.4 shows the spreadsheet for analysis set out to reflect the accounting equation. The new column is the one headed **provision for doubtful debts**. This is included in the assets section because it tells the user more about the asset of receivables (debtors), although it is the negative part of the asset. It causes some confusion to those who meet it for the first time because anything called a provision is usually reported under the heading of liabilities. However, on grounds of usefulness to readers and relevance to the provision of information about the asset, the provision for doubtful debts has special treatment in being included as a negative aspect within the asset section of the balance sheet.

It is quite a difficult matter for a company to be prudent in expressing doubt about a debtor while still pursuing the non-payer with a view to collection of the debt. To remove the debt from the record would be to admit defeat. Even to show a separate provision among the liability headings might lead other customers to think, 'Why not me also?' Some companies therefore do not disclose a separate provision for doubtful debts in a company's balance sheet. They deduct the provision from the full receivables (debtors)' list and report only the resulting net amount.

**Exhibit 9.4**

**Spreadsheet to analyse the effect of provision for doubtful debts at the end of Year 1, using the accounting equation**

| Date | Transaction or event | Assets | | | Ownership interest | |
|------|----------------------|--------|--|--|--------------------|--|
| Year 1 | | Receivables (debtors) | Provision for doubtful debts | Other assets | Ownership interest at start | Profit of the period |
| | | £ | £ | £ | £ | £ |
| Dec. 31 | Balance sheet first draft | 2,000 | | 7,000 | 1,800 | 7,200 |
| Dec. 31 | Recognition of doubtful debts | | (200) | | | (200) |
| Dec. 31 | Revised balance sheet | 2,000 | (200) | 7,000 | 1,800 | 7,000 |

The balance sheet after incorporating a provision for the doubtful debt would appear as in Exhibit 9.5.

There is no single method of calculating the provision for doubtful debts. Some companies consider separately the amount owed by each customer. To economise on time, most companies use previous experience to estimate a percentage of total receivables (debtors). A mixture of approaches could be used, with known problems being identified separately and a general percentage being applied to the rest.

**Exhibit 9.5**

**Balance sheet of Garden Pond Company showing the presentation of information on doubtful debts**

| Garden Pond Company Balance sheet at 31 December Year 1 | | |
|---|---|---|
| | £ | £ |
| Other assets | | 7,000 |
| Receivables (debtors) | 2,000 | |
| *Less:* provision for doubtful debts | (200) | |
| | | 1,800 |
| | | 8,800 |
| | | |
| Ownership interest at the start of the year | | 1,800 |
| Profit of the year | | 7,000 |
| | | 8,800 |

## 9.9.1    Change in a provision

During Year 2 matters take an upward turn and in July the customer who was showing signs of financial distress manages to pay the amount of £200 owed. The effect on the accounting equation is that the asset of cash is increased and the asset of debtor is reduced by £200. The provision for doubtful debts is now no longer required and could be transferred back to the income statement (profit and loss account), but in practice it tends to be left for tidying up at the end of the year.

The business continues and at the end of Year 2 the receivables (debtors) amount to £2,500. A review of the list of receivables (debtors) causes considerable doubt regarding an amount of £350. It is decided to create a new provision of £350. The old provision of £200 related to last year's receivables (debtors) and is no longer required.

Exhibit 9.6 shows the spreadsheet at the end of Year 2, before and after recording the new provision for doubtful debts. It is assumed that the other assets have grown to £10,000 and there is a profit of £3,500 before amending the provision for doubtful debts.

The income statement (profit and loss account) could show two separate entries, one being £200 increase in ownership interest and the other being £350 decrease in ownership interest. It is rather cumbersome in that form and most enterprises would report as an expense, in the income statement (profit and loss account), the single line:

Increase in provision for doubtful debts  £150

**Exhibit 9.6**
**Spreadsheet to analyse the effect of provision for doubtful debts at the end of Year 2, using the accounting equation**

| Date | Transaction or event | Assets | | | Ownership interest | |
|---|---|---|---|---|---|---|
| Year 2 | | Receivables (debtors) | Provision for doubtful debts | Other assets | Ownership interest at start | Profit of the period |
| | | £ | £ | £ | £ | £ |
| Dec. 31 | Balance sheet first draft | 2,500 | (200) | 10,000 | 8,800 | 3,500 |
| Dec. 31 | Elimination of provision no longer required | | 200 | | | 200 |
| Dec. 31 | Creation of new provision | | (350) | | | (350) |
| Dec. 31 | Revised balance sheet | 2,500 | (350) | 10,000 | 8,800 | 3,350 |

## 9.10 Prepayments

**Prepayments** arise when an item of expense is paid in advance of the benefit being received. A common example is the payment of an insurance premium. The payment is made in advance for the year ahead and the benefit is gradually used up as the year goes along. The balance sheet recognises the unexpired portion of the insurance premium as an asset, while the income statement (profit and loss account) reports the amount consumed during the period.

### Example

On 1 October Year 1 a company paid £1,200 for one year's vehicle insurance. At the balance sheet date of 31 December there have been three months' benefit used up and there is a nine-month benefit yet to come. The transactions relating to insurance would be reported as in Exhibit 9.7.

The effect of identifying the asset is to reduce the expense of the period from £1,200 to £300 and to hold the remaining £900 as a benefit for the next accounting period. In Year 2 the amount of £900 will be transferred from the prepayment column to the expense column, so that the decrease in the ownership interest is reported in the period in which it occurs.

**Exhibit 9.7**
**Spreadsheet recording prepayment of insurance at the balance sheet date**

| Date | Transaction or event | Assets | | Ownership interest |
|---|---|---|---|---|
| Year 2 | | Cash £ | Prepayment £ | Expense £ |
| Oct. 1 | Payment of premium | (1,200) | | (1,200) |
| Dec. 31 | Identification of asset remaining as prepayment | | 900 | 900 |
| | | (1,200) | 900 | (300) |

## 9.11 Revenue recognition

The sale of goods and services creates **revenue** for the business. Sometimes that revenue is referred to as **sales** or **turnover**. The term revenue may also be applied to rents received from letting out property, or interest received on investments made. In the conceptual frameworks of various countries, different views are held of the exact meaning and extent of the word *revenue*. The IASB defines revenue in terms of equity (ownership interest).

**Definition**

> **Revenue** is defined as the gross inflow of economic benefits during the period arising in the course of the ordinary activities of an enterprise when those inflows result in increases in equity, other than increases relating to contributions from equity participants.[8]

The main problem in recognition of revenue lies in the timing. Assets are recognised at a point in time but revenue is created over a period of time. What are the rules for deciding on the time period for which revenue should be reported? One suggestion has been that the **critical event** is the important factor.[9] When goods are produced or services are carried out, there is one part of the process which is critical to providing sufficient reassurance that the revenue has been earned by the efforts of the enterprise. For the sale of goods the point of delivery to the customer is the usual critical event which determines the date of revenue recognition. For a contract of service, the critical event is the production of the service.

### 9.11.1 Contract revenue

Where the service extends over more than one time period, the revenue may be split over the time periods involved. That may happen in a civil engineering or a building contract. In each year of the contract a portion of the revenue will be matched against costs of the period so as to report a portion of profit.

Take the example of a two-year bridge-building contract. The contract price is £60m. Two-thirds of the work has been completed in Year 1 and it is expected that the remainder will be completed in Year 2. The costs incurred in Year 1 are £34m and the costs expected for Year 2 are £17m.

The income statement (profit and loss account) of the business for Year 1 will report, in respect of this contract, turnover of £40m less costs of £34m giving profit of £6m. This gives a fair representation of the profit earned by the activity of the year (as two-thirds of the total). An independent expert, in this case an engineer, would confirm that the work had been completed satisfactorily to date. The effect on the accounting equation would be:

| Assets ↑↓ | – | Liabilities | = | Ownership interest ↑ |
|:---:|:---:|:---:|:---:|:---:|
| + £40m<br>– £34m | | | | + £6m |

Reporting contract revenue of £40m in Year 1 will increase the ownership interest by £40m. A matching asset will be reported, representing the value of the contract at that stage. The value of £40m shown for the construction contract represents the aggregate amount of costs incurred plus recognised profits to date.

In the income statement (profit and loss account) the expenses of £34m are reported in the usual way and a profit of £6m results. All being well, the income statement (profit and loss account) of Year 2 will report the remaining £20m of revenue minus £17m of expenses, leaving a profit of £3m. Over the two years the total profit of £9m will be reported.

Users of accounting information need to pay particular attention to contract revenue in a business and ask some careful questions. Has prudence been exercised in deciding what portion of revenue to report? Is there a risk that the future costs will escalate and there will be an overall loss? They should look carefully at the provisions section of the balance sheet (see Chapter 11).

Where the customer has paid money in advance as an instalment towards the final contract price, the effect on the accounting equation is to increase the asset of cash and create a liability towards the customer. These amounts received in advance from customers may be described as 'progress billings', 'payments on account', or 'payments in advance'. There is a liability because the business has an obligation to repay the customer if the contract is not completed on time or on specification. Although it might be expected that the liability towards the customer would appear in the current liabilities section of the balance sheet, that does not happen. The liability in respect of payments made in advance is deducted from the value of the contract and the resulting net figure is reported as *construction contracts* in the current assets section of the balance sheet. That may mean that, at first glance at the balance sheet, the reader does not realise the true size of the contract being undertaken for the customer. There is no guarantee that any better information will be found anywhere else in the financial statements, because turnover is aggregated for all activities. For the analyst as an expert user, construction contracts (long-term contracts) require a great deal of careful questioning if the underlying details are to be understood.

## 9.11.2    A continuing debate

There are problems in revenue recognition that continue to be debated. Consider three examples. In the first, a film production company sells a programme to a television company which agrees to pay royalties every time the programme is broadcast. In the second, a farmer sells a cow to a neighbour in return for five sheep. In the third, a mobile phone company charges customers a start-up fee that is 24 times the monthly rental and service charge. There is no specific accounting standard to cover any of these situations. One approach to each is to ask, 'Has the revenue been earned?' The companies would all answer, 'Yes, we have completed our side of the transaction.' So perhaps revenue should be recognised in all three cases. Another approach is to ask, 'Are there any risks related to recognising revenue?' The answer is, 'Yes – the programme may never be broadcast; we are not sure about the exchange values between cows and sheep; and the telephone company may not be able to provide the service for the long period implied by the high initial charge.' So perhaps the revenue should not be reported until the risks are diminished. Both views are being applied, with the result that there has been some lack of clarity and comparability as new types of business have emerged. It is necessary to pay careful attention to the accounting policy on revenue recognition.

## 9.12  Summary

- A **current asset** is an asset that satisfies any of the following criteria:
    (a) it is expected to be realised in, or is intended for sale or consumption in, the entity's normal operating cycle;
    (b) it is held primarily for the purpose of being traded;
    (c) it is expected to be realised within twelve months after the balance sheet date;
    (d) it is cash or a cash equivalent.
- **Working capital** is the amount which a business must provide to finance the current assets of a business, to the extent that these are not covered by current liabilities. It is calculated by deducting current liabilities from current assets.
- Inventories (stocks), receivables (debtors), investments and cash are commonly **recognised** in a balance sheet. If there is doubt attached to the expectation of economic benefit which creates the asset and to the reliability of measurement, then this is recognised by making a **provision** such as the provision for doubtful debts.
- Users need information about the working capital of the business to judge whether it is suitable to support the activities of the business. Information provided to help users includes: detailed notes of current assets and current liabilities; notes of accounting policy describing the valuation of current assets; and a discussion of working capital management in the operating and financial review.
- **Inventories** (stocks) are measured at the lower of cost and net realisable value.
- **Receivables** (debtors) are measured at the amount receivable on settlement less any provision for doubtful debts.
- **Prepayments** are amounts paid in advance for benefits expected. Prepayments are assets until the benefit is used up. The amount is then transferred from an asset to an expense.
- **Revenue** is defined as the gross inflow of economic benefits during the period arising in the course of the ordinary activities of an enterprise when those inflows result in increases in equity, other than increases relating to contributions from equity participants.
- If revenues are earned over more than one time period (e.g. on long-term contracts) then the revenue is allocated across time periods in proportion to the amount of work completed.

## QUESTIONS

The Questions section of each chapter has three types of question. 'Test your understanding' questions to help you review your reading are in the 'A' series of questions. You will find the answers to these by reading and thinking about the material in the book. 'Application' questions to test your ability to apply technical skills are in the 'B' series of questions. Questions requiring you to show skills in problem solving and evaluation are in the 'C' series of questions. A letter [S] indicates that there is a solution at the end of the book.

## A     Test your understanding

**A9.1**   What is the definition of a current asset? (Section 9.2)

**A9.2**   What is the working capital cycle? (Section 9.3)

**A9.3**   What are the features of raw materials, work-in-progress and finished goods which justify their recognition in a balance sheet? (Section 9.4.1)

**A9.4**   What information do users need about current assets? (Section 9.5)

**A9.5**   What is meant by FIFO, LIFO and the average cost method of pricing issues of goods? (Section 9.8.3)

**A9.6**   How is a provision for doubtful debts decided upon? (Section 9.9)

**A9.7**   What is a prepayment? (Section 9.10)

**A9.8**   What is meant by 'revenue recognition'? (Section 9.11)

**A9.9**   Why are there problems with revenue recognition? (Section 9.11.2)

**A9.10**  [S] The Sycamore Company has inventories which include the following four items:

| Description | Purchase cost | Selling price | Cost of selling |
|---|---|---|---|
| | £ | £ | £ |
| Engine | 6,500 | 8,250 | 350 |
| Chassis | 2,000 | 1,800 | 200 |
| Frame | 4,800 | 4,900 | 300 |

What amount should be reported as total inventory in respect of these three items?

**A9.11**  [S] On reviewing the company's financial statements, the company accountant discovers that items of year-end inventory of goods which cost £18,000 have been omitted from the record. What will be the effect on the income statement (profit and loss account) and the balance sheet when this omission is rectified?

**A9.12**  [S] On reviewing the financial statements, the company accountant discovers that an amount of £154,000 owed by a customer will be irrecoverable because the customer has fled the country. What will be the effect on the income statement (profit and loss account) and the balance sheet when this event is recognised?

## B     Application

**B9.1** [S]

During its first month of operations, a business made purchases and sales as shown in the table below:

| Date | Number of units purchased | Unit cost | Number of units sold |
|---|---|---|---|
| Jan. 5 | 100 | £1.00 | |
| Jan. 10 | | | 50 |
| Jan. 15 | 200 | £1.10 | |
| Jan. 17 | | | 150 |
| Jan. 24 | 300 | £1.15 | |
| Jan. 30 | | | 200 |

All sales were made at £2 each.

**Required**

Calculate the profit for the month and the stock value held at the end of the month using:

(a) the FIFO approach to the issue of units for sale, where:
   (i)   the calculation is carried out at the date of sale; and
   (ii)  the calculation is carried out at the end of the month without regard for the date of sale; and

(b) the LIFO approach to the issue of units for sale, where:
   (i)  the calculation is carried out at the date of sale; and
   (ii)  the calculation is carried out at the end of the month without regard for the date of sale; and
(c) the average-cost approach to the issue of units for sale, making the calculation at the end of the month without regard for the date of sale.

**B9.2** [S]
A company has a stock of goods consisting of four different groups of items. The cost and net realisable value of each group is shown in the table below.

| Group of items | Cost | Net realisable value |
|---|---|---|
| | £ | £ |
| A | 1,000 | 1,400 |
| B | 1,000 | 800 |
| C | 2,100 | 1,900 |
| D | 3,000 | 3,100 |

**Required**
Calculate the amount to be shown as the value of the company's stock.

**B9.3**
At the end of Year 3 the Bed Company has a balance sheet comprising £3,000 receivables (debtors), £8,000 other assets and £11,000 ownership interest, consisting of £2,000 ownership interest at the start of the period and £9,000 profit of the period. On the balance sheet date the manager of the company reviews the receivables (debtors) list and decides that debts amounting to £450 are doubtful because the customers have not replied to repeated requests for payment.

**Required**
(a) Prepare an accounting equation spreadsheet to show the effect of the provision. (See Exhibit 9.4 for an illustration.)
(b) Show the balance sheet information. (See Exhibit 9.5 for an illustration.)

**B9.4**
The Bed Company continues trading during Year 4. The balance sheet at the end of Year 4, in its first draft, showed receivables (debtors) as £4,850 and the provision for doubtful debts unchanged from Year 3 at £450. Enquiry showed that during Year 4 some of the receivables (debtors) at the end of Year 3 had been confirmed as bad. They amounted to £250 but nothing had yet been recorded. The management wish to make the provision £550 at the end of Year 4. Other assets amount to £12,000, ownership interest at the start of Year 4 is £10,550 and the profit is £5,750.

**Required**
Prepare an accounting equation spreadsheet to show the effect of the bad debt being recognised and of the decision to make a provision at the end of Year 4. (See Exhibit 9.6 for an illustration.)

**B9.5**
On 1 December Year 1 a company paid £2,400 as an insurance premium to give accident cover for the 12 months ahead. The accounting year-end is 31 December.

**Required**
Prepare an accounting equation spreadsheet to show the effect of the prepayment in the year ended 31 December Year 1.

## C    Problem solving and evaluation

**C9.1**
A fire destroyed a company's detailed stock records and much of the merchandise held in stock. The company accountant was able to discover that stock at the beginning of the period was £40,000, purchases up to the date of the fire were £250,000, and sales up to the date of the fire were £400,000. In past periods, the company has earned a gross profit of 35% of sales.

**Required**

Calculate the cost of the stock destroyed by the fire.

**C9.2**

It is the policy of Seaton Ltd to make provision for doubtful debts at a rate of 10% per annum on all debtor balances at the end of the year, after deducting any known bad debts at the same date. The following table sets out the total receivables (debtors) as shown by the accounting records and known bad debts to be deducted from that total. There is no provision at 31 December Year 0.

| Year-end | Debtor balances | Known bad debts |
|---|---|---|
| | £ | £ |
| 31 Dec. Year 1 | 30,000 | 2,000 |
| 31 Dec. Year 2 | 35,000 | 3,000 |
| 31 Dec. Year 3 | 32,000 | 1,500 |
| 31 Dec. Year 4 | 29,000 | 1,000 |

**Required**

(a) Calculate the total expense in the income statement (profit and loss account) in respect of bad and doubtful debts.

(b) Set out the balance sheet information in respect of receivables (debtors) and provision for doubtful debts at each year-end.

## Activities for study groups

Turn to the annual report of a listed company which you have used for activities in previous chapters. Find every item of information about current assets. (Start with the financial statements and notes but look also at the operating and financial review, chief executive's review and other non-regulated information about the company.)

As a group, imagine you are the team of fund managers in a fund management company. You are holding a briefing meeting at which each person explains to the others some feature of the companies in which your fund invests. Today's subject is current assets. Each person should make a short presentation to the rest of the team covering:

1 The nature and significance of current assets in the company.

2 The effect on profit of a 10% error in estimation of any one of the major categories of current asset.

3 The company's comments, if any, on its present investment in working capital and its future intentions.

4 The risks which might attach to the inventories of the company.

5 The liquidity of the company.

6 The trends in current assets since last year (or over five years if a comparative table is provided).

7 The ratio of current assets to current liabilities.

## Notes and references

1. IASB (1989), *Framework for the Preparation and Presentation of Financial Statements*, para. 49(a).
2. IASB (2004), IAS 1, para. 57.
3. IASB (2004), IAS 2 *Inventories*, para. 6.
4. IASB (2004), IAS 2 *Inventories*, para. 9.
5. IASB (2004), IAS 2 *Inventories*, para. 6.
6. IASB (2004), IAS 2 *Inventories*, para. 10.
7. IASB (2004), IAS 2 *Inventories*, para. 11.
8. IASB (2004), IAS 18, *Revenue*, para. 7.
9. J. H. Myers (1959) 'The critical event and recognition of net profit', *Accounting Review*, **34**, pp. 528–32; and ASB (1999) *Statement of Principles for Financial Reporting*, ch. 5, paras. 5.33–5.36.

# Bookkeeping entries for (a) bad and doubtful debts; and (b) prepayments

*The debit and credit recording aspects of inventories of raw materials and finished goods were explained in the Supplement to Chapter 6. That leaves, for this supplement, the recording of bad and doubtful debts as a new area where potential care is needed. Prepayments are also illustrated here.*

## Provision for doubtful debts

The following ledger accounts illustrate the recording of the transactions analysed in section 9.9. Look back to that section for the description and analysis of the transactions. The debit and credit analysis is shown in Exhibit 9.8. So that you will not be confused by additional information, the ledger accounts presented here show only sufficient information to illustrate the recording of transactions relating to doubtful debts. Leona comments on the main features.

**Exhibit 9.8**
**Analysis of debit and credit aspect of each transaction and event**

| Date | | Debit | Credit |
|---|---|---|---|
| Year 1 | | | |
| End of year | Manager identifies doubtful debts £200 | Profit and loss account £200 | Provision for doubtful debts £200 |
| Year 2 | | | |
| July | Customer who was doubtful pays £200 in full | Cash £200 | Receivables (debtors) £200 |
| End of year | Manager identifies new provision required £350 | Profit and loss account £350 | Provision for doubtful debts £350 |
| End of year | Former provision no longer required | Provision for doubtful debts £200 | Profit and loss account £200 |

The ledger accounts required are as follows:

| | | | |
|---|---|---|---|
| L1 | Receivables (debtors) | L3 | Cash |
| L2 | Provision for doubtful debts | L4 | Profit and loss account |

Also required to complete the double entry, but not shown here as a ledger account, is ledger account L5 Ownership interest.

The full list of transactions for the year would be too cumbersome to deal with here, so dots are used to show that the ledger account requires more information for completeness.

**L1 Receivables (debtors)**

| Date | Particulars | Page | Debit | Credit | Balance |
|------|-------------|------|-------|--------|---------|
| Year 1 | | | £ | £ | £ |
| | . . . | | . . . | | . . . |
| Dec. 31 | Balance at end of year | | | | 2,000 |
| Year 2 | | | | | |
| | . . . | | . . . | | . . . |
| July | Cash from customer | L3 | | 200 | . . . |
| | . . . | | . . . | | . . . |
| Dec. 31 | Balance at end of year | | | | 2,500 |

**LEONA:** *The ledger account for receivables (debtors) has no entries relating to doubtful debts. That is important because although there may be doubts from the viewpoint of the business, the customer still has a duty to pay and should be encouraged by all the usual means. Keeping the full record of amounts due is an important part of ensuring that all assets of the business are looked after.*

**L2 Provision for doubtful debts**

| Date | Particulars | Page | Debit | Credit | Balance |
|------|-------------|------|-------|--------|---------|
| Year 1 | | | £ | £ | £ |
| Dec. 31 | Profit and loss account – new provision | L4 | | 200 | (200) |
| Year 2 | | | | | |
| Dec. 31 | Profit and loss account – old provision | L4 | 200 | | nil |
| Dec. 31 | Profit and loss account – new provision | L4 | | 350 | (350) |

**LEONA:** *The provision for doubtful debts is a credit balance because it is the negative part of an asset. It keeps a separate record of doubt about the full value of the asset. A credit entry in the ledger account increases the amount of the provision and a debit entry decreases the amount of the provision.*

**L3 Cash**

| Date | Particulars | Page | Debit | Credit | Balance |
|------|-------------|------|-------|--------|---------|
| Year 2 | | | £ | £ | £ |
| | . . . | | . . . | | . . . |
| July | Cash from debtor | L1 | 200 | | |
| | . . . | | . . . | | . . . |

LEONA: *Receiving cash from the doubtful customer looks like any other transaction receiving cash. It is important that the cash is collected and the debt is removed by receiving the full amount due.*

**L4 Profit and loss account**

| Date | Particulars | Page | Debit | Credit | Balance |
|------|-------------|------|-------|--------|---------|
| Year 1 | | | £ | £ | £ |
| | . . . | | . . . | | . . . |
| Dec. 31 | Balance before provision for doubtful debts | | | | (7,200) |
| Dec. 31 | Provision for doubtful debts | L2 | 200 | | (7,000) |
| Dec. 31 | Transfer to ownership interest | L5 | 7,000 | | nil |
| Year 2 | | | | | |
| | . . . | | . . . | | . . . |
| Dec. 31 | Balance before provision for doubtful debts | | | | (3,500) |
| Dec. 31 | Removal of provision no longer required | L2 | | 200 | (3,700) |
| Dec. 31 | New provision for doubtful debts | L2 | 350 | | (3,350) |
| Dec. 31 | Transfer to ownership interest | L5 | 3,350 | | nil |

LEONA: *In Year 1 of this example the provision is established for the first time so there is one debit entry to establish an expense which decreases the profit (as a part of the ownership interest). In Year 2 of this example the old provision is removed and a new provision created. The overall effect is that the provision increases by £150. Some people would take a short-cut and make one entry of £150 to increase the provision from £200 to £350 but I am not keen on short-cuts. They sometimes lead to disaster. Separate entries make me think carefully about the effect of each.*

## Recording a doubtful debt which turns bad

Suppose that in July of Year 2 it was found that the doubtful debt turned totally bad because the customer was declared bankrupt. The effect on the accounting equation is that the asset of debtor is removed. That would normally reduce the ownership interest but on this occasion the impact on ownership interest was anticipated at the end of Year 1 and so the provision for doubtful debts is now used to match the decrease in the asset. The analysis of the transaction would be:

| Date | Transaction or event | Debit | Credit |
|---|---|---|---|
| Year 2 | | | |
| July | Doubtful debt becomes bad | Provision for doubtful debts £200 | Receivables (debtors) £200 |

The consequence of using the provision for doubtful debts is that there is no impact on the income statement (profit and loss account) of Year 2 of a bad debt which was known to be likely at the end of Year 1. However, when the provision for doubtful debts is reviewed at the end of Year 2 there is no reversal of the £200 because that has already been used during the year. The charge of £350 for Year 2 relates solely to the provision for doubt in respect of receivables (debtors) owing money at the end of Year 2.

## Prepayments

The prepayment transaction analysed in the chapter was as follows. On 1 October of Year 1 a company paid £1,200 for one year's vehicle insurance. At the balance sheet date of 31 December there have been three months' benefit used up and there is a nine-month benefit yet to come. (See Exhibit 9.9.)

**Exhibit 9.9**
**Analysis of prepayment of insurance, Year 1**

| Date | Transaction or event | Debit | Credit |
|---|---|---|---|
| Year 2 | | | |
| Oct. 1 | Payment of premium £1,200 | Expense (insurance) | Cash |
| Dec. 31 | Identification of asset remaining as a prepayment £900 | Asset (prepayment) | Expense (insurance) |

Ledger accounts required to record the prepayment are:

L6   Expense of insurance
L7   Prepayment

Not shown, but necessary for completion of the debit and credit record, are:

L3   Cash
L4   Profit and loss account

| | **L6 Expense of insurance** | | | | |
|---|---|---|---|---|---|
| Date | Particulars | Page | Debit | Credit | Balance |
| Year 1 | | | £ | £ | £ |
| Oct. 31 | Cash | L3 | 1,200 | | 1,200 |
| Dec. 31 | Prepayment | L7 | | (900) | 300 |
| Dec. 31 | Transfer to profit and loss account | L4 | | (300) | nil |

**LEONA:** *Although it is known in October that there will be a balance remaining at the end of the year, it is usually regarded as more convenient to debit the entire payment as an expense of the period initially. The expense is reviewed at the end of the year and £900 is found to be an asset which benefits the future. It is transferred to the asset account for prepayments, leaving only the expense of £300 relating to this period, which is transferred to the income statement (profit and loss account).*

**L7 Prepayment**

| Date | Particulars | Page | Debit | Credit | Balance |
|------|-------------|------|-------|--------|---------|
| Year 1 | | | £ | £ | £ |
| Oct. 31 | Insurance expense prepaid | L6 | 900 | | 900 |

**LEONA:** *The prepayment account is an asset account and therefore the balance remains in the account until the benefit asset is used up. During Year 2 the benefit will disappear and the asset will become an expense. The bookkeeping treatment will be to credit the prepayment account and debit the insurance expense account.*

## S  Test your understanding

**S9.1**  Record the transactions of question **B9.3** in ledger accounts for L1 Receivables (debtors), L2 Provision for doubtful debts, L3 Cash and L4 Profit and loss account.

**S9.2**  Record the transactions of question **B9.4** in ledger accounts for L1 Receivables (debtors), L2 Provision for doubtful debts, L3 Cash and L4 Profit and loss account.

**S9.3**  Record the transactions of question **B9.5** in ledger accounts for L6 Expense of insurance and L7 Prepayment.

# Chapter 10

# Current liabilities

## 19 Creditors: Amounts falling due within one year

| | Group | | Company | |
|---|---|---|---|---|
| | 2005 | Restated 2004 | 2005 | 2004 |
| | £'000 | £'000 | £'000 | £'000 |
| Loans and overdrafts | 71,994 | 16,274 | 67,499 | 15,000 |
| Trade creditors | 254,768 | 181,780 | – | – |
| Amounts owed to subsidiary undertakings | – | – | 353,007 | 314,152 |
| Corporation tax | 37,556 | 30,106 | – | – |
| Other taxes and social security costs | 33,612 | 26,668 | – | – |
| Other creditors | 44,648 | 38,988 | 11,296 | 1,230 |
| Accruals and deferred income | 120,893 | 106,546 | 4,784 | 6,293 |
| Proposed dividends | 10,968 | 7,869 | 10,968 | 7,869 |
| | 574,439 | 408,231 | 447,554 | 344,544 |

Prior year accruals and deferred income have been restated to reflect the reallocation of unearned insurance income of £8.1m which had previously been included in provisions for liabilities and charges (see note 22).

### Supplier payment policy

The Group's policy is to agree terms of transactions, including payment terms, with suppliers and, provided that suppliers perform in accordance with the agreed terms, it is the Group's normal practice that payment is made accordingly. The number of days outstanding between receipt of invoices and date of payment, calculated by reference to the amount owed to trade creditors at the period end as a proportion of the amounts invoiced by suppliers during the period, was 47 days (2004 – 42 days). The Company did not have any trade creditors at 2 April 2005 or 27 March 2004.

Source: The Carphone Warehouse Group plc, Annual Report 2005, pp. 49, 32.

### Discussion points

1 What do we learn about the group's policy of paying suppliers?

2 How significant is the amount of trade creditors in the current liabilities?

## Contents

## Learning outcomes

After studying this chapter you should be able to:

- Define a liability and explain the distinguishing feature of current liabilities.
- Explain the conditions for recognition of liabilities.
- Explain how the information presented in a company's balance sheet and notes, in relation to liabilities, meets the needs of users.
- Explain the features of current liabilities and the approach to measurement and recording.
- Explain the terms 'accruals' and 'matching concept' and show how they are applied to expenses of the period.
- Explain how liabilities for taxation arise in companies.

Additionally, for those who choose to study the Supplement:

- Prepare the ledger accounts to record accruals.

## 10.1   Introduction

The theme running through this textbook is the accounting equation:

| Assets | minus | Liabilities | equals | Ownership interest |
|---|---|---|---|---|

It was explained in Chapter 2 that the ownership interest is the residual amount found by deducting all liabilities of the company from total assets. Chapters 8 and 9 have taken you through aspects of non-current and current assets which are particularly significant to users of financial statements. Chapters 10 and 11 complete the left-hand side of the equation by providing a similar overview of current liabilities and non-current liabilities.

This chapter follows the approach established in Chapters 8 and 9:

- What are the principles for defining and recognising these items?
- What are the information needs of users in respect of the particular items?
- What information is currently provided by companies to meet these needs?
- Does the information show the desirable qualitative characteristics of financial statements?
- What are the principles for measuring, and processes for recording, these items?

## 10.2 Definitions

The definition of a liability, as provided in Chapter 2, is repeated here:

**Definition**

A **liability** is a present obligation of the entity arising from past events, the settlement of which is expected to result in an outflow from the entity of resources embodying economic benefits.[1]

A **current liability** is a liability which satisfies any of the following criteria:

(a) it is expected to be settled in the entity's normal operating cycle;
(b) it is held primarily for the purpose of being traded;
(c) it is due to be settled within twelve months after the balance sheet date.[2]

Supplement 7.1 to Chapter 7 sets out the information to be presented on the face of the balance sheet of companies using the IASB system in their financial statements. The only current liabilities listed there are item (j) trade and other payables, item (l) financial liabilities (where these are short-term loans) and (m) liabilities for current tax.

Supplement 7.2 to Chapter 7 sets out the information to be presented in the financial statements of companies that are using the UK Companies Act and UK ASB standards. There is one heading for current liabilities and a detailed list below. The list is as follows:

**E  Creditors: amounts falling due within one year**
1  Debenture loans
2  Bank loans and overdrafts
3  Payments received on account
4  Trade creditors
5  Bills of exchange payable
6  Amounts owed to group undertakings
7  Amounts owed to undertakings in which the company has a participating interest
8  Other creditors including taxation and social security
9  Accruals and deferred income

**Activity 10.1**

*Look back to Exhibit 2.3, which analyses some common types of liability. Set up on a blank sheet a similar table with four columns and headings for: type of liability; obligation; transfer of economic benefits; and past transaction or event. Then close the book and write down any ten liabilities you have come across during your study. Fill in all the columns as a check that, at this stage, you really understand what creates a liability.*

## 10.3  Recognition

The general conditions for recognition were set out in Chapter 2. An item that meets the definition of a liability should be recognised if there is sufficient evidence that the liability has been created and that the item has a cost or value that can be measured with sufficient reliability. In practice, recognition problems related to liabilities centre on ensuring that none is omitted which ought to be included. This is in contrast to the case of assets where there is a need, in practice, to guard against over-enthusiastic inclusion of items which do not meet the recognition conditions.

### 10.3.1  Risk of understatement of liabilities

The risk related to liabilities is therefore the risk of understatement. This is explained in Chapter 4 under the heading of prudence. The risk of understatement of liabilities is that it will result in overstatement of the ownership interest.

In recent years the standard-setting bodies have devoted quite strenuous efforts to discouraging companies from keeping liabilities (and related assets) off the balance sheet. This problem is called **off-balance sheet finance** and will be explained in Chapter 14.

### 10.3.2  Non-recognition: contingent liabilities

There are some obligations of the company which fail the recognition test because there is significant uncertainty about future events that may cause benefits to flow from the company. The uncertainty may be about the occurrence of the event or about the measurement of the consequences. These are called **contingent liabilities** because they are contingent upon (depend upon) some future event happening. Examples are:

- A company is involved in legal action where a customer is seeking damages for illness allegedly caused by the company's product. If the customer is successful, there will be more claims. The company does not believe that the customer will succeed.
- A parent company has given guarantees to a bank that it will meet the overdraft and loans of a subsidiary company if that company defaults on repayment. At the present time there is no reason to suppose that any default will take place.
- A company is under investigation by the Competition Commission for possible price-fixing within the industry in contravention of an order prohibiting restrictive practices. If there is found to be a restrictive practice, a penalty may be imposed.
- The company has acquired a subsidiary in Australia where the tax authorities have raised an action for tax due on a disputed transaction which occurred before the subsidiary was acquired. The action is being defended strenuously.

In each of these examples, the company is convinced that it will not have a liability at the end of the day, but the users of the financial statements may wish to have some indication of the upper bounds of the liability if the company's optimism proves unfounded. There may, however, be a problem for the company in publishing an estimate of the amount of the possible liability because it may be seen as admitting liability and furthermore may require disclosure of commercially sensitive confidential information.

Where a **contingent liability** is identified, the obligation is not recognised in the balance sheet but it may be important that users of the financial statements are aware of the problem. There will therefore be a note to the balance sheet reporting the circumstances of the contingent liability and sometimes giving an indication of the amount involved. Because of the confidentiality aspect, companies tend to give little information about the financial effect of a contingent liability, but some will try to set the outer limits of the liability.

A company should disclose a brief description of the nature of the contingent liability and, where practicable:

(a) an estimate of its financial effect;
(b) an indication of the uncertainties relating to the amount or timing of any outflow; and
(c) the possibility of any reimbursement.[4]

Rules about measurement are given in detail in the accounting standard. The detail is not necessary for an introductory course.

## 10.3.3 Changing thoughts on contingencies

In 2005 the IASB issued a proposal to eliminate the term 'contingent liability' because if the item cannot be recognised in a balance sheet then it cannot be a true liability. The proposal of the IASB was that items carrying an unconditional obligation should be recognised as a liability and measured at the best estimate. Any uncertain event affecting the measurement of the obligation would be explained in a note. Items that do not carry an unconditional obligation are seen as business risks. Such business risks would be reported as a note to the financial statements because they may have a significant effect on the carrying amount of assets and liabilities in the near future. These changing thoughts on contingencies do not change the overall amount of information to be disclosed about contingencies but the method of disclosure may change.

**Activity 10.2**

*Consider the four examples of contingent liability given at the start of this section. Based on the definition, explain why each is a contingent liability.*

# 10.4 Users' needs for information

There are two aspects of information in relation to liabilities. The first relates to the amount owed (sometimes called the **principal sum** or the **capital amount**) and the second relates to the cost of servicing the loan (usually the payment of **interest**).

In respect of current liabilities, other than a bank overdraft or bank loans repayable within the year, it is unlikely that interest will be payable, and so generally there will be no information about interest charges. The shareholders in the company will be concerned that there are adequate current assets to meet the current liabilities as they fall due. Those who supply goods and services will want to be reassured that payment will be made on the due date.

Owners of a company need to know how much the company owes to other parties because the owners are at the end of the queue when it comes to sharing out the assets of the company if it closes down. Many of those who supply goods and services are what is known as unsecured creditors, which means they come at the end of the list of creditors. They will also have an interest in the balance of long-term and current liabilities.

## 10.5 Information provided in the financial statements

The balance sheet of Safe and Sure plc, set out in Chapter 7, contains the following information in relation to current liabilities:

|  | Notes | Year 7 £m | Year 6 £m |
|---|---|---|---|
| **Current liabilities** | | | |
| Amounts payable (creditors) | 7 | (159.8) | (157.5) |
| Bank overdraft | 8 | (40.1) | (62.6) |
| | | (199.9) | (220.1) |

Notes to the balance sheet explain more about the balance sheet items. Note 7 lists the details of current liabilities.

**Note 7 Current liabilities: amounts payable**

|  | Year 7 £m | Year 6 £m |
|---|---|---|
| Deferred consideration on acquisition | 1.1 | 4.3 |
| Trade payables (trade creditors) | 23.6 | 20.4 |
| Corporation tax | 31.5 | 26.5 |
| Other tax and social security payable | 24.5 | 21.2 |
| Other payables (creditors) | 30.7 | 23.8 |
| Accruals and deferred income | 48.4 | 61.3 |
| | 159.8 | 157.5 |

Note 8 gives information on bank overdrafts due on demand and confirms that the interest charges incurred on these loans are payable at commercial rates:

**Note 8 Bank borrowings: current liabilities**

|  | Year 7 £m | Year 6 £m |
|---|---|---|
| *Bank overdrafts due on demand:* | 40.1 | 62.6 |

Interest on overdrafts is payable at normal commercial rates appropriate to the country where the borrowing is made.

The report of the finance director provides further insight into the currency spread of the bank borrowings:

*Foreign currency: £35.2m of foreign currency bank borrowings have been incurred to fund overseas acquisition. The main borrowings were £26.8m in US dollars and £8.4m in Japanese yen. The borrowings are mainly from banks on a short-term basis, with a maturity of up to one year, and we have fixed the interest rate on $20m of the US dollar loans through to November, Year 7, at an overall cost of 4.46%.*

*All material foreign currency transactions are matched back into the currency of the group company undertaking the transaction.*

David Wilson has already commented in Chapters 4 and 7 on some aspects of the liabilities in the financial statements of Safe and Sure plc. Here he is explaining to Leona, in the coffee bar at the health club, his views on current liabilities in particular.

**DAVID:** *Current liabilities are relatively similar in total to last year so there are no particular questions to ask there.*

*Then I start to think about the limits of risk. There is £40m due for repayment to the bank within the year. Will the company have any problem finding this amount? With £105m in cash and cash, it seems unlikely that there could be a problem. The entire current liabilities are £199.9m, all of which could be met from the cash and cash equivalents and receivables (debtors).*

*There is another risk that £40m shown as owing to the banks may be the wrong measure of the liability if exchange rates move against the company. Whenever I see foreign borrowings I want to know more about the currency of borrowings. You know from your economics class the theory of interest rates and currency exchange rates. It backs up my rule of thumb that borrowing in currencies which are weak means paying high rates of interest. Borrowing in currencies which are strong will mean paying lower rates of interest but runs a greater risk of having to use up additional pounds sterling to repay the loan if the foreign currency strengthens more. Information about the currency mix of loans is something I can probably get from the company if I need it. In this case, the finance director's report is sufficiently informative for my purposes. In past years, before finance directors started providing explanations in the annual report, we were asking these questions at face-to-face meetings.*

**LEONA:** *What you have described is similar in many respects to the analytical review carried out by the auditors. We do much more than merely check the bookkeeping entries and the paperwork. We are looking at whether the balance sheet makes sense and whether any items have changed without sufficient explanation.*

## 10.6  Measurement and recording

Liabilities are measured at the amount originally received from the lender of finance or supplier of goods and services, plus any additional charges incurred such as rolled-up interest added to a loan. This is generally agreed to be a useful measure of the obligation to transfer economic benefits from the company.

From the accounting equation it may be seen that an increase in a liability must be related either to an increase in an asset or a decrease in the ownership interest. Usually any related decrease in the ownership interest will be reported in the balance sheet as an expense.

The most significant current liabilities for most companies are bank borrowing and trade creditors. Both of these are essential sources of finance for small companies and are an important aspect, if not essential, for larger companies.

**Activity 10.3**

*Write down the documentation you would expect to see as evidence of the money amount of the following liabilities:*

- *bank overdraft;*
- *amount owing to a trade supplier.*

*Now read the next sections and find whether your answer matches the information in the text.*

### 10.6.1    Bank overdraft finance

Banks provide short-term finance to companies in the form of an overdraft on a current account. The advantage of an overdraft is its flexibility. When the cash needs of the company increase with seasonal factors, the company can continue to write cheques and watch the overdraft increase. When the goods and services are sold and cash begins to flow in, the company should be able to watch the overdraft decrease again. The most obvious example of a business which operates in this pattern is farming. The farmer uses the overdraft to finance the acquisition of seed for arable farming, or feed through the winter for stock farming and to cover the period when the crops or animals are growing and maturing. The overdraft is reduced when the crops or the animals are sold.

The main disadvantage of an overdraft is that it is repayable on demand. The farmer whose crop fails because of bad weather knows the problem of being unable to repay the overdraft. Having overdraft financing increases the worries of those who manage the company. The other disadvantage is that the interest payable on overdrafts is variable. When interest rates increase, the cost of the overdraft increases. Furthermore, for small companies there are often complaints that the rate of interest charged is high compared with that available to larger companies. The banks answer that the rates charged reflect relative risk and it is their experience that small companies are more risky.

### 10.6.2    Trade payables (trade creditors)

It is a strong feature of many industries that one enterprise is willing to supply goods to another in advance of being paid. Most suppliers will state terms of payment (e.g. the invoice must be paid within 30 days) and some will offer a discount for prompt payment. In the UK it has not been traditional to charge interest on overdue accounts but this practice is growing as suppliers realise there is a high cost to themselves of not collecting cash in good time. A supplier who is waiting to be paid is called a **trade creditor**.

Trade creditors rarely have any security for payment of the amount due to them, so that if a customer fails to pay the supplier must wait in the queue with other suppliers and hope for a share of some distribution. They are described as **unsecured creditors**. Some suppliers will include in the contract a condition that the goods remain the property of the supplier should the customer fail to pay. This is called retention of title (ROT) and will be noted in the balance sheet of a company which has bought goods on these terms. Retention of title may offer some protection to the unpaid supplier but requires very prompt action to recover identifiable goods in the event of difficulty.

Some suppliers send goods to a customer on a sale-or-return basis. If there are no conditions to prevent return then the goods will not appear as stock in the balance sheet of the customer and there will be no indication of a liability. This practice is particularly common in the motor industry where manufacturers send cars to showrooms for sale or return within a specified period of time. Omitting the inventories and the related potential liability is referred to as **off-balance sheet finance**, a topic explored further in Chapter 14.

Suppliers send **invoices** to the customer showing the amount due for payment. These invoices are used in the customer's accounts department as the source of information for liabilities. At the end of the month the suppliers send statements as a reminder of unpaid invoices. Statements are useful as additional evidence of liabilities to suppliers.

Measurement of trade creditors is relatively straightforward because the company will know how much it owes to short-term creditors. If it forgets the creditors, they will soon issue a reminder.

Recording requires some care because omission of any credit transaction will mean there is an understatement of a liability. In particular, the company has to take some care at the end of the year over what are called **cut-off procedures**. Take the example of raw materials provided by a supplier. The goods arrive at the company's store by delivery van but the invoice for their payment arrives a few days later by mail. The accounts department uses the supplier's invoice as the document which initiates the *recording* of the asset of stock and the liability to the supplier. In contrast, the event which *creates* the liability is the acceptance of the goods. (It is difficult for the accounts department to use the delivery note as a record of the liability because it shows the quantities but not the price of the goods delivered.) So, at the end of the accounting year the accounts department has to compare the most recent delivery notes signed by the storekeeper with the most recent invoices received from the supplier. If goods have been received by the company, the balance sheet must include the asset of stock and the related liability. Using a similar line of reasoning, if a supplier has sent an invoice ahead of delivery of the goods, it should not be recorded as a liability because there is no related asset.

The recording of purchases of goods for resale is shown in Chapter 6. In the illustration of the process for recording the transactions of M. Carter there is a purchase of goods from the supplier, R. Busby, on credit terms. Payment is made later in the month. The purchase of the goods creates the asset of stock and the liability to the supplier. Payment to the supplier reduces the asset of cash and eliminates the liability to the supplier.

## 10.7 Accruals and the matching concept

At the balance sheet date there will be obligations of the company to pay for goods or services which are not contained in the accounting records because no document has been received from the supplier of the goods or services. It is essential that all obligations are included at the balance sheet date because these obligations fall under the definition of liabilities even although the demand for payment has not been received. The process of including in the balance sheet all obligations at the end of the period is called the accrual of liabilities and is said to reflect the **accruals** basis or accruals concept (see Chapter 4).

**Definition**

> Under the **accruals basis**, the effects of transactions and other events are recognised when they occur (and not as cash or its equivalent is received or paid) and they are recorded in the accounting records and reported in the financial statements of the periods to which they relate.[5]

The argument contained in the previous paragraph is based on the definition of a liability, but some people prefer to arrive at the same conclusion using a different argument. They say that all expenses of the accounting period must be matched against the revenue earned in the period. If a benefit has been consumed, the effect must be recorded whether or not documentation has been received. This argument is referred to as the **matching concept**.

In the *Framework*, the IASB explains that in the income statement there is a direct association between the costs incurred and the earning of specific items of income. This process is called the matching of costs with revenues. As an example, the expenses that make up the cost of goods sold are recognised at the same time as the revenue derived from the sale of the goods.[6]

The accruals concept and the matching concept are, for most practical purposes, different ways of arriving at the same conclusion. (There are exceptions but these are well beyond the scope of a first-level text.)

## 10.7.1 The distinction between the expense of the period and the cash paid

A company starts business on 1 January Year 1. It has a financial year-end of 31 December Year 1. During Year 1 it receives four accounts for electricity, all of which are paid ten days after receiving them. The dates of receiving and paying the accounts are as follows:

| Date invoice received | Amount of invoice £ | Date paid |
|---|---|---|
| 31 Mar. Year 1 | 350 | 10 Apr. Year 1 |
| 30 June Year 1 | 180 | 10 July Year 1 |
| 30 Sept. Year 1 | 280 | 10 Oct. Year 1 |
| 31 Dec. Year 1 | 340 | 10 Jan. Year 2 |
| | 1,150 | |

The company has used electricity for the entire year and therefore should match against revenue the full cost of £1,150. Only three invoices have been paid during the year, the final invoice not being paid until the start of Year 2. That is important for cash flow but is not relevant for the measurement of profit. The transactions during the year would be recorded as shown in Exhibit 10.1. The arrival of the electricity invoice causes a record to be made of the increase in the liability and the increase in the expense (decreasing the ownership interest). The payment of the amount due requires a separate record to be made of the decrease in the liability and the decrease in the asset of cash.

**Exhibit 10.1**
**Spreadsheet analysis of transactions relating to the expense of electricity consumed, Year 1**

| Date | Transactions with electricity company | Asset | Liability | Ownership interest:profit of the period |
|---|---|---|---|---|
| | | Cash | Electricity company | Electricity expense |
| Year 1 | | £ | £ | £ |
| Mar. 31 | Invoice received £350 | | 350 | (350) |
| Apr. 10 | Pay electricity company £350 | (350) | (350) | |
| June 30 | Invoice received £180 | | 180 | (180) |
| July 10 | Pay electricity company £180 | (180) | (180) | |
| Sept. 30 | Invoice received £280 | | 280 | (280) |
| Oct. 10 | Pay electricity company £280 | (280) | (280) | |
| Dec. 31 | Invoice received £340 | | 340 | (340) |
| | Totals | (810) | 340 | (1,150) |

The payment made to the electricity company in January Year 2 is not recorded in Exhibit 10.1 because it is not a transaction of Year 1. It will appear in a spreadsheet for January Year 2. The totals at the foot of the spreadsheet show that the transactions of Year 1 have caused the cash of the company to decrease by £810. There remains a liability of £340 to the electricity company at the end of Year 1. The profit and loss account for the year will show an expense of £1,150. The spreadsheet satisfies the accounting equation because there is a decrease in an asset, amounting to £810, and an increase in a liability amounting to £340. These together equal the decrease of £1,150 in the ownership interest:

| Asset ↓ | – | Liability ↑ | = | Ownership interest ↓ |
|---|---|---|---|---|
| – £810 | | + £340 | | – £1,150 |

That one needs a little careful thought because several things are happening at once. You might prefer to think about it one stage at a time. You know from earlier examples in Chapters 2, 5 and 6 that a decrease in an asset causes a decrease in the ownership interest. You also know that an increase in a liability causes a decrease in the ownership interest. Put them together and they are both working in the same direction to decrease the ownership interest.

## 10.7.2 Accrual where no invoice has been received

Now consider what might happen if the final electricity invoice for the year has not been received on 31 December Year 1. If no invoice has been received then there will be no entry in the accounting records. That, however, would fail to acknowledge that the electricity has been consumed and the company knows there is an obligation to pay for that electricity. In terms of the matching concept, only nine months' invoices are available to match against revenue when there has been 12 months' usage. The answer is that the company must make an *estimate* of the accrual of the liability for electricity consumed. Estimates will seldom give the true answer but they can be made reasonably close if some care is taken. If the company keeps a note of electricity meter readings and knows the unit charge, it can calculate what the account would have been.

The entries in the spreadsheet at the end of the month are shown in Exhibit 10.2. They will be the same numerically as those in the final line of Exhibit 10.1 but the item shown at 31 December will be described as an accrual.

**Exhibit 10.2**
**Spreadsheet entry for accrual at the end of the month**

| Date | Transactions with electricity company | Asset | Liability | Ownership interest:profit of the period |
|---|---|---|---|---|
| | | Cash | Electricity company | Electricity expense |
| Year 1 | | £ | £ | £ |
| Dec. 31 | Accrual for three months | | 340 | (340) |

## 10.7.3 The nature of estimates in accounting

Making an accrual for a known obligation, where no invoice has been received, requires estimates. In the example given here it was a relatively straightforward matter to take a meter reading and calculate the expected liability. There will be other examples where the existence and amount of an expense are both known with reasonable certainty. There will be some cases where the amount has to be estimated and the estimate is later found to be incorrect. That is a normal feature of accounting, although not all users of financial statements realise there is an element of uncertainty about the information provided. If a liability is unintentionally understated at the end of a period, the profit will be overstated. In the next accounting period, when the full obligation becomes known, the expense incurred will be higher than was anticipated and the profit of that period will be lower than it should ideally be. If the error in the estimate is found to be such that it would change the views of the main users of financial statements, a prior year adjustment may be made by recalculating the profits of previous years and reporting the effect, but that is a relatively rare occurrence.

**Activity 10.4**

*Write down five types of transaction where you might expect to see an accrual of expense at the year-end. Against each transaction type write down the method you would use to estimate the amount of the accrued expense.*

## 10.8  Liabilities for taxation

In the balance sheet of a company there are two main categories of liability related directly to the company. The first is the **corporation tax** payable, based on the taxable profits of the period, the second is **deferred taxation**. Each of these will be discussed here. You will also see in the current liabilities section of a balance sheet the words 'other tax and social security payable'. This refers to the amounts deducted from employees' salaries and wages by the company on behalf of the Inland Revenue and paid over at regular intervals. In respect of such amounts the company is acting as a tax collecting agent of the Inland Revenue.

### 10.8.1  Corporation tax

Companies pay corporation tax based on the taxable profit of the accounting period (usually one year). The taxable profit is calculated according to the rules of tax law. That in itself is a subject for an entire textbook but one basic principle is that the taxable profit is based on profit calculated according to commercially accepted accounting practices. So, apart from some specific points of difference, the accounting profit is usually quite close to the taxable profit. Assume that the corporation tax rate is 30% of the taxable profit. (The tax rate each year is set by the Chancellor of the Exchequer.) Analysts will evaluate the tax charge in the profit and loss account as a percentage of taxable profit and start to ask questions when the answer is very different from 30%. The explanation could be that there are profits earned abroad where the tax rate is different, but it could also be that there has been some use of provisions or adjustments for accounting purposes which are not allowed for tax purposes. That will lead to more probing by the analysts to establish whether they share the doubts of the tax authorities.

Large companies must pay corporation tax by four quarterly instalments. A company with a year-end of 31 December Year 1 will pay on 14 July Year 1, 14 October Year 1, 14 January Year 2 and 14 April Year 2. The amount of tax due is estimated by making a forecast of the profit for the year. As the year progresses the forecast is revised and the tax calculation is also revised. This means that at the end of the accounting year there is a liability for half that year's tax bill. A 'large' company is any company that pays corporation tax at the full rate. Small companies, which have a special, lower, rate of corporation tax, pay their tax bill nine months after the end of the accounting period. The precise limits for defining 'large' and 'small' companies change with tax legislation each year. (You will be given the necessary information in any exercise that you are asked to attempt.) Suppose the taxable profit is £10m and the tax payable at 30% is £3m. During the year £1.5m is paid in total on the first two instalment dates. At the balance sheet date there will remain a liability of £1.5m to be paid in total on the final two instalment dates.

| Assets | – | Liabilities | = | Ownership interest |
|---|---|---|---|---|
| During year | ↓ £1.5m Cash | | | ↓ £1.5m (Tax expense) |
| At end of year | | ↓ £1.5m Tax liability | | ↓ £1.5m (Tax expense) |

### 10.8.2 Deferred taxation liability

It was explained earlier in this section that the taxable profit is based on the accounting profit unless there are taxation rules which indicate otherwise. There are taxation rules which allow companies to defer the payment of some taxation on the full accounting profit. ('Deferring' means paying much later than the normal period of nine months.) The deferral period might be for a few months or it might be for a few years. The obligation to pay tax eventually cannot be escaped but the liability becomes long term. This is reflected, in terms of the accounting equation, by reporting the decrease in ownership claim in the profit and loss account but showing the deferred liability as a separate item under **non-current liabilities**.

## 10.9 Summary

- A **current liability** is a liability which satisfies any of the following criteria:
    (a) it is expected to be settled in the entity's normal operating cycle;
    (b) it is held primarily for the purpose of being traded;
    (c) it is due to be settled within twelve months after the balance sheet date.
- The risk of understatement of liabilities is that it will result in overstatement of the ownership interest.
- **Off-balance sheet finance** means keeping liabilities (and related assets) off the balance sheet.
- There are some obligations of the company which fail the recognition test because there is significant uncertainty about future events that may cause benefits to flow from the company. These are reported as **contingent liabilities** in the notes to the financial statements.
- Users need to know about the existence of liabilities, the amount and timing of expected repayments, and interest charges payable on loans.
- Under the **accruals** basis, the effects of transactions and other events are recognised when they occur (and not as cash or its equivalent is received or paid) and they are recorded in the accounting records and reported in the financial statements of the periods to which they relate.
- Liabilities for unpaid expenses are often called **accruals**.
- The **matching concept** is the idea that all expenses of the accounting period must be matched against the revenue earned in the period. If a benefit has been consumed, the effect must be recorded whether or not documentation has been received.
- Companies pay corporation tax. The arrangements vary depending on the size of the company but there will usually be a liability for unpaid corporation tax in the current liabilities section of the balance sheet. Where government policy allows payment to be delayed for more than 12 months the liability is described as **deferred taxation**.

# QUESTIONS

The Questions section of each chapter has three types of question. 'Test your understanding' questions to help you review your reading are in the 'A' series of questions. You will find the answers to these by reading and thinking about the material in the book. 'Application' questions to test your ability to apply technical skills are in the 'B' series of questions. Questions requiring you to show skills in problem solving and evaluation are in the 'C' series of questions. A letter [S] indicates that there is a solution at the end of the book.

## A | Test your understanding

**A10.1** What is the definition of a liability? (Section 10.2)

**A10.2** What is the distinction between a long-term liability and a current liability? (Section 10.2)

**A10.3** What is the effect of understatement of liabilities? (Section 10.3.1)

**A10.4** What is a contingent liability? (Section 10.3.2)

**A10.5** What information do users of financial statements need to have concerning current liabilities of a company? (Section 10.4)

**A10.6** How are the current liabilities for (a) bank overdraft and (b) trade creditors measured? (Section 10.6)

**A10.7** What is meant by an accrual? How is it recorded? (Section 10.7)

**A10.8** Explain what is meant by the matching concept. (Section 10.7)

**A10.9** [S] On reviewing the financial statements, the company accountant discovers that a supplier's invoice for an amount of £10,000 has been omitted from the accounting records. The goods to which the invoice relates are held in the warehouse and are included in stock. What will be the effect on the profit and loss account and the balance sheet when this error is rectified?

**A10.10** [S] On reviewing the financial statements, the company accountant discovers that a payment of £21,000 made to a supplier has been omitted from the cash book and other internal accounting records. What will be the effect on the profit and loss account and the balance sheet when this omission is rectified?

**A10.11** [S] On reviewing the financial statements, the company accountant discovers that an invoice for the rent of £4,000 owed to its landlord has been recorded incorrectly as rent receivable of £4,000 in the company's accounting records. What will be the effect on the profit and loss account and the balance sheet when this error is rectified?

## B | Application

**B10.1** [S]
White Ltd commenced trading on 1 July Year 3 and draws up its accounts for the year ended 30 June Year 4. During its first year of trading the company pays total telephone expenses of £3,500. The three-month bill paid in May Year 4 includes calls of £800 for the quarter up to 30 April Year 4 and advance rental of £660 to 31 July Year 4. The bill received in August Year 4 includes calls of £900 for the quarter up to 31 July Year 4 and advance rental of £660 to 31 October Year 4.

**Required**
Show calculations of the telephone expense to be recorded in the profit and loss account of White Ltd for its first year of trading.

**B10.2** [S]

Plastics Ltd pays rent for a warehouse used for storage. The quarterly charge for security guard services is £800. The security firm sends an invoice on 31 March, 30 June, 30 September and 31 December. Plastics Ltd always pays the rent five days after the invoice is received. The security services have been used for some years. Plastics Ltd has an accounting year-end of 31 December.

**Required**

Prepare a spreadsheet to show how the transactions of one year in respect of security services are recorded.

**B10.3** [S]

The accountant of Brown Ltd has calculated that the company should report in its profit and loss account a tax charge of £8,000 based on the taxable profit of the period. Of this amount, £6,000 will be payable nine months after the accounting year-end but £2,000 may be deferred for payment in a period estimated at between three and five years after the accounting year-end. Using the accounting equation explain how this information will be reported in the financial statements of Brown Ltd.

## C   Problem solving and evaluation

**C10.1** [S]

The following file of papers was found in a cupboard of the general office of Green Ltd at the end of the accounting year. Explain how each would be treated in the financial statements and state the total amount to be reported as an accrued liability on the balance sheet date. The year-end is 31 December Year 1.

| Item | Description | Amount £ |
|---|---|---|
| 1 | Invoice dated 23 December for goods received 21 December. | 260 |
| 2 | Invoice dated 23 December for goods to be delivered on 3 January Year 2. | 310 |
| 3 | Foreman's note of electricity consumption for month of December – no invoice yet received from electricity supply company. | 100 |
| 4 | Letter from employee claiming overtime payment for work on 1 December and note from personnel office denying entitlement to payment. | 58 |
| 5 | Telephone bill dated 26 December showing calls for October to December. | 290 |
| 6 | Telephone bill dated 26 December showing rent due in advance for period January to March Year 2. | 90 |
| 7 | Note of payment due to cleaners for final week of December (to be paid on 3 January under usual pattern of payment one week in arrears). | 48 |
| 8 | Invoice from supplier for promotional calendars received 1 December (only one-third have yet been sent to customers). | 300 |
| 9 | Letter dated 21 December Year 1 to customer promising a cheque to reimburse damage caused by faulty product – cheque to be sent on 4 January Year 2. | 280 |
| 10 | Letter dated 23 December promising donation to local charity – amount not yet paid. | 60 |

## Activities for study groups

Turn to the annual report of a listed company which you have used for activities in previous chapters. Find every item of information about current liabilities. (Start with the financial statements and notes but look also at the operating and financial review, chief executive's review and other non-regulated information about the company.)

Divide into two groups. One group should take on the role of the purchasing director and one should take on the role of a company which has been asked to supply goods or services to this company on credit terms.

- *Supplier group*: What questions would you ask to supplement what you have learned from the annual report?
- *Purchasing director*: What questions would you ask about the supplier? What might you learn about the supplier from the annual report of the supplier's company?

### Notes and references

1. IASB (1989) *Framework*, para. 49(b).
2. IASB (2004) IAS 1, para. 60.
3. IASB (2004) IAS 37, *Provisions, Contingent Liabilities and Contingent Assets*, para. 10.
4. *Ibid.*, para. 86.
5. IASB (1989) *Framework*, para. 23.
6. IASB (1989) *Framework*, para. 95.

## Supplement to Chapter 10

# Bookkeeping entries for accruals

*In the main part of the chapter the accruals for electricity were analysed. Now consider the debit and credit recording. The following transactions are to be recorded.*

A company starts business on 1 January Year 1. It has a financial year-end of 31 December Year 1. During Year 1 it receives three accounts for electricity, all of which are paid ten days after receiving them. The dates of receiving and paying the accounts are as follows:

| Amount of invoice £ | Date invoice received | Date paid |
|---|---|---|
| 350 | 31 Mar. Year 1 | 10 Apr. Year 1 |
| 180 | 30 June Year 1 | 10 July Year 1 |
| 280 | 30 Sept. Year 1 | 10 Oct. Year 1 |

At 31 December the final invoice for the year has not arrived because of delays in the mail but the amount due for payment is estimated at £340.

**Activity 10.5**

*Before you read further, attempt to write down the debit and credit entries for: each of the three invoices received; the payments of those three invoices; and the estimated amount due for payment at the end of the year. You may find help in looking back to Exhibits 10.1 and 10.2.*

Exhibit 10.3 sets out the debit and credit aspect of each transaction and event. The amount of the liability to the supplier cannot be recorded until the invoice is received. The credit entry for the estimate of the amount owing to the supplier is therefore shown in a separate account called *accruals* which will be the basis for the amount shown in the balance sheet under that heading.

The ledger accounts required here are:

L1  Expense (electricity)
L2  Liability to supplier
L3  Accrual

Also required to complete the double entry, but not shown here as a ledger account, are:

L4  Cash
L5  Profit and loss account

**Exhibit 10.3**
**Analysis of debit and credit aspect of each transaction and event**

| Date | Transaction | Debit | Credit |
|------|-------------|-------|--------|
| Year 1 | | | |
| Mar. 31 | Receive invoice for electricity £350 | Expense (electricity) | Liability to supplier |
| Apr. 10 | Pay supplier £350 | Liability to supplier | Cash |
| June 30 | Receive invoice for electricity £180 | Expense (electricity) | Liability to supplier |
| July 10 | Pay supplier £180 | Liability to supplier | Cash |
| Sept. 30 | Receive invoice for electricity £280 | Expense (electricity) | Liability to supplier |
| Oct. 10 | Pay supplier £280 | Liability to supplier | Cash |
| Dec. 31 | Estimate amount owing to supplier £340 | Expense (electricity) | Accruals |

**L1 Expense (Electricity)**

| Date | Particulars | Page | Debit | Credit | Balance |
|------|-------------|------|-------|--------|---------|
| Year 1 | | | £ | £ | £ |
| Mar. 31 | Invoice from supplier | L2 | 350 | | 350 |
| June 30 | Invoice from supplier | L2 | 180 | | 530 |
| Sept. 30 | Invoice from supplier | L2 | 280 | | 810 |
| Dec. 31 | Estimated accrual | L3 | 340 | | 1,150 |
| Dec. 31 | Transfer to profit and loss account | L5 | | (1,150) | nil |

LEONA: *The electricity account for the year shows a full 12 months' expense which is transferred to the profit and loss account at the end of the year.*

**L2 Liability to supplier**

| Date | Particulars | Page | Debit | Credit | Balance |
|------|-------------|------|-------|--------|---------|
| Year 1 | | | £ | £ | £ |
| Mar. 31 | Invoice for electricity expense | L1 | | 350 | (350) |
| Apr. 10 | Cash paid | L4 | 350 | | nil |
| June 30 | Invoice for electricity expense | L1 | | 180 | (180) |
| July 10 | Cash paid | L4 | 180 | | nil |
| Sept. 30 | Invoice for electricity expense | L1 | | 280 | (280) |
| Oct. 10 | Cash paid | L4 | 280 | | nil |

**LEONA:** *The supplier's account is showing a nil liability because all invoices received have been paid. We know there is another invoice on the way but the bookkeeping system is quite strict about only making entries in the ledger when the documentary evidence is obtained. The document in this case is the supplier's invoice. Until it arrives the liability has to be recognised as an accrual rather than in the supplier's account.*

| | **L3 Accruals** | | | | |
|---|---|---|---|---|---|
| *Date* | *Particulars* | *Page* | *Debit* | *Credit* | *Balance* |
| *Year 1* | | | £ | £ | £ |
| Dec. 31 | Estimate of electricity expense | L1 | 340 | (340) | |

**LEONA:** *The balance sheet will record a nil liability to the supplier but will show an accrual of £340 for electricity. When the supplier's invoice arrives in January of Year 2, the debit and credit entries will be:*

| *Date* | *Transaction* | *Debit* | *Credit* |
|---|---|---|---|
| *Year 2* | | | |
| Jan. 4 | Receive invoice for electricity £340 | Accrual | Liability to supplier |

*In this way the liability remaining from Year 1 is recorded without affecting the expense account for Year 2. The credit balance on the accrual account at the end of Year 1 is eliminated by being matched against the debit entry at the start of Year 2.*

## S    Test your understanding

**S10.1**  Prepare bookkeeping records for the information in question **B10.1**.

**S10.2**  Prepare bookkeeping records for the information in question **B10.2**.

**S10.3**  Prepare bookkeeping records for the information in question **B10.3**.

**S10.4**  Prepare bookkeeping records for the information in question **C10.1**.

# Chapter 11

# Provisions and non-current (long-term) liabilities

## 30 Other provisions

| | Decommissioning | Environmental | Other | Group Total | Parent Other provisions |
|---|---|---|---|---|---|
| | | | | | $ million |
| At 1 January 2004 | 4,720 | 2,298 | 1,797 | 8,815 | 216 |
| Prior year adjustment – change in accounting policy | – | – | (216) | (216) | (216) |
| Restated | 4,720 | 2,298 | 1,581 | 8,599 | – |
| Exchange adjustments | 213 | 21 | 25 | 259 | – |
| New provisions | 294 | 588 | 298 | 1,180 | – |
| Write-back of unused provisions | – | (151) | (64) | (215) | – |
| Unwinding of discount | 118 | 55 | 23 | 196 | – |
| Change in discount rate | 434 | 40 | 1 | 475 | – |
| Utilized/deleted | (199) | (393) | (294) | (886) | – |
| At 31 December 2004 | 5,580 | 2,458 | 1,570 | 9,608 | – |

The group makes full provision for the future cost of decommissioning oil and natural gas production facilities and related pipelines on a discounted basis on the installation of those facilities. At 31 December 2004, the provision for the costs of decommissioning these production facilities and pipelines at the end of their economic lives was $5,580 million ($4,720 million). The provision has been estimated using existing technology, at current prices and discounted using a real discount rate of 2.0% (2.5%). These costs are expected to be incurred over the next 30 years. While the provision is based on the best estimate of future costs and the economic lives of the facilities and pipelines, there is uncertainty regarding both the amount and timing of incurring these costs.

### Decommissioning costs

The group holds provisions for the future decommissioning of oil and natural gas production facilities and pipelines at the end of their economic lives. The largest asset removal obligations facing BP relate to the removal and disposal of oil and natural gas platforms and pipelines around the world. The estimated discounted costs of dismantling and removing these facilities are accrued on the installation of those facilities, reflecting our legal obligations at that time. Most of these removal events are many years in the future and the precise requirements that will have to be met when the removal event actually occurs are uncertain. Asset removal technologies and costs are constantly changing, as well as political, environmental, safety and public expectations. Consequently, the timing and amounts of future cash flows are subject to significant uncertainty. The timing and amount of future expenditures are reviewed annually, together with the interest rate to be used in discounting the cash flows. The interest rate used to determine the balance sheet obligation at the end of 2004 was 2.0%, 0.5% lower than at the end of 2003. The interest rate represents the real rate (i.e. adjusted for inflation) on long-dated government bonds.

Source: BP Annual Report and Accounts 2004, pp. 67 and 34.

### Discussion points

1 Why is there a provision when the decommissioning will take place so far into the future?

2 What are the significant uncertainties in estimating the amount of the provision?

## Contents

## Learning outcomes

After studying this chapter you should be able to:

- Define a non-current (long-term) liability.
- Explain the needs of users for information about non-current (long-term) liabilities.
- Explain the different types of non-current (long-term) loan finance which may be found in the balance sheets of major companies.
- Understand the purpose of provisions and explain how provisions are reported in financial statements.
- Understand the nature of deferred income and explain how it is reported in financial statements.
- Know the main types of loan finance and capital instruments used by companies and understand the principles of reporting information in the financial statements.

Additionally, for those who choose to study the Supplement to this chapter:

- Prepare the ledger accounts to record provisions and deferred income.

## 11.1  Introduction

Supplement 7.1 to Chapter 7 sets out the information to be presented on the face of the balance sheet of companies using the IASB system in their financial statements. The non-current liabilities listed there are item (k) provisions, (l) financial liabilities (where these are loans due in more than one year's time) and (n) deferred tax liabilities.

Supplement 7.2 to Chapter 7 sets out the information to be presented in the financial statements of companies that are using the UK Companies Act and UK ASB standards. There is one heading for non-current liabilities, with a detailed list below, as follows:

**H Creditors: amounts falling due after more than one year**
1  Debenture loans
2  Bank loans and overdrafts
3  Payments received on account
4  Trade creditors
5  Bills of exchange payable
6  Amounts owed to group undertakings
7  Amounts owed to undertakings in which the company has a participating interest
8  Other creditors including taxation and social security
9  Accruals and deferred income

Comparing Supplements 7.1 and 7.2 it could appear that companies using the IASB system face fewer detailed rules. However those companies still produce a great deal of detailed information in practice because the IASB has other standards that require more detail.

In this chapter we follow the pattern established in earlier chapters by asking:

- What are the principles for defining and recognising these items?
- What are the information needs of users in respect of the particular items?
- What information is currently provided by companies to meet these needs?
- Does the information show the desirable qualitative characteristics of financial statements?
- What are the principles for measuring, and processes for recording, these items?

This chapter looks first at provisions, then turns to non-current (long-term) liabilities and finally covers deferred income. General principles of definition and recognition of liabilities are dealt with in Chapter 10 and you should ensure you have read and understood that chapter before embarking on this one. For convenience the definitions from Chapter 2 are repeated here.

**Definitions**

A **liability** is a present obligation of the entity arising from past events, the settlement of which is expected to result in an outflow from the entity of resources embodying economic benefits.[1]

A **current liability** is a liability which satisfies any of the following criteria:

(a) it is expected to be settled in the entity's normal operating cycle;
(b) it is held primarily for the purpose of being traded;
(c) it is due to be settled within 12 months after the balance sheet date.[2]

A **non-current liability** is any liability that does not meet the definition of a current liability.[3] Non-current liabilities are also described as **long-term liabilities**.

## 11.2  Users' needs for information

There are two aspects of information needed in relation to liabilities. The first relates to the amount owed (sometimes called the **principal sum** or the **capital amount**) and the second relates to the cost of servicing the loan (usually the payment of **interest**).

Owners of a company need to know how much the company owes to other parties because the owners are at the end of the queue when it comes to sharing out the assets of the company if it closes down. Lenders to the company want to know how many other lenders will have a claim on assets if the company closes down and how much the total claim of lenders will be. They may want to take a **secured loan**, where the agreement with the company specifies particular assets which may be sold by the lender if the company defaults on payment.

**Cash flow** is important to a range of users. Interest payments are an expense to be reported in the profit and loss account, but paying interest is a drain on cash as well as affecting the ownership interest by a reduction in profit. Owners of the company want to know if there will be sufficient cash left to allow them a **dividend** (or **drawings** for partnerships and sole traders) after interest has been paid. Lenders want to be reassured that the company is generating sufficient cash flow and profit to cover the interest expense.

Both owners and lenders want to see the impact of borrowing on future cash flows. They need to know the scheduled dates of repayments of loans (sometimes referred to as the **maturity profile of debt**), the currency in which the loan must be repaid and the structure of interest rates (e.g. whether the loan period is starting with low rates of interest which are then stepped up in future years).

Finally, owners and lenders are interested in the **gearing** of the company. This means the ratio of loan capital to ownership interest in the balance sheet or the ratio of interest payments to net profit in the profit and loss account. Chapter 13 will provide more detail on the calculation and interpretation of gearing.

| Activity 11.1 | *Imagine you are a shareholder in a company which is financed partly by long-term loans. Write down the information needed by users in the order of importance to you as a shareholder and explain your answer.* |
| --- | --- |

## 11.3  Information provided in the financial statements

The balance sheet of Safe and Sure plc, set out in Chapter 7, contains the following information in relation to non-current (long-term) liabilities:

|  | Notes | Year 7 £m | Year 6 £m |
| --- | --- | --- | --- |
| **Non-current liabilities** |  |  |  |
| Amounts payable (creditors) | 9 | (2.7) | (2.6) |
| Bank and other borrowings | 10 | (0.2) | (0.6) |
| Provisions | 11 | (20.2) | (22.2) |
| *Net assets* |  | 464.3 | 370.4 |

Notes to the balance sheet explain more about the balance sheet items. Note 9 gives some indication of the type of creditors due after more than one year.

**Note 9  Non-current liabilities: payables (creditors)**

|  | Year 7 £m | Year 6 £m |
|---|---|---|
| Deferred consideration on acquisition | 0.6 | – |
| Other payables (creditors) | 2.1 | 2.6 |
|  | 2.7 | 2.6 |

Note 10 distinguishes secured and unsecured loans among the borrowings due after one year and also gives a schedule of repayment over the immediate and medium-term or longer-term future. For this company, bank borrowings all mature within five years. Note 10 also confirms that commercial rates of interest are payable.

**Note 10  Non-current liabilities: bank and other borrowings**

|  | Year 7 £m | Year 6 £m |
|---|---|---|
| Secured loans | – | 0.3 |
| Unsecured loans | 0.2 | 0.3 |
|  | 0.2 | 0.6 |
| *Loans are repayable by instalments:* |  |  |
| Between one and two years | 0.1 | 0.2 |
| Between two and five years | 0.1 | 0.4 |
|  | 0.2 | 0.6 |

Interest on long-term loans, which are denominated in a number of currencies, is payable at normal commercial rates appropriate to the country in which the borrowing is made. The last repayment falls due in Year 11.

Note 11 gives information on provisions for liabilities which will occur at a future date, as a result of past events or of definite plans made.

**Note 11  Provisions**

|  | Year 7 £m | Year 6 £m |
|---|---|---|
| *Provisions for treating contaminated site:* |  |  |
| At 1 January | 14.2 | 14.5 |
| Utilised in the year | (2.2) | (0.3) |
| At 31 December | 12.0 | 14.2 |
| *Provisions for restructuring costs:* |  |  |
| At 1 January | 4.2 | – |
| Created in year | 1.0 | 4.3 |
| Utilised in year | (1.0) | (0.1) |
| At 31 December | 4.2 | 4.2 |
| *Provision for deferred tax:* |  |  |
| At 1 January | 3.8 | 2.7 |
| Transfer to profit and loss account | 0.5 | 1.2 |
| Other movements | (0.3) | (0.1) |
| At 31 December | 4.0 | 3.8 |
| Total provision | 20.2 | 22.2 |

Finally, note 33 sets out contingent liabilities. (Contingent liabilities are defined and explained in Chapter 10.) Two contingent items have the amount quantified. The impact of litigation (legal action) is not quantified. The company may think that to do so would be seen as an admission of legal liability.

> ### Note 33 Contingent liabilities
>
> The company has guaranteed bank and other borrowings of subsidiaries amounting to £3.0m (Year 6: £15.2m). The group has commitments, amounting to approximately £41.9m (Year 6: £28.5m), under forward exchange contracts entered into in the ordinary course of business.
>
> Certain subsidiaries have given warranties for service work. These are explained in the statement on accounting policies. There are contingent liabilities in respect of litigation. None of the actions is expected to give rise to any material loss.

The accounting policy statement contains three items relevant to liabilities:

### Accounting policies

*Deferred tax*
*The provision for deferred tax recognises a future liability arising from past transactions and events. Tax legislation allows the company to defer settlement of the liability for several years.*

*Warranties*
*Some service work is carried out under warranty. The cost of claims under warranty is charged against the profit and loss account of the year in which the claims are settled.*

*Deferred consideration*
*For acquisitions involving deferred consideration, estimated deferred payments are accrued in the balance sheet. Interest due to vendors on deferred payments is charged to the profit and loss account as it accrues.*

In this extract the word 'charge' appears several times. In relation to interest or taxes, the use of the word **charge** describes the reduction in ownership interest reported in the income statement (profit and loss account) due to the cost of interest and tax payable.

Because the level of borrowing is low in this company, and therefore would not create any concern for investors or new lenders, the finance director has very little to say about it in his report. To some extent the chairman takes the initiative earlier in the annual report:

### Finance
*Once again, during Year 7 we had a strong operating cash flow, amounting to £196.7m (up from £163.5m in Year 6). This funded expenditure of £24.6m on acquisition of other companies and businesses (after allowing for £3.1m received from a disposal of a company) and the group still ended the year with an increase in its cash balances.*

David Wilson has already commented in Chapters 4 and 7 on some aspects of the liabilities in the financial statements of Safe and Sure plc. Here he is explaining to Leona, in the coffee bar at the health club, his views on liabilities in particular.

DAVID: *Where do I start in explaining how I look at liabilities? Well, I always read the accounting policy notes before I look at any financial statements. This company provides three accounting policy notes relating to matters of liabilities. The policy on warranties is interesting because it confirms that the company does not record any expected liability on warranties. The first time I saw this in the annual report I was quite concerned about lack of prudence, but on my first visit to the company I was shown the warranty settlement file. There are very few claims under warranty because the company has lots of procedures which have to be followed by employees who carry out service work. Warranty claims are relatively unusual and unpredictable for this company so there is no previous pattern to justify setting up a liability in the form of a provision for future claims.*

*The deferred consideration arises because this company has acquired another business and wants to look into all aspects of the newly acquired investment before making full payment.*

*Deferred tax provisions are common to many companies. They are an attempt to line up the accounting profit with the tax charge based on taxable profits, which are usually different. I don't understand the technical details but my test of importance is to look at the amount charged to the profit and loss account for the year. It is less than 1% of the profit after tax, so I shan't be giving it much attention on this occasion.*

*Provisions for restructuring are my real headache. These are a measure of the costs expected when the company plans a restructuring such as changing the management structure with redefinition of the role of some employees and redundancy for others. It sounds reasonable to give warning of what all this will cost but the standard setters have to be strict about the details because in the past the use of provisions has been linked to some creative accounting in the profit and loss account. Do you know anything about that?*

**LEONA**: *Yes. On the one hand, you would like to know that a company is prudent in reporting in the profit and loss account now the likely losses which will arise in future years because of a decision to reorganise. On the other hand, you would not like to think that a company has loaded the profit and loss account with lots of bad news this year so that it can make next year look much better when the results are published. The accounting standard setter has prevented companies from being excessively prudent. I could explain more but not at this time on a Friday night. What do you see in the balance sheet and the other information provided by the company?*

**DAVID**: *After reading and thinking about the items in the accounting policy notes I look to the breakdown between current liabilities and longer-term liabilities. I also look to the amount of long-term finance compared with the amount of the equity holders' funds. The borrowings in this company are relatively low in relation to equityholders' funds, so there is not a high financial risk, but I still want to look for unexplained changes since the previous year. Again, there is nothing which springs to the eye.*

*The contingent liability note is usually quite interesting. One of my senior colleagues says that you should start at the end of the annual report and read it backwards. Then you find the best parts first. The contingent liability note is always near the end. I would be asking lots of questions about the forward exchange contracts, if I had not already asked the financial controller. He confirmed in more detail what the finance director says rather briefly. The forward exchange contracts are used as part of prudent financial management to put a limit on any potential loss through adverse currency movements on transactions in different countries.*

**LEONA**: *Much of what you say is reflected in what auditors carry out by way of analytical review. What we don't provide is a view to the future. What are your thoughts there?*

**DAVID**: *This is a cash-rich company and it has very little in the way of complicated financial structures. For a major company that is probably unusual, but it means I can concentrate on the operating aspects of the business and on whether it will continue to generate cash. It uses cash generated to buy other businesses and expand further, but I wonder what will happen when the scope for that expansion ceases. It is unlikely to be a problem in the near future because the company has a foothold in expanding markets in Asia. When that scope for expansion comes to an end the company may have to start borrowing to finance expansion rather than relying on internal cash flows.*

## 11.4 Provisions

Making a provision is an accounting process similar to that of making accrual for a known obligation.

| Definition | A **provision** is a liability of uncertain timing or amount.[4] |
|---|---|

The distinguishing feature of a provision often lies in the larger element of uncertainty which surrounds a provision. Such a provision will appear in the liabilities section of a balance sheet. (This book has already considered in Chapter 8 the provision for depreciation and in Chapter 9 the provision for doubtful debts. These are examples of what is regarded as an adjustment to the reported value of an asset, rather than an adjustment for significant uncertainty. They are therefore reported as adjustments to the asset and do not appear in the liabilities section.) The following are examples of provisions which may be found in the liabilities sections of published accounts:

- losses on contracts
- obsolescence of stock
- costs related to closure of a division of the company
- costs of decommissioning an oil rig
- cost of landscaping a site at the end of the period of use
- warranties given for repair of goods.

Recording a **provision** is relatively straightforward. The ownership interest is reduced by an expense in the profit and loss account and a liability is created under the name of the provision:

| Assets – **Liabilities** ↑ | equals | **Ownership interest** ↓ **(expense)** |
|---|---|---|

When the provision is no longer required it is released to the profit and loss account as an item of revenue which increases the ownership interest and the liability is reduced:

| Assets – **Liabilities** ↓ | equals | **Ownership interest** ↑ |
|---|---|---|

The provision may also be released to the profit and loss account so as to match an expense which was anticipated when the provision was made. The effect on the accounting equation is an increase in the ownership interest – the same effect as results from regarding the release of the provision as an item of revenue.

Of the topics covered in this chapter, provisions give the greatest scope for international variation in accounting treatment. In countries where the accounting system and the tax system are linked, there may be specific rules about the level and nature of provisions allowed. In countries that have a strong culture of **conservatism** (strong **prudence**) the provisions may be used to understate profit. The problem with such an approach is that the unnecessary provision may then be released in a year when profits would otherwise be lower. This has the effect of 'smoothing' out the peaks and troughs of profit. Both the IASB and the UK ASB believe that provisions should only be used under carefully defined conditions. This approach also applies in the USA.

The IASB has proposed[5] to change the description of provisions to become 'non-financial liabilities'. If consultation gives a favourable response, this change will take effect from 2007. The IASB has proposed that any items satisfying the definition of a liability should be recognised unless they cannot be measured reliably. Any unconditional obligation would be recognised so there would no longer be a need to estimate the likelihood of the obligation being implemented. Uncertainty about the amount or timing of the economic benefits required to settle the non-financial liability would be recognised in the measurement of the liability.

## Example

During the year ending 31 December Year 5, a company's sales of manufactured goods amounted to £1m. All goods carry a manufacturer's warranty to rectify any faults arising during the first 12 months of ownership. At the start of the year, based on previous experience, a provision of 2.5% of sales was made (estimating the sales to be £1m). During Year 5 repairs under warranty cost £14,000. There could be further repair costs incurred in Year 6 in respect of those items sold part-way through Year 5 whose warranty extends into Year 6.

Using the accounting equation, the effect of these events and transactions may be analysed. When the provision is established there is an increase in a liability and an expense to be charged to the profit and loss account:

| Assets | − | Liabilities ↑ | = | Ownership interest ↓ (expense) |
|---|---|---|---|---|
| | | +£25,000 | | −£25,000 |

As the repairs under warranty are carried out, they cause a decrease in the asset of cash and a decrease in the provision. They do not directly affect the profit and loss account expense:

| Assets ↓ | − | Liabilities ↓ | = | Ownership interest |
|---|---|---|---|---|
| −£14,000 | | −£14,000 | | |

The overall effect is that the profit and loss account will report an expense of £25,000 but the provision will only be used to the extent of £14,000, leaving £11,000 available to cover any further repairs in respect of Year 5 sales. The repairs, when paid for, decrease the asset of cash but are not seen as decreasing the ownership interest. They are seen as meeting a liability to the customer (rather like making a payment to meet a liability to a supplier). The creation of the provision establishes the full amount of the liability and the decrease in the ownership interest which is to be reported in the profit and loss account.

The spreadsheet for analysis is contained in Exhibit 11.1.

**Exhibit 11.1**
**Spreadsheet for analysis of provision for warranty repairs**

| Date | Transaction or event | Asset | Liability | Ownership interest |
|---|---|---|---|---|
| | | Cash | Provision | Profit and loss account |
| Year 5 | | £ | £ | £ |
| Jan. 1 | Provision for repairs | | 25,000 | (25,000) |
| Jan.–Dec. | Repairs under warranty | (14,000) | (14,000) | |
| | Totals | (14,000) | 11,000 | (25,000) |

**Activity 11.2**

*Test your understanding of the previous section by analysing the following information and entering it in a spreadsheet to show analysis of the impact of the information on the accounting equation:*

*Jan. 1 Year 1    Make a provision for repairs, £50,000.*
*During Year 1    Spend £30,000 against the provision and carry the rest forward.*
*Jan. 1 Year 2    Make a further provision for repairs, £10,000.*
*During Year 2    Spend £25,000 against the provision and carry the rest forward.*
*Jan. 1 Year 3    Reduce the remaining provision to £3,000.*

## 11.5  Deferred income

For companies located in areas of the country where there are particular problems of unemployment or a need to encourage redevelopment of the location, the government may award grants as a contribution to the operating costs of the company or to the cost of buying new fixed assets.

Consider the award of a government grant to a company, intended to help with the cost of training employees over the next three years. The asset of cash increases, but there is no corresponding effect on any other asset or liability. Consequently, the ownership interest is increased. The obvious label for this increase is **revenue**. However, the benefit of the grant will extend over three years and it would therefore seem appropriate to spread the revenue over three years to match the cost it is subsidising. The accounting device for producing this effect is to say that the cash received as an asset creates a liability called **deferred income**. This does not meet the definition of a liability stated at the start of this chapter because the practice of deferring income is dictated by the importance of **matching** revenues and costs in the profit and loss account. It is one of the cases where established custom and practice continues because it has been found to be useful although it does not fit neatly into the conceptual framework definitions.

### Example

A company receives a grant of £30,000 towards the cost of employee retraining. The retraining programme will last for three years and the costs will be spread evenly over the three years.

The profit and loss account will show revenue of £10,000 in each year. At the outset the deferred income will be recorded in the balance sheet as £30,000. By the end of Year 1 the deferred income will be reduced to £20,000. At the end of Year 2 the deferred income will be reduced to £10,000. At the end of Year 3 the deferred income is reduced to nil. The accounting records are shown in Exhibit 11.2.

Where grants are received towards the acquisition of fixed assets there is a similar approach of spreading the grant over the period during which the company will benefit from use of the asset. Some companies show the revenue as a separate item in the profit and loss account while others deduct it from the depreciation expense. This is a matter of presentation which makes no difference to the overall profit. The balance sheet treatment is more controversial. Some companies report separately the net book value of the asset and the deferred income. Others deduct the deferred income from the net book value of the asset. This does not affect the ownership interest but shows a lower amount in the fixed assets section of the balance sheet. In consequence, the user who calculates profit as a percentage of fixed assets or a percentage of total assets will obtain a higher answer where a company shows the lower amount for net assets. Most companies report the asset and deferred income separately, but some argue for

**Exhibit 11.2**
**Recording deferred income and transfer to revenue**

| Date | Transaction or event | Asset | Liability | Ownership interest |
|------|---------------------|-------|-----------|--------------------|
|      |                     | Cash  | Deferred income | Revenue |
| Year 1 |                   | £ | £ | £ |
| Jan. 1 | Receiving the grant | 30,000 | 30,000 | |
| Dec. 31 | Transfer to profit and loss account of first year's revenue | | (10,000) | 10,000 |
| Year 2 | | | | |
| Dec. 31 | Transfer to profit and loss account of second year's revenue | | (10,000) | 10,000 |
| Year 3 | | | | |
| Dec. 31 | Transfer to profit and loss account of third year's revenue | | (10,000) | 10,000 |

the **net** approach which sets one against the other. (Both methods are permitted by the international accounting standard and by the UK national standard. There is a view that the net approach may not be complying with the Companies Act 1985 and so relatively few UK companies have taken the net approach.) The choice will be set out in the notes on accounting policies. This is a useful illustration of the importance of reading the note on accounting policies.

**Activity 11.3**

*Consider a grant received as a contribution to staff retraining costs over the next three years. Write down three arguments in favour of reporting the entire grant in the profit and loss account in the year it is received and write down three arguments in favour of spreading the grant across the period of retraining. Which set of arguments do you find more persuasive?*

## 11.6 Non-current (long-term) liabilities

The balance sheet requires a separate heading for all liabilities payable after one year. Users of financial statements need information about when the liabilities will be due for repayment (the **maturity** pattern).

Users also need to know about the nature of the liability and any risks attaching to expected outflows of economic benefit from the liability. The risks lie in: the interest payable on the loan; the currency of the loan; and the eventual amount to be repaid to the lender. Interest payable may be at a fixed rate of interest or a variable rate of interest. The currency of borrowing is important when foreign exchange rates alter. Repayment amounts may equal the amount borrowed initially, in some cases. In other cases there may be a **premium** (an extra amount) payable in addition to the sum borrowed. There are some very complex accounting aspects to reporting non-current (long-term) liabilities, the technical aspects of which are well beyond the capacity of a first-level text, but they are all directed towards ensuring that liabilities are recorded in full and the matching concept is observed in relation to interest charges.

Users want to know about the risks of sacrificing particular assets if the loan is not repaid on the due date. A claim to a particular asset may be made by a creditor who has a loan **secured** on a particular asset or group of assets.

## 11.6.1   Recording and measurement

This section concentrates on the terminology of non-current (long-term) liabilities and the general issues of recording and measurement that they raise. The basic feature of non-current (long-term) loan finance is that it is:

- provided by a lender for a period longer than one year;
- who expects payment of interest at an agreed rate at agreed points in time; and
- expects repayment of the loan on an agreed date or dates.

The names given to loan capital vary depending on the type of lender, the possibility that the loan will be bought and sold like ordinary shares, the currency in which the loan has been provided and the legal form of the documents creating the loan. Some of the names you will see are: loan stock, debentures, bonds, commercial paper, loan notes and bank facility.

- **Loan stock**. The word **stock** is used in more than one context in accounting, which is potentially confusing. In Chapter 9 you saw the word used to describe goods held by a company for use or sale to customers. In the phrase **loan stock** it is used to describe an investment held by a lender. In the USA the problem has been avoided by using the word **inventories** to describe goods held for use or sale and using the word **bond** to describe loan stock. If a company shows loan stock in its balance sheet this usually indicates that the stock is available for purchase and sale, in a manner similar to the purchase and sale of shares in a company.
- **Debenture**. The legal meaning of the term **debenture** is a written acknowledgement of a debt. This means there will be a contract, in writing, between the company and the lender. The contract is called the debenture deed and is held by a trustee who is required to look after the needs of the lenders. If the company does not pay interest, or repay capital, on the due date, the trustee must take action to recover what is owed to the lenders. Debentures may be secured or unsecured, depending on what is stated in the debenture deed.
- **Bond** The term **bond** has been in common use in the USA for some time as a name for loan capital. It is now found increasingly frequently in the balance sheets of UK companies, particularly when they are raising finance in the international capital markets where the US terminology is more familiar.
- **Commercial paper**, **loan notes** and **bank facility**. These are all names of short- to medium-term financing provided by banks or similar organisations. The interest payable is usually variable and the loans are unsecured.

This is only a sample of the main variations of names given to loan finance. It is not exhaustive because the name does not matter greatly for the purposes of accounting records and interpretation. The essential information needed for the users of accounting information is the answer to five questions:

1  How much was borrowed (the **principal sum**)?
2  How much has to be repaid (the capital sum plus any additional interest charge)?
3  When is repayment required?
4  What are the interest payments required?
5  Has the lender sought any security for repayment of the interest and the principal sum?

For companies applying the IASB system of accounting, the relevant standard required companies to provide information about the extent and nature of financial liabilities, including the significant terms and conditions and the timing of future cash flows. For companies that do not apply the IASB system, the UK Companies Act required disclosure of the total amount in respect of which any security has been given, and an indication of the nature of the security, plus the interest payable and terms of repayment for each category of loan.

Under either set of rules you will find detailed notes to tbe balance sheet setting out the interest costs and repayment conditions for loans reported as liabilities.

### 11.6.2 Secured and unsecured loans

- **Unsecured loan**. An unsecured loan is one where the lender has no first claim on any particular assets of the company and, in the event of default, must wait for payment alongside all the other unsecured creditors. If there is no wording to indicate that the loan is secured, then the reader of financial statements must assume it is unsecured.
- **Secured loan**. Where any loan is described as **secured**, it means that the lender has first claim to named assets of the company. Where a debenture is secured, and the company defaults on payment, the trustee for the debenture will take possession of the asset and use it to make the necessary repayment. In the event of the company not being able to pay all the amounts it owes, secured lenders come before unsecured lenders in the queue for repayment.

**Activity 11.4**

*A financial weekly magazine contains the following sentence:*

Telecoms plc this week raised cash by selling $1m bonds with five-year and ten-year maturities.

*Explain each part of the sentence.*

### 11.6.3 Loan having a range of repayment dates

When a loan is made to a business, conditions will be negotiated regarding the amount and date of repayment. Some banks are willing to offer a range of repayment dates, say any time between 10 and 15 years hence, with the company being allowed to choose when it will repay. If the company needs the money and the interest rate is favourable, the company will borrow for the longest period allowed under the contract. If the company finds it no longer needs the money, or else the interest rate is burdensome, the company will repay at the earliest possible opportunity. For balance sheet purposes the preparer of accounts has to decide which date to use as a basis for classification.

The general principle is that if there is an obligation to transfer economic benefits, there will be a liability in the balance sheet. Where there is a range of possible dates for repayment, the maturity date will be taken as the earliest date on which the lender can require repayment.[6]

### 11.6.4 Change in the nature of finance source

Some types of finance provided to a business may be arranged so as to allow a change in the nature of the source during the period of financing. As an example, consider the case of convertible loans.

A **convertible loan** is a source of finance which starts its life as a loan but, at some point in the future, may be converted to ordinary shares in the company (e.g. the lender is promised five shares per £100 of loan capital). At the date of conversion, the lender becomes a **shareholder**. This kind of financial arrangement is attractive to those providing finance because it provides the reassurance of loan finance and a payment of interest in the early years of a new development, with the option of switching to shares if the project is successful. If the project is not successful and the share price does not perform as expected, then the lender will not convert and will look for repayment of the loan on the due date. For the company there are some tax advantages of issuing loan finance. Also, the rate of interest required by investors in a convertible loan is usually lower than that required for a straight (non-convertible) loan because investors see potential additional rewards in the convertible loan.

While a convertible loan remains unconverted it is reported as a loan. Companies are not allowed to say, 'We are almost certain there will be a conversion', and report the convertible loan as share finance from the outset. However, there is an awareness that the eventual conversion will dilute the existing shareholders' claim on future profits and so the company will report the earnings per share before and after taking into account the effect of this dilution. Consequently, you will see 'fully diluted earnings per share' at the foot of the profit and loss account.

## 11.6.5    Interest payable on the loan

Companies and their banks may negotiate a variety of patterns for interest payment on loans. The pattern of interest payment might be based on a low percentage charge in earlier years and a higher percentage charge in later years, because the company expects that profits will be low initially but will rise later to cover the higher interest payments. For many years the profit and loss account would have reported the interest charge based on the amount paid in each year, but now the standard setters require the interest charge to be reported as it would be if a compound interest rate were applied over the life of the loan. This is described as the **effective interest rate**.[7]

**Definition**

> The **effective interest rate** is the rate that exactly discounts estimated future cash payments or receipts through the expected life of the financial instrument.

The reasoning behind this approach is that, for purposes of reporting profit, the flexibility of negotiation of interest payment patterns makes comparability difficult to achieve. The banks will, however, ensure that they receive the overall compound interest they require and this gives a commercially relevant basis for comparability in the matching of interest charges against the profits of the period.

The general principle is that the amount shown as the expense of interest payable in the profit and loss account should be based on the compound rate of interest applying over the entire period of the loan. This will not always be the same as the amount of interest paid in cash during the period. The spreading of interest charges over the period of the loan is an application of the accruals or matching concept. As an example, consider stepped bonds and deep discount bonds.

### Stepped bonds

A **stepped bond** is a form of lending where the interest rate increases over the period of the loan. Take as an example a loan of £5m which carries a rate of interest of 8% per annum for the first three years, 10% per annum for the next three years and 13% per annum for the final four years. The cash payment for interest starts at £400,000 and by the tenth year has risen to £650,000. The overall payments may be shown to be equivalent to a compound rate of 10.06% per annum. Exhibit 11.3 shows that the profit and loss account charge of £503,000 would start higher than the cash amount, £400,000. By the final year the profit and loss account charge of £517,000 would be lower than the cash amount, £650,000. The pattern followed on each line of Exhibit 11.3 is to start with the amount owing, add interest at 10.06% and deduct the amount of the cash payment, leaving the amount owing at the end of the period which becomes the amount owing at the start of the next period. By the end of the ten years the amount owing is exactly £5,000,000, the amount required by the lender.

It may be seen from Exhibit 11.3 that the expense charged in the income statement (profit and loss account) has a smoother pattern than that of the cash payments. Over the life of the loan the total expense charged must equal the total of the cash payments. The accounting processes for recording these amounts are too complex for a first-level course. The important point to note is that all companies are required to use this approach in calculating the expense charged in calculating profit. The cash flow implications of interest payments may be quite different and it will be necessary to look to the cash flow statement for evidence of the cash flow effect.

**Exhibit 11.3**
**Calculation of expense charged in income statement (profit and loss account) for interest based on compound interest calculation**

| Year | Loan at start | Expense charged | Cash payment record | |
|---|---|---|---|---|
| | | Interest at 10.06% | Cash paid | Loan at end |
| | (a) | (b) | (c) | (a) + (b) − (c) |
| | £000s | £000s | £000s | £000s |
| 1 | 5,000 | 503 | 400 | 5,103 |
| 2 | 5,103 | 513 | 400 | 5,216 |
| 3 | 5,216 | 525 | 400 | 5,341 |
| 4 | 5,341 | 537 | 500 | 5,378 |
| 5 | 5,378 | 541 | 500 | 5,419 |
| 6 | 5,419 | 545 | 500 | 5,464 |
| 7 | 5,464 | 550 | 650 | 5,364 |
| 8 | 5,364 | 540 | 650 | 5,254 |
| 9 | 5,254 | 529 | 650 | 5,133 |
| 10 | 5,133 | 517 | 650 | 5,000 |
| Total | | 5,300 | 5,300 | |

## Deep discount bonds

A **deep discount bond** is issued at a price lower than (at a 'discount' to) its repayment amount. The interest rate (**coupon**) paid during the life of the loan may be very low (a 'low coupon' bond) or there may be no interest paid at all during the period of the loan (a 'zero coupon' bond). As an example, consider a zero coupon bond issued at £28m with a redemption value of £41m in four years' time. The cash payments of interest are zero but the profit and loss account would show an annual charge of 10% per annum (starting at £2.8m in Year 1 and rising to £3.73m by Year 4). If there were no pattern of annual interest the entire discount of £13m would be shown as an expense of Year 4, distorting the underlying pattern of trading profit. Exhibit 11.4 shows the pattern of interest charges for the profit and loss account.

**Exhibit 11.4**
**Schedule of interest charges for zero coupon bond**

| Year | Loan at start £m | Interest £m | Loan at end £m |
|---|---|---|---|
| 1 | 28.00 | 2.80 | 30.80 |
| 2 | 30.80 | 3.08 | 33.88 |
| 3 | 33.88 | 3.39 | 37.27 |
| 4 | 37.27 | 3.73 | 41.00 |
| Total | | 13.00 | |

In the balance sheet the amount recorded for the liability will start at £28m and rise to £41m as shown in the final column of Exhibit 11.4, so that the liability at the end represents the total amount due.

**Activity 11.5**

*A three-year loan of £100,000 will be repaid at the end of three years as £133,100. No interest is payable during the three-year period. The interest included in the loan repayment arrangement is equivalent to a compound annual charge of 10% per annum. Explain how this transaction would appear in the profit and loss account and balance sheet over the three-year period.*

## 11.6.6 Complex capital instruments

It is impossible to read the balance sheet of most major listed companies without realising rapidly that there is a bewildering array of capital instruments being used to raise money for business. The reasons are complex but lie in the need to provide conditions which are attractive to both borrower and lender when they may be based in different countries and may have different perspectives on interest rates and currency exchange rates. This section explains the term 'interest rate swaps', which are increasingly used by companies, and takes an illustration from a major company to indicate the variety of capital instruments (sources of finance) in use. Detailed descriptions and discussion are beyond the scope of this text but would be found in a finance manual.

### Interest rate swaps

Suppose there are two companies, A and B. Both have identical amounts of loan finance. Company A is paying fixed rates of interest, but would prefer to be paying variable rates, while Company B is paying variable rates of interest, but would prefer to be paying fixed rates. The reasons could be related to patterns of cash flow from trading, cash flow from investments or beliefs about future directions of interest rates. Whatever the reason, it would seem quite acceptable for them to swap (exchange) so that A pays the variable interest on behalf of B and B pays the fixed interest on behalf of A. This type of arrangement has to be explained carefully because neither company can escape from the legal obligation on the loans taken out initially. The explanation will usually be found in a note to the accounts which gives information on the legal obligation and on the actual impact on the profit and loss account of implementing the swap.

## Capital instruments of a listed company

The following illustration is based upon the balance sheet of a major UK listed company:

| Note on borrowings: | | Year 2 £m | Year 1 £m |
|---|---|---|---|
| Unsecured borrowings: | | | |
| $10^{1}/_{2}$% euro-sterling bonds Year 17 | | 100.0 | 100.0 |
| Loan stocks | | | |
| 13.625% | Year 16 | 25.0 | 25.0 |
| 5.675% – 9.3% | Year 3/Year 10 | 5.9 | 6.1 |
| Zero coupon bonds Year 3 | | 96.6 | 87.2 |
| Variable rate multi-option bank facility | | 15.8 | 155.2 |
| Bank loans, overdrafts, commercial paper, short- and medium-term notes | | 257.0 | 244.8 |

. . . the nominal value of the zero coupon bonds is £100m and the effective annual rate of interest is 10.85% . . .

*Comment.* The euro-sterling bonds and the loan stocks are reported at the amount due for repayment at the end of the loan period. The euro-sterling bonds are loans raised in the eurobond market, repayable in sterling. Those loans which have fixed rates of interest are indicated in the table by a fixed percentage rate. Zero coupon means a zero percentage rate of annual interest payable. That does not mean the company escapes interest payment altogether. The liability on the zero coupon bonds increases by 10.85% each year as indicated in the extract note at the foot of the table. It is presumably due for repayment part-way through Year 3 since the liability shown at the end of Year 2 is quite close to the £100m amount due (called the **nominal value** in the note). The remaining loans are variable rate and so the annual interest charge depends on current rates of interest. Professional investors might want to know more about the nature of the bank facility and also the breakdown of the various components of the figure £257m.

## 11.7 Summary

- A **non-current liability** is any liability that does not meet the definition of a current liability. Non-current liabilities are also described as **long-term liabilities**.

- Users need information about the **principal sum** repayable and the **interest** payable during the lifetime of a liability. They also need to know the dates on which significant payments will be required (called the **maturity profile of debt**).

- Detailed information about **non-current liabilities** is found in the notes to the financial statements.

- A **provision** is a liability of uncertain timing or amount. The amount of a provision is reported in the liabilities section of a balance sheet. Changes in provisions are reported in the income statement (profit and loss account).

- **Deferred income** arises where a business receives a government grant or receives cash for goods or services before these are provided. The cash received is reported as an increase in cash and an increase in a liability to represent the obligation to satisfy the conditions of the grant or provide the goods or services. When the conditions are satisfied the liability is reduced and the ownership interest is increased by recording the revenue.

# QUESTIONS

The Questions section of each chapter has three types of question. 'Test your understanding' questions to help you review your reading are in the 'A' series of questions. You will find the answers to these by reading and thinking about the material in the book. 'Application' questions to test your ability to apply technical skills are in the 'B' series of questions. Questions requiring you to show skills in problem solving and evaluation are in the 'C' series of questions. A letter [S] indicates that there is a solution at the end of the book.

## A   Test your understanding

**Skills outcomes**

**A11.1**   Explain why a provision may be required. (Section 11.4)

**A11.2**   Give three examples of situations which may lead to provisions. (Section 11.4)

**A11.3**   Explain how deferred income is recorded. (Section 11.5)

**A11.4**   Is it justifiable to report deferred income under the category of liability? (Section 11.5)

**A11.5**   Explain what is meant by each of the following terms: (Section 11.6)

    (a)   loan stock;
    (b)   debenture;
    (c)   bond;
    (d)   maturity date; and
    (e)   convertible loan stock.

**A11.6**   [S] On reviewing the financial statements, the company accountant discovers that a grant of £60,000 towards expenditure of the current year plus two further years has been reported entirely as revenue of the period. What will be the effect on the profit and loss account and the balance sheet when this error is rectified?

**A11.7**   [S] On reviewing the financial statements, the company accountant discovers that there has been no provision made for urgent repairs to external doors and window frames, already identified as being of high priority on grounds of health and safety. The amount of £50,000 should be provided. What will be the effect on the profit and loss account and the balance sheet when this error is rectified?

## B   Application

**B11.1** [S]
The Washing Machine Repair Company gives a warranty of no-cost rectification of unsatisfactory repairs. It has turnover from repair contracts recorded as:

| Year | Amount of turnover |
| --- | --- |
| | £ |
| 1 | 80,000 |
| 2 | 90,000 |

Based on previous experience the manager makes a provision of 10% of turnover each year for warranty costs. In respect of the work done during years 1 and 2, repairs under warranty are carried out as follows:

| Date of repair work | Amount in respect of Year 1 turnover | Amount in respect of Year 2 turnover | Total |
|---|---|---|---|
| | £ | £ | £ |
| 1 | 4,500 | | 4,500 |
| 2 | 3,200 | 4,800 | 8,000 |
| 3 | | 5,000 | 5,000 |

**Required**

(a) Show how this information would be recorded in the financial statements of the Washing Machine Repair Company.

(b) Explain how the financial statements would appear if the company made no provision for warranty costs but charged them to profit and loss account when incurred.

**B11.2 [S]**

General Engineering Ltd receives a government grant for £60,000 towards employee training costs to be incurred evenly over the next three years. Explain how this transaction will be reported in the financial statements.

## C    Problem solving and evaluation

**C11.1**

Explain why each of the following is recognised as a provision in the balance sheet of a telecommunications company:

(a) On 15 December Year 2, the Group announced a major redundancy programme. Provision has been made at 31 December Year 2 for the associated costs. The provision is expected to be utilised within 12 months.

(b) Because of the redundancy programme, some properties have become vacant. Provision has been made for lease payments that cannot be avoided where sub-letting is not possible. The provision will be utilised within 15 months.

(c) There is a legal claim against a subsidiary in respect of alleged breach of contract. Provision has been made for this claim. It is expected that the provision will be utilised within 12 months.

**C11.2**

(Refer also to Chapter 10, section 10.3.2, on Contingent liabilities.)

Explain why each of the following is reported as a contingent liability but not recognised as a provision in the balance sheet.

(a) Some leasehold properties which the group no longer requires have been sub-let to third parties. If the third parties default, the group remains responsible for future rent payments. The maximum liability is £200,000.

(b) Group companies are defendants in the USA in a number of product liability cases related to tobacco products. In a number of these cases, the amounts of compensatory and punitive damages sought are significant.

(c) The Department of Trade and Industry has appointed Inspectors to investigate the company's flotation ten years ago. The directors have been advised that it is possible that circumstances surrounding the flotation may give rise to claims against the company. At this stage it is not possible to quantify either the probability of success of such claims or of the amounts involved.

## Activities for study groups

Turn to the annual report of a listed company which you have used for activities in previous chapters. Find every item of information about liabilities. (Start with the financial statements and notes but look also at the operating and financial review, chief executive's review and other non-regulated information about the company.)

As a group, imagine you are the team of fund managers in a fund management company. You are holding a briefing meeting at which each person explains to the others some feature of the companies in which your fund invests. Today's subject is liabilities. Each person should make a short presentation to the rest of the team covering:

(a) The nature and significance of liabilities in the company.
(b) The effect on profit of a 10% error in estimation of any one of the major categories of liability.
(c) The company's comments, if any, on its future obligations.
(d) The risks which might attach to the liabilities of the company.
(e) The liquidity of the company.
(f) The trends in liabilities since last year (or over five years if a comparative table is provided).
(g) The ratio of current assets to current liabilities.

### Notes and references

1. IASB (1989), *Framework*, para. 49(b).
2. IASB (2004) IAS 1, para. 60.
3. IASB (2004) IAS 1, para. 60.
4. IASB (2004), IAS 37, *Provisions, Contingent Liabilities and Contingent Assets*, para. 10.
5. IASB (2005), Exposure draft of proposed amendments to IAS 37 Provisions, Contingent Liabilities and Contingent Assets, para. 1.
6. *Ibid.*, para. 34.
7. IASB (2004), IAS 39 *Financial Instruments: Recognition and Measurement*. Definitions section.

## Supplement to Chapter 11

# Bookkeeping entries for provisions and deferred income

## Provisions

In the main text of this chapter there is an example based on the recording of provision for repairs under warranty. The analysis of the transactions and events is set out in Exhibit 11.1. The ledger account will appear as follows:

| L3 Provision for warranty repairs | | | | | |
|---|---|---|---|---|---|
| Date | Particulars | Page | Debit | Credit | Balance |
| Year 5 | | | £ | £ | £ |
| Jan. 1 | Provision in respect of Year 5 | L2 | | 25,000 | (25,000) |
| Jan.–Dec. | Repairs carried out | L1 | 14,000 | | (11,000) |

LEONA: *At the start of the year (or possibly in practice at the end of each month) the provision is recorded by debiting the profit and loss account (L2) and crediting the provision. When the repairs are carried out there is a credit entry in the cash account (L1) and a debit entry in the provision account. Nothing is recorded as a profit and loss account expense at that time. The overall effect is that the profit and loss account carries an expense of £25,000 and the provision account shows a potential liability of £11,000 to cover any further repairs arising from work done during Year 5 (since some of the goods sold will remain under warranty into Year 6).*

## Deferred income

In the main text of this chapter there is an example based on the recording of deferred income arising under a grant. The analysis of the transactions and events is set out in Exhibit 11.2. The ledger account will appear as follows:

| L3 Deferred income (balance sheet) | | | | | |
|---|---|---|---|---|---|
| Date | Particulars | Page | Debit | Credit | Balance |
| Year 1 | | | £ | £ | £ |
| Jan. 1 | Grant received | L1 | | 30,000 | (30,000) |
| Dec. 31 | Transfer to profit and loss account | L2 | 10,000 | | (20,000) |
| Year 2 | | | | | |
| Dec. 31 | Transfer to profit and loss account | L2 | 10,000 | | (10,000) |
| Year 3 | | | | | |
| Dec. 31 | Transfer to profit and loss account | L2 | 10,000 | | nil |

LEONA: *The deferred income account is reported as a liability in the balance sheet. It is established by a credit entry matched by a debit in the cash account (L1). Each year there is a transfer of one-third to the profit and loss account (L2) so that the revenue is spread evenly over the period.*

## S | Test your understanding

**S11.1**  Prepare bookkeeping records for the information in question **B11.1**.

**S11.2**  Prepare bookkeeping records for the information in question **B11.2**.

# Chapter 12

# Ownership interest

**Balance sheets as at 29 January 2005**

| £ millions | Notes | Group | | Company | |
|---|---|---|---|---|---|
| | | **2005** | 2004 | **2005** | 2004 |
| **Capital and reserves** | | | | | |
| Called up share capital | 29 | **369.0** | 366.3 | **369.0** | 366.3 |
| Share premium account | 30 | **2,166.2** | 2,150.9 | **2,166.2** | 2,150.9 |
| Revaluation reserve | 30 | **611.7** | 441.3 | – | – |
| Non-distributable reserves | 30 | **159.0** | 159.0 | **2,934.2** | 2,934.2 |
| Profit and loss account | 30 | **1,615.6** | 1,286.2 | **808.3** | 836.7 |
| **Equity shareholders' funds** | 31 | **4,921.5** | 4,403.7 | **6,277.7** | 6,288.1 |
| Equity minority interests | | **2.7** | 2.9 | – | – |
| | | **4,924.2** | 4,406.6 | **6,277.7** | 6,288.1 |

## Property

Property income (primarily rent charged to B&Q on UK properties owned by the Group) grew at 28.2% to £41.4m (2004: £32.2m) reflecting rental inflation and some additional properties.

Kingfisher owns a significant property portfolio, substantially all of which is now used for trading purposes and which, at the year end, had a value of £2.4bn. Kingfisher has continued its normal practice of externally valuing, on an existing use basis, one-third of the property portfolio on a rolling basis, with internal valuations being performed for the other two-thirds. In both cases, these revalued amounts have been incorporated into the accounts, giving rise to a revaluation surplus in the year of £175.8m.

Source: Kingfisher Annual Report and Accounts 2004/5, pp. 29, 25.

## Discussion points

1 How did the group measure the revaluation of its property assets?

2 How did the group record the revaluation?

## Contents

## Learning outcomes

After reading this chapter you should be able to:
- Define ownership interest.
- Explain and demonstrate how the ownership interest is presented in company accounts.
- Understand the nature and purpose of the statement of changes in equity in the IASB system and also the UK ASB equivalents.
- Explain the needs of users for information about the ownership interest in a company.
- Read and interpret the information reported by companies in their annual reports, in respect of the ownership interest.
- Explain the accounting treatment of dividends.
- Understand the methods by which a company's shares may be issued when the company has a Stock Exchange listing.
- Show that you understand the impact of transactions and events on ownership interest in company accounts.

Additionally, for those who choose to study the Supplement:
- Record end-of-period adjustments as debit and credit adjustments to a trial balance taken from the ledger accounts and produce figures for financial statements.

## 12.1  Introduction

The final element of the accounting equation has been reached. It was explained in Chapter 2 that the ownership interest is the residual amount found by deducting all liabilities of the entity from all of the entity's assets:

| Assets | minus | Liabilities | equals | Ownership interest |
|--------|-------|-------------|--------|--------------------|

The terminology was also explained in Chapter 2. The words equity and net assets both appear in the press and in commentaries in connection with the ownership interest. **Equity** is a word used to describe the ownership interest in the assets of the business after all liabilities are deducted. This is also referred to as the **net assets**, calculated as the assets minus the liabilities.

The structure which has been adopted for Chapters 8 to 12 is based on a series of questions:

- What are the principles for defining and recognising these items?
- What are the information needs of users in respect of the particular items?
- What information is currently provided by companies to meet these needs?
- Does the information show the desirable qualitative characteristics of financial statements?
- What are the principles for measuring, and processes for recording, these items?

Each of these questions will be addressed in turn.

## 12.2  Definition and recognition

The definition of **ownership interest** was presented in Chapter 2 as: 'the residual amount found by deducting all of the entity's liabilities from all of the entity's assets'.

Because the ownership interest is the residual item of the equation, it can only increase or decrease if something happens to an asset or to a liability. Recognition conditions are applied to assets and liabilities but there cannot be any additional recognition criteria applied to the ownership interest.

Events which change assets or liabilities include:

- making a profit (or loss) through the operations of the business – earning revenue and incurring expenses;
- a contribution of cash by incoming shareholders purchasing new shares;
- holding an asset which increases or decreases in value;
- holding a liability which increases or decreases in value.

Each one of these events is important to the users of the financial statements and affects the claims of owners on the assets of the business. Since owners are the user group most interested in the ownership interest, this chapter will focus primarily on the information which is helpful to them. Reporting a profit or a loss has been dealt with in some length in previous chapters. In this chapter we concentrate on the issue of new shares and on the events which cause increases or decreases in assets and liabilities which are *not* reported in the profit and loss account.

## 12.3    Presentation of ownership interest

Chapters 7 to 11 have concentrated primarily on the limited liability company. For any limited liability company the **income statement (profit and loss account)** is the primary financial statement which reports the revenues and expenses of the business that arise through operations.

The change in value of an asset or liability while it is *held* by the company gives more cause for debate. If the asset has increased in value while still being held by the company, then there may be an increase in the valuation for financial reporting purposes. That is not a **realised** gain and so cannot be reported in the profit and loss account. There is another primary financial statement which companies must use to report **unrealised** gains. For companies using the IASB system in their financial statements, the unrealised gains are reported in a **statement of recognised income and expense** or a **statement of changes in equity**. For companies continuing to follow UK company law and standards the unrealised gains are reported in a **statement of total recognised gains and losses**.

### Example of an unrealised gain

A business buys a building at a cost of £10m. One year later similar buildings are selling for £13m. The business does not intend to sell but would like to report the potential increase in the market value of the asset. Because there is no sale, the £3m estimate of the increase in value is unrealised. It is not reported in the income statement (profit and loss account) but is reported in the statement of recognised income and expense (statement of total recognised gains and losses).

The presentation of the ownership interest is therefore a potentially complex affair, using more than one financial statement. There is information about the current position of the ownership interest contained in the balance sheet and the related notes to the accounts. There is information about changes in the ownership interest in the income statement (profit and loss account) and the statement of recognised income and expense (statement of total recognised gains and losses). The approach taken in this chapter is first of all to 'walk through' the early years of operating a limited liability company and the various types of ownership interest which arise.

### 12.3.1    Issue of shares at the date of incorporation

When the company first comes into existence it issues shares to the owners, who become **equity holders (shareholders)**. The date on which the company comes into existence is called the **date of incorporation**.

Each share has a *named value* which is called its **nominal value**. Sometimes it is referred to as the **par value**. This amount is written on the **share certificate** which is the document given to each owner as evidence of being a shareholder. Exhibit 12.1 shows the share certificate issued by a company which confirms that J. A. Smith is the owner of 100,000 ordinary shares of 25p nominal value each. This means that J. A. Smith has paid £25,000 to the company and that is the limit of this person's liability if the company fails.

All share certificates are recorded in the share register by the company secretary. The share certificate is a piece of paper which may be sold by the existing owner to another person who wishes to become a shareholder. The person who wishes to become a shareholder is often referred to as a **prospective investor**. That is not a legal term but is a useful way of indicating a person who has an interest in finding out more about the company, without having the legal rights of ownership. When the

**Exhibit 12.1**
**Share certificate issued by a company**

---

Certificate number 24516

## Public Company plc

## SHARE CERTIFICATE

This is to certify that

*J. A. Smith*

is the registered owner of 100,000 ordinary shares of 25 pence each.
Given under Seal of the Company the 15th day of August 20XX

Signed   *P McDowall*                           *J Jones*

Company Secretary                               *W Brown*

                                                Directors

---

new owner has acquired the shares, the term 'investor' may continue to be used as a description which emphasises that this person now has a financial interest in knowing that the company is performing well.

The issue of 100,000 shares at a price of 25 pence each will collect £25,000 cash for the company. The effect on the accounting equation is that the asset of cash increases by £25,000 and the ownership interest is increased by £25,000.

| Assets ↑ | – | Liabilities | = | Ownership interest ↑ |
|---|---|---|---|---|
| Increase in cash £25,000 | | | | Increase in nominal value of shares £25,000 |

For a company, the ownership interest created by the issue of new shares at their nominal value is recorded as **share capital**.

---

**Activity 12.1**

*Look at the financial pages of a newspaper. Find the daily list of share prices. What information does the newspaper provide about shares in each company? Which of these items of information would you expect to find in the annual report of the company? Give reasons for your answer.*

---

### 12.3.2   Retained earnings

Once the business is in operation it starts to make profits. The income statement (profit and loss account) shows the profit earned in a time period. This profit increases the ownership interest. The accumulation of past profits in the balance sheet is called **retained earnings**. The retained earnings represent the ownership interest in the net assets of the business. It is one type of **reserve**. At any point in time someone could ask the owner 'How much would you expect to receive if this business were to close down today?' The owner would look at the balance sheet and reply with the total of the **ownership interest**, shown by **equity share capital** plus all **reserves**.

You should be aware that the reserves are given different names in different countries. In some there is a legally defined reserve with a tax-deductible transfer to the reserve from the profit and loss account. It requires careful reading of the owner-ship interest section of the balance sheet.

### 12.3.3 Buying and selling shares

The company itself has no concern about the purchase and sale of shares from one owner to another, other than having to record the new owner's name in the share register. The purchase and sale may take place by private arrangement or may take place in an established **stock market** (also called a **stock exchange**) if the company is a public limited company. If the shares are traded in an established stock market they are called listed shares because the daily prices are listed on screens for buyers and sellers to see. If there is high demand for the shares, their price will rise. If there is little demand, the price will fall. The market price on any day will depend on investors' expectations about the future of the company. Those expectations will be influenced by announcements from the company, including financial information but also covering a much wider range of company news. The expectations may also be influenced by information about the industry in which the company operates. One of the main purposes of a well-regulated stock exchange is to ensure that all investors have access to the same information at the same time so that no one has an advantage.

### 12.3.4 Issue of further shares after incorporation

As time goes by, the company may wish to raise new finance and to issue new shares. This could be intended to buy new non-current (fixed) assets, or even to provide cash so that the company may purchase the shares of another company and create a larger group.

Although the **nominal value** remains the same, the **market value** may be quite different.

#### Example

Suppose a company has shares of nominal value 25 pence but finds that its shares are selling in the market at 80 pence each. If the company issues 200,000 new shares it will collect £160,000 in cash. That is the important piece of information for the company because it can use the cash to buy new assets and expand the activities of the business. The asset of cash has increased by £160,000 and the ownership interest has increased by £160,000.

The accounting records are required by company law to show separately the nominal value of the shares and any extra amount over the nominal value. The nominal value is 25 pence and the total amount collected per share is 80 pence. So the extra amount collected is 55 pence. This extra amount is called a **premium** (the word means 'something extra'). So the £160,000 increase in the ownership interest is recorded as two separate items, namely the **nominal value** of £50,000 and the **share premium** of £110,000.

| Assets ↑ | – | Liabilities | = | Ownership interest ↑→ |
|---|---|---|---|---|
| Increase in cash £160,000 | | | | Increase in nominal value of shares £50,000 |
| | | | | *and* increase in share premium £110,000 |

### 12.3.5 Revaluation of non-current (fixed) assets

Suppose a company buys a hotel costing £560,000. The hotel is run successfully for a period of three years and at the end of that period a professional valuer confirms that the hotel, if sold, would probably result in sale proceeds of £620,000 because of the change in property values and the reputation which the hotel has established. The directors of the company may wish to tell shareholders about this increased market value of the company's non-current (fixed) asset.

There are two ways of informing shareholders in the financial statements. One is to continue to record the balance sheet value at £560,000 (the historical cost) but to include a note to the balance sheet explaining that the market value has been confirmed as £620,000 by an expert. That information would allow the investor to think, 'That makes me feel better off by £60,000.'

This feeling of investor happiness is surrounded by a note of caution, because the gain in value is not **realised**. The asset has not in fact been sold in the market. It only needs a rumour of pollution on the local beach to depress the market value of all the hotels in the town. Some companies feel that this note of caution is conveyed by providing the information on the increase in value in the notes to the accounts rather than the balance sheet itself.

Other companies take a bolder view and decide that, in the interests of providing information which is relevant to the needs of users, the company should apply the accounting equation on behalf of the readers of the financial statement. These companies then have a problem of deciding on the name to be given to describe this £60,000 increase in the ownership interest. It cannot be called revenue and included in the profit and loss account because it has not been realised by the operations of the business. It represents a new ownership interest as a newly identified 'reserve' of wealth. The wealth lies in the asset, but the interest in that wealth is a claim which belongs to the owners. The increased wealth is caused by revaluation of the asset, and so the name chosen for this claim is **revaluation reserve**. In terms of the accounting equation there is an increase in the value of an asset and an increase in the ownership interest.

| **Assets** ↑ | – | Liabilities | = | **Ownership interest** ↑ |
|---|---|---|---|---|
| Increase in value of non-current (fixed) asset £60,000 | | | | Increase in revaluation reserve as part of the ownership interest £60,000 |

This section has explained the accounting processes for revaluing non-current (fixed) assets. You may see revaluation of non-current assets in some annual reports of UK companies. It is not compulsory but if companies choose to revalue then they must do so regularly. In contrast such revaluation is not allowed in the USA or Germany. In other countries, such as France, it is allowed but rarely used. Revaluation is permitted by the IASB but is not a requirement. So while the IASB system has brought standardisation of accounting practices across Europe it does not entirely take away the choices that may make comparisons less easy.

### Example

A company, Office Owner Ltd, is formed on 1 January Year 1 by the issue of 4m ordinary shares of 25 pence nominal value each. The cash raised from the issue is used on 2 January to buy an office block which is rented to a customer for an annual rent of £50,000. The tenant carries all costs of repairs. The company's administration costs for the year are £10,000. At the end of the year the office block is valued by an expert at £1,015,000. On the last day of the year the company issues a further 2 million ordinary shares at a price of 40 pence each, to raise cash in Year 2 for expansion plans.

**Activity 12.2** *For the analysis of each transaction you should look back to the previous sections where each type of transaction is dealt with in detail. Write down the effect of each transaction on the accounting equation. Check your answer against Exhibit 12.2. When you are satisfied that you understand Exhibit 12.2 look to Exhibit 12.3 where you will find the amounts entered in the spreadsheet.*

**Exhibit 12.2**
**Office Owner Ltd – analysis of transactions for Year 1**

| Date | Transaction or event | Effect on assets | Effect on ownership interest |
|---|---|---|---|
| Year 1 | | | |
| Jan. 1 | Issue of shares at nominal value | Increase asset of cash | Increase share capital at nominal value |
| Jan. 2 | Purchase of office block | Increase asset of property | Decrease asset of cash |
| Jan.–Dec. | Rent received | Increase asset of cash | Revenue of the period |
| Jan.–Dec. | Administration costs | Decrease asset of cash | Expense of the period |
| Dec. 31 | Revaluation of asset | Increase asset of property | Increase ownership interest by revaluation |
| Dec. 31 | Issue of further shares | Increase asset of cash | Increase share capital at nominal value and increase share premium |

**Exhibit 12.3**
**Office Owner Ltd – spreadsheet of transactions for Year 1**

| Date | Transaction or event | Cash | Office block | Share capital | Share premium | Income statement (profit and loss account) | Revaluation reserve |
|---|---|---|---|---|---|---|---|
| Year 1 | | £000s | £000s | £000s | £000s | £000s | £000s |
| Jan. 1 | Issue of shares | 1,000 | | 1,000 | | | |
| Jan. 2 | Purchase of office block | (1,000) | 1,000 | | | | |
| Jan.–Dec. | Rent received | 50 | | | | 50 | |
| Jan.–Dec. | Administration costs | (10) | | | | (10) | |
| Dec. 31 | Revaluation of asset | | 15 | | | | 15 |
| Dec. 31 | Issue of further shares | 800 | | 500 | 300 | | |
| | | 840 | 1,015 | 1,500 | 300 | 40 | 15 |

└─ 1,855 ─┘    └─ 1,855 ─┘

Entering the amounts in the spreadsheet of Exhibit 12.3 shows, in the final line, that the accounting equation is satisfied and allows a balance sheet to be prepared as in Exhibit 12.4.

**Exhibit 12.4**
**Office Owner Ltd – balance sheet at end of Year 1**

| Office Owner Ltd<br>Balance sheet at end of Year 1 | |
|---|---:|
| | £000s |
| *Non-current (fixed) asset*: Office block (at valuation) | 1,015 |
| Current asset: Cash | 840 |
| Net assets | 1,855 |
| Share capital | 1,500 |
| Share premium | 300 |
| Revaluation reserve | 15 |
| Retained earnings | 40 |
| | 1,855 |

**Activity 12.3**

*Suppose you note that a company has revalued its land and buildings as reported in the balance sheet. What evidence would you expect to see as justification for the amount of the revaluation? What questions might you ask about the basis of revaluation?*

## 12.3.6    Changes in exchange rates of foreign currency

All information in the financial statements of a UK company is shown in pound (£) sterling. Where exchange rates alter, a company may lose or gain purely because of the exchange rate movement. That loss or gain must be reported.

The accounting process is called translation. Translation from one currency to another is particularly important when the financial statements of companies in a group are added together and so must all be restated in a common currency. The word 'translation' is used because the process is comparable to translating words from one language to another.

There are different methods of reporting depending on the type of transaction or event. Two different stories are considered here. The first is the purchase of an asset located in a foreign country. The second is the purchase, by a group of companies, of the share capital of a company in a foreign country.

### Purchase of an asset

Take first of all the example of a UK company which buys a factory in Sweden. The factory is priced at Kr10,000,000. At the date of purchase of the factory the exchange rate is Kr10 = £0.70. The UK company has agreed to pay for the factory on the day of the transfer of legal title.

For accounting purposes the cost of the factory is recorded at the amount paid at the date of purchase. This is calculated as:

$$\frac{0.70}{10} \times Kr10,000,000 = £700,000$$

The effect of the transaction on the balance sheet of the UK company is:

| Assets ↑↓ | – | Liabilities | = | Ownership interest |
|---|---|---|---|---|
| Increase in asset of factory<br>£700,000 | | | | |
| Decrease in asset of cash<br>£700,000 | | | | |

That is the end of the story so far as the UK company is concerned. The exchange rate between the krona and the £ may fluctuate, and this may affect the company's view of the price for which the factory might eventually be sold, but that information will not appear in the financial statements of the UK company until such time as the factory is sold.

## Purchase of shares in another company

Suppose now that a UK group of companies has decided to purchase the entire share capital of a Swedish company whose only asset is the same factory. The purchase price is Kr10,000,000. The Swedish company distributes its entire profit as dividend each year so that the only item remaining in its balance sheet is the factory at a cost of Kr10,000,000. (This is a very simplistic example but is sufficient to illustrate the exchange rate problem.)

At the date of purchase of the investment, the factory will be recorded in the group balance sheet at £700,000.

| **Assets ↑↓** | – | Liabilities | = | Ownership interest |
|---|---|---|---|---|
| Increase in sterling equivalent of group's asset of factory £700,000<br><br>Decrease in group's asset of cash £700,000 | | | | |

One year later the exchange rate has altered to Kr10 = £0.68. The factory is the only asset of the subsidiary. In the Swedish accounts it remains at Kr10,000,000 but, translated into £ sterling, this now represents only £680,000:

$$\frac{0.68}{10} \times Kr10,000,000 = £680,000$$

This represents a potential loss of £20,000 on the translated value of the asset at the start of the year. The loss is unrealised but as a matter of prudence the fall in the translated asset value should be reported. However, there have been strong feelings expressed by companies over many years that the unrealised loss should not affect the reported profit of the period. Consequently the relevant accounting standard[1] allows the effect on the ownership interest to be shown in reserves.

| **Assets ↓** | – | Liabilities | = | **Ownership interest ↓** |
|---|---|---|---|---|
| Reduction in sterling equivalent of assets of subsidiary £20,000 | | | | Decrease in reserve £20,000 |

The reporting of the reduction in the asset value as a decrease in reserves is controversial because less attention is sometimes paid to reserves than is paid to the profit and loss account. This means that the impact on the ownership interest may pass unnoticed.

This practice of translation is required by the accounting standard on the subject. In group accounting there is considerable complexity to the technical aspects of which exchange rate effects must pass through the profit and loss account and which may pass through the reserves. The important message for the reader of the annual reports is to be alert to the possibility of exchange rate effects on the ownership interest being reported in reserves.

## 12.4 Additional primary financial statements

In Chapter 7 it was noted that the IASB specifies four primary financial statements:[2]

- a balance sheet
- an income statement (showing the profit or loss for the period)
- a statement of changes in equity, and
- a cash flow statement.

The balance sheet, income statement and cash flow statement were dealt with in Chapter 7. The statement of changes in equity is now explained.

### 12.4.1 Statement of changes in equity (IASB standards)

The **statement of changes in equity** must show on the face of the statement:

(a) The profit or loss for the period.
(b) Each item of income and expense for the period that is required by accounting standards to be recognised directly in equity.
(c) The effects of changes in accounting policies and corrections of errors.

If these are the only items reported then the statement of changes in equity is called a statement of **recognised** income and expenses.

An entity must also report, either in the statement of changes in equity or in the notes to the accounts:

(d) Transactions with equity holders (e.g. share capital issued, dividends paid).
(e) The balance of retained earnings at the start and end of the accounting period, and changes during the period.
(f) An explanation of the amounts of changes in each class of equity and each type of reserve.

If items (d), (e) and (f) are included on the face of the statement it is called a **statement of changes in equity**.

The reason for this flexibility of presentation is that different countries have applied different practices in the past. UK companies have been producing a **statement of total recognised gains and losses** for more than ten years while US companies have been presenting a **statement of changes in equity** for some years past. The annual report of Safe and Sure plc shown in Appendix I, presents a statement of total recognised gains and losses with the remaining movements on equity shown in a note to the financial statements.

### 12.4.2 Statement of total recognised gains and losses (UK ASB standards)

The statement of total recognised gains and losses (STRGL) was introduced by the UK ASB Standards Board[3] as a result of well-publicised company failures where it was apparent that important information about changes in the ownership interest had not been understood fully by the users of the financial statements. In particular, losses caused by exchange rate fluctuations had been reported in the notes on reserves, apparently without the expert observers pointing to the fact that these losses cancelled out the profits gained from operating activities.

As well as exchange rate gains and losses, the STRGL reports unrealised gains and losses arising on revaluation of non-current (fixed) assets of a period. Its purpose is to show the extent to which shareholders' funds have increased or decreased from all the various gains and losses recognised in the period.

### 12.4.3    Reconciliation of movements in shareholders' funds (UK ASB standards)

In addition to the statement of total recognised gains and losses the UK Accounting Standards Board also requires a reconciliation of movements in shareholders' funds. It may also be presented as a primary financial statement,[4] so that it has comparable prominence with other important information, or may be presented as a note to the financial statements. Most companies give this reconciliation the prominence of a primary financial statement.

## 12.5    Users' needs for information

The owners of a company, and potential investors in a company, are primarily interested in whether the business will make them better off or worse off. They also want to be reassured that the business has taken care of the resources entrusted to it (carrying out the function of **stewardship**). The first source of an increase in the ownership interest is the **profit** generated by the company. Professional investors will use the phrase **quality of earnings** to refer to the different components of profit. They tend to regard profits generated by the main operating activity as being of higher quality than windfall gains such as profits on the sale of non-current (fixed) assets which are not a regular feature of the company's activity.

Owners of a company expect to receive a reward for ownership. One form of reward is to watch the business grow and to know that in the future a sale of shares will give them a satisfactory gain over the period of ownership. That requires a long-term horizon. Some investors prefer to see the reward more frequently in the form of a dividend. They want to know that the ownership interest is adequate to support the dividend and yet leave sufficient assets in the business to generate further profits and dividends.

Creditors of a company know that they rank ahead of the shareholders in the event of the company being wound up, but they want to know that the company is generating sufficient wealth for the owners to provide a cushion against any adverse events. Therefore creditors will also be concerned with the ownership interest and how it is being maintained or is growing.

Employees, suppliers and customers similarly look for reassurance as to the strength of the business to continue into the future. The ownership interest is a convenient focus which summarises the overall impact of the state of assets and liabilities, although what employees are really interested in is the preservation of the earnings capacity of the business.

## 12.6    Information provided in the financial statements

In Chapter 7 the balance sheet of Safe and Sure plc was presented. The final section of that balance sheet presented information on the capital and reserves representing the claim of the shareholders on the assets.

|  |  | Year 7 £m | Year 6 £m |
|---|---|---|---|
| **Capital and reserves** |  |  |  |
| Called-up share capital | 12 | 19.6 | 19.5 |
| Share premium account | 13 | 8.5 | 5.5 |
| Revaluation reserve | 14 | 4.6 | 4.6 |
| Retained earnings | 15 | 431.6 | 340.8 |
| *Equity holders' funds* |  | 464.3 | 370.4 |

In the discussion contained in Chapter 7 it was emphasised that the most important feature of this information is that, in total, it represents the shareholders' legal claim. There is nothing to see, touch, count or hold. If the company were to cease trading at the balance sheet date, sell all its assets for the balance sheet amount and pay off all liabilities, the shareholders would be left with £464.3m to take away. The shareholders have the residual claim, which means that if the assets were to be sold for more than the balance sheet amount, the shareholders would share the windfall gain. If the assets were sold for less than the balance sheet amount, the shareholders would share the loss.

The total ownership interest is a claim which is described by this company as 'equity holders' funds'. It is equal to the **net assets** of the company. The total claim is subdivided so as to explain how the various parts of the claim have arisen. This section now considers each part of the claim in turn.

## 12.6.1 Share capital

The information shown by the company at note 12 is as follows:

**Note 12 Share capital**

|  | Year 7 £m | Year 6 £m |
|---|---|---|
| Ordinary shares of 2 pence each |  |  |
| Authorised: 1,050,000,000 shares |  |  |
| (Year 6: 1,000,000,000) | 21.0 | 20.0 |
| Issued and fully paid: 978,147,487 shares | 19.6 | 19.5 |

Certain senior executives hold options to subscribe for shares in the company at prices ranging from 33.40p to 244.33p under schemes approved by equity holders at various dates. Options on 3,479,507 shares were exercised during Year 7 and 66,970 options lapsed. The number of shares subject to options, the years in which they were purchased and the years in which they will expire are:

| Purchase | Expiry | Numbers |
|---|---|---|
|  | Year 8 | 13,750 |
| All | Year 9 | 110,000 |
| purchased | Year 10 | 542,500 |
| 10 years | Year 11 | 1,429,000 |
| before | Year 12 | 2,826,600 |
| expiry | Year 13/14 | 3,539,942 |
|  | Year 15 | 3,690,950 |
|  | Year 16 | 2,279,270 |
|  | Year 17 | 3,279,363 |
|  |  | 17,711,375 |

**Called-up** means that the company has called upon the shareholders who first bought the shares to make payment in full. When a new company is brought to the stock market for the first time, investors may be invited to buy the shares by paying an instalment now and the rest later. That was quite common in the 1980s when former nationalised industries, such as electricity and water companies, were being sold to the private sector. The **prospectus**, which is issued to invite the purchase of shares, specifies the dates on which the company would make a call for the rest of the share price due. After all the cash has been received by the company, the shares are described as **fully paid**.

Ordinary shareholders are entitled to vote at meetings, usually in proportion to the number of shares held. That means that the power of the individual shareholder depends on the number of shares held. For most large companies there are relatively small numbers of shareholders who control relatively large proportions of the share capital. A company which is part of a larger group of companies is required to report in the notes to the accounts the name and country of the ultimate parent company. Companies which are listed on the Stock Exchange are required to disclose in the directors' report the name of any shareholder interested in 3% or more of the company's issued share capital.

Before the directors of a company may issue new shares, they must be authorised to do so by the existing shareholders. The existing shareholders need to be aware that their claim will be diluted by the incoming shareholders. (If there are 50 shares owned equally by two persons, each controls 50% of the company. If 25 new shares are issued to a third person, then all three have 33.3% each, which dilutes the voting power of the first two persons.)

One of the controversial aspects of share capital in recent years has been the privilege of share options taken by directors and other employees (usually senior employees of the business but sometimes spreading to the wider employee range). A share option allows the person holding the option to buy shares in the company, at any future date up to a specified limit in time, at an agreed fixed price. The argument in favour of such an arrangement is that it gives senior management an incentive to make the company prosperous because they want the share price to increase above the price they have agreed to pay. The argument against it is that they have no very strong incentive because the worst that can happen to directors and other employees is that they decide not to take up the option when the share price has not performed well. Until 1995 there were also some personal tax advantages in taking options rather than a normal portion of salary, but since then, the tax rules have limited such benefits.

Major companies now disclose, in the directors' report, the options held by each of the directors.

### The analyst's view

David and Leona are on the plane flying from London to Aberdeen for a week's holiday in the Cairngorms. David has brought the annual report of Safe and Sure plc as a precaution against inclement weather disturbing their plans for outdoor activities. While they wait for lunch to be served, David turns to the annual report and finds it is quite helpful to have Leona alongside him.

**DAVID:** *At the present time nothing seems to excite more comment from the financial journalists than the salaries paid to the directors and the options they hold. I have to confess that it's something I look for in the annual report. Maybe I'm looking for my future earning potential! One of my more cynical colleagues says that directors can't lose on options. If the share price rises they make money, which we don't mind because our investment is rising in value. What happens if the share price falls? The directors take new options at the lower price and then wait for the market to rise again so that they make a profit! We can't do that for our investment.*

*I always look at the note on share capital to see whether new shares have been issued during the year. It reminds me to find out the reason. In this case the increase is £0.1m and the reason is explained in the accounts as being due entirely to the issue of options.*

### 12.6.2  Share premium

It was explained earlier in this chapter that when shares are issued by a company it may well be that the market price of the shares is greater than the nominal value. What really matters to the company is the amount of cash contributed by the new shareholders but company law insists that the claim of these new shareholders is split into a nominal amount and a share premium (the amount received in excess of the nominal amount).

**Note 13  Share premium account**

|  | Year 7 £m | Year 6 £m |
|---|---|---|
| At 1 January | 5.5 | 3.6 |
| Premium on shares issued during the year under the share option schemes | 3.0 | 1.9 |
| At 31 December | 8.5 | 5.5 |

DAVID: *I look at the share premium account only as a check on the amount of cash raised by issuing shares during the year. If I add the £3.0m shown in this note to the £0.1m shown as an increase in nominal value, then I know that £3.1m was raised in total by the issue of shares. I can check that in the cash flow statement.*

### 12.6.3  Revaluation reserve

Earlier in the chapter the effect of revaluing assets was explained in terms of the accounting equation. It was also explained that the effects of foreign currency exchange rates may appear in reserves. The note to the accounts of Safe and Sure plc appears as follows:

**Note 14  Revaluation reserve**

|  | Year 7 £m | Year 6 £m |
|---|---|---|
| At 1 January | 4.6 | 4.6 |
| At 31 December | 4.6 | 4.6 |

DAVID: *I always look at the reserves note to see what is happening to the overall share-holders' claim. There is no change in the reserve during Year 6 or Year 7 so does that mean the company has not revalued the non-current assets in that period?*

LEONA: *The directors are required to review the valuations at each balance sheet date. So if there is no change in the revaluation reserve there must have been no change in the value of the assets involved.*

### 12.6.4  Statement of total recognised gains and losses

**Safe and Sure plc**
**Statement of total recognised income and expense**

|  | Year 7 £m | Year 6 £m |
|---|---|---|
| Profit attributable to equity holders | 114.8 | 94.6 |
| Exchange rate adjustments | 5.5 | (6.0) |
| Total recognised gains for the year | 120.3 | 88.6 |

LEONA: *Let me take you through the Statement of total recognised income and expense. It brings together the items which cause an overall decrease or increase in the ownership interest. On the first line you can see the profit attributable to equity holders which comes from the income statement. On the next line there are the exchange rate adjustments that relate to translation of investments held in other currencies. In Year 6 the exchange rates worked against the interests of equity holders but in Year 7 there was a favourable effect.*

### 12.6.5  Reconciliation of movements in equity

**Safe and Sure plc**
**Reconciliation of movements in equity**

|                                          | Year 7 | Year 6 |
|------------------------------------------|--------|--------|
|                                          | £m     | £m     |
| Profit attributable to equity holders    | 114.8  | 94.6   |
| Dividends                                | (29.5) | (24.4) |
| New share capital issued                 | 3.1    | 2.0    |
| Exchange adjustments                     | 5.5    | (6.0)  |
| Net change in equity holders' funds      | 93.9   | 66.2   |
| Opening equity holders' funds            | 370.4  | 304.2  |
| Closing equity holders' funds            | 464.3  | 370.4  |

**LEONA:** *Now you really can start to tie things together. Look at the balance sheet. (See Chapter 7.) The final line there shows the closing equity holders' funds which appear as the final line in this reconciliation. Starting at the top line the profit attributable to equity holders comes from the income statement (profit and loss account). (See Chapter 7.) The next line shows the dividend of £29.5m paid during year 7. That dividend relates to the profits earned in Year 6. For the dividend recommended in respect of Year 7 we have to look at the Finance Director's review. On the next line we see that the new share capital issued is £3.1m which is a combination of the increase of £3.0m in share premium (Note 13) and the increase of £0.1m in nominal share capital (Note 12). That is really tricky to sort out from the Notes – it's very helpful to have the reconciliation give the information in one place. The exchange adjustments repeat the information shown in the statement of total recognised gains and losses.*

**DAVID:** *You have given me plenty to think about. I can see the drinks trolley on its way – what would you like?*

## 12.7  Dividends

Shareholders who invest in a company do so because they want the value of their shares to increase over time and return greater wealth when eventually sold. In the meantime the shareholders look for an income to spend each year. That comes to some of them by means of dividends.

Companies are not obliged to pay dividends and may decide not to do so if there is a shortage of cash or it is needed for other purposes. The directors make a recommendation to the shareholders in the annual general meeting. The shareholders may vote against taking the dividend but that happens only very rarely. Final dividend payments usually take place soon after the annual general meeting. Some companies also pay an interim dividend during the accounting year. Major UK companies have in past years ensured that a dividend was paid every year, however small, because it allowed the shares to be regarded as sufficiently 'safe' for investors such as trustees of charitable institutions.

When a company decides it wants to pay a dividend, there are two essential tests. The first is, 'Does the company have the cash resources to pay a dividend?' The second is, 'Has the company made sufficient profits, adding this year to previous years, to justify the dividend as being paid out of wealth created by the business?'

Even where the company has cash in the bank from which to pay the dividend, it must look forward and ensure that there are no other commitments in the near future which will also need cash. The company may decide to borrow short term to finance the dividend. In such a situation the company has to weigh the interest cost of borrowing against the risk of its shares being undervalued because of lack of interest from shareholders. These are all problems of cash management (more often called 'treasury management').

Company law imposes a different viewpoint. It takes the view that a company should not return to shareholders, during the life of the company, a part of the capital contributed by the shareholder body. Accordingly there is a requirement that dividends must be covered by accumulated reserves of past profit in excess of accumulated reserves of past losses. It is not required that the dividend is covered by the profit of the year. A company might choose to smooth things over by maintaining the dividend reasonably constant even where profits are fluctuating.

The dividend declared by the company is usually expressed in pence per share. Shareholders receive dividend calculated by multiplying the dividend in pence per share by the number of shares held. For the company there is a reduction in the asset of cash and a reduction in the ownership claim. The management of the company may regard the dividend as an expense of the business but it is more properly regarded as a reduction in the claim which the owners have on the net assets as a whole. The reduction in the ownership interest is reported in the statement of changes in equity because it is a transaction with the owners.

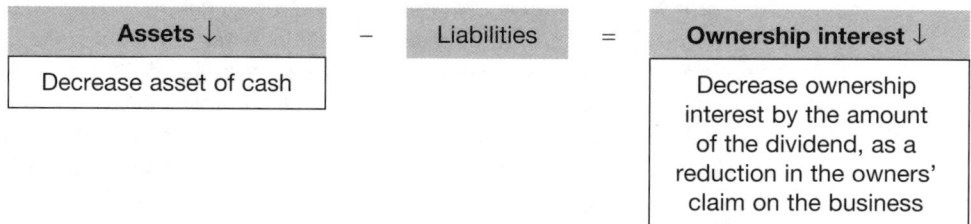

| **Assets ↓** | − | Liabilities | = | **Ownership interest ↓** |
|---|---|---|---|---|
| Decrease asset of cash | | | | Decrease ownership interest by the amount of the dividend, as a reduction in the owners' claim on the business |

At the end of the accounting period the company will calculate profit and then declare a recommended dividend. The dividend is recommended by the directors to the shareholders. The shareholders, in the annual general meeting, may accept or decline but are not allowed to increase the amount. At the balance sheet date there is no legal liability because the shareholders' meeting has not been held. Therefore there is no information reported in the financial statements. The directors' report, which is required by company law, will contain a statement of the recommended dividend for the year. There will probably also be information in the chairman's statement or on a 'highlights' page.

## 12.8  Issue of further shares on the Stock Exchange

Once a company has a listing on the Stock Exchange it may decide to issue further shares. There are different methods by which this may be done, depending on the company's motive for the action. This section describes an offer for sale, a capitalisation issue and a rights issue.

### 12.8.1  Offer for sale

When a company seeks a listing of its shares for the first time, it must offer those shares to the public (using the services of a member firm of the Stock Exchange as a sponsor) and issue a **prospectus** setting out information about itself. Some of the information to be included in the prospectus is required by the Companies Act but this is expanded upon by the **Listing Rules**. The prospectus is a highly informative document, revealing far more about a company than would be found in the annual report. There is a requirement for an accountant's report which includes a three-year history of the financial statements. In particular, there must be a specific statement confirming the adequacy of working capital.

There may also be a forecast of the expected profits for the next accounting period. The reporting accountants will be asked to give an opinion on the forecast. Particularly interesting are the assumptions on which the forecast is based. The reporting accountants will confirm that the amounts in the forecast are consistent with the assumptions but the reader will have to decide how appropriate the assumptions themselves are.

Exhibit 12.5 contains an example of a statement of assumptions taken from a company prospectus.

**Exhibit 12.5**
**Assumptions on which profit forecast is based**

> The forecasts have been prepared on a basis consistent with the accounting policies normally accepted by the Group and on the following principal assumptions:
>
> (i)  there will be no changes in taxation or other legislation or government regulations or policies which will have a significant effect on the Group; and
> (ii) the operations of the Group and its suppliers will not be significantly affected by weather conditions, industrial action or civil disturbances.

You may be surprised to learn that the wording in Exhibit 12.5 is extracted from the prospectus of a company retailing high quality chocolates. You may be further surprised to learn that very similar wording appeared in the prospectus of a company offering dry cleaning services. There is no regulation which says that the statement of assumptions has to be helpful to the user of the annual report.

### 12.8.2 Capitalisation issue

After the shares have been listed for some time, the market value may have grown to the point where the shares are less marketable because the price of each is too large for convenient trading in small lots. The company may decide to increase the number of shares held by shareholders without making any change to the assets or liabilities of the company. One way of achieving this is to convert reserves into share capital. Take the simplified balance sheet in Exhibit 12.6. The company decides to convert £1m of reserves into share capital. It writes to each shareholder saying, 'You will receive one new share for each share already held'. The balance sheet now becomes as shown in Exhibit 12.7.

The shareholder now holds twice as many shares by number but is no better or worse off financially because the total value of the company has not changed. The shares will each be worth one-half of the market price of an old share at the moment of issue. This process is sometimes referred to as a bonus issue because the shareholders receive new share certificates, but in reality there is no bonus because no new wealth is created.

**Exhibit 12.6**
**Balance sheet of company prior to capitalisation**

|  | £m |
|---|---|
| Assets | 7 |
| Liabilities | (4) |
|  | 3 |
| Share capital, in shares of 25 pence each | 1 |
| Reserves | 2 |
|  | 3 |

**Exhibit 12.7**
**Balance sheet of company after capitalisation**

|  | £m |
|---|---|
| Assets | 7 |
| Liabilities | (4) |
|  | 3 |
| Share capital, in shares of 25 pence each | 2 |
| Reserves | 1 |
|  | 3 |

In terms of the accounting equation the effect on the balance sheet is:

| Assets | – | Liabilities | = | Ownership interest ↑↓ |
|---|---|---|---|---|
|  |  |  |  | Increase in share capital £1m |
|  |  |  |  | Decrease in reserves £1m |

### 12.8.3    Rights issue

Once a company has a market listing it may decide that it needs to raise further finance on the stock market. The first people it would ask are the existing shareholders, who have already shown their commitment to the company by owning shares in it. Furthermore, it is desirable to offer them first chance because if strangers buy the shares the interests of the existing shareholders may be diluted. Suppose the company in Exhibit 12.6 wishes to raise £3m new finance. It will offer existing shareholders the right to pay for, say, 2 million new shares at 150 pence each. There are already 4 million shares of 25p nominal value in issue, so the letter to the shareholders will say: 'The company is offering you the right to buy 1 new share at a price of 150p for every 2 existing shares you hold.' Existing shareholders will be attracted by this offer provided the market price stays above 150 pence for existing shares. They may take up the rights themselves or sell the right to someone else. In either event, the company will receive £3m cash, the company will issue 2 million new shares at 150 pence each and the balance sheet will appear as in Exhibit 12.8.

**Exhibit 12.8**
**Balance sheet after rights issue**

|  | £m |
|---|---|
| Assets | 7.0 |
| New cash | 3.0 |
|  | 10.0 |
| Liabilities | (4.0) |
|  | 6.0 |
| Share capital, in shares of 25 pence each | 1.5 |
| Share premium | 2.5 |
| Reserves | 2.0 |
|  | 6.0 |

The issue price of 150 pence is split for accounting purposes into the nominal value of 25 pence and the premium of 125 pence. In terms of the accounting equation the effect of the rights issue on the balance sheet is:

| Assets ↑ | – | Liabilities | = | Ownership interest ↑ |
|---|---|---|---|---|
| Increase in cash £3m | | | | Increase in share capital £0.5m Increase in share premium £2.5m |

**Activity 12.4** *Look in the financial section of a newspaper for the list of recent issues of new shares. Obtain the address of one company from a trade directory and write politely to ask for a copy of the prospectus. If you are sufficiently fortunate to obtain a copy of a prospectus, look at the accounting information and compare it with the amount and type of information published in the annual report. Why are they not the same?*

## 12.9 Summary

- **Ownership interest** is the residual amount found by deducting all of the entity's liabilities from all of the entity's assets.

- Unrealised gains are reported in a **statement of recognised income and expense** or a **statement of changes in equity** in the IASB system. They are reported in a **statement of total recognised gains and losses** in the UK ASB system.

- Each share has a named value when the company is formed. This is called its nominal value. It does not change unless the shareholders agree to split shares into smaller units.

- When the shares are sold on a stock market they have a **market value**. The market value of frequently traded shares changes daily with the forces of supply and demand.

- The difference between the nominal value and the market value is called the **share premium**. When the company issues further shares at market price the share premium is recorded separately from the nominal value.

- When non-current assets are revalued, the **unrealised** increase in value is recorded in the **revaluation reserve**.

- **Dividends** paid to shareholders reduce the ownership interest. The effect on the accounting equation is reported when dividends are paid. Dividends proposed to be paid in future are described in the directors' report.

- When a company issues more shares after incorporation it may be through a capitalisation issue, an offer for sale or a rights issue. A **capitalisation issue** gives more shares to equity shareholders. It changes the relationship between share capital and reserves but brings no new resources into the business. An **offer for sale** increases the ownership interest and brings in new cash. A **rights issue** also increases the ownership interest and brings in new cash but it gives the existing shareholders the first choice of maintaining their proportionate interest in the company.

# QUESTIONS

The Questions section of each chapter has three types of question. 'Test your understanding' questions to help you review your reading are in the 'A' series of questions. You will find the answers to these by reading and thinking about the material in the book. 'Application' questions to test your ability to apply technical skills are in the 'B' series of questions. Questions requiring you to show skills in problem solving and evaluation are in the 'C' series of questions. A letter [S] indicates that there is a solution at the end of the book.

## A    Test your understanding

**A12.1**    Why may it be said that the ownership interest is the residual item in the accounting equation? (Section 12.1)

**A12.2**    What is the definition of ownership interest? (Section 12.2)

**A12.3**    What is the effect on the accounting equation where new shares are issued for cash? (Section 12.3.1)

**A12.4**    Why does the company not record the buying and selling of shares in its balance sheet? (Section 12.3.3)

**A12.5**    What is a share premium? How is it recorded? (Section 12.3.4)

**A12.6**    How is the revaluation of a non-current (fixed) asset reported? (Section 12.3.5)

**A12.7**    Why may the revaluation of a non-current (fixed) asset not be reported in the profit and loss account? (Section 12.3.5)

**A12.8**    Where may the reader of the annual report find out about the effect of movements in foreign exchange rates? (Section 12.3.6)

**A12.9**    What is the purpose of the statement of total recognised income and expenses? (Section 12.6.4)

**A12.10**   What is the purpose of the reconciliation of movements in equity? (Section 12.6.5)

**A12.11**   How do the directors report their recommended dividend for the financial period, to be agreed at the shareholders' meeting? (Section 12.7)

**A12.12**   What is meant by:

(a)  offer for sale; (section 12.8.1)
(b)  capitalisation issue; and (section 12.8.2)
(c)  rights issue? (section 12.8.3)

Explain the effect of each of the above on the balance sheet of a company.

## B    Application

**B12.1** [S]
Explain the effect on the accounting equation of each of the following transactions:

(a)  At the start of Year 1, Bright Ltd issues 200,000 shares at nominal value 25 pence per share, receiving £50,000 in cash.
(b)  At the end of Year 2, Bright Ltd issues a further 100,000 shares to an investor at an agreed price of 75 pence per share, receiving £75,000 in cash.
(c)  At the end of Year 3 the directors of Bright Ltd obtain a market value of £90,000 for a company property which originally cost £70,000. They wish to record this in the balance sheet.

**B12.2** [S]
Explain the effect on the accounting equation of the following transactions and decisions regarding dividends:

(a)  The company pays a dividend of £20,000 during the accounting period.
(b)  The directors recommend a dividend of £30,000 at the end of the accounting year. It will be paid following shareholder approval at the Annual General Meeting, held two months after the accounting year-end.

**B12.3** [S]
The following is a summarised balance sheet of Nithsdale Ltd.

|  | £000s |
|---|---|
| Cash | 20 |
| Other assets less liabilities | 320 |
|  | 340 |
|  |  |
| Ordinary shares (400,000 of 25 pence each) | 100 |
| Share premium | 40 |
| Reserves of retained profit | 200 |
|  | 340 |

The company is considering three possible changes to its capital structure:

(a)  issue for cash 50,000 additional ordinary shares at £1 per share, fully paid; or
(b)  make a 1 for 4 capitalisation issue of ordinary shares; or
(c)  make a 1 for 5 rights issue at £3 per share.

Show separately the impact of each change on the balance sheet of the company.

**B12.4** [S]
Fragrance plc has owned a factory building for many years. The building is recorded in the balance sheet at £250,000, being historical cost of £300,000 less accumulated depreciation of £50,000. The recent report of a professional valuer indicated that the property is valued at £380,000 on an open market basis for its existing use. Explain the effect this information will have on the reported financial statements.

**B12.5** [S]
Suppose the factory building in question **B12.4** was valued by the professional expert at £240,000. What effect would this information have on the reported financial statements?

## C    Problem solving and evaluation

*This question reviews your understanding of Chapters 8–12 and the effect of transactions on ownership interest.*

**C12.1**
Set out below is a summary of the accounting records of Titan Ltd at 31 December Year 1:

| | £000s | £000s |
|---|---|---|
| **Assets** | | |
| Land and buildings | 200 | |
| Plant and machinery | 550 | |
| Investment in shares | 150 | |
| Stock | 250 | |
| Trade receivables (debtors) | 180 | |
| Cash | 150 | |
| **Liabilities** | | |
| Trade payables (creditors) | | 365 |
| Debenture loan 10% nominal rate of interest | | 250 |
| **Ownership interest** | | |
| Share capital | | 600 |
| Retained earnings at 1 Jan. Year 1 | | 125 |
| **Revenue** | | |
| Sales | | 1,815 |
| Cost of goods sold | 1,505 | |
| **Expenses** | | |
| Overhead expenses | 145 | |
| Debenture interest paid | 25 | |
| Totals | 3,155 | 3,155 |

The summary of the accounting records includes all transactions which have been entered in the ledger accounts up to 31 December, but investigation reveals further adjustments which relate to the accounting period up to, and including, that date.

The adjustments required relate to the following matters:

(i)   No depreciation has been charged for the year in respect of buildings, plant and machinery. The depreciation of the building has been calculated as £2,000 per annum and the depreciation of plant and machinery for the year has been calculated as £55,000 for the year.

(ii)  The company is aware that electricity consumption during the months of November and December, Year 1, amounted to around £5,000 in total, but no electricity bill has yet been received.

(iii) Overhead expenses include insurance premiums of £36,000 which were paid at the start of December, Year 1, in respect of the 12-month period ahead.

(iv) The stock amount is as shown in the accounting records of items moving into and out of stock during the year. On 31 December a check of the physical stock was made. It was discovered that raw materials recorded as having a value of £3,000 were, in fact, unusable. It was also found that an employee had misappropriated stock worth £5,000.

(v)  The company proposes to pay a dividend of £30,000.

(vi) The corporation tax payable in respect of the profits of the year is estimated at £45,000, due for payment on 30 September, Year 2.

**Required**

(a) Explain how each of the items (i) to (vi) will affect the ownership interest.

(b) Calculate the amount of the ownership interest after taking into account items (i) to (vi).

(*Hint*: First calculate the profit of the year.)

## Activities for study groups

Turn to the annual report of a listed company which you have used for activities in earlier chapters. Find every item which relates to the ownership interest (including any discussion in the non-regulated part of the annual report).

As a group, imagine you are shareholders in this company. You are holding a meeting of the shareholders' action group calling for clarity of information about your total interest in the business. Make lists of the good points and weak points in the quality of information available to you and then arrange the weak points in descending order of importance. Then draft an action plan for improved communication with shareholders which you would propose sending to the company.

## Notes and references

1. IASB (2004), IAS 21, *The effects of changes in foreign exchange rates*, International Accounting Standards Board.
2. IASB (2004), IAS 1, *Presentation of Financial Statements*, para. 8.
3. ASB (1992), Financial Reporting Standard (FRS 3), *Reporting Financial Performance*, Accounting Standards Board; and ASB (1999), *Statement of Principles for Financial Reporting*, ch. 7.
4. ASB (1992), FRS 3, para. 59.

# A spreadsheet for adjustment to a trial balance at the end of the accounting period

## End-of-period adjustments and the ownership interest

If you look back to Chapter 6 you will see that it finished with a trial balance and a promise that the trial balance would be used later as the starting point for preparation of financial statements. The moment has now arrived where the trial balance is used as a starting point for making end-of-period adjustments to show the change in the ownership interest during the period.

The accruals concept (or the parallel argument of matching in the profit and loss account) requires all items relevant to the period to be included in the financial statements of the period. Most items will be included because they will have been recorded in the ledger and hence in the financial statements. However, there will be some items of information, emerging from enquiry at the end of the period, which have not yet resulted in a transaction but which are undoubtedly based on events relevant to the period.

The enquiry will take a routine form of:

- estimating the depreciation of non-current (fixed) assets where this has not already been recorded;
- examining non-current (fixed) assets for signs of obsolescence beyond the amount allowed for in the depreciation charge;
- counting the inventory (stock) of raw materials, work-in-progress and finished goods, for comparison with the accounting record;
- evaluating the doubtful debts;
- checking files for any purchase invoices received but not yet recorded;
- checking files for any sales invoices for goods sent out but not yet recorded;
- considering whether any resource has been consumed, or service received, for which a supplier has not yet sent an invoice.

Returning to the trial balance contained in Exhibit 6.15 of Chapter 6, it may be noted that the depreciation for the month has been charged, there are no trade receivables (debtors) and therefore no concerns about doubtful debts, and it would appear from the list of transactions for the month that all sales and purchases have been recorded carefully. Suppose, however, that when M. Carter checks the inventory (stock) of goods at the end of the month it is found that the roof has been leaking and rainwater has damaged goods worth £500. Furthermore, the business uses gas to heat a water boiler and it is estimated that consumption for the month amounts to £80.

These items of information are called *end-of-period adjustments*. Both events could, and would, be recorded in the ledger accounts by the business. If you were presented with this information as a class exercise, or you were the auditor taking the trial balance and adjusting it for this further information, you would use a spreadsheet which set out the trial balance and then provided further columns for the end-of-period adjustments. The spreadsheet for this example is set out in Exhibit 12.9 but before looking at that you should read through the next section which explains the recording of end-of-period adjustments. In this case a one-month period is covered and so the adjustments are referred to as month-end adjustments.

## Analysis of the month-end adjustments

Before any entries may be made in the adjustments columns of the spreadsheet, the effect of each adjustment on the accounting equation must be considered so that the debit and credit entries may be identified.

### (a) At the end of the month it is found that the roof has been leaking and rainwater has damaged goods worth £500

| Assets ↓ | – | Liabilities | = | Ownership interest ↓ |
|---|---|---|---|---|
| Inventory (stock) decreases by £500 | | | | Expense of £500 for inventory (stock) damaged |

The loss of inventory (stock) causes the ownership interest to decrease and is recorded as a debit entry in the expense of cost of goods sold. The decrease in the inventory (stock) is recorded as a credit entry in the ledger account.

| | | | |
|---|---|---|---|
| Dr | Cost of goods sold | £500 | |
| Cr | Inventory (stock) of goods | | £500 |

### (b) The business uses gas to heat a water boiler and it is estimated that consumption for the month amounts to £80

| Assets | – | Liabilities ↑ | = | Ownership interest ↓ |
|---|---|---|---|---|
| | | Obligation to pay for gas consumed £80 | | Expense of £80 for gas consumed |

The event of consuming the gas causes the ownership interest to decrease and is recorded as a debit entry in an expense account for gas consumed. The obligation to pay for the gas at a future time is recorded as a credit entry in the ledger account for accruals.

| | | |
|---|---|---|
| Dr Expense of gas | £80 | |
| Cr Accruals | | £80 |

### The spreadsheet

Exhibit 12.9 contains, in the left-hand pair of debit and credit columns, the trial balance of Exhibit 6.15 from Chapter 6. The next pair of columns contains the debit and credit entries necessary for the end-of-period adjustments. The third pair of columns shows the resulting amounts on each line of profit and loss account items. The final pair of columns shows the resulting amounts on each line of balance sheet items. The entire spreadsheet could be thought of as a series of ledger accounts stretched across the page, with one line for each ledger account.

The debit and credit entries identified by the foregoing analysis are shown in the adjustments columns of the spreadsheet with identifying letters in brackets alongside. Where no suitably named line exists, a new line may be inserted. The use of a new line is shown here for accruals and the expense of gas. If the exercise is being carried out using a computer spreadsheet package, the insertion of an extra line is not a problem. For a handwritten exercise it may be necessary to leave spaces at possible insertion points.

Once all adjustments have been entered, each of the adjusted amounts can be carried across to one of the final four columns, depending on whether the item belongs

**Exhibit 12.9**

**Trial balance of M. Carter at the end of May, before month-end adjustments**

| Ledger account title | | Trial balance | | Adjustments | | Income (profit) statement | | Balance sheet | |
|---|---|---|---|---|---|---|---|---|---|
| | | Dr | Cr | Dr | Cr | Expense | Revenue | A | L + OI |
| | | £ | £ | £ | £ | £ | £ | £ | £ |
| L3 | Buildings | 30,000 | | | | | | 30,000 | |
| L4 | Equipment | 5,750 | | | | | | 5,750 | |
| L5 | Inventory (stock) of goods | 8,000 | | | 500 (a) | | | 7,500 | |
| L11 | R. Welsby | nil | | | | | | | |
| L1 | Cash | 6,400 | | | | | | 6,400 | |
| | Accruals | | | | 80 (b) | | | | 80 |
| L6 | R. Busby | | nil | | | | | | |
| L2 | Ownership interest | | 49,000 | | | | | | 49,000 |
| | Subtotal | 50,150 | 49,000 | | | | | 49,650 | 49,080 |
| | *Difference: profit of the month* | | | | | | | | 570 |
| L10 | Sales | | 7,000 | | | | 7,000 | | |
| L9 | Cost of goods sold | 3,500 | | 500 (a) | | 4,000 | | | |
| L7 | Electricity | 100 | | | | 100 | | | |
| | Gas | | | 80 (b) | | 80 | | | |
| L8 | Wages | 2,000 | | | | 2,000 | | | |
| L12 | Depreciation | 250 | | | | 250 | | | |
| | Subtotal | 5,850 | 7,000 | | | 6,430 | 7,000 | | |
| | *Difference: profit of the month* | | | | | 570 | | | |
| | Total of each column | 56,000 | 56,000 | 580 | 580 | 7,000 | 7,000 | 49,650 | 49,650 |

to the profit and loss account or the balance sheet. Each pair of columns is added and the difference between the totals in the profit and loss account columns should equal the difference between the totals in the balance sheet columns. If that is not the case, it means that an error has taken place at some point in the spreadsheet and must be found.

## Revised statement of profit

The statement of profit before adjustments is shown in section 6.6.2 of Chapter 6 and the balance sheet is in section 6.6.3. From the final four columns of the spreadsheet in Exhibit 12.9, these could now be restated as follows:

**M Carter, Wholesaler**
**Income statement (profit and loss account) (adjusted)**
**for the month of May Year XX**

|  | £ | £ |
|---|---|---|
| Revenue (sales) |  | 7,000 |
| Cost of goods sold |  | (4,000) |
| Gross profit |  | 3,000 |
| *Other expenses* |  |  |
| Wages | (2,000) |  |
| Electricity | (100) |  |
| Gas | (80) |  |
| Depreciation | (250) |  |
|  |  | (2,430) |
| Net profit |  | 570 |

## Statement of financial position: the balance sheet

**M Carter, Wholesaler**
**Balance sheet (adjusted) at 31 May Year XX**

|  | £ |
|---|---|
| **Non-current (fixed) assets** |  |
| Buildings | 30,000 |
| Equipment | 6,000 |
|  | 36,000 |
| Depreciation | (250) |
| Depreciated cost of non-current (fixed) assets | 35,750 |
| **Current assets** |  |
| Inventory (stock) | 7,500 |
| Cash at bank | 6,400 |
|  | 13,900 |
| Accruals | (80) |
| Net current assets | 13,820 |
| Net assets | 49,570 |
| **Ownership interest** |  |
| Capital at start | 50,000 |
| Add profit | 570 |
| Less drawings | (1,000) |
| **Total ownership interest** | 49,570 |

This completes the study of double entry bookkeeping in this book. You are now in a position to be able to carry out the following tasks in relation to the business of a sole trader:

- record transactions in ledger accounts
- prepare a trial balance
- make end-of-period adjustments to the trial balance
- prepare a profit and loss account and balance sheet.

## S    Test your understanding

**S12.1** (a) Using the information provided in question **C12.1**, prepare a spreadsheet containing a trial balance, adjustment and resulting figures for profit and loss account and balance sheet items. (Exhibit 12.9 provides a pattern to follow.)

(b) Present the profit and loss account for the year and the balance sheet at the end of the year in an informative and useful manner.

# Chapter 13

# Ratio analysis

## Five year summary

| | 2005 £'000 | 2004 £'000 | 2003* £'000 | 2002 £'000 | 2001* £'000 |
|---|---|---|---|---|---|
| **Consolidated profit and loss account** | | | | | |
| Turnover – continuing operations | **187,704** | 178,746 | 167,095 | 163,800 | 159,921 |
| **Profit before interest** | **10,520** | 9,584 | 9,444 | 10,410 | 10,148 |
| Net interest payable | **(2,366)** | (2,578) | (3,049) | (3,296) | (4,063) |
| **Profit before taxation** | **8,154** | 7,006 | 6,395 | 7,114 | 6,085 |
| Taxation | **(2,584)** | (2,037) | (1,972) | 238 | (1,570) |
| **Profit after taxation** | **5,570** | 4,969 | 4,423 | 7,352 | 4,515 |
| Dividends | **(4,460)** | (4,426) | (4,422) | (4,435) | (4,490) |
| **Retained profit** | **1,110** | 543 | 1 | 2,917 | 25 |

| | 2005 £'000 | 2004 £'000 | 2003 £'000 | 2002 £'000 | 2001 £'000 |
|---|---|---|---|---|---|
| **Group balance sheet and key ratios** | | | | | |
| Net assets | **42,728** | 41,406 | 41,668 | 43,015 | 40,097 |
| Net borrowings | **(18,843)** | (15,930) | (19,191) | (28,139) | (36,299) |
| Net debt | **(29,171)** | (25,996) | (28,864) | (37,193) | (44,515) |
| Gearing ratio | **68.3%** | 62.8% | 69.3% | 86.5% | 111.0% |
| Additions to fixed assets | **11,204** | 10,359 | 6,813 | 5,379 | 6,142 |
| Basic earnings per share (excluding exceptional items) | **8.6p** | 7.6p | 6.8p | 11.2p | 6.8p |
| Dividends per share | **6.80p** | 6.80p | 6.80p | 6.80p | 6.80p |
| Net assets per share | **64.1p** | 62.2p | 62.5p | 64.6p | 60.2p |
| Number of outlets – continuing operations | | | | | |
| Own stores | **369** | 378 | 389 | 395 | 400 |
| Franchises | **216** | 203 | 198 | 181 | 163 |

### Dividends and shareholder returns

Basic earnings per share have increased by 11.9% from 7.64p per share to 8.55p per share. Despite the increase in profits, the level of dividend cover remains low and, therefore, the Directors are recommending that the fully year dividend per share should remain at 6.80p per share which means that a final dividend of 4.85p per share will be paid in November.

Source: Thorntons plc Annual Report 2005, pp. 43, 5.

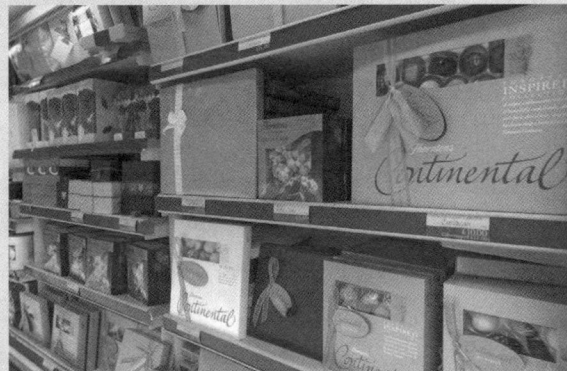

### Discussion points

1 What does the reader learn from the ratios and performance measures presented by the company?

2 What major ratios are not shown in this summary?

## Contents

## Learning outcomes

After reading this chapter you should be able to:

● Define, calculate and interpret ratios that help analyse and understand (a) performance for investors, (b) management performance, (c) liquidity and working capital, and (d) gearing.

● Explain investors' views of the balance of risk and return, and the risks of investing in a geared company when profits are fluctuating.

● Explain how the pyramid of ratios helps integrate interpretation.

● Describe the uses and limitations of ratio analysis.

● Carry out a practical exercise of calculating and interpreting ratios.

## 13.1  Introduction

Ratios are widely used as a tool in the interpretation of financial statements. The ratios selected and the use of the resulting information depend on the needs of the person using the information. What investors really want to do is choose the best moment to sell shares when the share price is at its highest. To choose that best moment, the investors will monitor the company's performance. Bankers lending to the company will also monitor performance, and look for indicators of solvency and ability to repay interest and capital.

Many users will rely on others to monitor ratios on their behalf. Employees will look to their advisers, perhaps union officials, to monitor performance. Small private investors with limited resources will rely heavily on articles in the financial sections of newspapers. Professional fund managers will look to their own research resources and may also make use of the analysts' reports prepared by the brokers who act for the fund managers in buying and selling shares. Each broker's analyst seeks as much information as possible about a company so that he or she can sell information which is of better quality than that of any other broker's analyst. There is fierce competition to be a highly rated analyst because that brings business to the broking firm and high rewards for the analyst.

In monitoring performance the expert analysts and fund managers will use ratios rather than absolute amounts. A figure of £100m for sales (revenue) means nothing in isolation. The reader who knows that last year's sales (revenue) amounted to £90m sees immediately an increase of 11.1%. The reader who knows that fixed (non-current) assets remained constant at £75m knows that the fixed (non-current) assets this year have earned their value in sales (revenue) 1.33 times (100/75 = 1.33) whereas last year they earned their value in sales (revenue) 1.2 times (90/75 = 1.2). Ratios show changes in relationships of figures which start to create a story and start to generate questions. They do not provide answers.

The fund managers and analysts all have their own systems for calculating ratios and some keep these a carefully guarded secret so that each may hopefully see an important clue before the next person does so. That means there is no standard system of ratio analysis. There are, however, several which are used frequently. A selection of these will be used here as a basic framework for analysis. As you start to read more about company accounts you will find other ratios used but you should discover that those are largely refinements of the structure presented here.

## 13.2 A note on terminology

Ratio analysis is not a standardised exercise. It is often taught in finance courses and management accounting courses as well as in financial accounting courses. Businesses use ratios to describe their own performance. There is a tendency towards creating ratios that suit the purpose and towards using descriptions that are personal choices of the presenter. This chapter gives commonly used names for ratios (such as 'gross profit percentage') and links these to the terminology of the IASB system of accounting by using additional descriptions in brackets. For example, the title 'gross profit percentage' is used as a name for a ratio and it is defined as follows:

$$\frac{\text{Gross profit}}{\text{Sales (revenue)}} \times 100\%$$

In the denominator of this ratio the word 'sales' describes the activity that creates gross profit; the additional word (revenue) in brackets reminds you that the information will be found in financial statements under 'revenue'. Similarly 'fixed assets (non-current assets)' uses the commonly established words 'fixed assets' with the addition of (non-current assets) in brackets to remind you of where the information will be found in the balance sheet.

## 13.3 Systematic approach to ratio analysis

A systematic approach to ratio analysis seeks to establish a broad picture first of all, and then break that broad picture down until there are thumbnail sketches of interesting areas. Four key headings commonly encountered in ratio analysis are:

1 *Investor ratios.* Ratios in this category provide some measure of how the price of a share in the stock market compares to key indicators of the performance of the company.

2 *Analysis of management performance.* Ratios in this category indicate how well the company is being run in terms of using assets to generate sales (revenue) and how effective it is in controlling costs and producing profit based on goods and services sold.

3 *Liquidity and current assets.* The management of cash and current assets and the preservation of an adequate, but not excessive, level of liquidity is an essential feature of business survival especially in difficult economic circumstances.

4 *Gearing (referred to in American texts as 'leverage').* Gearing is a measure of the extent to which there is financial risk indicated in the balance sheet and in the profit and loss account (see section 13.4 on risk and return). Financial risk means the risk associated with having to pay interest and having an obligation to repay a loan.

In the following sections key ratios for each of these aspects of a systematic analysis are specified by the name of the ratio and the definition in words. Below each definition there is a brief discussion of the meaning and interpretation of the ratio.

### 13.3.1    Investor ratios

Investors who buy shares in a company want to be able to compare the benefit from the investment with the amount they have paid, or intend to pay, for their shares. There are two measures of benefit to the investors. One is the profit of the period (usually given the name **earnings** when referring to the profit available for equity holders (ordinary shareholders)). The other is the **dividend** which is an amount of cash that is paid to the shareholders. Profit indicates wealth created by the business. That wealth may be accumulated in the business or else paid out in the form of dividend. Four ratios are presented with a comment on each.

| Earnings per share | $\dfrac{\text{Profit after tax for ordinary equity holders}}{\text{Number of issued ordinary shares}}$ |
|---|---|

*Comment.* **Earnings per share** is the most frequently quoted measure of company performance and progress. The percentage change from year to year should be monitored for the trend. Criticisms are that this strong focus on annual earnings may cause 'short-termism' among investors and among company managers. The IASB and the UK ASB would like to turn the attention of preparers and users of accounts away from reliance on earnings per share as a single performance measure, but the earnings per share remains a strong feature of comments on company results.

| Price–earnings ratio | $\dfrac{\text{Share price}}{\text{Earnings per share}}$ |
|---|---|

*Comment.* The **price–earnings ratio** (often abbreviated to 'p/e ratio') compares the amount invested in one share with the earnings per share. It may be interpreted as the number of years for which the currently reported profit is represented by the current share price. The p/e ratio reflects the market's confidence in future prospects of the company. The higher the ratio, the longer is the period for which the market believes the current level of earnings may be sustained.

In order to gain some feeling for the relative magnitude of the p/e ratio of any individual company, it should be compared with the average p/e ratio for the industry, given daily in the *Financial Times*. The p/e ratio is quite commonly used as a key item of input information in investment decisions or recommendations.

| Dividend per share | $\dfrac{\text{Dividend of the period}}{\text{Number of issued ordinary shares}}$ |
| --- | --- |

*Comment*. The **dividend per share** is one of the key measures announced by the company at the end of the financial year (and sometimes as an interim dividend during the year as well). Shareholders immediately know how much to expect in total dividend, depending on the number of shares held. The figure of dividend per share is the cash amount paid by the company. It may or may not be subject to tax in the hands of the recipient, depending on whether or not the recipient is a taxpayer.

The dividend of the period is equal to any interim dividend paid plus the final recommended dividend (see section 12.7). To find the recommended dividend you will have to look beyond the financial statements. The Directors' Report will contain a note on the recommended dividend which is to be paid to shareholders following their agreement at the annual general meeting. There may also be a description of the recommended dividend in the Chairman's Statement, or a Highlights Statement, or the Operating and Financial Review (OFR).

| Dividend cover (payout ratio) | $\dfrac{\text{Earnings per share}}{\text{Dividend per share}}$ |
| --- | --- |

*Comment*. Companies need cash to enable them to pay dividends. For most companies the profits of the business must generate that cash. So the dividend decision could be regarded as a two-stage question. The first part is, 'Have we made sufficient profits?' and the second stage is, 'Has that profit generated cash which is not needed for reinvestment in fixed or current assets?' The **dividend cover** helps in answering the first of these questions. It shows the number of times the dividend has been covered by the profits (earnings) of this year. It could be said that the higher the dividend cover, the 'safer' is the dividend. On the other hand, it could be argued that a high dividend cover means that the company is keeping new wealth to itself, perhaps to be used in buying new assets, rather than dividing it among the shareholders.

The dividend policy of the company is a major decision for the board of directors. Many companies like to keep to a 'target' dividend cover with only minor fluctuations from one year to the next. The evidence from finance research is that company managers have two targets, one being the stability of the dividend cover but the other being a desire to see the dividend per share increase, or at least remain stationary, rather than decrease. Dividends are thought to carry a signal to the market of the strength and stability of the company.

| Dividend yield | $\dfrac{\text{Dividend per share}}{\text{Share price}} \times 100\%$ |
| --- | --- |

*Comment*. The **dividend yield** is a very simple ratio comparing dividend per share with the current market price of a share. It indicates the relationship between what the investor can expect to receive from the shares and the amount which is invested in the shares. Many investors need income from investments and the dividend yield is an important factor in their decision to invest in, or remain in, a company. It has to be noted that dividends are not the only benefit from share ownership. Section 13.4 on risk and return presents a formula for return (yield) which takes into account the growth in share price as well as the dividend paid. Investors buy shares in expectation of an increase in the share price. The directors of many companies would take the view that the dividend yield should be adequate to provide an investment income, but it is the wealth arising from retained profits that is used for investment in new assets which in turn generate growth in future profits.

### 13.3.2    Analysis of management performance

Management of a business is primarily a function requiring **stewardship**, meaning careful use of resources for the benefit of the owners. There are two central questions to test this use of resources:

1  How well did the management make use of the investment in assets to create sales (revenue)?
2  How carefully did the management control costs so as to maximise the profit derived from the sales (revenue)?

| Return on shareholders' equity | $\dfrac{\text{Profit after tax for ordinary equity holders}}{\text{Share capital + Reserves}} \times 100\%$ |
|---|---|

*Comment.* A key measure of success, from the viewpoint of shareholders, is the success of the company in using the funds provided by shareholders to generate profit. That profit will provide new wealth to cover their **dividend** and to finance future expansion of the business. The **return on shareholders' equity** is therefore a measure of company performance from the shareholders' perspective. It is essential in this calculation to use the profit for ordinary equity holders, which is the profit after interest charges and after tax. The formula uses the phrase **equity holders** which will probably be the wording that you see in the financial statements. It has the same meaning as **ordinary shareholders**.

| Return on capital employed | $\dfrac{\text{Operating profit (before interest and tax)}}{\text{Total assets – Current liabilities}} \times 100\%$ |
|---|---|

| Return on capital employed | $\dfrac{\text{Operating profit (before interest and tax)}}{\text{Ordinary share capital + reserves + long-term loans}} \times 100\%$ |
|---|---|

*Comment.* **Return on capital employed** (ROCE) is a broader measure than return on shareholders' equity. ROCE measures the performance of a company as a whole in using all sources of long-term finance. Profit before interest and tax is used in the numerator as a measure of operating results. It is sometime called 'earnings before interest and tax' and is abbreviated to EBIT. Return on capital employed is often seen as a measure of management efficiency. The denominator can be written in two ways, as shown in the alternative formulae. Think about the accounting equation and rearrange it to read:

Total assets – current liabilities = Ordinary share capital plus
reserves plus long-term loans

The ratio is a measure of how well the long-term finance is being used to generate operating profits.

| Return on total assets | $\dfrac{\text{Operating profit (before interest and tax)}}{\text{Total assets}} \times 100\%$ |
|---|---|

*Comment.* Calculating the **return on total assets** is another variation on measuring how well the assets of the business are used to generate operating profit before deducting interest and tax.

| Operating profit as % of sales (revenue) | $\dfrac{\text{Operating profit (before interest and tax)}}{\text{Sales (revenue)}} \times 100\%$ |
|---|---|

*Comment.* The ratio of operating profit as a percentage of sales (revenue) is also referred to as the **operating margin**. The aim of many successful business managers is to make the margin as high as possible. The margin reflects the degree of competitiveness in the market, the economic situation, the ability to differentiate products and the ability to control expenses. At the end of this section it is shown that companies are not obliged to seek high **margins**. Some cannot, because of strong competitive factors. Yet they still make a satisfactory return on capital employed by making efficient use of the equipment held as fixed (non-current) assets.

| Gross profit percentage | $\dfrac{\text{Gross profit}}{\text{Sales (revenue)}} \times 100\%$ |
|---|---|

*Comment.* The gross profit as a percentage of sales (revenue) is also referred to as the **gross margin**. It has been seen in earlier chapters that the gross profit is equal to sales (revenue) minus all cost of sales. That gross profit may be compared with sales (revenue) as shown above. The gross profit percentage concentrates on costs of making goods and services ready for sale. Small changes in this ratio can be highly significant. There tends to be a view that there is a 'normal' value for the industry or for the product that may be used as a benchmark against which to measure a company's performance.

Because it is such a sensitive measure, many companies try to keep secret from their competitors and customers the detailed breakdown of gross profit for each product line or area of activity. Companies do not want to give competitors any clues on how much to undercut prices and do not want to give customers a chance to complain about excessive profits.

| Total assets usage | $\dfrac{\text{Sales (revenue)}}{\text{Total assets}} \times 100\%$ |
|---|---|

*Comment.* **Total assets usage** indicates how well a company has used its fixed and current assets to generate sales (revenue). Such a ratio is probably most useful as an indication of trends over a period of years. There is no particular value which is too high or too low but a sudden change would prompt the observer to ask questions.

| Fixed assets (non-current assets) usage | $\dfrac{\text{Sales (revenue)}}{\text{Fixed assets (non-current assets)}} \times 100\%$ |
|---|---|

*Comment.* **Fixed assets usage** is a similar measure of usage, but one which concentrates on the productive capacity as measured by fixed assets, indicates how successful the company is in generating sales (revenue) from fixed assets (non-current assets). The ratio may be interpreted as showing how many £s of sales (revenue) have been generated by each £ of fixed assets.

### 13.3.3 Liquidity and working capital

**Liquidity** is a word which refers to the availability of cash in the near future after taking account of immediate financial commitments. Cash in the near future will be available from bank deposits, cash released by sale of stocks and cash collected from customers. Immediate financial commitments are shown in current liabilities. The first ratio of liquidity is therefore a simple comparison of current assets with current liabilities.

| Current ratio | Current assets:Current liabilities |
|---|---|

*Comment*. If the current assets amount to £20m and the current liabilities amount to £10m the company is said, in words, to have 'a current ratio of 2 to 1'. Some commentators abbreviate this by saying 'the current ratio is 2'. Mathematically that is incorrect wording but the listener is expected to know that the words 'to 1' have been omitted from the end of the sentence.

The current ratio indicates the extent to which short-term assets are available to meet short-term liabilities. A current ratio of 2:1 is regarded, broadly speaking, as being a reasonable order of magnitude. As with other ratios, there is no 'best' answer for any particular company and it is the trend in this ratio which is more important. If the ratio is worsening over time, and especially if it falls to less than 1:1, the observer would look closely at the cash flow. A company can survive provided it can meet its obligations as they fall due. Some companies therefore operate on a very tight current ratio because they are able to plan the timing of inflows and outflows of cash quite precisely.

Companies which generate cash on a daily basis, such as retail stores, can therefore operate on a lower current ratio. Manufacturing businesses which have to hold substantial stocks would operate on a higher current ratio.

| Acid test | Current assets minus inventories (stock):Current liabilities |
|---|---|

*Comment*. In a crisis, where short-term creditors are demanding payment, the possibility of selling stocks (inventories) to raise cash may be unrealistic. The **acid test** takes a closer look at the liquid assets of the current ratio, omitting the stocks (inventories). For many companies this ratio is less than 1:1 because it is unlikely that all creditors will require payment at the same time. As with the current ratio, an understanding of the acid test has to be supported by an understanding of the pattern of cash flows. Analysts in particular will often ask companies about the peak borrowing requirements of the year and the timing of that peak in relation to cash inflows.

| Stock holding period (inventories holding period) | $\dfrac{\text{Average inventories (stock) held}}{\text{Cost of sales}} \times 365$ |
|---|---|

*Comment*. The **stock holding period** (inventories holding period) measures the average period during which stocks (inventories) of goods are held before being sold or used in the operations of the business. It is usually expressed in days, which is why the figure of 365 appears in the formula. If months are preferred, then the figure 12 should be substituted for the figure 365. One point of view is that the shorter the period, the better. An opposite point of view is that too short a period may create a greater risk of finding that the business is short of a stock item.

In calculating the stock holding period it is preferable to use the average of the stock (inventories) held at the start of the year and the stock (inventories) held at the end of the year. Some analysts use only the year-end figure if the start-of-year figure is not available. Whatever variation is used, it is important to be consistent from one time period to the next.

| Customers (trade debtors) collection period | $\dfrac{\text{Trade receivables (trade debtors)}}{\text{Credit sales (revenue)}} \times 365$ |
|---|---|

*Comment*. The **customers'** (trade debtors') **collection period** measures the average period of credit allowed to credit customers. An increase in this measure would indicate that a company is building up cash flow problems, although an attempt to decrease the period of credit allowed might deter customers and cause them to seek a competitor who gives a longer period of credit. It is important to be aware of the normal credit period for the industry. Some companies offer discount for prompt payment. Any offer of discount should weigh the cost of the discount against the benefit of earlier receipt of cash from customers. When you are looking for information in the annual report of companies using the IASB system you will probably have to start on the face of the balance sheet with the heading 'trade and other receivables' and then read the corresponding Note to the balance sheet to find the amount of trade receivables. If you are looking at the balance sheet of a company that does not use the IASB system you will have to find the Note to the balance sheet that gives detailed information about trade debtors.

| Suppliers (trade creditors) payment period | $\dfrac{\text{Trade payables (trade creditors)}}{\text{Credit purchases}} \times 365$ |
| --- | --- |

*Comment.* The **suppliers'** (trade creditors') **payment period** measures the average period of credit taken from suppliers of goods and services. An increase in this measure could indicate that the supplier has allowed a longer period to pay. It could also indicate that the company is taking longer to pay, perhaps because of cash flow problems. If payment is delayed then the company may lose discounts available for prompt payments. A reputation for being a slow payer could make it more difficult to obtain supplies in future. Some large companies have gained a reputation for delaying payment to smaller suppliers. Company law now requires company directors to make a statement of policy in relation to creditor payment.

Companies do not usually report **purchases** directly, so the figure must be calculated as follows:

$$\text{Purchases} = \text{Cost of goods sold} + \text{Closing stock} - \text{Opening stock}$$

Analysts often use **cost of goods** sold rather than calculate purchases, arguing that stock levels are broadly similar at corresponding period-ends.

| **Working capital cycle** | Stock (inventories) holding period PLUS Customers (trade debtors) collection period MINUS Suppliers (trade creditors) payment period |
| --- | --- |

*Comment.* You saw in Chapter 9 (Exhibit 9.1) the **working capital cycle** whereby stocks (inventories) are purchased on credit, then sold to customers who eventually pay cash. The cash is used to pay suppliers and the cycle starts again. We can now put some timings into the diagram. The working capital represents the long-term finance needed to cover current assets that are not matched by current liabilities. The longer the total of the stock holding period and customer collection period, compared to the suppliers payment period, the greater the need for working capital to be financed long term.

### 13.3.4  Gearing

The term **gearing** is used to describe the mix of loan finance and equity finance in a company. It is more properly called **financial gearing** and in American texts is called **leverage**. There are two main approaches to measuring gearing. The first looks at the balance sheet and the second looks at the profit and loss account.

| Debt/equity ratio | $\dfrac{\text{Long-term liabilities plus Preference share capital*}}{\text{Equity share capital + reserves}} \times 100\%$ |
| --- | --- |

* where preference share capital is in existence

*Comment.* From the balance sheet perspective the **gearing** measure considers the relative proportions of long-term (non-current) loans and equity in the long-term financing of the business. The precise meaning of long-term liabilities will vary from one company to the next. It is intended to cover the loans taken out with the aim of making them a permanent part of the company's financing policy. As they come due for repayment, they are replaced by further long-term finance. The starting point is the loans (but not the provisions) contained in the section headed *non-current liabilities*. However the accounting rules require separate reporting of loans due for repayment within one year, reported as current liabilities. It is necessary to look in the *current liabilities* for bank loans that are becoming due for repayment. In some companies the bank overdraft is a semi-permanent feature and so is included in this ratio calculation.

Preference share capital is included in the numerator because it has the characteristics of debt finance even although it is not classed as debt in company law. The preference shareholders have the first right to dividend, before the ordinary shareholders receive any dividend. This is why they are called 'preference' shares. The amount of the dividend is usually fixed as a percentage of nominal value of shares. The amount repaid to preference shareholders on maturity is the amount of the share capital only. They do not normally take a share of accumulated profits.

Different industries have different average levels, depending on the types of assets held and the stability or otherwise of the stream of profits. A low gearing percentage indicates a low exposure to financial risk because it means that there will be little difficulty in paying loan interest and repaying the loans as they fall due. A high gearing percentage indicates a high exposure to financial risk because it means that there are interest charges to be met and a requirement to repay the loans on the due date.

| Interest cover | $\dfrac{\text{Operating profit (before interest and tax)}}{\text{Interest}}$ |
|---|---|

*Comment.* The importance of being able to meet interest payments on borrowed funds is emphasised by measuring gearing in terms of the profit and loss account. If the profit generated before interest and tax is sufficient to give high cover for the interest charges, then it is unlikely that the company is overcommitting itself in its borrowing. If the interest cover is falling or is low, then there may be increasing cause for concern.

**Activity 13.1**   *Write down the name of each ratio given in this section. Close the book and test your knowledge by writing down the formula for each ratio. Then write one sentence for each ratio which explains its purpose. Be sure that you know each ratio and understand its purpose before you proceed with the rest of the chapter.*

## 13.4  Investors' views on risk and return

Uncertainty about the future means that all investments contain an element of risk. For investors who are averse to risk, there is a fear of income falling below an acceptable level and a fear of losing the capital invested in the company. Given a choice between two investments offering the same expected return, risk-averse investors will choose the least risky investment.

### 13.4.1 Return

The word **return** has many meanings but for an investor the basic question is, 'What have I gained from owning these shares?' One simple formula which answers that question is:

$$\frac{(Market\ price\ of\ share\ today - Price\ paid\ for\ share) + Dividends\ received}{Price\ paid\ for\ share} \times 100\%$$

Investors in a company which is in a low-risk industry may be willing to accept a low rate of return. Investors in a company which is in a high-risk industry will be seeking a higher rate of return to compensate for the additional risk they take.

Research has shown that share prices react very rapidly to any item of information which is sufficiently important to affect investors' decisions. This phenomenon is sometimes referred to as the **efficient markets hypothesis**, which is a statement that share prices react immediately to make allowance for each new item of information made available. The annual results of a listed company are announced through the Stock Exchange by means of a document called a **preliminary announcement**, issued approximately two months after the accounting year-end. The annual report then goes to the printers and is distributed to shareholders about three months after the related year-end.

When investors evaluate share price by calculating return, they take the most up-to-date price available.

### 13.4.2 Risk

There are two main types of risk: operating risk and financial risk.

**Operating risk** exists where there are factors which could cause sales (revenue) to fluctuate or cause costs to increase. Companies are particularly vulnerable to operating risk when they have a relatively high level of fixed operating costs. These fixed costs are incurred independently of the level of activity. If sales (revenue) fall, or the direct costs of sales increase, the fixed costs become a greater burden on profit.

**Financial risk** exists where the company has loan finance, especially long-term loan finance where the company cannot relinquish its commitment. Loan finance carries an obligation to pay interest charges and these create a problem similar to the fixed costs problem. If the sales (revenue) are strong and the direct costs of sales are well under control, then interest charges will not be a problem. If sales (revenue) fall, or the direct costs of sales rise, then a company may find that it does not have the cash resources to meet the interest payments as they fall due. Repaying the loan could become an even greater worry.

Both operating risk and financial risk are important to the company's shareholders because they have the residual claim on assets after all liabilities are met. If the company's assets are growing then these risks will not pose a problem but if the business becomes slack then the combination of high fixed operating costs and high interest charges could be disastrous. As a rule of thumb, investors look for low financial risk in companies which have high operating risk and, conversely, will tolerate a higher level of financial risk where there is relatively low operating risk.

The terms **operating gearing** and **financial gearing** are frequently used to describe the extent of operating risk and financial risk. (Financial gearing has been explained in the previous section.) In terms of the profit and loss account they are defined as follows:

| | |
|---|---|
| Operating gearing | $\dfrac{Profit\ before\ fixed\ operating\ costs}{Fixed\ operating\ costs}$ |

| Financial gearing | $\dfrac{\text{Profit before interest charges}}{\text{Interest charges}}$ |
|---|---|

In analysis of published accounting information, it is not possible to estimate the operating gearing because detailed information on fixed costs is not provided. Thus the term **gearing** is applied only in measuring financial gearing. Despite the lack of published information, professional investors will be aware of the importance of operating gearing and will try to understand as much as possible about the cost structure of the company and of the industry. The next section illustrates the benefits to shareholders of having gearing present when operating profits are rising and the risks when operating profits are falling.

### 13.4.3 Impact of gearing when profits are fluctuating

In a situation of fluctuating profits the presence of a fixed charge, such as an interest payment, will cause the profit for ordinary shareholders to fluctuate by a greater percentage. Exhibit 13.1 sets out data to illustrate this fluctuation. Company X has no gearing but company Y has loan finance in its capital structure.

**Exhibit 13.1**
**Data to illustrate the effect of gearing on profits for ordinary shareholders**

|  | X plc £m | Y plc £m |
|---|---|---|
| *Summary balance sheet* | | |
| Total assets minus current liabilities | 1,000 | 1,000 |
| Ordinary shares (£1 nominal value per share) | 1,000 | 500 |
| Loan stock (10% per annum) | – | 500 |
|  | 1,000 | 1,000 |
| *Expected level of profit* | | |
| Operating profit | 100 | 100 |
| Interest | – | (50) |
| Net profit for ordinary shareholders (A) | 100 | 50 |

Exhibit 13.2 uses the data to ask 'what happens to earnings per share if there is an increase or a decrease in operating profit?'

**Exhibit 13.2**
**Fluctuations in profit**

| | | |
|---|---|---|
| *(a) Effect of 20% decrease in operating profit* | | |
| Operating profit | 80 | 80 |
| Interest | | (50) |
| Net profit for ordinary shareholders (B) | 80 | 30 |
| Percentage decrease of (B) on (A) | 20% | 40% |
| *(b) Effect of 20% increase in operating profit* | | |
| Operating profit | 120 | 120 |
| Interest | – | (50) |
| Net profit for ordinary shareholders (C) | 120 | 70 |
| Percentage increase of (C) on (A) | 20% | 40% |

The conclusion to be drawn from Exhibit 13.2, panels (a) and (b), is that a 20% increase or decrease in operating profit causes a corresponding 20% increase or decrease in profit for ordinary shareholders in the ungeared company but a 40% increase or decrease in profit for ordinary shareholders in the geared company. It would appear preferable to be a shareholder in a geared company when profits are rising but to be a shareholder in an ungeared company when profits are falling.

## 13.5 Pyramid of ratios

The various ratios which contribute to the analysis of management performance may be thought of as forming a pyramid, as in Exhibit 13.3.

**Exhibit 13.3**
**Pyramid of ratios for analysis of management performance**

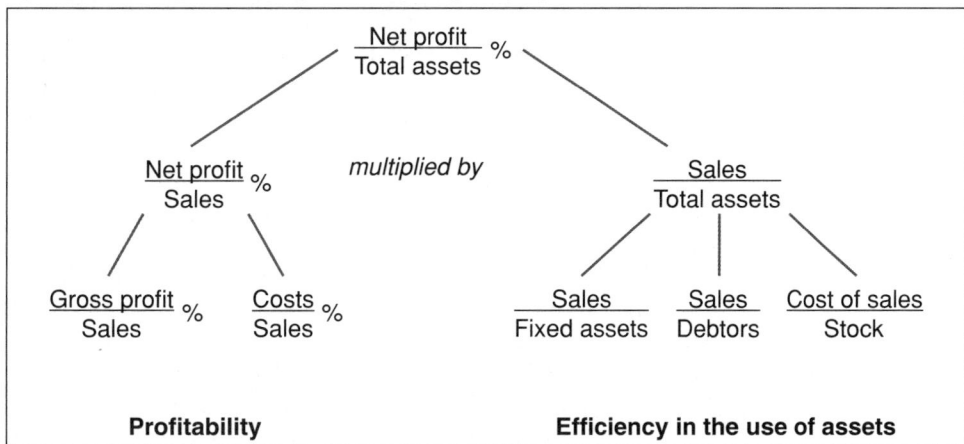

At the apex is the **return on capital employed** (measuring capital employed here as total assets). As the pyramid spreads out there are more detailed explanations of how the pyramid is built up. Net profit as a percentage of total assets has two components. One is the net profit as a percentage of sales (revenue) and the other is sales (revenue) as a multiple of total assets. Multiply these two together and you return to the net profit as a percentage of total assets. This relationship indicates that there could be two quite different types of business, both of which may be highly successful. One business trades on low margins, charging prices which look highly competitive, and succeeds by having a high level of sales (revenue) so that the assets are being used very effectively. The other business trades on high margins and sells goods or services less frequently. You could contrast the discount furniture store on the outskirts of town, where the car park is always full and the prices are unbeatable, with the old-world charm of the retail furnisher in the town centre whose prices look high but which attracts customers preferring extra service and attention. Both businesses are able to earn sufficient return on total assets to satisfy the owners.

The pyramid then spreads out into two areas: profitability and efficiency in the use of assets. The relationships here are additive – each component explains a little of the profitability of sales (revenue) or the efficiency in the use of assets. The pyramid is a useful tool of detective work to trace the cause of a change in return on capital employed.

## 13.6 Use and limitations of ratio analysis

The important feature of ratios is that they indicate trends and deviations from expected patterns. Ratios taken in isolation for a single company or a single period of time are of limited usefulness. The first requirement is to find a benchmark against which to compare ratios calculated for one period only.

### 13.6.1 Evaluating ratios by comparison

The comparison could be made with any or all of the following:

● the company's prior expectations of the outcome
● external observers' prior expectations of the outcome
● ratios based on previous years' figures for this company
● ratios calculated from this year's figures for other companies
● ratios calculated from previous years' figures for other companies
● industry averages published by commercial organisations.

The company's prior expectations are set out in a budget which is usually kept confidential. It is therefore unlikely that the user of the financial statements will have access to such a high-quality source of comparison. External observers may also have prior expectations. Professional analysts make forecasts of profits to help them or their clients in making investment decisions. The forecasts may be sent to clients of professional advisers, by way of investment advice bulletins. There are directories which publish such forecasts.

In the absence of information based on expectations, the user of the annual report may have to rely on the past as a possible predictor of the future, or on comparisons with other companies and industry norms. Professional investment advisers will collect data from annual reports and calculate ratios in their preferred manner. Advisory services will process the information and sell the results in the form of directories, on-line search facilities or CD-ROM with regular updates. One of the most widely used sources of ratio analysis of company accounts is Datastream, available in many colleges and universities and also used commercially. Organisations such as Reuters publish regular analyses of company information but usually charge a commercial fee. Newspapers and weekly journals such as the *Financial Times* and the *Investors Chronicle* are yet another source of information which will include ratios.

It could be argued that companies should themselves publish the norms against which their own particular results may be compared, but most would claim that their business is unique and no comparisons would be entirely valid.

### 13.6.2 Limitations

No two companies are exactly alike in the nature of their operations. Comparisons must make allowances for differences in the types of business or the relative weighting of different types of business. Many companies operate in more than one industry so that comparison with industry norms has to be treated with care.

Accounting numbers are used in ratio analysis and it has been a theme of the preceding chapters that accounting numbers may be affected by different accounting policies. The most common causes of variation due to accounting policy differences lie in depreciation and stock valuation, both of which are highly subjective.

Ratios are primarily a starting point from which to identify further questions to ask about the present position and future directions of the operations and the financing of a company. They do not provide answers in themselves.

## 13.7 Worked example of ratio analysis

In the following worked example, information is provided about a company buying and selling television and video equipment. Data are given for the current year in the first pair of columns and there are comparative figures for the previous year in the second pair of columns. Ratios are calculated for the two years as an indication of trends. Tentative comments are provided as to the possible interpretation of the resulting figures.

### 13.7.1 Financial statements to be analysed

**Peter (Television) plc**
**Profit and loss account**
**for the year ended 31 December Year 2**

|  | Year 2 | | Year 1 | |
| --- | --- | --- | --- | --- |
|  | £m | £m | £m | £m |
| Revenue |  | 720 |  | 600 |
| Cost of sales |  | (432) |  | (348) |
| Gross profit |  | 288 |  | 252 |
| Distribution costs | (72) |  | (54) |  |
| Administrative expenses | (87) |  | (81) |  |
|  |  | (159) |  | (135) |
| Operating profit |  | 129 |  | 117 |
| Interest payable |  | (24) |  | (24) |
| Profit before taxation |  | 105 |  | 93 |
| Taxation |  | (42) |  | (37) |
| Profit for the period for ordinary equity holders |  | 63 |  | 56 |

**Balance sheet as at 31 December Year 2**

|  | £m | £m | £m | £m |
| --- | --- | --- | --- | --- |
| Non-current (fixed) assets: |  |  |  |  |
| Land and buildings |  | 600 |  | 615 |
| Plant and equipment |  | 555 |  | 503 |
|  |  | 1,155 |  | 1,118 |
| Current assets: |  |  |  |  |
| Inventories (stock) | 115 |  | 82 |  |
| Trade receivables (debtors) | 89 |  | 61 |  |
| Prepayments | 10 |  | 9 |  |
| Bank | 6 |  | 46 |  |
|  | 220 |  | 198 |  |
| Current liabilities |  |  |  |  |
| Trade payables (creditors) | (45) |  | (30) |  |
| Taxation | (21) |  | (19) |  |
| Accruals | (29) |  | (25) |  |
|  | (95) |  | (74) |  |
| Net current assets |  | 125 |  | 124 |
|  |  | 1,280 |  | 1,242 |
| 6% debentures |  | (400) |  | (400) |
|  |  | 880 |  | 842 |
| Ordinary shares of £1 each |  | 500 |  | 500 |
| Retained earnings |  | 380 |  | 342 |
| Share capital and reserves |  | 880 |  | 842 |

**Extract from directors' report**

The directors propose a dividend of 6.0 pence per share in respect of Year 2 (Year 1: 5.0 pence), amounting to £30m in total (Year 1: £25m).

**Notes to the financial statements: Reconcilation of movements in equity**

|  | £m |
|---|---|
| Share capital and reserves at the end of year 1 | 842 |
| Less dividend paid in respect of year 1 | (25) |
| Add profit for year 2 | 63 |
| Share capital and reserves at the end of year 2 | 880 |

### 13.7.2    Share price information

When investors evaluate share price, they take the most up-to-date price available. However, for the exercise of comparing financial ratios it is useful to take the share prices immediately after the preliminary announcement at the end of February or beginning of March, representing the market's opinion when the accounting information has not become too much out of date.

Market price at 1 March Year 2    202 pence
Market price at 1 March Year 3    277 pence

### 13.7.3    Presenting the ratio calculations

Because there are so many variations on the methods of calculating ratios in accounting, it is extremely important to practise a useful and informative layout. That must include, at a minimum:

- the name of each ratio
- the formula in words
- the workings to show how the formula has been applied
- the value of the ratio
- a narrative comment.

Exhibits 13.4 to 13.7 present this information in a set of ratio calculations for Peter (Television) plc, each exhibit covering one of the main headings explained earlier. The calculations are given first for the more recent year, Year 2, followed by the comparative figures for Year 1. A commentary is provided for each exhibit.

**Activity 13.2**

*Use the ratios explained in section 13.6 to carry out a full analysis of the Year 2 column of the accounts of Peter (Television) plc. Prepare your analysis before you read Exhibits 13.4 to 13.7. When you have finished, compare your analysis with the ratios calculated. Where your answers differ, be sure that you understand whether it is due to an arithmetic error or a more fundamental point. Keep a note of your score of the number of items calculated correctly.*

*Then go back to Year 1 and repeat the exercise. Hopefully your score of correct items will have increased.*

**Exhibit 13.4**
**Investor ratios**

| Ratio | Definition in words | Year 2 Workings | Year 2 Result | Year 1 Workings | Year 1 Result |
|---|---|---|---|---|---|
| Earnings per share | $\dfrac{\text{Profit after tax for ordinary equity holders}}{\text{Number of issued ordinary shares}}$ | $\dfrac{63}{500}$ | 12.6 pence | $\dfrac{56}{500}$ | 11.2 pence |
| Price earnings ratio | $\dfrac{\text{Share price}}{\text{Earnings per share}}$ | $\dfrac{277}{12.6}$ | 22 | $\dfrac{202}{11.2}$ | 18 |
| Dividend per share | $\dfrac{\text{Dividend of the period}}{\text{Number of issued ordinary shares}}$ | $\dfrac{30}{500}$ | 6.0 pence | $\dfrac{25}{500}$ | 5.0 pence |
| Dividend cover (payout ratio) | $\dfrac{\text{Earnings per share}}{\text{Dividend per share}}$ | $\dfrac{12.6}{6.0}$ | 2.1 times | $\dfrac{11.2}{5.0}$ | 2.24 times |
| Dividend yield | $\dfrac{\text{Dividend per share}}{\text{Share price}} \times 100$ | $\dfrac{6.0}{277} \times 100\%$ | 2.17% | $\dfrac{5.0}{202} \times 100\%$ | 2.48% |

*Comment*: Earnings per share increased over the period, indicating an improved profit performance for shareholders. The price earnings ratio rose, indicating greater confidence in the stock market about the sustainability of this new level of profit. The dividend cover has fallen marginally, but is still more than twice covered. This marginal decrease in dividend cover is caused by increasing the dividend per share from 5 pence to 6 pence. The dividend yield has fallen, despite the increased dividend per share, because the market price has risen. The fall in yield may not be significant if it reflects a general trend in the market where, possibly, all shares have risen in price over the year. To say anything more about these ratios requires comparative figures for the industry and for the market as a whole. Both types of data would be found in the *Financial Times*.

**Exhibit 13.5**
**Analysis of management performance**

| Ratio | Definition in words | Year 2 | | Year 1 | |
|---|---|---|---|---|---|
| | | Workings | Result | Workings | Result |
| Return on shareholders' equity | $\dfrac{\text{Profit after tax for ordinary equity holders}}{\text{Share capital + Reserves}} \times 100\%$ | $\dfrac{63}{880} \times 100\%$ | 7.2% | $\dfrac{56}{842} \times 100\%$ | 6.7% |
| Return on capital employed | $\dfrac{\text{Operating profit (before interest and tax)}}{\text{(Total assets − Current liabilities)}} \times 100\%$ | $\dfrac{129}{1{,}280} \times 100\%$ | 10.1% | $\dfrac{117}{1{,}242} \times 100\%$ | 9.4% |
| Operating profit on sales (revenue) | $\dfrac{\text{Operating profit (before interest and tax)}}{\text{Sales (revenue)}} \times 100\%$ | $\dfrac{129}{720} \times 100\%$ | 17.9% | $\dfrac{117}{600} \times 100\%$ | 19.5% |
| Gross profit percentage | $\dfrac{\text{Gross profit}}{\text{Sales (revenue)}} \times 100\%$ | $\dfrac{288}{720} \times 100\%$ | 40% | $\dfrac{252}{600} \times 100\%$ | 42% |
| Total assets usage | $\dfrac{\text{Sales (revenue)}}{\text{Total assets}} \times 100\%$ | $\dfrac{720}{(1{,}155 + 220)}$ | 0.52 times | $\dfrac{600}{(1{,}118 + 198)}$ | 0.46 times |
| Fixed assets (non-current assets) usage | $\dfrac{\text{Sales (revenue)}}{\text{Fixed assets (non-current assets)}} \times 100\%$ | $\dfrac{720}{1{,}155}$ | 0.62 times | $\dfrac{600}{1{,}118}$ | 0.54 times |

*Comment*: The return on shareholders' equity and the return on capital employed both show an improvement on the previous year. This is due to an improvement in the use of assets (total assets and fixed assets) which more than offsets a fall in the operating profit as a percentage of sales (revenue). The gross profit percentage fell by a similar amount, which suggests that the price charged for goods and services is not keeping pace with increases in costs. The company should look carefully at either increasing prices or attempting to control costs of goods sold more effectively.

**Exhibit 13.6**
**Liquidity and working capital**

| Ratio | Definition in words | Year 2 | | Year 1 | |
|---|---|---|---|---|---|
| | | Workings | Result | Workings | Result |
| Current ratio | Current assets:Current liabilities | 220:95 | 2.3:1 | 198:74 | 2.7:1 |
| Acid test | (Current assets – Inventories):Current liabilities | (220 – 115):95 | 1.11:1 | (198 – 82):74 | 1.11:1 |
| Stock holding period (inventories holding period) | $\dfrac{\text{Average inventories (stock held)}}{\text{Cost of sales}} \times 365$ | $\dfrac{(115 + 82)/2}{432} \times 365$ | 83.2 days | $\dfrac{(*82 + 82)/2}{348} \times 365$ | 86 days |
| Customers' (trade debtors') collection period | $\dfrac{\text{Trade receivables (trade debtors)}}{\text{Credit sales (revenue)}} \times 365$ | $\dfrac{89}{720} \times 365$ | 45.1 days | $\dfrac{61}{600} \times 365$ | 37.1 days |
| Suppliers' (trade creditors') payment period | $\dfrac{\text{Trade payables (trade creditors)}}{\text{Credit purchases}} \times 365$ | $\dfrac{45}{432 + 115 - 82} \times 365$ | 35.3 days | $\dfrac{30}{348 + 82 - {*}82} \times 365$ | 31.5 days |

*Note:* \*Assuming the opening inventories are the same as the closing inventories.

*Comment:* The current ratio has fallen over the period while the acid test ratio remains constant. The ratios appear relatively high and are probably still within acceptable ranges (although this needs to be confirmed by comparison with industry norms). One cause of the relatively high current ratio at the start and end of the period appears to be in the combination of stock holding period and customers collection period compared to the suppliers payment period. The period of credit taken by customers has increased and this should be investigated as a matter of urgency. There is a marginal decrease in the stock holding period but it remains relatively long, compared to the creditors payment period. The acid test remains similar because there is an increase in the number of customer days for payment and a similar increase in the number of supplier days for payment.

**Exhibit 13.7**
**Gearing (leverage)**

| Ratio | Definition in words | Year 2 | | Year 1 | |
|---|---|---|---|---|---|
| | | Workings | Result | Workings | Result |
| Debt/equity ratio | $\dfrac{\text{Long-term liabilities plus Preference share capital}}{\text{Equity share capital + reserves}} \times 100\%$ | $\dfrac{400}{880} \times 100\%$ | 45.5% | $\dfrac{400}{842} \times 100\%$ | 47.5% |
| Interest cover | $\dfrac{\text{Operating profit (before interest and tax)}}{\text{Interest}}$ | $\dfrac{129}{24}$ | 5.38 times | $\dfrac{117}{24}$ | 4.88 times |

*Comment*: Gearing in the balance sheet has remained almost constant and the interest cover has increased marginally. The relative stability of the position indicates that there is probably no cause for concern but the ratios should be compared with those for similar companies in the industry.

## 13.8  Linking ratios to the cash flow statement

In Chapter 7 the cash flow statement of a company was illustrated and discussed. Any ratio analysis which seeks to interpret liquidity, management performance or financial structure should be related to the information provided by the cash flow statement. Ratios give a measure of position at a particular point in time while the cash flow statement gives some understanding of the movements in cash and cash-related items.

The operating cash flow will be explained by a note showing the movements in working capital and these may usefully be linked to changes in the rate of movement of stock or the period of credit allowed to customers and taken from suppliers. The ratio will give the change in terms of number of days, while the cash flow statement will indicate the overall impact on liquid resources.

If the efficiency in the use of fixed assets appears to have fallen, it may be that new assets were acquired during the year which, at the balance sheet date, were not fully effective in generating sales. That acquisition will appear in the cash flow statement. If the gearing has changed, the impact on cash flow will be revealed in the cash flow statement.

**Activity 13.3**    *Read again the sections of Chapters 3, 4 and 7 on cash flow statements. What is the purpose of the cash flow statement? What are the main headings? Which ratios may be used in conjunction with the cash flow statement to help understand the financial position of the company?*

### 13.8.1  Explanation of a cash flow statement

The cash flow statement in Exhibit 13.8 is calculated from the balance sheets and profit and loss account of Peter (Television) plc (see section 13.6). It is presented using headings similar to those of Safe and Sure in Chapter 7. The headings are taken from the international accounting standard IAS 7.

In Chapters 3, 5 and 6 you saw simple cash flow statements prepared using the information entered in the cash column of a spreadsheet. Those were examples of what is called the **direct method** of preparing a cash flow statement because the figures came directly from the cash column of the transaction spreadsheet. The cash flow statement in Exhibit 13.8 is said to be prepared using the **indirect method** because it takes an indirect route of starting with an accruals-based profit figure and then making adjustments to arrive at the cash figure. Consider each line in turn.

One purpose of the cash flow statement is to answer the question, 'Why do we have a cash problem despite making an operating profit?' We saw in Exhibit 3.7 of Chapter 3 that profit and cash flow can be different because the cash generated in making a profit is spent in various ways. The cash flow statement emphasises ways in which cash has come into, or moved out of, the company. So we start with profit before taxation of £129m.

Depreciation is an expense in the profit and loss account which represents cost being shared across accounting periods. There is no cash flow and so there should be no deduction for this item. To correct the position, depreciation of £50m is 'added back' as an adjustment to the accounting profit.

Next we consider how changes in working capital have affected cash flow. Looking first at current assets, we find that the inventories (stocks) have increased from £82m to £115m. Allowing inventories (stocks) to increase has reduced the cash available for other purposes. Trade receivables (debtors) have increased from £61 to £89. This means the cash is flowing less fast and so cash is reducing. Prepayments have increased

**Exhibit 13.8**
**Cash flow statement**

---

**Peter (Television) plc**
**Cash flow statement**
**for the year ended 31 December Year 2**

Notes: Assume depreciation charge for year is £50m.
　　　No non-current (fixed) assets were sold.

*[The words and figures printed in italics are not normally shown in published cash flow statements – they are to help you with interpretation.]*

|  | £m | £m |
|---|---|---|
| **Cash flows from operating activities** |  |  |
| Profit before taxation |  | 129 |
| Adjustment for items not involving a flow of cash: |  |  |
| 　Depreciation |  | 50 |
|  |  | 179 |
| Increase in inventories (stocks) *(115 – 82)* | 33 |  |
| Increase in trade receivables (debtors) *(89 – 61)* | 28 |  |
| Increase in prepayments *(10 – 9)* | 1 |  |
| *Reduction in cash due to increases in current assets* | 62 |  |
| Increase in trade payables (creditors) *(45 – 30)* | (15) |  |
| Increase in accruals *(29 – 25)* | ( 4) |  |
| *Increase in cash due to increases in liabilities* | (19) |  |
| *Reduction in cash due to working capital changes* |  | (43) |
| Cash generated from operations |  | 136 |
| Interest paid |  | (24) |
| Taxes paid *(42 +19 – 21)* |  | (40) |
| *Net cash inflow from operating activities* |  | 72 |
|  |  |  |
| **Cash flows from investing activities** |  |  |
| Capital expenditure *(1,155 – 1,118 + 50)* |  | (87) |
|  |  | (15) |
|  |  |  |
| **Cash flows from financing activities** |  |  |
| Equity dividends paid *(dividend proposed at end of Year 1)* |  | (25) |
| Decrease in cash |  | (40) |
| *Check in balance sheet Decrease in bank (46 – 6) = 40* |  |  |

---

from £9m to £10m. This is also using up cash. In total the increases in current assets have used up £62m of the cash generated in making profit.

Looking next at current liabilities, we see that trade payables (creditors) have increased from £30m to £45m. If payables (creditors) are increasing, it means they are not being paid. This helps cash flow by not spending it. Accruals have increased by £4m, again helping cash flow by not making a payment. It is not a good idea to help cash flow indefinitely by not paying creditors, but where stocks and debtors are expanding to use up cash flow, it is helpful if current liabilities are expanding in a similar way to hold back cash flow.

Interest paid is taken from the profit and loss account as £24m. There is no liability for unpaid interest at either the start of end of the period so the amount in the profit and loss account must equal the amount paid.

The taxation payment involves more calculation. Cash has been required to meet the liability of £19m remaining in the Year 1 balance sheet, and also to pay half of the tax expense of Year 2, which is £21m. The calculation is: tax expense of the year as shown in the income statement (profit and loss account), minus liability at the end of the year (balance sheet), plus liability at the start of the year (balance sheet).

Capital expenditure is calculated by comparing the book values at the beginning and end of the year and adjusting for changes during the year. We are told there were no sales of fixed assets so any increase must represent an addition. The balance started at £1,118m, fell by £50m for depreciation, increased by the unknown figure for additions, and finished at £1,155m. The missing figure is calculated as £87m.

The dividend paid during year 2 was the dividend proposed at the end of Year 1. If you look back to section 13.7.1, you will see the dividend paid as an entry in the 'reconciliation of movements on equity'.

Finally the right-hand column of the cash flow statement is added and produces a figure of £40m which is then checked against the balance sheet figures. This shows that cash has fallen from £46m to £6m and so the calculation is confirmed as being correct.

## 13.8.2 Analyst's commentary

Here is the comment made by one analyst in a briefing note to clients.

> Despite making a profit before taxation of £129,000, the cash balances of the company have decreased by £40,000 during the year.
>
> The cash generated by operating profit is calculated by adding back depreciation of £50,000 because this is an accounting expense which does not involve an outflow of cash. The resulting cash flow of £179,000 was eroded by allowing current assets to increase by more than the increase in current liabilities. This suggests that we should ask questions about the rate of usage of inventories (stocks) and the period of credit allowed to credit customers (debtors). Our analysis [see section 13.7] shows that the inventories (stocks) holding period reduced marginally from 86 to 83 days, which is not unexpected in the industry. The period of credit taken from suppliers increased by 4 days but the customers collection period increased by 8 days. Our attention should focus on the control of credit customers to look for any weaknesses of credit control and a potential risk of bad debts.
>
> After paying interest charges and taxation the company was still in cash surplus at £72,000 but swung into cash deficit through capital expenditure of £87,000. Taking in the dividend payment of £25,000 the positive cash flow of £72,000 changed to a negative cash flow of £40,000.
>
> We take the view that in the short run it is reasonable to run down cash balances in this way. The company probably had excessive liquidity at the end of Year 1. However if there is to be a further major investment in fixed assets we would want to see long-term finance being raised, either through a share issue or through a new long-term loan.

## 13.8.3 EBITDA

EBITDA stands for earnings before interest, taxation, depreciation and amortisation. It is increasingly used by analysts as an approximate measure of cash flow because it removes the non-cash expenses of depreciation and amortisation from profit. Instead of a price–earnings multiple based on earnings per share, the analyst will relate share price to EBITDA. The reason appears to be a desire to get away from the subjectivity of accruals-based profit and closer to cash flow as something objectively measured.

## 13.8.4 Free cash flow

'Free cash flow' is a phrase that you may encounter in company reports, particularly in the narrative discussions by the chief executive and the finance director. It is a term that is used differently by different people and so you have to read it in the setting where it is used. A common theme is to say, 'We have calculated our operating cash flow and allowed for investment in working capital and we have deducted the amount of cash invested in capital expenditure.' How much cash does that leave free to pay dividends or to invest in new ideas for expansion?

Following this theme, the calculation of free cash flows generally start with the net cash flow generated from operations (operating cash flow after tax) and then deducts the capital expenditure of the period. This leaves an amount of 'free' cash (in the sense of 'freely available' for future planning). The free cash is available to pay dividends to shareholders and to pay for further investment to expand the business. Directors have to decide their priorities and allocate the cash accordingly. If the free cash flow is a negative figure then the company will need to borrow to pay dividends or finance expansion.

## 13.9 Summary

The main areas of ratio analysis explained in this chapter are:

● investor ratios (summarised in Exhibit 13.4)
● analysis of management performance (summarised in Exhibit 13.5)
● liquidity and working capital (summarised in Exhibit 13.6)
● gearing (summarised in Exhibit 13.7).

Section 13.8 explains how the interpretation of ratios may be linked to an understanding of cash flows.

It is essential to treat ratio analysis with great caution and to understand the basis of calculation and the nature of the data used. For that reason the illustrations have been set out in detail using a layout that allows you to demonstrate your knowledge of the formula, your ability to collect data for calculation, and the result of that calculation which can then be interpreted. In this chapter all the information has been made available to you as and when you required it. In Chapter 14 we move on to consider published financial statements where more exploration may be required to find the most useful information.

The general principles explained in this chapter can be applied to the annual report of any profit-seeking business. The precise formulae may require adaptation to suit particular national characteristics. However international comparison requires great caution. Accounting policies and practices are not yet harmonised entirely. If the underlying data are not comparable then neither are the ratios.

The key is to ask first, 'What value do we expect for this ratio?' Then calculate the ratio and seek an interpretation of the similarity or difference.

## QUESTIONS

The Questions section of each chapter has three types of question. 'Test your understanding' questions to help you review your reading are in the 'A' series of questions. You will find the answers to these by reading and thinking about the material in the book. 'Application' questions to test your ability to apply technical skills are in the 'B' series of questions. Questions requiring you to show skills in problem solving and evaluation are in the 'C' series of questions. A letter [S] indicates that there is a solution at the end of the book.

## A  Test your understanding

**A13.1** Which ratios provide information on performance for investors? (Section 13.3.1)

**A13.2** Which ratios provide information on management performance? (Section 13.3.2)

**A13.3** Which ratios provide information on liquidity and working capital? (Section 13.3.3)

**A13.4** Which ratios provide information on gearing? (Section 13.3.4)

**A13.5** What is the view of investors on risk and return? (Section 13.4)

**A13.6** Why is financial gearing riskier for a company which has fluctuating profits? (Section 13.4.3)

**A13.7** Explain the use of the pyramid of ratios in analysis of performance. (Section 13.5)

**A13.8** What are the limitations of ratio analysis? (Section 13.6)

## B  Application

**B13.1** [S]
The following financial statements relate to Hope plc:

### Income statement (profit and loss account) for the year ended 30 June Year 4

|  | £000s | £000s |
|---|---|---|
| Revenue |  | 6,200 |
| Cost of sales |  | (2,750) |
| Gross profit |  | 3,450 |
| Administration and selling expenses |  | (2,194) |
| Operating profit |  | 1,256 |
| Debenture interest |  | (84) |
| Profit before taxation |  | 1,172 |
| Taxation |  | (480) |
| Profit for equity holder |  | 692 |

The directors have recommended a dividend of 36.7 pence per share in respect of Year 4, to be paid following approval at the next annual general meeting.

### Balance sheet as at 30 June Year 4

|  | £000s | £000s | £000s |
|---|---|---|---|
| Non-current (fixed assets) net of depreciation |  |  | 1,750 |
| Current assets: |  |  |  |
| Stocks and work-in-progress | 620 |  |  |
| Trade receivables (debtors) | 1,540 |  |  |
| Cash | 200 | 2,360 |  |
| *less*: Current liabilities: |  |  |  |
| Trade payables (creditors) | (300) |  |  |
| Other creditors and accruals | (940) | (1,240) |  |
| Net current assets |  |  | 1,120 |
| Total assets *less* current liabilities |  |  | 2,870 |
| Non-current liabilities |  |  |  |
| 6% debentures |  |  | (1,400) |
| Total net assets |  |  | 1,470 |
| Share capital and reserves |  |  |  |
| Issued share capital: |  |  |  |
| 900,000 ordinary shares of 50p nominal value |  |  | 450 |
| Retained earnings |  |  | 1,020 |
|  |  |  | 1,470 |

**Required**

(a) Calculate ratios which measure:
   (i) liquidity and the use of working capital;
   (ii) management performance; and
   (iii) gearing.
(b) Explain how each ratio would help in understanding the financial position and results of the company.
(c) The market price is currently 1,100 pence per share. Calculate ratios which are useful to investors.

**B13.2**

The following financial statements relate to Charity plc:

**Profit and loss account for year ended 30 September Year 4**

|  | £000s | £000s |
|---|---|---|
| Revenue |  | 2,480 |
| Cost of sales |  | (1,100) |
| Gross profit |  | 1,380 |
| Administration and selling expenses |  | (678) |
| Operating profit |  | 702 |
| Debenture interest |  | (31) |
| Profit before taxation |  | 671 |
| Taxation |  | (154) |
| Profit for equity holders |  | 517 |

Note: The directors have recommended a dividend of 11.4 pence per share in total in respect of Year 4, to be paid following approval at the next annual general meeting.

**Balance sheet as at 30 September Year 4**

|  | £000s | £000s | £000s |
|---|---|---|---|
| Non-current assets, net of depreciation |  |  | 785 |
| Current assets: |  |  |  |
| Inventories (stocks) | 341 |  |  |
| Trade receivables (debtors) | 801 |  |  |
| Cash | 110 | 1,252 |  |
| *less*: Current liabilities |  |  |  |
| Trade payables (creditors) | (90) |  |  |
| Other payable and accruals | (654) | (744) |  |
| Net current assets |  |  | 508 |
| Total assets *less* current liabilities |  |  | 1,293 |
| Non-current liabilities |  |  |  |
| 7% debentures |  |  | (440) |
| Total net assets |  |  | 853 |
| Share capital and reserves |  |  |  |
| Issued share capital |  |  |  |
| (1,360,000 ordinary shares of 25p nominal value) |  |  | 340 |
| Retained earnings |  |  | 513 |
|  |  |  | 853 |

**Required**

(a) Calculate ratios which measure:
   (i) liquidity and the use of working capital;
   (ii) management performance; and
   (iii) gearing.
(b) Explain how each ratio would help in understanding the financial position and results of the company.
(c) The market price of one share is 800 pence. Calculate ratios which will be of interest to investors.

## C    Problem solving and evaluation

**C14.1**

Carry out a ratio analysis of Safe and Sure plc, using the financial statements set out in Appendix I (at the end of this book) and applying the method of analysis set out in section 13.6. Making a comparison of Year 7 with Year 6, write a short commentary on each ratio separately and then summarise the overall themes emerging from the ratios. Assume a share price of 260 pence is applicable at 31 December Year 7 and a share price of 210 pence is applicable at 31 December Year 6.

# Chapter 15

# Reporting cash flows

### Review of the period: cash flow

There was a net cash inflow from operating activities of £119m during the half year. The operating profit of £483m and depreciation of £162m were partially offset by an increase in working capital requirements of £333m, reflecting higher debtors associated with the increase in average revenue and an increase in slab stock ahead of next year's blast furnace reline at IJmuiden. Interest payments were £71m in the first half of the year. Taxation paid was £113m reflecting the improvements in overseas profits. A net outflow of £170m was incurred on investing activities. Capital expenditure increased to £167m (2004: £139m) as the Group continued with its investment programme, including the completion of UK Restructuring capital expenditure in the period. After taking account of a £3m outflow on financing activities, cash and cash equivalents decreased by £54m (£58m including the impact of foreign exchange rate changes).

Source: Corus Group Plc Interim Report 2005, pp. 4–5.

### Discussion points

1 How does the discussion of cash flow reflect the three main sections of the cash flow statement (operating, investing and financing flows)?

2 The explanation refers to increased revenue causing higher debtors. Is that a sign of progress or of problems?

## Contents

## Learning outcomes

After reading this chapter you should be able to:

- Explain why cash flow statements are regarded as providing useful information
- Explain the meaning of cash and cash equivalents
- Explain the direct and the indirect forms of presentation of cash flow statements
- Prepare a cash flow statement using the direct and the indirect method.

## 15.1  Introduction

The cash flow statement is one of the primary financial statements. It provides information that can not be seen in the balance sheet and income statement (profit and loss account) alone. Users of financial statements want to know about changes in financial position. This involves providing information about an entity's ability to generate cash flows and the entity's use of those cash flows.

Chapter 3 gives a very simple introduction to cash flow statements. In particular it shows why cash flow and profit differ because of the different timings of cash flow and profits. Chapter 9 indicates the working capital cycle through which inventories are acquired from suppliers on credit and sold to customers on credit. The cash eventually received from customers is used to pay suppliers and the cycle starts again. Chapter 13 illustrates a cash flow statement prepared from the balance sheets and income statement of the illustrative company used in that chapter. The case study of Safe and Sure plc runs throughout several chapters with outline discussion of the cash flow statement in Chapter 4.

This chapter provides a more thorough explanation of cash flow statements as presented in the IASB system. It explains in sections 15.2 and 15.3 the nature of the two choices – the 'direct' and the 'indirect' methods. Section 15.4 explains the nature and purpose of each line item of a cash flow statement prepared using the indirect system. Section 15.5 explains the nature and purpose of each line item of a cash flow statement prepared using the direct system. Section 15.6 presents a worked example for those who wish to practise preparation of a cash flow statement based on the IASB system.[1]

## 15.2 Cash and cash equivalents

The IASB system[2] presents a cash flow statement that explains changes in **cash** and **cash equivalents**.

**Definitions**

**Cash** comprises cash on hand and demand deposits.

**Cash equivalents** are short-term, highly liquid investments that are readily convertible to known amounts of cash and which are subject to an insignificant risk of changes in value.[3]

Cash is relatively easy to understand – it is cash that is immediately available. Cash equivalents are investments that are held to meet short-term commitments. To qualify as a cash equivalent the investment must be readily convertible to a known amount of cash and there must be an insignificant risk of changes in value. An investment qualifies as a cash equivalent only when it has a short maturity of, say, three months or less from the date of acquisition.[4]

Bank borrowings are generally considered to be financing activities. However bank overdrafts that are repayable on demand are part of the cash management of a business. The bank balance fluctuates from a positive balance to an overdrawn balance at different times of the year.[5]

## 15.3 The direct method and the indirect method

There are two approaches to presenting the cash flows arising from operations. The direct method presents cash inflows from customers and cash outflows to suppliers and employees, taken from the entity's accounting records of cash receipts and payments. The indirect method starts with the operating profit and makes a series of adjustments to convert profit to cash. The data in Exhibit 15.1 and Exhibit 15.2 is used to illustrate each method.

**Exhibit 15.1**
**Income statement (profit and loss account), Year 2**

|  | £ |
|---|---|
| Revenue | 100 |
| Cost of sales: materials | (40) |
| Wages | (20) |
| Depreciation | (10) |
| Operating profit | 30 |

**Exhibit 15.2**
**Balance sheets, end of years 1 and 2**

|  | Year 2 | | Year 1 | |
|---|---|---|---|---|
|  |  | £ |  | £ |
| **Non-current assets** |  | 90 |  | 100 |
| **Current assets** |  |  |  |  |
| Inventory (stock) of materials | 55 |  | 40 |  |
| Trade receivables (debtors) | 12 |  | 15 |  |
| Cash | 35 |  | 10 |  |
|  | 102 |  | 65 |  |
|  |  |  |  |  |
| **Current liabilities** |  |  |  |  |
| Trade payables (creditors) | (11) |  | (14) |  |
| Current assets net of current liabilities |  | 91 |  | 51 |
|  |  |  |  |  |
| **Non-current liabilities** |  |  |  |  |
| Long-term loans |  | (100) |  | (100) |
| Net assets |  | 81 |  | 51 |
|  |  |  |  |  |
| **Ownership interest** |  | 81 |  | 51 |

## 15.3.1    Direct method

The direct method reports the cash inflows from customers and cash outflows to suppliers, employees and other aspects of operations. This information is contained in the cash book or in the cash receipts and cash payments records used as input to the bookkeeping records in the general ledger. The direct method calculation is presented in Exhibit 15.3. It is followed by a comment on each line in the calculation.

**Exhibit 15.3**
**Direct method**

| **Operating cash flow, Year 1** | |
|---|---|
|  | £ |
| Cash received from customers | 103 |
| Cash paid to suppliers | (58) |
| Wages paid | (20) |
| Operating cash flow | 25 |

*General comment*: In the direct method the cash flows are taken from the cash records. The cash records have to be analysed into categories suitable for the cash flow statement. In Chapters 5 and 6 you have seen spreadsheets in which the cash record is the 'cash at bank' column. That column was used as the basis for the simple cash flow statements on the direct method illustrated in those chapters (see sections 5.5.1 and 6.6.1). This chapter does not provide the detail of the cash records of receipts and payments but the following comments explain how the cash figures can be confirmed from the information in the balance sheet and the income statement (profit and loss account).

*Cash received from customers*: The cash inflows from customers may be confirmed by starting with the revenue earned in the period. Some of the revenue has been earned from selling to customers on credit. The amounts receivable from customers (debtors) at the start of the period will have been collected in cash during the period. The amounts shown as receivable from customers (debtors) at the end of the period are the revenue not yet collected in cash. This analysis is presented in the following calculation:

|                                           | £m    |
|-------------------------------------------|-------|
| Revenue of the period                     | 100   |
| Add receivables at the start of the period| 15    |
| Less receivables at the end of the period | (12)  |
| Cash received from customers              | 103   |

*Cash paid to suppliers*: The cash outflows to suppliers may be confirmed by starting with the materials purchased in the period. Some of the purchases have been obtained from suppliers on credit. The amounts payable to suppliers (creditors) at the start of the period will have been paid in cash during the period. The amounts shown as payable to suppliers (creditors) at the end of the period are the payments not yet made.

The next question is – how to confirm the figure for purchases?

The purchases of materials are needed to supply the goods sold and to provide an inventory at the end of the period. If there is an inventory (stock) at the start of the period this reduces the need to make purchases. This analysis is presented in the following calculation:

|                                           | £m    |
|-------------------------------------------|-------|
| Cost of materials sold in the period      | 40    |
| Add inventory at the end of the period    | 55    |
| Less inventory at the start of the period | (40)  |
| Purchases of materials                    | 55    |

Then the payment to suppliers is calculated.

|                                           | £m    |
|-------------------------------------------|-------|
| Purchases of the period                   | 55    |
| Add payables at the start of the period   | 14    |
| Less payables at the end of the period    | (11)  |
| Cash paid to suppliers                    | 58    |

*Wages paid*: Usually the wages are paid as soon as the work is done so the amount shown for wages in the income statement (profit and loss account) is the same as the cash payment. To confirm the wages payment, if any amount of wages remains unpaid at the start or end of the period then the wages cost must be adjusted for these unpaid amounts in a manner similar to the calculation of cash paid to suppliers.

## 15.3.2   Indirect method

The indirect method starts with the operating profit and makes adjustments to arrive at cash flow from operations. The indirect method calculation is presented in Exhibit 15.4. It is followed by an explanation of each line in the calculation.

**Exhibit 15.4**
**Indirect method**

| Operating cash flow, Year 1       |       |
|-----------------------------------|-------|
|                                   | £     |
| Operating profit                  | 30    |
| Add back depreciation             | 10    |
|                                   | 40    |
| (Increase) in inventory           | (15)  |
| Decrease in receivables           | 3     |
| (Decrease) in payables            | (3)   |
| Operating cash flow               | 25    |

*Operating profit*: This figure is taken from the income statement in Exhibit 15.1.

*Add back depreciation*: **Depreciation** is an accounting expense that does not involve any flow of cash. It is an **allocation** of the cost of the non-current (fixed) asset. So if we are looking for the cash generated by making profits, this depreciation needs to be excluded. It was deducted as an expense to calculate profit, so now it is added back to exclude it.

*(Increase) in inventory*: When a business acquires inventory it uses up cash. The cash is recovered when the inventory is sold. The greater the build-up of inventory, the greater the amount of cash that the business is waiting to recover. So an increase in inventory uses cash. A decrease in inventory releases cash and so is a source of cash.

*Decrease in receivables*: When a business sells goods or services to customers on credit it has to wait to collect the cash. The greater the increase in receivables (debtors) the greater is the amount of cash that the business is waiting to collect. So an increase in receivables has the effect of decreasing cash flow. A decrease in receivables releases cash and so is a source of cash.

*(Decrease) in payables*: When a business buys goods or services from suppliers on credit it delays payment of the cash. The greater the increase in payables (creditors) the greater is the amount of cash payment that the business is delaying. So an increase in payables has the effect of increasing cash flow by postponing payments. A decrease in payables means that suppliers are being paid sooner and so is equivalent to a use of cash.

*Change in cash in the balance sheet*: Finally it is important to check that the cash flow matches the change in cash in the balance sheet. Looking at the balance sheets in Exhibit 15.2 you will see that the cash has increased from £10m to £35m which equals the positive cash flow of £25m calculated by both the direct and the indirect method.

### 15.3.3  Which to choose – direct or indirect?

When students are asked at this point whether they prefer the direct or the indirect method they usually choose the direct method because it looks less cumbersome. In practice almost all companies choose the indirect method because it can be prepared from the opening and closing balance sheets and the income statement (profit and loss account). Some supporters also argue that it is useful to highlight the effect of working capital on cash flows.

The direct method needs more work to identify all the operating flows from the cash records. Bookkeeping records, as illustrated in the supplements to previous chapters in this book, are based on ledger accounts which include non-cash items. The sales ledger account, for example, combines cash sales and credit sales. All expense accounts combine expenses paid in cash and expenses obtained on credit. In practice the direct method creates additional work in analysing the accounting records, because there are many aspects to operating cash flow. Supporters of cash flow reporting advocate the direct method because it gives a clearer picture of cash flows. It also provides information on details of cash flows that is not available under the indirect method.

The standard setters recognise that there are valid arguments for and against each method and so continue to permit both. The IASB 'encourages' entities to report cash flow from operating activities using the direct method[6] but this encouragement appears to have been ineffective in many cases.

## 15.4 Preparing a cash flow statement: the indirect method

Most companies prepare their cash flow statement using the **indirect method**. This means they start with the reported operating profit and then make adjustments to work back to the cash amounts that are incorporated in profit and in working capital. This section explains the indirect method. A format for a cash flow statement is presented in Exhibit 15.5. Line numbers have been added at the left-hand side. Each line is explained in the section following Exhibit 15.5.

**Exhibit 15.5**
**Format for cash flow statement, indirect method**

| Line | | £m | £m |
|---|---|---|---|
| 1 | **Cash flows from operating activities** | | |
| 2 | Profit before taxation | | xx |
| 3 | Adjustment for items not involving a flow of cash: | | |
| 4 | Depreciation, amortisation, gain or loss on disposal of non-current assets etc | | xx |
| 5 | *Adjusted profit* | | xx |
| 6 | (Increase)/decrease in inventories | xx | |
| 7 | (Increase)/decrease in trade receivables | xx | |
| 8 | (Increase)/decrease in prepayments | xx | |
| 9 | *Increase/(decrease) in cash due to (increases)/decreases in current assets* | xx | |
| 10 | Increase/(decrease) in trade payables | xx | |
| 11 | Increase/(decrease) in accruals | xx | |
| 12 | *Increase/(decrease) in cash due to increases/(decreases) in liabilities* | xx | |
| 13 | *Increase/(decrease) in cash due to working capital changes* | | xx |
| 14 | Cash generated from operations | | xx |
| 15 | Interest paid | | (xx) |
| 16 | Taxes paid | | (xx) |
| 17 | *Net cash inflow from operating activities* | | xx |
| 18 | **Cash flows from investing activities** | | |
| 19 | Purchase of non-current assets | xx | |
| 20 | Proceeds from sale of non-current assets | xx | |
| 21 | Interest received | xx | |
| 22 | Dividends received | xx | |
| 23 | *Net cash used in investing activities* | | xx |
| 24 | **Cash flows from financing activities** | | |
| 25 | Proceeds from issue of share capital | xx | |
| 26 | Proceeds from long-term borrowing | xx | |
| 27 | Dividends paid | xx | |
| 28 | *Net cash used in financing activities* | | xx |
| 29 | Increase/(decrease) in cash and cash equivalents | | xx |
| 30 | **Cash and cash equivalents at the start of the period** | | xx |
| 31 | **Cash and cash equivalents at the end of the period** | | xx |

### Line 1 Cash flows from operating activities

This line indicates the start of the first major section of the cash flow statement, showing how cash flows are generated from the operations of the business.

### Line 2 Profit before taxation

The indirect method always starts with the operating profit *before* deducting interest and taxation, taken from the income statement (profit and loss account). This is because interest is seen as a separate payment to reward lenders and taxation is seen as a separate outflow of cash to government which need to be emphasised. If the operating profit includes any investment income or interest received this must also be removed because it is reported in the separate section for investing activities (see lines 21 and 22). So the following checklist should be used to ensure the correct starting point:

|  | £m |
|---|---|
| Operating profit before taxes | xx |
| *Is there any interest expense included in this figure? If so add it back to arrive at:* | xx |
| Operating profit before deducting interest payable and taxes | xx |
| *Is there any interest received/receivable or any dividends received in this figure? If so deduct it to arrive at:* | (xx) |
| Operating profit before deducting interest payable and taxes and before including interest receivable and dividends received. | xx |

### Line 3 Adjustment for items not involving a flow of cash

The finance director now looks at the profit figure and asks, 'Are there any items in here that do not involve a flow of cash? If so we want to remove these so that we can get closer to cash.' Most income statements (profit and loss accounts) contain depreciation and amortisation, which have no effect on cash. Other items to look out for are changes in provisions, unrealised gains and losses on foreign currency translation.

### Line 4 Adding back depreciation, amortisation, gain or loss on disposal etc

So the depreciation and amortisation are 'added back' to remove them from the profit figure. This usually causes some problems for readers of cash flow statements. If it worries you, just ask yourself – how did the depreciation get in there in the first place? The answer is that it was deducted as an expense, so if we add it back we exclude the expense. Other items that could come under this heading of 'not involving a flow of cash' are changes in provisions charged through income statement and gains or losses calculated on disposal of a non-current (fixed) asset. The following table summarises the action to be taken in the cash flow statement:

| Item in calculation | Reason |
|---|---|
| *Add back* any **expenses** that do not involve a flow of cash (e.g. depreciation, amortisation, loss on disposal of non-current assets). | These expenses reduced the profit but they do not involve any flow of cash and so must be excluded by adding back. |
| *Deduct* any **revenue** that does not involve a flow of cash (e.g. gain on disposal of non-current assets). | These revenues increased the profit but they do not involve any flow of cash and so must be excluded by deducting. |

### Line 5 Adjusted profit

In some presentations of the cash flow statement this line is not shown separately, but it it is a useful subtotal to remind yourself that you have now removed all non-cash items and you are ready to think about how working capital changes affect cash flow from operations.

### Line 6 (Increase)/decrease in inventories (stocks)

When a business buys inventories of raw materials or produces work-in-progress and finished goods, it uses up cash. The cash is only recovered when the inventories are sold. While the inventories are increasing the cash invested in them is increasing and there is a negative impact on cash flow.

The following table summarises the action to be taken in the cash flow statement:

| Item in calculation | Reason |
|---|---|
| *Deduct* increase in inventories | Allowing inventories to increase takes up more cash in paying for them, or prevents cash being obtained through sale. |
| *Add* decrease in inventories | Allowing inventories to decrease reduces the cash needed to pay for them, or allows cash to be obtained through sale. |

### Line 7 (Increase)/decrease in trade receivables (debtors)

When a business sells goods and services on credit to customers, these customers are given some time to pay. They become debtors of the business until they pay cash. Selling goods and services on credit encourages customers to buy from the business but it delays the flow of cash to the business. The longer the period of credit taken by customers, the longer the delay. The danger of allowing the period of credit to increase is that the customer may become increasingly reluctant to pay. Chapter 13 explains how to estimate the average period of credit taken by credit customers.

The following table summarises the action to be taken in the cash flow statement:

| Item in calculation | Reason |
|---|---|
| *Deduct* increase in receivables | Allowing amounts of receivables to increase means that cash is not being collected from credit customers. |
| *Add* decrease in receivables | Allowing amounts of receivables to decrease means that cash is being collected faster from credit customers. |

### Line 8 (Increase)/decrease in prepayments

When a business makes payments for expenses in advance of enjoying the benefit of the payment, there is an outflow of cash. Examples are rent in advance or insurance premiums in advance (see Chapter 9 for the accounting treatment of prepayments). If the business is making more prepayments, there is a greater outflow of cash. If the business reduces its prepayments the cash flow position improves.

The following table summarises the action to be taken in the cash flow statement:

| Item in calculation | Reason |
|---|---|
| *Deduct* increase in prepayments | If prepayments increase then more cash is being used to make payments in advance. |
| *Add* decrease in prepayments | If prepayments decrease then less cash is being used to make payments in advance. |

### Line 9 Increase/(decrease) in cash due to (increases)/decreases in current assets

This line adds all the increases in current assets and deducts all the decreases in current assets. If the current assets have increased in total then the cash flow has decreased.

If the current assets have decreased in total then the cash flow has increased. It is good practice to delete the alternative words here that do not apply to the particular circumstances of the company. Some published cash flow statements leave all the words in the statement but this can be very confusing to readers.

### Line 10 Increase/(decrease) in trade payables (creditors)

When a business buys goods or services on credit, the supplier often allows a period of credit. This helps the cash flow of the business in the gap between buying inputs and selling outputs of goods or services. The longer the period of credit taken from the supplier, the better the effect on cash flow. The danger of delaying payment beyond an agreed date is that the supplier may refuse to supply more goods or services and may even begin legal action for recovery of amounts owing. Chapter 13 explains how to calculate the average period of credit taken from suppliers.

The following table summarises the action to be taken in the cash flow statement:

| Item in calculation | Reason |
|---|---|
| Deduct decrease in payables | Allowing amounts of payables to decrease means that more cash is being paid to suppliers and other creditors. |
| Add increase in payables | Allowing amounts of payables to increase means that less cash is being paid to suppliers and other creditors. |

### Line 11 Increase/(decrease) in accruals

**Accruals** is the general description for unpaid expenses. If a business delays paying expenses there is a benefit for cash flow. If the accruals increase then there is a greater benefit for cash flow. The danger of delaying payment beyond an agreed dates is that the supplier may refuse to supply more goods or services and may even begin legal action for recovery of amounts owing.

The following table summarises the action to be taken in the cash flow statement:

| Item in calculation | Reason |
|---|---|
| Deduct decrease in accruals | Allowing amounts of unpaid expenses (accruals) to decrease means that more cash is being paid to settle these obligations. |
| Add increase in accruals | Allowing amounts of unpaid expenses (accruals) to increase means that less cash is being paid to settle these obligations. |

### Line 12 Increase/(decrease) in cash due to increases/(decreases) in liabilities

This line adds all the increases in current liabilities and deducts all the decreases in current liabilities. If the current liabilities have increased in total then the cash flow has benefited – less cash has been paid to settle current liabilities. If the current liabilities have decreased in total then the cash flow has suffered – more cash has been paid to settle liabilities. It is good practice to delete the alternative words here that do not apply to the particular circumstances of the company. Some published cash flow statements leave all the words in the statement but this can be very confusing to readers.

### *Line 13 Increase/(decrease) in cash due to working capital changes*

This line shows the result of comparing the change in current assets with the change in current liabilities. There are several combinations of increases and decreases in current assets and liabilities so the easiest way to think about the outcome is to ask 'what has happened to working capital (current assets less current liabilities) overall?

| |
|---|
| If the working capital has *increased*, then cash flow has *decreased*. |
| If the working capital has *decreased*, then cash flow has *increased*. |

### *Line 14 Cash generated from operations*

This is a subtotal combining the cash flow effect of the adjusted profit and the cash flow effect of the changes in working capital.

### *Line 15 Interest paid*

Interest must be paid on loans. If it is not paid on time the lender will take action to demand payment of the interest and might even demand immediate repayment of the loan in full, depending on the conditions of the loan agreement. The interest expense in the income statement represents the interest cost of the accounting period but if the payment dates fall outside the accounting period there may be an accrual of unpaid interest in the balance sheet. A calculation is required to arrive at the amount of cash paid during the accounting period.

| *Item in calculation* | *Reason* |
|---|---|
| Interest expense in income statement | We are starting with the expense in the income statement, to adjust it to a cash figure. |
| *minus* liability at end of period | This is the part of the expense that has not yet been paid in cash. |
| *plus* liability at start of period | During this period the liability at the start of the period has been paid. |
| *equals* cash paid to lenders | |

### *Line 16 Taxes paid*

There is a corporation tax expense in the income statement (profit and loss account). The due dates for payment depend on the size of the company, as explained in Chapter 10. Any unpaid taxation at the start or end of the period will appear as a liability in the balance sheet. A calculation is required to arrive at the amount of tax paid in the accounting period.

| *Item in calculation* | *Reason* |
|---|---|
| Taxation expense in income statement | We are starting with the expense in the income statement, to adjust it to a cash figure. |
| *minus* liability at end of period | This is the part of the expense that has not yet been paid in cash. |
| *plus* liability at start of period | During this period the liability at the start of the period has been paid. |
| *equals* cash paid to tax authorities | |

### Line 17  Net cash inflow from operating activities

This is a subtotal that indicates the end of the first major section of the cash flow statement.

### Line 18  Cash flows from investing activities

This line starts the second major section of the cash flow statement showing how cash has been used for making new investment in non-current assets and also released from sales of existing investment in non-current assets.

### Line 19  Purchase of non-current assets

In many cases the amount spent on non-current assets will be known from the accounting records. However if you are preparing a cash flow statement using only the balance sheet and income statement plus some notes, you may find that you need to calculate the amount spent on non-current assets. The following table summarises the calculation of changes in non-current assets which includes the cash payment. It assumes that all assets of one type are recorded together as one category (e.g. vehicles; plant and machinery). The following table summarises the calculation of changes in non-current assets which includes the cash payment for additions to non-current assets.

| Item in calculation | Reason |
|---|---|
| Original cost of non-current assets in a specified category at start of period | Begin with the amount of the assets at the start of the period. |
| **plus cash paid for additions** | **Cash is spent during the period on additions to the assets.** |
| Minus disposals at original cost | Assets are removed – see later calculation of gain or loss on disposal. |
| *equals* Non-current assets at end of period | The result is the amount of the assets at the end of the period. |

### Line 20  Proceeds from sale of non-current assets

This line reports the cash received from sale or disposal of non-current assets. It is important to use the cash received from the disposal of the asset and not the gain or loss on disposal recorded in the income statement (profit and loss account). Look back to Chapter 8 and you will see that the gain or loss on disposal arises only when the cash received is different from the book value. If the depreciation had been calculated with perfect foresight then the net book value would be equal to the cash received and there would be no gain or loss. A gain or loss on disposal is the result of estimating depreciation at the start of the asset's life when the proceeds on disposal have to be estimated.

The following table summarises the calculation relating to the sale or disposal of non-current assets which includes the cash received.

| Item in calculation | Comment |
|---|---|
| Original cost of non-current asset at start of period | This item of information is shown as 'disposal' in the 'cost' section of the schedule of non-current assets. |
| *Minus* accumulated depreciation of non-current asset at start of period | This item of information is shown as 'disposal' in the 'accumulated depreciation' section of the schedule of non-current assets. |
| **Minus cash received on disposal** | **This is the amount of cash received for the asset sold.** |
| *equals* gain or loss on disposal | The gain or loss on disposal is reported in the income statement. |

### Line 21  Interest received

Interest received is a reward for investment and so it is regarded as part of the cash flows relating to investing activities. Look back to the calculations in the workings for line 2 and you will see the item:

> Is there any interest received/receivable or any dividends received in this figure? If so deduct it.

The interest receivable is removed in calculating operating profit at line 2 so that interest received can be inserted at line 21. The following table summarises the action to be taken in the cash flow statement:

| Item in calculation | Reason |
|---|---|
| Interest receivable in the income statement | We are starting with the revenue reported in the income statement, to adjust it to a cash figure. |
| *minus* asset at end of period | This is the part of the revenue that has not yet been received in cash. |
| *plus* asset at start of period | During this period the asset at the start of the period has been received. |
| *equals* interest received in cash | |

### Line 22  Dividends received

The dividends received relate to equity investments held by the company. The calculation is very similar to that for interest received.

| Item in calculation | Reason |
|---|---|
| Dividend receivable in the income statement | We are starting with the revenue reported in the income statement, to adjust it to a cash figure. |
| *minus* asset at end of period | This is the part of the revenue that has not yet been received in cash. |
| *plus* asset at start of period | During this period the asset at the start of the period has been received. |
| *equals* dividend received in cash | |

### Line 23 Net cash used in investing activities

This sub-total indicates the end of the second major section of the cash flow statement. It will usually be a negative figure showing that the business is expanding through more investment in non-current assets. Less commonly, a business may be selling off existing investments to raise cash for future plans. Having the separate sub-total draws attention to the magnitude and direction of investing activities.

### Line 24 Cash flows from financing activities

This line starts the third and final major section of the cash flow statement showing how cash has been raised from financing activities. This usually means issuing new share capital and raising or repaying long-term loans.

### Line 25 Proceeds from issue of share capital

Chapter 12 explains the process of issuing share capital, both when the business starts and when it looks for more finance some time later. In many cases the shares are issued at market price which is higher than nominal value. The difference is called a share premium. The total cash raised is measured in terms of the market price but company law requires separate reporting of the change in nominal value and the changes in the share premium. The calculation required is as follows:

| Item in calculation | Reason |
|---|---|
| *Increase* in nominal value of share capital. *Increase* in share *plus* premium reserve. *equals* cash received from issue of shares. | The amount of cash raised by issuing shares at market price is the nominal value plus the share premium. |

### Line 26 Proceeds from long-term borrowings

The proceeds from long-term borrowings can be seen from the change in the balance sheet figures for long-term borrowings, after allowing for any long-term borrowings that have changed category to short term in the accounting period.

| Item in calculation | Reason |
|---|---|
| Long-term borrowing in balance sheet at the start of the period. | We are starting with amount reported in the balance sheet at the start of the accounting period. |
| *minus* long-term reclassified as short-term during the period. | This is the part of loan that is reclassified but remains in the balance sheet. |
| *plus* new loans taken up in cash. | Cash received. |
| *minus* loans repaid. | Cash paid out. |
| *equals* Long-term borrowing in balance sheet at the end of the period. | The amount reported in the balance sheet at the end of the accounting period. |

### Line 27 Dividends paid

The dividend paid during the period may be a combination of the dividend paid in respect of the previous year's profit plus an interim dividend for the current year.

Chapter 12 explains in more detail the accounting procedures for reporting dividends. The amount of dividend paid will appear in the statement of changes in equity.

### Line 28  Net cash used in financing activities

This sub-total indicates the end of the third section of the cash flow statement.

### Line 29  Increase/(decrease) in cash and cash equivalents

This line is the arithmetic total of the three separate sections as reported in lines 17 + 23 + 28.

### Lines 30 and 31  Cash and cash equivalents at the start and end of the period

This is the moment of truth where you find out whether you have made errors on the way through the cash flow statement. Lines 30 and 31 are taken from the balance sheet. If your cash flow statement is correct then line 29 plus line 30 will equal line 31. The following table is used to record the information extracted from the balance sheet.

|  | Start of period | End of period |
|---|---|---|
| Cash on hand and balances with banks | xx | xx |
| Short-term investments | xx | xx |
| Cash and cash equivalents | xx | xx |

## 15.5  Preparing a cash flow statement: the direct method

**Exhibit 15.6**
**Format for cash flow statement, direct method**

| Line |  | £m | £m |
|---|---|---|---|
| 1 | **Cash flows from operating activities** | | |
| 2 | Cash receipts from customers | | xx |
| 3 | Cash paid to suppliers | | xx |
| 4 | Cash paid to employees | | xx |
| 5–13 | *(Lines not used)* | | |
| 14 | Cash generated from operations | | xx |
| 15 | Interest paid | | (xx) |
| 16 | Taxes paid | | (xx) |
| 17 | *Net cash inflow from operating activities* | | xx |
| 18 | **Cash flows from investing activities** | | |
| 19 | Purchase of non-current assets | xx | |
| 20 | Proceeds from sale of non-current assets | xx | |
| 21 | Interest received | xx | |
| 22 | Dividends received | xx | |
| 23 | *Net cash used in investing activities* | | xx |
| 24 | **Cash flows from financing activities** | | |
| 25 | Proceeds from issue of share capital | | |
| 26 | Proceeds from long-term borrowing | | |
| 27 | Dividends paid | | |
| 28 | *Net cash used in financing activities* | | |
| 29 | Increase/(decrease) in cash and cash equivalents | | |
| 30 | **Cash and cash equivalents at the start of the period** | | |
| 31 | **Cash and cash equivalents at the end of the period** | | |

*Line 1  Cash flows from operating activities*

This line indicates the start of the first major section of the cash flow statement, showing how cash flows are generated from the operations of the business.

*Line 2  Cash receipts from customers*

This line reports the total cash received from customers in the period. Some customers may have paid immediate cash for goods and services. Others may have taken credit and paid later.

*Line 3  Cash paid to suppliers*

This line reports the total cash paid to suppliers in the period. The business may have paid immediate cash for some goods and services. In other cases the suppliers may have allowed a period of credit to be paid later.

*Line 4  Cash paid to employees*

This line reports the total cash paid to employees in the period. Usually the employees are paid promptly each week or each month and so the cash payments are closely related to the wages expense.

Lines 14 to 31 have the same meaning as described for these lines in Section 15.4.

## 15.6  Interpretation of cash flow information

The cash flow information is useful in itself in showing trends in the company's cash resources. Some businesses operate on cycles lasting several years where the cash position moves from negative to positive. The industry position is often a useful starting point for understanding company cash flows. If the industry is cyclical and all companies in the sector have negative cash flow then we might expect any company in the sector to show the same trends. Equally, any company in the sector should be showing signs of improvement as the cycle moves upwards.

For the indirect method, which reports the cash flow effects of working capital, it may be useful to link the increases or decreases in working capital items to the number of days in the working capital cycle. The calculation of the working capital cycle appears in Chapter 13. For example, if there is an increase in cash invested in inventory there are two possible causes: one is a lengthening of the stock holding period and the other is an increase in sales volume causing more inventory to be held. The stock holding period helps to narrow down the possible cause. If the trade receivables increase there are two possible causes. One is that customers are taking longer to pay and the other is that credit sales are increasing. The period of credit given to customers helps to narrow down the cause here.

The amount of cash invested in capital expenditure is an important sign of the continuing development of the business. Ratios are used by analysts in comparing capital expenditure to depreciation and comparing capital expenditure to the existing asset base.

## 15.7  Illustration

The following information is used to illustrate the indirect method and then compare the direct method of preparing and presenting a cash flow statement.

*Income statement Year 2*

| | £m |
|---|---|
| Revenue | 246 |
| Cost of sales | (110) |
| Gross profit | 136 |
| Investment income – interest received | 4 |
| Gain on disposal of equipment | 5 |
| Depreciation | (30) |
| Administrative and selling expenses | (10) |
| Operating profit before interest | 105 |
| Interest expense | (15) |
| Profit after deducting interest | 90 |
| Taxation | (30) |
| Profit after tax | 60 |

**Balance sheets at 31 December**

| | Year 2 | | Year 1 | |
|---|---|---|---|---|
| | £m | £m | £m | £m |
| **Non-current assets** | | | | |
| Property, plant and equipment at cost | | 150 | | 100 |
| Accumulated depreciation 40 + 30 − 10 | | (60) | | (40) |
| | | 90 | | 60 |
| Investments | | 100 | | 100 |
| **Current assets** | | | | |
| Inventory (stock) | 20 | | 15 | |
| Trade receivables (debtors) | 18 | | 16 | |
| Cash and cash equivalents | 32 | | 5 | |
| | 70 | | 36 | |
| **Current liabilities** | | | | |
| Trade payables (creditors) | (14) | | (13) | |
| Interest payable | (6) | | (7) | |
| Taxes payable | (8) | | (7) | |
| | (28) | | (27) | |
| | | 42 | | 9 |
| **Non-current liabilities** | | | | |
| Long-term loans | | (20) | | (15) |
| Net assets | | 212 | | 154 |
| **Capital and reserves** | | | | |
| Share capital | | 140 | | 130 |
| Share premium | | 20 | | 18 |
| Retained earnings | | 52 | | 6 |
| | | 212 | | 154 |

*Further information*
1 The dividend paid during Year 2 was £14m. The retained earnings increased by £60m profit of the period and decreased by the amount of the dividend £14m.
2 During Year 2 the company acquired property, plant and equipment costing £80m.
3 During Year 2 the company sold property, plant and equipment that had an original cost of £30m and accumulated deprecation of £10m. The proceeds of sale were £25m.

### 15.7.1  Indirect method

A cash flow statement using the indirect method is presented in Exhibit 15.7.

**Exhibit 15.7**
**Cash flow statement using the indirect method**

| Notes | | £m | £m |
|---|---|---:|---:|
| | **Cash flows from operating activities** | | |
| 1 | Profit before taxation | | 101 |
| | Adjustment for items not involving a flow of cash: | | |
| 2 | Depreciation | 30 | |
| 3 | Gain on disposal of equipment | (5) | |
| | | | 25 |
| | *Adjusted profit* | | 126 |
| 4 | (Increase) in inventories | (5) | |
| 5 | (Increase) in trade receivables | (2) | |
| 6 | Increase in trade payables | 1 | |
| | *Increase/(decrease) in cash due to working capital changes* | | (6) |
| | Cash generated from operations | | 120 |
| 7 | Interest paid | | (16) |
| 8 | Taxes paid | | (29) |
| | *Net cash inflow from operating activities* | | 75 |
| | **Cash flows from investing activities** | | |
| 9 | Purchase of non-current assets | (80) | |
| 10 | Proceeds from sale of non-current assets | 25 | |
| 11 | Interest received | 4 | |
| | *Net cash used in investing activities* | | (51) |
| | **Cash flows from financing activities** | | |
| 12 | Proceeds from issue of share capital | 12 | |
| 13 | Proceeds from long-term borrowing | 5 | |
| 14 | Dividends paid | (14) | |
| | *Net cash used in financing activities* | | 3 |
| | Increase/(decrease) in cash and cash equivalents | | 27 |
| 15 | **Cash and cash equivalents at the start of the period** | | 5 |
| 15 | **Cash and cash equivalents at the end of the period** | | 32 |

*Working note 1*

| | £m |
|---|---:|
| Operating profit before taxes | 90 |
| Is there any interest expense included in this figure? If so add it back to arrive at: | 15 |
| Operating profit before deducting interest payable and taxes | 105 |
| Is there any interest received/receivable or any dividends received in this figure? If so deduct it to arrive at: | (4) |
| Operating profit before deducting interest payable and taxes and before including interest receivable and dividends received. | 101 |

*Working note 2*

The depreciation is seen in the income statement (profit and loss account). It is added back to exclude the effect of a non-cash item.

*Working note 3*

The gain on disposal is seen in the income statement (profit and loss account). It is added back to exclude the effect of a non-cash item.

*Working note 4*

There is an increase in inventory seen by comparing the balance sheets at the end of year 1 and year 2. This decreases the cash flow.

*Working note 5*

There is an increase in trade receivables (debtors) seen by comparing the balance sheets at the end of year 1 and year 2. This decreases the cash flow.

*Working note 6*

There is an increase in trade payables (creditors) seen by comparing the balance sheets at the end of year 1 and year 2. This has a positive effect on the cash flow by increasing the amount unpaid.

*Working note 7*

Interest paid is calculated from the profit and loss account expense £15m plus the unpaid interest at the start of the year £7m minus the unpaid interest at the end of the year, £6m.

*Working note 8*

Taxes paid are calculated from the profit and loss account charge £30m plus the unpaid liability at the start of the year £7m minus the unpaid liability at the end of the year £8m.

*Working note 9*

The purchase cost of non-current assets is given in the further information. It can be checked by taking the cost at the start of the year £100m, adding £80m and deducting the £30m cost of the disposal to leave £150m as shown in the balance sheet at the end of the year.

*Working note 10*

The proceeds of sale £25m are given in the further information. This can be checked by taking the net book value of the asset sold (£30m − £10m = £20m) and adding the gain on disposal £5m shown in the income statement.

*Working note 11*

The interest received is taken from the income statement. There is no interest receivable shown in the balance sheet so the profit and loss account figure must be the same as the cash figure.

*Working note 12*

The proceeds from the share issue are the total of the increase in share capital £10m plus the increase in share premium £2m.

*Working note 13*

The proceeds from long-term borrowings are the increase in long-term loans calculated by comparing the opening and closing balance sheets.

*Working note 14*

The dividend paid is given in the further information. It can be checked by taking the retained earnings at the start of the period £6m, add the profit of the period £60m and deduct dividend £14m to arrive at the retained earnings at the end of the period, £52m.

*Working note 15*

The cash and cash equivalents at the start and end of the period are taken from the balance sheet.

## 15.7.2   Direct method

A cash flow statement presented by the direct method is presented in Exhibit 15.8.

**Exhibit 15.8**
**Cash flow statement using the direct method**

| Notes | | £m | £m |
|---|---|---:|---:|
| | **Cash flows from operating activities** | | |
| 1 | Cash receipts from customers | | 244 |
| 2 | Cash paid to suppliers and employees | | (114) |
| 3 | Cash paid for administrative and selling expenses | | (10) |
| | Cash generated from operations | | 120 |
| 4 | Interest paid | | (16) |
| 5 | Taxes paid | | (29) |
| | *Net cash inflow from operating activities* | | 75 |
| | **Cash flows from investing activities** | | |
| 6 | Purchase of non-current assets | (80) | |
| 7 | Proceeds from sale of non-current assets | 25 | |
| 8 | Interest received | 4 | |
| | *Net cash used in investing activities* | | (51) |
| | **Cash flows from financing activities** | | |
| 9 | Proceeds from issue of share capital | 12 | |
| 10 | Proceeds from long-term borrowing | 5 | |
| 11 | Dividends paid | (14) | |
| | *Net cash used in financing activities* | | 3 |
| | Increase/(decrease) in cash and cash equivalents | | 27 |
| 12 | **Cash and cash equivalents at the start of the period** | | 5 |
| 12 | **Cash and cash equivalents at the end of the period** | | 32 |

In practice the cash receipts from customers and cash payments to suppliers and employees are taken from the records of cash received and paid, which requires analysis of the cash records. In this relatively straightforward situation the figures may be confirmed from the information in the balance sheet and income statement (profit and loss account).

### Working note 1

The cash receipts from customers may be confirmed from revenue £246m plus receivables at the start of the period £16m minus receivables at the end of the period £18m equals £244m.

### Working note 2

There are two stages to the confirmation of cash paid to suppliers. First the purchases are calculated from cost of sales £110m plus inventory at the end £20m minus inventory at the start £15m = £115m. Next the payment to suppliers is confirmed from purchases £115m plus liability at the start £13m minus liability at the end £14m equals £114m. It is assumed that the wages are all paid when the work is done so there is no accrual.

### Working note 3

The administrative and selling expenses are seen in the income statement. There is no accrual indicated in the balance sheet and so the cash figure equals the expense figure.

### Working notes 4 to 12

See working notes 7 to 15 for the indirect method.

### 15.7.3 Comment on cash flow statement

The cash flow from operating activities amounted to £75m. The purchase of non-current (fixed) assets cost £80m but this was offset by £25m proceeds of sale of non-current assets no longer required and was also helped by the £4m interest received from investments. The net outflow from investments was £51m. This left £24m of cash flow available to increase cash resources but £14m was required for dividend payments. The remaining £10m was added to the proceeds of a share issue, £12m and an increase in long-term loans, £5m, giving an overall cash inflow of £27m.

## 15.8 Summary

- The cash flow statement provides information about changes in financial position that adds to the understanding of the business obtainable from the balance sheet and income statement (profit and loss account).
- It explains changes in cash and cash equivalents arising from operating activities, investing activities and financing activities.
- **Cash** comprises cash on hand and demand deposits.
- **Cash equivalents** are short-term, highly liquid investments that are readily convertible to known amounts of cash and which are subject to an insignificant risk of changes in value.
- The **indirect method** and the **direct method** are alternative approaches to calculating the cash flow arising from operating activities.
- The **indirect method** starts with the profit from operations, eliminates non-cash expenses such as depreciation, and adds on or deducts the effects of changes in working capital to arrive at the cash flow arising from operating activities.
- The **direct method** takes each item of operating cash flow separately from the cash records to arrive at the cash flow arising from operating activities.
- The cash flow is useful in analysis when combined with ratio analysis that shows relationships of liquidity, working capital management, rates of investment in non-current assets and financial gearing.

### Further reading

The following standard is too detailed for a first level course but the definitions section may be helpful and the Appendices give illustrations of cash flow statements.

IASB (2004), IAS 7, *Cash flow statements*, International Accounting Standards Board.

## QUESTIONS

The Questions section of each chapter has three types of question. 'Test your understanding' questions to help you review your reading are in the 'A' series of questions. You will find the answers to these by reading and thinking about the material in the book. 'Application' questions to test your ability to apply technical skills are in the 'B' series of questions. Questions requiring you to show skills in problem solving and evaluation are in the 'C' series of questions. A letter [S] indicates that there is a solution at the end of the book.

## A    Test your understanding

**A15.1**    What is the definition of 'cash'? (Section 15.2)

**A15.2**    What is the definition of 'cash equivalent'? (Section 15.2)

**A15.3**    What is meant by the 'direct method' of calculating operating cash flow? (Section 15.3.1)

**A15.4**    What is meant by the 'indirect method' of calculating operating cash flow? (Section 15.3.2)

**A15.5**    Why is depreciation 'added back' to operating profit in the indirect method of calculating operating cash flow? (Section 15.3.2)

**A15.6**    What is the effect on cash flow of an increase in inventory levels? (Section 15.3.2)

**A15.7**    What is the effect on cash flow of an increase in trade receivables (debtors)? (Section 15.3.2)

**A15.8**    What is the effect on cash flow of an increase in trade payables (creditors)? (Section 15.3.2)

**A15.9**    What are the relative benefits of the direct method compared to the indirect method? (Section 15.3.3)

**A15.10**    What are the three main sections of a cash flow statement? (Section 15.4)

**A15.11**    What kinds of items in a profit and loss account do not involve a flow of cash? (Section 15.4)

**A15.12**    What happens to cash flow when working capital increases? (Section 15.4)

**A15.13**    How is taxation paid calculated from the taxation payable and the taxation liability at the start and end of the period? (Section 15.4)

**A15.14**    How is the cash paid for additions to fixed assets if we know the opening and closing balances and there are no disposals? (Section 15.4)

**A15.15**    Explain how the proceeds of sale of a non-current asset differ from the net book value. (Section 15.4)

**A15.16**    Explain how the cash proceeds of a share issue are calculated from knowledge of the share capital and the share premium reserve. (Section 15.4)

**A15.17**    Explain how cash received from customers is calculated if we know the sales of the period and the receivables (debtors) at the start and end of the period. (Section 15.5)

**A15.18**    Explain how the purchases of goods or materials is calculated if we know the cost of goods sold and the inventory (stock) at the start and end of the period. (Section 15.5)

**A15.19**    Explain how the cash paid to suppliers is calculated if we know the purchases and the payables (creditors) at the start and end of the period. (Section 15.5)

## B    Application

**B15.1** [S]
Sales on credit during Year 2 amount to £120m. The trade receivables (debtors) at the start of Year 2 were £8. The trade receivables (debtors) at the end of Year 2 were £10. What is the amount of cash received from customers during Year 2?

**B15.2** [S]
Purchases on credit during Year 3 amount to £20m. The trade payables (creditors) at the start of Year 3 were £6m. The trade payables (creditors) at the end of Year 3 were £4m. What is the amount of cash paid to suppliers during Year 3?

**B15.3** [S]

The equipment at cost account at the start of Year 2 records a total of £34m. The equipment at cost account at the end of Year 2 records a total of £37m. An asset of original cost £5m was sold during the period. What was the amount spent on acquisition of equipment?

**B15.4**

A vehicle costing £20m and having accumulated depreciation of £12m was sold for £5m. How will this information be reported in the cash flow statement?

**B15.5**

The share capital account increased by £40m during Year 4. The share premium reserve increased by £20m. What amount of cash was raised by the issue of shares?

**B15.6**

The corporation tax charge in the income statement (profit and loss account) for Year 2 was £30m. The tax liability in the balance sheet at the start of Year 2 was £6m. The tax liability in the balance sheet at the end of Year 2 was £10m. What was the amount of cash paid in taxation during Year 2?

**B15.7**

D Ltd has an operating profit of £12m, which includes a depreciation charge of £1m. During the year the trading stock has increased by £4m, trade debtors have increased by £3m and trade creditors have increased by £5m. Prepare a statement of cash flow from operations.

**B15.8**

E Ltd has an operating profit of £16m, which includes a depreciation charge of £2m. During the year the trading stock has increased by £1m, trade debtors have decreased by £3m and trade creditors have decreased by £2m. Prepare a statement of cash flow from operations.

## C    Problem solving and evaluation

**C15.1** [S]

The directors of Transport plc produced the following income statement (profit and loss account) for Year 2 and balance sheet at the end of Year 2.

**Income statement for year 2**

|  | £m |
|---|---|
| Revenue | 320 |
| Cost of sales | (143) |
| Gross profit | 177 |
| Investment income – interest received | 5 |
| Gain on disposal of equipment | 7 |
| Depreciation | (39) |
| Administrative and selling expenses | (13) |
| Operating profit before interest | 137 |
| Interest expense | (20) |
| Profit after deducting interest | 117 |
| Taxation | (35) |
| Profit after tax | 82 |

**Balance sheets at 31 December**

|  | Year 2 | | Year 1 | |
| --- | --- | --- | --- | --- |
|  | £m | £m | £m | £m |
| **Non-current assets** | | | | |
| Vehicles at cost | | 195 | | 130 |
| Accumulated depreciation | | (79) | | (52) |
| | | 116 | | 78 |
| Investments | | 100 | | 80 |
| **Current assets** | | | | |
| Inventory (stock) | 26 | | 20 | |
| Trade receivables (debtors) | 23 | | 21 | |
| Cash and cash equivalents | 43 | | 6 | |
| | 92 | | 47 | |
| **Current liabilities** | | | | |
| Trade payables (creditors) | (18) | | (13) | |
| Interest payable | (8) | | (7) | |
| Taxes payable | (10) | | (7) | |
| | (36) | | (27) | |
| | | 56 | | 20 |
| **Non-current liabilities** | | | | |
| Long-term loans | | (26) | | (18) |
| Net assets | | 246 | | 160 |
| **Capital and reserves** | | | | |
| Share capital | | 152 | | 120 |
| Share premium | | 26 | | 23 |
| Retained earnings | | 68 | | 17 |
| | | 246 | | 160 |

*Further information*

1  The dividend paid during Year 2 was £31m. The retained earnings increased by £82m profit of the period and decreased by the amount of the dividend £31m.
2  During Year 2 the company acquired vehicles costing £90m.
3  During Year 2 the company sold vehicles that had an original cost of £25m and accumulated depreciation of £12m. The proceeds of sale were £20m.

**Required**

1  Prepare a cash flow statement using (a) the direct method and (b) the indirect method of calculating operating cash flow.
2  Write a comment on the cash flow of the period.

**C15.2**

Consider the following:

|  | £m |
| --- | --- |
| Revenue | 320 |
| Cost of sales | (143) |
| Gross profit | 177 |
| Investment income – interest received | 5 |
| Loss on disposal of equipment | (8) |
| Depreciation | (39) |
| Administrative and selling expenses | (13) |
| Operating profit before interest | 122 |
| Interest expense | (6) |
| Profit after deducting interest | 116 |
| Taxation | (39) |
| Profit after tax | 77 |

## Balance sheets at 31 December

| | Year 2 | | Year 1 | |
|---|---|---|---|---|
| | £m | £m | £m | £m |
| Property, plant and equipment at cost | | 225 | | 150 |
| Accumulated depreciation | | (90) | | (60) |
| | | 135 | | 90 |
| Investment | | 70 | | 100 |
| Inventory (stock) | 30 | | 22 | |
| Trade receivables (debtors) | 27 | | 24 | |
| Cash and cash equivalents | 48 | | 8 | |
| | 105 | | 54 | |
| Trade payables (creditors) | (21) | | (20) | |
| Interest payable | (9) | | (11) | |
| Taxes payable | (12) | | (9) | |
| | (42) | | (40) | |
| | | 63 | | 14 |
| Long-term loans | | (20) | | (15) |
| Net assets | | 248 | | 189 |
| Share capital | | 144 | | 140 |
| Share premium | | 26 | | 23 |
| Retained earnings | | 78 | | 26 |
| | | 248 | | 189 |

*Further information*

1  The dividend paid during Year 2 was £25m. The retained earnings increased by £77m profit of the period and decreased by the amount of the dividend, £25m.
2  During Year 2 the company acquired property, plant and equipment costing £94m.
3  During Year 2 the company sold for scrap property, plant and equipment that had an original cost of £19m and accumulated depreciation of £9m. The proceeds of disposal were £2m.
4  Investments were sold during the year for cash proceeds of £30m. There were no purchases of investments.

**Required**

1  Prepare a cash flow statement using (a) the direct method and (b) the indirect method of calculating operating cash flow.
2  Write a comment on the cash flow of the period.

## Notes and references

1. Cash flow statements in published financial statements are often prepared for a group as a whole. The details of group cash flow statements are too complex for a first level text but in general appearance they are similar to those for individual companies.
2. IASB (2004), IAS 7 *Cash flow statements*.
3. IAS 7 para. 6.
4. IAS 7 para. 7.
5. IAS 7 para. 8.
6. IAS 7 para. 18a.

# Chapter 16

# Functions of management accounting

## REAL WORLD CASE

This case study describes the role of the management accountant. Read it now, but only attempt the discussion points after you have finished studying the chapter.

The day of the 'bean counter' has gone forever.

Line managers responsible for the day-to-day profitability of their business operations use sophisticated software to analyse the financial consequences of their decisions. Financial record-keeping and analysis are automated. And financial accountability has become a key part of every executive's job description.

Meanwhile, to maintain the growth rates that capital markets demand, business leaders are compelled to make increasingly risky decisions. They look to their finance people to support and participate in these decisions to help them understand the risks and likely consequences and to help manage the rapid change that their organisations must then undergo.

This means that management accountancy skills influence every area of a business, are internationally recognised and are valued in every business and industry sector.

Source: 'Your career', website of the Chartered Institute of Management Accountants, 2005, www.cimaglobal.com/main/prospective/career/

## Discussion points

1 What does the phrase 'bean counter' mean?

2 How do line managers and business leaders use management accountants to help them in their management activities?

**Contents**

**Learning outcomes**

After studying this chapter you should be able to:

- Explain how the definition of 'accounting' represents the subject of management accounting.
- Explain the needs of internal users of accounting information.
- Describe the management functions of planning, decision making and control and show how these are related within a business activity.
- Describe the roles of management accounting in directing attention, keeping the score and solving problems.
- Analyse simple cases where management accounting may contribute to making judgements and decisions.
- Understand that the terminology of management accounting is less well defined than that of financial accounting, so that you will need to be flexible in interpreting the use of words.

## 16.1    Introduction

In Financial Accounting, section 1.1, accounting was defined as follows:

**Definition**

> **Accounting** is the process of identifying, measuring and communicating financial information about an entity to permit informed judgements and decisions by users of the information.[1]

The process of identifying, measuring and communicating financial information has been explained and illustrated in Parts 1 to 5, Financial Accounting, by reference to communicating with users external to the entity. However, many would argue that the foremost users of accounting information about an organisation must be those who manage it on a day-to-day basis. This group is referred to in broad terms as **management**, which is a collective term for all those persons who have responsibilities for making judgements and decisions within an organisation. Because they have close involvement with the business, they have access to a wide range of information (much of which may be confidential within the organisation) and will seek those aspects of the information which are most relevant to their particular judgements and decisions. Because this group of users is so broad, and because of the vast amount of information potentially available, a specialist branch of accounting has developed, called **management accounting**, to serve the particular needs of management.

**Activity 16.1**

*Imagine that you are in charge of a cycle hire business in a holiday resort. You have 50 cycles available for hire. Some customers hire cyles for one day; others take them for up to one week. Write down any three decisions that you might make as a manager, where accounting information would be helpful in making the decision.*

### 16.1.1    Applying the definition

Consider the following three scenarios which are typical of comments in the 'management' section of the financial press. As you read each scenario, think about how it relates to the definition of 'accounting' given at the start of this section. Then read the comment following the scenario and compare it with your thinking.

> **Scenario 1.1**
>
> 'In the 12 months to June 30, net profits dropped from £280m to £42m, depressed by hefty investments, increased paper costs and poor advertising spending . . . The chief executive has explained the company's plans for improving its margins to the average level for the industry. The directors are also committed to getting the assets to work creatively together.'
> [*Report on a magazine publishing company*]

Scenario 1.1 indicates decision making related to **profit margins** and the effective use of assets. The profit margins will be improved either by improving **sales**, or by controlling **costs**, or through a mixture of both. **Assets** will be used more effectively if they create more profit or higher sales. Achieving these targets requires a range of managerial skills covering sales, production and asset management. Identifying the relevant **costs** and **revenues**, measuring the achievement of targets and communicating the outcomes within the organisation are all functions of management accounting. The chief executive will need to form a judgement on whether the decisions taken are likely to satisfy investors and maintain their confidence in the management team.

## Scenario 1.2

Salespersons at a car manufacturer's dealership noticed business was slow in April. They reacted by encouraging customers to take more time in deciding whether to buy a car. What was the reason? They were paid a monthly bonus where sales exceeded a specified target. They could see that the April sales would not reach the target and so encouraged customers to wait until May, to increase the likely volume of May sales. In a brewing company the sales manager set a low sales target, in the hope of exceeding it easily. This caused the company to reduce production, so that when demand for beer rose to a higher level because of good weather, the company could not provide adequate supplies. [*Journalist's comment on how unrealistic targets can distort achievement of company objectives*]

Scenario 1.2 shows that at some point in the past a decision was taken to create employee incentives by setting quantifiable targets. Unfortunately this has led to a narrow focus on measuring the achievement of the targets. There was a problem in allowing the employees too much freedom to influence either the setting of the target or the achievement of the target. There was no judgement about the best interests of the company. A further decision is now required to balance the motivation of the employees against the best interests of the company. Communication is an important feature of getting the decision right.

## Scenario 1.3

'Engineers are challenging the assumption that companies are run by number-crunchers. . . . The hidden skill of engineers is their ability to be analytical and numerate. As someone who has to evaluate and sit on the boards of information technology and software development companies, I have the ability to understand the basics of their business.' [*Managing director of a venture capital company, qualified engineer*]

The term 'number-cruncher' tends to be used as a somewhat uncomplimentary description of an accounting specialist. The engineer quoted in Scenario 1.3 has related to the measurement aspect of accounting and has identified the need to make judgements ('evaluate') using analytical skills. However this quotation has made no mention either of communication or of decision making. There is an increasing expectation that the management accountants in an organisation will work with the engineers or other technical specialists, and will try to understand the nature of the business and will ensure that the judgements are communicated to the experts so that cost-effective decisions can be made.

## 16.1.2 Matching the approach to the judgements or decisions

Management accounting methods have developed in a variety of ways depending on the judgements or decisions required. This is sometimes described in terms of a **contingency theory** of management accounting. The management accounting approach is conditioned by (is 'contingent upon') the situation. Management accounting methods have been developed within particular industries. In the UK economy approximately 75% of output is provided by service industry with only 25% of output being provided by manufacturing industry. However management accounting began to develop in the twentieth century at a time when manufacturing industry dominated. As the service sector has grown, management accounting has developed to meet its particular needs. What remains of the manufacturing sector has moved from being labour intensive to being capital intensive. In some parts of the world, manufacturing remains labour intensive. The agricultural sector may be stronger. All these differences lead to different judgements and decisions, and hence different approaches to identifying, measuring and communicating accounting data. The following chapters will explain management accounting techniques that have been developed to meet particular needs in making judgements and decisions.

### 16.1.3    Strategic management accounting

The traditional approach to management accounting has been to regard internal decision makers as inward looking. This has led to developing techniques for identifying, measuring and communicating costs where only internal comparisons have been thought relevant. Those techniques remain useful in some cases and are sufficiently widely used to justify studying them in an introductory course. However the later years of the twentieth century brought an increasing awareness that company managers must be outward looking. They must form a strategy for their business that has regard to what competitors are achieving. This requires management accounting to identify, measure and communicate data on the company relative to data for other similar companies. Managers must consider competitive forces such as the threat of new entrants, substitute products or services, rivalry within the industry and the relative bargaining strength of suppliers and customers. Managers must also consider how their organisation adds value in creating its product. There is a flow of business activity from research and development through production, marketing, distribution and after-sales support. This chain of activities creates costs which must be compared with the value added by the organisation. The term **strategic management accounting** applies to the identification, measurement and communication of cost data in all these situations where the organisation is being judged against the performance of competitors.

## 16.2    Meeting the needs of internal users

Although the definition of accounting remains appropriate for internal reporting purposes, its application will be different because internal users need to form judgements and make decisions that are different from those of external users. External users form judgements on the overall performance of the entity and make decisions about their relationship with it. Their decisions are of the type: 'Shall I invest money in this business?', 'Shall I continue to be an investor in this business?', 'Shall I supply goods to this business?', 'Shall I continue to supply goods to this business?', 'Shall I become a customer of this business?', 'Shall I continue to be a customer of this business?'

The internal users make different types of judgements and different types of decisions. They may have to judge the performance of the various products of the organisation as compared with those of competitors. They may have to judge the performance of different divisions within the organisation. Their decisions are of the type: 'Shall I invest in manufacturing more soap powder, or do I switch resources into toothpaste?', 'Shall I continue offering a television repair service as support for my sales of televisions?', 'Is it cost effective to have three separate locations at which my tenants can pay their rent?', 'Will this investment in a new factory pay for itself over the next ten years?' There is great variety in the judgements and decisions made by those who manage the business. Their needs are so wide ranging that management accounting has developed as a separate discipline, within the overall 'accounting' umbrella, in order to serve the particular needs of management.

The use of accounting as a tool which will assist in the management of a business raises two significant questions:

1  What types of informed judgements are made by management and about management?
2  What types of decisions are made by management?

It is presumed that many of those reading this text for the first time may not have a great deal of experience of the types of judgements and decisions made in business. This chapter therefore devotes space to four case study illustrations of management situations where management accounting will have a contribution to make. The case studies are uncomplicated so that the management accounting applications are intuitively obvious. After each case study outline there is a comment on the management accounting aspects. You will then meet Fiona McTaggart, a management accounting consultant, who explains how she sees the management accountant's contribution to the management issues raised in each of the four case studies.

Before exploring the case studies, this chapter sets out, in section 16.3, some basic categories of management functions and then outlines, in section 16.4, the role of management accounting in helping to meet the information needs of those management functions.

## 16.3    Management functions

This section describes three management functions: planning, decision making and control.

To be effective, each of these functions requires the application by management of communication and motivation skills. To ensure that the entity's operations are effective, those who work in the entity must be persuaded to identify with its objectives. Managers require the skills to motivate those for whom they are responsible, creating a sense of teamwork. The communication process is a vital part of creating a sense of teamwork and ensuring that all the players understand the role they play in achieving targets. They must also be motivated to want to achieve the targets. Management accounting has a particularly important role in that process of communication and motivation.

### 16.3.1    Planning

**Planning** is a very general term which covers longer-term strategic planning and shorter-term operational planning. These two types of planning differ in the time scale that they cover. **Strategic planning** involves preparing, evaluating and selecting *strategies* to achieve objectives of a long-term plan of action. **Operational planning** relates to the detailed plans by which those working within an organisation are expected to meet the short-term objectives of their working group.

Strategic planning is based on objectives set by those who manage the entity at a senior level. If the entity is a legal entity such as a limited liability company or a public sector corporation, objectives will be set for the corporate entity which will require high-level **corporate strategic planning**. Within the company or corporation there will be major divisions of activities into key business areas, each with their own objectives requiring **business strategic planning**.

The corporate entity may contain many different businesses and those who manage the corporate entity as a whole must manage the entire collection of businesses. They must decide which businesses to develop in the corporate interest, which to support when in temporary difficulties, and which to dispose of as no longer contributing to the corporate well-being. Business strategic planning focuses on each of the separate businesses which have to consider not only their position within the corporate group of businesses but also their position within the industry or sector to which the business belongs.

Shorter-term operational planning is also referred to as **functional strategic planning**. It concentrates on the actions of specific functions within the business. Although these functions may have a longer-term existence they must also plan their activity in shorter-term periods so that achievement of targets may be monitored regularly.

At a practical level, managers find that they have to plan ahead in making major decisions on such things as **sales**, **production** and **capital expenditure**. Such planning is required for the immediate future and for the longer term. Businesses will typically make a detailed plan for the year ahead and a broader plan for a two- to five-year period. Plans for sales require decisions on which products to sell, which markets to target and what price to charge. Plans for production require decisions on the mix of resources, including labour, the source of raw materials or component parts, the level of stock of raw materials and finished goods to hold and the most effective use of productive capacity. Plans for capital expenditure require a longer-term perspective, taking into account the expected life of the capital equipment acquired. As well as investing in **fixed assets**, the business will need **working capital** as a base for a new project. Decisions will be required on the level of working capital which is appropriate. If the enterprise is to move ahead, plans must lead to decisions.

### 16.3.2    Decision making

**Decision making** is central to the management of an enterprise. The manager of a profit-making business has to decide on the manner of implementation of the objectives of the business, at least one of which may well relate to allocating resources so as to maximise profit. A non-profit-making enterprise (such as a department of central or local government) will be making decisions on resource allocation so as to be economic, efficient and effective in its use of finance. All organisations, whether in the private sector or the public sector, take decisions which have financial implications. Decisions will be about resources, which may be people, products, services or long-term and short-term investment. Decisions will also be about activities, including whether and how to undertake them. Most decisions will at some stage involve consideration of financial matters, particularly cost. Decisions may also have an impact on the working conditions and employment prospects of employees of the organisation, so that cost considerations may, in making a final decision, be weighed against social issues. Where the owners are different persons from the manager (e.g. shareholders of a company as separate persons from the directors), the managers may face a decision where there is a potential conflict between their own interests and those of the owners. In such a situation cost considerations may be evaluated in the wider context of the responsibility of the managers to act in the best interests of the owners.

### 16.3.3    Control

Once a decision has been taken on any aspect of business activity, management must be in a position to **control** the activity and to have a view on whether the outcome is in accordance with the initial plans and with the objectives derived from those plans. This might involve identifying areas in the business where managers are in a position to control and account for costs and, in some cases, profit. To implement the control process, individual managers will require timely, relevant and accurate information about the part of the business for which they are responsible. Measurement, including cost measurement, is therefore an important ingredient in carrying out the control function.

To carry out the control function, a management control system is needed. A useful definition of a management control system is the following:

**Definition**

A **management control system** is a system involving organisational information-seeking and gathering, accountability and feedback designed to ensure that the enterprise adapts to changes in its substantive environment and that the work behaviour of its employees is measured by reference to a set of operational sub-goals (which conform with overall objectives) so that the discrepancy between the two can be reconciled and corrected for.[2]

This definition points to some of the aspects of control which will be encountered in later chapters. It acknowledges the process of seeking and gathering information but emphasises the importance of adaptation and meeting operational goals. Later chapters will refer to feedback processes and also to techniques for measuring differences between actual performance and sub-goals set for that performance.

The information provided to individual management is an essential part of the communication process within a business. For effective communication, there must be an organisational structure which reflects the responsibility and authority of management. Communication must cascade down through this organisational structure and the manner of communication must have regard for the motivation of those who are part of the control process. For control to be effective there must also be a reverse form of communication upwards so that management learn of the concerns of their staff. Motivation, expectations and personal relationships are all matters to be considered and to be harnessed effectively by the process of control.

| Activity 16.2 | *Think of an organised activity in which you participate at college or at home. To what extent does this activity involve planning, decision making and control? Who carries out the planning? Who makes the decision? Who exercises control?* |
|---|---|

### 16.3.4  An organisation chart

Exhibit 16.1 presents a simple organisation chart showing various types of relationships in a manufacturing company. It illustrates line relationships within the overall finance function of the business, showing separately the management accounting and financial accounting functions. In most medium to large companies, the management accounting function will be a separate area of activity within the finance function. The term 'management accountant' is used here as a general term, but a brief perusal of the 'situations vacant' pages of any newspaper or professional magazine advertising accountancy posts would indicate the range of titles available and the versatility expected (see Case 16.1 at the end of the chapter). Two other functions have been shown in the chart as 'project accountant' and 'systems accountant'. Such specialists have specific roles in the internal accounting process within the enterprise which are relevant, although not exclusive, to the management accounting function.

The organisation chart shows individual people, each with a different job to do. Each person has a specialisation indicated by the job title, but he or she also has responsibilities to others higher in the structure and with authority over others lower in the structure. In the interests of the business as a whole, individuals must communicate up and down the line relationships and also across the horizontal relationships.

Taking one line relationship as an example, the finance director must make plans for the year ahead which are communicated to the financial controller. The financial controller must consult the systems accountant to ensure that the accounting systems are in place to record and communicate these plans within the organisation. The financial controller must also consult the project accountant to ensure that there is an evaluation of any capital investment aspects of the finance director's plans. The management accountant will prepare accounting statements showing how the plans will be implemented. The financial controller will bring together the details supplied by each person, summarising and evaluating the main factors so that the results may be relayed to the finance director.

Horizontal relationships can be more difficult when communications channels are being planned, because there are so many potential combinations. It is a responsibility of management to decide which horizontal relationships have the greatest communication needs. Continuing the planning theme, the finance director will be expected to

**Exhibit 16.1**

**Part of an organisation chart for a manufacturing company, illustrating line relationships within the overall finance function of the business**

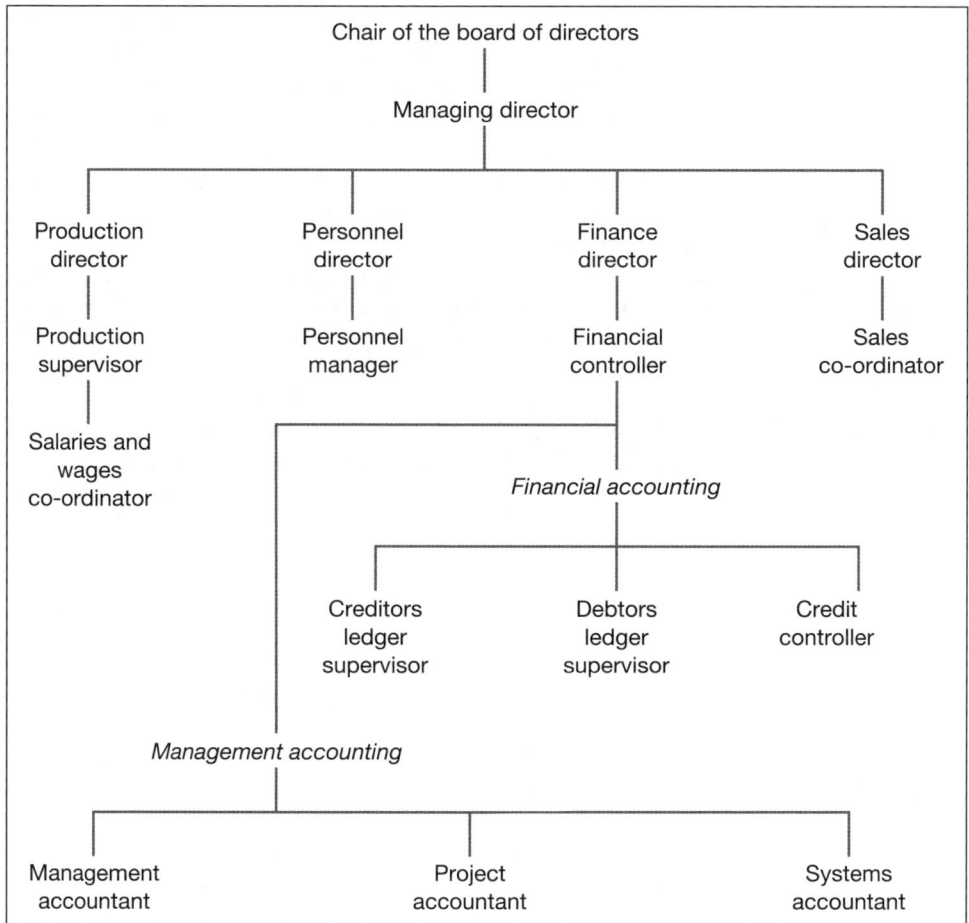

communicate the financial plan to the other members of the board of directors, who in turn will want to see that it fits the board's overall strategy and that it is compatible with the capacity of their particular areas of activity in the business. The financial plan will depend on the projected level of sales and will reflect strategy in production and personnel management. The plan will therefore need to be communicated to the sales co-ordinator, the production supervisor and the personnel manager. The sales co-ordinator, production supervisor and personnel manager will in turn provide feedback to the financial controller. The detailed analysis of the plans for the period, and the expected impact of those plans, will be evaluated by the management accountant, project accountant and systems accountant. They will report back to the financial controller who in turn will channel information to the finance director and the rest of the board of directors.

**Activity 16.3**

*Think again about the organised activity which you identified in Activity 16.2. Prepare an organisation chart to include all the persons involved in the activity. Draw green lines with arrows to show the direction of communication. Draw red lines with arrows to show the direction of responsibility. What does the pattern of red and green lines tell you about communication and co-ordination in the organisation? What is the mechanism for motivation? Does it use the communication network?*

16.3.5 ## Illustration of the interrelationships

The three management functions of **planning**, **decision making** and **control** are all interrelated in the overall purpose of making judgements and decisions. Exhibit 16.2 shows how a company owning a chain of shops supplying motor-cycle spares might go about the business of planning to open a new shop in the suburbs of a city. The shop will sell motor-cycle spares and will also provide advice on basic repair work which motor cyclists can safely undertake themselves.

**Exhibit 16.2**
**Managing a decision on the location of a new business**

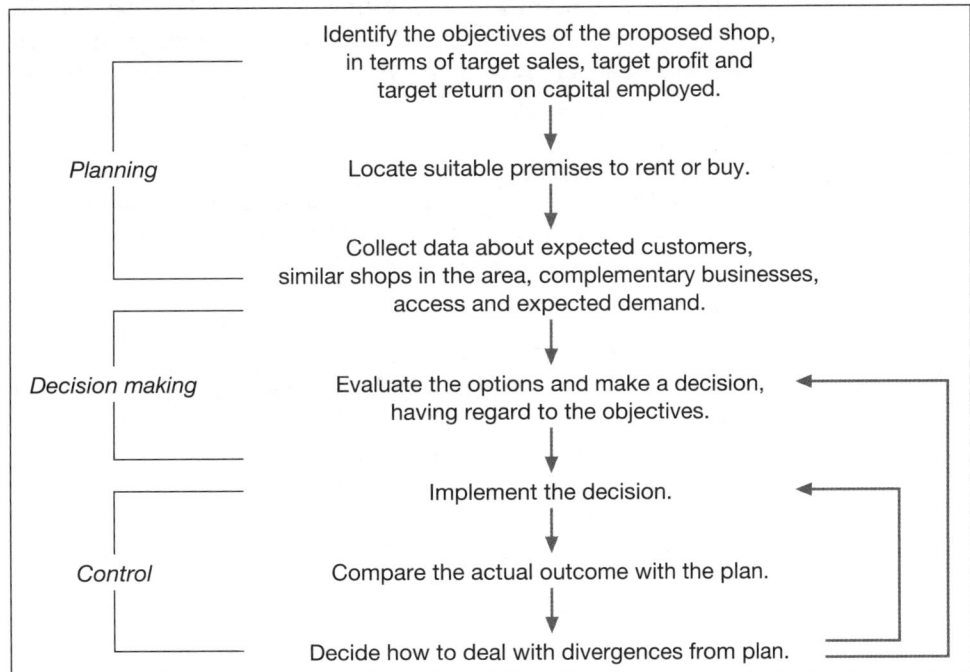

The shop's objectives will be concerned with achieving target sales and profit, and with making an adequate return on the capital invested in establishing the shop. Because of the desire to offer an advice service as well as selling spare parts, there will be non-financial objectives expressed in terms of customer satisfaction. These non-financial objectives will have indirect financial implications because satisfied customers will lead to increased sales and increased profits. The location of the shop, other types of shop close by, hours and days of opening and approach to stock control are all factors which are considered in the planning process. The choice of shop premises will depend upon the rent to be paid, any costs associated with the property, such as refurbishment and repairs, access for delivery and collection, and security. If the shop is to trade successfully there will need to be parking facilities, good access by road, and preferably public transport backup for those who need spare parts but whose motor cycles are too much in need of repair to be used as transport to the shop. Location requires careful consideration. Is it preferable to have the shop in a neighbourhood where a high proportion of residents own motor cycles or to locate it on a main road along which they travel to work? Evaluation for decision-making purposes will require information about planned costs and revenues, although non-cost factors may also influence the decision.

Knowing the objectives and planning to meet those objectives will result in a decision, but the decision to start up the shop is not the end of the story. There has to be a continuing judgement as to whether the shop is successful and, eventually, there may be another decision on expanding or contracting the shop's activity. The continuing exercise of judgement will require a management accounting information outcome of the judgement. Any future decision to expand or contract will similarly include a requirement for information on planned costs and revenues.

Planning, decision making and control are shown on the diagram in Exhibit 16.2 as separate parts of the total activity. Communication is shown by arrows from one stage to the next. Motivation is not easily shown on a diagram, so there is no attempt to do so, but it remains an important part of the communication process. The greater the number of communication trails built into the process, the more effective will be the understanding and motivation of those who carry out the work of the business at various levels of management. Ideally, the diagram would be criss-crossed with communication trails so that all participants are well informed.

| Activity 16.4 | *Imagine that you want to set up a business as a travel agent booking low-cost holidays with the emphasis on good value. List two activities that you might carry out in each of the stages of planning, decision making and control.* |
| --- | --- |

## 16.4  Role of management accounting

In the previous illustration of planning where to open a new shop, there is work for the management accountant: first, in directing attention to accounting information which is relevant to making plans and taking the decision; second, in keeping the score for making judgements on the effectiveness of decisions; and third, in helping to solve problems which arise when the results of decision making do not work out as expected. So there are three roles that management accounting could play in this exercise that will be found to be general features of any decision-making situation encountered by management. These are: directing attention, keeping the score and solving problems.

### 16.4.1  Directing attention

**Directing attention** is a matter of being able to answer questions such as 'Who should take action?' or 'Whose responsibility is this loss?' or 'Who is to be congratulated on this favourable result?' Managers are busy people. They do not always have time to consider every detail of cost information about the operation or process they control. They look to the management accountant to direct their attention to the exceptional points of interest, be these good or bad. One way of carrying out that function is to highlight those costs which have departed from expectations – provided everyone understands at the outset what the expectations are. Words such as *fairness* and *timeliness* are almost bound to be involved in attention-directing processes.

Managers are also sensitive people. They do not like being blamed unjustly for something they see as being beyond their control. So the management accounting information has to be presented in such a way as to relate to the level of responsibility and degree of authority held by the manager concerned. On the other side of the coin, managers enjoy being praised for achievements and may welcome management accounting information which helps them to demonstrate their accountability for the resources entrusted to them.

In any organisation emphasising strategic management, it will be part of the role of management accounting to direct the attention of management towards information about competitors. Competitive forces include: the threat posed by new entrants to the industry, the emergence of substitute products or services, the relative strength of suppliers and customers in controlling prices and conditions in the industry and the intensity of rivalry within the industry. Such information is often well known on an anecdotal basis. The management accountant may be required to collect and present information in a useful and focused manner.

The role of management accounting in directing attention will therefore depend on how managers wish their attention to be directed. A business which retains an inward-looking approach to management will expect management accounting to direct attention inwards. A business which is thinking strategically about its position in the market for goods and services will expect management accounting to include an outward-looking perspective.

**Strategic management accounting** has been defined as:

**Definition** | The provision and analysis of financial information on the firm's product markets and competitors' costs and cost structures and the monitoring of the enterprise's strategies and those of its competitors in these markets over a number of periods.[3]

The practical effects of the different types of management accounting approaches are summarised in Exhibit 16.3.

**Exhibit 16.3**
**Contrasting an inward and outward focus of management**

| Possible limitations of an inward focus for management | Benefits of an outward focus for management |
|---|---|
| A risk of placing too much emphasis on evaluating past actions. | Management accounting includes a prospective element evaluating the potential outcomes of various strategies. |
| A risk of focusing on the business entity alone. | Management accounting sets information about the business entity in the context of other businesses in the sector. |
| A tendency to focus on a single reporting period. | Management accounting sets the results of one period in a longer-term analysis. |
| Directing attention towards separate single issues of decision making. | Management accounting directs attention towards sequences and patterns in decision making. |
| Directing attention to the outcome of the manufacturing or service activity of the particular organisation. | Management accounting directs attention to the competition for the manufacturing or service activity. |
| A tendency to concentrate on existing activities. | Management accounting is expected to look also to prospective activities. |
| Risk of not considering linkages within the organisation or potential for effective linkages beyond. | Management accounting is expected to direct attention to effective linkages which will improve competitive position. |

### 16.4.2   Keeping the score

**Keeping the score** is very much a case of being able to answer the questions 'How much?' or 'How many?' at any point in time. It requires careful record keeping and a constant monitoring of accounting records against physical quantities and measures of work done. The emphasis is on *completeness* but also on *fairness*. Questions such as 'How much?' may involve sharing, or allocating, costs. Accounting is concerned with allocations of various types, all concerned with aspects of *matching*. That could require matching costs to a time period, matching costs to an item of output, or matching costs against revenue for the period. For this matching process to be effective, information must be complete and the basis of allocation must be fair.

For the business which has a strong emphasis on strategic management, score keeping will include being able to answer questions such as 'How much of the market share?' or 'How many compared to our competitors?' Questions of fairness of allocation within the business may be important but it may be even more important to understand the performance of the business in relation to others. Such questions will be answered by both financial and non-financial measures.

### 16.4.3   Solving problems

**Solving problems** involves a different type of question. It might be 'Why did that plan go well?' or 'Why did that action fail?' or 'Which of these three choices is the best to take?' In solving problems of this type, *relevance* is an important issue. People who have taken a decision are often reluctant to admit that it has not turned out as expected and may continue making worse mistakes unless someone points out that past events are of little or no relevance to decisions on future action. Where choices are concerned, those choices will involve people, each of whom may have different motives for preferring one choice above others. Management accounting information may have a role in providing an objective base for understanding the problem to be solved, even where at the end of the day a decision is based on non-accounting factors.

Some problems resemble making a jigsaw, or perhaps deciding which piece of the jigsaw has gone missing. Other problems are like solving crosswords where the answers must interlock but some of the clues have been obliterated. In solving any problem of that type, logical reasoning is essential. No one can memorise the answer to every conceivable question which might arise. You will find that management accounting tests your powers of logical reasoning in that every problem you encounter will never entirely resemble the previous one.

Exhibit 16.4 illustrates a combination of the management accounting functions of directing attention, keeping the score and solving problems. It shows the cycle of profit planning and control, starting with the measurement of existing performance, which is an example of the score-keeping aspects of management accounting. From the measurement of existing performance the cycle moves through an examination of the future environment of the business, where techniques of economic analysis would be used. In developing objectives, the management accountant would provide accounting information on targets to be achieved. Formulating a strategy is a management task but the management accountant is then expected to provide detailed budgets which translate that strategy into operating plans. When the plans are implemented the management accountant must be ready to measure the results and compare these with the outcome expected when the operating plans were set. From there the cycle is repeated.

**Activity 16.5**   *Look back to your list from Activity 1.4 for planning, decision making and control in setting up a travel agency business. Make another list of ways in which management accounting will help in directing attention, keeping the score and solving problems.*

**Exhibit 16.4**
**Stages in the cycle of profit planning and control**

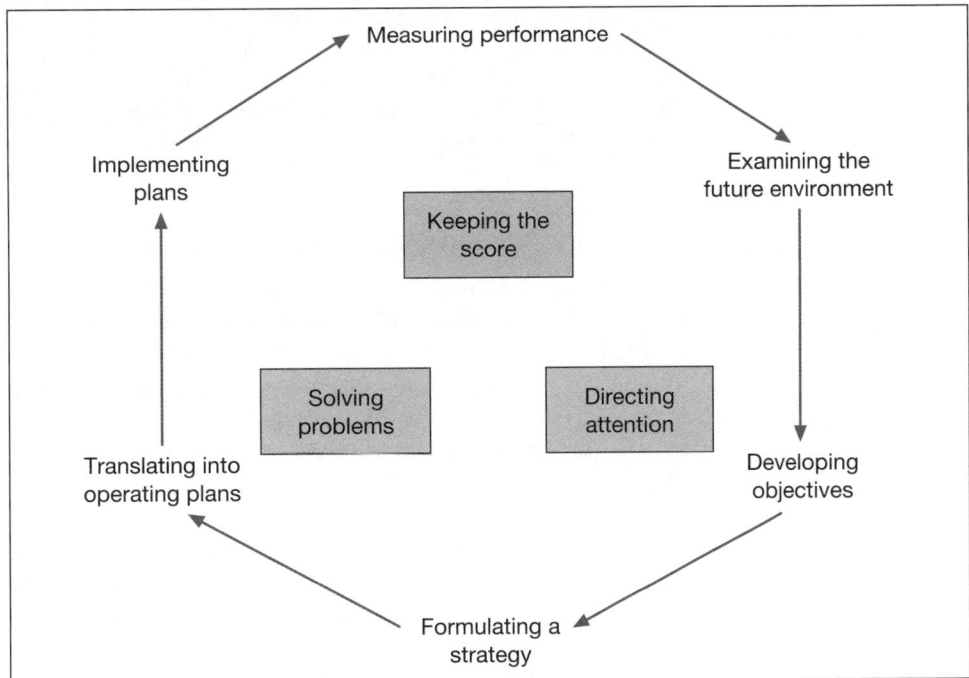

## 16.5 Judgements and decisions: case study illustrations

You are now presented with four cases in which there is a need for decisions and for judgements. After each case study there is a brief analysis of the decisions and judgements which will arise in each.

These four cases indicate areas where management accounting could serve as a tool to provide information which is relevant to decision making and to the formation of judgement at all levels within an organisation. Hopefully, you will have recognised some situations in each case where accounting information will be of help.

The organisation chart in Exhibit 16.1 includes an expert management accountant. It has already been explained that most medium to large companies include specialist management accountants on their staff. However, from time to time a consultant may be called in to give a wider and more frank appraisal than might be feasible for a paid employee. In this and subsequent chapters you will meet Fiona McTaggart, a freelance management accountant, who is prepared to offer advice on a variety of case study situations. In practice, the management accountant within the organisation might provide similar advice, but this text uses the management consultant so that her comments are not unduly constrained by existing limitations within the business.

Fiona explains what she could offer from her management accounting experience in each of these four case study situations. Read her explanations and in each case identify the places where she is hinting at directing attention, keeping the score or solving problems.

**Activity 16.6** *Read the text of the case study (set out in the box at the beginning of each case) and then make a note of the way in which you think management accounting may help each person. Compare your answer with the discussion which follows each case.*

## 16.5.1    Case study: John Smith

> John Smith has taken early retirement at the age of 50 in order to develop his hobby of model shipbuilding into a full-time business. He has several models already assembled and has advertised in the model builders' weekly journal. Interested enquiries are starting to come in and he realises that he does not know what price to charge for the models.

### Analysis of decisions and judgements

John Smith needs to make a decision about pricing policy. That will involve many factors such as looking at what competitors are charging, having regard to the type of customer he expects to attract, and making sure that the price covers the cost of making and selling the models. After he has decided on a pricing policy he will need to measure its success by making judgements on the level of **sales** achieved and on the **profitability** of the product in relation to the capital he has invested in the business.

FIONA: *John Smith needs to know the cost of the models he is making. That sounds easy – he has a note of the money he has spent on materials for the models and he has detailed plans which tell him exactly how much material is used for each one. But that's not the end of the story. John puts a tremendous amount of time into the model building. He says it is all enjoyment to him, so he doesn't treat that time as a cost, but I have to persuade him that making the models represents a lost opportunity to do something else. The cost of his time could be measured in terms of that lost opportunity.*

*Then there are his tools. He has a workshop at the end of the garage and it's stacked high with tools. They don't last for ever and the cost of depreciation should be spread over the models produced using those tools. He needs heat to keep the workshop warm, power for the electric tools and packing material for the models sent in response to a postal enquiry. He has paid for an advertisement in the model builders' magazine and there is stationery, as well as postage and telephone calls, to consider.*

*Costs never seem to end once you start to add them up. It can all be a bit depressing, but it is much more depressing to sell something and then find out later that you've made a loss. I could help John work out his costs and make sure the price he charges will leave a profit so that he builds up his investment in the business.*

*Making the decision on selling price would not be the end of my involvement. I would continue to measure costs each month and compare these with sales. I would give John reports on profit and cash flow and warnings if working capital was starting to build up. If he gives credit he'll need to keep an eye on the level of debtors, and there will always be a stock, either of raw materials or of finished goods or of both. Trade creditors will fund some of the stock but working capital mismanagement has been the downfall of many a business which tried to expand too fast.*

*I will also need to keep John down to earth in ensuring that what has until now been a hobby can become a successful business. I will direct his attention to professional business reports for this kind of specialist service. I will encourage him to subscribe to information services and I will incorporate such information in my reports to John so that he can take a realistic view of his performance compared with what might be expected in the general business of special craft work.*

In advising John Smith, Fiona McTaggart will direct attention to the costs which are relevant to the pricing decision, she will keep the score by calculating profits once the business is in production and will help solve problems by monitoring the working capital position.

## 16.5.2   Case study: Jennifer Jones

> Jennifer Jones has been operating a small hairdressing business for several months. She would like to expand by employing an assistant and by purchasing new dryers and washing equipment. She cannot decide whether the investment would be justified.

### Analysis of decisions and judgements

Jennifer Jones will be taking a longer-term view in making a decision about investing in new equipment. That equipment must generate cash flows over its expected life. Jennifer's decision to invest will take into account the number of customers she expects, the prices she is able to charge them, and the cost of paying the proposed assistant, projected ahead for several years. It will also take into account the percentage **return** expected on the capital invested in the equipment.

If she decides to invest, she will need to monitor the success of that investment by making judgements on the profitability of the product in relation to the capital she has invested in it, and on whether the **return on the investment** is adequate in the light of having expanded the business.

FIONA: *Jennifer Jones needs help in taking a longer-term perspective. To assess the profitability of the new equipment and the assistant, I'll first of all need Jennifer to tell me how many customers she can realistically expect and what she will be able to charge them. I'll need those estimates over the life of the equipment, which will probably be around five years.*

*Once I have the estimates of cash inflows from customers over the five years, I can set against that the cash outflows in terms of payments for all the costs of providing the service, including the wages of the intended assistant. Then I will apply to those cash flows a factor which makes an allowance for uncertainty in the future and also takes account of the rate of interest Jennifer could earn if she invested her money in financial markets rather than hairdryers. I'll then compare the expected cash flows with the initial cost of acquiring the equipment, to see whether it's a good idea. Of course, if Jennifer gets the cash flow estimates wrong, then the answer won't mean very much, but that's not my problem.*

*If Jennifer makes the decision to invest, I'll be needed after that to monitor the success of the project. I can measure the cash flows after the event and give an indication of how well they met expectations. I can compare the cost of the assistant with the revenue generated by the extra work available.*

*Problems might arise if there is a change of fashion and everyone decides they prefer short straight hair. That could cause chaos in the hairdressing industry and might make some of the washing equipment surplus to requirements. There is a great temptation in such situations to hang on to the past because of the cash which was sunk into it. That's often the wrong thing to do because it brings disaster ever closer. It may be better to cut off the activity altogether and limit the losses. I can give a dispassionate view based on cost rather than sentiment and emotion.*

Fiona McTaggart will provide information which is relevant to the investment decision by drawing attention to the cost in comparison with the expected cash inflows. She will keep the score on the cash inflows and outflows once the project is established and she will help in problem solving by evaluating the losses arising if an unsuccessful project continues in operation.

## Case study: Central Ltd

Central Ltd is a small business manufacturing and assembling plastic components for use in car manufacture. It has been drawn to the attention of the financial controller that one of the plastic components could be purchased elsewhere at a price less than the cost of manufacture. What action should the production director take?

### Analysis of decisions and judgements

The production director of Central Ltd needs to decide whether to continue manufacturing the component within the business or to cease production and buy the component elsewhere. To make that decision requires a knowledge of the full cost of manufacture and reassurance that the cost has been calculated correctly. It also depends on the relative aims and objectives of the financial controller and the production director, who may be in conflict and who may be putting their own point of view at the expense of the overall good of the business. Costs of ceasing manufacture will also need to be taken into account. Beyond the accounting costs there are human costs and business risks. Is there alternative employment for the staff released from this internal production? Will there be redundancy costs? Is it safe to rely on this outside supplier? What are the risks to Central Ltd if supplies dry up?

Whatever decision is taken, there will be a subsequent need for judgement in monitoring the effectiveness of the decision and its impact on profitability. In the decision and in the subsequent judgements of the effectiveness of that decision, there will be a need for communication and interaction between the financial controller and the production director.

**FIONA:** *Central Ltd is an example of the football game situation where sometimes the players in a team forget that they are on the same side. I saw a game last week when the home team won on the away team's own goals. The same thing could happen for Central. When people have a defined role in an organisation they can be too closely involved in their own work to see the bigger picture. The financial controller sees the costs of manufacturing and assembling the parts and has identified a cost saving based on a simple comparison. It's hard for the production director to fight the logic of that argument but I can see he's worried.*

*What I can do is turn his worries into cost arguments which should be considered alongside the direct make-or-buy comparison. The costs may not be capable of such precise calculation but I'll give estimates of the risk to the business and the sensitivity of the situation. I'll give particular attention to the quality issues and to the risk of disruption of supply. It's more than likely that the financial controller and the production director will still not agree even when they have the information, so I'll present my information in a way which the board of directors can relate to the overall objectives and strategy of the company. Whatever decision is taken, I'll establish a monthly reporting system, to be operated by the financial controller, which will give the earliest possible warning of whether the decision remains in the best interests of the company.*

*That is the traditional management accounting role which I am happy to provide. However, I will also indicate, in conversation with the financial controller and the production director, that it would be important to discover first of all what their competitors are doing about this problem. The competitors will not answer the question directly but potential suppliers of the components may be willing to indicate that there is a similar demand emerging elsewhere. If the problem here is that production costs are too high in relation to the rest of the industry then perhaps the board of directors has to focus on cost reduction rather than external purchase. If the price is lower externally, someone somewhere has apparently found a better approach to cost control.*

Fiona McTaggart will provide information directly relevant to the make-or-buy decision. She will help in problem solving by setting out the information in such a way that others in the organisation can be satisfied that a decision will be in the best interests of the company as a whole. Finally, she will establish a score-keeping system which continues to monitor the effectiveness of the decision taken.

## 16.5.4    Case study: Ann Brown

Ann Brown is a hospital manager having responsibility for ensuring that the cost of treatment is recovered in full by invoicing the patient or the appropriate organisation which is financing the patient care. Pricing policy is dictated at a more senior level.

### Analysis of decisions and judgements

Ann Brown has no direct decision-making responsibility but the information she collates and the records she keeps, in relation to identifying costs and charging these costs to patients, will be used in the decision-making process at a more senior level. It will also be used as a tool of judgement on the effectiveness of the hospital's cost control and charging policy for the various treatments and services provided. In this case the criteria for the judgement may be rather different in that there may be less emphasis on **profitability** and more on the quality of service in relation to the cost of providing that service.

FIONA: *Ann Brown doesn't have direct decision-making responsibility. She is a smaller cog in a large machine. However, the efficiency with which she carries out her job will have a direct impact on the performance of the hospital and will have an impact on future decision making at a more senior level. Charging out to patients the cost of their care is a difficult matter and requires very careful record keeping. Patients who are ill don't question their treatment at the time, but when they are convalescing they have lots of time to look through the bill, especially if the medical insurance company is asking questions. Some patients may be paid for through the health service but at the end of the line there is a fundholder who wants to ensure that the funds are used to best advantage.*

*The cost of, say, major surgery can be the least difficult to work out because the time in theatre will be known, the staff on duty will be listed and their salary costs can be apportioned over the time taken. But when the patient is back on the ward recovering, there have to be records kept of the type of nursing care, the specialist equipment and supplies, food costs and the hotel-type services associated with providing a bed. Then there have to be charges to cover the overhead costs of heating, maintaining and cleaning the buildings.*

*Ann Brown needs an effective recording system which is accurate in terms of care for each patient but is not so cumbersome to apply that the nurses' time is entirely taken up with clerical recording. Many costs can be applied to patient care on a predetermined charge-out rate based on previous experience. A computerised cost recording system, with a carefully thought out coding system for each cost, is essential. Of the four cases I have considered here, this will be the most time-consuming to set up, but it will give satisfaction all round when it is working and seen to be fair to patients in terms of individual charge-out costs as well as giving the hospital reassurance that all costs are being recovered.*

*The cost-recording system will provide information for the decision-making process in relation to future pricing policy and also for the more difficult decisions as to which specialised medical functions at the hospital are cost effective and which functions do not fully cover costs. There are bound to be problems within the hospital if decisions are needed on expanding or cutting back. Everyone hates the accountant at those times, but at least I can design a system which provides an objective starting point even though non-financial factors are eventually the determining factor.*

Fiona McTaggart is describing here the score-keeping aspects of management accounting. That score keeping will be used as information for the decision-making process and may also have a problem-solving aspect if disputes arise where medical decisions have a cost impact.

## Comment

These case study discussions have given some insight into how the management account-ant has a role to play in contributing to the management of an organisation. Three general themes have been explored, namely **keeping the score**, **directing attention** and **solving problems**. The case studies have shown that within each of these three themes there are many different approaches to be taken, depending on the circumstances. By way of illustration of the scope of management accounting activity, Fiona McTaggart has the following list of special studies she has undertaken, as an adviser on manage-ment accounting, where problem-solving skills have been required:

- product cost comparisons
- evaluation of product profitability
- alternative choices of resource usage
- asset management
- labour relations
- capital investment
- investigation on behalf of customer for contract pricing purposes
- directing attention to the activities of competitors.

All of these, and other problem situations, will be encountered in subsequent chapters. This chapter ends with a warning that there will be some new terminology to learn and a summary of the role of the management accountant.

## 16.6 The language of management accounting

Management accounting is not a difficult subject but to understand it requires a logical mind. To be successful, methods of management accounting must reflect a reasoned approach to a judgement on a situation problem and a logical basis for making decisions. If reason and logic are strong, then it should not be difficult to understand the approach.

Unfortunately, as with most specialist subjects, management accounting has grown a language of its own, which is helpful to those who work closely with the subject but can sometimes cause problems at the outset for newcomers. This chapter has avoided using specialist terminology, relying on intuitive ideas. However, progress in understanding management accounting will be limited without the use of that terminology, so subsequent chapters will introduce the technical terms, each of which will be explained. End-of-chapter questions will help you to test your understanding of new terminology before you move on to each new chapter.

One important difference from financial accounting is that there is no official regulatory process governing management accounting. This is very different from the framework of company law, accounting standards and other regulatory processes which are found throughout financial reporting to external users. Consequently there is relative freedom in management accounting to tailor the accounting process to the management function. That does not mean that management accounting is any less rigorous professionally than other forms of accounting reporting. In the UK there is a professional body, the Chartered Institute of Management Accountants (CIMA), which provides guidance to its members on good practice in management accounting. That guidance includes a wide range of publications ranging from definitions of terminology to reports on newly emerging techniques. Similar professional bodies having a management accounting specialism exist in other countries.

## 16.7  Summary

You have seen from the discussion in section 16.1.3 and the case studies that management accounting should direct attention towards strategic issues of surviving and prospering in a competitive environment. The remaining chapters of this book will introduce the various techniques that have been developed in management accounting for keeping the score, directing attention and solving problems. The traditional techniques are described, with current thinking and developments explained and contrasted as relevant.

Key themes in this chapter are:

- Management accounting is concerned with reporting accounting information within a business, for management use only.
- Management takes its widest meaning in describing all those persons (managers) responsible for the day-to-day running of a business.
- The managers of a business carry out functions of **planning**, **decision making** and **control**.
- Management accounting supports these management functions by **directing attention**, **keeping the score** and **solving problems**.
- The **contingency theory** of management accounting explains how management accounting methods have developed in a variety of ways depending on the judgements or decisions required.
- **Strategic management accounting** pays particular attention to the provision and analysis of financial information on the firm's product markets and competitors' costs and cost structures, and the monitoring of the enterprise's strategies and those of its competitors in these markets over a number of periods.

### Further reading

CIMA (2000) *Management Accounting Official Terminology*, Chartered Institute of Management Accountants.

# QUESTIONS

The Questions section of each chapter has three types of question. 'Test your understanding' questions to help you review your reading are in the 'A' series of questions. You will find the answers to these by reading and thinking about the material in the book. 'Application' questions to test your ability to apply technical skills are in the 'B' series of questions. Questions requiring you to show skills in problem solving and evaluation are in the 'C' series of questions. A letter [S] indicates that there is a solution at the end of the book.

## A   Test your understanding

**A16.1**  Define 'management accounting'. (Section 16.1)

**A16.2**  Explain why management decisions will normally require more than a management accounting input. (Section 16.1.1)

**A16.3**   What is meant by a 'contingency theory' of management accounting? (Section 16.1.2)

**A16.4**   Why is management accounting required to take on an outward-looking role of contributing to business strategy by identifying, measuring and communicating financial information about a wider business community? (Section 16.1.3)

**A16.5**   Explain the needs of internal users for management accounting information. (Section 16.2)

**A16.6**   Explain, giving a suitable example in each case, what is meant by the management functions of:

(a)  planning; (Section 16.3.1)
(b)  decision making; (Section 16.3.2) and
(c)  control. (Section 16.3.3)

**A16.7**   Explain, giving a suitable example in each case, how management accounting may serve the purposes of:

(a)  directing attention; (Section 16.4.1)
(b)  keeping the score; (Section 16.4.2) and
(c)  solving problems. (Section 16.4.3)

**A16.8**   Describe, and explain each stage of, the cycle of profit planning and control. (Section 16.4.3)

**A16.9**   In the chapter there are four case studies where Fiona McTaggart explains what she is able to offer in four situations, using her management accounting experience. Her advice is primarily inward looking and based on the traditional approaches to planning, control and decision making. Add two sentences to each of Fiona's explanations in order to present a more strategic awareness of the activities of competitors. (Section 16.5)

**A16.10**  Suggest reasons for the lack of an agreed set of standard words in the language of management accounting. (Section 16.6)

## B    Application

**B16.1**
(a)  Imagine you are the finance director of a company which is planning to open a new supermarket chain. Prepare a chart similar to that shown in Exhibit 16.2 which sets out key aspects of the planning, decision making and control.
(b)  Give two examples of financial objectives and two examples of non-financial objectives which you might expect of the sales manager of the new supermarket chain.
(c)  Explain how management accounting skills would be required in providing product costs comparisons when the supermarket chain becomes operational.

**B16.2**
A record company is planning to launch an internet music service. Subscribers who pay £15 per month will be allowed to download 100 songs per month to a personal computer. If the subscription lapses, access to the music will be lost. The quality of the file transfer is guaranteed to be high. Legal advice has been obtained to confirm that the arrangement is within copyright regulations. Royalties will be paid to recording artistes based on the number of times that a song is requested.

(a)  Identify the judgements and decisions to be made here.
(b)  Explain how management accounting may help in directing attention, keeping the score or solving problems.

**B16.3**
A group of doctors operates a joint surgery. They are planning to provide a private clinic where minor surgery can be performed on a day basis (no overnight facilities will be offered).

The project will require investment in a new building and operating theatre. Three theatre nurses will be required and three healthcare assistants will be employed. Admissions will be dealt with by the existing medical secretaries. The fees charged will cover costs plus a profit percentage based on cost.

(a) Identify the judgements and decisions to be made here.
(b) Explain how management accounting may help in directing attention, keeping the score or solving problems.

### B16.4

A recently retired police officer has received a lump sum award and a pension. She has a hobby of making soft toys which have for some years been sold to friends and colleagues at a price to cover the cost of materials. She now wishes to turn this into a commercial venture and to sell them through a children's clothing shop which has agreed to provide shelf space for the sale of 20 toys per month. She is not concerned initially about making a high profit and will be satisfied with covering costs. The shop will take a fee of 5% of the sale price of each toy sold.

(a) Identify the judgements and decisions to be made here.
(b) Explain how management accounting may help in directing attention, keeping the score or solving problems.

## C    Problem solving and evaluation

### C16.1

You have been invited to write a proposal for the development of a new production line to process dog food. The production of dog food will take up space previously devoted to cat food. Write 250 words (approx.) explaining how management accounting would be used to justify any decision by the production manager to replace cat food with dog food in the production process.

### C16.2

Chris and Alison Weston have been manufacturing and selling children's toys from a workshop attached to their house. Alison has carried out the manufacturing activity and Chris has provided the marketing and financial support. The scale of customers' orders has reached a point where they must make a decision about renting a production unit on a nearby trading estate and employing two assistants. One assistant would be required to help make the toys and the other would carry out routine record keeping, allowing Chris to spend more time on marketing. Write 250 words (approx.) explaining (a) the main judgements and decisions which will arise; and (b) the kind of advice that could be offered by a management accounting expert.

### C16.3

Set out below is a selection of advertisements for posts in management accounting. Read the text of the advertisement and relate the specified requirements to the three management accounting roles set out in this chapter, namely:

(a) directing attention;
(b) keeping the score; and
(c) solving problems.

## PLANNING AND REPORTING CONTROLLER

Reporting to the group finance director, your key task will be to drive a step change in all areas of corporate reporting and planning and provide analytical impetus to the development of business strategy. Responsibilities will include:

- ownership and control of the quality of reporting and forecasting throughout the business;
- managing the group's quarterly strategic business unit review, forecasting and annual planning cycles;
- managing the day to day treasury processes including cash-flow forecasting;
- supporting the finance director in all corporate activities including financing, acquisitions, presentations and ad hoc projects as required.

This is a high profile role which interfaces directly with directors, shareholders, advisers, banks, head office functions and divisions.

The ideal candidate will be an ambitious graduate qualified accountant with a minimum of four years' post-qualified experience. First class communication skills and good systems knowledge will complement your proven technical expertise.

## HEAD OF MANAGEMENT INFORMATION

Reporting to the financial director, you will be responsible for:

- developing and automating the production of management accounts and contract cash reporting;
- implementing and managing a robust process for all contract valuations;
- managing all aspects of budgeting, forecasting and group reporting;
- developing relationships with operational teams to improve controls and increase commercial awareness;
- full review of financial processes and implementation of new systems and controls.

The successful candidate will be commercially minded and profit-motivated with the ability to manage a strong team.

## MANAGEMENT ACCOUNTANT

This is a major support services organisation, supplying services and products to government agencies and commercial businesses worldwide. Working closely with the commercial teams, you will provide them with full financial support at every stage of the contract life cycle. Main responsibilities include:

- assisting with the compilation of new bids and tenders;
- ongoing contract monitoring including budgeting and forecasting;
- development of key performance indicators for the business;
- production of monthly management accounts, analysis and commentary.

You will need to have excellent business acumen and highly developed communication skills.

## MANAGEMENT ACCOUNTANT
### (*charitable organisation*)

This is a leading charity providing safe, secure and affordable housing for young people and working with homeless young people to provide safe shelter. Reporting to the head of finance, the role involves working closely with various departments identifying areas of concern and solutions.

Key responsibilities include:

1　Reviewing of trial balance and generation and review of management accounts; identifying and resolving any issues and offering a business support function.
2　Attending committee meetings to present the accounts to the trustees.
3　Identifying trends in the management accounts and advising management as to recommendations.
4　Development of budgets and forecasts.
5　Investigating and improving financial performance in the operations of the residential centres.

This role would suit an individual who is looking to shape the continuing development of the work of the charity.

## HEAD OF MANAGEMENT ACCOUNTS
### (*the finance office of a university*)

You will be responsible for the setting, monitoring, control and reporting on budgets and the regular production of management accounts. In addition, you will ensure the provision of a comprehensive payroll service and be responsible for arranging and accounting for capital finance.

## PRINCIPAL MANAGEMENT ACCOUNTANT
### (*public sector organisation*)

This is one of the most successful police forces in the country. With 2,000 employees and an annual budget of over £80 million, it is essential that the organisation has appropriate and well-maintained financial management and information systems to support the demands of modern policing.

We now require a dynamic team leader to ensure the continued development of these systems and to provide a comprehensive financial advice/support service to senior managers.

The successful candidate will be closely involved in the production of medium-term financial plans, annual budgets, financial information systems upgrades as well as the training and development of non-technical staff on financial management.

You will be self-reliant and able to work to tight deadlines whilst maintaining high standards, be capable of clearly communicating financial concepts in a persuasive and effective manner and have a suitable professional qualification with three years' experience in financial management.

## Cases for study groups

### Case 16.1

Form a study group of four to six persons who are to act out the role of the finance director and related staff on the accounting team of a company planning to open a new supermarket chain at an out-of-town location. Give a ten-minute presentation to the rest of the class explaining the major issues you will be expected to deal with in making a contribution to the decision and the subsequent monitoring of that decision.

### Case 16.2

Form a study group of four to six persons who are to negotiate the development of a new production line to process canned peas. The canned peas will replace an existing product, canned carrots. Half of the team will argue on behalf of the canned peas while the other half will argue on behalf of the canned carrots. Give a ten-minute presentation to the class (five minutes for each half of the team) explaining how management accounting information will help you to justify the decision you propose and to monitor the implementation of the decision.

### Notes and references

1. AAA (1966), *A Statement of Basic Accounting Theory*, American Accounting Association, Evanston, Illinois, p. 1.
2. Lowe, E. A. (1971), 'On the idea of a management control system', *Journal of Management Studies*, **8** (1), pp. 1–12.
3. Bromwich, M. (1990), 'The case for strategic management accounting: the role of accounting information for strategy in competitive markets', *Accounting, Organizations and Society*, **15** (1/2), pp. 27–46.

The following chapters are from:
*Managerial Accounting for Business Decisions*
Third Edition
by Ray Proctor

# Cost behaviour

## Introduction

As a manager, you might find yourself asking your accountant for the cost of one of your products. The answer you expect to be given is probably a specific amount of money, e.g. £49.55. If your accountant replies 'Why do you want to know?' you may think he (or she) is being unnecessarily awkward and assume that he is in a bad mood for some reason or other. However, the accountant's reply is actually very sensible, even though it would have been better for him to reply 'The answer depends on why you want to know.' At first, this may seem very strange to you but a product has several different costs, each of which serves a different purpose. As you will see in the next few chapters of this book, there are several different costing systems in existence, each giving a different answer to your original question.

The absorption costing system gives the absorption cost; the variable costing system gives the variable cost; and the activity-based costing system gives the activity-based cost. They all give the correct cost in the context of their own system. Each system is a financial model based on its own rules and assumptions. Different rules and assumptions result in different numerical answers. For example, the product in question may have an absorption cost of £49.55, a variable cost of £20.95 and an activity-based cost of £142.00. **Each of these three answers is correct.**

The word 'cost' is a general word and is often used in a general sense. However, when a manager asks an accountant for the cost of a product, the manager usually has a specific purpose in mind. The reason why the accountant replied 'Why do you want to know?' is that he wanted to determine the manager's specific purpose so that he could give the right answer. He was actually trying to be helpful rather than awkward! In this chapter, we will look at the different ways in which costs can behave and see how some of these form the bases of the different costing systems.

## Learning objectives

**Having worked through this chapter you should be able to:**

- explain the difference between manufacturing, trading and providing services;
- explain the difference between product and period costs;
- explain the difference between variable and fixed costs;
- explain what semi-variable costs and stepped fixed costs are;
- find fixed and variable elements of semi-variable costs using the high–low method;
- draw a scattergraph based on periodic cost and output data and interpret it;
- explain **in outline** what regression analysis is;
- explain the difference between direct and indirect costs;
- compare variable cost analysis with absorption cost analysis;
- explain the basis for analysing activity-based costs;
- say what relevant costs are used for.

## Types of business

There are three main categories of businesses: manufacturers, traders and service businesses. Manufacturers make the goods they sell by converting raw materials into finished products. Traders buy in goods and sell them without altering them in any significant way (they may be repackaged and re-presented). Service businesses create

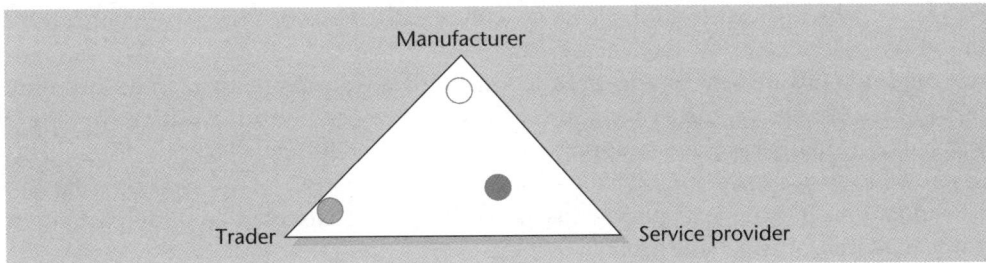

Figure 1.1 **Business orientations**

intangible products – for example, banks, accountants, lawyers, financial advisers, freight companies, railways, theatrical agents, education and training institutions. So costs can be described as manufacturing costs, trading costs or service costs.

It is worth noting that the type of organization affects the format of the financial accounts. Gross profit is meaningful for a manufacturer or trader but much less so for a service business. Production accounts (to calculate the cost of production) are essential for manufacturers but not applicable to traders or service businesses. However, it is wise not to be too pedantic about this as services tend to be mainly intangible but often include minor tangible items such as chequebooks, sets of accounts, property deeds, share certificates, bills of lading, rail tickets, contracts of employment and degree certificates. In these cases you would probably agree that gross profit is inappropriate.

On the other hand, manufacturers often include a small service element in their products. When you buy a new car, the first two services may be free of charge and there may be a three-year warranty. The price of a new computer usually includes the right to use a selection of software applications for word processing, spreadsheets, databases, etc.

But what about pubs, restaurants and clubs? Are they manufacturers, traders or service providers? The answer is, of course, that they can be all three. The meals are created on the premises, the drinks are bought in and waiting at table, pouring drinks, etc., are pure services. The same applies to residential health clubs and activity holidays where you learn to produce something tangible such as a painting or a piece of pottery.

Figure 1.1 illustrates the relationship between these different types of organization. The darker-coloured circle shows the approximate position of a restaurant. The empty circle represents firms such as furniture makers, and the lighter-coloured circle could represent a national chain of off-licences.

## Product and period costs

There are two ways of including costs in the profit and loss account. First, they can be included as part of the production cost of the products made. The production cost of all goods sold in the period gives the total *cost of sales* figure, which is deducted from *sales revenue* to give *gross profit*. Closing stock of finished goods is also valued at production cost. This is how production costs of goods unsold at the year-end are carried forward to the year in which they are sold. (This complies with the accounting rule/concept of realization.) These costs are known as *product costs*.

Second, the full amount of non-production overheads for marketing, administration, etc. appears directly in the profit and loss account of the period in which they were incurred. No attempt is made to apportion them to different financial years. These costs are known as *period costs*.

Product and period costs will be discussed further in Chapter 11, 'Comparison of profits under absorption and variable costing'.

## Variable and fixed costs

### Variable costs

These are costs which vary **in total** with a measure of activity – for example, the total cost of raw materials increases as output increases (see Figure 1.2b). Take the example of a business making furniture – if the number of chairs produced doubles then the cost of raw materials also doubles.

[Note: Direct labour is always a variable cost when calculating product costs. However, when looking at the overall total costs of a business, it is often thought of as a fixed cost (provided operatives are employed on a 'permanent' basis, e.g. paid monthly).]

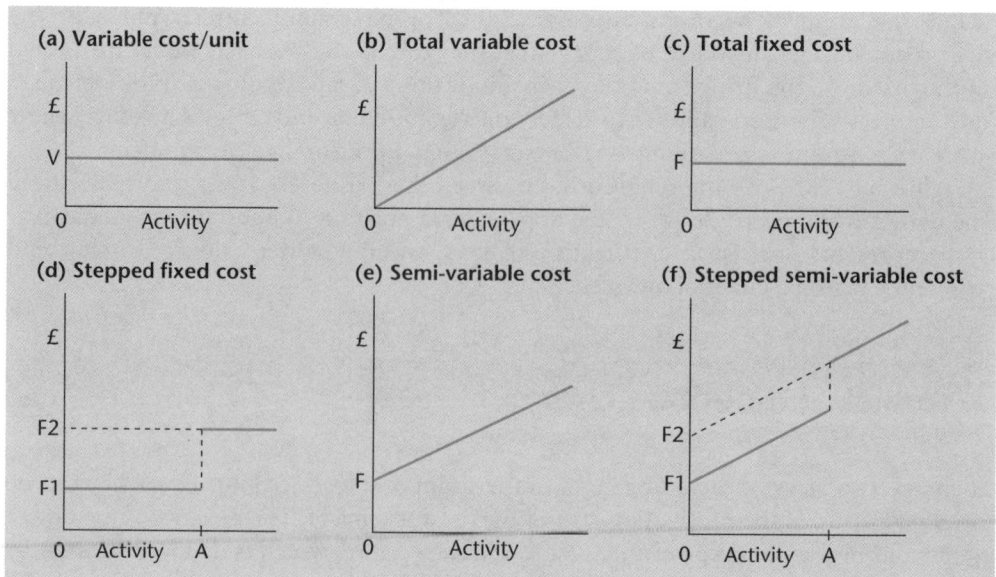

Figure 1.2 **Patterns of variable and fixed cost behaviour**

## Fixed costs

These are costs incurred for a period of time, which, within a given range of production and/or sales activity, do not change (see Figure 1.2c). Continuing the furniture-making example above, if the number of chairs produced doubles, the business rates on the premises do **not** change.

Note that variable costs can be calculated per unit of output but that fixed costs refer to the business as a whole. Variable costing assumes that the variable cost **per unit** stays the same over a range of activity (see Figure 1.2a). This means that **total** variable costs increase linearly with activity (see Figure 1.2b).

Great care must be taken if *fixed cost per unit* is used in calculations. This measure will change every time the number of units changes, i.e. fixed cost per unit is **not** fixed!

## Stepped fixed costs

When a certain level of production and/or sales activity is reached, there is a sudden increase in fixed costs from F1 to F2 (see Figure 1.2d). For example, when output increases significantly, it may be necessary to put on an extra work shift. This occurs at activity level A and entails extra costs for items such as supervision, security, heating and lighting, etc.

## Semi-variable costs

Although there are several costs which are either purely variable or purely fixed, many costs are semi-variable. The utilities, such as telephone and electricity, often have a fixed cost element such as line rental or a standing charge which has to be paid irrespective of usage. In addition, there is also a cost per unit used. The graph of the semi-variable cost (see Figure 1.2e) combines the features of graphs (b) and (c).

If the semi-variable cost covers a range of activity including a stepped fixed cost, it would behave as shown in graph (f). This graph is obtained by combining graphs (b) and (d).

---

*Self-assessment question S1.1*

*Try the following question for yourself (answer at the end of the chapter).*

Match the following cost descriptions to the appropriate graph in Figure 1.3.

a) This graph shows a variable cost with a price discount activated after a certain quantity has been purchased.
b) This graph shows a semi-variable cost which reaches a maximum at a specified quantity of purchases.
c) This graph shows a variable cost with 10 free units for every 100 bought.
d) This graph shows the fixed cost per unit.
e) This graph shows a variable cost which has a minimum charge.
f) This graph shows the variable cost of a scarce item. When local supplies have been exhausted, it has to be purchased abroad, entailing extra transport costs.

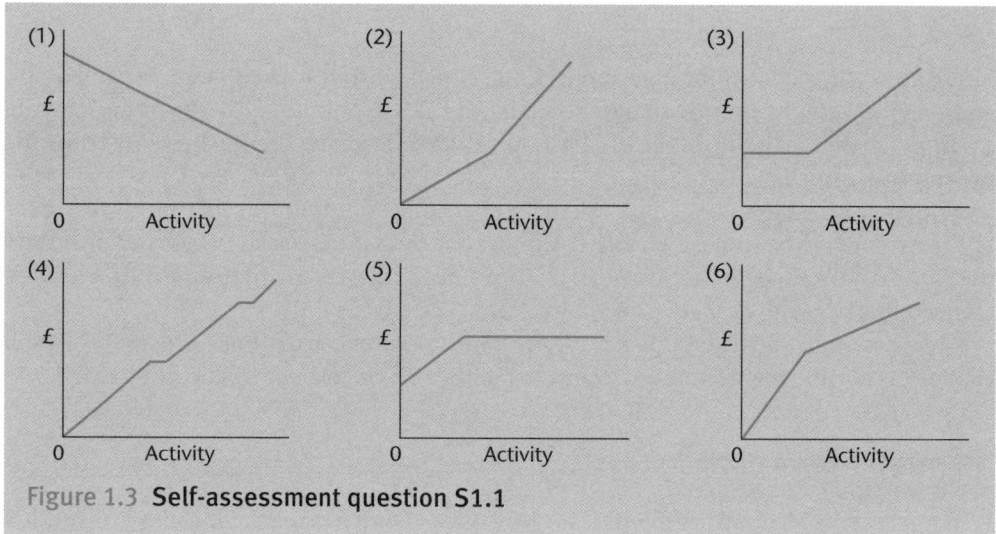

Figure 1.3  **Self-assessment question S1.1**

## Analysis of semi-variable costs into their fixed and variable elements

It is not just the utilities that have semi-variable costs. Many other costs, such as security and maintenance, also follow this pattern. Often, only the **total** amounts of these semi-variable costs are known and the fixed and variable elements have to be worked out mathematically. Three alternative ways of doing this are shown below.

### The high–low method

Figure 1.4 shows the machine maintenance costs and the output level of products for the first six monthly periods of the year.

Only two sets of monthly information are used, one from the highest-output month (month 3 = 600 units) and the other from the lowest-output month (month 6 = 500 units).

| Month | Output (units) | Maintenance cost (£) |
|-------|----------------|----------------------|
| 1 | 586 | 12,340 |
| 2 | 503 | 11,949 |
| 3 | 600 | 12,400 |
| 4 | 579 | 12,298 |
| 5 | 550 | 12,075 |
| 6 | 500 | 12,000 |

Figure 1.4  **Monthly maintenance costs**

|  | Highest (month 3) | 600 units | £12,400 |
|---|---|---|---|
| Less: | Lowest (month 6) | 500 units | £12,000 |
|  | Difference | 100 units | £400 |

Since both the £12,400 and the £12,000 include the fixed cost element, this is eliminated by the subtraction and the £400 difference is due solely to the variable cost of the 100 units difference.

**Variable cost per unit produced = £400/100 units = £4/unit**

Using this in month 6:

**Variable cost of 500 units = 500 × £4 =  £2,000**
**Total cost of 500 units                = £12,000**
**Therefore, fixed cost of 500 units     = £10,000**

These cost elements can be checked by applying them to the other month used, month 3:

**Variable cost of 600 units = 600 × £4 =  £2,400**
**Fixed cost of 600 units                 = £10,000**
**Therefore, total cost of 600 units      = £12,400**

This shows the calculations to be correct. However, if any of the other months **not** used in the calculation is chosen to test the results, it will probably not work! This is because the high–low method uses the information from only two months. It ignores all the other information. It assumes that the relationship between the cost and production output is a linear one, i.e. if all the monthly points were plotted on a graph, they would all be points on the same straight line. In fact, this is not so, as you can probably see from Figure 1.4. For instance, month 2 has a higher output (503 units) than month 6 (500 units) but a lower maintenance cost.

It can be seen that the high–low method is a fairly crude way of estimating the fixed and variable cost elements of a semi-variable cost. However, its advantage is that it is easy to understand and easy to calculate.

## Scattergraphs

If the monthly information shown above (in the high–low method) was plotted on a graph it would look like Figure 1.5.

The line of best fit is drawn on the graph by eye. The intersection of this line and the vertical cost axis gives the fixed cost element. This is **read** from the graph and should be close to £10,000.

The slope of the line,

$$\frac{\text{change in cost}}{\text{change in output}} = 2{,}384/600 = £3.97$$

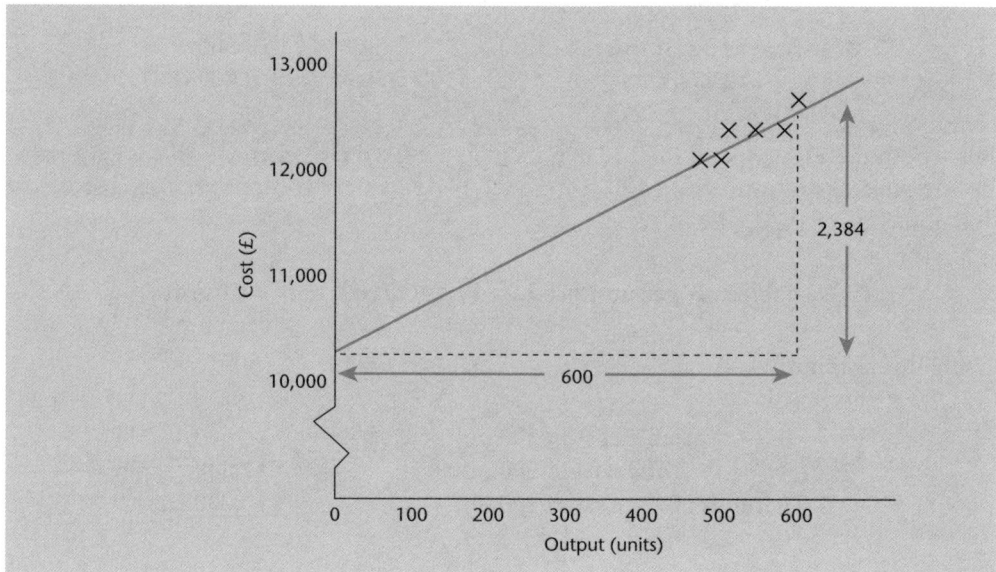

Figure 1.5 **A scattergraph**

gives the variable cost per unit. You may remember the equation for a straight line is

$$y = a + bx$$

where *a* is the intersection with the vertical axis and *b* is the slope of the line. In this context, the fixed cost is *a* and the variable cost per unit is *b*.

The disadvantage of this method is that drawing the line of best fit by eye is subjective and different individuals will produce slightly different lines. However, it does have the advantage of using all the available information and, like the high–low method, a scattergraph will give a workable estimate and is easy to understand.

## Regression analysis

This method is similar to the scattergraph but the line of best fit is not drawn by eye. The equation for the line is calculated by a statistical technique called *regression analysis*. It is sometimes known as *least squares regression*. It is more precise than the other two methods but it is much more complex mathematically. The technique of regression analysis is not covered by this book. It is sufficient for you to know of its existence and availability if needed.

The most important thing to remember is that, although it is more precise than the high–low and scattergraph methods, it still only gives an estimate of the fixed and variable cost elements. The extra complexity involved may not be worth the improvement in accuracy gained.

*Self-assessment question S1.2*

*Try the following question for yourself (answer at the end of the chapter).*

As the manager of an Indian restaurant with a take-away service, you have been asked to prepare a detailed budget for next year. To help you with this, you need to know the fixed and variable cost elements of your delivery cost to customers' homes.

The following information is available from the monthly accounts. Calculate the fixed and variable cost elements using the *high–low* method.

| Month | No. of deliveries | Total delivery cost (£) |
|---|---|---|
| July | 403 | 662.70 |
| August | 291 | 561.90 |
| September | 348 | 613.20 |
| October | 364 | 627.60 |
| November | 521 | 768.90 |
| December | 387 | 648.30 |

# Absorption costs: direct and indirect

## Direct cost

This is expenditure which can be economically identified with, and specifically **measured** in, a product.

Consider an advertising agency specialising in the production of television adverts. The cost of hiring a celebrity to appear in one such advert is a measurable direct cost of that advert. Similarly, if the company is a furniture manufacturer, the cost of materials used to make a chair and the pay of the operative assembling it are measurable direct costs of that chair.

## Indirect cost (or overhead)

This is expenditure which **cannot** be economically identified with, and specifically **measured** in, a product.

There are many, many different overheads including expenses such as the supervisor's pay, depreciation of fixed assets, business rates and insurance. Somehow, a proportion of these non-measurable expenses has to be included in the total product cost. Absorption costing is one way of doing this. It is based on the assumption that costs can be analysed into their 'direct' and 'indirect' components. For each product, the direct cost is measured but the indirect cost is estimated.

Absorption cost = direct cost + indirect cost

The estimates of indirect costs are usually based on some connection or correlation between the cost and a measure such as machine hours used, direct labour hours used or total cost of direct materials used. Absorption costing is the subject of Chapter 9.

## Comparison of alternative cost analyses

Variable costing analyses total costs into fixed and variable components. Absorption costing analyses total costs into direct and indirect components. In itself, this is not problematical as these two systems of costing, variable and absorption, are independent financial models. However, it is not unusual to be confused by these terms and how they interrelate. The aim of Figure 1.6 is to clarify these relationships.

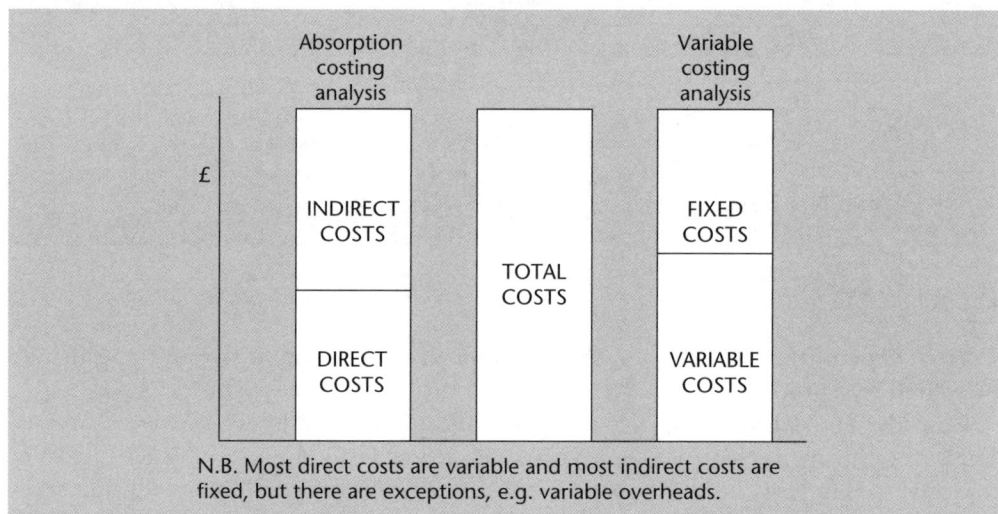

Figure 1.6  **Alternative cost analysis**

## Cost analysis by activity

This analysis is based on the principle that costs are **caused** by activities and that activities are caused by products or services. The activity-based cost of a product is a result of determining the costs of all the activities caused by that product. This principle is fundamentally different from the correlation principle used in absorption costing.

Activities are identified and their costs calculated before being attached to products via a measure of the activity called a *cost driver*. Activity-based costing gives significantly more accurate product costs than absorption costing but it has difficulties of its own and does not give 100% accurate costs. This subject is discussed at length in Chapter 10.

# Relevant and irrelevant costs

This analysis of costs is very useful in decision making. In brief, it differentiates between those costs which affect a decision (i.e. relevant costs) and those that do not (irrelevant costs). This approach to decision making is discussed further in Chapter 7.

*Summary*

- Each product can have several different costs.
- The cost of a product depends on the purpose for which this information is required.
- Business types can be divided into three categories: manufacturing, trading and providing services.
- Period costs are written off to the profit and loss account of the period for which they were incurred.
- Product costs are built into the production cost of manufactured items and are accounted for by either the cost of sales figure for the year in which they were incurred or carried forward to the next period in the closing stock valuation figure.
- Total cost can be analysed into variable and fixed cost elements.
- Semi-variable costs have both variable and fixed cost elements.
- Fixed costs are stable only up to a certain level of activity; above this, they step up to a higher level.
- There are three ways of analysing semi-variable costs into their fixed and variable components: the high–low method, scattergraphs and regression analysis.
- Total cost can be analysed into direct and indirect cost elements.
- Costs can be analysed causally according to production activities and activities can be analysed causally by products.
- As an aid to decision making, costs can be analysed into relevant and irrelevant types.
- Direct and indirect costs are similar to, but different from, variable and fixed costs.

## Further reading

Anderson, M. C., Banker, R. D. and Janakiraman, S. N. (2003) 'Are selling, general, and administrative costs "sticky"?', *Journal of Accounting Research*, Vol. 41, Issue 1, March.

Drury, C. (2004) *Management and Cost Accounting*, 6th edition, Thomson Learning, London. See chapter 'An introduction to cost terms and concepts'.

Horngren, C., Bhimani, A., Datar, S. and Foster, G. (2002) *Management and Cost Accounting*, Prentice Hall Europe, Harlow. See chapter 'Determining how costs behave'.

Liu, L. and Robinson, J. (2002) 'Double measure', *Financial Management (CIMA)*, October.

Upchurch, A. (2003) *Management Accounting, Principles and Practice*, 2nd edition, Financial Times/Prentice Hall, Harlow. See chapter 'Cost estimation'.

Weetman, P. (2002) *Management Accounting, an Introduction*, 3rd edition, Financial Times/Prentice Hall, Harlow. See chapter 'Classification of costs'.

## Answers to self-assessment questions

### S1.1 Cost behaviour graphs

a) Graph 6
b) Graph 5
c) Graph 4
d) Graph 1
e) Graph 3
f) Graph 2

### S1.2 Indian take-away delivery costs

Only two sets of monthly information are used, one from the highest-activity month (November = 521 deliveries) and the other from the lowest-activity month (August = 291 deliveries).

|  | | | |
|---|---|---|---|
|  | Highest (November) | 521 deliveries | £768.90 |
| Less: | Lowest (August) | 291 deliveries | £561.90 |
|  | Difference | 230 deliveries | £207.00 |

**Variable cost per delivery = £207.00/230 = £0.90/delivery**

Using this in November:

$$\text{Variable cost of deliveries} = 521 \times £0.90 = £468.90$$
$$\text{Total cost of 521 deliveries} = £768.90$$
$$\text{Therefore, Fixed cost of 521 deliveries} = £300.00$$

These cost elements can be checked by applying them to the other month used, August:

$$\text{Variable cost of 291 deliveries} = 291 \times £0.90 = £261.90$$
$$\text{Fixed cost of 291 deliveries} \qquad\qquad = £300.00$$
$$\text{Therefore, Total cost of 291 deliveries} \qquad = \underline{\underline{£561.90}}$$

## Review questions

1  Explain the difference between manufacturing, trading and providing services.
2  Explain the difference between product costs and period costs.
3  Explain the difference between variable and fixed costs.
4  Explain what semi-variable costs and stepped fixed costs are.
5  Describe the advantages and disadvantages of finding the fixed and variable elements of semi-variable costs using the high–low method.
6  Describe the advantages and disadvantages of finding the fixed and variable elements of semi-variable costs using a scattergraph.
7  Explain **in outline** what regression analysis is.
8  Explain the difference between direct and indirect costs.
9  Compare variable cost analysis with absorption cost analysis.
10  Explain the underlying theory of activity-based costing.
11  Explain the difference between relevant and irrelevant costs.

*The answers to all these questions can be found in the text of this chapter.*

# CHAPTER 5

# Variable costing and breakeven analysis

**Chapter contents**

## Introduction

Sometimes there are ways of doing things which are so simple they seem almost too easy, too good to be true. Variable costing is one of these. But do not be fooled by its simplicity – it is a very powerful technique. It is used mainly for short-term decision making and calculating the effect of production and sales levels on profitability. Short-term decision making is the subject of the next chapter. This chapter concentrates on the relationship between profit and activity (i.e. production and sales), commonly known as breakeven analysis.

At some point in your life you will probably think seriously about starting your own business. If the type of business you have in mind involves providing the same item for many different customers, breakeven analysis will be very useful to you. Suppose you decide to open a driving school, offering lessons to learner drivers. After much careful thought you will be able to estimate your total annual cost. Dividing this amount by the number of lessons (**estimated conservatively**) will give you the cost per lesson. But what are you going to charge your customers for each lesson? How do you know if you will make a profit or a loss? And how much is it likely to be? These are very important questions for anyone going into business on their own. Breakeven analysis is the financial model designed to answer these questions.

Note: Variable costing is also known as *marginal costing* and *cost–volume–profit (CVP) analysis*.

| Learning objectives | Having worked through this chapter you should be able to: |
|---|---|

**Having worked through this chapter you should be able to:**

- differentiate between variable and fixed costs;
- define contribution;
- explain the relationship between contribution, fixed costs and net profit;
- calculate contribution;
- calculate breakeven point;
- draw traditional and contribution breakeven charts;
- define and calculate the margin of safety;
- evaluate different cost structures in terms of their operational gearing;
- calculate the activity level to produce a target profit;
- draw and use a profit–volume chart;
- discuss the assumptions and limitations of breakeven analysis.

## Cost behaviour

This section is a brief revision of Chapter 2. Variable costing is based on the difference between fixed and variable costs, which are defined as follows and illustrated in Figure 5.1.

**Variable costs – Costs which vary with output (e.g. raw materials)**
**Fixed costs – Costs which do not change when output changes (e.g. business rates)**
**Semi-variable costs – Costs which are partly fixed and partly variable (e.g. telephone)**

Although there are several costs which are either purely variable or purely fixed, many costs are semi-variable. The utilities, such as telephone and electricity, often have a fixed cost element, such as line rental or a standing charge, which has to be paid irrespective of usage. In addition, there is also a cost per unit used. The graph of the semi-variable cost combines the features of the other two graphs. Sometimes, only the total amounts of semi-variable costs are known for successive periods and the fixed and variable elements have to be worked out. (One way of doing this is the 'high–low method' as detailed in Chapter 1, on cost behaviour.)

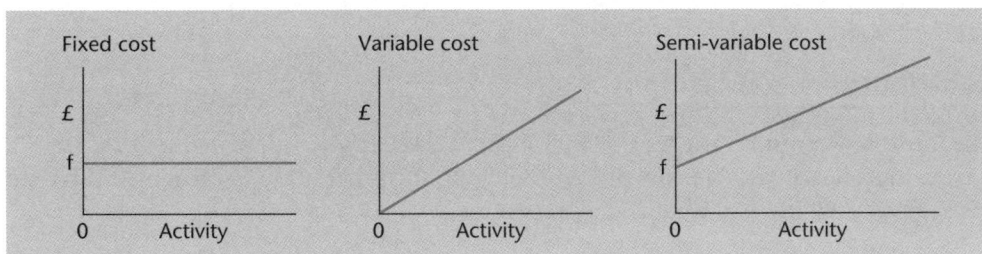

Figure 5.1  **Patterns of cost behaviour**

## Contribution

In the introduction to this chapter, it was pointed out that ignoring fixed costs is sometimes the correct thing to do. As fixed costs cannot be changed **in the short term**, there is no point considering them for short-term decision making. This approach results in something that is like 'profit' but is not 'profit'. To avoid confusion, this new entity is called 'contribution'.

Contribution is defined as the excess of sales revenue over the variable costs.

It can be thought of as the contribution towards paying for the fixed costs. Once all fixed costs have been covered, any further contribution is all net profit, as shown in Figure 5.2.

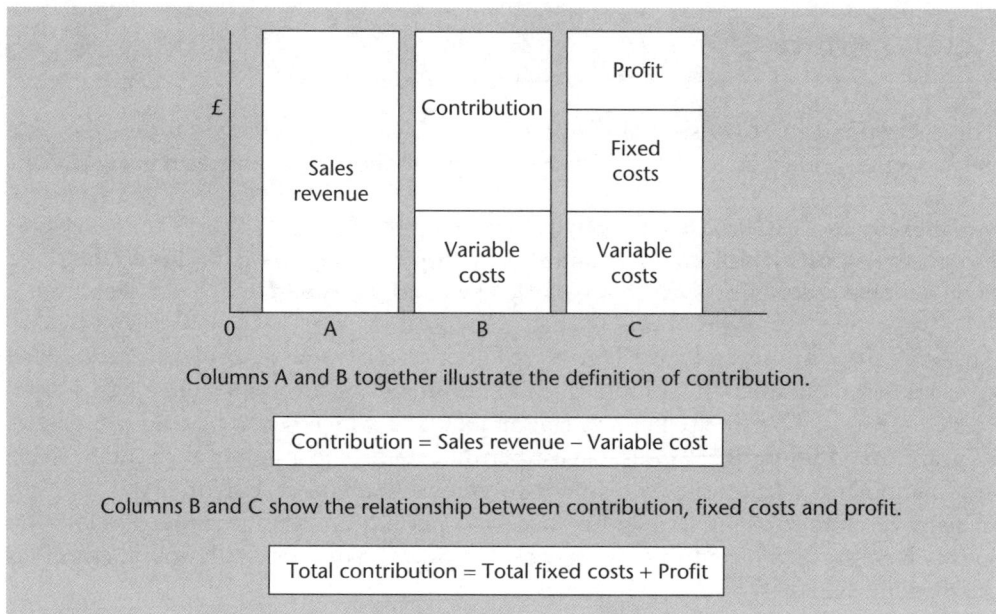

Figure 5.2  **Contribution relationships**

## Contribution calculations

The Grubsteaks restaurant sells 18,000 meals a year at a standard selling price of £5. If each meal has a variable cost of £2, what annual contribution is earned? If the fixed costs are £30,000 in total, what is the net profit?

$$
\begin{aligned}
&\qquad\qquad\qquad £\\
\text{Sales revenue} &= 90,000 \quad (18,000 \times £5)\\
\text{Variable costs} &= \underline{36,000} \quad (18,000 \times £2)\\
\text{Contribution} &= 54,000\\
\text{Fixed costs} &= \underline{30,000}\\
\text{Net profit} &= \underline{\underline{24,000}}
\end{aligned}
$$

Alternatively, the contribution per unit could have been calculated first to give £3 (= £5 − £2). Multiplying this by 18,000 meals gives the total contribution of £54,000.

**Self-assessment question S5.1**

*Try the following question for yourself (answer at the end of the chapter).*

The Good Health drinks tent at a local horse-race meeting sells all its drinks at £2.50 each. The variable cost of each drink is £1.00 and the fixed cost for the one-day event is £2,700. If 4,000 drinks are sold in the day, what is (a) the total contribution, and (b) the net profit?

## Breakeven point

### Definition and calculation

The total contribution increases as more units are sold. A point will come when the total contribution is just enough to cover the fixed costs. At this precise level of sales, all the costs have been covered and the next unit sold will produce the first profits for the business. This critical point, where the business makes neither a profit nor a loss, is known as the *breakeven point* (BEP). This is a useful concept for planning and control purposes.

$$\text{At BEP, Total contribution} = \text{total fixed costs}$$

Continuing with the example used above: the Grubsteaks restaurant sells 18,000 meals a year at a standard selling price of £5 and a variable cost of £2 with fixed costs of £30,000; how many meals will it need to sell to break even?

Let breakeven occur when $N$ meals have been sold – in other words, when $N$ lots of unit contributions have been received.

$$\text{Total contribution} = \text{total fixed costs}$$
$$N \times \text{unit contribution} = \text{total fixed costs}$$
$$N \times (5-2) = 30{,}000$$
$$N = 30{,}000/3$$
$$N = 10{,}000 \text{ meals}$$

The relationship between costs and revenues can be illustrated graphically by *breakeven charts*. Figure 5.3 gives the basic structure; this is then added to in two alternative ways in Figures 5.4 and 5.5. It is these two alternatives that are normally seen and used in practice.

Figure 5.4 shows the total cost broken down into its fixed and variable elements.

Figure 5.5 also shows the fixed and variable elements, but with their positions reversed. This enables the contribution to be clearly illustrated by the shaded area. (This is not possible on the traditional breakeven chart.)

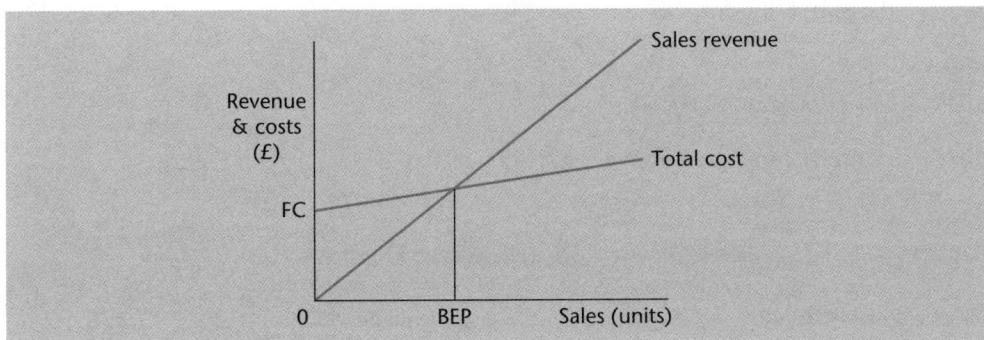

Figure 5.3 **Fundamental structure**

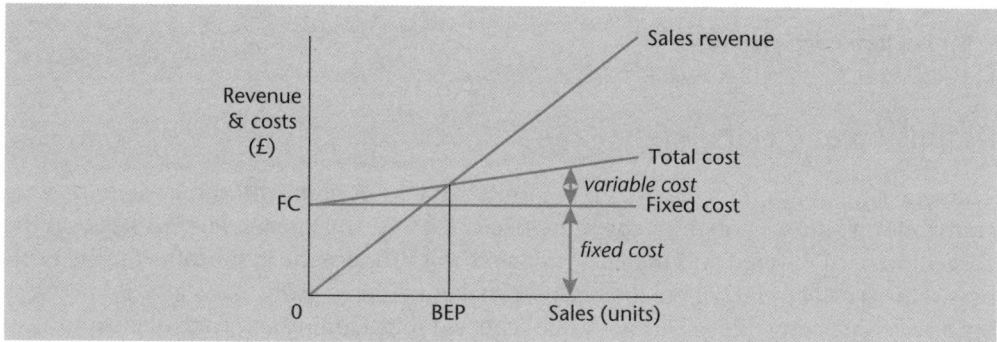

Figure 5.4 **Traditional breakeven chart**

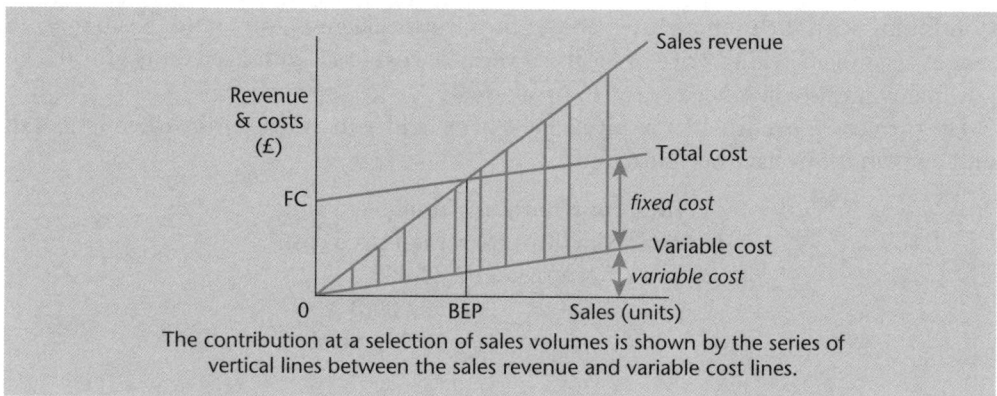

The contribution at a selection of sales volumes is shown by the series of vertical lines between the sales revenue and variable cost lines.

Figure 5.5 **Contribution breakeven chart**

*Self-assessment question S5.2*

*Try the following question for yourself (answer at the end of the chapter).*

Continuing with S5.1 above: the Good Health drinks tent at a local horse-race meeting sells all its drinks at £2.50 each. The variable cost of each drink is £1.00 and the fixed cost for the one-day event is £2,700. How many drinks does it need to sell to break even?

## Graphical representation

The restaurant example used above can be illustrated by the chart in Figure 5.6.

*Self-assessment question S5.3*

*Try the following question for yourself (answer at the end of the chapter).*

Using your answers from S5.1 and S5.2 above, draw a contribution breakeven chart (to scale) for the Good Health drinks tent.

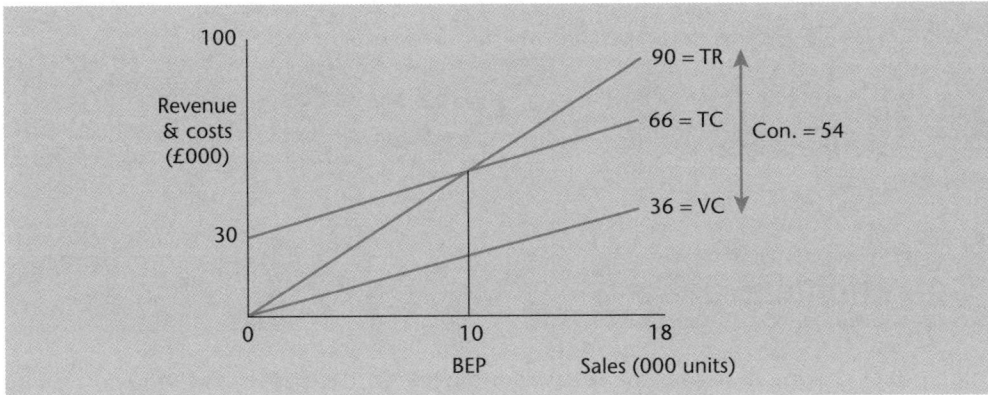

Figure 5.6  **Contribution breakeven chart for the Grubsteaks restaurant**

# Margin of safety

This is a measure of the amount by which sales can fall before profit turns to loss, i.e. the excess of actual sales over breakeven sales. This can be expressed as a number of units or as a percentage of sales and is illustrated by Figure 5.7.

For the Grubsteaks restaurant example:

$$\text{Actual number of meals sold} = 18,000$$
$$\text{Breakeven level of sales} = \underline{10,000}$$
$$\text{Margin of safety} = \underline{\ 8,000\ }\text{ meals}$$

$$\text{or,}\quad \frac{\text{Margin of safety in units}}{\text{Actual sales in units}} \times 100 = \frac{8,000}{18,000} \times 100 = 44\% \text{ of sales}$$

So sales could fall by 44% before losses occurred.

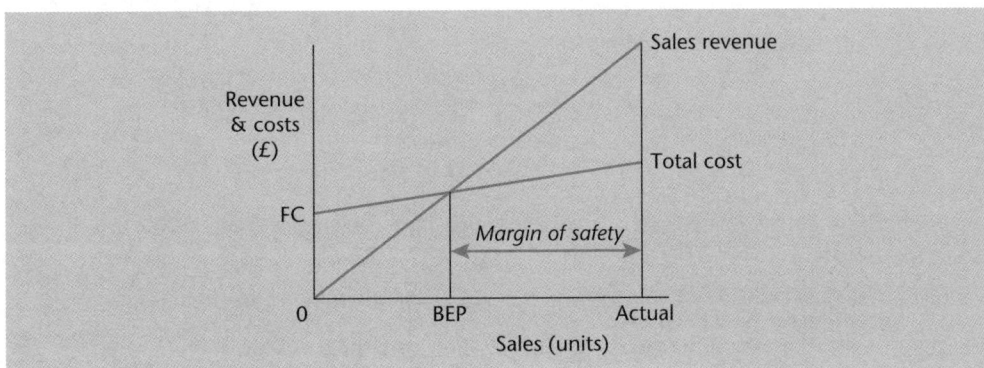

Figure 5.7  **Margin of safety**

**Self-assessment question S5.4**

*Try the following question for yourself (answer at the end of the chapter).*

Calculate the margin of safety for the Good Health drinks tent example in S5.3, (a) in units, and (b) as a percentage of sales.

## Operational gearing

Operational gearing describes the relationship between fixed costs and total costs. The greater the amount of fixed costs, expressed as a percentage of total costs, the greater the operational gearing. The greater the operational gearing, the greater is the effect of changes in sales volume on contribution and profit. The following formula expresses this numerically:

$$\text{Operational gearing} = \frac{\text{change in contribution or profit}}{\text{change in output}}$$

Consider the following situation where two separate businesses make and sell the same item at the same price. They both make cardboard 'outer' boxes to contain, for example, 48 packets of cereal. These large outers are used to transport large volumes of goods around the country.

Business A keeps fixed costs to a minimum but has a high proportion of variable costs. It uses simple bending and gluing devices operated by 12 employees and buys in large sheets of ready-made cardboard as its raw material. On the other hand, business B has invested heavily in automated machinery whose first process is to make its own cardboard sheet. This needs only two people to operate but causes a much larger amount of depreciation (i.e. fixed cost) than in business A. Its raw material is shredded recycled paper and other fibres which are much cheaper to buy than ready-made cardboard. Consequently, business B has a much higher proportion of fixed costs than variable costs compared with A. (See Figure 5.8 and notice the change in slope of the total cost line.)

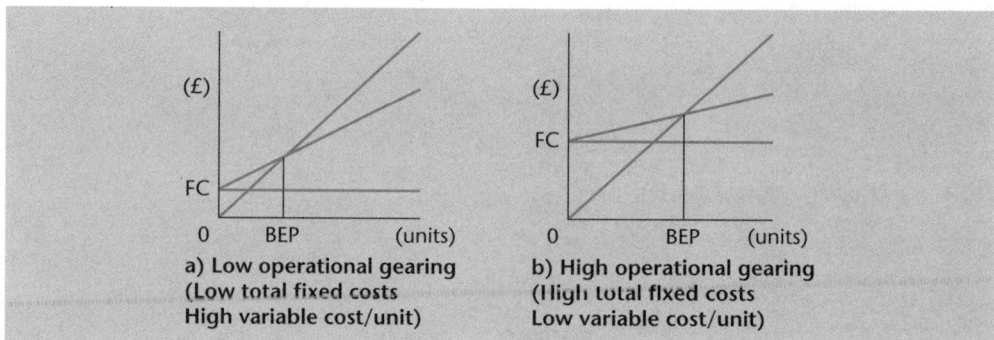

Figure 5.8 **Operational gearing**

As an example, for one outer:

|  | A | B |
|---|---|---|
|  | £ | £ |
| Selling price | 5 | 5 |
| Variable cost | 3 | 1 |
| Contribution | 2 | 4 |
| Annual fixed cost | £100,000 | £300,000 |

If there is a new order for 3,000 outers the profit will increase by £6,000 (3,000 × £2) for business A but by £12,000 (3,000 × £4) for business B. B will do better than A.

However, if a customer decides to purchase its outers elsewhere and cancels an order for 3,000 outers, the profit will decrease by £6,000 (3,000 × £2) for business A but by £12,000 (3,000 × £4) for business B. This time, A will do better than B.

The greater the operational gearing, the greater is the effect of changes in sales volume on profit. In other words, the greater the operational gearing, the greater the risk.

When starting a new business, and sales are not very predictable, low operational gearing is preferable to high operational gearing. Low gearing means that there are fewer fixed costs to be covered before reaching profitability. This strategy helps to minimize risk.

On the other hand, as shown in the above example, provided the business is making profits, high gearing gives a greater increase in profit for each extra item sold.

## Activity levels for target profits

Another useful calculation is to determine the number of items that has to be sold to achieve a given net profit. Figure 5.2 at the start of this chapter illustrates the following relationship:

$$\text{Total contribution} = \text{total fixed costs} + \text{profit}$$

If the unit contribution, the total fixed cost and the target profit are known, the activity level can be calculated. Suppose you were given the following information:

|  | £/unit |
|---|---|
| Direct materials | 4 |
| Direct labour | 7 |
| Variable overhead | 3 |
| Selling price | 24 |
| Total fixed cost | £5,000 |

How many items need to be sold for the business to make a profit of £10,000?

$$\text{Unit contribution} = \text{sales revenue} - \text{variable costs}$$
$$= 24 - (4 + 7 + 3) = 10$$

Let the number of items needed $= N$.

$$\text{Total contribution} = \text{total fixed costs} + \text{profit}$$
$$N \times 10 = 5{,}000 + 10{,}000$$
$$10N = 15{,}000$$
$$N = 1{,}500$$

**1,500 items need to be sold to achieve a profit of £10,000.**

---

| **Self-assessment question S5.5** | *Try the following question for yourself (answer at the end of the chapter).* |
|---|---|

*A new style of electric bass guitar is about to be launched by a well-known instrument company. The materials for each guitar total £25 and 2.5 hours of labour (paid at £12/hour) are needed to assemble one. Variable overheads are charged at £2/labour hour and the associated fixed costs are £600 per month. If the selling price is set at £160, how many guitars need to be sold to achieve an annual profit of £20,000?*

## Profit–volume relationships

Sometimes it is preferable to bypass the details of sales and costs and compare profit directly with the volume of activity. The profit–volume chart shown in Figure 5.9 has the same horizontal axis as the breakeven chart but the vertical axis is for profit only. The breakeven point is where the profit line crosses the horizontal axis.

In order to draw a profit–volume graph, two points are needed to determine the position of the profit line. One of these points is easy to find. When activity is zero, the loss being made is exactly equal to the total of fixed costs. For the other point, a calculation is needed. The following relationship is used (see Figure 5.2):

$$\text{Total contribution} = \text{total fixed costs} + \text{profit}$$

Assuming the total of fixed costs is given, the amount of profit can be calculated for a chosen activity level if the total contribution at that level can be found.

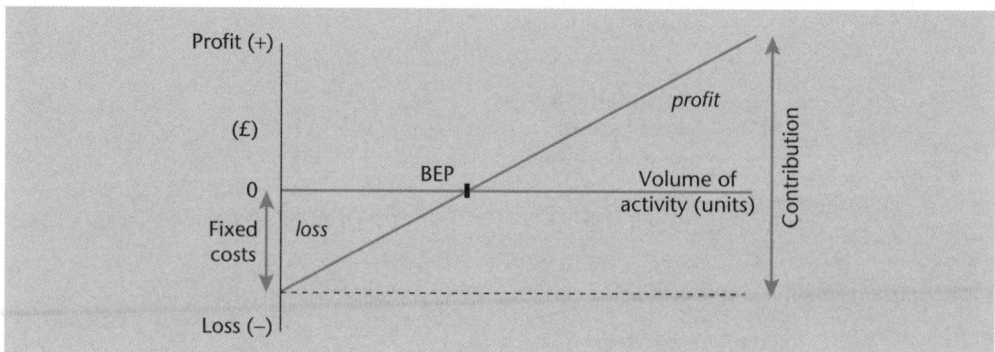

Figure 5.9 **Profit–volume chart**

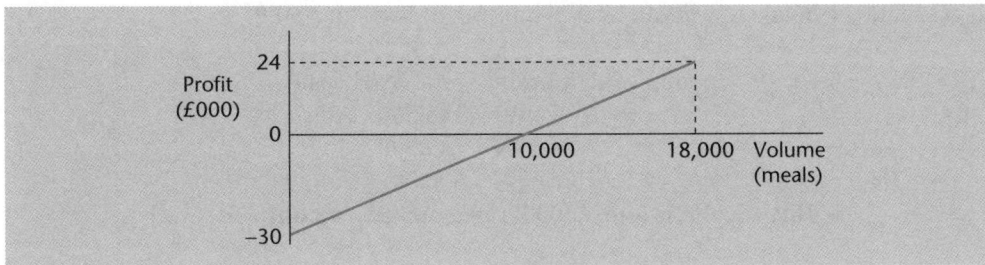

**Figure 5.10  Profit–volume chart for the Grubsteaks restaurant**

The Grubsteaks restaurant example earlier in this chapter showed the application of this formula. At the activity level of 18,000 meals a year the profit was calculated to be £24,000 (see Figure 5.10).

The advantage of the profit–volume chart over the breakeven chart is that the profit can be determined for any level of activity within the range of the graph. This is done simply by reading the graph.

*Try the following question for yourself (answer at the end of the chapter).*

Using the answer to S5.1, draw a profit–volume graph for the Good Health drinks tent. From this graph, **read** the profit for sales of (a) 1,200 drinks and (b) 2,500 drinks.

*Self-assessment question S5.6*

## Effect of alternative sales mixes

The vast majority of businesses sell more than one product and many of these sell lots of different products. As different products tend to have different unit contributions and no one knows for sure the sales mix that will occur in the next period, it is impossible to determine the breakeven level of output for the whole business. Different sales mixes will have different breakeven points. However, if the sales mix tends not to change much, it is possible to make an estimate with some degree of reliability.

Consider a business with just two products, As and Bs. Product B has a higher price and unit contribution, but a lower volume, than product A. The current sales mix is three As are sold for every B (A:B = 3:1).

| Product | A | B | Total |
|---|---|---|---|
| Sales price | 10 | 18 | |
| Variable cost | 4 | 9 | |
| Unit contribution | 6 | 9 | |
| Quantities | 30,000 | 10,000 | 40,000 |
| Total contribution | 180,000 | 90,000 | 270,000 |
| Total fixed costs | | | 148,500 |
| Profit | | | 121,500 |

To calculate the breakeven point, let $N$ = number of Bs sold at BEP:

$$\text{Total contribution} = \text{total fixed cost}$$
$$3N(6) + N(9) = 148{,}500$$
$$27N = 148{,}500$$
$$N = 5{,}500$$

**At BEP, 16,500 As and 5,500 Bs are sold (22,000 units in total)**

But if the sales mix is changed to 2:1 (= A:B),

$$\text{Total contribution} = \text{total fixed cost}$$
$$2N(6) + N(9) = 148{,}500$$
$$21N = 148{,}500$$
$$N = 7{,}071$$

**At BEP, 14,142 As and 7,071 Bs are sold (21,243 units in total)**

*Note that this is 757 items less in total than the previous sales mix.*

What if the original volume was sold in total (40,000 units) but in the new sales mix of 2:1?

| Product | A | B | Total |
|---|---|---|---|
| Sales price | 10 | 18 | |
| Variable cost | 4 | 9 | |
| Unit contribution | 6 | 9 | |
| Quantities | 26,667 | 13,333 | 40,000 |
| Total contribution | 160,002 | 119,998 | 280,000 |
| Total fixed costs | | | 148,500 |
| Profit | | | 131,500 |

*Note that this is £10,000 greater than with the original sales mix.*

---

**Self-assessment question S5.7**

*Try the following question for yourself (answer at the end of the chapter).*

Hoffman Limited makes and sells only two types of portable cooking stove, the Lightweight (L) and the Megarange (M). The Megarange is more sophisticated and sells for more than twice as much as the Lightweight which is very popular. Consequently, nine Ls are sold for every M. The selling prices for Ls and Ms respectively are £8.20 and £19.40; their variable costs are £3.70 and £10.90. The budget for next year shows 50,000 stoves sold altogether with fixed overheads costing £150,000 in total.

For next year, calculate:

1 Profit if sales mix remains L:M = 9:1.
2 Breakeven point if sales mix remains L:M = 9:1.
3 Breakeven point if sales mix becomes L:M = 15:1.
4 Profit if sales mix becomes L:M = 15:1.

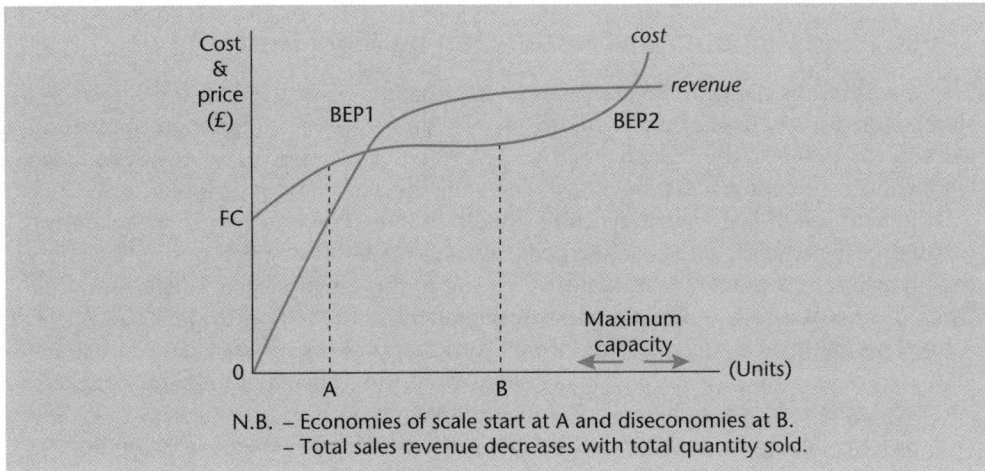

N.B. – Economies of scale start at A and diseconomies at B.
 – Total sales revenue decreases with total quantity sold.

Figure 5.11 **Economist's cost–volume chart**

# Limitations of variable costing

The relationship between sales income and quantity sold may not be linear. Beyond a certain point, it may be necessary to reduce the selling price in order to achieve further sales. The previously straight sales revenue line starts to curve beyond this point. (See Figure 5.11.)

The relationship between total costs and quantity produced may not be linear. The greater the quantity of units produced, the lower may be the price per unit of materials purchased. The straight total cost line also turns into a curve. (See Figure 5.11.)

Contribution analysis can be unreliable outside the relevant range (the range of activity levels for which the curves approximate to straight lines). At very high (close to maximum capacity) and very low activity levels, costs and revenues may not be representative of normal values (see Figure 5.11).

Breakeven analysis is not very useful for multi-product businesses as different breakeven points are produced for different sales mixes. Because different products have different unit contributions, different sales mixes for the same overall activity will have different breakeven points.

It is difficult to measure activity for 'jobbing' businesses, where every item produced is different. Breakeven calculations and charts are applicable to firms which make large volumes of the same product. They are of no use to firms which make only one or a few of each item. This would include civil engineering firms producing public buildings and boatyards producing to customer specification only.

It is assumed that all the items made are sold, i.e. there is no increase or decrease in stock levels over the period. But stock levels may change over a financial period. When this is the case, the production activity will not be the same as the sales activity. Which of these two activity levels should be used for breakeven purposes? As breakeven is based on contribution (sales revenue – variable cost), the sales activity level should be used. 'Variable cost' is the variable cost of the items sold, not the items made.

# The manager's point of view (written by Nigel Burton)

Breakeven analysis can provide vital financial information, particularly for small, relatively simple companies. It also has a role to play in larger, more complex organizations, although its potential applications tend to be limited. In all companies, however, it can help managers to understand the cost/price/volume relationships in their businesses.

The main use of breakeven analysis in single-product companies is to calculate the number of items to be sold before a profit can be made. Most small businesses know exactly where this point is, and it becomes one of the driving forces of the business. Once this point is reached, managers know that they are starting to generate profit. A small businessman of my acquaintance reckons that he works on Mondays to pay the taxman, Tuesdays to pay the VAT man, Wednesday and Thursday to pay his suppliers, and only starts working for himself on Friday. He knows nothing about accounting, and his logic may be slightly suspect, but his little joke demonstrates that, even if he doesn't realize it, he has grasped the principles of breakeven analysis!

The same basic technique is employed for various purposes in large companies. It is commonly used, in conjunction with other measurements, in capital appraisals. All formal proposals for capital projects will be accompanied by supporting financial data, which will inevitably demonstrate that a satisfactory rate of return and payback period can be expected. But are the numbers reasonable? It is possible that the underlying assumptions about projected sales, capital expenditure and operating costs are all at their most optimistic limits, and could spell disaster if just one of them failed to materialize. To test the figures, therefore, it is useful to carry out a sensitivity analysis, calculating the impact on the rate of return of, say, a 10% reduction in sales, or a 20% overspend in capital expenditure. One of the key calculations here is the breakeven point, which represents the 'least acceptable' position. What level of inaccuracy in the numbers will bring the project down to its breakeven level? This neatly puts all the alternative scenarios into context and allows management to assess the robustness of the proposed figures.

Some years ago, breakeven principles played an important part in another type of major project, this time the sale of a business. We were instructed by our American parent company to shed a particular product line, and achieve a specified net gain for the company. The matter was greatly complicated when the favoured purchaser decided to buy only the trading assets, i.e. customer lists, product know-how and working capital, but not the fixed assets, i.e. land, buildings and plant. As a result, we were obliged to close down the factory, leading to significant expenditure which had not been envisaged when the sale of the business had first been authorized. This included decommissioning of the plant, building demolition, environmental testing, land remediation, and redundancy, among many others. Against these we had several unforeseen items of revenue, such as sale of plant and the disposal of the land. Our job was to ensure that the ultimate sale of the land covered all the net expenditure, leaving the American parent company with the profit it expected from the sale of the business. We used a breakeven model to monitor progress on this project, initially using estimated figures, and replacing them with the actual numbers as they became confirmed. In this way we were able to monitor constantly the proceeds required from the sale of the land to break even, and keep an eye on the property market to see if this level was achievable. Unfortunately, when we were ready to sell, the property market was in a slump, so we retained the land for a further five years until the market had recovered sufficiently to enable us to reach our breakeven point.

These examples will hopefully illustrate that breakeven principles can be used in a variety of different ways, even if the determination of sales volume, especially in small companies, remains its most common application. However, in large companies, the breakeven point of individual items is rather muddied by the multiplicity of products being sold; if you sell more of Product A than you expected, thus recovering a higher level of overhead, the breakeven point on Product B may go down. That is why we found ourselves concentrating more on the overall level of marginal income being generated by groups of products, and the contribution that they made towards fixed costs. The concept of contribution is a useful way of focusing on profit, and analysing the elements which are causing you to over- or underachieve the profit target. By increasing volume, or by changing the mix of sales towards the higher margin products, more marginal income will be generated. This additional contribution should fall straight through to the bottom line profit, assuming that the fixed costs remain fixed. In practice, of course, they rarely do. There are always spending variances to be managed, but this merely demonstrates another opportunity for effective profit generation. If you can reduce the level of fixed costs, at the same time as increasing marginal income, the gearing effect on the profit line can be significant.

Finally, the concept of contribution can sometimes show expenditure in a startling light. For instance, how big a deal do your American salespeople have to make, in order to pay for the managing director's first-class flight to New York to sign the final contract? The contribution calculation will tell you this, although you may not wish to point it out to the MD! Perhaps a more relevant question is: 'Will the contribution generated by the New York sale cover all the costs associated with it, and still leave a satisfactory profit?' Consider not only the variable costs of materials, labour, variable overhead and freight, but also other related costs, such as warehousing, export documentation, currency risks from $ invoicing, extended credit terms and bank charges, as well as the cost of customer visits and technical support. The MD's visit could be the final straw which pushes this piece of business into loss!

*Summary*

- Costs can be analysed into variable and fixed.
- Contribution is sales revenue minus variable cost, either per unit or in total.
- Total contribution equals total fixed cost plus profit.
- At breakeven point (profit = 0) total contribution equals total fixed cost.
- There are two types of breakeven charts, traditional and contribution.
- The margin of safety shows how far above breakeven point a firm is operating.
- Operational gearing affects the amount of profit due to changes in sales volume.
- Activity levels can be calculated for target profits.
- The profit–volume chart is an alternative to the breakeven chart.

## Further reading

Horngren, C. T. (2004) 'Management accounting: some comments', *Journal of Management Accounting Research*, Vol. 16.

Horngren, C., Bhimani, A., Datar, S. and Foster, G. (2002) *Management and Cost Accounting*, 2nd edition, Prentice Hall Europe, Harlow. See Chapter 8, 'Cost–volume–profit relationships'.

Upchurch, A. (2003) *Management Accounting, Principles and Practice*, 2nd edition, Financial Times/Prentice Hall, Harlow. See Chapter 6, 'Cost/volume/profit analysis'.

Weetman, P. (2002) *Management Accounting, an Introduction*, 3rd edition, Financial Times/Prentice Hall, Harlow. See chapter 'Profit measurement and short-term decision making'.

## Answers to self-assessment questions

### S5.1  Good Health drinks tent

$$
\begin{array}{rl}
& £ \\
\text{Sales revenue} = & 2.50/\text{unit} \\
\text{Variable costs} = & \underline{1.00}/\text{unit} \\
\text{Unit contribution} = & 1.50/\text{unit} \\
\text{Number of units} = & \underline{4,000} \\
\text{Total contribution} = & 6,000 \\
\text{Fixed costs} = & \underline{2,700} \\
\text{Net profit} = & \underline{3,300}
\end{array}
$$

a)  Total contribution = £6,000
b)  Net profit = £3,300

### S5.2  Good Health drinks tent

Let BEP occur when B drinks have been sold.

$$
\begin{array}{l}
\text{Total contribution} = \text{total fixed costs} \\
\text{B} \times \text{unit contribution} = \text{total fixed costs} \\
\text{B} \times (2.50 - 1.00) = 2,700 \\
\text{B} = 2,700/1.50 \\
\text{Breakeven point, B} = 1,800 \text{ drinks}
\end{array}
$$

## S5.3  Contribution breakeven chart for the drinks tent

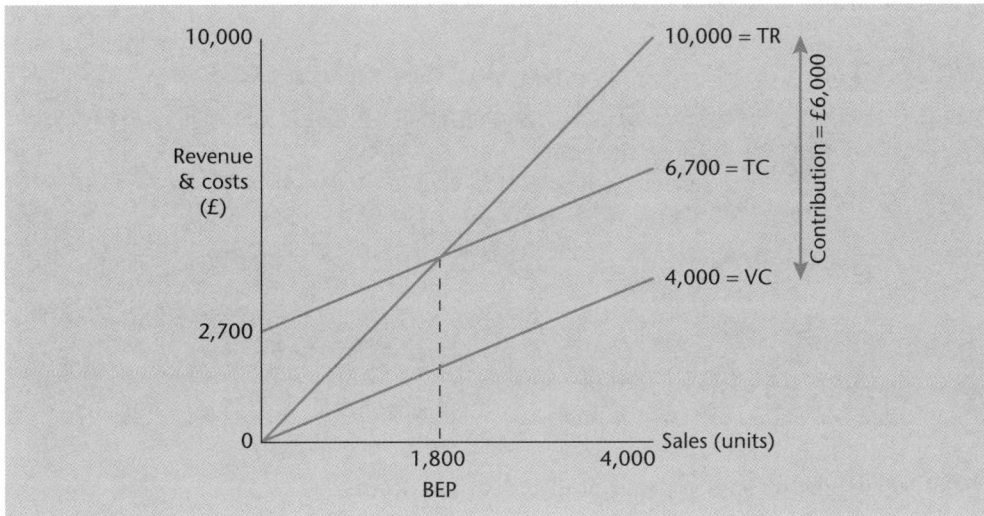

## S5.4  For the Good Health drinks tent example

a) Actual number of drinks sold = 4,000
Breakeven level of sales = 1,800
Margin of safety = 2,200 drinks

b) $\dfrac{\text{Margin of safety in units}}{\text{Actual sales in units}} \times 100 = \dfrac{2,200}{4,000} \times 100 = 55\%$

So, sales could fall by 55% before losses occurred.

## S5.5  Variable costs

| | | |
|---|---|---|
| Materials | 25 | |
| Labour | 30 | $(2.5 \times 12)$ |
| Overheads | 5 | $(2.5 \times 2)$ |
| Total | 60 | |
| Sales price | 160 | |
| Unit contribution | 100 | |

Let the number of items needed = $N$
Total contribution = total fixed costs + profit
$N \times 100 = (600 \times 12) + 20,000$
$N = 27,200/100$
$N = 272$

So, 272 bass guitars need to be sold to create a net profit of £20,000.

## S5.6  Profit–volume chart for the Good Health drinks tent

a)  If 1,200 drinks are sold, a **loss** of £900 would occur.

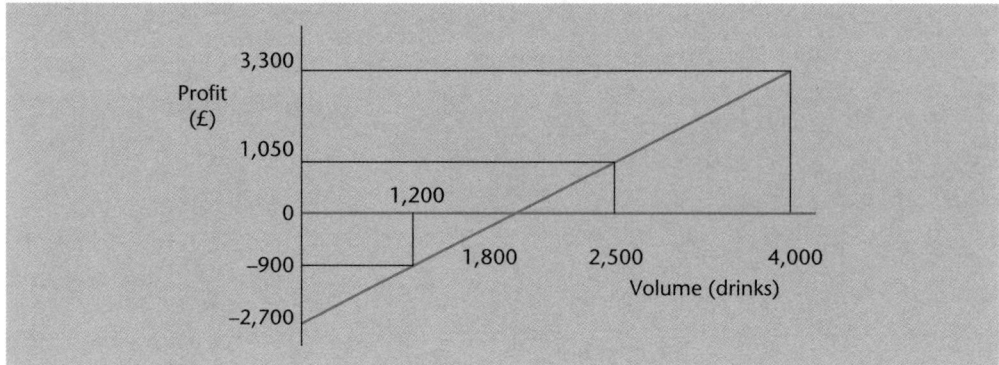

b)  If 2,500 drinks are sold, a **profit** of £1,050 would occur.

## S5.7  Hoffman Ltd

The current sales mix is 9 Ls are sold for every M (L:M = 9:1).

| Product | L | M | Total |
|---|---|---|---|
| Sales price | 8.20 | 19.40 | |
| Variable cost | 3.70 | 10.90 | |
| Unit contribution | 4.50 | 8.50 | |
| Quantities | 45,000 | 5,000 | 50,000 |
| Total contribution | 202,500 | 42,500 | 245,000 |
| Total fixed costs | | | 150,000 |
| Profit | | | 95,000 |

To calculate the breakeven point, let $N$ = number of Bs sold at BEP:

$$\text{Total contribution} = \text{total fixed cost}$$
$$9N(4.50) + N(8.50) = 150,000$$
$$49N = 150,000$$
$$N = 3,061$$
**At BEP: 27,549 Ls and 3,062 Ms are sold (30,611 stoves in total)**

But if the sales mix changed to 15:1 (= L:M),

$$\text{Total contribution} = \text{total fixed cost}$$
$$15N(4.50) + N(8.50) = 150,000$$
$$76N = 150,000$$
$$N = 1,974$$
**AT BEP:29,610 Ls and 1,974 Ms are sold (31,584 stoves in total)**

*Note that this is 973 stoves more in total than the previous sales mix.*

What if the original volume was sold in total (50,000 stoves) but in the new sales mix of 15:1?

| Product | L | M | Total |
|---|---|---|---|
| Sales price | 8.20 | 19.40 | |
| Variable cost | 3.70 | 10.90 | |
| Unit contribution | 4.50 | 8.50 | |
| Quantities | 46,875 | 3,125 | 50,000 |
| Total contribution | 210,937 | 26,563 | 237,500 |
| Total fixed costs | | | 150,000 |
| Profit | | | 87,500 |

*Note that this is £8,000 less than with the original sales mix.*

| CASE STUDY 1 | The Hutton Vinification Company |

HVC Ltd is based in north Somerset and has a financial year starting on 1 August. It produces wine from bulk grape juice bought from vineyards in southern England. In 2006/07 it made and sold 90,000 litres of wine in standard-sized 750 millilitre bottles to customers located throughout the UK. The maximum annual output of its plant is estimated to be 98,000 litres. Demand has grown steadily over the last 10 years in step with increased interest in, and knowledge of, wine in the UK. Home market production has been encouraged by the recent gradual warming of the climate.

However, the number of complaints received by HVC Ltd has risen sharply over the last two years and, if nothing is done to correct this, sales and profits are expected to fall next year. The directors attribute the complaints to the difficulty in controlling the quality of the 'must' (bought-in grape juice). The managing director has suggested that it would be easier to control the quality of harvested grapes rather than processed must. This means that HVC Ltd would have to acquire wine-pressing equipment to process the purchased grapes. Despite the extra temporary labour involved in pressing the grapes, the resulting self-pressed must is expected to have a variable cost equal to only 60% of bought-in must. The necessary grape-pressing machinery will cost £440,000 and will last 10 years before being scrapped (at zero value).

The managing director's remuneration is £42,000 p.a. and the sales director's is £38,000 p.a. In addition to the two directors, HVC Ltd has five full-time employees, whose pay in 2006/07 totalled £89,000. This included £25,000 annual salary for the production manager and basic annual pay of £10,000 for each of four operatives. This remuneration is considered to be a fixed cost but the remainder, which was earned as overtime by the four operatives, is considered to be a variable cost.

The total cost of must purchased in 2006/07 was £45,000. The average cost of the bottle, cork and label is £0.20 a bottle and delivery costs average £0.10 a bottle. HVC Ltd has a policy of having zero stocks at the end of July (this is also the company's financial year-end). Apart from a negligible amount, it has managed to achieve this for the last few years.

With effect from 1 August 2007 the directors will be entitled to a profit-related bonus dependent on the annual increase in net profit. Naturally, they are both very keen to earn a good bonus. With this in mind, the managing director has analysed the costs for 2006/07 (which was a typical year) as follows:

| Fixed costs | £ | Variable costs | £ |
|---|---|---|---|
| Salaries and wages | 145,000 | Must | 45,000 |
| Depreciation | 88,000 | Overtime pay | 24,000 |
| Production costs | 47,000 | Bottle, cork and label | 24,000 |
| Selling costs | 33,000 | Delivery | 12,000 |
| Administration costs | 29,000 | | £105,000 |
| Interest | 8,000 | | |
| | £350,000 | | |

The sales director is not entirely convinced that the managing director's idea is the best solution. She thinks it would be better to go further south than at present, into central France, in order to purchase better-quality must. She believes that the effect of this would be to increase the must cost by 25% but this would be more than covered by her proposed 5% increase in the sales price.

### HVC Ltd: Profit and loss account for y/e 31 July 2007

| | £000 | £000 |
|---|---|---|
| Sales | | 504 |
| Must | 45 | |
| Operatives' wages | 64 | |
| Bottles, corks and labels | 24 | |
| Production depreciation | 53 | |
| Other production costs | 47 | |
| Manufacturing costs of goods sold | | 233 |
| Gross profit | | 271 |
| Salaries | 105 | |
| Depreciation | 35 | |
| Selling costs | 33 | |
| Delivery costs | 12 | |
| Administration costs | 29 | |
| Bank interest | 8 | |
| Total overheads | | 222 |
| Net profit | | 49 |

*Tasks:*

1 For 2006/07:
  1 Calculate the breakeven point in litres.
  2 Calculate the net profit if HVC Ltd had made and sold 95,000 litres.
  3 How many litres would have to be sold to increase net profit by 50%?

(20 marks)

2 If the MD's plan to buy and press grapes (instead of purchasing grape must) is put into operation for 2007/08 and output increases to 95,000 litres and the selling price increases by 5%:
  a) What would the revised breakeven point be?
  b) What would the revised profit be?

(20 marks)

3  Alternatively, if the sales director's plan to buy better-quality grape must is put into operation for 2007/08 and output increases to 95,000 litres and the selling price increases by 5%:

a)  What would the revised breakeven point be?

b)  What would the revised profit be?

(20 marks)

4  Evaluate the directors' plans and recommend a course of action for 2008/09. You may wish to use chart(s) to illustrate your answer.

(40 marks)

(Total 100 marks)

The Muesli Company

The Muesli Company (TMC) is a small business which makes and sells muesli. It was started two years ago by Rosemary Helms on the basis of her family's liking for the homemade mixture of cereals, nuts and dried fruits she had created for personal consumption. When a new farm shop opened nearby, she enquired if it would be interested in selling her muesli. The shop agreed to give it a try and found that it sold sufficient quantities to justify a permanent place in the shop. Rosemary now has five outlets and is considering selling her muesli on the Internet.

The business has reached a point where decisions have to be made concerning product type and distribution channel. The original recipe used nine different ingredients which were sourced from supermarkets and local shops. However, in recent months, Rosemary has created a new simplified recipe which uses only organic ingredients. Her idea is to appeal to the growing health food market which is willing to pay premium prices for organic foods. However, she has discovered that, if she wishes to use the word 'organic' on the label, she must register with the Soil Association and pay an annual fee of £440. As the business is just starting up, she is undecided as to whether this cost is worthwhile. She could continue with the current labels (omitting the word 'organic') while still using the organic ingredients to improve the taste.

While searching for organic materials, she discovered a wholesaler based 25 miles (40 km) away which delivers direct to its customers. The minimum quantities purchased are much higher but the prices are significantly lower than local shops. Rosemary now saves time and effort by using this supplier for all her ingredients. The supplier has pointed out that she could get even better prices if she ordered in greater quantities (about five times what she orders now). Although she is tempted by these low prices, she is not sure if she should buy her ingredients in these quantities.

Her son, who is something of a computer expert, has suggested creating a website to sell the muesli over the Internet. She is not too sure about this but is investigating the possibility and thinking about the consequences. How much would it cost to set up? What would the minimum delivery size have to be? How much extra would customers be prepared to pay for postage and packing? Could she cope if demand surged? How much would she need to sell to break even? Are there any 'hidden' costs?

In a two-and-a-half-hour session, she makes 12 kg of muesli. The product is packed in individual 500 g bags and special scales are needed to ensure that the weight is accurate. (To ensure that no bag is underweight, each one is slightly overfilled.) The Internet orders would be for a 'parcel' of seven bags. She thinks the website would last for about five years before a complete overhaul would be necessary. Although it is a few years old, she could use her present computer, but she would need to purchase broadband access. The current selling price is £2.00 a bag to her retail outlets who sell it to their customers for £3.00 a bag. For the Internet business, direct to the consumer, she thinks she will charge £21.00 a parcel (7 bags @ £3.00).

While doing this exercise, Rosemary realizes that she does not know what her current breakeven point is and decides to calculate it. Also, it will serve as a useful comparison with the proposed Internet business. She does not use a computer for the local farm shop business and she uses her own car to deliver orders. It is difficult to be precise but she estimates that her average delivery is 12 bags, takes one hour and costs her £1.80 in petrol. She has recently purchased scales and a bag-sealing machine. Her costs are shown below.

| For all sales: | £ |
| --- | --- |
| Cereals | 0.20/500 g bag |
| Nuts | 0.45/500 g bag |
| Dried fruits | 0.50/500 g bag |
| Plastic bags and sealing tape | 0.01/500 g bag |
| Labels | 0.05/500 g bag |
| Bag-sealing machine | 45.00 |
| Weighing scales | 235.00 |
| | |
| For Internet sales only: | |
| Creation of website | 250.00 |
| Maintenance of website | 50.00 per month |
| Internet payment company charges | 30.00 per month |
| Broadband access | 20.00 per month |
| Packing materials | 0.42/parcel of 3.5 to 4.0 kg |
| Postage | 7.21/parcel of 3.5 to 4.0 kg |

At the moment she is only selling about 12 bags a week and wants to expand in order to create more income. Her objective is to make a profit of approximately £10,000 a year by working no more than 20 hours a week for 50 weeks a year on her muesli business.

*Tasks:*

*Without the use of 'organic' labels – Soil Association fee not paid:*

1 Calculate the breakeven point of her current 'farm shop' business (in numbers of bags). Assume all sales are through farm shops and Internet sales are zero.

(15 marks)

2 If Internet sales caused the volume to increase sufficiently, the bulk purchase of edible ingredients would be justified, giving a 25% saving on current costs. Calculate the breakeven point (in numbers of bags) if this was so. Assume all sales are over the Internet and farm shop sales are zero.

(15 marks)

3 Assuming the 25% bulk saving was in operation, how many bags would Rosemary need to sell in order to make a profit of £10,000 a year? Assume all sales are over the Internet and farm shop sales are zero.

(15 marks)

*With the use of 'organic' labels only – Soil Association fee paid:*

4   Repeat task 1.

(5 marks)

5   Repeat task 2.

(5 marks)

6   Repeat task 3.

(5 marks)

*General*

7   Advise Rosemary about the possible expansion of her business to achieve her desired level of profit.

(40 marks)

(Total 100 marks)

# Questions

An asterisk * on a question number indicates that the answer is given at the end of the book. Answers to the other questions are given in the Lecturer's Guide.

## Q5.1*  Bodgit Ltd

Bodgit Ltd makes 200 wooden kitchen chairs every month and sells them for £50 each. Fixed monthly overheads are £3,000 and the standard cost of one chair is as follows:

|  | £ |
|---|---|
| Materials | 15 |
| Direct labour | 8 |
| Variable overheads | 7 |

*Tasks:*

1  Calculate for one month:
   a)  the variable cost of one chair;
   b)  the breakeven point;
   c)  the profit if 200 chairs are sold;
   d)  the number of chairs sold to give a profit of £4,000.
2  In an attempt to boost sales, Bodgit plans to reduce the selling price to £48, improve the quality by spending 20% more on materials and increase its advertising by £1,000 a month. Calculate:
   a)  the new breakeven point;
   b)  the profit if 350 chairs are sold;
   c)  the margin of safety (expressed as a % of sales) if 350 chairs are sold;
   d)  the number of chairs sold to give a profit of £4,000.
3  Explain why your answers to the above questions should be seen as estimates rather than exact answers.

## Q5.2*  Concord Toy Company

The Concord Toy Company has two separate strategic business units. A draft plan, incorporating a target return on capital employed (ROCE) of 20% per annum, has been created by the managing director. Aware that the toy industry is a volatile one, the board of directors wishes to review the flexibility of the profit forecast shown by the plan. In preparation for the board meeting to discuss the plan, certain questions have been posed for each operating unit (see below).

*Operating Unit 1 – novelty pens*

This unit produces novelty pens. Most of these are based on popular cartoon characters. Variable costs are taken as raw materials and royalties. All other costs are assumed to be fixed in the short term. The following forecasts have been made:

| | |
|---|---|
| Selling price per pen | £2 |
| Variable cost per pen | £1.50 |
| Sales revenue | £800,000 |
| Average capital employed | £300,000 |

Within the output range 300,000 to the maximum capacity of 450,000 pens, the fixed costs are £150,000.

*Operating Unit 2 – dolls' accessories*

This unit produces three main products – a doll's buggy, a doll's scooter and a doll's personal stereo. In the past, the company has exported most of its products but, in its drive to develop home sales, it has recently obtained a contract to supply a national chain store. The store's toy buyer has requested the company to supply a doll's convertible car in addition to its existing products.

**Forecast accounts**

| Product | Buggy | Scooter | Personal stereo | Total |
|---|---|---|---|---|
| Selling price | £20 | £10 | £10 | |
| Unit sales (000) | 100 | 100 | 100 | |
| Sales (£000) | 2,000 | 1,000 | 1,000 | 4,000 |
| Variable costs (£000) | 600 | 200 | 400 | 1,200 |
| Contribution (£000) | 1,400 | 800 | 600 | 2,800 |
| Fixed costs (£000) | 700 | 700 | 700 | 2,100 |
| Profit/loss (£000) | 700 | 100 | (100) | 700 |

Fixed costs are apportioned on the basis of unit sales. The average capital employed is estimated at £3.6 million. To make a doll's convertible car would require new plant, financed in full by a bank loan.

*Tasks re. Unit 1:*

1  What is the breakeven point in sales volume and value?
2  What is the margin of safety shown by the forecast?
3  Will the operating unit achieve a 20% return on capital employed?
4  What will be the profit if production output increases to maximum capacity? Qualify your answer.
5  How many pens must be sold to make a profit of £60,000?
6  What actions can be taken to improve profitability?

*Tasks re. Unit 2:*

1  Will this operating unit achieve a 20% return on capital employed on the existing sales forecast?
2  If the sales mix remains at equal volumes of the three products, what is the breakeven point in sales volume and value?
3  What will the operating profit be if the sales volume on each product falls
   a)  10% below forecast?
   b)  20% below forecast?

4  Should Concord stop producing and selling the personal stereo?

5  Should the selling price of the personal stereo be increased to £12 to cover the full costs?

6  What further information is required to decide whether or not to make a doll's convertible car?

## Q5.3* Rover's 'last chance saloon'

The following comments were broadcast on a television news programme in the first week of February 1999:

> *Rover's future depends on the success of their latest model, codename R75. They intend to attract buyers away from Audi and Volvo to what they describe as the best car they have ever built. They claim to have paid more attention to detail than ever before on this upmarket saloon car. This may be why the launch has been put back from autumn 1998 to the summer of 1999.*
>
> *Selling prices will be a crucial element in their battle for market share and are expected to range from £18,000 to £26,000. Rover say they need to sell 140,000 cars a year to break even and acknowledge that this is a significant challenge. However, this is one test they cannot afford to fail. It is no coincidence that the R75 has been nicknamed 'the last chance saloon'!*

*Investigation*

Assume:

> The retail selling price is £22,000 (average of £18,000 and £26,000)
> The trade selling price is 75% of the retail price
> The total cost is 80% of the trade selling price
> The variable cost is $X$% of the total cost

*Tasks:*

1  Calculate the total fixed costs for the R75 project if $X$ is
   a)  50%
   b)  65%
   c)  80%.
   As well as an annual total, express your answers in £/day.

2  Assuming the variable cost is 65% of total cost, how many R75s need to be sold for profit to be £100 million?

3  If 200,000 R75s were sold in the year, assuming the variable cost is 65% of total cost, how much profit would they make?

4  If the total capital employed on the R75 project is £10,000 million and Rover's owners wanted a 20% return on capital employed (ROCE), how many cars would have to be sold?

## Q5.4 SACCUS

SACCUS is a local charity which decides to hold an outdoors fund-raising event in mid-summer. The secretary has a connection with an entertainments company which puts on musical laser light shows for the public. For charities, it charges a reduced rate of £375 all-inclusive. The venue would be provided free of charge by a local farmer. A barbecue would be put on and the food and drink would be included in the ticket price. It is estimated that the food would cost £2 a head and the drink £1 a head. Also, a special licence for the sale of alcohol would be needed at a cost of £25. Based on the experience of similar events, SACCUS expects to sell 500 tickets at £5 each.

However, the treasurer (who has a degree in business studies) is a little concerned about this plan and proposes an alternative. She suggests hiring a nationally known West Indian steel band at the special rate of £100 plus £50 transport costs. The ticket price would remain at £5 and food would be provided as before. However, no drink would be provided, the audience being invited to bring their own. The number of people attending is expected to be half that for the laser show.

*Tasks:*

1 Advise SACCUS as to which event it should stage.
2 Illustrate your answer by sketching a contribution breakeven chart for each event.

## Q5.5 Royal Hotel

Jim Culf is the manager of the Royal Hotel, Bigtown-on-Sea. In anticipation of preparing next year's budget, he has analysed his recent costs and income. His findings are summarized below.

|  | £/week |
|---|---|
| Staff salaries | 2,000 |
| Head office charge | 400 |
| Depreciation of equipment and fittings | 875 |
| Heating | 425 |

For each guest the average variable cost of food, drink, linen and sundries totals £100 per week. Jim considers all other overheads to be semi-variable and has produced the following data from his records:

| Week no. | Occupancy (no. of guests) | Other overheads (£) |
|---|---|---|
| 13 | 75 | 7,050 |
| 14 | 94 | 8,200 |
| 15 | 70 | 6,980 |
| 16 | 61 | 6,500 |
| 17 | 57 | 6,350 |
| 18 | 83 | 7,590 |
| 19 | 85 | 7,700 |

The average price charged for a week's stay is £240 per guest. Since it is a seaside hotel, the vast majority of its customers stay for either one or two weeks at a time.

*Tasks:*

1  Calculate the average number of guests needed each week to avoid making a loss.
2  The hotel can accommodate a maximum of 120 people. How much is the weekly profit if the average occupancy level is:
   a)  70%?
   b)  80%?
   c)  90%?
3  Jim has been invited by an international tour company to quote a competitive price for a group of 20 Japanese tourists who wish to stay in the area for two weeks. They are due to arrive in 10 days' time.
   a)  Calculate the lowest price Jim can quote if he is to avoid making a loss on the tour. (Assume that the hotel is currently 70% booked for the two weeks in question.)
   b)  If Jim wants to make a profit of £2,000 from this tour, what price should he quote?

## Q5.6 Hughes Healthfoods

Hughes Healthfoods makes and sells two types of diet supplement, Slim Quick (SQ) and Healthy Living (HL). It has a single production line on which the two products are made alternately in batches. Some details from next year's budget are shown below:

| Product | Unit selling price (£) | Unit variable cost (£) | Annual sales volume (units) |
|---------|----------------------|----------------------|----------------------------|
| SQ | 5.00 | 2.00 | 800,000 |
| HL | 9.00 | 4.00 | 200,000 |

The annual total fixed cost is £2.9 million and the production facility has an absolute maximum capacity of 1.1 million units a year.

*Tasks:*

1  Calculate the budgeted profit.
2  Determine the breakeven point. (Assume the budgeted sales mix is stable throughout the year.)
3  Is it possible for the business to double its profit while maintaining the budgeted sales mix?
4  Is it possible for the business to double its profit if the budgeted sales mix changed to two SQs being sold for every HL?

## Review questions

1 Define variable and fixed costs.
2 Define contribution.
3 Explain the relationship between contribution, fixed costs and net profit.
4 Define breakeven point.
5 Draw traditional and contribution breakeven charts.
6 Define the margin of safety.
7 Explain operational gearing.
8 Draw a profit–volume chart.
9 Discuss the assumptions and limitations of breakeven analysis.

*The answers to all these questions can be found in the text of this chapter.*

# Short-term decisions using variable costing

## Introduction

Suppose you were a director of a well-known international passenger airline whose main route was London–New York. You operate this route with a fleet of several large aircraft, each with a capacity to carry 450 passengers. However, due to the number of competitors flying the same route, there is much surplus capacity and your aircraft often fly with more than 100 of their seats empty. Your standard return fare is £500, which is based on the total cost of £400 per available seat plus a 25% profit margin. The £400 total cost includes items such as depreciation of aircraft, fuel, on-board food and drink for passengers, rent of airport facilities, staff pay, training and administration costs.

Unexpectedly, a well-known holiday company offers to purchase 50 seats on every one of your flights for the next six weeks but is only willing to pay £100 a seat – only one-quarter of the total cost! What would your response be? Would you, politely but firmly, inform the holiday company that its offer is far too low or would you accept gladly and get the contract signed as soon as possible?

To solve this problem, you need to think about how your net income would change if you accepted the offer. Obviously, your revenue would increase by £100 for each of the 50 seats. But what about your costs? Which of the costs listed in the previous paragraph would increase? Most of them would not change at all! Only the cost of the on-board food and drink for passengers would increase. If this costs £10 per person, you would be increasing your net income by £90 a seat or £4,500 per return flight. If there were 100 flights during the six-week period, the net income from the contract would be £450,000. This is the case even though each seat is sold at £300 less than total cost. This is because most of the costs are 'fixed' and only the food and drink are 'variable' (see Chapter 1 on cost behaviour if you do not understand this). Your positive decision to accept the offer is based on your knowledge of variable costing and your company is nearly half a million pounds better off because of it! An understanding of variable costing will enable you to make similar, good, profitable decisions in your business career.

Note: This use of variable costing for short-term decision making is also known as contribution analysis.

**Having worked through this chapter you should be able to:**

- advise whether or not to cease certain activities;
- advise on the order of production when one of the resources used is scarce;
- advise whether or not to accept one-off contracts;
- advise whether to produce or buy in components used in your products;
- discuss the limitations of decision making using variable costing.

**Learning objectives**

## Cessation of activities

The previous chapter dealt with the application of variable costing to breakeven analysis. We will now concentrate on commercial decision making in the short term, i.e. the immediate future. This aspect of variable costing is also known as *contribution analysis*. Four typical situations will be considered.

The first situation is where a financial analysis shows that a product line or profit centre is making a net loss and a proposal is made to close it down. A contribution analysis is performed to confirm or deny this course of action.

Provided the selling price of a product is greater than its variable cost, each sale will create a positive contribution towards the organization's fixed costs. This is so even when the product is making a net loss. Cessation of that product would mean that fewer of the fixed costs were covered **and the loss would be greater than before**. Remember that fixed costs are, by definition, costs which do not change with the level of activity, even if that level falls to zero. In other words, fixed costs cannot be eliminated **in the short term**.

Take the example of the Top Ski Holiday Company, which offers specialist skiing holidays in Norway, Spain and Italy. A financial analysis of last season in which 3,000 holidays were sold (1,000 for each country) shows the following:

| | Norway | Italy | Spain | Total |
|---|---|---|---|---|
| | £000 | | | |
| Total cost | 950 | 700 | 450 | 2,100 |
| Sales revenue | 700 | 650 | 800 | 2,150 |
| Net profit | (250) | (50) | 350 | 50 |

The company would like to increase its selling prices but believes this to be unwise as its competitors are offering very similarly priced holidays in those countries. Alternatively, it has been suggested that if the Norwegian and Italian holidays for next season were withdrawn (starting in the near future) Top Ski would increase its profits from £50,000 to £350,000 by eliminating the losses for those two countries. This is based on the reasonable assumption that 1,000 holidays will continue to be sold for Spain.

A more detailed examination of the financial analysis reveals that the total fixed costs for last season were £600,000. These were for items such as brochures, advertising, directors' salaries and head office administration costs. These fixed costs were spread evenly over all the holidays. As 3,000 holidays had been sold, fixed costs of £200 (£600,000/3,000) were absorbed into each holiday. A contribution analysis of the above figures reveals the following:

| | | Norway | Italy | Spain | All |
|---|---|---|---|---|---|
| | | £000 | | | |
| | Total cost | 950 | 700 | 450 | 2,100 |
| Less: | Total fixed costs | 200 | 200 | 200 | 600 |
| | Variable cost | 750 | 500 | 250 | 1,500 |
| | Sales revenue | 700 | 650 | 800 | 2,150 |
| | Contribution | (50) | 150 | 550 | 650 |
| Less: | Total fixed costs | | | | 600 |
| | Net profit | | | | 50 |

If the Norwegian and Italian holidays did cease, the analysis would change as follows:

| | | Norway | Italy | Spain | All |
|---|---|---|---|---|---|
| | | £000 | | | |
| | Contribution | 0 | 0 | 550 | 550 |
| Less: | Total fixed costs | | | | 600 |
| | Net profit/(Loss) | | | | (50) |

So, instead of the profit increasing by £300,000, it would actually decrease by £100,000 to give a net **loss** of £50,000. The situation would be much worse than if no action had been taken and the Norwegian and Italian holidays sold as before.

The contribution analysis shows that, although the Italian holidays are making a loss, they are still making a positive contribution to the company's fixed costs. However, the

Norwegian holidays are making a negative rather than positive contribution. Every time one of these is sold the company loses money it otherwise would not lose. Thus, it does seem a good idea to cease the Norwegian holidays.

If this happened and the Italian holidays continued, the analysis would be as follows:

| | Norway | Italy | Spain | All |
|---|---|---|---|---|
| | | **£000** | | |
| Contribution | 0 | 150 | 550 | 700 |
| Less: Total fixed costs | | | | 600 |
| Net profit | | | | 100 |

The rule is, in order to improve profitability, cease activities with negative contributions. (This assumes that these negative contributions cannot be made positive in the short term.)

Of course, **in the long term**, maybe the fixed costs could be reduced or maybe an alternative holiday venue could be found. In the long term **anything** is possible. However, for short-term decisions, the correct course of action comes from a contribution analysis. Although a sudden cessation of the Norwegian and Italian holidays seemed a reasonable proposition at first sight, it would have been a disaster for Top Ski Holidays if they had both been withdrawn.

From a business point of view, other aspects of the situation should always be taken into account. In particular, are the products interrelated? Consider a company selling three products: a basic food processor, a grating attachment and a coffee grinding attachment. Suppose the company stops making the coffee grinder because the accounting system shows that it is making a loss while the other two items are making a profit. Those potential customers who would have bought the processor and the grinder will not now do so. As the products are interdependent, sales of related items will be lost. Suppose it was the processor making the loss instead of the grinder. Anyone suggesting that production of the processor should cease should be asking themselves if they are in the right job.

*Self-assessment question S6.1*

*Try the following question for yourself (answer at the end of the chapter).*

The V&A Group is made up of four operating subsidiaries: A, B, C and D. Its corporate accounting system has produced the following figures which show the group has made a loss of £1,000. Analyse them and state which operations (if any) you would recommend for closure in order to return the group to profitability.

Summarized profit and loss accounts for last year (£000):

| | A | B | C | D | Group |
|---|---|---|---|---|---|
| Sales | 180 | 420 | 500 | 900 | 2,000 |
| Raw materials | 41 | 95 | 202 | 370 | 708 |
| Direct labour | 62 | 89 | 37 | 105 | 293 |
| Direct cost | 103 | 184 | 239 | 475 | 1,001 |
| Gross profit | 77 | 236 | 261 | 425 | 999 |
| Total overheads | 90 | 210 | 250 | 450 | 1,000 |
| Net profit | (13) | 26 | 11 | (25) | (1) |

*Note: Fixed overheads have been apportioned according to the amount of sales revenue from each operation. Overheads are considered to be 90% variable and 10% fixed.*

> *Tasks:*
>
> a) State which operations you recommend closing and why.
> b) What would the group's profit be if your recommendations were actioned?
> c) What would the group's profit be if A and D were closed?

## Scarce resources

The usual factor limiting an organization's activities is the number of products it can sell. However, occasionally, a shortage of something it uses in its operations means that it cannot sell as many items as it otherwise would have. The item in short supply is known as a *scarce resource*. It is usually either a raw material or a particular type of specialized labour. For example, if there were an unforeseen shortage of crude oil due to some international dispute, the refining companies would not be able to make as much petrol as they could normally sell. In this case, in order to maximize profits, they would concentrate on the products which gave them the largest amount of contribution per barrel of oil.

The highest contribution might come from high-octane kerosene for jet engines. When the refining companies had produced all the aviation fuel that they could sell, they would concentrate on the product with the next-highest contribution per barrel, which might be unleaded petrol for cars. If there were any crude oil left after this, they would choose the next-highest-contribution product, and so on. In this way, they would ensure that they made the best use of every barrel of crude oil, i.e. every unit of their scarce resource. Here is a numerical example.

The following information has been extracted from the budget of Lonestar Petroleum:

| | Contribution per 000 litres (£) | Barrels of crude per 000 litres | Sales forecast for month 5 (000 litres) | Quantity required (barrels) |
|---|---|---|---|---|
| Unleaded petrol | 15.00 | 4.0 | 35,000 | 140,000 |
| Diesel | 12.00 | 3.0 | 18,000 | 54,000 |
| Kerosene | 20.00 | 4.0 | 8,000 | 32,000 |
| Paraffin | 8.00 | 5.0 | 7,000 | 35,000 |
| | | | | 261,000 |

Due to an unexpected worldwide shortage of oil, the quota of crude oil available to Lonestar for month 5 has been set at 200,000 barrels.

Obviously, Lonestar will not be able to make all it planned to in month 5; it is 61,000 barrels short. One answer is to cut back production of all products pro rata but this would not maximize its profits. As crude oil is scarce, it needs to maximize the profit from each barrel. This is done by producing the highest-contribution-**per-barrel** product first, then the next highest, etc. **Lonestar needs to put its products into order according to their *contribution per unit of scarce resource* and produce in this order.**

Care must be exercised here for the contributions shown in the budget information are per thousand litres of finished product, not per unit of scarce resource which is a barrel of crude oil. To solve the problem, the contributions per barrel of crude oil must be calculated for each of the four products.

|  | Contribution per 000 litres (£) | Order | Barrels of crude per 000 litres | Contribution per barrel (£) | Order |
|---|---|---|---|---|---|
| Kerosene | 20.00 | 1 | 4.0 | 20/4 = 5.00 | 1 |
| Unleaded petrol | 15.00 | 2 | 4.0 | 15/4 = 3.75 | 3 |
| Diesel | 12.00 | 3 | 3.0 | 12/3 = 4.00 | 2 |
| Paraffin | 8.00 | 4 | 5.0 | 8/5 = 1.60 | 4 |

So, the order of production would be kerosene, diesel, unleaded petrol and paraffin, until the quota of crude oil was all used up. Production in this new order gives the following results:

|  | Order | Quantity required (barrels) | Cumulative quantity (barrels) | Actual quantity (barrels) | Contribution/ barrel (£) | Total contribution (£) |
|---|---|---|---|---|---|---|
| Kerosene | 1 | 32,000 | 32,000 | 32,000 | 5.00 | 160,000 |
| Diesel | 2 | 54,000 | 86,000 | 54,000 | 4.00 | 216,000 |
| Unleaded petrol | 3 | 140,000 | 226,000 | 114,000 | 3.75 | 427,500 |
| Paraffin | 4 | 35,000 | 261,000 | – |  | – |
|  |  | 261,000 |  | 200,000 |  | 803,500 |

It is clear from the cumulative column that not all the unleaded petrol and none of the paraffin will be able to be produced. The total contribution for month 5 is £803,500. After the kerosene has been produced in full, any other order of production will give a smaller total contribution (and so a smaller profit). To prove this, the following table shows the result of producing in the incorrect order of contribution per thousand litres of output:

|  | Order | Quantity required (barrels) | Cumulative quantity (barrels) | Actual quantity (barrels) | Contribution/ barrel (£) | Total contribution (£) |
|---|---|---|---|---|---|---|
| Kerosene | 1 | 32,000 | 32,000 | 32,000 | 5.00 | 160,000 |
| Unleaded petrol | 2 | 140,000 | 172,000 | 140,000 | 3.75 | 525,000 |
| Diesel | 3 | 54,000 | 226,000 | 28,000 | 4.00 | 112,000 |
| Paraffin | 4 | 35,000 | 261,000 | – |  | – |
|  |  | 261,000 |  | 200,000 |  | 797,000 |

This total contribution is £6,500 lower than before.

The decision-making rule here is to produce in the order of the highest **contribution per unit of scarce resource** until it is used up.

From a business point of view, other aspects of the situation should always be taken into account. Are the sales of the products related? Would the lack of paraffin cause any customers to purchase their petrol or diesel elsewhere? These are not easy questions to answer but in-depth knowledge of the customers should go a long way in arriving at the correct answers.

*Self-assessment question S6.2*

*Try the following question for yourself (answer at the end of the chapter).*

Your company manufactures three products, Alpha, Beta and Gamma. The following information refers to next month:

|  | Alpha | Beta | Gamma |
|---|---|---|---|
| Sales demand (units) | 50 | 150 | 200 |
| Raw materials/unit | £100 | £150 | £80 |
| Direct labour hours/unit | 5 | 10 | 2 |
| Fixed overheads/unit | £30 | £60 | £12 |

Direct labour is paid at £3.00 per hour. Variable overhead is equal to 10% of the cost of materials. Fixed overheads are attached to the products at the rate of 200% of the total direct labour cost. The selling price is calculated by doubling the prime cost (= total direct cost).

*Tasks:*

1  Calculate the contribution per unit for each product and rank them.
2  Using the ranking from the previous answer, prepare a forecast of the profit for each product and in total for next month if only 1,650 direct labour hours are available.
3  Calculate the contribution per direct labour hour for each product and rank them.
4  Using the ranking from the previous answer, prepare a forecast of the profit for each product and in total for next month if only 1,650 direct labour hours are available.
5  Quantify the difference between the answers to 2. and 4. and comment on your findings.

# One-off contracts

Occasionally, in addition to their 'normal' business, organizations are offered work which is of a 'one-off' nature. Take the example of Goodtime Holiday Centre plc (GHC) whose normal business is to provide package holidays in the UK at its custom-built holiday village in Cornwall. All accommodation, meals and entertainment are included in the holiday price, which averages £350 per person per week. The centre can accommodate a maximum of approximately 500 people and holidays are offered between the beginning of May and the end of September. The winter months are taken up with maintenance and new projects. GHC has been approached by an international charity to provide a one-week holiday for 500 refugee children during the last week of April. The charity is willing to pay a total of £50,000 (£100 per child). In deciding whether to accept the offer, GHC must bear in mind its duty to its shareholders to maximize their wealth.

The following information is from GHC's management accounting system and is used to determine its holiday prices.

| Annual costs | £000 | £000 |
|---|---|---|
| Marketing and advertising | 600 | |
| Depreciation of equipment, vehicles, etc. | 538 | |
| Administration staff (permanent) | 132 | |
| Insurance | 80 | |
| Local rates | 90 | |
| | | 1,440 |
| **Holiday season\* costs** | | |
| Other staff (temporary) | 470 | |
| Food and drink | 310 | |
| Other holiday running costs | 120 | |
| | | 900 |
| Total | | 2,340 |

\* The holiday season lasts for 20 weeks.

The total cost of providing one week's holiday = £2,340,000/20 = £117,000
The price for one week's holiday offered by the charity = 500 × £100 = £50,000
It may appear that acceptance of the proposition will lead to a loss of = £67,000

However, before a decision is made, GHC should calculate the **contribution** arising from this one-off proposal.

Variable costs of special holiday:

| | £000 |
|---|---|
| Other staff (temporary) | 470 |
| Food and drink | 310 |
| Other holiday running costs | 120 |

| | £000 | |
|---|---|---|
| Total variable costs for 20 weeks | 900 | |
| Total variable costs for 1 week | 45 | (900/20) |
| Total sales revenue from the charity | 50 | |
| Contribution for the special holiday week | + 5 | (50 − 45) |

GHC should accept the offer because **profit will increase by £5,000**.

This positive contribution means that GHC will not be £67,000 worse off by agreeing to the special holiday but will, in fact, be **£5,000 better off**. This is because the remaining costs of £1,440,000 are **fixed** and will occur whether the special holiday goes ahead or not. If the fixed costs do not affect the financial outcome, they should not be used to make the decision. The fixed costs are absorbed into, and recovered by, the sales revenue from the 'normal holidays'.

The decision-making rule for one-off propositions is that **they should be accepted if they have a positive contribution and rejected if they do not**.

From a business point of view, other aspects of the situation should always be taken into account. For example, if the contract is a trial for a possible much larger order to follow, it should be made clear to the customer that the price is also a one-off and will not be sustainable in the long term. Also, any possible effects on normal sales should be considered. If a regular customer finds out that you have produced and sold a very similar product to the one it purchases from you but at a lower price for someone else, the customer may insist on renegotiating the price. The customer may even place future orders with a competitor.

<table>
<tr><td>

**Self-assessment question S6.3**

</td><td>

*Try the following question for yourself (answer at the end of the chapter).*

a) Abacus Inc. is a small one-product firm which plans to make and sell 1,000 ornamental abacuses a year at a price of $250 each. How much profit does Abacus expect to make in a year if the standard cost of one abacus is as follows?

|                                           | $/unit |
|-------------------------------------------|--------|
| Materials                                 | 100    |
| Direct labour                             | 25     |
| Variable overheads                        | 20     |
| Variable cost                             | 145    |
| Fixed cost (based on a budget of 1,000)   | 75     |
| Total cost                                | 220    |

b) An export order is received for 200 abacuses modified by the addition of some semi-precious stones. The effect of this is a 30% increase in the cost of materials and a 40% increase in the cost of direct labour. Also, special export insurance will cost $5 for each modified abacus shipped. However, the customer is not willing to pay more than $44,000 in total for this large order. Should Abacus Inc. accept this order?

</td></tr>
</table>

## Make or buy

Products and services are often made up of several component parts. A CD-player consists of an amplifier, motor, speakers, laser and casing. A holiday may consist of travel, accommodation, courier, food and drink. Businesses have a choice of creating these components themselves or buying them in from outside. Some very successful companies buy a significant proportion of their components from 'outside' companies. The world-leaders in aero engines, Rolls-Royce, buy in about 75% of parts included in their turbine-driven engines, enabling it to concentrate on the technology-critical areas. When reviewing their costs, organizations should compare the cost of making each component with that of buying it in. Sometimes, they are offered the chance of buying a component instead of making it. How should they decide?

Take the example of a meals-on-wheels service run by a local authority. It provides 100,000 meals a year from kitchens also used to prepare school dinners. Its costings for the meals-on-wheels service are as follows:

|                                        | £       |
|----------------------------------------|---------|
| Depreciation of kitchen equipment*     | 20,000  |
| Depreciation of delivery vehicles      | 30,000  |
| Catering staff wages*                  | 30,000  |
| Drivers' wages                         | 90,000  |
| Food and drink                         | 50,000  |
| Vehicle running costs                  | 80,000  |
| Total cost                             | 300,000 |

\* Based on proportion of total time used for meals-on-wheels.

An independent firm of caterers has offered to cook all the meals on its own premises and provide them to the authority for £0.90 each.

The cost of preparing the meals is:

|                                        | £       |
|----------------------------------------|---------|
| Depreciation of kitchen equipment      | 20,000  |
| Catering staff wages                   | 30,000  |
| Food and drink                         | 50,000  |
| Total cost                             | 100,000 |

As 100,000 meals are provided a year, each one costs £1.00 (£100,000/100,000). This is £0.10 more than the price being offered by the outside caterers, whose offer looks very attractive in this light. However, in order to make the best decision, the **variable** costs should be determined as they will be the only ones that change if the offer is accepted.

Assuming the number of part-time catering staff and the hours they work can be easily adjusted, the variable cost of meals-on-wheels is:

|                                        | £       |
|----------------------------------------|---------|
| Catering staff wages                   | 30,000  |
| Food and drink                         | 50,000  |
| Total variable cost                    | 80,000  |

As 100,000 meals are provided a year, each one has a variable cost of £0.80 (£80,000/100,000). The fixed cost of kitchen depreciation will now have to be borne in full by the school dinners.

If the authority accepts the offer, it will be £10,000 worse off than before. This is because the offer price is £0.10 greater than the variable cost per meal. So the authority should not accept the offer.

The decision rule for make-or-buy situations is that **a component should be bought in only if its price is below the variable cost of producing it.**

From a business point of view, other aspects of the situation should always be taken into account. Will the supply of components be adequate and reliable? Will the quality of components be satisfactory? Will the price of components escalate in future? How easy would it be to start making the components again if the buying-in arrangement goes wrong?

*Try the following question for yourself (answer at the end of the chapter).*

Vendco manufactures a variety of vending machines which have a number of common components. As part of a cost review, Vendco has found an external supplier who will supply it with one of these parts (which has a standard cost of £90 – see below) for £75.

|                    | £  |
|--------------------|----|
| Direct labour      | 25 |
| Direct materials   | 30 |
| Variable overheads | 5  |
| Fixed overhead     | 30 |
| Standard cost      | 90 |

Advise Vendco whether it should continue to make this part or to buy it in at £75.

# Limitations of short-term decision making using variable costing

All the above decision-making techniques have been used strictly within the confines of the variable costing model. This is the accounting part of decision making. It provides a good basis for solving the problem. However, do not forget that making decisions is essentially a management function. The role of accountancy is to provide good information to help managers make the right decisions. Remember, the reality of the situation being faced is always more complex than the assumptions from which the financial model is constructed.

The next chapter, on relevant costing, builds on what you have learnt in this chapter. It, also, is about making decisions but its context is widened to include any other effects caused by those decisions. For example, your contribution analysis may indicate that you should stop making one of your products. However, this may cause a significant number of redundancies to be made at a cost of hundreds of thousands of pounds. Whereas the variable costing model would not take this into account, relevant costing would include the redundancy costs because its boundary of cause and effect is so much wider. To find out more, have a look at the next chapter.

## The manager's point of view (written by Nigel Burton)

Like most manufacturing concerns, my chemical company carried out periodic business reviews to consider withdrawing products which were no longer generating a satisfactory profit. There are many reasons why profitability might be in decline on individual items – perhaps a mature product has reached the end of its natural life, and been superseded by new technology, or fierce competition from Far Eastern suppliers has caused prices to fall to uneconomic levels. Management had to decide whether there was any course of action which would bring these products back into profitability, or whether they should be terminated, to allow the company to concentrate its resources on the newer, more profitable products.

The decision often hinged on the impact of a product's withdrawal on the recovery of fixed overhead. If a product is making a marginal loss (i.e. its variable cost is greater than its selling price) and therefore making no contribution to fixed overhead, the decision is simple. But if the product is making a marginal profit, although not enough to cover all the overheads attributed to it by the costing system, the decision is rather more complicated. If it is terminated, and there is no accompanying reduction in fixed overhead, the contribution will be lost and the company will be worse off. The fixed overhead attributed to the product will simply be reallocated to the next product. This may then become unprofitable as well, and be terminated in its turn, and so it goes on, until the domino effect wipes out the business! In the short term, fixed overheads cannot easily be reduced, so it may well be wise to persevere with the product until longer-term actions can be taken.

In this situation, variable costing is clearly crucial in preventing you from making inappropriate short-term decisions, although you will still have uncovered a problem which needs resolution in the longer term, probably by fixed overhead reductions. The decision to terminate a product is a long-term issue, which will change the future shape of the business. However, variable costing is also valuable in assessing the appropriateness of temporary actions, as a situation in our chemical factory demonstrates.

One of our plants made a high-volume product for use in the paper industry. The plant had been built in the 1970s, and despite one or two capacity improvements, the demand had grown so much by the late 1980s that we were unable to cope, even with continuous shift working. At this point, we were faced with two options: we could increase capacity by building a second plant, or we could concentrate our existing resources on the most profitable pieces of business. An analysis of the business showed that some of the sales generated a relatively low marginal income, and that, by eliminating these and accepting only the higher margin business, the profitability of the group would continue to rise.

This strategy was successful in the short term, and profitability improved. But it was an unsatisfactory way to run a business. Nobody likes to turn away business. It alienates the customer and sends them to the competition. The rejected business may have been at a lower margin, but it was still making a reasonable contribution to profit. The problem was that, at the time, there was insufficient business available to justify the cost of building a new plant. Fortunately, this changed over a period of time, and the growth in demand of both high- and low-margin business reached a point where the numbers started to add up. Accordingly, a new plant was built, doubling the capacity.

Now we had another problem. We had too much capacity for the present demand, and our sales projections showed that we would not be able to fill the plant for several years. At this point we had an enquiry from a large paper company, which needed a volume of product which roughly equated to 30% of our new plant's capacity. The margin on this product was lower than we would normally have accepted, but after much debate, we concluded that it did indeed make a positive contribution towards both fixed overheads and labour, which would otherwise have remained idle. We therefore accepted the business.

Such decisions are not as easy to make as they may seem. There are both quantifiable and unquantifiable issues to take into account. For instance, how fixed is the labour? If we do not accept this business, can we switch the labour on to cheaper single shifts, or is the volume of other business sufficient to require continuous shift-working anyway? What is the impact on the cover provided by other departments, such as maintenance, quality control or the canteen? What about the level of raw material and finished goods stocks that will be needed, with the consequent warehousing and interest costs? Are we happy that the product costs on which we are basing this significant decision are sufficiently accurate in the first place? We certainly do not want to discover too late that the new business is actually draining profit from the company. And there are also the less quantifiable issues to consider, such as the extent of management input required, or the impact on the company's ability to accept unexpected, but more profitable orders that may arise in the near future.

Once you have decided that it is in your company's interests to accept low-margin business, it is imperative that all parties are fully aware of the implications. Our American parent used marginal income percentage as one of the key measurements of our group's performance. The inclusion of a substantial piece of low-margin business naturally caused the marginal income percentage to decline, so it was important to ensure that the parent understood both the rationale and the effect of it, and that, if we chose not to do the business the following year, the parent would understand the reasons for a fluctuating sales line.

Such business should always be regarded as a one-off, separate piece of business which is outside the normal course of the company's activities. The business does not cover its share of the overheads, and is therefore technically unprofitable. We only consider accepting it when the overheads are already covered by other more profitable business. If there were a temptation to repeat this low-margin business year after year, perhaps a more advantageous course of action for the company would be to pursue a reduction in the level of fixed overheads.

There is also a risk in accepting low-margin business, in that it might encourage salespeople to chase more and more of it. After all, isn't any sale with a positive marginal income making a contribution towards overhead? Well, maybe, if you are a supermarket, where high sales volumes may well compensate for low margins and be sufficient to generate a satisfactory return. In manufacturing companies, however, capacity constraints will tend to limit the opportunity for substantial volume increases, so primary concentration on high-margin business is essential.

*Summary*

- Cease activities only if there is a negative contribution.
- Produce in the order of 'contribution per unit of scarce resource'.
- Decide whether to accept one-off contracts on the basis of their contribution.
- Buy in components if their price is less than the variable cost of manufacturing.
- Do not forget to take into account the factors outside the variable costing model. (The next chapter looks at this in greater depth.)

# Further reading

Horngren, C., Bhimani, A., Datar, S. and Foster, G. (2002) *Management and Cost Accounting*, 2nd edition, Prentice Hall Europe, Harlow. See Chapter 8, 'Cost–volume–profit relationships'.

Upchurch, A. (2003) *Management Accounting, Principles and Practice*, 2nd edition, Financial Times/Prentice Hall, Harlow. See chapter 'Cost/volume/profit analysis'.

Weetman, P. (2002) *Management Accounting, an Introduction*, 3rd edition, Financial Times/Prentice Hall, Harlow. See chapter 'Profit measurement and short-term decision making'.

# Answers to self-assessment questions

## S6.1 V&A Group

|  | A | B | C | D | Group |
|---|---|---|---|---|---|
| Total overheads | 90 | 210 | 250 | 450 | 1,000 |
| Variable overheads (90%) | 81 | 189 | 225 | 405 | 900 |
| Fixed overheads (10%) | 9 | 21 | 25 | 45 | 100 |
| **Variable costs** | | | | | |
| Raw materials + direct labour | 103 | 184 | 239 | 475 | 1,001 |
| Add: Variable overheads | 81 | 189 | 225 | 405 | 900 |
| Variable costs | 184 | 373 | 464 | 880 | 1,901 |
| Sales income | 180 | 420 | 500 | 900 | 2,000 |
| Contribution | (4) | 47 | 36 | 20 | 99 |

**(a) Close factory A only**
If A is closed:

|  | A | B | C | D | Group |
|---|---|---|---|---|---|
| Contribution | – | 47 | 36 | 20 | 103 |
| Less: Fixed costs | | | | | 100 |
| **(b) Net profit** | | | | | 3 |

If A and D are closed:

|  | A | B | C | D | Group |
|---|---|---|---|---|---|
| Contribution | – | 47 | 36 | – | 83 |
| Less: Fixed costs | | | | | 100 |
| (c) Net loss | | | | | (17) |

## S6.2  Alpha, Beta, Gamma

| | Alpha | Beta | Gamma | Total |
|---|---|---|---|---|
| Direct costs: | | | | |
| Raw materials | 100 | 150 | 80 | |
| Direct labour | 15 | 30 | 6 | |
| Prime cost | 115 | 180 | 86 | |
| Variable overhead | 10 | 15 | 8 | |
| Variable cost | 125 | 195 | 94 | |
| Fixed overhead | 30 | 60 | 12 | |
| Total cost/unit | 155 | 255 | 106 | |
| Fixed overhead/unit | 30 | 60 | 12 | |
| Sales demand (units) | 50 | 150 | 200 | |
| Total fixed overhead | 1,500 | 9,000 | 2,400 | 12,900 |

| 1 | Alpha | Beta | Gamma | |
|---|---|---|---|---|
| Selling price | 230 | 360 | 172 | (200% of prime cost) |
| Variable cost | 125 | 195 | 94 | |
| Contribution/unit | 105 | 165 | 78 | |
| Ranking | 2 | 1 | 3 | |

| 2 | Alpha | Beta | Gamma | Total |
|---|---|---|---|---|
| Labour hours/unit | 5 | 10 | 2 | |
| No. of labour hours | 150 | 1,500 | – | 1,650 |
| No. of units sold | 30 | 150 | – | |
| Contribution/unit | 105 | 165 | 78 | |
| Total contribution | 3,150 | 24,750 | – | 27,900 |
| Less: Fixed costs | | | | 12,900 |
| **Net profit** | | | | **£15,000** |

| 3 | | | | |
|---|---|---|---|---|
| Contribution/unit | 105 | 165 | 78 | |
| Labour hours/unit | 5 | 10 | 2 | |
| Contribution/labour hour | **21.0** | **16.5** | **39.0** | |
| Ranking | **2** | **3** | **1** | |

| 4 | | | | Total |
|---|---|---|---|---|
| Labour hours/unit | 5 | 10 | 2 | |
| No. of labour hours | 250 | 1,000 | 400 | 1,650 |
| No. of units sold | 50 | 100 | 200 | |
| Contribution/unit | 105 | 165 | 78 | |
| Total contribution | 5,250 | 16,500 | 15,600 | 37,350 |
| Less: Fixed costs | | | | 12,900 |
| Net profit | | | | **£24,450** |

5  Using the contribution per direct labour hour ranking gives £9,450 more profit than the contribution per unit ranking. So, using the contribution per unit of scarce resource does give the highest profit.

## S6.3  Abacus Inc.

(a)  Normal activity

|  | $ |
|---|---|
| Sales price | 250 |
| Variable cost | 145 |
| Contribution | 105/unit |

|  |  | $ |
|---|---|---|
| Total contribution = 1,000 × $105 = | | 105,000 |
| Less: Fixed costs  = 1,000 × $75  = | | 75,000 |
| **Net profit** | | = **$30,000** |

(b)  Export order

|  | $ |
|---|---|
| Materials | 130 ($100 + 30%) |
| Direct labour | 35 ($25 + 40%) |
| Variable overheads | 20 |
| Export insurance | 5 |
| Variable cost | 190/unit |
| Sales price | 220 ($44,000/200) |
| Contribution | +30/unit |
| Total contribution = | +$6,000 (200 × $30) |

**Recommend acceptance of the export order as it has a positive contribution.**

## S6.4  Vendco

Compare the relevant variable costs of manufacture with the buying-in cost. Remember that fixed overheads will still have to be paid for in the short term so these are irrelevant to the decision.

|  | £ |
|---|---|
| Variable production costs | |
| Direct labour | 25 |
| Direct materials | 30 |
| Variable overheads | 5 |
| Total | 60 |
| Buy-in price | 75 |

**Therefore, buying in is not recommended (in the short term).**

| CASE STUDY | Sara Wray Enterprises |
|---|---|

Sara Wray lives in the Cotswolds, an area of outstanding natural beauty in central-southwest England. She started her working life as a teacher of French and art but, after several years, she gave this up to have a family. As her children grew older, she went back to work on a part-time basis, not as a teacher but as an administrator of a local art gallery. Her children are now adults with jobs of their own and Sara is the driving force behind a successful business offering language tuition and cultural holidays to non-UK residents.

Her business actually started seven years ago when she decided to gain a Teaching English as a Foreign Language (TEFL) qualification. Having achieved this, she provided English language tuition to foreign students in the summer months. Two students would come to stay in her home at any one time, receiving formal tuition in the morning and going out for visits to local places of interest in the afternoon and evenings with Sara. During her first summer season, she had a total of nine students, eight staying for two weeks and one staying for one month. This was a total of 20 student-weeks' tuition. She established a good reputation and the number of students grew each year.

After a few years, Sara branched out by offering one-week Tours of the Cotswolds for groups of approximately 16 adults without any formal language tuition element. Her success with these tours is based on her organisational ability and her experience of arranging local trips for her language students. As well as general tours, she now offers two specialized ones: English Gardens and Arts and Crafts. Sara still sees her English language courses as the basis of her operations as many of her tours include some people who have been students of hers or have been recommended by them. However, most of her tour customers come from her advertisements in France, Holland, Germany, Italy and Spain.

Current demand for her TEFL courses is such that she now employs seven other qualified teachers, each taking two students at a time. The students live in the teachers' homes and are taught there in the mornings but join together for the visits and eat out together each evening at a different venue. For these outings, Sara hires an 18-seater minibus and driver for her 12-week season (mid-June to mid-September). Her non-tuition tours start in May and finish in October but do not take place every week. These tour customers stay in local hotels which are block-booked in advance by Sara. She hires the same type of minibus and driver for her tour parties and she also hires a guide to accompany them.

Up to now, there has been no difficulty finding guides of the right quality. Unfortunately, her regular garden tour guide, Rose, is about to move to Paris due to her partner's unexpected relocation and will no longer be available to guide these tours. However, one of the TEFL teachers, Mary, is also an expert gardener and has volunteered her services as garden tour guide. As Mary speaks reasonably good French, Spanish and German, she would be an ideal choice for this job. But the two planned garden tours are scheduled to take place during the TEFL season and Sara would have to find a replacement teacher for those weeks. Most of the other good TEFL teachers living in the area have contracted with the many English language schools based in nearby Oxford and Sara is finding it impossible to find a suitable replacement. As the season is just about to start, it looks as though Sara will have to cancel either two teacher-weeks of English tuition or two one-week garden tours. She is unsure whether to use Mary as a TEFL teacher or a garden tour guide.

While she is pondering this dilemma, Sara receives a letter from one of her previous students, Michael, who lives in Munich. Michael wants Sara to arrange a one-week 'Beer and Brewing' tour to include five beer-related visits for himself and 15 of his friends. When he was brushing up his English last year with Sara, he was very impressed with several local beers he tasted in the Cotswold area. He is offering to pay Sara £5,600 (16 @ £350 per person) for local accommodation, food, transport, brewery visit fees and knowledgeable guide. He will organize the travel between Munich and the Cotswolds.

Sara's friend, David, is a member of the Campaign for Real Ale (CamRA) and says that he would be willing to give up a week of his holidays to guide this tour for £500. Sara estimates admission fees at £650 and other costs the same as for a general or gardens tour. She does not see any reason why this tour should not go ahead. The only thing concerning her is that the price offered seems so low that the tour will make a loss. The lowest cost of her other tours is £6,000 (see below). She thinks she will probably have to contact Michael and refuse his offer.

As well as all this, she notices that the financial analysis prepared by her accountant shows that, although the general and gardens tours are profitable, the arts and crafts tours are making a loss (see below). Although they are more costly to run, she is reluctant to drop them but, on the other hand, does not want to run any of her activities at a loss. She is reluctant to increase her prices as she is aware of a firm in nearby Oxford which offers very similar arts tours at the price of £385 per person.

Sara wants to increase her profit next year by at least £3,000 by expanding either the English teaching or the tours but she is unsure what she needs to do to achieve this.

## Financial analysis of TEFL activities

Maximum activity for season is 8 teachers for 12 weeks = 96 teacher-weeks
Each teacher has two students each week. Each student pays £400/week
Fixed costs (minibus hire, insurance, advertising, etc.) for TEFL total £19,200

| For one teacher-week | £ |
|---|---|
| 2 hours' tuition/day for 5 days = 10 h @ £15/h = | 150 |
| Agent's commission, 2 students @ £25 = | 50 |
| Accommodation, 5 nights @ £20 × 2 students = | 200 |
| Evening meals, £5 × 2 students × 5 days = | 50 |
| Admission fees, £5 × 2 students × 5 days = | 50 |
| Total variable cost = | 500 |
| Fixed cost (£19,200/12 weeks/8 teachers) = | 200 |
| Total cost = | 700 |
| Sales revenue (2 @ £400) = | 800 |
| Net profit = | 100 |

## Financial analysis of tour activities

Tours planned: 3 general, 2 gardens and 2 arts and crafts
Maximum of 16 per tour, each person paying £400
Fixed costs (administration, insurance, advertising, etc.) for tours total £12,810

| Per tour (16 people) | General/Gardens £ | Arts and Crafts £ |
|---|---|---|
| Minibus and driver | 800 | 800 |
| Guide fees | 350 | 500 |
| Hotel, bed, breakfast & evening meal | 2,620 | 2,620 |
| Admission fees | 400 | 800 |
| Total variable costs | 4,170 | 4,720 |
| Fixed costs | 1,830 | 1,830 |
| Total cost | 6,000 | 6,550 |
| Sales revenue (16 × £400) | 6,400 | 6,400 |
| Net profit | 400 | (150) |

*Tasks:*

Advise Sara on the decisions facing her:

1 Is it better to use Mary as a garden tour guide or English teacher for two weeks?

(25 marks)

2 Should she decline Michael's offer of £5,600 for a Beer and Brewing tour?

(25 marks)

3 Should she stop offering the Arts and Crafts tours?

(25 marks)

4 Next year, should she expand the English teaching or the tours?

(25 marks)
(Total 100 marks)

## Questions

An asterisk * on a question number indicates that the answer is given at the end of the book. Answers to the other questions are given in the Lecturer's Guide.

### Q6.1* Burgabar Corporation

Burgabar Corporation owns and operates a range of fast food outlets throughout the East End of London. A summary of next year's budget (before head office costs are taken into account) is given below:

| Branch | Sales revenue £ | Variable costs £ | Salaries & wages £ | Fixed costs £ |
|---|---|---|---|---|
| West Ham | 100,000 | 20,000 | 32,000 | 30,000 |
| Hackney | 120,000 | 24,000 | 32,000 | 30,000 |
| Forest Gate | 120,000 | 24,000 | 34,000 | 32,000 |
| Mile End | 140,000 | 28,000 | 34,000 | 34,000 |

The administrative head office of Burgabar Corporation is at Epping. Its running costs of £96,000 a year are apportioned to branches on the basis of sales revenue.

Concern is being expressed about the West Ham branch as it is showing a loss (after head office costs have been deducted). One director has suggested that the branch is closed as soon as possible and a new branch opened, possibly in the Ilford area. However, it would take approximately 12 months to open a new branch. The closure of the West Ham branch would reduce head office costs by £10,000 p.a. with immediate effect. Also, although West Ham's salaries and wages bill would disappear immediately, redundancy pay of £8,000 would be payable.

*Task:*

Advise the directors of Burgabar Corporation.

### Q6.2* Profoot Ltd

Profoot currently makes and sells two types of protective shoe, model P1 and model P2.

|  | P1 | P2 |
|---|---|---|
| Annual sales demand (pairs) | 14,000 | 10,000 |
| Selling price | £40 | £40 |
| Variable costs per pair: |  |  |
| Materials | £15 | £15 |
| Labour – Machining (£8/hour) | £2 | £2 |
|     – Assembly (£7/hour) | £3.50 | £3.50 |
|     – Packing (£6/hour) | £0.50 | £0.50 |

Annual total fixed costs are currently £300,000.

For the next financial year, Profoot intends to keep model P1 as it is but to upgrade model P2 by the use of better materials. The materials cost for P2 is expected to be £20 a pair (an increase of £5 a pair) and its new selling price will be £50 a pair. Also, the amount of time spent machining P2s will double and the cost of this will increase to £4 a pair.

Also, next year, Profoot intends to introduce the PDL, a top-of-the-range model with a selling price of £65. Labour costs for machining will be £4 a pair, assembly £7 a pair and packing £0.50 a pair. Materials will cost £32.50 a pair.

Demand for the P1, P2 and PDL next year is predicted to be 14,000, 7,000 and 5,000 pairs respectively. Annual fixed costs are expected to increase by 2% next year.

*Tasks:*

1 Calculate the annual net profit for the current year.
2 Calculate the annual net profit for next year assuming the predicted demand is met in full.
3 If the maximum number of machine hours available next year is 8,500, create a production plan to maximize net profit. (Clearly show the quantity of each model produced and calculate the net profit.)
4 Profoot could purchase an additional machine costing £420,000 which would last for 10 years and have no residual value at the end of that period. This machine could be used for a maximum of 1,750 hours a year. How would the purchase of this machine affect next year's net profit?

## Q6.3* King & Co.

The current annual budget for King & Co., makers of baseball caps, is summarized as follows:

|  | £000 |
|---|---|
| Sales (1 million caps @ £5 each) | 5,000 |
| Less manufacturing cost of caps sold | 3,000 |
| Gross margin | 2,000 |
| Less sales and administration expenses | 1,500 |
| Operating income | 500 |

King's fixed manufacturing costs were £2.0 million and its fixed sales and administration costs were £1.0 million. Sales commission of 5% of sales is included in the sales and administration expenses. It is approaching the end of the current financial year and looks as though it will exceed its budgetary targets.

King's has just been asked by its local first division football club to make a special order of 50,000 caps in the club colours to celebrate their promotion to the Premier league; they are willing to pay £4 a cap. However, a special badge of the club's emblem would have to be made for each cap.

Even though King & Co. has the necessary capacity to produce the order, the managing director has decided to reject the club's offer of £200,000 for the 50,000 caps. He explained his decision by saying, 'The club's offer is too low. I know we would save the sales commission but the badges alone will cost twice as much as that, and it costs us £4.50 to make our ordinary caps. I'm willing to cut our usual 10% profit margin to 5%, or even less, to get this order but I'm not prepared to do it for nothing and I'm certainly not prepared to make a loss on the deal.'

*Task:*

Comment on the managing director's decision.

## Q6.4  Parfumier Jean-Paul

Jean-Paul Cie (J-P) is a world-famous haute-couture fashion house based in Paris. It also manufactures a range of perfumes, all made from secret recipes. Only one ingredient called 'maylarnge', a mixing agent, is used in all their products. Maylarnge is obtained from SML Laboratoire in Brussels and the quantity used varies with the particular perfume recipe.

Due to temporary processing difficulties, SML have informed J-P that it can supply only €13,100 worth of maylarnge over the next three months.

The budget below relates to the quarter in question under normal circumstances. The shortage of the mixing agent means that the budget will have to be revised.

| Perfume | Passion | Entice | Magique | Exotique |
|---|---|---|---|---|
| Sales volume (50 ml bottles) | 6,000 | 5,500 | 6,500 | 4,500 |
| Variable costs per bottle | € | € | € | € |
| Maylarnge | 1.00 | 0.80 | 1.20 | 0.60 |
| Ingredients (as per recipe) | 2.00 | 3.10 | 2.60 | 1.90 |
| Selling price | 12.90 | 15.70 | 16.10 | 14.50 |

Fixed costs for the quarter amount to €133,300 (including all wages and salaries).

*Tasks:*

1  What would the quarter's profit be if there was no shortage of maylarnge?
2  Calculate the profit for this period of shortage if the perfumes were manufactured in the order of their contribution per bottle until they ran out of maylarnge.
3  Calculate the revised sales budget and profit assuming J-P wishes to maximize its profit for this period of shortage.

## Q6.5  MPB Ltd

Marie and Peter Bridge run a business manufacturing and selling sets of the popular French game, boules. The boules are turned from aluminium, packaged in a neat carrying case and sold for £22 a set. The raw materials cost £8 a set and each set takes 20 minutes of turning by skilled operatives who are paid £9.00 an hour. The fixed costs of the business are £480,000 a year. This year, they plan to produce 80,000 sets.

*Tasks:*

1  Calculate:
   a)  the variable cost of a set of boules;
   b)  the absorption cost of a set of boules;
   c)  the breakeven point;
   d)  the profit or loss if 80,000 sets are sold.

2  A large French champagne house has asked MPB Ltd if it will produce 5,000 boule sets for a worldwide promotion. Each set has to be engraved with the French company's logo and the carrying case must bear its brand name. The extra work involved in this will cost £2.50 a set. It has offered to pay a total of £75,000 for the order. Should MPB accept this offer?

3  A Chinese company has proposed to MPB that it should manufacture the finished boule sets in China and supply them to MPB for £14 delivered. This price would apply to the first 50,000 sets, but after this it would reduce to £10 a set. MPB appreciates that this would change its function to trading only and it would be able to eliminate its manufacturing facilities, saving £180,000 a year.
   a)  Advise MPB whether or not it should accept this proposition.
   b)  List the points MPB should consider carefully before accepting this proposition.

## Q6.6

BBQ Ltd manufactures two types of barbecue – the Deluxe BBQ and the Standard BBQ. Both undergo similar production processes and use similar materials and types of labour. However, a shortage of direct labour has been identified and this is limiting the company's ability to produce the required number of barbecues for the year ending 31 May 2002. Labour capacity is limited to 235,000 labour hours for the year ending 31 May 2002 and this is insufficient to meet total sales demand.

BBQ Ltd has stated that the standard selling price and standard prime cost for each barbecue for the forthcoming year are as follows:

|                                   | Deluxe BBQ | Standard BBQ |
|-----------------------------------|------------|--------------|
| Selling price                     | £100       | £50          |
| Direct material                   | £50        | £11          |
| Direct labour (rate £5 per hour)  | £25        | £20          |
| Estimated sales demand (units)    | 10,000     | 50,000       |

It has been company policy to absorb production overheads on a labour hour basis. The budgeted information for the year ending 31 May 2002 is as follows:

| Fixed production overhead    | £188,000                  |
|------------------------------|---------------------------|
| Variable production overhead | £2 per direct labour hour |

Non-production costs for the year ending 31 May 2002 are estimated to be:

*Selling and distribution overhead:*
   Variable                                10% of selling price
   Fixed                                   £35,000
*Administrative overhead:*
   Fixed                                   £50,000

*Required:*

a) Calculate the production plan that will maximize profit for the year ending 31 May 2002.

*(7 marks)*

b) Based on the production plan that you have recommended in part (a), present a profit statement for the year ending 31 May 2002 in a marginal costing format.

*(9 marks)*

c) Discuss two problems that may arise as a result of your recommended production plan.

*(4 marks)*

d) Explain why the contribution concept is used in limiting factor decisions.

*(5 marks)*
*(Total = 25 marks)*

CIMA Foundation: Management Accounting Fundamentals, May 2001.

## Review questions

1  Explain how to tell whether or not to cease certain activities.
2  Explain how to determine the order of production when one of the resources used is scarce.
3  Explain how to tell whether or not to accept one-off contracts.
4  Explain how to tell whether to produce or buy in components used in your products.
5  Discuss the limitations of decision making using variable costing.

*The answers to all these questions can be found in the text of this chapter.*

# Short-term decisions using relevant costing

## Introduction

Managers should take decisions that result in maximum benefit for the organization **as a whole**. This means taking into account **indirect** effects as well as the direct ones. Suppose that a lawn mower manufacturer decides to buy in a particular component, e.g. the motor, instead of making it, the justification being that the £15 purchase price of the motor is less than its £17 variable cost of manufacture. If the company uses 10,000 motors a year then the annual saving should be £20,000.

This looks like a good decision. But suppose that one indirect effect of this was to make five jobs redundant in the motor production section. If the average redundancy pay was £12,000, it would take three years before the total redundancy pay of £60,000 was covered by the savings made!

The point is that **all** the known quantifiable effects of a decision should be part of the analysis, not just the obvious ones. Relevant costing is particularly appropriate for managers as they are more likely to be aware of the indirect effects than the accountants. This applies even more so to the consideration of the qualitative factors involved. The voice of the manager should be paramount in these decisions.

**Having worked through this chapter you should be able to:**
- describe relevant costing;
- distinguish between relevant and irrelevant costs;
- identify avoidable costs, opportunity costs, sunk costs, committed costs, non-cash costs and opportunity benefits;
- quantify the relevant cost of decisions;
- discuss the importance of qualitative factors;
- give good advice based on relevant costing.

## Definition of relevant cost/revenue

Relevant costs/revenues have three criteria. They are **always**:

- **avoidable** – they are caused by a positive decision and would not happen if the decision was negative;
- **future** – costs/revenues that have already happened cannot be altered by a decision not yet taken;
- **cash** – the net change in cash (not profit) is used to measure the decision's effects.

**All three criteria must be fulfilled.** If only one or two criteria are met, the cost/revenue is not relevant.

The topic of 'relevant costing' is really about **relevant cash flows** (which would be a better title due to its descriptive nature). These relevant cash flows can be 'in' (revenues) or 'out' (costs).

## Types of relevant cost

The two main types of relevant costs are *avoidable costs* and *opportunity costs*.

## Avoidable costs

These will only be incurred if a certain course of action is followed, otherwise they will not occur. If a positive decision means that a new lorry will be purchased for £22,000 then a negative decision means that expenditure of £22,000 will be **avoided**.

## Opportunity costs

These are a measure of the net cash **benefit** foregone from the next most desirable alternative course of action. Even though these do not appear on the profit and loss account, they are real and relevant for decision making.

For example, if some **scarce** specialised labour (like a high-level relational database programmer) is reassigned due to a positive decision, the opportunity cost will be the net cash benefit sacrificed due to the discontinuation of the programmer's current assignment. If there are plenty of these programmers in the organization the opportunity cost will not arise as both projects can be performed at the same time.

## Types of irrelevant cost

The three main types of irrelevant costs are sunk costs, committed costs and non-cash costs.

## Sunk costs

These relate to the proposal under consideration but are incurred **prior** to the decision being made. A good example is the cost of market research undertaken to help make decisions about a new product. Sunk costs are also known as 'past costs'.

## Committed costs

These are costs that have not been paid at the time of making the decision but a legal obligation exists to pay them at some time in the future; for example, lease payments of premises for the project under consideration if that lease is already in existence but the premises are currently unoccupied. As the lease payments must be made whether the decision is positive or negative, these costs are also called 'common costs'. (They are common to both the 'yes' and 'no' decision as to whether the project goes ahead or not.)

## Non-cash costs

The most usual example of these is the depreciation charged in the profit and loss account. Depreciation is a legitimate cost; indeed the net profit figure would be incorrect if depreciation had not been deducted from gross profit together with the other overheads. However, depreciation does **not** cause any movement of cash and therefore cannot be a relevant cost.

Example
7.1

# Relevant costing

Frank Jeffery Limited is a manufacturer of reproduction antique furniture. Three months ago it tendered for a one-off order from English Heritage to make a copy of a four-poster bed that was once slept in by Queen Elizabeth I. The cost of preparing this tender was estimated to be £250. The specification would use 5 cubic metres ('cubes') of English oak, a timber in regular use in the factory. Its current price is £400 a cube. There are three cubes in stock at the moment, which were bought in at £375 a cube.

Business is good and the factory is working at full capacity. To make the bed would need three skilled craftworkers for two weeks each. The company operates a 40-hour week and pays skilled craftworkers at the rate of £10 per hour. It is estimated that the normal work lost due to this order would produce a net cash contribution for the company totalling £3,000.

The machinery involved would depreciate by £400 in the two weeks and the cost of electricity to run the machines would be £80. The machines would be in continual use whether or not the tender was successful. Fixed production overheads are absorbed at the rate of £25 per direct labour hour.

One month ago, a new advanced type of hand-held router was purchased at the cost of £750 as it would be very useful if the bid was selected by English Heritage. (This was a bargain introductory offer for last month only; its price is now £899.) The company's policy is to write off in full hand tools costing less than £1,000 to the profit and loss account in the year of purchase.

What is the relevant cost to Frank Jeffery Limited of making the four-poster bed?

## Solution

| Item | Avoidable | Future | Cash | Note | Amount | Relevant |
|---|---|---|---|---|---|---|
| Tender preparation | | | X | 1 | | – |
| English oak | X | X | X | 2 | 5 cubes × £400 | 2,000 |
| Craftworker's pay | | X | X | 3 | | – |
| Cash contribution lost | X | X | X | 4 | | 3,000 |
| Machine depreciation | | X | | 5 | | – |
| Machine electricity | | X | X | 6 | | – |
| Fixed production overhead | | X | | 7 | | – |
| New router | | | X | 8 | | – |
| | | | | | **Relevant cost** | **£5,000** |

Notes:
1 Sunk cost.
2 As oak is in regular use, 5 cubes will need to be replaced at the current price.
3 Craftworkers are assumed to be permanent employees paid on a time basis.
4 Opportunity cost of next best alternative.
5 Depreciation is not a **cash** cost. It is a book entry not causing any cash to flow.
6 Common cost. The machines will be running irrespective of the tender.
7 Overhead absorption is a book entry. It does not change the overheads **incurred**.
8 Sunk cost.

*Self-assessment question S7.1*

*Try the following question for yourself (answer at the end of the chapter).*

Welgrow Ltd is a manufacturer of garden seed compost. At the moment, it makes six different types and is considering adding a new basic compost to its range. Initially, it will make a batch of 10,000 kg and has listed the following costs involved.

1 Exclusive use of the company's mixing machine will be needed for one week. The depreciation of this machine is included as a production overhead at £520 per year.
2 The trial batch will need 7,000 kg of vermiculite. Welgrow does not use this material and does not have any of it in stock at present; its market price is £1.00 per kg.
3 Several years ago Welgrow bought a large quantity of black sand at £0.10 per kg for a special project. A left-over surplus of 3,000 kg is currently in stock as it has proved impossible to resell. Welgrow has no alternative use for this surplus other than as an ingredient in the new compost.
4 To ensure successful marketing of this new product at the right time, a contract for advertising space with a total cost of £500 has been signed. A deposit of 20% has been paid and the balance is due one month before launch next spring.
5 An aluminium storage bin, which was due to have been offered for sale at the realistic price of £100, will be used for the new compost.

Consider each item and state why you think it is relevant or not. Calculate the relevant cost to Welgrow of the decision to go ahead. Also, calculate the breakeven selling price of the new compost.

## Opportunity benefits

These benefits, or savings, may be created by taking a positive decision to go ahead with a project. For example, some redundancy costs which were about to be incurred may be avoided by going ahead.

**The avoidance or prevention of a cash cost is equivalent to cash income.**

Opportunity benefits are relevant to the decision and must be taken into account.

## Relevant cost of materials

The relevant cost of a material is not what it cost to buy it in the first place, i.e. a sunk or committed cost. If a material is in regular use, its relevant cost is its **replacement** cost. This is the **future, avoidable, cash flow** caused by the decision to use it.

But if the material was already owned and would not be replaced if used (i.e. it was not in regular use) its relevant cost is the **greater** of:

a) its current realisable value (i.e. the amount received from selling it) and
b) the value obtained from alternative uses.

You should recognize this as its opportunity cost.

---

## Relevant cost of materials

Example 7.2

Birch Brothers is a low-volume, high-specification bicycle manufacturer based in South Yorkshire. It has been requested to quote for producing a special pedal-powered vehicle for promoting bicycle use in the UK. The vehicle has four pedalling positions at the front and four at the rear. In between these is a three-dimensional platform structure for advertising the various benefits of cycling. It is approximately the size of a small lorry.

Birch Brothers is currently short of work and is operating at well below its maximum capacity. Unfounded rumours of possible redundancies are circulating among the 20-strong workforce and morale is not good. No additional labour or overtime would be needed to build this 'promotional platform'. This order would provide some very welcome work for the business.

However, the contract would need the following materials:

a) New materials not normally used, e.g. a trailer chassis for the central advertising platform. These would total £5,000.
b) Materials currently in regular use and in stock, e.g. wheels, pedals, etc. These have a book value of £1,780 but would cost £2,000 to buy now.
c) 80 metres of stainless steel tube: Birch Brothers has 60 metres of this disused item in stock left over from a discontinued model. This stock has a resale value of £500 but it is planned to use it all for an export order commencing in four months' time in place of a very similar specification tube which would cost £12.50 a metre. The current price of stainless steel tube is £20 a metre.
d) 95 square metres of aluminium sheet: it has just this amount in stock. It was left over from the manufacture of a batch of bike-trailers, a product that was unsuccessful for the company. Birch Brothers has tried reselling these sheets but not a single buyer was found. The sheeting is taking up a lot of workshop space and it was decided last week to pay £200 to have it removed in the near future.
e) 8 sets of brakes: the company has 20 sets of old-fashioned brakes that are perfectly functional although there is no demand for them. The original cost of these was £12 a set. Whatever is left of this stock item will be thrown in the bin at the financial year-end stocktake.

## Solution

| Item | Avoidable | Future | Cash | Note | Amount | Relevant |
|------|-----------|--------|------|------|--------|----------|
| a) New materials | X | X | X | 1 | £5,000 | 5,000 |
| b) Regular materials | X | X | X | 2 | £2,000 | 2,000 |
| c) 60 m st. steel tube | X | X | X | 3 | 60 m × £12.50 | 750 |
| d) 20 m st. steel tube | X | X | X | 4 | 20 m × £20 | 400 |
| e) Aluminium sheet | X | X | X | 5 | £200 | (200) |
| f) Old-fashioned brakes | | | | 6 | – | |
| | | | | | **Relevant cost** | **£7,950** |

Notes:
1  At current buying-in market price (= replacement cost).
2  At replacement cost.
3  First 60 metres at opportunity cost (= cost saved by use for export order).
4  Next 20 metres need to be bought in (at current replacement price).
5  This is an opportunity **benefit**. By using the sheeting, the company is saving the cost of its disposal.
6  No cash flows of any sort are caused by using these brakes.

Note also that there are no relevant labour costs. The labour force would be paid whether the contract is obtained or not. This is a common cost.

**Self-assessment question S7.2**

*Try the following question for yourself (answer at the end of the chapter).*

Tilly Ltd has been approached by a customer who wants a special job done and is willing to pay £20,000 for it. The job would require the following materials:

| Material | Total units required | Units in stock | Book value of units in stock (£/unit) | Realizable value (£/unit) | Replacement cost (£/unit) |
|----------|---------------------|----------------|---------------------------------------|---------------------------|---------------------------|
| A | 1,000 | 0 | – | – | 6 |
| B | 1,000 | 600 | 2 | 2.5 | 5 |
| C | 1,000 | 700 | 3 | 2.5 | 4 |
| D | 200 | 200 | 4 | 6 | 9 |
| E | 500 | 500 | 5 | – | – |

Material B is regularly used by Tilly Ltd in the manufacture of its standard products.

Materials C and D are specialist materials, in stock due to previous overbuying. No other use can be found for material C. However, the stock of material D could be used in another job as a substitute for 300 units of material M. Tilly has no stock of material M at present but it can be purchased locally at £5 a unit.

Since the stock of material E was acquired, its sale has been banned by the government (although previously acquired stocks are allowed to be used up). It is a toxic chemical and Tilly is expecting to pay £500 in the near future for its safe disposal as it has no other use for it.

*Task:*

To help Tilly Ltd decide whether or not to accept the job, calculate the relevant cost of materials needed.

# Qualitative factors

Although relevant costing is a numerical or quantitative analysis technique, only a poor manager would ignore the non-numerical or qualitative factors involved in a decision. These are just as important, if not more so, and should be given serious consideration before the decision is made.

Take the case of an advertising agency that currently handles the Mars UK account being offered the chance to pitch for the business of Cadbury's Chocolate. Before doing so, it should think very carefully about the reaction of Mars UK to its acting for a major competitor. Would Mars UK see it as a conflict of interests and take its business elsewhere?

Although no **definite** numerical answers are attainable in such cases, organizations should be aware of the possible risks involved and act accordingly.

# Limitations of decision making using relevant costing

The context of relevant costing is broader than that of variable costing (discussed in the last chapter). This lack of artificial boundaries makes it much more realistic. It also makes it more useful, as decisions usually have indirect consequences which should be included in the decision-making process. The main limitation of relevant costing is the difficulty in foreseeing all the indirect consequences arising from the decision in question.

Take the example used in the 'Limitations' section of the previous chapter on variable costing. This described the decision, based on an analysis of product contributions, to cease manufacturing one of several products. The indirect consequence of multiple redundancies and associated payments occurring had been foreseen and taken into account in the cessation decision. However, it may be that the dropping of that particular product would enhance the market's perception of the company as the product was considered to be outmoded and unattractive. Cessation may improve the 'positioning' of the company in the eyes of its customers and sales may increase accordingly. This particular indirect effect is much more difficult to foresee than the ensuing redundancies but its consequences are just as real.

This emphasizes the point that making decisions is essentially a management, rather than an accounting, function. The role of accountancy is to provide good information to assist managers make the right decisions. But the manager always has a limited time frame in which to make the decision. During that short time, it is impossible to foresee **all** the consequences of the decision. Even when you have made the best decision you possibly could, events may yet overtake you. Being aware of this will make you a wiser and better manager.

## The manager's point of view (written by Nigel Burton)

Business decisions need to be taken in the round, giving thought to all the relevant factors and potential consequences of any actions taken. The decisions based on variable costing, as discussed in Chapter 6, would in practice never be taken on the arithmetic alone, but on their total impact on the business. While some of this will be quantifiable, much of it will not, and will require the input of judgement, inspiration and informed guesswork. Nevertheless, the starting point for most decisions remains the arithmetic. The way in which the quantifiable factors are handled in practice is perhaps best illustrated by the Capital Investment Appraisal procedures adopted by our company.

In every capital investment decision, the fundamental issue is: What is the total impact on my business of making this investment? To answer this question from a financial standpoint, we have to compare the consequences of making the investment with the consequences of not making it. Our capital appraisal model required a 'Before Case', which consisted of a 10-year income statement showing the results which would be expected if no capital investment was made, and an 'After Case', which showed the forecast position after the investment had been made. The 'Before Case' might, for example, see a flat sales line due to capacity constraints, or perhaps a declining sales line if perseverance with the old plant results in increased downtime for maintenance. Perhaps the old plant has been condemned for environmental reasons, so without the investment sales will be reduced to nil, and redundancies will ensue. All the costs and quantifiable implications of refusing the investment are considered here, including committed costs and opportunity costs, the latter being opportunities which would have been seized but for the project.

The 'After Case', on the other hand, might reflect continued sales growth arising from increased capacity, or reduced marginal costs due to more process automation, larger batch sizes or higher yields. Also shown here are the expected fixed overheads following the investment, including any changes to areas such as selling and administration. In producing these two sets of figures, the principles of relevant costing are regularly utilized. Is a particular cost directly attributable to the project, or would we have incurred it anyway? Many costs will be incurred regardless of the project, and therefore will appear in both Cases.

Then, by deducting the 'Before Case' numbers from the 'After Case' numbers, we arrive at the 'Incremental Case'. This represents exactly the expected impact of the initial investment on each line of the income statement for each of the next 10 years, i.e. the net increase in sales, the net reduction in marginal costs, the additional selling expenses, and so on. From this basic data, we can calculate both the rate of return and the number of years needed to pay back the initial investment, two of the key indicators used by management to assess the viability of the project.

This Capital Investment Appraisal procedure neatly captures and displays the quantifiable elements of an investment decision. These elements may tell a good financial story, but it may well be non-quantifiable issues which cause management ultimately to approve or reject the investment proposal. Another example from my chemical business illustrates the kinds of issues which may have an influence on the decision.

One of our products had been used for many years by both the petroleum and plastics industries. It had always been profitable, not least because none of our competitors had quite managed to duplicate it, despite the fact that the patents had expired many years previously. Cheaper, but inferior, alternatives had become available on the market, but our business maintained its competitive edge.

The plant, and the technology on which it was based, was some 40 years old. Over the years, there had been many repairs and part replacements, but eventually the time came when a number of considerations, among them environmental concerns, brought us to the point when substantial changes were necessary. Failure to improve the environmental performance was ultimately likely to result in the plant's closure, although the timescales involved in this were indeterminate. We were also aware that the demand for the product from the petroleum companies might decline at some stage in the future as alternative technologies became available, although sales to the plastics industry were likely to continue. The timing of any decline was again largely a matter of guesswork.

Our options were: (a) to do nothing, and subcontract manufacturing when the plant was closed; (b) to patch up the plant once again, with a view to temporarily satisfying the environmental concerns, until such time as the petroleum business died a natural death, then sub-contract; or (c) to build a new plant, incorporating state-of-the-art technology. The financial implications of each of these scenarios were reasonably easy to establish. The 'Before Case' represented option (a), and included the costs of closing down and decommissioning the plant, as well as the redundancy costs of surplus staff. It also reflected the additional cost of buying in the material from a sub-contractor, for which role the most likely candidates were in India and China. Our first 'After Case' scenario (option (b)) was clearly the cheapest, but would provide us with only a short-term solution to our environmental problems. If the petroleum business did not decline within five years, a further patching-up project would almost certainly be required. Moreover, if the product turned out to have a much longer life than we anticipated, we might end up putting up a new plant anyway. Our second 'After Case' scenario (option (c)) was a high-cost, high-risk strategy, because if the petroleum demand turned out to be short term, we could find ourselves left with a relatively new but largely redundant plant. It would, however, solve all our environmental issues at a stroke.

Interestingly, neither of the capital investment scenarios (options (b) and (c)) produced a satisfactory Incremental Case when compared against option (a). This was not because either of the proposals themselves were non-viable, but because the cost of contracting out manufacture turned out, rather unexpectedly, to be much less than expected. The additional cost of buying in from a sub-contractor was substantially offset by overhead and labour savings, so a satisfactory level of profitability could more or less be maintained without any capital investment. The financial advantages offered by the two 'After Case' scenarios were therefore relatively small, and did not appear to justify the capital outlays. The financial arguments clearly pointed towards sub-contracting as a solution to our plant problem, but here the non-quantifiable aspects came into play. Did we really want to divulge our company secrets to a third party? Could we trust any confidentiality agreement signed by the sub-contractor? Was it worth the risk? After all, the product might yet have many years of life left with the petroleum industry and would anyway still be in demand from the plastics companies.

So we had to balance the risks of losing control of our know-how, and then possibly finding our business under threat from our own product coming in cheaply from the East, against the possibility of a white elephant of a plant if the petroleum companies converted in the near future. After much deliberation, we decided to carry out the full plant renewal (option (c)). Our 'Before Case' was changed to reflect our new assumption that we would lose business to the Eastern threat, and on this basis the figures showed an acceptable return and payback period. Now, several years later, the petroleum companies are still using the product, the capital outlay has already been paid back and the environmental problems are a thing of the past. There is still talk that the petroleum companies may soon discontinue their use of the product, but the new plant has already justified its existence.

So our gamble has paid off, but we hit upon the right solution not because we followed the direction pointed out by the financial information, but because we took our decision in the light of wider business considerations. The financials, however, built up on relevant costing principles, provided an essential basis for further decision making. Sound financials, plus informed judgement, experience, and a little bit of luck, can minimize risk, and bring you to the correct conclusion.

## Summary

- Relevant costing is a financial model to aid managers with decision making.
- Its objective is to maximize future net cash inflows to the business.
- It considers the indirect, as well as direct, effects of decisions.
- Its method is to identify the relevant costs and benefits **caused by** the decision.
- Relevant costs are avoidable **and** future **and** cash.
- The two types of relevant cost are *avoidable* and *opportunity* costs.
- The three types of irrelevant cost are *sunk, committed* and *non-cash* costs.
- Opportunity benefits must be taken into account.
- Qualitative factors are important and should be seriously considered.
- Relevant costing is more realistic than variable costing but it is not perfect.

## Further reading

Balakrishnan, R. and Sivaramakrishnan, K. (2002) 'A critical overview of the use of full-cost data for planning and pricing', *Journal of Management Accounting Research*, Vol. 14.

Drury, C. (2004) *Management and Cost Accounting*, 6th edition, Thomson Learning, London. See chapter 'Measuring relevant costs and revenues for decision making'.

Horngren, C., Bhimani, A., Datar, S. and Foster, G. (2002) *Management and Cost Accounting*, 2nd edition, Prentice Hall Europe, Harlow. See chapter 'Revenues, costs and the decision process'.

Upchurch, A. (2003) *Management Accounting, Principles and Practice*, 2nd edition, Financial Times/Prentice Hall, Harlow. See chapter 'Relevant costs and benefits for decision making'.

## Answers to self-assessment questions

### S7.1  Welgrow Ltd

| Item | Avoidable | Future | Cash | Note | Amount | Relevant |
|---|---|---|---|---|---|---|
| 1  Mixing machine | | X | | 1 | | – |
| 2  Vermiculite | X | X | X | 2 | 7,000 @ £1 | 7,000 |
| 3  Black sand | | | | 3 | | – |
| 4  Advertising space | | | X | 4 | | – |
| 5  Storage bin | X | X | X | 5 | | 100 |
| | | | | | **Relevant cost** | **£7,100** |

For the batch of 10,000 kg, the breakeven selling price is **£0.71 per kg.**

*Notes*:
1 Depreciation is a non-cash expense.
2 Vermiculite needs to be bought in at replacement cost.
3 Sunk cost with no alternative use.
4 The 20% deposit is sunk and the 80% remainder is committed.
5 Opportunity cost.

### S7.2  Tilly Ltd

| Item | Avoidable | Future | Cash | Note | Amount | Relevant |
|---|---|---|---|---|---|---|
| Material A | X | X | X | 1 | 1,000 × £6 | 6,000 |
| Material B | X | X | X | 2 | 1,000 × £5 | 5,000 |
| Material C | X | X | X | 3 | 700 × £2.50 | 1,750 |
| Material C | X | X | X | 4 | 300 × £4 | 1,200 |
| Material D (200 units) | X | X | X | 5 | 300 × £5 | 1,500 |
| Material E | X | X | X | 6 | £500 | (500) |
| | | | | | **Relevant cost** | **£14,950** |

*Notes*:
1 All 1,000 units need buying in at replacement cost.
2 600 units from stock need replacing and 400 need buying at replacement cost.
3 Opportunity cost = resale value.
4 Remaining 300 units bought in at replacement cost.
5 Opportunity cost is greatest of resale value of £1,200 (200 × 6) and saving the purchase of 300 units of M, £1,500 (300 × £5).
6 Opportunity **benefit**: using the stock of E in production avoids disposal costs of £500.

| CASE STUDY | Roverco |
|---|---|

Roverco plc manufactures and markets a house-cleaning robot. At present, it is in the middle of a project to develop a voice-controlled robot from a laboratory prototype. The prototype was built from a patent which the company acquired for £50,000. The inventor agreed to accept payment in five equal instalments, three of which have now been paid.

At a recent board meeting, it was revealed that sales of Roverco's standard product had taken an unforeseen downturn and that this would have a knock-on effect on profitability and liquidity. This situation is partly due to increased competition from Housemouse Ltd, a dynamic new entrant to the market which specialises in the application of the very latest technology to its products. Also, Roverco's two long-established rivals, Cleanbot plc and Nomess plc, have been competing on price for the last year or so. Roverco decided against joining in the price war, hoping that it would soon be over. However, the market has responded positively to the price reductions, with increased orders going to Cleanbot and Nomess, causing Roverco to lose market share.

During the meeting, there was a heated discussion concerning the voice-controlled robot project. The project manager presented a financial statement (shown below) and reported that progress was slower than expected due to snags with the voice-recognition system. In connection with this, he recommends that a specialist electronic engineer be employed for the duration of the project, which he estimates will now continue for the next 18 months. The salary would be £28,000 p.a. on a fixed-term contract basis. Without this additional appointment, it is very doubtful that the project will be completed.

### Project manager's financial statement

|  |  | £ |
|---|---|---|
| Costs to date |  | 42,000 |
| Estimated costs for completion of project: |  |  |
| Final payment for patent | 20,000 |  |
| Gross salaries of two development engineers | 75,000 |  |
| Gross salary of new engineer | 42,000 |  |
| Materials and equipment (including M4411) | 19,000 |  |
| Overheads | 65,000 |  |
|  |  | 221,000 |
| Total cost of project |  | 263,000 |
| Budgeted cost of project |  | 218,000 |
| Requested increase in budget |  | 45,000 |

Following this, the finance director shocked the meeting into silence by proposing that the project be abandoned. She justified this course of action by pointing out that Roverco's share price had been falling slowly but steadily for the last three months and that in her regular meeting with share analysts from the big City firms, scheduled for next month, she feels it would be wise to issue a profits warning. The effect of this would be a steeper fall in the share price which, in turn, would make the company more vulnerable to a takeover bid. However, to avoid this, she believes the downwards profit trend can be quickly reversed by abandoning the voice-controlled project and putting the savings of £191,000 into price cuts on the existing product range.

The chairman is not sure what to do. He postpones the discussion for one week and asks you for advice. You ascertain the following information:

1  Market research costing £35,000 was commissioned for the project. This predicted that the optimum price/volume relationship was a selling price of £999, creating sales of 6,000 robots a year. The product life cycle was estimated as four years, at which point a major redesign would be needed to remain competitive.

2  Roverco's accountant has estimated that the new production facility fixed assets for the voice-controlled robot will cost £900,000 and will have a resale value of £400,000 after four years. Other fixed overhead costs of £340,000 p.a. will be incurred; these are caused solely by this product and include depreciation of £90,000 p.a. for the production facility. The variable cost of producing each robot will be £917.

3  A special miniature hydraulic mechanism will be used in the robot's production. Roverco has a stock of 9,000 of these left over from a previous product. They were originally bought at a 'bargain price' of £9 each (the current market price is £15 which is included in the £917 total variable cost). They could probably be sold as a job lot for £45,000. Roverco has no other use for these items.

4  If the project is abandoned, two development engineers will have to be made redundant at a cost to Roverco of £18,000 each.

5  Some specialized voice-control testing equipment could be sold for £8,500 in its present condition, or for £2,500 at the end of the project. The rest of the equipment has no resale value.

6  A £6,000 order (order no. M4411) for bespoke electronic components was placed last month for delivery in two months' time; three months' credit is normally allowed by the supplier. A legal contract was signed for this order which Roverco is not able to cancel.

7  The project overheads of £65,000 include £15,000 for depreciation of the buildings used for product development and a general administration charge of £3,000 (nominally for services from the rest of the company). They also include £17,000 as a proportion of the project manager's pay.

*Task:*

Identify the relevant cash flows and advise the chairman whether, on purely financial grounds, the project should continue or be abandoned. Support your calculations with clear statements as to why particular items have been included or excluded and state any assumptions that you make.

## Questions

An asterisk * on a question number indicates that the answer is given at the end of the book. Answers to the other questions are given in the Lecturer's Guide.

### Q7.1*  Burton Brothers

Burton Brothers manufactures machine tools for metal-based industries. One of its customers, Wey Ltd, has placed a £590,000 order for a machine, including £10,000 for delivery and installation. Wey paid a deposit of £180,000 and has since paid instalments totalling £150,000. Unfortunately, Burton Brothers has received a letter from a solicitor informing it that Wey Ltd has gone into liquidation and is unlikely to be able to pay any of its debts. This project has incurred the following costs to date:

|                                              | £       |
|----------------------------------------------|--------:|
| Engineering design                           | 70,000  |
| Materials                                    | 129,000 |
| Direct labour (760 hours @ £10/h)            | 7,600   |
| Production overheads (760 hours @ £88/dlh)   | 66,880  |
|                                              | 273,480 |

The production overheads are all fixed costs and it is company policy to absorb them on the basis of direct labour hours (dlh).

Another customer, Bridge & Co., has expressed an interest in the machine, provided some additions are made to the specification, and is willing to pay a price of £400,000. To complete the machine to the original specification, it is estimated that a further 2,000 direct labour hours (at £10/hour) and a further £204,000 of materials will be needed. Contracts for £24,000 of these materials have already been signed but no money has yet been paid. The contract provides for a cancellation fee of £6,000 provided cancellation is confirmed in the next 11 days. These materials are components made especially to order for this machine and have no other use or value. The rest of the materials are in regular use by Burton Brothers. Twenty-five per cent of the £204,000 of materials are currently in the stores.

The additions requested by Bridge & Co. will need a further £45,000 of materials and 400 hours of direct labour. Some of these additional materials, which have an estimated purchase price of £13,500, could be replaced by similar material currently in the stores. This was left over from a previous contract and has no other use. It originally cost £9,500, which is its current stock valuation, but if it were to be sold on the open market it would fetch £12,000.

Burton Brothers is itself in a precarious position as it has no new orders on its books. If this job is abandoned, its direct workforce will be put on standby, which means they will be sent home and paid a rate of £4 an hour to retain their services. However, if this were to happen, the directors believe that some of these skilled workers would find permanent work elsewhere and would leave the company.

If no customer is found for the machine, it will be sent for scrap; this is expected to produce £6,000 income.

*Task:*

Burton Brothers is unsure whether or not to accept the offer from Bridge & Co. Consider each of the above items and advise the company accordingly.

## Q7.2* Eezikum

Eezikum is a duo of rap artists currently touring the UK. They still have 11 venues remaining when they are asked to fill in at short notice on a tour of the USA, starting in two days' time. They will be the first act on stage to warm up the audience in preparation for the big American star whose tour it is. They know that this could establish them in the lucrative North American market but are not sure of the financial implications. There is a cancellation fee of £10,000 for each abandoned concert. Each time they perform in the UK they are paid a fee of £15,000 and their out-of-pocket expenses amount to £2,500. At present, they have no future work commitments once the UK tour is over.

If they join the tour of the USA, they will need to buy new equipment compatible with the American electricity supply and safety standards. The cost of this is estimated at £100,000 but it could be sold for £40,000 at the end of the nine-month tour, on their return to the UK. The money is not a problem as they currently have more than £1 million in a deposit account earning interest of 12% a year.

The US tour consists of 125 performances, each paying fees of £10,000 and having associated out-of-pocket expenses of £2,000. The airfare for the whole entourage, including a considerable amount of luggage, is £14,500 each way. Additional health insurance will cost £6,000 for the duration of the tour. Travel insurance is £9,000 (three-quarters of their existing annual worldwide policy, which carries a premium of £12,000).

*Task:*

Calculate the relevant benefit/cost of accepting the US tour.

## Q7.3* Carbotest Corporation

Carbotest Corporation manufactures equipment to test for the presence of carbon monoxide in confined spaces. It has just been offered a contract to build some specialised monitoring equipment to test for the presence of carbon dioxide in the freight containers of lorries and railway wagons. The contract offers to pay £152,000 for 1,000 sets of testing equipment, which must be delivered in six months' time. Carbotest has looked into this opportunity and has produced the following information.

*Materials*

The contract will need 40,000 components which Carbotest does not currently use; these cost £3 each. However, it could use up old stock of 5,000 components that it recently tried to sell without success. But £1 will need to be spent on each of them to make them into suitable replacements for 5,000 of the 40,000 components needed. This old stock originally cost £20,000 but now has a scrap value of only £1,000. Each testing set also needs a carrying harness identical to those used for the carbon monoxide testing equipment. Carbotest has 600 of these currently in stock, valued at their cost price of £8 each. The suppliers of this harness have just increased their price to £9, which Carbotest will have to pay for future orders.

*Labour*

The contract will use five skilled operatives full time for six months. These operatives are paid £1,400 a month gross and are presently employed on the carbon-monoxide-testing production. They will have to be redeployed from this work to the new contract. Their combined output for the six-month period is estimated to have a sales revenue of £60,000, a variable cost of £48,000 and to absorb £8,000 of fixed overheads. It is thought that one of the factory supervisors (currently with a light workload) could manage the project for 50% of his time. His annual gross pay is £24,000. Carbotest is working at full capacity and has enough orders to keep it busy for 15 months.

*Machinery*

Three years ago, Carbotest bought a machine for a similar project, which had to be abandoned after two years. It cost £25,000 and was estimated to have a useful life of five years, with a zero residual value. (Carbotest uses the straight-line method of depreciation for all its fixed assets.) The machine has been 'mothballed' for the last 12 months and has been stored out of the way. Carbotest was just about to advertise it for sale at the very reasonable price of £5,000. It is thought that this intensive contract will effectively wear it out. To meet the six-month deadline, Carbotest plans to lease an identical machine for six months at a cost of £500 a month.

*Accommodation*

Employees have to park their cars on the road outside the factory. As the company is located in a busy area, this is often difficult, with cars having to be parked some distance away. Carbotest is just about to convert a rough piece of land in one corner of its site into an employees' car park. It hired a professional firm of surveyors to obtain planning permission for this and their invoice for £2,200 has recently been received but not yet paid. The cost of building the car park is £28,000. But if the contract is accepted, this land will have to be used for a temporary building to house the necessary machinery. The construction of this building will cost £8,000 and when the contract is completed, it will be demolished at a cost of £2,000. The car park will then go ahead.

*Fixed overheads*

Carbotest's absorption costing system attaches fixed overheads to production on a machine hour basis. The contract is expected to absorb £10,000 of fixed overhead.

*Tasks:*

State whether each of the above items is relevant or irrelevant to Carbotest's acceptance of the contract and explain your reasoning. Advise it whether or not to accept the contract. Discuss any other factors the company should take into consideration when making this decision.

## Q7.4  Murray Polls

Murray Polls Limited recently contracted to conduct an opinion poll concerning global warming and its causes. Its costing for this job is shown below:

|  |  | £ |
|---|---|---:|
| Planning | 100 hours @ £12 | 1,200 |
| Questioning | 800 hours @ £7 | 5,600 |
| Travel and subsistence |  | 4,800 |
| Telephone | 30,000 minutes @ £0.02/min | 600 |
| Analysis of results & report | 60 hours @ £12 | 720 |
| Fixed overheads | 800 hours @ £25 | 20,000 |
| Total cost |  | 32,920 |
| Profit @ 20% mark-up |  | 6,584 |
| Price to client |  | £39,504 |

(Overheads are absorbed on the basis of questioning hours.)

The client paid a deposit of £5,000 and contracted to pay the remainder within one month of receiving the report. Unfortunately, Murray has just been informed that its client has gone into liquidation and is not expected to be able to meet any of its debts.

At this point, Murray has completed all the planning and 75% of the questioning; travel and subsistence so far total £3,700 and 50% of the telephoning has been completed. No analysis has yet been done. If the poll is abandoned, two of the 10 researchers involved will have to be paid a cancellation fee of £200 each.

The managing director of Murray immediately suspends all work on the contract and decides to attend an international conference on the environment, taking place in Stockholm next week. He is hopeful of finding another client for this project as he will be able to offer the completed poll and report at a greatly reduced price. His airfares, hotel bills and out-of-pocket expenses for the five-day Stockholm trip are expected to be £2,200. His rate of pay works out at £400 a day.

*Task:*

Calculate the lowest price the managing director can quote without making his firm worse off and advise him accordingly. State your reasons for including or excluding the above factors in your calculation.

## Q7.5  Eldave Advertising Agency

The Eldave Advertising Agency has been working on a campaign for Greenpoint Leisure Limited for the last four months. The campaign is for Greenpoint's eco-friendly holidays in South America and uses both TV and Sunday-paper magazines. The adverts have almost been completed and the campaign launch date is in six weeks' time. The estimated cost of completion is £2,400 (two people @ £400/week for three weeks). Greenpoint has signed a contract to pay Eldave £50,000 (for advert production) plus media space at cost.

Eldave has just received a letter from a firm of solicitors stating that Greenpoint has ceased trading with immediate effect and that its creditors are unlikely to receive any of the money they are owed. Fortunately, Eldave has received a non-returnable deposit of

£25,000 (50% of the production fee) from Greenpoint but a summary of its account reveals an overall balance owing of £61,000 for work to date. This includes a general fixed overheads charge of £6,000 apportioned on the basis of total direct cost.

In order to minimize Eldave's losses, Eloise Thompson, the partner in charge of the Greenpoint account, has contacted three other travel firms specializing in the South American market. She has shown them the adverts and tried to persuade them to take over the work-in-progress for the special price of £25,000. One of these three, Trek Hols Limited, has offered £12,000 for the appropriately modified and completed adverts on condition that the campaign starts in two weeks' time.

Eldave has provisionally booked advertising space for eight consecutive weeks starting in six weeks' time. The cost of this is £30,000 a week, for which it has paid £12,000 (a 5% non-returnable deposit included in the £61,000). It has also booked a one-quarter-page colour space in the *Independent on Sunday* magazine for the same eight weeks. Each of these spaces costs £9,000 but, although a contract has been signed, no money has yet been paid (not included in the £61,000). The contract allows for a 50% reduction if cancellation occurs less than four weeks before publication. This reduction increases to 75% if cancellation occurs more than four weeks before publication. Although Trek Hols is happy to take over Greenpoint's media slots, it also wants the same weekly coverage for the four weeks immediately prior to the original launch date. Trek Hols insists the campaign must start in two weeks' time and agrees to pay for all the media space in full, at cost.

In order to complete the adverts for launch in two weeks' time, Eldave will have to redeploy two of its employees (gross pay £400 a week each) for one and a half weeks, at the end of which the adverts will be delivered to the media. As a result of this, the job these two are currently doing will be one and a half weeks late and Eldave will incur a financial penalty of '£1,000 a week or part-week'.

*Tasks:*

Identify the **relevant costs and income** and advise Eldave as to whether it should accept Trek Hols' offer. Your calculations must clearly show the reasons why each of the above items has been included or excluded. State any assumptions that you make.

## Q7.6  MOV plc

MOV plc produces custom-built sensors. Each sensor has a standard circuit board (SCB) in it. The current average contribution from a sensor is £400. MOV plc's business is steadily expanding and in the year just ending (2001/2002), the company will have produced 55,000 sensors. The demand for MOV plc's sensors is predicted to grow over the next 3 years:

| Year | Units |
|------|-------|
| 2002/03 | 58,000 |
| 2003/04 | 62,000 |
| 2004/05 | 65,000 |

The production of sensors is limited by the number of SCBs the company can produce. The present production level of 55,000 SCBs is the maximum that can be produced without overtime working. Overtime could increase annual output to 60,500, allowing production of sensors to also increase to 60,500. However, the variable cost of SCBs produced in overtime would increase by £75 per unit.

Because of the pressure on capacity, the company is considering having the SCBs manufactured by another company, CIR plc. This company is very reliable and produces products of good quality. CIR plc has quoted a price of £116 per SCB, for orders greater than 50,000 units a year.

MOV plc's own costs per SCB are predicted to be:

|  | £ |  |
|---|---|---|
| Direct material | 28 | |
| Direct labour | 40 | |
| Variable overhead | 20 | (based on labour cost) |
| Fixed overhead | 24 | (based on labour cost and output of 55,000 units) |
| Total cost | 112 | |

The fixed overheads directly attributable to SCBs are £250,000 a year; these costs will be avoided if SCBs are not produced. If more than 59,000 units are produced, SCBs' fixed overheads will increase by £130,000.

In addition to the above overheads, MOV plc's fixed overheads are predicted to be:

| Sensor production in units: | 54,001 to 59,000 | 59,001 to 64,000 | 64,001 to 70,000 |
|---|---|---|---|
| Fixed overhead: | £2,600,000 | £2,900,000 | £3,100,000 |

MOV plc currently holds a stock of 3,500 SCBs but the production manager feels that a stock of 8,000 should be held if they are bought in; this would increase stockholding costs by £10,000 a year. A purchasing officer, who is paid £20,000 a year, spends 50% of her time on SCB duties. If the SCBs are bought in, a liaison officer will have to be employed at a salary of £30,000 in order to liaise with CIR plc and monitor the quality and supply of SCBs. At present, 88 staff are involved in the production of SCBs at an average salary of £25,000 a year: if the SCBs were purchased, 72 of these staff would be made redundant at an average cost of £4,000 per employee.

The SCB department, which occupies an area of 240 × 120 square metres at the far end of the factory, could be rented out, at a rent of £45 per square metre a year. However, if the SCBs were to be bought in, for the first year only MOV plc would need the space to store the increased stock caused by outsourcing, until the main stockroom had been reorganized and refurbished. From 2003/04, the space could be rented out; this would limit the annual production of sensors to 60,500 units. Alternatively the space could be used for the production of sensors, allowing annual output to increase to 70,000 units if required.

*Required:*

a) Critically discuss the validity of the following statement. It was produced by Jim Elliot, the company's accountant, to show the gain for the coming year (2002/03) if the SCBs were to be bought in.

| Saving in: | £ |
|---|---:|
| Manufacturing staff – salaries saved: 72 staff × £25,000 | 1,800,000 |
| Purchasing officer – time saved | 10,000 |
| Placing orders for SCB materials: 1,000 orders × £20 per order | 20,000 |
| Transport costs for raw materials for SCBs | 45,000 |
| Cost saved | 1,875,000 |
| Additional cost per SCB: (£116 – £112) × 58,000 units | 232,000 |
| Net gain if SCBs purchased | 1,643,000 |

*(10 marks)*

b) i) Produce detailed calculations that show which course of action is the best financial option for the three years under consideration. (Ignore the time value of money.)

*(12 marks)*

   ii) Advise the company of the long-term advantages and disadvantages of buying in SCBs.

*(3 marks)*
*(Total = 25 marks)*

CIMA Intermediate: Management Accounting – Decision Making, May 2002

## Review questions

1 Describe relevant costing.
2 Distinguish between relevant and irrelevant costs.
3 Explain the terms: avoidable costs, opportunity costs, sunk costs, committed costs, non-cash costs and opportunity benefits.
4 Discuss the importance of qualitative factors.

*The answers to all these questions can be found in the text of this chapter.*

# CHAPTER 8

# Capital investment appraisal for long-term decisions

- Answers to self-assessment questions
- Case study 1: Nufone
- Case study 2: The Private Healthcare Group
- Questions
- Review questions
- Present value factor table
- Cumulative present value factor table (annuities)

## Introduction

Imagine that you are a director of a large business which urgently needs to replace one of its large old machines. Preliminary investigation has narrowed down your choice to two alternatives.

The first machine costs £3.2 million, is guaranteed for three years, is four times as productive as the present machine and can be sold back to its supplier for £0.5 million after five years. The second machine costs £2.5 million, is guaranteed for one year, is three times as productive as the present machine and cannot be sold back to its supplier. How do you decide which machine is the best one to buy?

Capital investment appraisal is the decision-making process used by businesses to decide which fixed assets to purchase. Vehicles, machines and buildings can be very expensive so it is important to make the best decision possible from the information available at the time.

Correcting a bad capital investment decision can be very costly. Consider a company that has a choice between buying a large piece of plant from either Atlas Ltd or Tyrell & Co. If it spends £3.2 million on an Atlas machine and three months later finds out it would have been better to buy a Tyrell machine, correcting this decision will entail significant extra costs. For a start, the Atlas machine will now be second-hand and will have lost value. There may not be a ready market for this type of machine and the price will have to be reduced further to sell it. Also, there is the cost of uninstalling and removing it. And how about the lost production caused by this change?

Because of the importance of these long-term decisions, managers normally seek help from their management accountants. Over the years several methods for determining the best choice have been established. This chapter looks at the four most popular of these (see Figure 8.1). Note that one uses profits but all the others use cash flows.

| Method | Base |
|---|---|
| Accounting rate of return (ARR) | Profits |
| Payback period (PBP) | Cash flows |
| Net present value (NPV) | Discounted cash flows |
| Internal rate of return (IRR) | Discounted cash flows |

Figure 8.1 **Summary of capital investment appraisal methods**

For each of these methods it is necessary to **estimate** future profits or cash flows arising from the new investments. However, when we do this, we usually get it wrong. The quality of the investment decision will depend on the quality of these estimates. You may think it is not worth bothering if the answers will probably involve such significant errors but the alternative is to make these decisions by tossing a coin. It is better to attempt some analysis than none at all. Often, the objective is to choose between alternative fixed assets. As the same assumptions are made for each alternative, the results become more valid.

**Having worked through this chapter you should be able to:**

- calculate the accounting rate of return (ARR);
- convert profits to cash flows;
- justify the exclusion of working capital from cash flows;
- reconcile cash flows with profits over the lifetime of a project;
- calculate the payback period (PBP);
- discount future cash flows to today's values;
- calculate the net present value (NPV);
- calculate the internal rate of return (IRR);
- discuss the limitations of the four methods;
- compare NPV with IRR;
- criticize the discounted payback approach;
- discuss the choice of available methods;
- appreciate the usefulness of sensitivity analysis in managing risk;
- explain why the financing decision is excluded from the investment decision;
- discuss the importance of relevant qualitative factors.

## Method 1: accounting rate of return (ARR)

The accounting rate of return attempts to express the return on the investment as an annual percentage of the cost of that investment. This is similar to comparing interest-bearing bank and building society accounts with each other when deciding where to invest your money. Businesses using this method usually set a minimum threshold rate which must be equalled or exceeded by the ARR. For example, a company may be earning an average of 18% a year from all its current activities. It may use this as a threshold or target rate for any new investments. If the calculations for a possible new investment showed its ARR to be only 15%, the investment would not go ahead. This is because if it were adopted it would **reduce** the 18% currently achieved by the company as a whole. On the other hand, if the potential ARR was 20%, the investment would be considered further.

If Maniff plc (threshold ARR = 24%) had to choose between machines M1 (ARR = 29%), M2 (ARR = 22%) and M3 (ARR = 33%), it would disregard M2 and further consider M1 and M3. If ARR was the only technique it used, it would choose M3 as it produces the greatest return on investment (i.e. the greatest profitability).

Unfortunately, there are several ways of calculating ARR. However, as there is very little to choose between them, we will use the least complicated. The formula used in this book is as follows:

$$ARR = \frac{\text{Average annual profit}}{\text{Initial investment}} \times 100$$

Note that sometimes the **average** investment is used instead of the **initial** investment.

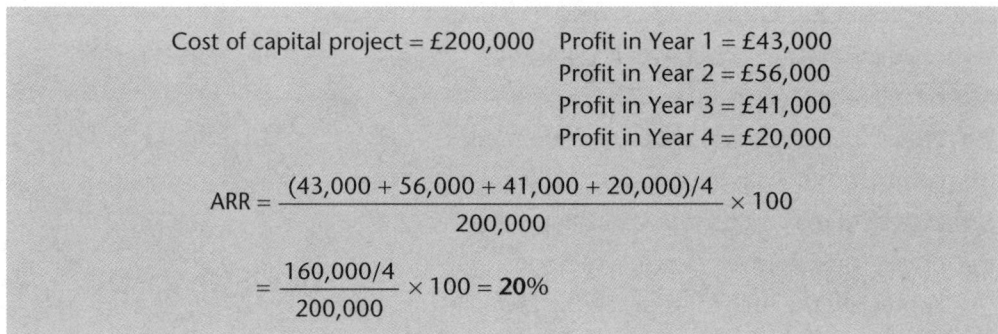

Cost of capital project = £200,000    Profit in Year 1 = £43,000
Profit in Year 2 = £56,000
Profit in Year 3 = £41,000
Profit in Year 4 = £20,000

$$ARR = \frac{(43,000 + 56,000 + 41,000 + 20,000)/4}{200,000} \times 100$$

$$= \frac{160,000/4}{200,000} \times 100 = \mathbf{20\%}$$

Figure 8.2 **Example of an ARR calculation**

*Self-assessment question S8.1*

*Try the following question for yourself (answer at the end of the chapter).*

You have the chance to open a manicure parlour in your local shopping centre at an initial cost of £25,000. For each manicure, the sales price will be £10 and the direct cost £6. The annual total of indirect costs (i.e. overheads) is estimated to be £16,000. Market research has estimated demand for manicures to be:

|        |              |
|--------|--------------|
| Year 1 | 5,000 units  |
| Year 2 | 6,000 units  |
| Year 3 | 7,000 units  |
| Year 4 | 8,000 units  |
| Year 5 | 6,500 units  |

What is the ARR for the project?

## Limitations of ARR

One reservation concerning profit-based ARR is that profits can vary much more than cash flows. Remember that the profit figure depends on many subjective estimates such as depreciation, stock valuation and provision for doubtful debts. On the other hand, the cash figure is theoretically measurable and therefore more objective. Thus, the ARR tends to be less reliable than the cash flow-based methods.

## Converting profits to cash flows

Having considered ARR, we will now look at the other three methods. These are all based on the relevant cash flows (not profits). A relevant cash flow is one **caused by the project**. If a cash flow will still occur whether we go ahead or not, it is not caused by the project, and so it is not relevant to our decision. Exclude irrelevant cash flows from your calculations.

Very often the starting point in these calculations is a profit and loss account rather than a cash flow forecast. In this case the first thing we have to do is to convert the profits to cash flows. This is done by **adding back any non-cash expenses** to the net profit. The most common of these is depreciation, see Figure 8.3. (If you are not sure about this, have a look at Chapter 2 on the difference between profit and cash.)

*Self-assessment question S8.2*

*Try the following question for yourself (answer at the end of the chapter).*

A building company is considering branching out into the mobile crane hire business. It is thinking of buying a 42-tonne model similar to ones it has often hired in the past. This will cost £190,000 and should last for nine years, after which time it will have an estimated scrap value of £10,000. The profits from this venture are expected to be as shown below. Calculate the associated cash flows.

| Year | Profit (£) | Year | Profit (£) | Year | Profit (£) |
|---|---|---|---|---|---|
| 1 | 10,000 | 4 | 30,000 | 7 | 30,000 |
| 2 | 18,000 | 5 | 35,000 | 8 | 20,000 |
| 3 | 24,000 | 6 | 38,000 | 9 | 10,000 |

## Reconciliation of cash flows with profits

**Over the whole lifetime of a project**, the total of profits will equal the total of cash flows. (Note that this is **not** true for any one year within the lifetime.) This enables you to check the accuracy of your cash flow calculations. Look at Figure 8.3 to check this; the lifetime total is £11.5 million.

N.B. Beware of situations where fixed assets are sold for more or less than their written down value. This will give a 'profit or loss on disposal' which must be included in the profit of the disposal year for the above statement to be true.

A company is considering launching a new product requiring the purchase of new plant and machinery costing £5.5 million. The additional profits resulting directly from this five-year project are as follows:

| Year | Profit/(Loss) |
|---|---|
| 1 | (0.5) |
| 2 | 1.0 |
| 3 | 4.0 |
| 4 | 5.0 |
| 5 | 2.0 |

The company uses straight line depreciation and expects to be able to sell the plant for £0.5 million at the end of the project. What are the project's cash flows?

**Answer**

$$\text{Annual depreciation charge} = \frac{\text{Fall in value over project's lifetime}}{\text{Lifetime in years}}$$

$$= \frac{£(5.5 - 0.5)\text{m}}{5} = £1.0\text{m a year}$$

| Year | Profit/(Loss) | Annual depreciation | Other items | Cash in/(out)flow |
|---|---|---|---|---|
| 0 | 0.0 | 0.0 | plant purchase (5.5) | (5.5) |
| 1 | (0.5) | 1.0 | 0.0 | 0.5 |
| 2 | 1.0 | 1.0 | 0.0 | 2.0 |
| 3 | 4.0 | 1.0 | 0.0 | 5.0 |
| 4 | 5.0 | 1.0 | 0.0 | 6.0 |
| 5 | 2.0 | 1.0 | sale of scrap 0.5 | 3.5 |
| | 11.5 | | | 11.5 |

N.B. 'Year 0' is the equivalent of *now*, i.e. the start of the project.

Figure 8.3 **Example of converting profits to cash flows**

## Method 2: payback period (PBP)

This calculates how long it will take for the business to recover the initial **cash** outflow to purchase the fixed asset. The answers are given in units of time, usually years. If the investment decision was a choice between several alternative capital projects, the one with the shortest PBP would be recommended. Most people agree that uncertainty increases the further you go into the future. Thus, choosing the project with the shortest PBP is a way of minimizing risk. An example of a PBP calculation is shown in Figure 8.4.

Note that we have assumed the cash to flow **evenly** throughout the year. For example, an annual net cash flow of £120,000 is assumed to occur at the rate of £10,000 a month. In reality, this is most unlikely, especially for seasonal businesses. However, unless we can forecast more accurately, this is the assumption we have to make.

Initial cash outflow (i.e. project cost) = £240,000

| Year | Net cash in £ | Cumulative £ |
|---|---|---|
| 1 | 93,000 | 93,000 |
| 2 | 107,000 | 200,000 Payback not reached |
| 3 | 120,000 | 320,000 Payback occurs in year 3 |
| 4 | 80,000 | 400,000 |

$$PBP = 2 + \frac{\text{amount still needed}}{\text{total inflow in payback year}}$$

$$PBP = 2 + \frac{(240{,}000 - 200{,}000)}{120{,}000}$$

$$= 2 + \frac{40{,}000}{120{,}000}$$

$$= 2.33 \text{ years}$$

*or* = **2 years 4 months**   (0.33 years × 12 months/year = 4 months)

Figure 8.4 **Example of a payback period calculation**

*Self-assessment question S8.3*

*Try the following question for yourself (answer at the end of the chapter).*

Calculate the payback period for the manicure parlour project in S8.1 if the only non-cash expense included in the annual fixed costs was depreciation of £2,000.

## Limitations of payback period

One limitation of this technique is that it takes no account of the cash flows occurring after the payback point has been reached. Project A in Swindon may be chosen in preference to project B in Oxford because it has a shorter payback period. But the total of net cash inflows over the projects' lifetimes may be much greater for project B than for project A.

Thus, choosing project A may be the wrong decision for the business. It depends on how risky the project is perceived to be. If it is thought to be a high-risk investment, then project A may be the best decision after all as it is more likely to recover its initial cost. One reason for the relative popularity of the payback period method is that many business decisions are considerably risky. Another reason is that the concept is easy to understand.

# Discounting cash flows

## The time value of money

If I were to offer you either £900 now **or** £900 in 12 months' time, which would you choose? I suspect you would choose the £900 now.

Alternatively, if I were to offer to give you either £900 now **or** £945 12 months from now, which would you choose? This is a more difficult choice. To help you with your decision, you are told that the bank interest rate is currently 5% a year. If you accepted the £900 now and invested it for 12 months at 5% a year, it would be worth £945 in a year's time. This implies that the two alternatives are really the same, provided interest rates remain constant for the year.

The significance of this is that the value of money changes with time because it is possible to invest and earn interest on it over a period. Check your understanding of this by considering the following question.

If the interest rate changed to 3% a year and I offered you either £945 in 12 months' time or £900 now, which would you choose? The answer is that £900 invested now at 3% gives £927 in 12 months' time. So, on this occasion, it is worth waiting for the £945.

A sum of money **now** has a greater value than the same sum in a year's time because it can be invested for that year to earn interest.

**Thus, a £ in one year is NOT worth the same as a £ in another year.**

This concept is known as the 'time value of money'.

When looking at cash flows over a number of years, **to be sure of comparing like with like**, future amounts should be reduced by the business's interest or 'cost of capital' rate. In simple terms, it can be thought of as the overall rate of interest applying to a business. It is also referred to as the *discount rate*. The discounted cash flow technique is:

**All future cash flows should be discounted to *present values*.**

## Compounding and discounting

Compounding is the effect of repeatedly adding interest earned to the lump sum invested so that interest will be paid on larger and larger amounts as time passes (see Figure 8.5).

What is the value of £751 invested at 10% p.a. for 3 years?
(To increase a number by 10%, multiply it by the decimal 1.10)

Year 1      £751 × 1.10 = £826
Year 2      £826 × 1.10 = £909
Year 3      £909 × 1.10 = £1,000

The answer is £1,000.

Figure 8.5 **Example of a compounding calculation**

You own a machine which will produce a cash income of £1,000 p.a. for each of the next three years. What is the present value of this income stream if the discount rate is 10% p.a.?

| Year | Cash | 10% Discount factor | Present value |
|------|------|---------------------|---------------|
| 1 | 1,000 | 1.0000/1.10 = 0.9091 | 909 |
| 2 | 1,000 | 0.9091/1.10 = 0.8264 | 826 |
| 3 | 1,000 | 0.8264/1.10 = 0.7513 | 751 |
| | | Total present value = | £2,486 |

Figure 8.6 **Example of a discounting calculation**

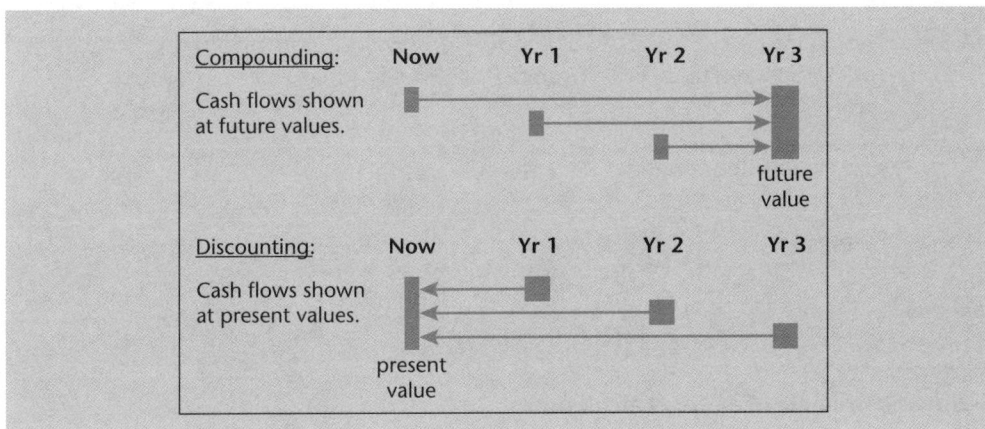

Figure 8.7 **Diagrammatic illustration of compounding and discounting**
*Source*: From P. Atrill and E. McLaney (1994) *Management Accounting: An Active Learning Approach*, Blackwell Publications Ltd., Oxford, with permission.

*Try the following question for yourself (answer at the end of the chapter).*

If £500 is invested at 7.5% p.a. compound, how much is it worth at the end of four years?

*Self-assessment question S8.4*

Discounting can be viewed as the opposite process to compounding (see Figure 8.7). If the interest rate was 10% p.a. (as in Figure 8.5), instead of multiplying by 1.10, you divide by 1.10 (see Figure 8.6).

An alternative method of obtaining discount factors is to use a present value table. These show the factors for different discount rates for a number of years. Their disadvantage is that they may not include the rate or the number of years you wish to use. A present value table has been included at the end of this chapter. Practise using it by finding the factor for year 9 at a discount rate of 17%. You should find 0.243. Now try finding the factor for year 18 at a discount rate of 12.5%.

*Self-assessment question S8.5*

*Try the following question for yourself (answer at the end of the chapter).*

Discount the cash flows of the manicure parlour (see answer to S8.3) to the present time using a rate of 3% p.a. What is the total of these present values?

# Method 3: net present value (NPV)

The net present value is the *sum total* of all the present values of all the cash flows caused by the project (see Figure 8.8).

A vending machine costs £2,500. It will produce positive net cash inflows of £1,000 a year for each of the next three years (residual value = nil). What is the NPV if the discount rate is 10% p.a.?

| Year | Cash in/(out) | 10% discount factors | Present value |
|------|---------------|----------------------|---------------|
| 0 | (2,500) | 1.0000 | (2,500) |
| 1 | 1,000 | 1.0000/1.10 = 0.9091 | 909 |
| 2 | 1,000 | 0.9091/1.10 = 0.8264 | 826 |
| 3 | 1,000 | 0.8264/1.10 = 0.7513 | 751 |
| | | | NPV = £(14) |

Figure 8.8  **Example of an NPV calculation**

## NPV calculation procedure

1  Calculate the annual **net cash flows** (inflows are positive, outflows are negative).
2  Determine the discount rate.
3  Discount future cash flows to present values (calculate the factors or use PV tables).
4  Combine all the annual PVs to give the Net PV for the whole project period.

## Interpreting the results

- If NPV is positive, accept the project.
- If NPV is negative, reject the project.
- If several projects are being considered of which only one can be accepted (mutually exclusive projects), accept the project with highest positive NPV.

*Self-assessment question S8.6*

*Try the following question for yourself (answer at the end of the chapter).*

You are considering investing in production facilities for a new product with an estimated life span of four years. The fixed assets will cost £49,500 and the net cash inflows will be £20,000 for each of the first two years and £10,000 for each of the last two years. If the company's cost of capital is 10% p.a., what is the NPV of the project? Would you recommend going ahead? (Use three decimal places for your PV factors.)

## Annuities

When projects have a long lifetime and their net cash flows are the same each year, the concept of an annuity can be used to make the NPV calculation easier. An 'annuity' is defined as a fixed periodic (e.g. annual) cash flow which continues for a defined period of time (or until a specified event occurs). Consider the following example.

**Example 8.1**

# Eastshore Airport, NPV calculation

Eastshore Airport is considering installing 50 'iris-recognition' devices to improve its security. These devices will cost a total of £2,500,000 and will have the effect of making 25 jobs redundant. The annual cost of each of these employees is £22,000. Fifteen of these employees will be redeployed and the average redundancy payment for the others is estimated at £30,000 each.

It is thought that these devices will have an effective life of 20 years before being replaced with more up-to-date technology. Their collective residual value in 20 years' time will be £250,000. Annual running costs will be £1,000 per device for the first half of their life but this will increase to £3,000 for the second half due to the increase in maintenance required.

Assuming Eastshore's cost of capital is 15% a year, calculate the NPV of this project. (Use the Annuities Present Value Table to determine the appropriate discount factors.)

### Solution (£000)

|  | Years 1–10 | Years 11–20 |
|---|---|---|
| Annual savings | 25 × 22 = 550 | 25 × 22 = 550 |
| Less annual running costs | 50 × 1 =  50 | 50 × 3 = 150 |
| Net annual savings | 500 | 400 |

Determine the discount factors needed by reading the annuities table at the end of this chapter. A single factor can be used for years 1 to 10 as the annual savings (equal to relevant income) are £500,000; this is a 10-year annuity. Look at the 15% column and read off the factor of 5.019 for year 10. (Check this by adding up the ten annual factors in the 'normal' single-value table for years 1 to 10.)

For years 11 to 20, the factor cannot just be read from the table as this would also include years 1 to 10. To obtain the correct factor, in the 15% column, deduct the 10-year factor from the 20-year factor, 6.259 − 5.019 = 1.240.

|  | Year | Cash in/(out) | 15% factors | Present values |
|---|---|---|---|---|
| Equipment | 0 | (2,500) | 1.000 | (2,500.00) |
| Redundancy | 0 | (300) | 1.000 | (300.00) |
| Net savings | 1–10 | 500 | 5.019 | 2,509.50 |
| Net savings | 11–20 | 400 | 1.240 | 496.00 |
| Residual value | 20 | 250 | 0.061 | 15.25 |
|  |  |  |  | **NPV = 220.75** |

Note that 18 lines of calculation are avoided by making use of the annuity factors.

<table><tr><td>*Self-assessment question S8.7*</td><td>*Try the following question for yourself (answer at the end of the chapter).*

The New English Wine Company is considering automating its operations by investing in some new bottling plant. It has a choice of two machines, A and B. Machine A costs £40,000 and will have a residual value at the end of its 10-year life of £1,000. Machine B costs £20,000 and will have a residual value at the end of its 10-year life of £500. Machine A will save £10,000 a year in labour costs but machine B will only save £6,000 a year. If the company's cost of capital is 20% a year, which machine would you advise the company to buy?</td></tr></table>

## Limitations of NPV

For NPV calculations, all cash flows (except for the initial project cost outflows) are assumed to occur **on the last day of the year.** This is due to discounting being the opposite of compounding **once a year.** In reality, this means cash flows throughout the year, not just at its end. This is a weakness of the model.

A further weakness is that the cost of capital is assumed to remain constant over the whole lifetime of the project. The longer the time period involved, the less likely this is to be true.

## Method 4: internal rate of return (IRR)

The IRR is the average annual rate of return that the project is expected to produce; it is calculated using cash flows adjusted for the time-value of money. It is expressed as a percentage and is determined by calculating the discount rate that gives the project an NPV of zero.

When organizations use IRR to evaluate capital investment proposals they set a threshold or 'hurdle' rate (usually equal to or higher than their ROCE). This is the minimum acceptable IRR for the project to go ahead. In theory, this threshold is set equal to the organization's cost of capital or discount rate. In other words, the cash **generated** by the project must be at least equal to the cost of financing the project. In practice, to allow for risk and inherent approximation in the IRR calculations, it may be set at a rate greater than the cost of capital.

If several mutually exclusive projects are being considered, the one with the greatest IRR is chosen. An example of an IRR calculation is shown in Figure 8.9. This mathematical technique is known as **interpolation.**

### Procedure for calculating the IRR

1  Perform the NPV process using your best guess of the discount rate which will give an NPV of zero.
2  If your NPV is positive, repeat the process using a higher discount rate in order to give a negative NPV. (If first NPV is negative, try a lower rate to find a positive NPV.)
3  When you have one positive and one negative NPV, use *interpolation* to find the rate giving NPV = 0.

A project costs £28,000 and produces net cash flows as shown. What is the IRR?

| Year | Cash inflow | 60% factor | PV | 61% factor | PV |
|------|------------|-----------|------|-----------|------|
| 0 | (28,000) | 1.0000 | (28,000) | 1.0000 | (28,000) |
| 1 | 18,000 | 0.6250 | 11,250 | 0.6211 | 11,180 |
| 2 | 21,000 | 0.3910 | 8,211 | 0.3858 | 8,102 |
| 3 | 24,000 | 0.2440 | 5,856 | 0.2396 | 5,750 |
| 4 | 18,000 | 0.1530 | 2,754 | 0.1488 | 2,679 |
| | | | 71 | | (289) |

$$\text{IRR} = 60\% + [71/(71 + 289) \times 1\%] = 60\% + [71/360]\% = \underline{60.2\%}$$

| 60% | IRR | gap = 1% | 61% |
|------|------|----------|------|
| +71 | 0 | gap = 360 | (289) |

Figure 8.9  **Example of an IRR calculation**

N.B. This is an **iterative** technique using **trial and error**. Most spreadsheets and some calculators have dedicated functions to calculate PV, NPV and IRR but they do the calculations using the same method.

*Try the following question for yourself (answer at the end of the chapter).*

Find the IRR of the project detailed in S8.6.

*Self-assessment question S8.8*

## Inherent approximation

Interpolation assumes that the NPV changes linearly with the discount rate. Mathematically, this is not true because the relationship is correctly represented by a curve rather than a straight line. Figure 8.10 illustrates this as follows.

Line B interpolates between NPVs of +325 (at 10%) and −125 (at 30%) and gives an IRR of 27%.

Line A interpolates between NPVs of +95 (at 15%) and −105 (at 25%) and gives an IRR of 21%.

The actual IRR is 19%.

## Limitations of IRR

Consider two alternative projects, one in Sheffield and the other in Lincoln. The Sheffield project may have an IRR of 25% and the Lincoln project may have an IRR of 50%, so the Lincoln project would be chosen. But which project produces most money? 25% of £800,000 is greater than 50% of £300,000! IRR is a **relative** measure. (In contrast, NPV is an **absolute** measure giving monetary answers rather than percentages.)

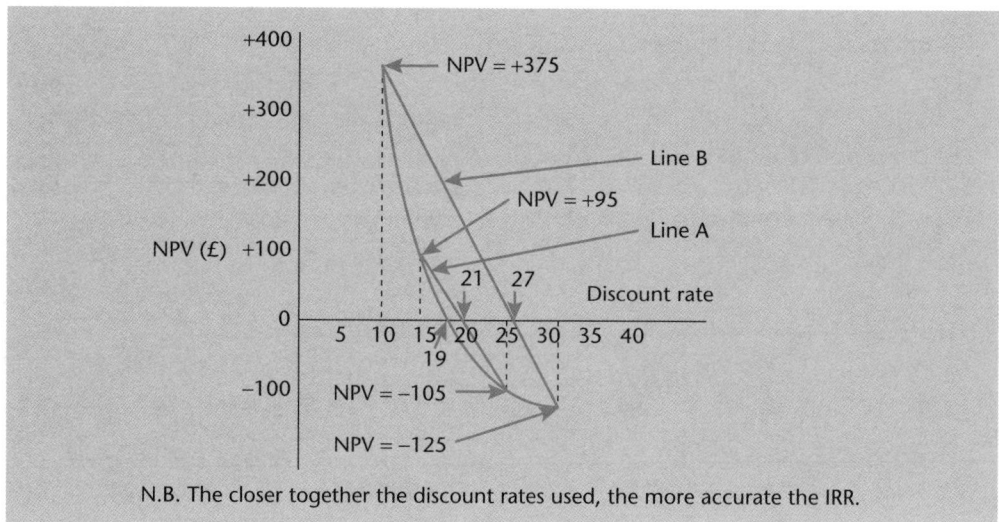

Figure 8.10  **Effect of discount rate choice**

Also, due to the mathematics involved, if any of the cash flows after year zero are net outflows, there may be **more than one value** of the IRR. (This is similar to the square root of 9 having two answers, +3 and −3.)

## Comparing NPV with IRR

Suppose a business has a choice between the Arundel project (A) and the Brighton project (B), what guidance can it gain from calculating their NPVs and IRRs? Assuming that they have different cash flows, the situation is represented in Figure 8.11 as follows:

- The Brighton project has the higher IRR (Z%).
- At a discount rate of 25%, Brighton has a higher NPV than Arundel.
- At a discount rate of 5%, Arundel has a higher NPV than Brighton.

To the right of the crossover point (X%), IRR and NPV will both recommend adopting the Brighton project. However, to the left of this point, IRR and NPV will conflict and recommend different projects.

N.B. If the IRR decision conflicts with the NPV, the NPV decision should be used as it is technically more sound. Remember that IRR is a **relative** measure but NPV is an **absolute** measure (see 'Limitations of IRR' above).

## Capital rationing and the profitability index

At any point in time, an organization may have identified several projects in which it is worthwhile investing as they each have a positive NPV. Unfortunately, it may not be able to raise sufficient funds to invest in all of them. This situation is referred to as 'capital

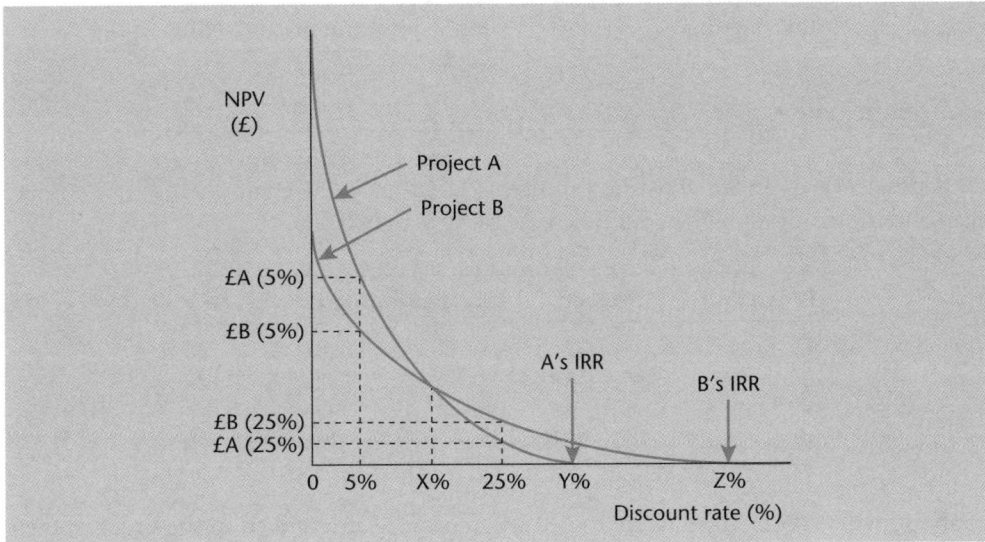

Figure 8.11 **Mutually exclusive projects**

rationing' and the problem it poses is how the business decides in which of the available projects to invest.

A good way of approaching this decision is to calculate the 'profitability index' of each project. This is defined by the formula

$$PI = \frac{\text{Present Value of Future Cash Inflows}}{\text{Initial Investment}}$$

This is effectively a 'benefit to cost' ratio. (The present value of future cash inflows excludes the initial investment, year 0 in NPV calculations.)

The decision rule is for the company to accept the projects with the greatest PIs until the funds run out. (This assumes all PIs are greater than 1.0 which means they have a positive NPV.) Consider the following example of a company with a maximum of £200,000 of funds to invest in the five different projects shown in the table below. (All figures are in £000s.)

| Project | Initial investment | PV of future cash inflows | NPV | PI | PI ranking | NPV ranking |
|---|---|---|---|---|---|---|
| A | 78 | 105 | 27 | 1.35 | 2 | 3 |
| B | 55 | 70 | 15 | 1.27 | 3 | 4 |
| C | 200 | 250 | 50 | 1.25 | 4 | 1 |
| D | 66 | 94 | 28 | 1.42 | 1 | 2 |
| E | 72 | 79 | 7 | 1.10 | 5 | 5 |

If projects are ranked according to the size of their NPVs, only project C is able to be undertaken which has a total NPV of £50,000.

| NPV ranking | Project | Initial investment | NPV |
|---|---|---|---|
| 1 | C | 200 | 50 |
| Total | | 200 | 50 |

But if projects are ranked according to their PIs, projects D, A and B would be under-taken and the resulting NPV would increase by 40% to £70,000.

| PI ranking | Project | Initial investment | NPV |
|---|---|---|---|
| 1 | D | 66 | 28 |
| 2 | A | 78 | 27 |
| 3 | B | 55 | 15 |
| Total | | 199 | 70 |

A suboptimal result is normally obtained when projects are ranked in the order of their absolute NPVs. This is because the largest projects tend to be selected due to their high individual NPVs. However, their combined NPV is usually lower than that of those projects selected by their PI ranking.

**Self-assessment question S8.9**

*Try the following question for yourself (answer at the end of the chapter).*

Invest Quest plc has a maximum of £700 million to invest in new capital projects. Advise which of the following five projects should be chosen. (All figures are in £m.)

| Project | Initial investment | PV of future cash inflows |
|---|---|---|
| A | 185 | 269 |
| B | 197 | 260 |
| C | 81 | 137 |
| D | 210 | 299 |
| E | 282 | 352 |

# Discounted payback period?

It may have occurred to you that it is possible to discount the cash flows used in payback calculations. The effect of this is to lengthen the period and so show more caution in the estimate of the time needed for the project to pay for itself.

At first sight this approach may seem an improvement on the basic payback period. However, the simplicity of PBP, which is one of its main attractions, is significantly diminished by it. Also, as PBP concentrates on the early years of a project, the benefit of discounting is limited.

More importantly, PBP assumes cash to flow evenly throughout each year but discounting assumes the annual cash flow to occur on the last day of the financial year. These two **contradictory assumptions** render this financial model theoretically unsound and its use inadvisable.

## Choice of method

Having four methods of appraising capital investments at your disposal, how do you choose which one to use? Fortunately, you do not have to answer this question because you do not have to use only one method. Indeed, it is preferable to employ a variety of approaches to see how much consensus they produce. After all, each method tells you something different.

ARR tells you the percentage profit return on your investment. PBP tells you how long it will take to recoup your initial investment. NPV tells you the current cash value of the project measured in today's money. IRR tells you the average annual growth rate of your cash investment. As a starting point to your final discussion and recommendation, it is helpful to create a summary table of the results from all the methods employed. This makes the comparison of the findings relatively easy.

However, it is important not to overlook the limitations of the techniques you have used. Will the assumptions of the various methods impinge more on some projects than others or is the effect likely to be the same for all of them?

Finally, you should think more as a manager than an accountant. There will always be some qualitative factors to consider. Factors such as the availability of skilled labour, the ease of distribution to the market and the enhancement of the product range should not be ignored.

## Sensitivity analysis

Sensitivity analysis is used to evaluate the risk from each of the factors involved in the project. Once the non-starters have been eliminated and only the possible projects remain, each factor can be analysed to see how much it would need to change before the project would no longer be viable (NPV = 0). Even where one single project has been chosen, it is wise to perform a sensitivity analysis to identify the factors which need to change least to cast doubt on the viability of the project. Sensitivity analysis is illustrated in the following example.

## Sensitivity analysis

**Example 8.2**

The **Freeway Driving School** is considering expanding its operations by employing one further instructor and car. The car will cost £15,000 (including the addition of dual controls), will be used for three years and then scrapped (for zero value). Fixed costs such as insurance, vehicle licence duty, servicing, etc., will be £4,600 a year and the annual cost of the instructor is £20,000. Instructors are expected to give a maximum of six lessons a day for five days a week and to work for 50 weeks a year. However, it is estimated that the take-up rate for lessons will be 90% of the maximum, i.e. 27 lessons a week ($5 \times 6 \times 90\%$). The selling price of each lesson is £32 and the petrol cost is £5. Freeway has calculated that their cost of capital is 12.5% p.a. Calculate the net present value of this three-year project and perform a sensitivity analysis to identify the relative sensitivity of the factors involved.

## Suggested solution

Contribution/lesson = lesson price − petrol cost = 32 − 5 = £27
Annual contribution = weeks worked × lessons/week × contribution/lesson
= 50          × 27          × 27      = £36,450
Fixed cost        = insurance etc. + salary = 4,600 + 20,000 = £24,600
Annual Net Cash Inflow                                            = £11,850

*NB: Depreciation is ignored as it is a non-cash cost; NPV uses only cash flows.*

### NPV calculation

| Year | Annual cash contribution | Initial & fixed costs | Net cash in/(out) flow | 12.5% Discount factors | Present value |
|------|-------------------------|----------------------|------------------------|------------------------|---------------|
| 0 | 0 | 15,000 | −15,000 | 1.000 | −15,000 |
| 1 | 36,450 | 24,600 | 11,850 | 0.889 | 10,533 |
| 2 | 36,450 | 24,600 | 11,850 | 0.790 | 9,363 |
| 3 | 36,450 | 24,600 | 11,850 | 0.702 | 8,323 |
| | | | | | NPV = 13,219 |

If all assumptions prove to be correct, NPV = £13,219

### Sensitivity analysis – annual cash contribution

| Year | Annual cash contribution | Initial & fixed costs | Net cash in/(out) flow | 12.5% Discount factors | Present value |
|------|-------------------------|----------------------|------------------------|------------------------|---------------|
| 0 | 0 | 15,000 | −15,000 | 1.000 | −15,000 |
| 1 | 30,900 | 24,600 | 6,300 | 0.889 | 5,600 |
| 2 | 30,900 | 24,600 | 6,300 | 0.790 | 4,987 |
| 3 | 30,900 | 24,600 | 6,300 | 0.702 | 4,425 |
| | | | | | NPV = 2 |

*By trial and error, it is found that the annual cash contribution must reduce to £30,900 for the NPV to equal zero. (An NPV of 2 is considered to be effectively equal to zero as the NPV model makes some significant assumptions which cause its numerical answers to be estimates rather than 100% accurate figures.)*

Sensitivity of 'annual cash contribution' factor $= (36{,}450 - 30{,}900)/36{,}450$
$= 0.15226 = \mathbf{15\%}$
However, *annual contribution = weeks worked × lessons/week × contribution/lesson*
and *reduced annual contribution = 0.85 × weeks worked × lessons/week × contribution/lesson*
So the 15% factor applies to each of these three components (taken in isolation).
This means that the weeks worked/year would have to fall to 42.5 ($50 \times 0.85$) for
NPV = 0, or the number of lessons given a week would have to fall to 23 ($27 \times 0.85$)
for NPV = 0, or the contribution/lesson would have to fall to 23 ($27 \times 0.85$) for
NPV = 0.

However, contribution/lesson can be analysed by lesson price and petrol cost:

| | Contribution/lesson = lesson price − petrol cost | |
|---|---|---|
| Base position: | $= \quad 32 - 5$ | $= 27$ |
| Lesson price: | $= \quad 28 - 5$ | $= 23$ |
| Petrol cost: | $= \quad 32 - 9$ | $= 23$ |
| Lesson price: | $[(32 - 28)/32] \times 100 = (4/32) \times 100 = \mathbf{13\%}$ | |
| Petrol cost: | $[(9 - 5)/5] \times 100 = (4/5) \times 100 \quad = \mathbf{80\%}$ | |

### Sensitivity analysis – fixed costs

| Year | Annual cash contribution | Initial & fixed costs | Net cash in/(out) flow | 12.5% Discount factors | Present value |
|---|---|---|---|---|---|
| 0 | 0 | 15,000 | −15,000 | 1.000 | −15,000 |
| 1 | 36,450 | 30,150 | 6,300 | 0.889 | 5,600 |
| 2 | 36,450 | 30,150 | 6,300 | 0.790 | 4,978 |
| 3 | 36,450 | 30,150 | 6,300 | 0.702 | 4,425 |
| | | | | | NPV = 2 |

The fixed costs have to increase to £30,150 for NPV = 0, so the sensitivity factor is:

$$[(30{,}150 - 24{,}600)/24{,}600] \times 100 = 22.561 = \mathbf{23\%}$$

### Sensitivity analysis – discount rate

| Year | Annual cash contribution | Initial & fixed costs | Net cash in/(out) flow | 59.5% Discount factors | Present value |
|---|---|---|---|---|---|
| 0 | 0 | 15,000 | −15,000 | 1.000 | −15,000 |
| 1 | 36,450 | 24,600 | 11,850 | 0.627 | 7,429 |
| 2 | 36,450 | 24,600 | 11,850 | 0.393 | 4,658 |
| 3 | 36,450 | 24,600 | 11,850 | 0.246 | 2,920 |
| | | | | | NPV = 8 |

The discount rate has to increase to 59.5% for NPV = 0, so the sensitivity factor is:

$$[(59.5 - 12.5)/12.5] \times 100 = \mathbf{376\%}$$

**Sensitivity analysis – initial cost of car**

| Year | Annual cash contribution | Initial & fixed costs | Net cash in/(out) flow | 12.5% Discount factors | Present value |
|---|---|---|---|---|---|
| 0 | 0 | 28,219 | −28,219 | 1.000 | −28,219 |
| 1 | 36,450 | 24,600 | 11,850 | 0.889 | 10,533 |
| 2 | 36,450 | 24,600 | 11,850 | 0.790 | 9,363 |
| 3 | 36,450 | 24,600 | 11,850 | 0.702 | 8,323 |
| | | | | | NPV = 0 |

For NPV = 0, the initial cost of the car would have to increase by £13,219 (the NPV value at year 0) to £28,219. The sensitivity factor of this is:

$$[(28,219 - 15,000)/15,000] \times 100 = (13,219/15,000) \times 100 = \textbf{88\%}$$

**Summary table of changes needed to produce a negative NPV (most sensitive factors listed first)**

| Factor | Change |
|---|---|
| Lesson price | 13% |
| Weeks worked/year | 15% |
| Lessons given/week | 15% |
| Fixed costs | 23% |
| Petrol cost | 80% |
| Initial cost of car | 88% |
| Discount rate | 376% |

Findings

As the table shows, the lesson price is the most sensitive factor and the discount rate the least sensitive. The assumptions and forecasts underlying the most sensitive factors should be carefully checked and reconsidered. (In the 'Freeway Driving School' example above, the lesson price, the number of weeks worked a year and the number of lessons given a week should be carefully scrutinized.) To reduce the investment risk involved, managers may think it wise to take a more pessimistic view of these factors in order to re-evaluate the validity of the capital investment project under consideration.

# The financing decision

## Project loans and interest payments

Obtaining a bank loan is one way of financing a capital investment project. All the cash flows associated with the loan (initial sum, interest payments and final repayment of sum) should be **excluded** from the cash flows used in capital investment appraisal. This is because the decision on how to finance a project is separate from the decision whether or not to accept the project. The decision to accept or reject a project should be made first. Only if this is positive will the choice of finance need to be made. (The financing decision is outside the scope of this book.)

*If the effect of interest charges is not eliminated from the cash flows for DCF purposes, double counting will occur. This is because the discounting process automatically allows for the time value of money, which is firmly based on the ability of money to earn interest.*

To eliminate the effect of interest from the calculations, the annual interest charges are added back to profits to give the **cash flows before interest**.

N.B. Concerning the 'Reconciliation of cash flows with profits' subsection we looked at earlier in this chapter, the position is modified as follows. **Over the whole lifetime of a project**, the total of profits (**before interest**) will equal the total of cash flows (**ignoring loans, interest and repayments**). (Note that this is not true for any one year within the project's lifetime.)

## Qualitative factors

The management accountant's role is to provide the calculations and a recommendation. The manager's role is to apply experience and knowledge of the industry, weigh up the risks involved and make the decision. The work of the management accountant is important but it is only the starting point of the appraisal process. Other factors, many of which are not numerically quantifiable but still affect the decision, should be taken into account. Remember, the final decision should be a management decision, not an accounting one.

## Limitations of capital investment appraisal techniques

The limitations of the four techniques have already been discussed at the end of each of their sections. However, it is worth pointing out that all capital investment appraisals are only as good as the forecasts of profit or cash flow on which they are based. The long-term nature of capital investment appraisal compounds this weakness. The further into the future the forecast goes, the less reliable it becomes.

Also, these techniques cannot tell companies when, and in what, they should be investing. For example, the petrol company Shell announced record profits of £9.8 billion pounds in 2004, an all-time record for a European company! But Shell's stated total of oil reserves was only nine years which compared badly with its rivals BP and Exxon which had each identified sufficient oil to keep them in business for the next 14 years. This was an excellent opportunity to plough as much of the 'excess' profit as possible back into the company to finance increased exploration activities or research into alternative energy sources. After all, if it did not find any more oil or develop new products, it would be out of business in less than 10 years. However, Shell decided that it would spend its 'windfall' profits on paying a one-off special dividend to shareholders and buying back its own shares on the stock-market in order to keep its share price high rather than invest in its long-term future.

## The manager's point of view (written by Nigel Burton)

Capital investment decisions are among the most challenging issues faced by management. The sums of money involved can be very large, and the decision to invest or not to invest can have a profound influence on the future of the business. Large projects are often turning points in the life of a company. Success can raise the business on to a new plane. Failure can bring it down altogether. Moreover, the decision has to be taken largely on the basis of estimates of what might happen in the future. Different assumptions about future circumstances will lead to different patterns of projected profits and cash flow. Management has to decide on the most likely outcome of the project, and ensure that the proposed level of capital expenditure is compatible with this outcome. Capital appraisal techniques are designed to rationalize all the relevant information and present management with a reasonable comparison between the options available.

Preparing a capital expenditure proposal is an iterative process. It is rather like budgeting. All the contributors to the process – the engineer, salesman, raw material purchaser, production and technical representatives, etc. – draw up proposals relating to their areas, but without seeing the overall picture. As in budgeting, therefore, everyone starts by specifying their requirements with their own particular agendas in mind, while preparing to make concessions only if it is found that the figures do not ultimately add up. For instance, engineers will tend, perhaps rightly, to aim in the first instance for state-of-the-art technology, as they feel this will keep the company in the forefront of the industry. Salespeople, being optimistic by nature, may have a tendency to overestimate what their talents can achieve, so their projected sales levels may appear to support the high capital expenditure proposals. A decision to go for expensive plant under these circumstances would be very tempting, but it may be based on a false assumption of future cash flows and could in fact be quite the wrong option for the company.

A similar pattern of optimism and aspiration is likely to be repeated throughout the departments involved, so that, when all the figures are put together for the first time, the initial view may be completely distorted. It is likely to be quite different from the final article when the iterative process is complete. Every number in the financial statements must be challenged. Are the proposed sales volumes reasonable? Will the competition bring a better product to the market during the lifespan of the project? Are the proposed selling prices supportable? Will the increased capacity in the marketplace, created by the project itself, have an impact on prices? And so on. For every question asked, there will be a variety of inconclusive answers, more like statements of probabilities. But every discussion will give you a better feel for the robustness of a particular number. In the end, you can only go with one set of figures, but it is useful to bear in mind the best-case and worst-case scenarios, so that you develop an understanding of the risks inherent in the project.

Throughout the iterative process, the capital appraisal techniques outlined in this chapter provide a common point of comparison between the different financial scenarios which each set of circumstances throws up. They will help you to answer critical questions such as: 'Will the business support a full replacement of the plant, or is refurbishment the more viable option?' and 'Is it worth going for the expense of a bigger expansion now, so that we do not have to put up with the upheaval of a further expansion project in three, five or ten years' time?' The internal rate of return calculation takes into account the cash flows for the whole of a project's lifespan, and reduces it to a single figure which can be compared not only with alternative options, but also with the company's required benchmark.

Cash is a scarce commodity for many companies, so the payback period is also a critical measurement. If we make the capital investment today, how many years of cash inflow will it take to get our money back? In other words, how soon will we be making a genuine profit on our investment? If the profit arrives a long way into the future, we could be better off by simply keeping our funds on deposit. At the very least, we should consider alternative projects which give a quicker return.

For some years, my corporation's strategy had been aimed at raising the company's overall return on capital employed to 20%, a high target, but an attainable one for a speciality chemical business. In order to achieve this, the company set a minimum IRR of 20% and a maximum payback period of three years for all capital expenditure proposals. Any project with better returns than these had a good chance of success. Since it was a multinational corporation, however, competition for capital funds was always intense. If we submitted our project at a time when other subsidiaries were putting forward even better proposals, we could find ourselves being either turned down or deferred. There was always a temptation, therefore, to go forward with optimistic figures, and while optimism is fine, there is always the risk that it may spill over into fantasy land, with disaster following closely behind.

One of our fellow subsidiaries had proposed a major expansion to one of its plants. The engineers determined that the capital cost would be $9.6 million. This included a number of specific pieces of plant for which firm quotations had been obtained, but the majority of it was based on estimates. In view of these uncertainties, it is common to add a general contingency into the cost, usually amounting to 10%. This contingency, at $960,000, was therefore completely non-specific. Yet this amount alone was larger than most other capital projects routinely undertaken by the subsidiary, all of which were subjected to the normal, detailed capital appraisal scrutiny. Much concern was expressed at the time over how this amount was to be controlled, but the engineers insisted that it represented only a buffer amount, and very little of it would actually be used. However, due to inaccurate estimating in the first place, and inadequate control during the installation process, especially over subcontractors, the actual capital cost of the project spiralled, finally amounting not to $9.6 million, but $12.3 million. If this level of cost had been incorporated into the original financial appraisal, the IRR and payback would have been insufficient, and the project would never have been approved. As it was, the problem emerged too late for any remedial action to be taken. The business group concerned was left to carry an enormous burden, which severely inhibited its profitability for several years, and might well have caused the business to collapse.

This story demonstrates how critical the capital appraisal process can be to the well-being of the business. It will result in the business making a substantial commitment, not only in terms of capital, which can be significant, but also in respect of its future, strategic direction. Once the decision is made, the die is cast. It is critical, therefore, that the optimism inherent in capital proposals is tempered with a good dose of realism, or at least an element of conservatism. This is where the sensitivity analyses described earlier play an important part. They will demonstrate the robustness of the project if specific estimates, such as capital cost or sales levels, prove to be inaccurate.

When the project is approved and under way, it is also important that all the managers contributing to the appraisal process are held to account for their commitments. Post-completion audits are a good way to focus their minds. These can take place at any time in the life of a project, but usually occur after a period of several years, when the pattern of the business has been established. Although the threat of audit can sharpen the minds of managers, the disadvantage is that they happen so far after the event that any problems unearthed will almost certainly be beyond rectification. There is no substitute therefore for detailed analysis and testing of the basic assumptions underlying the capital appraisal, followed by close control of the project at every stage of its development. The potential risk to the business of unsound assumptions is simply too great to permit the slightest lack of rigour in the management review process.

*Summary*

- There are four alternative ways of appraising large investments in fixed (or capital) assets: ARR, PBP, NPV and IRR.
- They all use cash flow except ARR, which uses profit.
- Cash flows can be calculated by adding back depreciation to profits.
- Due to the long time periods involved, it is appropriate to discount future cash flows to present values for NPV and IRR.
- Discounting is the opposite process to the compounding of interest.
- Several methods should be used to aid decision making as each one considers a different aspect of the project.
- Each method is based on assumptions and has its limitations.
- The interpolation process for calculating IRR contains inherent approximations.
- It is possible for the NPV and IRR decisions to contradict each other. If this occurs, it is preferable to use the NPV recommendation.
- Sensitivity analysis helps to identify the major risk factors.
- The cash flows arising from the financing decision should **not** be included in the calculations.
- The final decision should take account of qualitative factors as well as the quantitative results of the methods used.
- Each method has its own limitations/weaknesses.
- All capital investment appraisal is limited by the inaccuracy of the cash flow/profit forecasts used.

## Further reading

Atkinson, A., Banker, R., Kaplan, R. and Young, S. (2001) *Management Accounting*, 3rd edition, Prentice Hall, Harlow. See chapter 'Using management accounting information for investment decisions'.

Borgonovo, E. and Peccati, L. (2004) 'Sensitivity analysis in investment project evaluation', *International Journal of Production Economics*, July, Vol. 90, Issue 1.

Boston, J. (2002) 'Purer speculation', *Financial Management* (CIMA), March.

Cohn, E. (2003) 'Benefit-cost analysis: a pedagogical note', *Public Finance Review*, September, Vol. 31, Issue 5.

Horngren, C., Bhimani, A., Datar, S. and Foster, G. (2002) *Management and Cost Accounting*, 2nd edition, Prentice Hall Europe, Harlow. See Chapter 13, 'Capital investment decisions'.

McDermott, T., Stainer, A. and Stainer, L. (2002) 'Environmental sustainability and capital investment appraisal', *International Journal of Environmental Technology & Management*, Vol. 2, Issue 4.

Otley, D. (1987) *Accounting Control and Organisational Behaviour*, Heinemann Professional Publishing Ltd. See Chapter 8, 'Capital budgeting'.

Pogue, M. (2004) 'Investment appraisal: a new approach', *Managerial Auditing Journal*, April, Vol. 19, Issue 4.

Upchurch, A. (2003) *Management Accounting, Principles and Practice*, 2nd edition, Financial Times/Prentice Hall, Harlow. See chapter 'Capital investment appraisal'.

Weetman, P. (2002) *Management Accounting, an Introduction*, 3rd edition, Financial Times/Prentice Hall, Harlow. See chapter 'Capital budgeting'.

## *Answers to self-assessment questions*

### S8.1

| Year | Units | Profit before fixed costs | Fixed costs | Net profit |
|------|-------|---------------------------|-------------|------------|
| 1 | 5,000 | 20,000 | 16,000 | 4,000 |
| 2 | 6,000 | 24,000 | 16,000 | 8,000 |
| 3 | 7,000 | 28,000 | 16,000 | 12,000 |
| 4 | 8,000 | 32,000 | 16,000 | 16,000 |
| 5 | 6,500 | 26,000 | 16,000 | 10,000 |

$$\text{ARR} = \frac{(4 + 8 + 12 + 16 + 10)/5}{25} \times 100$$

$$= \frac{10}{25} \times 100$$

$$= 40\%$$

### S8.2

$$\text{Annual depreciation charge} = \frac{\text{Fall in value over project's lifetime}}{\text{Lifetime in years}}$$

$$= \frac{(190,000 - 10,000)}{9}$$

$$= £20,000$$

**(Figures shown in £000s)**

| Year | Profit/(Loss) | Annual depreciation | Other items | Cash flow in/(out) |
|---|---|---|---|---|
| 0 | 0 | 0 | (190) buy crane | (190) |
| 1 | 10 | 20 | 0 | 30 |
| 2 | 18 | 20 | 0 | 38 |
| 3 | 24 | 20 | 0 | 44 |
| 4 | 30 | 20 | 0 | 50 |
| 5 | 35 | 20 | 0 | 55 |
| 6 | 38 | 20 | 0 | 58 |
| 7 | 30 | 20 | 0 | 50 |
| 8 | 20 | 20 | 0 | 40 |
| 9 | 10 | 20 | 10 sell scrap | 40 |
|   | **215** | | | **215** |

## S8.3

| Year | Profit | Depreciation | Cash flow | Cumulative |
|---|---|---|---|---|
| 1 | 4,000 | 2,000 | 6,000 | 6,000 |
| 2 | 8,000 | 2,000 | 10,000 | 16,000 |
| 3 | 12,000 | 2,000 | 14,000 | 30,000 |
| 4 | 16,000 | 2,000 | 18,000 | 48,000 |
| 5 | 10,000 | 2,000 | 12,000 | 60,000 |

$$\text{Payback period} = 2 + \frac{(25-16)}{14} = 2 + \frac{9}{14} = 2.64 \text{ years} = \text{2 years 8 months}$$

## S8.4

£500 invested for 4 years at 7.5% p.a. compound:

| Year | Amount £ | Factor | Total £ |
|---|---|---|---|
| 1 | 500.00 | 1.075 | 537.50 |
| 2 | 537.50 | 1.075 | 577.81 |
| 3 | 577.81 | 1.075 | 621.15 |
| 4 | 621.15 | 1.075 | **£667.73** |

## S8.5

Discounting cash flows at 3% p.a.:

| Year | Cash flow £ | 3% discount factor | Present value £ |
|---|---|---|---|
| 1 | 6,000 | 1/1.03 = 0.97087 | 5,825 |
| 2 | 10,000 | 0.97087/1.03 = 0.94260 | 9,426 |
| 3 | 14,000 | 0.94260/1.03 − 0.91514 | 12,812 |
| 4 | 18,000 | 0.91514/1.03 = 0.88849 | 15,993 |
| 5 | 12,000 | 0.88849/1.03 = 0.86261 | 10,351 |
|   | **£60,000** | | Total **£54,407** |

S8.6

| Year | Cash in/(out) | 10% factors | Present value |
|---|---|---|---|
| 0 | (49,500) | 1.000 | (49,500) |
| 1 | 20,000 | 0.909 | 18,180 |
| 2 | 20,000 | 0.826 | 16,520 |
| 3 | 10,000 | 0.751 | 7,510 |
| 4 | 10,000 | 0.683 | 6,830 |
| | | | NPV = (460) |

Recommendation: Do not go ahead with project.

S8.7

**Machine A**

| Year | Cash in/(out) £ | 20% factor | Present value £ |
|---|---|---|---|
| 0 | (40,000) | 1.000 | (40,000) |
| 1–10 | 10,000 | 4.192 | 41,920 |
| 10 | 1,000 | 0.162 | 162 |
| | | | NPV = 2,082 |

**Machine B**

| Year | Cash in/(out) £ | 20% factor | Present value £ |
|---|---|---|---|
| 0 | (20,000) | 1.000 | (20,000) |
| 1–10 | 6,000 | 4.192 | 25,152 |
| 10 | 500 | 0.162 | 81 |
| | | | NPV = 5,233 |

Machine B appears to be a much better investment than machine A.

S8.8

| Year | Cash in/(out) | 10% factor | PV | 9% factor | PV |
|---|---|---|---|---|---|
| 0 | (49,500) | 1.000 | (49,500) | 1.000 | (49,500) |
| 1 | 20,000 | 0.909 | 18,180 | 0.917 | 18,340 |
| 2 | 20,000 | 0.826 | 16,520 | 0.842 | 16,840 |
| 3 | 10,000 | 0.751 | 7,510 | 0.772 | 7,720 |
| 4 | 10,000 | 0.683 | 6,830 | 0.708 | 7,080 |
| | | | NPV = (460) | | NPV = 480 |

By interpolation:

$$\text{IRR} = 9\% + \frac{480}{(480 + 460)} \times 1\% = 9.51\%$$

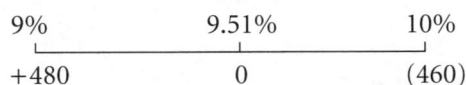

| 9% | 9.51% | 10% |
|---|---|---|
| +480 | 0 | (460) |

## S8.9

Calculate the NPV, PI and rankings for all projects.

| Project | Initial investment | PV of future cash inflows | NPV | PI | PI ranking | NPV ranking |
|---|---|---|---|---|---|---|
| A | 185 | 269 | 84 | 1.45 | 2 | 2 |
| B | 197 | 260 | 63 | 1.32 | 4 | 4 |
| C | 81 | 137 | 56 | 1.69 | 1 | 5 |
| D | 210 | 299 | 89 | 1.42 | 3 | 1 |
| E | 282 | 352 | 70 | 1.25 | 5 | 3 |

If projects are ranked according to the size of their NPVs, projects D, A and E are undertaken giving a total NPV of £243 m.

| NPV ranking | Project | Initial investment | NPV |
|---|---|---|---|
| 1 | D | 210 | 89 |
| 2 | A | 185 | 84 |
| 3 | E | 282 | 70 |
| **Total** | | **677** | **243** |

But if projects are ranked according to their PIs, projects C, A, D and B would be undertaken and the resulting NPV would increase by £49 m to £292 m.

| PI ranking | Project | Initial investment | NPV |
|---|---|---|---|
| 1 | C | 81 | 56 |
| 2 | A | 185 | 84 |
| 3 | D | 210 | 89 |
| 4 | B | 197 | 63 |
| | | **673** | **292** |

Based on the figures alone, IQ plc should consider investing in projects A, B, C and D.

<table>
<tr><td>**CASE<br>STUDY<br>1**</td><td>Nufone</td></tr>
</table>

Nufone plc is considering the launch of a new product, the latest in its range of mobile phones. Its major selling point is a modified microwave technology which will significantly improve the quality of the voice output and the robustness of the connection. Its inventor has approached Nufone plc with a view to selling it the patent and has given the company one week before he offers it elsewhere. The patent will cost £5 million. The profit estimates below are based on a market research survey for a similar concept which Nufone commissioned four months ago from an independent bureau.

If the project goes ahead, a new factory will have to be built at a cost of £2 million plus £6 million for machinery. The company is currently negotiating for a suitable site on which to build; it expects to have to pay £3 million for it. Nufone plc's depreciation policy is to use the equal instalment (straight-line) method with residual values always assumed to be zero. Patents are decreased in value (amortized) in the same way but land is not depreciated. It is assumed the patent will have no value in 10 years' time.

It is estimated that the product will have a life of ten years, at the end of which time it will be obsolete. It is also assumed that the factory building will then be demolished. The cost of the demolition will be exactly covered by the sale proceeds of the ten-year-old machinery. Also, the land will be sold for an estimated £3 million.

The financing of the project will be assisted by a bank loan, which will incur interest of £300,000 p.a., payable in arrears at the end of each year. The working capital (stock, debtors and creditors) needed to run this project is estimated to be £1.2 million.

The profits shown below are **after** charging depreciation, interest on the bank loan and launch costs (£1.5 million, all in year one).

| Year | Profit/(loss) £m | Year | Profit/(loss) £m |
|------|------------------|------|------------------|
| 1 | (2.3) | 6 | 10.0 |
| 2 | 1.5 | 7 | 8.0 |
| 3 | 6.0 | 8 | 6.0 |
| 4 | 8.0 | 9 | 4.0 |
| 5 | 10.0 | 10 | 2.0 |

(The project detailed above will be known as project T.)

Having seen the above project proposal from the technical director, the financial director suggests that they should lease an existing factory instead of building one. She estimates that the lease will cost £1.4 million to purchase (payable in advance) followed by ten annual payments of £800,000 (payable in arrears). The machinery will still have to be purchased as before. (This alternative project will be known as project F.)

The sales director has come up with a third alternative. This is to go ahead with a new design of phone with a modified casing. In this case it would not be necessary to purchase the patent. As less new technology is involved, the production could take place in the present factory by putting on a night shift. However, £4 million would still need to be spent on new machinery, although the bank loan would be unnecessary. Working capital would be reduced to £0.8 million. The profits from this phone, after charging depreciation on the new machinery, are estimated as follows:

| Year | Profit/(loss) £m | Year | Profit/(loss) £m |
|------|------------------|------|------------------|
| 1 | 2.1 | 6 | 2.6 |
| 2 | 3.6 | 7 | 2.6 |
| 3 | 3.6 | 8 | 1.6 |
| 4 | 3.6 | 9 | 1.6 |
| 5 | 2.6 | 10 | 0.6 |

(This alternative project will be known as project S.)

*Notes:*

1  Nufone plc's cost of capital (or discount rate) is 12.5% p.a.
2  Work to the nearest £000 when performing your calculations.
3  You are expected to use a word-processor and a spreadsheet for this assignment.
4  When performing your calculations, **show your workings** and do not use the dedicated functions for PV, NPV and IRR provided by spreadsheets and some calculators.

*Tasks:*

1  For each of the three alternatives, calculate the following:
   a)  the cash flows;
   b)  the accounting rate of return (using the initial cost);
   c)  the payback period;
   d)  the net present value;
   e)  the internal rate of return (using the 'interpolation' method).

(50%)

2  **On no more than two sides of A4 paper,** create an executive summary report for Nufone plc's board of directors, appraising the capital investment decision facing them. Justify any recommendations you make and discuss any reservations you have concerning the application and interpretation of the techniques used. *(Any work in excess of the first two pages will be ignored.)*

(50%)
(Total 100%)

| CASE STUDY 2 | The Private Healthcare Group |
|---|---|

The Private Healthcare Group (PHG) was started nine years ago by three doctors previously employed by the National Health Service. It is based in London and specializes in cosmetic surgery. It now operates four clinics: two in London, one in Bristol and one in Cardiff. It is considering opening a new clinic in the Birmingham area.

An initial feasibility study has been carried out and several alternative ways forward have been identified. The two most likely are to erect a new building and to convert an existing one. The conversion is likely to be cheaper to build but more expensive to run.

The study was based on a clinic with a capacity of 20 beds open for business seven days a week. A new building would be operational for 50 weeks a year but a converted building for only 48 weeks a year due to the additional amount of building maintenance work needed on a regular basis. Any improvement work thought necessary could also be carried out during this shutdown period.

However, the fee to be charged to the clients (on a daily basis) and the annual occupancy rate are more difficult to determine due to the price elasticity of demand. A market research report, commissioned as part of the feasibility study, is shown below (see Table A). It predicts annual bed occupancy rates at various fee levels.

PHG thinks that the considerable entry barriers, such as high initial building costs, will result in a relatively low competitive environment for about five years. Competitors are likely to be offering equivalent treatments by then so PHG will probably sell the business and pursue other more profitable ventures. PHG has calculated that its accounting rate of return (ARR) for the whole group was 21.4% in the previous financial year.

The cost of building the clinic from scratch is estimated at £6.0 m. A suitable existing building has been identified and is on the market at £3.0 m but a further £2.2 m would need to be spent to convert it to meet the clinic's building specification. In addition to this, in both cases, specialized medical equipment would need to be purchased and installed at a cost of £2.8 m. They have been advised by an independent professional property company that the resale value of the new building in five years' time will probably be 10% lower than its initial cost and that the converted building should maintain its value of £5.2 m over the same period.

PHG's accounting policy on depreciation is to use the straight-line method, buildings over 25 years and equipment (including vehicles) over five years, assuming all residual values to be zero. The variable costs, such as food and drink, are estimated to be £40 per client per day. A schedule of fixed costs (excluding depreciation) has been drawn up by the group accountant (see Table B).

The Chief Executive Officer of PHG has decided to ask for some calculations to be done regarding this project. Having had his fingers burned in a similar situation a few years earlier, he is particularly concerned about the reliability of answers resulting from the application of accounting techniques.

As most of the funding for this project would be provided by a debenture, PHG estimates that the cost of capital for the new clinic will be 16.5% a year. PHG's current approach to capital projects is to stipulate that their IRRs must equal or exceed a 'hurdle rate' of 24% a year.

**Table A: Market research data**

| Daily fee (£) | Annual Occupancy Rate (%) |
|---|---|
| 500 | 94 |
| 600 | 91 |
| 700 | 82 |
| 800 | 77 |
| 900 | 67 |
| 1,000 | 55 |

**Table B: Annual fixed costs other than depreciation**

| Item | New build (£) | Conversion (£) |
|---|---|---|
| Medical salaries | 1,320,000 | 1,320,000 |
| Admin salaries | 170,000 | 170,000 |
| Building maintenance | 50,000 | 120,000 |
| Heat, light and air conditioning | 70,000 | 100,000 |

*Tasks:*

1 Calculate the annual operating contribution and profit for each of the price/occupancy rate combinations in the market research report and identify the 'maximum' profit for a) a new building and b) a converted building.

(20 marks)

*NB: For the following tasks, use only the price/occupancy rate combination which gives the maximum profit for a) a new building, and b) a converted building (as identified in 1 above).*

2 Calculate the first year's Return on Capital Employed for a) a new building, and b) a converted building. (Use **initial** capital employed.)

(6 marks)

3 Calculate the Payback Period of the project for a) a new building, and b) a converted building.

(10 marks)

4 Calculate the Net Present Value (NPV) of the project for a) a new building, and b) a converted building.

(14 marks)

5 Calculate the IRR of a) a new building, and b) a converted building. Show your workings; do NOT use the automatic IRR function on a calculator or computer.

(14 marks)

6  For the New Building option only, perform a sensitivity analysis on the following three factors: end value of building, number of operational weeks and discount rate.

(12 marks)

7  Advise the PHG directors on proceeding with the new clinic.

(15 marks)

8  Justify to the Chief Executive Officer (who is a medic with only a little knowledge of accountancy) why PHG should use Capital Investment Appraisal. *(A discussion of CIA's limitations or a comparison of methods is not required.)*

(9 marks)
(Total 100 marks)

## Questions

An asterisk * on a question number indicates that the answer is given at the end of the book. Answers to the other questions are given in the Lecturer's Guide.

### Q8.1*  Frynas & Co.

Frynas & Co. are considering buying a mobile drilling rig to expand the range of services they provide for the water, gas and oil industries. The rig would cost £620,000 and last for four years, at the end of which it would be sold for £20,000. The estimated profits for each of the four years are shown below. (The company uses the straight-line method of calculating depreciation. Its latest set of accounts showed its return on capital employed to be 11.1 %.)

| Year | Profit/(Loss) |
|------|---------------|
|      | £             |
| 1    | (50,000)      |
| 2    | 50,000        |
| 3    | 150,000       |
| 4    | 50,000        |

*Tasks:*

1  Calculate and comment on the accounting rate of return (using the initial investment).
2  Calculate the payback period.
3  Calculate the net present value if Frynas' cost of capital is 10.0%.
4  Calculate the internal rate of return.
5  Comment on your findings.

### Q8.2*  Binley Blades Ltd

Binley Blades specializes in the manufacture of rotor blades for helicopters. It has just spent £50,000 developing a new type of blade based on a mixture of carbon fibre and naturally occurring resins. These blades can withstand 80% more stress than the company's standard blades but will cost approximately 50% more to manufacture. It now has to decide whether to go ahead and build a new production facility for its new blades. Unfortunately, the net present value analysis (reproduced below) indicates that it would be most unwise to go ahead with this project.

| Year | 0 | 1 | 2 | 3 | 4 | 5 |
|---|---|---|---|---|---|---|
| COSTS (£000) | | | | | | |
| Plant & equipment | 2,000 | 0 | 0 | 0 | 0 | 0 |
| Research & development | 0 | 10 | 10 | 10 | 10 | 10 |
| Materials usage | 0 | 500 | 500 | 500 | 500 | 500 |
| Direct labour | 0 | 200 | 200 | 200 | 200 | 200 |
| Indirect labour | 0 | 20 | 20 | 20 | 20 | 20 |
| Working capital | 150 | 0 | 0 | 0 | 0 | 0 |
| Depreciation | 0 | 200 | 200 | 200 | 200 | 200 |
| Production overheads | 0 | 40 | 40 | 40 | 40 | 40 |
| Sales & administration overheads | 0 | 60 | 60 | 60 | 60 | 60 |
| Finance overhead | 0 | 200 | 200 | 200 | 200 | 200 |
| **Total costs** | 2,150 | 1,230 | 1,230 | 1,230 | 1,230 | 1,230 |
| REVENUES (£000) | | | | | | |
| Sales revenue | 0 | 1,450 | 1,450 | 1,450 | 1,450 | 1,450 |
| Disposal of plant & equipment | 0 | 0 | 0 | 0 | 0 | 1,000 |
| **Total revenue** | 0 | 1,450 | 1,450 | 1,450 | 1,450 | 2,450 |
| **NET TOTAL REVENUE** | −2,150 | 220 | 220 | 220 | 220 | 1,220 |
| **10% Discount factors** | 1 | 0.9 | 0.8 | 0.7 | 0.6 | 0.5 |
| **Present values** | −2,150 | 198 | 176 | 154 | 132 | 610 |
| **NET PRESENT VALUE** | **−880** | | | | | |

*Notes:*

1 It is company policy to write off research and development costs over the lifetime of the product.

2 It is company policy to use straight-line depreciation over 10 years, with a zero residual value, for plant and equipment.

3 The company is currently developing an even stronger blade which uses a very different technology. Binley thinks it will take a further five years before it is ready for production. Thus, it considers that the carbon fibre/resin project will have a life of five years, at the end of which the plant and equipment will be sold off at 25% of its original cost.

4 The necessary plant and equipment will be purchased for £2 million, financed in full by a bank loan for this amount, bearing interest at 10% a year (shown above as 'Finance overhead').

5 The working capital consists of carbon fibre and resin material stocks.

6 Only half of the indirect labour costs will be actually caused by this project. The other half is a redistribution from standard blade production.

7 Only 12.5% of the production overheads will be actually caused by this project. The remainder is a redistribution from standard blade production.

8 Binley believes that its current marketing and administration departments will be able to cope with any increased workloads. The overheads shown are a redistribution from standard blade production.

*Task:*

Redraft the above schedule, correcting any mistakes you find. Comment briefly on your results.

## Q8.3* Stobo plc

Stobo plc is a well-known national chain of high-street chemists. Its traditional markets of pharmaceuticals and beauty products are becoming increasingly competitive due to the aggressive entry of certain supermarkets. To counter this, it is considering expanding its services to the public. It plans to make more effective use of some of its retail space and storerooms by introducing some sort of personal healthcare service. A few stores have been chosen in specially selected locations for a five-year pilot scheme. They intend to choose one of the three following alternative possibilities:

| | |
|---|---|
| SR | Stress relief, including aromatherapy, massage and reflexology |
| OHC | Oral hygiene and chiropody |
| PF | Personal fitness using multigym equipment. |

Each of these would involve an initial cash outlay on appropriate equipment and the employment of specialist personnel. Market research and a financial analysis have been carried out for each alternative; an extract of the findings is shown below.

| (All figures in £000) | SR | OHC | PF |
|---|---|---|---|
| Initial cash outlay | <u>44</u> | <u>40</u> | <u>44</u> |
| Net cash flow: | | | |
| Year 1 | 16 | 8 | 12 |
| Year 2 | 14 | 10 | 12 |
| Year 3 | 12 | 12 | 12 |
| Year 4 | 10 | 14 | 12 |
| Year 5 | <u>8</u> | <u>16</u> | <u>12</u> |
| | <u><u>60</u></u> | <u><u>60</u></u> | <u><u>60</u></u> |
| Internal rate of return | 13% | 13% | 11% |

*Tasks:*

1  Calculate the payback period for each alternative.
2  Calculate the net present value of each alternative if Stobo's cost of capital is 10%.
3  Advise Stobo which of the three alternatives it should concentrate on.

## Q8.4 Fiesole Ltd

Fiesole Ltd is considering the selection of one of a pair of mutually exclusive capital investment projects. Both would involve the purchase of machinery with a life of five years. Fiesole uses the straight-line method for calculating depreciation and its cost of capital is 15% per year.

Project 1 would generate annual net cash inflows of £400,000; the machinery would cost £1,112,000 and have a scrap value of £112,000.

Project 2 would generate annual net cash inflows of £1,000,000; the machinery would cost £3,232,000 and have a scrap value of £602,000.

*Tasks:*

1 For each project, calculate:
   a) the accountancy rate of return (using the initial investment);
   b) the payback period;
   c) the net present value.
2 State which project, if any, you would recommend for acceptance.

   Give your reasons.

## Q8.5 The Adaptor Company

The Adaptor Company has recently invested £40,000 in a market research survey to determine the demand for its new product, the AdaptAll. The bill for this survey has not yet been paid. Adaptor is encouraged by the survey and now has to decide whether or not to go ahead.

The AdaptAll cost £50,000 to develop and if it goes ahead will need a further £10,000 spent on packaging development before it can be put on the market. The equipment needed to produce it will cost £180,000.

The product will only have a four-year life. In years 1 and 2, annual sales will be 30,000 units, falling to 20,000 units in year 3 and 10,000 units in year 4. The selling price will be £12 per unit.

The costs of producing the AdaptAll are as follows:

**Materials** – One unit of AdaptAll requires one unit of raw material. The company has 15,000 units of material in stock. This material originally cost £2 per unit but could be sold immediately for £3 per unit. The material could not be used by the Adaptor Company for any other of its products. If the AdaptAll project does not go ahead, the material will be sold. The current market price of material is £4 per unit.

**Labour** costs are £2 for each AdaptAll.

**Fixed overheads** – The company will need to rent a new factory unit to produce the AdaptAll, at a cost of £50,000 per annum. It does not advertise its products individually but sends out a company catalogue every two months with details of all its products. The catalogue incorporates details of all existing and new products, including the AdaptAll. The catalogue costs £1,000,000 per annum to produce and distribute, and it is company policy to allocate an equal share of this cost to each of its products. AdaptAll will therefore bear its share, amounting to £10,000 a year.

**Variable overheads** amount to £1 for each AdaptAll.

At the end of the four years the machinery will be sold for £20,000. The company uses straight-line depreciation for all its assets.

The company has a cost of capital of 10%, although projects are normally expected to achieve an IRR hurdle rate of at least 20%.

*Tasks:*

1 Calculate the net present value (NPV) of the AdaptAll project.
2 Estimate the effect on NPV of a reduction in sales volume of 10% per year, and use this to assess the % fall in volume that will reduce the NPV to zero.
3 Advise the company on whether or not it should proceed with the AdaptAll project, raising any other issues you feel should be considered in the decision. Your advice should incorporate comments on the use of the 20% hurdle rate as a decision rule.

## Q8.6 MN plc

MN plc has a rolling programme of investment decisions. One of these investment decisions is to consider mutually exclusive investments A, B and C. The following information has been produced by the investment manager.

| | Investment decision A £ | Investment decision B £ | Investment decision C £ |
|---|---|---|---|
| Initial investment | 105,000 | 187,000 | 245,000 |
| Cash inflow for A: years 1 to 3 | 48,000 | | |
| Cash inflow for B: years 1 to 6 | | 48,000 | |
| Cash inflow for C: years 1 to 9 | | . | 48,000 |
| Net present value (NPV) at 10% each year | 14,376 | 22,040 | 31,432 |
| Ranking | 3rd | 2nd | 1st |
| Internal rate of return (IRR) | 17.5% | 14% | 13% |
| Ranking | 1st | 2nd | 3rd |

*Required:*

a) Prepare a report for the management of MN plc which includes:
   - a graph showing the sensitivity of the three investments to changes in the cost of capital;
   - an explanation of the reasons for differences between NPV and IRR rankings – use investment A to illustrate the points you make;
   - a brief summary which gives MN plc's management advice on which project should be selected.

*(18 marks)*

b) One of the directors has suggested using payback to assess the investments. Explain to him the advantages and disadvantages of using payback methods over IRR and NPV. Use the figures above to illustrate your answer.

*(7 marks)*
*(Total = 25 marks)*

CIMA Intermediate: Management Accounting – Decision Making, November 2001

## Q8.7 CAF plc

CAF plc is a large multinational organization that manufactures a range of highly engineered products/components for the aircraft and vehicle industries. The directors are considering the future of one of the company's factories in the UK which manufactures product A. Product A is coming to the end of its life but another two years' production is planned. This is expected to produce a net cash inflow of £3 million next year and £2.3 million in the product's final year.

*Product AA*

CAF plc has already decided to replace product A with product AA which will be ready to go into production in two years' time. Product AA is expected to have a life of eight years. It could be made either at the UK factory under consideration or in an eastern European factory owned by CAF plc. The UK factory is located closer to the markets and therefore, if product AA is made in eastern Europe, the company will incur extra transport costs of £10 per unit. Production costs will be the same in both countries. Product AA will require additional equipment and staff will need training; this will cost £6 million at either location. 200,000 units of product AA will be made each year and each unit will generate a net cash inflow of £25 before extra transport costs. If product AA is made in the UK, the factory will be closed and sold at the end of the product's life.

*Product X*

Now, however, the directors are considering a further possibility: product X could be produced at the UK factory and product AA at the eastern European factory. Product X must be introduced in one year's time and will remain in production for three years. If it is introduced, the manufacture of product A will have to cease a year earlier than planned. If this happened, output of product A would be increased by 12.5% to maximum capacity next year, its last year, to build stock prior to the product's withdrawal. The existing staff would be transferred to product X.

The equipment needed to make product X would cost £4 million. 50,000 units of product X would be made in its first year; after that, production would rise to 75,000 units a year. Product X would earn a net cash flow of £70 per unit. After three years' production of product X, the UK factory would be closed and sold. (Product AA would not be transferred back to the factory in the UK at that stage; production would continue at the eastern European site.)

*Sale of factory*

It is expected that the UK factory could be sold for £5.5 million at any time between the beginning of year 2 and the end of year 10. If the factory is sold, CAF plc will make redundancy payments of £2 million and the sale of equipment will raise £350,000.

CAF plc's cost of capital is 5% each year.

*Required:*

a) Prepare calculations that show which of the three options is financially the best.

*(15 marks)*

b) The directors of CAF plc are unsure whether their estimates are correct. Calculate and discuss the sensitivity of your choice of option in (a) to:

i) changes in transport costs;

*(3 marks)*

ii) changes in the selling price of the factory.

*(3 marks)*

c) Briefly discuss the business issues that should be considered before relocating to another country.

*(4 marks)*

*(Total = 25 marks)*

CIMA Intermediate: Management Accounting – Decision Making, May 2002

## Review questions

1  Define the accounting rate of return (ARR).
2  Justify the exclusion of working capital from cash flows.
3  Define the payback period (PBP).
4  Explain why future cash flows should be discounted to today's values.
5  Define the net present value (NPV).
6  Define the internal rate of return (IRR).
7  Discuss the limitations of the four methods.
8  Compare NPV with IRR.
9  Criticize the discounted payback approach.
10  Describe the usefulness of sensitivity analysis in managing risk.
11  Explain why the financing decision is excluded from the investment decision.
12  Discuss the importance of relevant qualitative factors.

*The answers to all these questions can be found in the text of this chapter.*

# Present value factor table

This table is used to calculate the present value of an amount received a number of years in the future, discounted at a given percentage rate.

Example 1: at the discount rate of 5%, a sum of £1 received in 25 years' time is currently worth £0.295.

Example 2: at the discount rate of 5%, a sum of £1,000 received in 25 years' time is currently worth £295.00.

| Discount rate Years | 1% | 2% | 3% | 4% | 5% | 6% | 7% | 8% | 9% | 10% | 11% | 12% | 13% | 14% | 15% | 16% | 17% | 18% | 19% | 20% |
|---|---|---|---|---|---|---|---|---|---|---|---|---|---|---|---|---|---|---|---|---|
| 1 | 0.990 | 0.980 | 0.971 | 0.962 | 0.952 | 0.943 | 0.935 | 0.926 | 0.917 | 0.909 | 0.901 | 0.893 | 0.885 | 0.877 | 0.870 | 0.862 | 0.855 | 0.847 | 0.840 | 0.833 |
| 2 | 0.980 | 0.961 | 0.943 | 0.925 | 0.907 | 0.890 | 0.873 | 0.857 | 0.842 | 0.826 | 0.812 | 0.797 | 0.783 | 0.769 | 0.756 | 0.743 | 0.731 | 0.718 | 0.706 | 0.694 |
| 3 | 0.971 | 0.942 | 0.915 | 0.889 | 0.864 | 0.840 | 0.816 | 0.794 | 0.772 | 0.751 | 0.731 | 0.712 | 0.693 | 0.675 | 0.658 | 0.641 | 0.624 | 0.609 | 0.593 | 0.579 |
| 4 | 0.961 | 0.924 | 0.888 | 0.855 | 0.823 | 0.792 | 0.763 | 0.735 | 0.708 | 0.683 | 0.659 | 0.636 | 0.613 | 0.592 | 0.572 | 0.552 | 0.534 | 0.516 | 0.499 | 0.482 |
| 5 | 0.951 | 0.906 | 0.863 | 0.822 | 0.784 | 0.747 | 0.713 | 0.681 | 0.650 | 0.621 | 0.593 | 0.567 | 0.543 | 0.519 | 0.497 | 0.476 | 0.456 | 0.437 | 0.419 | 0.402 |
| 6 | 0.942 | 0.888 | 0.837 | 0.790 | 0.746 | 0.705 | 0.666 | 0.630 | 0.596 | 0.564 | 0.535 | 0.507 | 0.480 | 0.456 | 0.432 | 0.410 | 0.390 | 0.370 | 0.352 | 0.335 |
| 7 | 0.933 | 0.871 | 0.813 | 0.760 | 0.711 | 0.665 | 0.623 | 0.583 | 0.547 | 0.513 | 0.482 | 0.452 | 0.425 | 0.400 | 0.376 | 0.354 | 0.333 | 0.314 | 0.296 | 0.279 |
| 8 | 0.923 | 0.853 | 0.789 | 0.731 | 0.677 | 0.627 | 0.582 | 0.540 | 0.502 | 0.467 | 0.434 | 0.404 | 0.376 | 0.351 | 0.327 | 0.305 | 0.285 | 0.266 | 0.249 | 0.233 |
| 9 | 0.914 | 0.837 | 0.766 | 0.703 | 0.645 | 0.592 | 0.544 | 0.500 | 0.460 | 0.424 | 0.391 | 0.361 | 0.333 | 0.308 | 0.284 | 0.263 | 0.243 | 0.225 | 0.209 | 0.194 |
| 10 | 0.905 | 0.820 | 0.744 | 0.676 | 0.614 | 0.558 | 0.508 | 0.463 | 0.422 | 0.386 | 0.352 | 0.322 | 0.295 | 0.270 | 0.247 | 0.227 | 0.208 | 0.191 | 0.176 | 0.162 |
| 11 | 0.896 | 0.804 | 0.722 | 0.650 | 0.585 | 0.527 | 0.475 | 0.429 | 0.388 | 0.350 | 0.317 | 0.287 | 0.261 | 0.237 | 0.215 | 0.195 | 0.178 | 0.162 | 0.148 | 0.135 |
| 12 | 0.887 | 0.788 | 0.701 | 0.625 | 0.557 | 0.497 | 0.444 | 0.397 | 0.356 | 0.319 | 0.286 | 0.257 | 0.231 | 0.208 | 0.187 | 0.168 | 0.152 | 0.137 | 0.124 | 0.112 |
| 13 | 0.879 | 0.773 | 0.681 | 0.601 | 0.530 | 0.469 | 0.415 | 0.368 | 0.326 | 0.290 | 0.258 | 0.229 | 0.204 | 0.182 | 0.163 | 0.145 | 0.130 | 0.116 | 0.104 | 0.093 |
| 14 | 0.870 | 0.758 | 0.661 | 0.577 | 0.505 | 0.442 | 0.388 | 0.340 | 0.299 | 0.263 | 0.232 | 0.205 | 0.181 | 0.160 | 0.141 | 0.125 | 0.111 | 0.099 | 0.088 | 0.078 |
| 15 | 0.861 | 0.743 | 0.642 | 0.555 | 0.481 | 0.417 | 0.362 | 0.315 | 0.275 | 0.239 | 0.209 | 0.183 | 0.160 | 0.140 | 0.123 | 0.108 | 0.095 | 0.084 | 0.074 | 0.065 |
| 16 | 0.853 | 0.728 | 0.623 | 0.534 | 0.458 | 0.394 | 0.339 | 0.292 | 0.252 | 0.218 | 0.188 | 0.163 | 0.141 | 0.123 | 0.107 | 0.093 | 0.081 | 0.071 | 0.062 | 0.054 |
| 17 | 0.844 | 0.714 | 0.605 | 0.513 | 0.436 | 0.371 | 0.317 | 0.270 | 0.231 | 0.198 | 0.170 | 0.146 | 0.125 | 0.108 | 0.093 | 0.080 | 0.069 | 0.060 | 0.052 | 0.045 |
| 18 | 0.836 | 0.700 | 0.587 | 0.494 | 0.416 | 0.350 | 0.296 | 0.250 | 0.212 | 0.180 | 0.153 | 0.130 | 0.111 | 0.095 | 0.081 | 0.069 | 0.059 | 0.051 | 0.044 | 0.038 |
| 19 | 0.828 | 0.686 | 0.570 | 0.475 | 0.396 | 0.331 | 0.277 | 0.232 | 0.194 | 0.164 | 0.138 | 0.116 | 0.098 | 0.083 | 0.070 | 0.060 | 0.051 | 0.043 | 0.037 | 0.031 |
| 20 | 0.820 | 0.673 | 0.554 | 0.456 | 0.377 | 0.312 | 0.258 | 0.215 | 0.178 | 0.149 | 0.124 | 0.104 | 0.087 | 0.073 | 0.061 | 0.051 | 0.043 | 0.037 | 0.031 | 0.026 |
| 21 | 0.811 | 0.660 | 0.538 | 0.439 | 0.359 | 0.294 | 0.242 | 0.199 | 0.164 | 0.135 | 0.112 | 0.093 | 0.077 | 0.064 | 0.053 | 0.044 | 0.037 | 0.031 | 0.026 | 0.022 |
| 22 | 0.803 | 0.647 | 0.522 | 0.422 | 0.342 | 0.278 | 0.226 | 0.184 | 0.150 | 0.123 | 0.101 | 0.083 | 0.068 | 0.056 | 0.046 | 0.038 | 0.032 | 0.026 | 0.022 | 0.018 |
| 23 | 0.795 | 0.634 | 0.507 | 0.406 | 0.326 | 0.262 | 0.211 | 0.170 | 0.138 | 0.112 | 0.091 | 0.074 | 0.060 | 0.049 | 0.040 | 0.033 | 0.027 | 0.022 | 0.018 | 0.015 |
| 24 | 0.788 | 0.622 | 0.492 | 0.390 | 0.310 | 0.247 | 0.197 | 0.158 | 0.126 | 0.102 | 0.082 | 0.066 | 0.053 | 0.043 | 0.035 | 0.028 | 0.023 | 0.019 | 0.015 | 0.013 |
| 25 | 0.780 | 0.610 | 0.478 | 0.375 | 0.295 | 0.233 | 0.184 | 0.146 | 0.116 | 0.092 | 0.074 | 0.059 | 0.047 | 0.038 | 0.030 | 0.024 | 0.020 | 0.016 | 0.013 | 0.010 |

# Cumulative present value factor table (annuities)

This table is used to calculate the present value of future, consecutive, equal, annual amounts, all discounted at the same percentage rate.
Example 1: at the discount rate of 5%, a sum of £1 received each year for 25 years is currently worth £14.094.
Example 2: at the discount rate of 5%, a sum of £1,000 received each year for 25 years is currently worth £14,094.00.

| Discount rate Years | 1% | 2% | 3% | 4% | 5% | 6% | 7% | 8% | 9% | 10% | 11% | 12% | 13% | 14% | 15% | 16% | 17% | 18% | 19% | 20% |
|---|---|---|---|---|---|---|---|---|---|---|---|---|---|---|---|---|---|---|---|---|
| 1 | 0.990 | 0.980 | 0.971 | 0.962 | 0.952 | 0.943 | 0.935 | 0.926 | 0.917 | 0.909 | 0.901 | 0.893 | 0.885 | 0.877 | 0.870 | 0.862 | 0.855 | 0.847 | 0.840 | 0.833 |
| 2 | 1.970 | 1.942 | 1.913 | 1.886 | 1.859 | 1.833 | 1.808 | 1.783 | 1.759 | 1.736 | 1.713 | 1.690 | 1.668 | 1.647 | 1.626 | 1.605 | 1.585 | 1.566 | 1.547 | 1.528 |
| 3 | 2.941 | 2.884 | 2.829 | 2.775 | 2.723 | 2.673 | 2.624 | 2.577 | 2.531 | 2.487 | 2.444 | 2.402 | 2.361 | 2.322 | 2.283 | 2.246 | 2.210 | 2.174 | 2.140 | 2.106 |
| 4 | 3.902 | 3.808 | 3.717 | 3.630 | 3.546 | 3.465 | 3.387 | 3.312 | 3.240 | 3.170 | 3.102 | 3.037 | 2.974 | 2.914 | 2.855 | 2.798 | 2.743 | 2.690 | 2.639 | 2.589 |
| 5 | 4.853 | 4.713 | 4.580 | 4.452 | 4.329 | 4.212 | 4.100 | 3.993 | 3.890 | 3.791 | 3.696 | 3.605 | 3.517 | 3.433 | 3.352 | 3.274 | 3.199 | 3.127 | 3.058 | 2.991 |
| 6 | 5.795 | 5.601 | 5.417 | 5.242 | 5.076 | 4.917 | 4.767 | 4.623 | 4.486 | 4.355 | 4.231 | 4.111 | 3.998 | 3.889 | 3.784 | 3.685 | 3.589 | 3.498 | 3.410 | 3.326 |
| 7 | 6.728 | 6.472 | 6.230 | 6.002 | 5.786 | 5.582 | 5.389 | 5.206 | 5.033 | 4.868 | 4.712 | 4.564 | 4.423 | 4.288 | 4.160 | 4.039 | 3.922 | 3.812 | 3.706 | 3.605 |
| 8 | 7.652 | 7.325 | 7.020 | 6.733 | 6.463 | 6.210 | 5.971 | 5.747 | 5.535 | 5.335 | 5.146 | 4.968 | 4.799 | 4.639 | 4.487 | 4.344 | 4.207 | 4.078 | 3.954 | 3.837 |
| 9 | 8.566 | 8.162 | 7.786 | 7.435 | 7.108 | 6.802 | 6.515 | 6.247 | 5.995 | 5.759 | 5.537 | 5.328 | 5.132 | 4.946 | 4.772 | 4.607 | 4.451 | 4.303 | 4.163 | 4.031 |
| 10 | 9.471 | 8.983 | 8.530 | 8.111 | 7.722 | 7.360 | 7.024 | 6.710 | 6.418 | 6.145 | 5.889 | 5.650 | 5.426 | 5.216 | 5.019 | 4.833 | 4.659 | 4.494 | 4.339 | 4.192 |
| 11 | 10.368 | 9.787 | 9.253 | 8.760 | 8.306 | 7.887 | 7.499 | 7.139 | 6.805 | 6.495 | 6.207 | 5.938 | 5.687 | 5.453 | 5.234 | 5.029 | 4.836 | 4.656 | 4.486 | 4.327 |
| 12 | 11.255 | 10.575 | 9.954 | 9.385 | 8.863 | 8.384 | 7.943 | 7.536 | 7.161 | 6.814 | 6.492 | 6.194 | 5.918 | 5.660 | 5.421 | 5.197 | 4.988 | 4.793 | 4.611 | 4.439 |
| 13 | 12.134 | 11.348 | 10.635 | 9.986 | 9.394 | 8.853 | 8.358 | 7.904 | 7.487 | 7.103 | 6.750 | 6.424 | 6.122 | 5.842 | 5.583 | 5.342 | 5.118 | 4.910 | 4.715 | 4.533 |
| 14 | 13.004 | 12.106 | 11.296 | 10.563 | 9.899 | 9.295 | 8.745 | 8.244 | 7.786 | 7.367 | 6.982 | 6.628 | 6.302 | 6.002 | 5.724 | 5.468 | 5.229 | 5.008 | 4.802 | 4.611 |
| 15 | 13.865 | 12.849 | 11.938 | 11.118 | 10.380 | 9.712 | 9.108 | 8.559 | 8.061 | 7.606 | 7.191 | 6.811 | 6.462 | 6.142 | 5.847 | 5.575 | 5.324 | 5.092 | 4.876 | 4.675 |
| 16 | 14.718 | 13.578 | 12.561 | 11.652 | 10.838 | 10.106 | 9.447 | 8.851 | 8.313 | 7.824 | 7.379 | 6.974 | 6.604 | 6.265 | 5.954 | 5.668 | 5.405 | 5.162 | 4.938 | 4.730 |
| 17 | 15.562 | 14.292 | 13.166 | 12.166 | 11.274 | 10.477 | 9.763 | 9.122 | 8.544 | 8.022 | 7.549 | 7.120 | 6.729 | 6.373 | 6.047 | 5.749 | 5.475 | 5.222 | 4.990 | 4.775 |
| 18 | 16.398 | 14.992 | 13.754 | 12.659 | 11.690 | 10.828 | 10.059 | 9.372 | 8.756 | 8.201 | 7.702 | 7.250 | 6.840 | 6.467 | 6.128 | 5.818 | 5.534 | 5.273 | 5.033 | 4.812 |
| 19 | 17.226 | 15.678 | 14.324 | 13.134 | 12.085 | 11.158 | 10.336 | 9.604 | 8.950 | 8.365 | 7.839 | 7.366 | 6.938 | 6.550 | 6.198 | 5.877 | 5.584 | 5.316 | 5.070 | 4.843 |
| 20 | 18.046 | 16.351 | 14.877 | 13.590 | 12.462 | 11.470 | 10.594 | 9.818 | 9.129 | 8.514 | 7.963 | 7.469 | 7.025 | 6.623 | 6.259 | 5.929 | 5.628 | 5.353 | 5.101 | 4.870 |
| 21 | 18.857 | 17.011 | 15.415 | 14.029 | 12.821 | 11.764 | 10.836 | 10.017 | 9.292 | 8.649 | 8.075 | 7.562 | 7.102 | 6.687 | 6.312 | 5.973 | 5.665 | 5.384 | 5.127 | 4.891 |
| 22 | 19.660 | 17.658 | 15.937 | 14.451 | 13.163 | 12.042 | 11.061 | 10.201 | 9.442 | 8.772 | 8.176 | 7.645 | 7.170 | 6.743 | 6.359 | 6.011 | 5.696 | 5.410 | 5.149 | 4.909 |
| 23 | 20.456 | 18.292 | 16.444 | 14.857 | 13.489 | 12.303 | 11.272 | 10.371 | 9.580 | 8.883 | 8.266 | 7.718 | 7.230 | 6.792 | 6.399 | 6.044 | 5.723 | 5.432 | 5.167 | 4.925 |
| 24 | 21.243 | 18.914 | 16.936 | 15.247 | 13.799 | 12.550 | 11.469 | 10.529 | 9.707 | 8.985 | 8.348 | 7.784 | 7.283 | 6.835 | 6.434 | 6.073 | 5.746 | 5.451 | 5.182 | 4.937 |
| 25 | 22.023 | 19.523 | 17.413 | 15.622 | 14.094 | 12.783 | 11.654 | 10.675 | 9.823 | 9.077 | 8.422 | 7.843 | 7.330 | 6.873 | 6.464 | 6.097 | 5.766 | 5.467 | 5.195 | 4.948 |

# Product costs using absorption costing

## Introduction

At some stage in your career, you may find yourself responsible for controlling costs. The object of this exercise is to minimize the costs of your products, which should enable you to keep their selling prices competitive. Hopefully, the result of this will be increased numbers of items sold and good levels of profit. Cost control is an important activity for all organizations. So how is it achieved?

The first step is fundamental. In order to control a cost, you have to have an accurate measurement of it, i.e. you need to know exactly how much the cost is. Without this information your task is impossible.

Another good reason for determining product costs is that, from time to time, you may be required to make decisions concerning your products. For example, if you do not know the cost of a product when setting its selling price, you may unknowingly set the price lower than cost. The obvious consequence of this is that you will trade at a loss rather than at a profit.

A further important reason for knowing your product costs is that they are used to value the cost of sales and stock in the periodic accounts of organizations. Indeed, the ninth statement of standard accounting practice (SSAP 9) prescribes that production and stock must be valued at the 'absorption' production cost for accounts which are accessible to owners and other interested people **outside** the organization. In effect, if this is not done, the Companies Act is breached and the company is acting illegally and should expect to suffer the adverse consequences.

Note: This chapter applies to those organizations which perform work on their raw materials to convert them into finished products. It does not apply to merchanting or trading companies which buy at one price and sell for a higher price without changing the products in any way.

| Learning objectives | **Having worked through this chapter you should be able to:** |
|---|---|
| | • explain the difference between direct and indirect costs; |
| | • list the constituent parts of an absorption cost; |
| | • allocate and apportion overheads to cost centres; |
| | • calculate overhead absorption rates using a variety of different bases; |
| | • use overhead absorption rates to attach overheads to products. |

## Direct and indirect costs

(This section first appears in Chapter 1 but is repeated here for your convenience.) The absorption cost of a product is based on the assumption that costs can be analysed into their 'direct' and 'indirect' components which are defined as follows.

### Direct cost

This is expenditure which can be economically identified with, and specifically measured in respect to, a relevant cost object or product. Consider an advertising agency specializing in the production of television adverts. The cost of hiring a celebrity to appear in one such advert is a measurable direct cost of that advert. Similarly, if the company is a furniture manufacturer, the cost of materials used to make a chair and the pay of the operative assembling it are measurable direct costs of that chair.

## Indirect cost (or overhead)

This is expenditure on labour, materials or services which cannot be economically identified with a specific saleable cost unit or product. There are many, many different overheads, including supervisors' pay, depreciation of fixed assets, business rates and insurance. Remember,

$$\text{Total absorption cost} = \text{direct cost} + \text{indirect cost}$$

---

*Try the following question for yourself (answer at the end of the chapter).*

Macframe Ltd makes photograph frames and sells them to national retail chains. The following costs are incurred in connection with its manufacturing process. Decide whether each cost is direct or indirect and give your reasons.

1  Picture frame moulding.
2  Pay of assembly department's supervisor.
3  Heating oil used for cutting department.
4  Pay of employees assembling frames.
5  Dab of glue put in each corner joint of frame.

*Self-assessment question S9.1*

---

## The absorption cost of products

The way the product cost is determined in absorption costing is illustrated in Figure 9.1. This shows that as well as the total of direct costs (prime cost) the production overheads

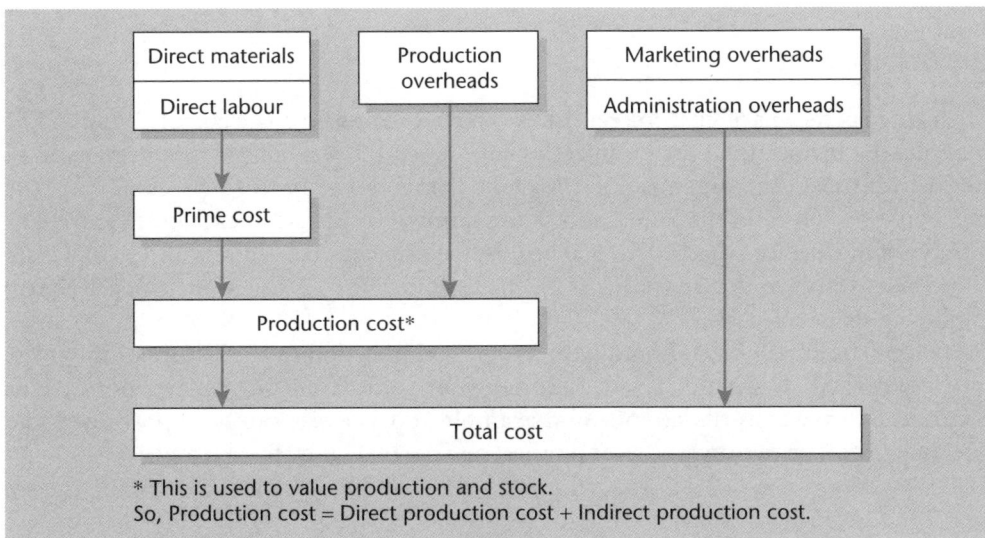

Figure 9.1  **Outline of the absorption costing system**

are included in the production cost (in accordance with SSAP 9). Stock of finished goods is unsold production so it is logical to value it at production cost. Note that all other overheads, although part of the total cost, are excluded from the production cost. These other overheads are treated as 'period' costs and are listed in the profit and loss account as deductions from the gross profit.

The objective of absorption costing is to ensure that both the direct and indirect costs of production are included in the production cost. The CIMA *Management Accounting Official Terminology* (2000) describes absorption costing as 'a method of costing that, in addition to direct costs, assigns . . . production overhead costs to cost units by means of . . . overhead absorption rates'.

Determining the direct production costs is relatively simple as the amount of them in each product can be measured. But how do we know how much of the production director's pay, depreciation of equipment, etc., to include in the cost of a specific product or service? These indirect costs cannot be measured so there has to be some other mechanism for attaching them to products. This is achieved by allocation, apportionment and absorption of overheads.

## Attaching overheads to products

### Allocation

This is the assigning of **whole** items of cost, or revenue, to a single cost unit or centre. For example, in a company making furniture, an invoice for 50 kilograms of sausage meat can be safely allocated **in total** to the canteen cost centre. However, if the company produced processed foods, further investigation would be necessary. If the sausage meat was an ingredient of one of the company's products, it would be a direct cost and not an overhead.

### Apportionment

This is the spreading of costs or revenues over two or more cost centres or units. For example, the invoice total for flu injections for all employees should be spread over all the cost centres in the organization. But how is this done? In this particular case, the total could be spread in the same ratio as the number of people in each cost centre. For example, if the invoice was £500 for 500 people, the dispatch cost centre with 12 employees would receive twice the amount (£12) apportioned to the site security cost centre employing six people (£6).

An apportionment base should have a logical connection to the nature of the overhead concerned. It should have a rationality of some kind but it need not give as 'accurate' an answer as the flu injection example above. Costs can be apportioned in a 'fair' way to cost centres by means of physical or financial units. For example:

| Costs | Basis of apportionment |
|---|---|
| Personnel department | Number of employees |
| Business rates | Area |
| Heating and lighting | Area **or** volume |
| Insurance | Net book value **or** cost of assets |
| Maintenance | Number of machines |
| Central stores | Value of production **or** number of stores issues |
| Production planning | Value of production |

## Absorption

This is the attaching of overheads to products or services by means of overhead absorption rates (OARs) using some measure of activity. For example,

£/direct labour hour      % of total labour cost
£/machine hour          % of prime cost

## Overhead attachment procedure (illustrated in Figure 9.2)

### Step 1

Allocate or apportion the overheads to the production and service cost centres (by reasonable bases of apportionment).

### Step 2

The total cost of the service centres is apportioned first to other service centres which use their service, and second to the production centres so that all overheads end up in production centres.

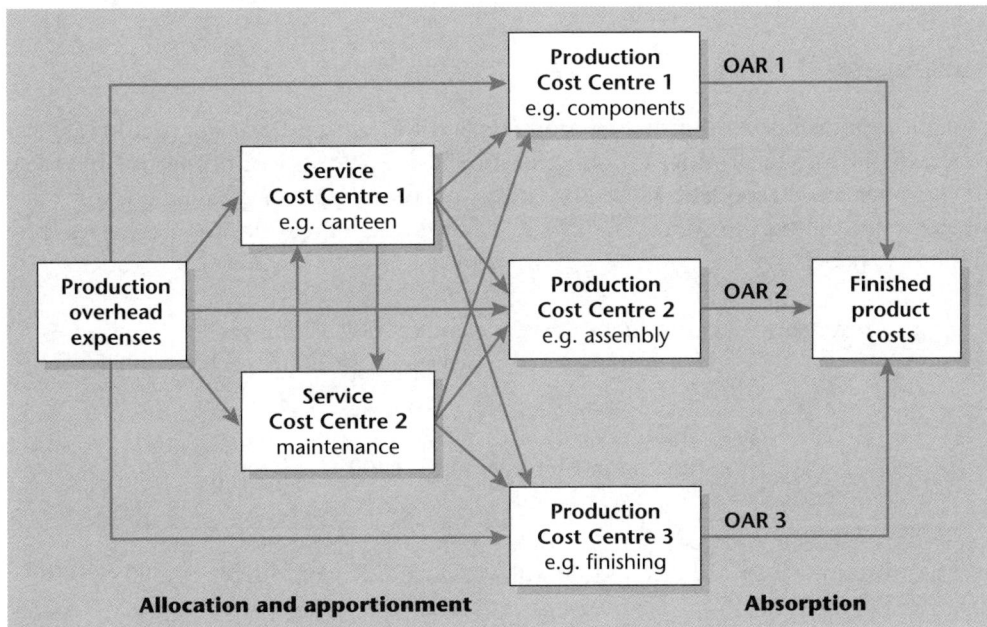

Figure 9.2 **Production overhead attachment**

## Step 3

The total amount of each production centre is divided by some measure of activity (e.g. machine hours) to derive the overhead absorption rate (OAR).

Note that production overheads are absorbed only from production cost centres or departments. All service centre overheads must be transferred into production cost centres. Where service cost centres service each other, the easiest way of dealing with this is to determine the order in which it happens and transfer the costs in that order. It may not exactly reflect reality but, unless the overheads involved are a very large proportion of total overheads, it will do the job. Remember that the nature of apportionment leads to estimates rather than perfect 'accuracy'.

## Single- and multi-product companies

To illustrate these two alternative scenarios, a fork-lift truck driver's pay of £200/week is used as an example of a production overhead.

### Single-product company

If a factory makes only one product, and makes 40 of them each week, the overhead absorption rate is

$$\text{OAR} = \frac{\text{estimated pay for period}}{\text{number of items made}} = \frac{200}{40} = \textbf{£5/unit}$$

### Multi-product company

If a factory makes several different products, a different method is needed to absorb overheads into each product on an equitable basis. One way of doing this is to use the number of direct labour hours (dlh) for each type of product. Suppose a company makes two products, G and K, each G taking 10 dlh and each K taking 25 dlh to make.

$$\text{If estimated weekly production} = 30 \times \text{product G @ 10 dlh each} = 300 \text{ dlh}$$
$$4 \times \text{product K @ 25 dlh each} = \underline{100} \text{ dlh}$$
$$\underline{\underline{400}} \text{ dlh}$$

$$\text{OAR} = \frac{\text{estimated pay for period}}{\text{output in dlh}} = \frac{\text{£200}}{400 \text{ dlh}} = \textbf{£0.50/dlh}$$

Each G would have £5 (10 dlh × £0.50/dlh) and each K would have £12.50 (25 dlh × £0.50/dlh) of the fork-lift truck driver's pay attached to it.

This approach is then extended to include all overheads. If these totalled £6,000 a week, then:

$$OAR = \frac{\text{estimated total overhead cost for period}}{\text{output in dlh}}$$

$$= \frac{£6,000}{400} = £15/\text{dlh}$$

In a machine-intensive, automated manufacturing environment, machine hours would probably be used instead of direct labour hours. (Remember that other factors may be used for OARs, such as multiples of the material cost or wages cost.)

# Overhead attachment

Example 9.1

Maykit Ltd manufactures plastic chairs. It has two production departments (Moulding and Assembly) and one service department (Canteen). The following information is taken from this year's budget:

|  | Moulding | Assembly | Canteen |
|---|---|---|---|
| Direct labour hours | 10,000 | 50,000 | – |
| Machine hours | 15,000 | 5,000 | – |
| Direct labour pay (£) | 100,000 | 200,000 | – |
| Indirect labour pay (£) | 3,030 | 5,220 | 4,000 |

**Fixed factory overheads (per year)**

|  | £ |
|---|---|
| Rent and rates | 15,000 |
| Depreciation of machinery (straight line) | 7,200 |
| Heat and light | 4,800 |
| Protective clothing | 6,500 |

**Other information**

|  | Moulding | Assembly | Canteen |
|---|---|---|---|
| Number of employees | 2 | 8 | 3 |
| Area (square metres) | 3,000 | 5,000 | 2,000 |
| Cost of machinery (£) | 60,000 | 36,000 | 24,000 |

*Tasks:*

1  Calculate the total overhead cost for each department.
2  Attach the service department overhead to the production departments.
3  Calculate the most appropriate overhead absorption rate for each production department.
4  What value of production overheads would be absorbed by a batch of chairs taking two machine hours to mould and three direct labour hours to assemble?

## Solution

**Apportionment of rent and rates (total cost £15,000):**

Most rational basis of apportionment is 'area'. Total area 10,000 sq. m.

|  | Moulding | Assembly | Canteen | Total |
|---|---|---|---|---|
| Proportion | 3,000/10,000 | 5,000/10,000 | 2,000/10,000 | 10,000/10,000 |
|  | = 3/10 | = 5/10 | = 2/10 | = 10/10 |
| Overhead cost | £15,000 | £15,000 | £15,000 | £15,000 |
| Apportionment | **£4,500** | **£7,500** | **£3,000** | **£15,000** |

**Apportionment of protective clothing (total cost £6,500):**

Most rational basis of apportionment is 'number of employees' = 13.

|  | Moulding | Assembly | Canteen | Total |
|---|---|---|---|---|
| Proportion | 2/13 | 8/13 | 3/13 | 13/13 |
| Overhead cost | £6,500 | £6,500 | £6,500 | £6,500 |
| Apportionment | **£1,000** | **£4,000** | **£1,500** | **£6,500** |

| 1 | Moulding | Assembly | Canteen | Total |
|---|---|---|---|---|
| Indirect pay | 3,030 | 5,220 | 4,000 | 12,250 |
| Rent and rates (area) | 4,500 | 7,500 | 3,000 | 15,000 |
| Depreciation of machinery (cost) | 3,600 | 2,160 | 1,440 | 7,200 |
| Heat and light (area) | 1,440 | 2,400 | 960 | 4,800 |
| Protective clothing (employees) | 1,000 | 4,000 | 1,500 | 6,500 |
| **Total overhead cost** | **13,570** | **21,280** | **10,900** | **45,750** |

| 2 | | | | |
|---|---|---|---|---|
| Canteen overheads (employees) | 2,180 | 8,720 | (10,900) | – |
| **Service overhead attachment** | **15,750** | **30,000** | – | **45,750** |

| 3 | Moulding | Assembly |
|---|---|---|
| Machine hours | 15,000 | – |
| Direct labour hours | – | 50,000 |
| **OAR** | 15,750/15,000 | 30,000/50,000 |
|  | = £1.05/mh | = £0.60/dlh |

| 4  Batch of chairs | 2 mh | 3 dlh | |
|---|---|---|---|
| **Batch overhead** | **£2.10** | **£1.80** | Total £3.90 |

*Try the following question for yourself (answer at the end of the chapter).*

Cayten Ltd produces domestic robots to perform household chores. Its manufacturing facilities consist of three production departments and two service departments. The following information is taken from the company's current annual budget.

|  | Production cost centres | | | Service cost centres | |
|---|---|---|---|---|---|
|  | PA | PB | PC | SD | SE |
| Indirect labour (£) | 80,850 | 87,750 | 36,600 | 45,900 | 42,400 |
| Direct labour (£) | 100,000 | 110,000 | 140,000 | | |
| Direct labour hours (dlh) | 90,000 | 120,000 | 90,000 | | |
| Machine hours (mh) | 80,000 | 90,000 | 75,000 | | |

| Production overheads | £ |
|---|---|
| Business rates | 8,000 |
| Electricity to run machines | 6,000 |
| Heating and lighting | 4,800 |
| Insurance for machinery ('like for like' policy) | 2,700 |
| Depreciation of machinery (straight line over 10 years) | 19,000 |
| Total | 40,500 |

The following information relates to the cost centres:

|  | PA | PB | PC | SD | SE |
|---|---|---|---|---|---|
| Number of employees | 20 | 35 | 25 | 12 | 8 |
| Original cost of machinery (£) | 60,000 | 70,000 | 40,000 | 20,000 | – |
| Machinery written-down value (£) | 20,000 | 40,000 | 25,000 | 5,000 | – |
| Machinery power rating (joules) | 350 | 450 | 250 | 150 | – |
| Floor area (square metres) | 12,000 | 8,000 | 5,000 | 3,000 | 4,000 |

*Required:*

a) Calculate the total overhead for each cost centre.
b) Reassign service cost centre overheads to production cost centres on the following basis:

|  | PA | PB | PC |
|---|---|---|---|
| SD | 30% | 50% | 20% |
| SE | 25% | 40% | 35% |

c) Calculate an overhead absorption rate for each production cost centre using the following bases:

| PA | machine hour basis |
|---|---|
| PB | direct labour hour basis |
| PC | percentage of direct pay |

d) Calculate the total of production overheads absorbed by an order requiring the following resources:

|  | PA | PB | PC |
|---|---|---|---|
| Machine hours | 7,000 | 2,100 | 900 |
| Direct labour hours | 600 | 9,800 | 2,000 |
| Direct wages (£) | 2,700 | 45,000 | 11,600 |

# Limitations of absorption costing

Absorption costing is approximately a hundred years old. It was devised for a manufacturing era whose products relied upon direct labour much more than they do today. Volume production in the twenty-first century is based on computer-controlled automatic machinery. Compare a car production line from the 1930s with one 70 years later and the difference is quite astonishing. From a distance, the old line would look something like an ant's nest, with men scurrying about doing all kinds of job. The machinery used by them consisted to a great extent of hand-tools such as screwdrivers and spanners. The latest lines are often quite devoid of people apart from the occasional machine minder. The robotic machinery being overseen probably cost millions of pounds, which causes a commensurately large amount of depreciation (a production overhead). The trend over the last 50 years has been an increase in the importance of overheads. The proportion of overheads in the total production cost is far greater now than it was in the past.

Absorption costing was not designed for the modern automated technological environment. Overhead absorption rates are a crude device for attaching overheads to products. The absorption costing system is mathematically sound and ensures that all the production overheads are absorbed by all the production. In the days when overheads were only a small part of the total costs, it did not matter that it was not particularly accurate. Today, when overheads often represent well over 50% of total costs, it does matter. Fortunately, activity-based costing now exists to fill that gap. Having said all this, many businesses still use absorption costing. Like many aspects of business life, there is a reluctance to change from a tried-and-tested system to something new. However, the pressures of competitive marketplaces will drive the change. Absorption costing will be used less and less as time passes.

## The manager's point of view (written by Nigel Burton)

No single costing system is ever likely to provide the perfect answer to a company's costing requirements. However, all systems, by providing views of the business from different angles, will produce some information of greater or lesser value to management. In certain circumstances, absorption costing may indeed prove to be the best available solution, although its inherent drawbacks will render it inappropriate for many companies.

Absorption costing is essentially simple and is therefore best suited to companies with simple processes. Consider, for example, a paint blending operation, consisting of a wide range of end products being produced on a number of standard blending machines. The blending process is simple, identical for each product, and unlikely to require significant levels of overhead. In this case, the simple spreading of overhead across all products, on a volume (i.e. number of units produced) or machine hours basis, may be perfectly adequate, particularly as overhead is likely to be a relatively small component of the overall product cost.

As companies become more complex, the simple principles of absorption costing may give a distorted picture of product costs. If our paint blender were to decide to backward-integrate into paint manufacture, and, at the same time, diversify into paint can production, its previous practice of spreading overhead simply across products would clearly no longer be valid. It would need to introduce more sophistication into its costing system to match the needs of the more complicated business. As complexity grows, the problems with absorption costing become more apparent.

Imagine a large manufacturing company, with multiple production cost centres, each producing a range of products, by differing processes, on various items of plant. The absorption costing system first requires the allocation of expenses to cost centres. Consider electricity. How many companies can accurately attribute electricity usage to individual production areas, as opposed to equipment in the maintenance department, or heating in the offices, or lighting in the factory yard? Larger companies may have it all metered, but most will need to determine some kind of apportionment. This may apply not only to utilities like electricity, but also to other items such as supervisors' salaries where the supervisors work in more than one cost centre. This is a general problem, and not necessarily specific to the absorption costing method, but it does introduce a measure of inaccuracy which absorption costing compounds.

Then the service centre costs have to be reapportioned to production cost centres. These costs, which may include maintenance, quality control, waste treatment, general factory expenses, etc., can be relatively high, so the basis of apportionment is critical. Take the cost of maintaining machinery: 'number of machines' or 'machine hours' may be a reasonable basis, but the likelihood is that Machine A is continually breaking down, while Machine B runs perfectly smoothly. Some processes place much greater physical demands on the equipment than others. For example, a very corrosive process will wear out the equipment much more quickly than a non-corrosive process. So, perhaps actual time spent on these machines by the maintenance department in the past may be a better basis for reapportioning service centre costs – though not of course if the attention given to Machine A has finally fixed a long-running problem! Similar issues surround the allocation of all service departments, and have the potential to cause major distortions.

Finally, a basis is needed to attribute production cost centres to products. These cost centres now include the reapportioned service department costs, so the numbers are significant. The use of direct labour hours as a basis is very common, but this too can be troublesome. For instance, it does not take proper account of Product C, which requires a large amount of machine time (e.g. for cooling, drying or processing) but with minimum labour input. The use of direct labour hours will seriously undercost this product. On the other hand, using machine hours may substantially undercost Product D, which requires constant supervision throughout its production cycle and consequently uses a disproportionate amount of departmental resource.

A great deal of care is required in identifying the most appropriate bases of apportionment, but a similar amount of attention needs to be given to the flaws inherent in these bases. In arriving at the final cost of our products, we have had to resort to apportionments at every level. This raises some awkward questions. First, does the final product cost contain the correct overall charge for electricity? Answer: We have no idea! Second, is the product cost correct? Answer: We do not know! Third, what level of confidence do we have in the accuracy of the product cost? Answer: We are not sure!

The key to cost apportionment is to ensure that the bases are agreed and accepted as valid by all sides. For organizational reasons, many companies divide their products into logical groupings, or product lines, each with its own business manager. Each product line has its own sales department and production cost centre, but factory management and general administration remain centralised. The apportionment of overheads will have a direct impact on the profitability of individual product lines. And in a competitive world, where demands from senior management for higher returns grow ever louder, the two options available to the business manager are either to increase sales or to cut costs. The easiest way for a business manager to increase profits at a stroke is to convince the accountant that the overhead apportionments are unfair, and that some of the costs should consequently be transferred to other product lines. In my experience, this has proved to be a recurring cause of irritation, argument and management time consumption. For this reason it is essential that the cost apportionment bases are defensible. However, this is not an easy position to achieve in a conventional absorption costing environment.

Finally, while considering the impact of overhead apportionments on the profits of individual business groups, there is another area of legitimate concern for managers. In a single-business-group company, indirect expenses, such as the factory manager's salary, security and business rates, are genuinely fixed costs which do not change as sales levels grow. In a two-business-group company, these expenses will be apportioned between the businesses on the basis of, say, direct labour hours. Similarly, non-production expenses, such as general administration, will also have an arbitrary basis, perhaps sales or volume. If the two businesses grow at the same rate, the proportion of costs assigned to each will remain the same from year to year. But suppose one business ran into trouble, and its sales halved. This would result in a switch of overhead from the failing business to the successful business. Through no fault of its own, and without any increase in the overall level of expenses, the successful business will suffer a substantial increase in its fixed costs. Is this fair? I think not. It seems to me that the failing group should suffer the full impact on profits of its reduced income.

The same situation exists if the sales of the successful business forge ahead. If its apportionment of overhead were to go up proportionately, it would be tantamount to treating fixed costs as variable! Some reapportionment may well be desirable over time, but this could perhaps best be achieved by small changes over a number of years. Business group managers, and indeed all other users of financial information, are looking for consistency, fairness and clarity. Nothing is more frustrating than finding the impact of one's sales achievements being eroded by the blind application of accounting principles, which may be mathematically correct, but logically flawed. Senior managers judge businesses on their ability to produce consistent profit growth over a number of years, and the accounting principles adopted should serve to support this objective. Absorption accounting may do the job for you, but always be aware of its limitations, and treat the results with a due measure of caution.

My purpose here is not to devalue absorption costing as a valid accounting tool, but merely to highlight the potential pitfalls. These difficulties are evident in any accounting system which requires a measure of apportionment. But absorption costing can compound the margin of error through its broadbrush approach, to the point that the information provided is so inaccurate that it risks leading management into making erroneous decisions.

*Summary*

- The absorption cost is the sum of the direct and indirect costs.
- Absorption costing treats production overheads as product costs.
- Overheads are assigned to cost centres via allocation and apportionment.
- Apportionment uses bases which are rational but not necessarily accurate.
- Service cost centre totals are reapportioned to production cost centres.
- Overheads are absorbed into production costs via overhead absorption rates.
- Overhead absorption rates are usually different for each production cost centre.
- Absorption costing is becoming less relevant to advanced technological production.

## Further reading

Atkinson, A., Banker, R., Kaplan, R. and Young, S. (2001) *Management Accounting*, 3rd edition, Prentice Hall, Harlow. See chapter 'Traditional cost management systems'.

Drury, C. and Tayles, M. (2005) 'Explicating the design of overhead absorption procedures in UK organizations', *British Accounting Review*, Vol. 37, Issue 1, March.

Johnson, H. and Kaplan, R. (1987) *Relevance Lost, the Rise and Fall of Management Accounting*, Harvard Business School Press, Boston, MA. This provides a fascinating history of traditional cost accounting and states the case for a new direction.

Lucas, M. (2000) 'The reality of product costing', *Management Accounting*, February.

Upchurch, A. (2003) *Management Accounting, Principles and Practice*, 2nd edition, Financial Times/Prentice Hall, Harlow. See chapter 'Absorption of overheads'.

Weetman, P. (2002) *Management Accounting, an Introduction*, 3rd edition, Financial Times/Prentice Hall, Harlow. See chapter 'Accounting for materials, labour and overheads'.

## Answers to self-assessment questions

### S9.1 Macframe Ltd

1 Picture frame moulding is a direct cost – identifiable and measurable.

2 Pay of assembly department's supervisor is an indirect cost – not specifically identifiable in product.

3 Heating oil used for cutting department is an indirect cost – not specifically identifiable in product.

4 Pay of employees assembling frames is a direct cost – identifiable and measurable.

5 Dab of glue put in each corner joint of frame is, in theory, a direct cost as it is identifiable and measurable. However, in practice, this would be treated as an indirect cost as the cost of measuring and valuing the dab of glue would be far greater than the value of the information gained. Accounting activities should always be carried out in a commercially sensible manner.

### S9.2  Cayten Ltd

|  | PA | PB | PC | SD | SE | Total |
|---|---|---|---|---|---|---|
| Indirect labour | 80,850 | 87,750 | 36,600 | 45,900 | 42,400 | 293,500 |
| Business rates (area) | 3,000 | 2,000 | 1,250 | 750 | 1,000 | 8,000 |
| Power (joules) | 1,750 | 2,250 | 1,250 | 750 | – | 6,000 |
| Light and heat (area) | 1,800 | 1,200 | 750 | 450 | 600 | 4,800 |
| Insurance (WDV) | 600 | 1,200 | 750 | 150 | – | 2,700 |
| Depreciation (orig. cost) | 6,000 | 7,000 | 4,000 | 2,000 | – | 19,000 |
| Sub-totals | **94,000** | **101,400** | **44,600** | **50,000** | **44,000** | **334,000** |
| Adj. SD | 15,000 | 25,000 | 10,000 | (50,000) | – | – |
| Adj. SE | 11,000 | 17,600 | 15,400 | – | (44,000) | – |
| Total overheads | **120,000** | **144,000** | **70,000** | – | – | **334,000** |

| PA | PB | PC |
|---|---|---|
| $\dfrac{120,000}{80,000}$ | $\dfrac{144,000}{120,000}$ | $\dfrac{70,000}{140,000} \times 100$ |
| $= £1.50/\text{mh} \times 7,000 \text{ mh}$ | $= £1.20/\text{dlh} \times 9,800 \text{ dlh}$ | $= 50\% \text{ of direct labour cost} \times £11,600$ |
| $= £10,500$ | $= £11,760$ | $= £5,800$ |

**Total absorbed = £28,060** (10,500 + 11,760 + 5,800)

| CASE STUDY | Travelsound |
|---|---|

Travelsound Ltd was started five years ago by three friends who had just graduated from university. They had lived in the same house for two years and were all passionate about music. During their many late-night discussions they talked much about music and, as two of them were electronic engineers, they often discussed the latest equipment for sound reproduction and how it could be improved. The third person had a joint degree in finance and marketing and saw the opportunity for a business venture involving state-of-the-art sound systems.

They started out in a garage at the home of one of their parents and soon found that ideas alone were not enough to run a business. Most of their work in the first two years consisted of upgrading and constructing personal computers and laptops. Through their contacts, they also gained from their old university several one-off contracts concerned with upgrading software and hardware (a perennial occupation for universities). At this stage in their development they employed five assistants.

Towards the end of their second year they bid for a contract to manufacture small quantities of an experimental mobile phone for a European electronics group. To their delight, they were awarded the contract and have produced several versions of this phone over the last few years. By the start of their fourth year they had 27 employees. In that year they gained the right to produce, under licence, mini-disc players for a Japanese company. This contract has gone very well despite the very tight profit margins involved. In fact, the sales price was slightly below the original estimated absorption production cost. They decided to go ahead on the assumption that they would be able to reduce their costs as they gained experience of manufacturing this product. (Although they were not aware of it, this was the reason they were awarded the contract, as other more established firms had turned it down as they believed it was not profitable.) Fortunately, Travelsound had made the right decision and this work currently has a positive net profit margin of around 3%.

However, in recent months, relations with this company have deteriorated, mainly due to a change in the pound/yen exchange rate. In fact, the three Travelsound directors believe that their licence will be revoked at the next renewal date in two months' time unless they are willing to trade in euros instead of UK pounds. They are apprehensive about this as the euro/pound exchange rate has been falling consistently for over a year. It would not be difficult for this work to be moved to mainland Europe where a significant amount of overcapacity exists.

Throughout their five-year history, they maintained an active interest in the improvement of sound systems. What little spare time the two engineering directors had was spent on developing a new method of sound reproduction. They are now at the point where, with the help of an agent, they have applied for a patent on their invention. They currently employ 88 people and made a net profit last year of £45,000. Their annual production rate is now 10,000 phones and 38,000 mini-disc players. They wish to grow in size and profitability but are unsure of how to do it. As an organisation, they are now approaching a crisis point. One alternative is for them to replace the mini-disc player production with a new product using their own new technology.

This product has been named the MNP, short for Music Net Phone. It combines a WAP phone with their own miniaturized sound reproduction system which is also able to play mini-discs. They have tentatively approached the European electronics group for whom they manufacture mobile phones, with a view to its marketing the MNP. The European company is very interested but needs some indication of price before taking the idea any further.

Travelsound now needs to cost the MNP using the absorption costing system. The directors decide to do this using next year's budget, which is based on continuing production of mobile phones and mini-disc players. They assume the overheads will be the same if the mini-disc player is replaced by the MNP. The following information comes from this budget.

Travelsound has three production cost centres and three service cost centres. The former are electronic components, plastic cases and assembly. The latter are the canteen, material stores and quality control. The quality controllers inspect goods received into the stores as well as the output of each production cost centre. The assembly shop uses the manufactured components, plastic cases and items from material stores to produce the finished items ready for delivery. The estimated cost for one MNP is £12.20 for materials and £9.80 for direct labour. A single materials store serves only the three production departments. The canteen is situated just inside the factory entrance.

The production overheads are shown as:

|  | £ |
|---|---|
| Factory rent and rates | 150,000 |
| Depreciation of machinery (straight line) | 89,250 |
| Machinery insurance (like-for-like basis) | 53,000 |
| Cost centre managers' pay | 80,000 |
| Materials storekeepers' pay | 19,125 |
| Quality controllers' pay | 32,000 |
| Heating and lighting | 14,000 |
| Canteen costs | 29,920 |
| Factory security | 25,000 |
|  | 492,295 |

The managers of the components, cases and assembly cost centres earn salaries of £30,000, £25,000 and £25,000 respectively. Factory security is provided by a local firm patrolling inside and outside the factory at intervals throughout the night. One quality controller earns £20,000 p.a., spending 30% of his time on stores materials and 70% on components. The other quality controller, who works part time, earns £12,000 p.a. and divides her time equally between cases and assembly. Any quality control costs other than pay should be considered proportional to the amounts of quality controllers' pay incurred by each cost centre. All employees eat in the canteen.

Other information:

| | Canteen | Stores | Quality control | Assembly | Cases | Components |
|---|---|---|---|---|---|---|
| Area (sq. metres) | 550 | 600 | 25 | 1,900 | 795 | 1,130 |
| Employees | 6 | 3 | 2 | 36 | 12 | 29 |
| Number of stores issues | – | – | – | 51,000 | 10,200 | 2,550 |
| Direct labour hours | – | – | – | 120,309 | 33,410 | 99,281 |
| Direct labour cost (£) | – | – | – | 611,404 | 148,596 | 450,000 |
| Machine hours | – | – | – | 100,973 | 51,236 | 453,791 |
| Machinery cost (£000) | – | – | – | 340 | 510 | 1,700 |
| Machinery WDV (£000) | – | – | – | 250 | 350 | 1,400 |

*Tasks:*

1 Calculate the overhead absorption rate (OAR) for each production cost centre. The bases used should be direct labour hours for assembly, machine hours for components and a percentage of direct labour cost for cases.

(40 marks)

2 Calculate the absorption production cost for one MNP if a batch of 100 MNPs takes 9,000 machine hours in the component shop, 667 direct labour hours in the assembly shop and has a direct labour cost of £1,100 in the case shop.

(10 marks)

3 **On no more than two sides of A4,** discuss the situation and advise Travelsound Ltd on its future course of action.

(50 marks)
(Total 100 marks)

## Questions

An asterisk * on a question number indicates that the answer is given at the end of the book. Answers to the other questions are given in the Lecturer's Guide.

### Q9.1* Lewington Ltd

Lewington Ltd makes a variety of kitchen fittings and equipment. It uses a three-stage process involving cutting, assembly and finishing. The following figures are extracted from its budget for the current year:

|  | Cutting | Assembly | Finishing |
|---|---|---|---|
| Production overheads (£000) | 1,600 | 2,000 | 1,400 |
| Machine hours | 40,000 | 25,000 | 14,000 |
| Direct labour hours | 10,000 | 40,000 | 20,000 |

The company uses an absorption costing system for calculating its costs.

A batch of 300 'DX' workstations has just been produced using £3,300 of materials, £4,500 of direct labour and the following quantities of time:

|  | Cutting | Assembly | Finishing |
|---|---|---|---|
| Machine hours | 50 | 25 | 10 |
| Direct labour hours | 20 | 45 | 20 |

*Tasks:*

Calculate the unit production cost and the total production cost of the batch of 'DX' workstations using the following three alternative bases:

1  All overhead absorption rates are calculated on a machine hour basis.
2  All overhead absorption rates are calculated on a direct labour hour basis.
3  The Cutting overhead absorption rate is calculated on a machine hour basis but the Assembly and Finishing rates are calculated on a direct labour hour basis.

Comment on your findings.

## Q9.2* Graham and Sara

Graham and Sara are partners in a clothes manufacturing firm. Graham manages menswear and Sara controls ladies fashions. They have just received last year's accounts which are summarized below.

| | Mens £000 | Womens £000 | Total £000 |
|---|---|---|---|
| Materials | 78 | 26 | 104 |
| Direct labour | 18 | 30 | 48 |
| Variable overheads | 4 | 4 | 8 |
| Variable production cost | 100 | 60 | 160 |
| Fixed production overheads | 10 | 6 | 16 |
| Total production cost | 110 | 66 | 176 |
| Increase in stock | 2 | 1 | 3 |
| Cost of sales | 108 | 65 | 173 |
| Marketing overheads | 8 | 4 | 12 |
| Administration overheads | 4 | 4 | 8 |
| Total cost | 120 | 73 | 193 |
| Sales revenue | 118 | 78 | 196 |
| Profit/(loss) | (2) | 5 | 3 |

Naturally, Sara is pleased with the results but Graham is not so happy. On questioning their accountant he finds that the fixed production overheads have been apportioned on the basis of variable production costs. He wonders how the results would change if they were apportioned on different bases.

*Tasks:*

1  Redraft the above statement if the fixed production overheads were apportioned on the basis of:
   a)  direct material cost;
   b)  direct labour cost;
   c)  variable overhead cost.
2  What do your answers tell you about the absorption costing system?

## Q9.3* Stellar Showers

Stellar Showers Co. Ltd manufactures domestic electric showers. It moulds its own plastic casings but buys in the other components from a variety of sources. In addition to 54 production operatives, it employs two quality controllers and four stores operatives. The company's production facility consists of three production cost centres (moulding, assembly and packaging) and two service cost centres (quality control and material stores). Quality control inspects work in the three production centres as well as goods received into the materials store. The store services the three production centres only.

Stellar's annual budget lists the following production overheads:

|  | £ |
|---|---|
| Electricity to run machines and equipment | 40,000 |
| Material stores running costs | 80,000 |
| Heating (oil-fired boiler) | 13,000 |
| Lighting | 4,000 |
| Supervision | 65,000 |
| Production manager | 35,000 |
| Business rates | 16,000 |
| Fire insurance | 10,000 |
| Quality controllers' pay | 30,000 |
| Depreciation (straight line) | 18,000 |

The supervision overhead consists of an assembly supervisor (£25,000 p.a.), a moulding supervisor (£20,000 p.a.) and a packaging supervisor (£20,000 p.a.).

The following information is also available:

|  | Moulding | Assembly | Packaging | Quality control | Stores |
|---|---|---|---|---|---|
| Head count | 12 | 36 | 6 | 2 | 4 |
| Machine wattage | 4,500 | 1,200 | 300 | – | – |
| Stores issue notes | 2,000 | 14,500 | 3,500 | – | – |
| Area (sq. metres) | 300 | 800 | 500 | 50 | 350 |
| Volume (cu. metres) | 1,200 | 2,100 | 2,000 | 100 | 1,100 |
| Fixed assets – cost | 50,000 | 40,000 | 20,000 | – | 10,000 |
| Fixed assets – WDV | 22,000 | 18,000 | 9,000 | – | 1,000 |
| Added value (£000) | 800 | 5,700 | 500 | – | – |
| Machine hours | 34,967 | 24,080 | 3,944 | – | – |
| Direct labour hours | 20,016 | 63,986 | 10,998 | – | – |
| Quality control (hrs/wk) | 6 | 18 | 6 | 4 | 6 |

*Tasks:*

1  Calculate the most appropriate overhead absorption rate for each production cost centre.
2  Calculate the unit production cost of an SS40T shower if a batch of 800 uses the following resources:

| Direct materials | £16,000 |
|---|---|
| Direct labour | £8,800 |
| Machine hours in moulding | 1,500 |
| Machine hours in assembly | 900 |
| Machine hours in packaging | 170 |
| Direct labour hours in moulding | 1,200 |
| Direct labour hours in assembly | 3,500 |
| Direct labour hours in packaging | 1,000 |

## Q9.4  Medley Ltd

Medley Ltd makes dishwashers. There are three production departments: machining, assembly and finishing; and two service departments: maintenance and stores.

Costs are as follows:

|  | Machining | Assembly | Finishing | Maintenance | Stores |
|---|---|---|---|---|---|
| Direct materials | £240,000 | £160,000 | £40,000 | – | – |
| Direct wages | £200,000 | £150,000 | £100,000 | – | – |
| Indirect wages | £9,000 | £8,000 | £8,000 | £11,000 | £8,000 |
| Indirect materials | – | – | – | £4,000 | – |

Factory overheads are:

| | |
|---|---|
| Business rates | £30,000 |
| Factory manager's salary | £30,000 |
| Heat and light | £20,000 |
| Depreciation of machinery | £40,000 |

Production statistics are:

|  | Machining | Assembly | Finishing | Maintenance | Stores |
|---|---|---|---|---|---|
| Personnel | 20 | 15 | 10 | 4 | 1 |
| Area (sq. metres) | 8,000 | 4,000 | 4,000 | 1,000 | 3,000 |
| Kilowatt hours (000) | 100 | 40 | 30 | 10 | 20 |
| Machinery cost (£000) | 100 | 50 | 50 | – | – |
| Direct labour hours (000) | 40 | 30 | 20 | – | – |
| Machine maintenance hours | 850 | 600 | 200 | – | – |
| Material issue notes | 1,800 | 1,000 | 500 | 100 | – |

*Tasks:*

1  Calculate an overhead absorption rate based on direct labour hours for each production department.
2  A standard dishwasher uses 4, 3 and 2 direct labour hours in machining, assembly and finishing respectively. If all direct labour is paid £5.00/hour and the cost of materials for one dishwasher is £48, what is the production cost of one dishwasher?

## Q9.5  Ugur Ltd

Ugur Ltd makes three different types of marine compass: Type A, Type D and Type N. Each compass passes through two production departments: assembling and finishing. Ugur absorbs its overheads on the basis of direct labour hours.

Production overheads for the next 12 months are expected to be

|  | £ |
|---|---|
| Factory power | 80,000 |
| Depreciation | 60,000 |
| Fixed asset insurance | 3,600 |
| Supervisors' pay | 40,000 |
| Factory rent | 70,400 |
|  | 254,000 |

The following information for next year is also available:

|  | Assembly | Finishing |
|---|---|---|
| Number of direct operatives | 30 | 20 |
| Floor space (sq. metres) | 16,000 | 9,000 |
| Book value of fixed assets (£000) | 60 | 30 |
| Machine hours | 15,000 | 30,000 |
| Power (kilowatt hours used) | 30,000 | 20,000 |
| Supervisory staff | 1 | 1 |

Times per product (hours):

|  | Assembly | | Finishing | |
|---|---|---|---|---|
|  | Labour | Machine | Labour | Machine |
| Type A | 1.0 | 0.75 | 0.75 | 0.50 |
| Type D | 1.5 | 0.50 | 1.00 | 0.40 |
| Type N | 2.5 | 0.25 | 1.50 | 0.30 |

Each operative is expected to work 36 hours a week for 46 weeks a year.

*Tasks:*

1 Calculate the total overheads for each department.
2 Calculate the overhead absorption rate for each department (to three decimal places).
3 Calculate the overhead cost attached to each type of compass.
4 Recalculate your answers to tasks 2 and 3 if overheads were absorbed on a machine hour basis and comment on your findings.

## Review questions

1 Explain the difference between direct and indirect costs.
2 List the constituent parts of an absorption cost.
3 Explain the difference between allocating and apportioning overheads to cost centres.
4 Explain the different bases that can be used by overhead absorption rates.

*The answers to all these questions can be found in the text of this chapter.*

# Comparison of profits under absorption and variable costing

## Introduction

Because the annual profit figure is such an important piece of information ('the bottom line') it is advisable to monitor profit throughout the year. Knowing how things are progressing enables you to take corrective action when necessary and avoid unpleasant surprises at the financial year-end. Most organizations do this by producing monthly or quarterly management accounts.

As the idea is to help meet the annual profit target, it seems sensible to use the same rules by which the annual profit is calculated. One of these is that fixed production overheads must be treated as **product** costs and not as **period** costs (see SSAP 9). In other words, annual accounts intended for public circulation are based on absorption costing. This works well for monthly accounting, provided that the pattern of trading is reasonably predictable over the year. However, for businesses whose trading pattern is difficult to predict, profits may be distorted. This also applies, to some extent, to seasonal businesses.

Distortions of profit do not help these businesses to monitor their real performance. So, it is not surprising that they sometimes decide to use a system which avoids this distortion. This alternative approach uses variable (also known as marginal) costing. Variable costing treats fixed production overheads as period costs rather than product costs. This is opposite to absorption costing used in the audited accounts **and will produce a different profit total**. However, at the end of the year, the internally reported 'variable profits' can be reconciled to the externally reported 'absorption profits'.

These two alternative financial models can be applied to a single set of commercial transactions, resulting in two different profit figures. This chapter shows you how to calculate the profits for a trading period in two different ways and how to reconcile them to each other.

**Learning objectives**

**Having worked through this chapter you should be able to:**

- explain the difference between a product cost and a period cost;
- use budget information to predetermine an overhead absorption rate;
- explain why predetermined OARs are used in preference to actual OARs;
- explain how under- and overabsorption of overheads occur;
- adjust profit and loss accounts for under- and overabsorption of overheads;
- calculate 'absorption' profit and 'variable' profit;
- reconcile 'absorption' profit to 'variable' profit;
- explain the limitations of both systems.

## Treatment of fixed production overheads

As stated above, absorption costing treats fixed production overheads as production costs and variable costing treats them as period costs. A production cost is the total direct cost (prime cost) plus absorbed production overhead (see Figure 11.1a). A period cost is one which relates to a time period rather than to the output of products or services (see Figure 11.1b).

## Predetermination of overhead absorption rates

The previous chapter showed how overhead absorption rates (OARs) are calculated via allocation, apportionment and an appropriate choice of the base. These OARs are used to determine the production cost and stock valuations for period-end accounts. The

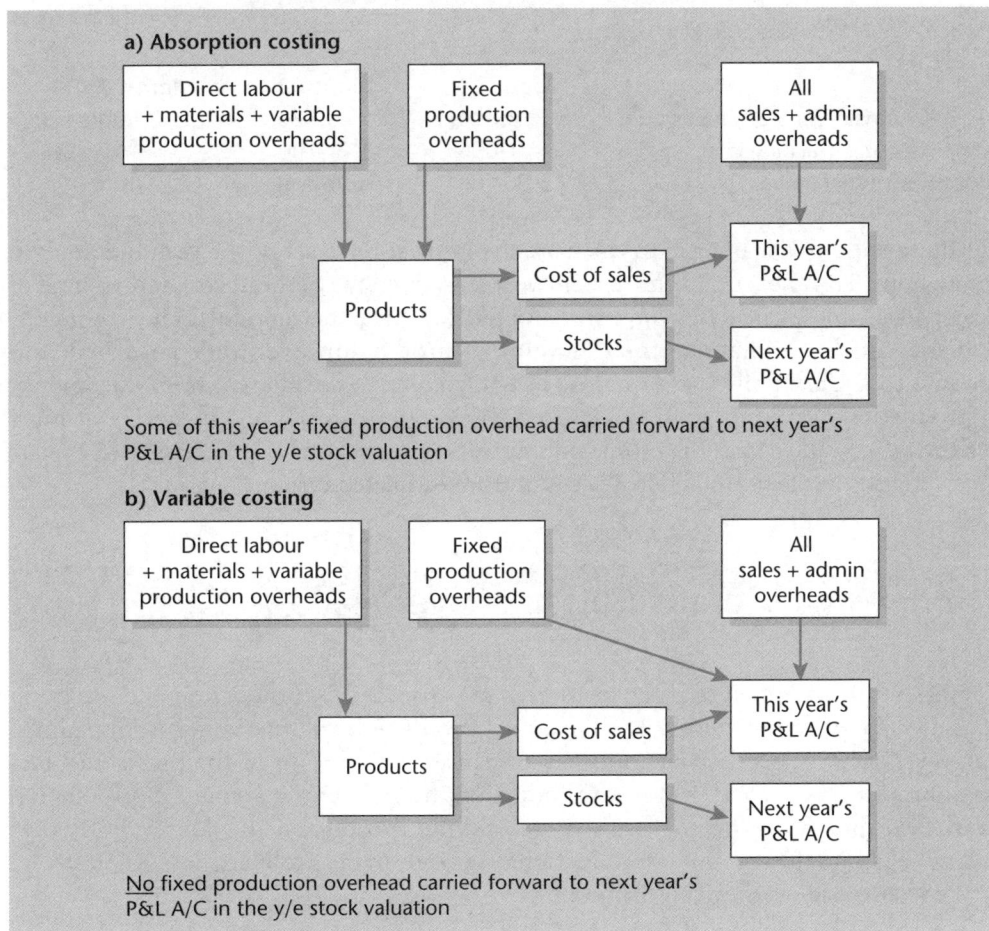

Figure 11.1  **Tracing overhead costs to the profit and loss account**

practice is to use predetermined rates rather than actual rates. After all, the actual rates could only be determined after the period has ended, so selling prices could not be based on actual absorption costs. One possibility is to use the actual rates of the last-but-one month so that rates were fairly up to date. However, this would cause monthly fluctuations in the product cost figures (see below). If selling prices were based directly on costs, they would be changed every month. Prices going up and down at each month-end would give the impression of instability and incompetence in the eyes of customers.

Annual basis:

> Estimated annual fixed production overheads = £36,000
> Estimated annual volume of activity = 12,000 machine hours
> Overhead absorption rate = £36,000/12,000 mh = £3.00/mh

Monthly basis:

|  | **Month 1** | **Month 2** | **Month 3** |
|---|---|---|---|
| Actual overheads incurred | 3,000 | 3,520 | 2,500 |
| Actual machine hours | 1,000 | 1,100 | 909 |
| Monthly actual OAR | £3.00/mh | £3.20/mh | £2.75/mh |

For these reasons it is normal to calculate the OAR at the start of the year and apply it throughout. This means that the current year's production overhead cost and volume of activity used in the calculation are estimates rather than actual amounts. The major consequence of this is that the total amount of production overheads absorbed into product costs during the year is almost certainly going to be different from the amount of production overheads actually incurred. However, the profit and loss account must use the actual rather than the estimated figure. So an adjustment is necessary to change the overheads in the profit and loss account from estimated to actual amounts.

## Under- and overabsorption of overheads

The first thing to note is that the overheads are absorbed by production and are in no way affected by sales volumes. Thus, if actual production volumes differ from planned volumes, either too much or too little overhead will end up in the profit and loss account. (The greater the volume of production, the greater the amount of production overheads absorbed.) If actual sales volumes differ from planned volumes, no change will be caused to the amount of production overheads in the profit and loss account.

Predetermined overhead absorption rate:

> Estimated annual fixed production overheads = £500,000
> Estimated annual volume of activity = 100,000 direct labour hours
> Overhead absorption rate = £500,000/100,000 dlh = £5.00/dlh

If either of these estimates is incorrect (as they almost certainly will be) the amount of production overheads in the profit and loss account will be inaccurate.

i)  Actual annual fixed production overheads = £525,000
    Actual annual volume of activity = 100,000 direct labour hours
    Overhead absorbed by production = 100,000 × £5.00
    $$= £500,000$$
    **Underabsorption** of overheads = £25,000 (500,000 − 525,000)
    **Unless this adjustment is made, profit will be overstated by £25,000.**

ii) Actual annual fixed production overheads = £500,000
    Actual annual volume of activity = 112,000 direct labour hours
    Overhead absorbed by production = 112,000 × £5.00
    $$= £560,000$$
    **Overabsorption** of overheads = £60,000 (560,000 − 500,000)
    **Unless this adjustment is made, profit will be understated by £60,000.**

# The Jinasy Umbrella Company

Example 11.1

The Jinasy Umbrella Company makes an up-market all-purpose umbrella. It produces management accounts for internal use on a quarterly basis. Its fixed production overheads are budgeted at £20,000 a quarter (£80,000 a year) and its marketing and administration overheads at £19,000 a quarter (£76,000 a year). The production plan is for 4,000 umbrellas each quarter (16,000 a year). The selling price is £20 and the variable cost of each umbrella is £8. There are 1,000 umbrellas in stock at the start of the first quarter. The actual results for last year, expressed in numbers of umbrellas, are as follows:

|  | Q1 | Q2 | Q3 | Q4 | Year |
|---|---|---|---|---|---|
| Sales | 4,000 | 2,000 | 1,000 | 8,000 | 15,000 |
| Production | 4,000 | 4,000 | 3,000 | 6,000 | 17,000 |

Calculate the quarterly and annual profits (i) using absorption costing and (ii) using variable costing. (iii) Explain why the profits differ. (Assume the total of actual overheads incurred was as forecast.)

Under both systems, stocks of finished umbrellas are valued at production cost.

| Production cost: | Variable costing<br>variable cost<br>£8 | Absorption costing<br>variable cost + fixed production overhead<br>£8 + (£20,000/4,000 units) = £13 |
|---|---|---|

Physical stock changes (number of umbrellas):

|  | Q1 | Q2 | Q3 | Q4 | Year |
|---|---|---|---|---|---|
| Opening stock | 1,000 | 1,000 | 3,000 | 5,000 | 1,000 |
| Actual production | 4,000 | 4,000 | 3,000 | 6,000 | 17,000 |
| Actual sales | 4,000 | 2,000 | 1,000 | 8,000 | 15,000 |
| Closing stock | 1,000 | 3,000 | 5,000 | 3,000 | 3,000 |

i) Absorption costing (£000)

|  | Q1 | Q2 | Q3 | Q4 | Year |
|---|---|---|---|---|---|
| Opening stock | 13 | 13 | 39 | 65 | 13 |
| Add: Production cost | 52 | 52 | 39 | 78 | 221 |
| Less: Closing stock | (13) | (39) | (65) | (39) | (39) |
| Under-/(over)absorption | – | – | 5 | (10) | (5) |
| Cost of sales | 52 | 26 | 18 | 94 | 190 |
| Sales revenue | 80 | 40 | 20 | 160 | 300 |
| Gross profit | 28 | 14 | 2 | 66 | 110 |
| Non-production overhead | 19 | 19 | 19 | 19 | 76 |
| Net profit | 9 | (5) | (17) | 47 | 34 |

ii)  Variable costing (£000)

|  | Q1 | Q2 | Q3 | Q4 | Year |
|---|---|---|---|---|---|
| Opening stock | 8 | 8 | 24 | 40 | 8 |
| Add: Production cost | 32 | 32 | 24 | 48 | 136 |
| Less: Closing stock | (8) | (24) | (40) | (24) | (24) |
| Cost of sales | 32 | 16 | 8 | 64 | 120 |
| Sales revenue | 80 | 40 | 20 | 160 | 300 |
| Gross profit | 48 | 24 | 12 | 96 | 180 |
| Production overheads | 20 | 20 | 20 | 20 | 80 |
| Non-production overhead | 19 | 19 | 19 | 19 | 76 |
| Total fixed overheads | 39 | 39 | 39 | 39 | 156 |
| Net profit | 9 | (15) | (27) | 57 | 24 |

iii)  Reconciliation of profits (£000)

|  | Q1 | Q2 | Q3 | Q4 | Year |
|---|---|---|---|---|---|
| Absorption net profit | 9 | (5) | (17) | 47 | 34 |
| Variable net profit | 9 | (15) | (27) | 57 | 24 |
| **Difference** | – | **10** | **10** | **(10)** | **10** |
| Increase in stock (units) | – | 2,000 | 2,000 | (2,000) | 2,000 |
| **Production overheads in stock increase (@ £5 a unit)** | – | **10** | **(10)** | **10** | **10** |

### Annual results

The total of fixed production overheads charged in this year's 'variable' profit and loss account is the total incurred in this period, £80,000 (see Figure 11.1b). Variable profits are £24,000.

On the other hand, the net effect in this year's 'absorption' profit and loss account is that the amount of production overheads is reduced by £10,000, as follows:

> **Production overheads brought forward from last year (in opening stock) into this year = 1,000 units @£5 = £5,000**
> **Production overheads carried forward from this year (in closing stock) into next year = 3,000 units @£5 = £15,000**

The total of fixed production overheads charged in this year's 'absorption' profit and loss account is £70,000 (see Figure 11.2a).

The net reduction of £10,000 in production overhead charged will increase net profit from £24,000 (variable) to £34,000 (absorption).

Similar explanations and profit reconciliations can be made for each quarter (the process is summarized by Figure 11.3 below).

a) Less overheads are brought into the current year in the value of opening stock than are carried forward into next year in the value of closing stock

Fixed production overhead incurred in current year = £80,000

Opening stock =
1,000 units
@£5 = £5,000

Closing stock =
3,000 units
@£5 = £15,000

Fixed production overhead charged
in current year's profit & loss account
£5,000 + £80,000 − £15,000 = £70,000

b) More overheads are brought into the current year in the value of opening stock than are carried forward into next year in the value of closing stock

Fixed production overhead incurred in current year = £80,000

Opening stock =
3,000 units
@£5 = £15,000

Closing stock =
1,500 units
@£5 = £7,500

Fixed production overhead charged
in current year's profit & loss account
£15,000 + £80,000 − £7,500 = £87,500

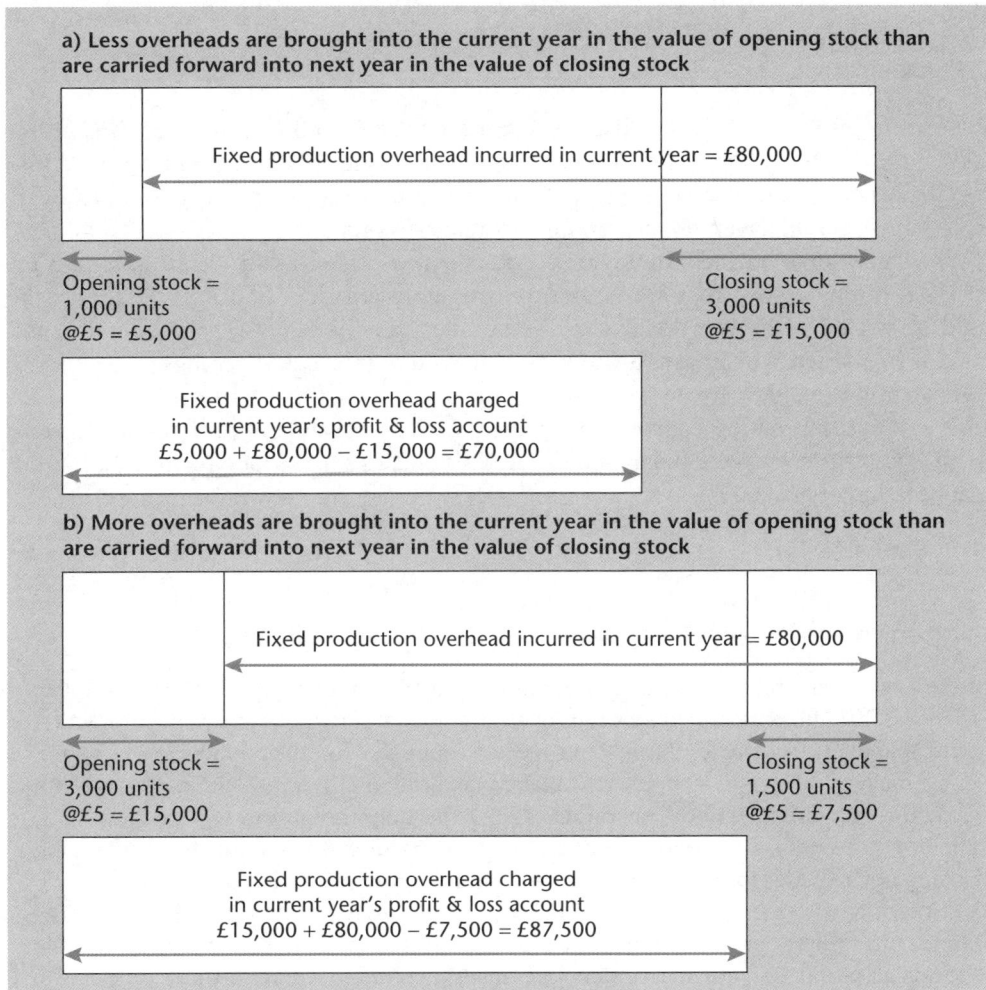

Figure 11.2 **Production overhead charged to the profit and loss account**

*Try the following question for yourself (answer at the end of the chapter).*

Hiphoptop Ltd produces music CDs. Internal management accounts are drawn up on a quarterly basis. The company plans to produce and sell 12,000 CDs each quarter and have a stock of 2,000 CDs at the start of quarter 1. The selling price is £6 and the variable cost of each CD is £1. The production and non-production overheads are estimated at £24,000 and £30,000 a quarter respectively. The actual results for the year, expressed in numbers of CDs, are as follows:

| | Q1 | Q2 | Q3 | Q4 | Year |
|---|---|---|---|---|---|
| Sales | 9,000 | 16,000 | 6,000 | 13,000 | 44,000 |
| Production | 14,000 | 12,000 | 11,000 | 10,000 | 47,000 |

Calculate the quarterly and annual profits (a) using absorption costing and (b) using variable costing. (c) Explain why the profits differ. (Assume the total of actual overheads incurred was as forecast.)

## Limitations

Absorption profits make the realistic assumption that, in most years, most businesses will sell most of their stock. However, if the stock of finished goods brought forward into the current year proves to be unsaleable, absorption costing will bring forward overheads which should have been charged in last year's accounts.

When a seasonal business builds up stocks for next period's sales (as in quarter 3 for Jinasy) it can be argued that absorption profits avoid creating 'fictitious' losses for the build-up period. However, the greater the number of periods between production and sales (as in quarter 2 for Jinasy) the less convincing this argument becomes.

Absorption profits may be increased by producing extra units in order to increase stock levels rather than to enable sales. In certain cases, absorption profits may decrease even though the sales volume has increased. This creates some scope for the short-term manipulation of profits.

### The manager's point of view (written by Nigel Burton)

Senior managers tend to be busy people who, if not financially orientated, want to spend as little time as possible poring over interim statements of account. In practice, most managers will already have a gut feeling about the current period's performance, or alternatively will have been able to obtain an indication of it from data readily available from the computer. Periodic accounts often serve only to confirm what they already know. Once again, the need for consistency, clarity and accuracy in the accounts is paramount, in order to minimize any time-consuming queries arising from them.

Unfortunately, the application of SSAP 9 principles may not help in this regard. The standard requires, quite rightly, that the valuation of products in inventory should include all production costs, including overheads incurred in bringing those products to their current condition. As this is the required basis for year-end accounts, it is logical that the same basis should be used for interim internal accounts. We have already seen how absorption costing and variable costing can generate significantly different profits, and the last thing management want to see is a substantial year-end adjustment as the inventory valuation is switched from one accounting basis to the other.

But the adoption of SSAP 9 in interim accounts can itself lead to confusion, particularly for periods as short as one month. Absorption costing may be precisely correct in principle, in that it matches costs to sales by transferring cost into inventory when the product goes into stock, and releasing it back into the profit and loss account when the product is sold. (This results directly from the application of the accruals or matching-up principle of accounting.) But this also means that a simple increase or decrease in the level of production will have a direct impact on the level of profitability, which is especially significant in view of that all-important yardstick, the budget.

In the vast majority of companies, the budget is the principal tool used by management to set targets and monitor performance. The budget predicts not only the levels of sales and costs, but also how these will be phased throughout the year. Unless there are special factors to consider, such as seasonal influences, it would be a reasonable assumption that, in any given month, production will match sales volumes, thus keeping inventory at a constant level. But life rarely turns out as planned. In some months, sales will exceed production, causing a net transfer of period cost out of inventory into the profit and loss account. Conversely, when production exceeds sales, there will be a net transfer of period costs out of the profit and loss account into inventory. And in an exceptionally poor sales month, profitability can apparently be improved by increasing production levels and transferring more overhead into inventory; this is probably the exact reverse of management's correct course of action, which should be to reduce production to reflect the lower demand. I stress that there is nothing wrong with these period cost transfers, which accurately reflect the movements of stock in and out of inventory. But when these movements take place against a fixed overhead monthly budget, the value of this budget as a control tool is diminished.

A solution to this problem is to use a combination of absorption and variable costing. The production overheads are fixed costs, incurred over a period of time, and it would be fair to argue that they should be written off in that period, in exactly the same way as non-production expenses such as marketing or administration. The marginal income generated by sales in the period (i.e. sales less variable costs) can then be set against the total period costs relating to that period, producing an easily understandable 'variable' net profit. The requirements of SSAP 9 can be satisfied by a 'below-the-line' adjustment, transferring the necessary amount to or from inventory, before striking a final reportable 'absorption' net profit for the month. In this way, we are structuring a set of figures which achieve all our objectives: they provide data of sufficient clarity for management purposes, meet the requirements of the standard, and also highlight separately the 'accountants' adjustment', which need concern only those who understand it!

The following example relates to the Jinasy Umbrella Company illustration earlier in the chapter.

Variable costing statement:

|  | Q1 | Q2 | Q3 | Q4 | Year |
|---|---|---|---|---|---|
| Opening stock | 8 | 8 | 24 | 40 | 8 |
| Add: Production cost | 32 | 32 | 24 | 48 | 136 |
| Less: Closing stock | (8) | (24) | (40) | (24) | (24) |
| Cost of sales | 32 | 16 | 8 | 64 | 120 |
| Sales revenue | 80 | 40 | 20 | 160 | 300 |
| Gross profit | 48 | 24 | 12 | 96 | 180 |
| Production overheads | 20 | 20 | 20 | 20 | 80 |
| Non-production overhead | 19 | 19 | 19 | 19 | 76 |
| Total fixed overheads | 39 | 39 | 39 | 39 | 156 |
| Variable net profit | 9 | (15) | (27) | 57 | 24 |
| 'Below-the-line' adjustment: | | | | | |
| Adjustment for production overheads in stock increase | – | 10 | 10 | (10) | 10 |
| Absorption net profit | 9 | (5) | (17) | 47 | 34 |

This monthly adjustment for period cost in inventory needs to be carefully monitored. In most systems, the use of budgeted expenditure and budgeted levels of production to calculate overhead recovery rates will be quite adequate for the purposes of internal monthly accounts. But for final audited accounts, the period costs held in inventory must be valued on actual experience, rather than budget. In a normal year, where expenditure and production run close to budget, the adjustment to actual may be minimal, but, in an abnormal year, the company could be in for a nasty surprise. For instance, if the year had been going extremely well, and production had exceeded budget by 25%, the actual overhead rate would be recalculated at 20% (= 25/125) below the budgeted rate. If, at the same time, the production overhead budget was underspent by 10%, the overhead rate would decrease in total by nearly 30%. This would result in a substantial reduction of total overhead in inventory, and a corresponding increase in the charge written off in the profit and loss account. The accountants would not be popular unless this situation had been foreseen and communicated to management well in advance!

In practice, auditors will accept that the valuation of period costs in inventory should be based on normal levels of production and normal levels of expenditure. This will eliminate, or at least diminish, the impact of unusual or non-recurring events. For instance, if production had been halved in the last quarter as a result of serious plant failure, it would be wrong to double the period costs on products manufactured in that period as the situation was abnormal. The impact of such an event should be a write-off of any unrecovered overhead directly to the profit and loss account. Acceptable norms can perhaps best be established by looking at production and expenditure over a longer period of time. In my company, we used the average production over the last three years, which had the effect of smoothing out any anomalies, without discarding them altogether. We also used actual expenditure in the year, as this was usually fairly constant. The most appropriate method of establishing norms is a matter for agreement with the auditors, and may vary from company to company. But, once agreed, it will be expected that this method will be applied consistently in future years.

There is one final point to mention in connection with period cost in inventory. As one moves across a year-end into a new financial year, the overhead absorption rates will be recalculated on the basis of the new budget. Unless your system is such that you can identify the overhead costs attributed to each individual item held in stock, you will have to revalue the whole of the inventory on to the new cost basis. Otherwise you will have some products going into stock at last year's cost, and coming out at this year's higher cost, resulting in an undervaluation of inventory. The revaluation of the period cost in inventory will produce a surplus (or deficit) which will have to be written off to future profit and loss accounts, complicating the period cost in inventory adjustment line still further. In my view, therefore, it is highly desirable to isolate the adjustment below the line, where it will not confuse non-financial users of the interim accounts.

*Summary*

- The choice between absorption profits and variable profits only exists for internal reporting (external reporting must use absorption profits).
- No change in stock level (P = S): absorption profit equals variable profit.
- Increase in stock level (P > S): absorption profit greater than variable profit.
- Decrease in stock level (P < S): absorption profit less than variable profit. (where P = production volume and S = sales volume)
- The more volatile the business, the more suitable are variable profits for internal reporting.
- The less volatile the business, the more suitable are absorption profits for internal reporting.

The process by which the absorption profit is reconciled to the variable profit is shown in Figure 11.3.

It is important to note that variable profit depends solely on sales volume, but absorption profit depends on both sales volume **and** production volume. The implication of this is that absorption profits can be improved by increasing production! The effect of increasing production is to increase closing stock. Remember that absorption profits are the ones that must be used for external reporting. In the short term, profits can be manipulated upwards by this strategy **without breaking any accounting rules**. In the medium/long term, high stock levels due to excess production will return to normal and the effect on profit will be downwards.

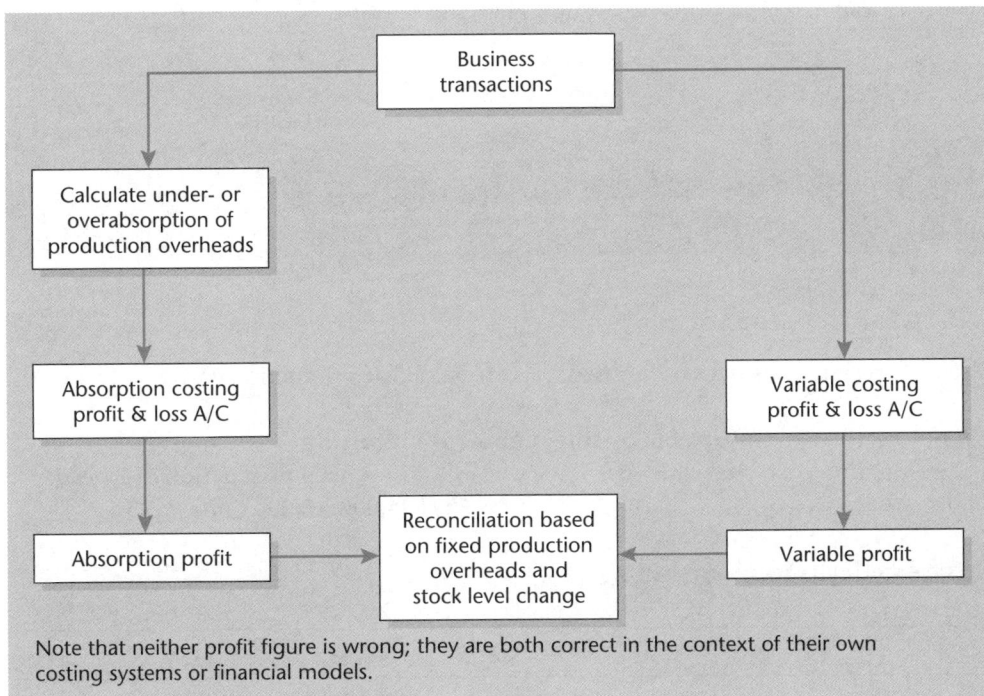

Note that neither profit figure is wrong; they are both correct in the context of their own costing systems or financial models.

Figure 11.3 **Reconciliation of absorption and variable costing profits**

## *Further reading*

Baxter, W. T. (2005) 'Direct versus absorption costing: a comment', *Accounting, Business & Financial History*, Vol. 15, Issue 1, March.

Dugdale, D. and Jones, T. C. (2003) 'Battles in the costing war: UK debates, 1950–75', *Accounting, Business & Financial History*, Vol. 13, Issue 3, November.

Dugdale, D. and Jones, T. C. (2005) 'Direct versus absorption costing: a reply', *Accounting, Business & Financial History*, Vol. 15, Issue 1, March.

Horngren, C., Bhimani, A., Datar, S. and Foster, G. (2002) *Management and Cost Accounting*, 2nd edition, Prentice Hall Europe, Harlow. See Chapter 7, 'Income effects of alternative stock costing methods'.

Upchurch, A. (2003) *Management Accounting, Principles and Practice*, 2nd edition, Financial Times/Prentice Hall, Harlow. See chapter 'Absorption costing and marginal costing'.

Weetman, P. (2002) *Management Accounting, An Introduction*, 3rd edition, Financial Times/Prentice Hall, Harlow. See chapter 'Profit, performance and current developments', section on 'Absorption costing and variable costing'.

## *Answer to self-assessment question*

### 1. S11.1 Hiphoptop Ltd

Under both systems, stocks of finished CDs are valued at production cost.

| | Variable costing | Absorption costing |
|---|---|---|
| Production cost: | variable cost | variable cost + fixed production overhead |
| | £1 | £1 + £2 (£24,000/12,000 units) = £3 |

Physical stock changes (number of CDs):

| | Q1 | Q2 | Q3 | Q4 | Year |
|---|---|---|---|---|---|
| Opening stock | 2,000 | 7,000 | 3,000 | 8,000 | 2,000 |
| Actual production | 14,000 | 12,000 | 11,000 | 10,000 | 47,000 |
| Actual sales | 9,000 | 16,000 | 6,000 | 13,000 | 44,000 |
| Closing stock | 7,000 | 3,000 | 8,000 | 5,000 | 5,000 |

Under-/(over)absorption of overheads:

|                                      | Q1      | Q2      | Q3      | Q4      | Year    |
|--------------------------------------|---------|---------|---------|---------|---------|
| Planned production level             | 12,000  | 12,000  | 12,000  | 12,000  | 48,000  |
| Actual production level              | 14,000  | 12,000  | 11,000  | 10,000  | 47,000  |
| Under-/(over)absorption in units     | (2,000) | 0       | 1,000   | 2,000   | 1,000   |
| Under-/(over)absorption @ £2/unit    | (4,000) | 0       | 2,000   | 4,000   | 2,000   |

a)  Absorption costing (£000)

|                          | Q1       | Q2      | Q3       | Q4       | Year     |
|--------------------------|----------|---------|----------|----------|----------|
| Opening stock            | 6,000    | 21,000  | 9,000    | 24,000   | 6,000    |
| Add: Production cost     | 42,000   | 36,000  | 33,000   | 30,000   | 141,000  |
| Less: Closing stock      | (21,000) | (9,000) | (24,000) | (15,000) | (15,000) |
| Under-/(over)absorption  | (4,000)  | –       | 2,000    | 4,000    | 2,000    |
| Cost of sales            | 23,000   | 48,000  | 20,000   | 43,000   | 134,000  |
| Sales revenue            | 54,000   | 96,000  | 36,000   | 78,000   | 264,000  |
| Gross profit             | 31,000   | 48,000  | 16,000   | 35,000   | 130,000  |
| Non-production overhead  | 30,000   | 30,000  | 30,000   | 30,000   | 120,000  |
| Net profit               | 1,000    | 18,000  | (14,000) | 5,000    | 10,000   |

b)  Variable costing (£000)

|                          | Q1      | Q2      | Q3       | Q4      | Year     |
|--------------------------|---------|---------|----------|---------|----------|
| Opening stock            | 2,000   | 7,000   | 3,000    | 8,000   | 2,000    |
| Add: Production cost      | 14,000  | 12,000  | 11,000   | 10,000  | 47,000   |
| Less: Closing stock      | (7,000) | (3,000) | (8,000)  | (5,000) | (5,000)  |
| Cost of sales            | 9,000   | 16,000  | 6,000    | 13,000  | 44,000   |
| Sales revenue            | 54,000  | 96,000  | 36,000   | 78,000  | 264,000  |
| Gross profit             | 45,000  | 80,000  | 30,000   | 65,000  | 220,000  |
| Production overheads     | 24,000  | 24,000  | 24,000   | 24,000  | 96,000   |
| Non-production overhead  | 30,000  | 30,000  | 30,000   | 30,000  | 120,000  |
| Total fixed overheads    | 54,000  | 54,000  | 54,000   | 54,000  | 216,000  |
| Net profit               | (9,000) | 26,000  | (24,000) | 11,000  | 4,000    |

c)  Reconciliation of profits (£000)

|                                              | Q1      | Q2      | Q3       | Q4      | Year    |
|----------------------------------------------|---------|---------|----------|---------|---------|
| Absorption net profit                        | 1,000   | 18,000  | (14,000) | 5,000   | 10,000  |
| Variable net profit                          | (9,000) | 26,000  | (24,000) | 11,000  | 4,000   |
| **Difference**                               | **10,000** | **(8,000)** | **10,000** | **(6,000)** | **6,000** |
| Increase in stock (units)                    | 5,000   | (4,000) | 5,000    | (3,000) | 3,000   |
| **Production overheads in stock**            |         |         |          |         |         |
| **increase (@ £2 a unit)**                   | **10,000** | **(8,000)** | **10,000** | **(6,000)** | **6,000** |

# CASE STUDY

# Canco Foods

Canco Foods specializes in the preparation and canning of three different products: new potatoes, mincemeat and ham. The company has three divisions (one for each product), each with its own production and sales facilities. It so happens that each division has the same cost structure for manufacturing and marketing its product. For each division, the annual fixed production overheads are £200,000 and the annual fixed administration and sales overheads combined are £80,000. These are incurred evenly over the year. Also, each division has an annual budget of 20,000 cases bought and sold; all stocks are zero on 1 January. The selling price is £50 a case and the delivery costs are £2.50 a case.

The preparation and canning of new potatoes starts in February and is completed by mid-June, but sales are evenly spread over the year. Mincemeat is produced at the same rate throughout the year but sales only occur between September and December, mainly for the Christmas mince pie market. Ham is produced and sold at a steady rate with very little variation from month to month. (Stocks of all three products are zero at 1 January.)

| Costs per case for each product are: | £ |
|---|---|
| Direct material and direct labour | 21 |
| Variable production overhead | 3 |
| Variable production cost | 24 |

Activity (number of cases):

| | | January–June | July–December | Year |
|---|---|---|---|---|
| Potatoes | Production | 20,000 | – | 20,000 |
| | Sales | 10,000 | 10,000 | 20,000 |
| Mincemeat | Production | 10,000 | 10,000 | 20,000 |
| | Sales | – | 20,000 | 20,000 |
| Ham | Production | 10,000 | 10,000 | 20,000 |
| | Sales | 10,000 | 10,000 | 20,000 |

*Tasks:*

1 Prepare summarized profit and loss accounts for each half-year and the whole year for each division using absorption costing.

(25 marks)

2 Prepare summarized profit and loss accounts for each half-year and the whole year for each division using variable costing.

(25 marks)

3 Reconcile the profits for each of the three periods by producing a statement involving a 'below-the-line' adjustment as shown in 'The manager's point of view' section of this chapter.

(10 marks)

4 **On no more than two sides of A4,** discuss the use of absorption costing and variable costing for the periodic, internal reporting of profitability.

(40 marks)
(Total 100 marks)

## Questions

An asterisk * on a question number indicates that the answer is given at the end of the book. Answers to the other questions are given in the Lecturer's Guide.

### Q11.1* Clamco

Clamco makes car clamps. The following information is from January's budget, which is based on a production volume of 6,000 clamps:

|  | £ |
|---|---|
| Opening stock of clamps | 0 |
| Fixed manufacturing overhead | 72,000 |
| Variable manufacturing overhead | 18,000 |
| Selling and administrative expenses (all fixed) | 25,000 |
| Direct labour | 120,000 |
| Direct materials used | 90,000 |
| Selling price (per unit) | 64 |

The actual production and sales volumes for the first three months of the year were as follows:

| Number of clamps: | January | February | March | Quarter |
|---|---|---|---|---|
| Production level | 6,000 | 5,000 | 7,000 | 18,000 |
| Sales | 4,000 | 6,000 | 7,000 | 17,000 |

Actual variable costs per unit and total fixed overheads incurred were exactly as forecast.

*Tasks:*

1. Calculate the profit for each month and for the quarter
   a) using absorption costing;
   b) using variable costing.
2. Reconcile the profits for each month and for the quarter. Explain why they differ.

### Q11.2* Rivilin plc

Rivilin is a uni-product firm with the following budgeted amounts:

|  | £ |
|---|---|
| Unit selling price | 60 |
| Unit variable cost | 20 |
| Fixed production overhead per month | 9,600 |

Rivilin's planned level of production is 800 units a month. However, actual activity was as follows:

|                | April | May | June |
|----------------|-------|-----|------|
| Units produced | 800   | 750 | 820  |
| Units sold     | 800   | 700 | 850  |

There was no opening stock at 1 April.

The actual fixed production overhead incurred was accurately predicted at £9,600 a month.

The non-production fixed overheads are £10,000 a month.

*Required:*

1 A variable costing profit statement for each month.
2 An absorption costing profit statement for each month.
3 An explanation of the difference in profits between the two statements.

## Q11.3* The Valley Fireworks Corporation

The Valley Fireworks Corporation manufactures special firework display kits to sell to responsible organizations only. The following information is taken from its budget for 2002:

**Opening stock of kits = closing stock of kits = 20 kits**
**Annual production = annual sales = 1,200 kits**

|                                 | £ per unit | £ per year |
|---------------------------------|------------|------------|
| Selling price                   | 500        |            |
| Direct materials                | 60         |            |
| Direct labour                   | 180        |            |
| Variable production overhead    | 10         |            |
| Variable distribution overhead  | 20         |            |
| Fixed production overhead       |            | 96,000     |
| Fixed non-production overhead   |            | 144,000    |

The actual production and sales volumes for 2002 were:

| (Units)       | Q1  | Q2  | Q3  | Q4  | Year  |
|---------------|-----|-----|-----|-----|-------|
| Opening stock | 10  | 290 | 550 | 690 | 10    |
| Production    | 300 | 300 | 200 | 300 | 1,100 |
| Sales         | 20  | 40  | 60  | 980 | 1,100 |
| Closing stock | 290 | 550 | 690 | 10  | 10    |

The variable costs per kit and the total fixed costs were as forecast.

*Tasks:*

1 Prepare profit statements for each of the four quarters and the year,
   a) using absorption costing;
   b) using variable costing.

2 Reconcile the two profit figures for each quarter and prepare a summary statement in the following format:

|  | Qtr 1 | Qtr 2 | Qtr 3 | Qtr 4 | Year |
|---|---|---|---|---|---|
| Net profit using variable costing | | | | | |
| Adjustment for fixed production | | | | | |
|   overheads in stock change | | | | | |
| Net profit using absorption costing | | | | | |

3 Explain how both sets of profit figures can be useful to the management of The Valley Fireworks Corporation.

## Q11.4 Nalpo Ltd

Nalpo Ltd manufactures and markets a small table that attaches to ladders. The following annual budget is based on 75,000 units made and sold:

|  | Per unit | | Total | |
|---|---|---|---|---|
|  | £ | £ | £ | £ |
| Sales revenue | | 5 | | 375,000 |
| Sales | | | | |
| Production cost of sales: | | | | |
|   Variable | 3 | | 225,000 | |
|   Fixed | 1 | | 75,000 | |
|  | | 4 | | 300,000 |
| Gross profit | | 1 | | 75,000 |
| Selling and admin costs: | | | | |
|   Variable (10% of sales) | 0.5 | | 37,500 | |
|   Fixed | | | 30,000 | |
|  | | | | 67,500 |
|  | | | | 7,500 |

Actual production figures for 2001 and 2002 were as follows:

|  | 2001 | 2002 |
|---|---|---|
| Opening stock | 0 | 15,000 |
| Production | 85,000 | 70,000 |
| Sales | 70,000 | 80,000 |
| Closing stock | 15,000 | 5,000 |

*Tasks:*

You are required to:

1 Prepare budgeted statements of profitability on the basis of:
   a) absorption costing;
   b) variable costing.
2 Reconcile the difference in profit in the two statements produced for part 1.

## Q11.5 Brafire Ltd

Brafire manufactures small, portable electric fires. It has operated an absorption costing system since it started many years ago. However, the new managing director (who is studying part time for an MBA) has recently learned of the possibility of using a variable costing system as an alternative to the company's usual approach. He decides to investigate this further by applying both systems to next quarter's budget (shown below). To provide a good comparison, the output will be shown at both a constant level and a fluctuating one.

    Budget for quarter 3 (units):

|  | July | August | September | Total |
|---|---|---|---|---|
| Sales volume | 3,000 | 3,000 | 6,500 | 12,500 |
| Constant output | 4,500 | 4,500 | 4,500 | 13,500 |
| Fluctuating output | 4,500 | 4,000 | 5,000 | 13,500 |

There will be 500 fires in stock on 1 July. The selling price is £30 and the cost structure is as follows:

|  | £/unit |
|---|---|
| Direct materials | 4.00 |
| Direct labour | 1.50 |
| Variable production overheads | 0.50 |
| Fixed production overheads* | 6.00 |
| Fixed marketing overheads* | 4.00 |
| Total cost | 16.00 |

     * These figures are based on a constant monthly production level of 4,500 fires.

*Tasks:*

Produce a budgeted profit and loss account for internal management reporting using the following four bases:

1 Absorption costing and constant output levels.
2 Variable costing and constant output levels.
3 Absorption costing and fluctuating output levels.
4 Variable costing and fluctuating output levels.

Comment on your findings.

## Q11.6 P Ltd

P Ltd manufactures a specialist photocopier. Increased competition from a new manufacturer has meant that P Ltd has been operating below full capacity for the last two years.

The *budgeted information* for the last two years was as follows:

|  | Year 1 | Year 2 |
|---|---|---|
| Annual sales demand (units) | 70 | 70 |
| Annual production (units) | 70 | 70 |
| Selling price (for each photocopier) | £50,000 | £50,000 |
| Direct costs (for each photocopier) | £20,000 | £20,000 |
| Variable production overheads (for each photocopier) | £11,000 | £12,000 |
| Fixed production overheads | £525,000 | £525,000 |

*Actual results* for the last two years were as follows:

|  | Year 1 | Year 2 |
|---|---|---|
| Annual sales demand (units) | 30 | 60 |
| Annual production (units) | 40 | 60 |
| Selling price (for each photocopier) | £50,000 | £50,000 |
| Direct costs (for each photocopier) | £20,000 | £20,000 |
| Variable production overheads (for each photocopier) | £11,000 | £12,000 |
| Fixed production overheads | £500,000 | £530,000 |

There was no opening stock at the beginning of year 1.

*Required:*

(a) Prepare the actual profit and loss statements for each of the two years using:
- absorption costing;
- marginal costing

(14 marks)

(b) Calculate the budgeted breakeven point in units and the budgeted margin of safety as a percentage of sales for year 1 and then again for year 2.

(6 marks)

(c) Explain how the change in cost structure (as detailed in the budgeted information) has affected the values you have calculated in your answer to part (b).

(5 marks)

(Total = 25 marks)

CIMA Foundation: Management Accounting Fundamentals, November 2001

## Review questions

1 Explain the difference between a product cost and a period cost.
2 Explain why predetermined OARs are used in preference to actual OARs.
3 Explain how under- and overabsorption of overheads occurs.
4 Explain how to reconcile 'absorption' profit to 'variable' profit.
5 Discuss the limitations of both systems.

*The answers to all these questions can be found in the text of this chapter.*

## Introduction

One of the most important decisions that any business has to make is what prices to charge for its products and services. If it sets them too low, its profits may be insufficient for it to survive in the medium/long term. If it sets them too high, sales may be lost to competitors and profits may again be insufficient. In short, if it gets its pricing wrong it may go out of business!

So, how are selling prices calculated? Is there one best method? Or does it depend on each firm's business environment?

This chapter looks at three different points of view before attempting to integrate them into a practical pricing strategy. The viewpoints examined are those of the economist, the accountant and the marketer.

**Having worked through this chapter you should be able to:**

- explain the economist's pricing model;
- explain the accountant's pricing model;
- compare these by the use of charts;
- describe the optimum level of output;
- describe price elasticity of demand;
- explain cost-plus pricing;
- discuss the dangers of cost-plus pricing;
- discuss the marketer's view of pricing;
- explain the pricing strategies of skimming and penetration;
- explain target pricing as an integrating mechanism;
- discuss the limitations of pricing theory.

# The economist's view

## Optimum level of output

This is a simplified explanation based on economic theory. It is presented as an extension to breakeven analysis, which is covered in Chapter 5. Towards the end of that chapter there is a section detailing the limiting assumptions of that technique. Two of these limiting assumptions are that neither the variable cost, nor the selling price, change when the volume of output changes. This means that the total revenue and total cost lines on breakeven charts are **straight** and the total revenue line goes through the origin. The relationships between revenue, costs and volume are assumed to be linear (see Figures 12.1 and 12.3).

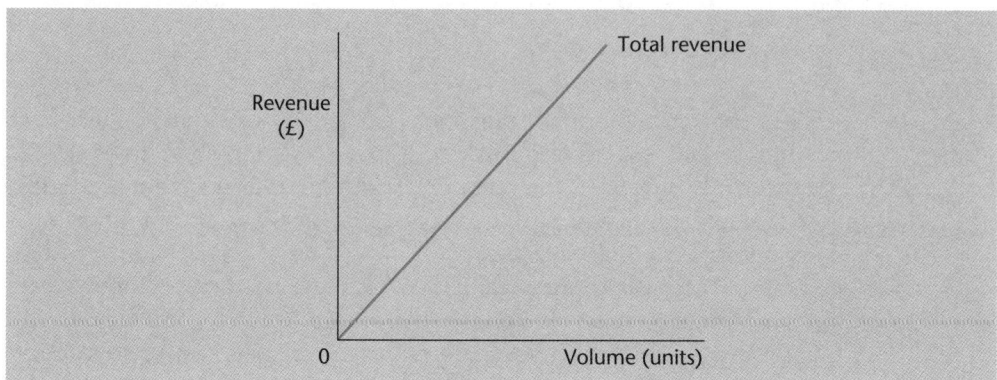

Figure 12.1 **Unit selling price remains the same for all volumes**

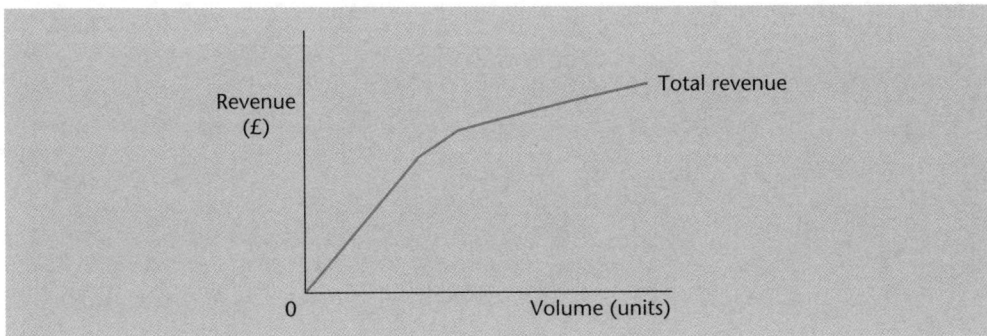

Figure 12.2  **Unit selling price reduces as volume increases**

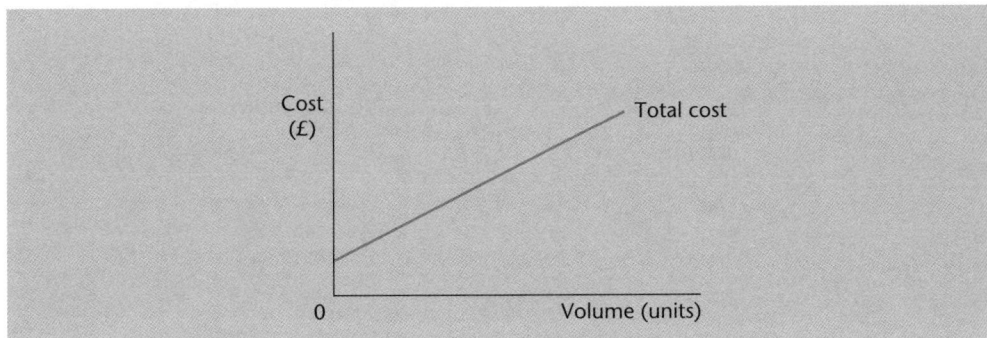

Figure 12.3  **Variable cost per unit remains the same for all volumes**

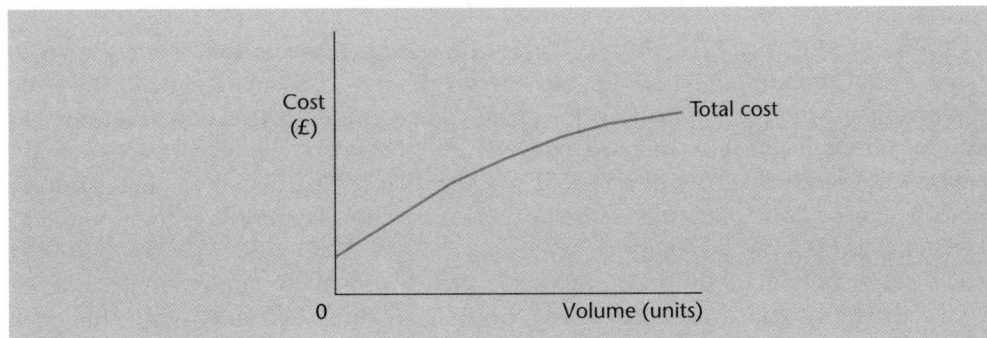

Figure 12.4  **Variable cost per unit reduces as volume increases**

However, economists recognise that these simple relationships do not hold for all volumes of activity. Beyond a certain point, in order to increase the volume of sales, the unit selling price has to be reduced (see Figure 12.2). Economists quantify this relationship between price and quantity through the concept of price elasticity of demand. Also, beyond a certain point, the cost per unit should reduce due to bulk-buying discounts and other economies of scale (see Figure 12.4). The effect of these different assumptions is that the lines on the charts are now curved (at least beyond a certain volume).

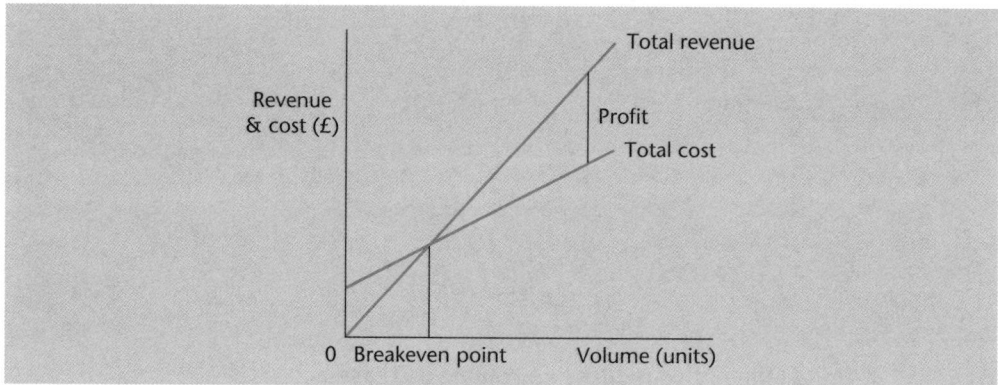

Figure 12.5 **Profit continues to increase with volume**

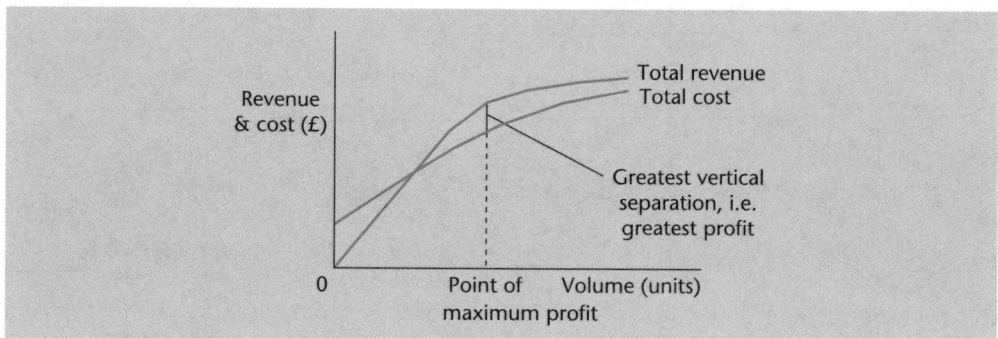

Figure 12.6 **Profit is maximized at one level of activity**

Combining Figures 12.1 and 12.3 gives the familiar breakeven chart shown in Figure 12.5. Combining Figures 12.2 and 12.4 gives the economist's view of the same relationships. Note the implication for profit. The accountant's version (Figure 12.5) shows profit continuing to increase with volume. However, the economist's version (Figure 12.6) shows that maximum profit is achieved at one particular volume of output and, therefore, at one particular selling price. This is how economic theory is used to determine the optimum selling price.

The major problem with this approach is that it is virtually impossible to forecast accurately the revenue and cost curves shown in Figures 12.2 and 12.4. This is an unavoidable consequence of attempting to predict the future in an ever-changing world. Economic analysis can be insightful when applied to historical data but it is of limited practical use for setting future prices. Fortunately, there are several alternative ways of approaching this problem, as you will see later in this chapter.

**Self-assessment question S12.1**

*Try the following question for yourself (answer at the end of the chapter).*

Here is a profit–volume chart as used by accountants. Redraw it, showing how it might look from an economist's point of view.

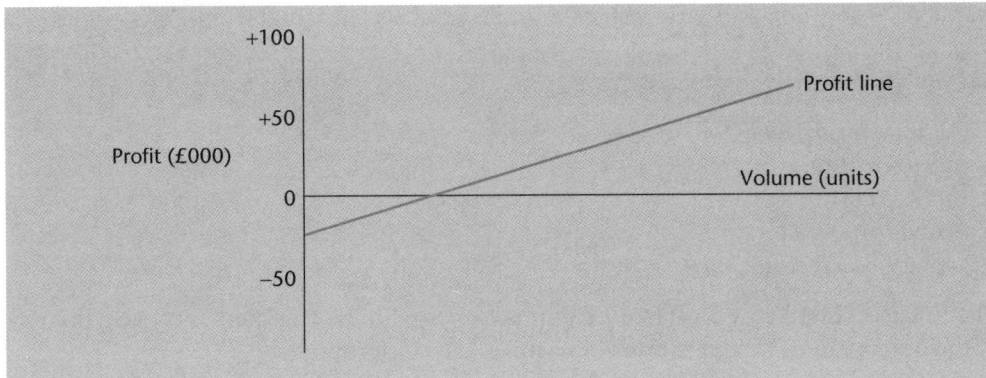

## Price elasticity of demand

Another useful concept from the field of economics is that of *price elasticity of demand*. This concerns the rate at which the amount sold changes relative to the rate of change of the selling price. For products which are essentials or necessities, a large increase in price may only produce a small decrease in sales volume. For example, if petrol prices increased by 5%, the amount of petrol sold might decrease by only 2%. In this case, petrol can be described as having a 'low elasticity of demand' or being relatively 'price inelastic'. This reflects the small amount of change (or *stretching*) in demand relative to the amount of change in price. (Implicit in Figure 12.1 is the assumption that the price elasticity of demand is infinity.)

However, for other items, a small increase in price may produce a large decrease in sales volume. For example, a 5% increase in the price of coffee may produce a 10% decrease in the amount of coffee sold. In this case coffee could be described as having high elasticity of demand. The amount of coffee sold changes more than its price. One of the reasons for this is that coffee substitutes are more easily obtainable than petrol substitutes. It is easier to change from coffee to tea than to change your vehicle from petrol to diesel. When setting selling prices, it is very useful to have a reasonable idea of the product's price elasticity of demand as this will help to predict the revenue curve (see Figure 12.2). (Implicit in Figure 12.2 is the assumption that the price elasticity of demand is greater than 1.0 as total revenue continues to rise with output.)

## The accountant's view

### Cost-plus pricing

When setting the price of a product, the first thing an accountant usually thinks of is its cost. It is a fundamental rule of business that, in order to make a profit, prices have to be greater than costs. So, the product cost is first established and then a profit margin is added to give the selling price. But, as can be seen from earlier chapters, the concept of *product cost* is far from straightforward. There are at least three types of costing (variable, absorption and activity-based) and several specific costs within these types. So, which is the best cost to use?

Here are some of the choices:

- manufacturing cost;
- full absorption cost;
- variable cost;
- prime cost;
- activity-based cost.

The full absorption cost is often used as it is perceived to be the safest approach, but any of the others can be used if the business thinks them appropriate.

The next question is how to set the profit margin. What percentage should be added to the cost? The answer to this comes from the business's corporate plan. In this should be stated the required *return on capital employed*. This enables the required annual profit to be estimated and from this the percentage profit margin can be calculated.

For example, if Kryptomatic Limited aims to achieve a 20% return on capital employed and its latest figure of total capital is £1 million, then its annual profit needs to be £200,000. If its budget for next year shows that its total costs will be £600,000, then its total sales revenue needs to be £800,000.

Below is an extract from Kryptomatic's budget for next year:

|  | £000 |
|---|---|
| Direct materials | 150 |
| Direct labour | 50 |
| **Prime cost** | **200** |
| Variable production overheads | 25 |
| Fixed production overheads | 75 |
| **Manufacturing cost** | **300** |
| Administration overheads | 120 |
| Marketing overheads | 180 |
| **Total cost** | **600** |
| **Required profit** | **200** |
| **Total revenue** | **800** |

If it adopted a **prime-cost-plus** approach, the 'plus' margin added would be:

$$\frac{800 - 200}{200} = \frac{600}{200} = +300\%$$

If it adopted a **manufacturing-cost-plus** approach, the 'plus' margin added would be:

$$\frac{800 - 300}{300} = \frac{500}{300} = +167\%$$

If it adopted a **full-cost-plus** approach, the 'plus' margin added would be:

$$\frac{800 - 600}{600} = \frac{200}{600} = +33\%$$

*Try the following question for yourself (answer at the end of the chapter).*

Codex Ltd has a target return on capital employed of 40% p.a. and its latest balance sheet shows its capital employed is £15 million. The following figures are from next year's budget.

Calculate the cost-plus percentage Codex should use based on (a) prime cost, (b) manufacturing cost and (c) total cost.

|  | £m |
|---|---|
| Direct materials | 8 |
| Direct labour | 12 |
| **Prime cost** | 20 |
| Variable production overheads | 1 |
| Fixed production overheads | 3 |
| **Manufacturing cost** | 24 |
| Administration overheads | 2 |
| Marketing overheads | 4 |
| **Total cost** | 30 |

## The absorption cost suicide spiral

The main drawback of cost-plus pricing is that it ignores the demand aspects of a competitive environment. It assumes that all product demand is completely price inelastic. This is very unrealistic for the vast majority of products. Figure 12.7 illustrates the potential danger of blindly following the cost-plus approach.

The amount of fixed cost attached to each unit is calculated by dividing the total of fixed costs by the planned number of units. Every time the price is increased, the volume sold goes down, which causes an increase in fixed cost per unit and, consequently, a further price increase. If this downward spiral were allowed to happen, the company would very soon cease trading.

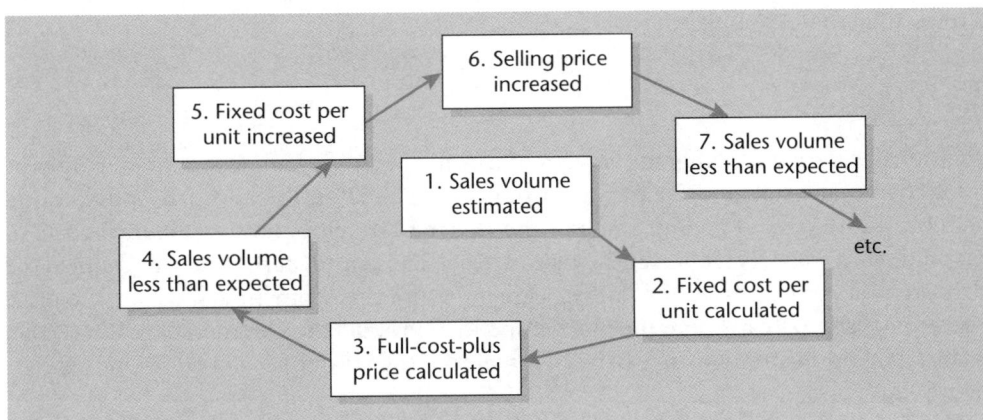

Figure 12.7 **The absorption cost suicide spiral**

Here is a numerical example. Blinkered Ltd produces a standard saddle. Its total annual fixed costs are £1 million and the variable cost of each saddle is £80. It prices the saddle by adding a 40% mark-up to its absorption cost.

1  Sales volume estimated at 50,000 units.
2  Fixed cost per unit = £20 (£1,000,000/50,000).
3  Absorption cost = £100 (£80 + £20); selling price = £140 (£100 + 40%).
4  Actual sales volume = 40,000 saddles.
5  Fixed cost per unit = £25 (£1,000,000/40,000).
6  Absorption cost = £105 (£80 + £25); selling price = £147 (£105 + 40%).
7  Sales volume falls to 33,000 saddles due to price increase.
8  etc.

Blinkered Ltd's profits diminish at an ever-increasing rate due to the downward spiral of sales volume. Before long, its losses will be unsustainable and it will have to cease trading.

## The marketer's view

### Existing products

No organization functions in isolation. Trading takes place in the competitive environment of the marketplace, which means that firms cannot charge whatever they wish for their products. They have to set their prices in relation to those set by their competitors. This is particularly true for products that have been in existence for a while. The cost-plus method may suggest a selling price of £25 but, if a competitor has a very similar product on the market for £19, it would be very risky to stick with the £25 price tag. Maybe the price should be reduced to £18 or £21; maybe the product should be discontinued. Maybe it should be altered in some way that clearly differentiates it from the competition, resulting in a perceived higher value in the eyes of the customer. If this is achieved, it may even be possible to set the selling price successfully above £25! This is an example of *product positioning* in which the selling price is an important factor. The point is that market considerations (not cost-plus calculations) should have the final say in the setting of the selling price.

### New products

Occasionally, a product different enough to be called 'new' is launched into an empty or unsatisfied market. The price of new products depends on the company's marketing strategy. If it desires to recoup some of the research, development and launch costs of the product, it may decide to set the price artificially high to start with. This targets the **early-adopters** or **trend-setters** market segment. Once this segment is satisfied, the price is reduced, especially as there may be competitive products in the market by that time, encouraged by the high selling price. This marketing strategy is called *skimming* (see Figure 12.8).

The shape of the unit cost line reflects the **learning curve** concept based on the belief that during the initial period of a new process the operatives usually significantly

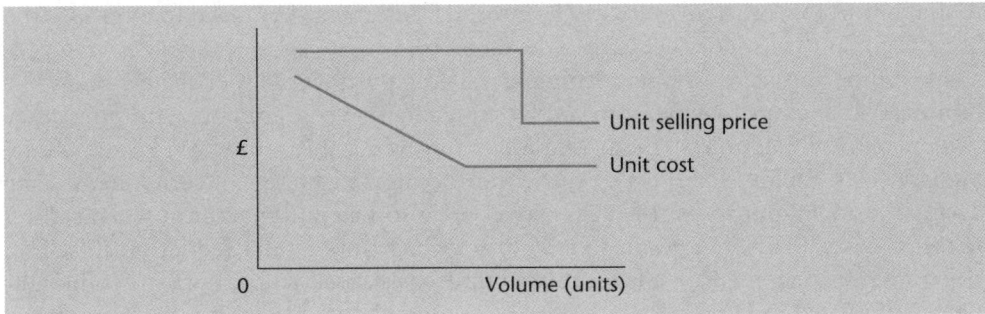

Figure 12.8 **Skimming pricing policy**

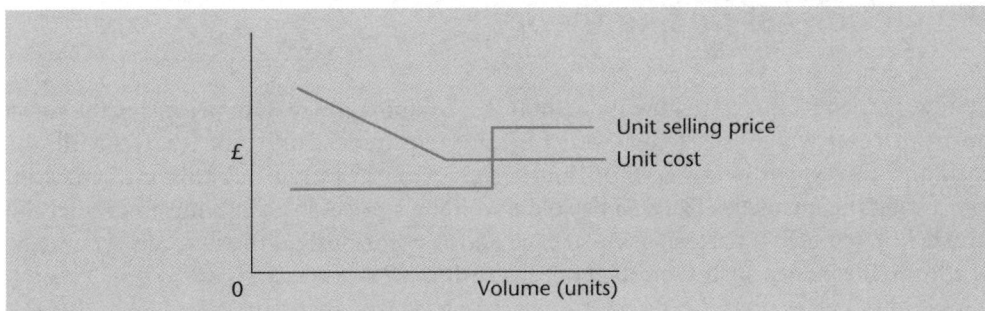

Figure 12.9 **Penetration pricing policy**

improve its efficiency. For example, in month one, 500 items may be produced but, due to learning curve effects, 1,200 may be produced in month two.

An alternative approach to skimming is to set an artificially low initial price to gain the maximum number of customers as quickly as possible. The object is to establish brand loyalty so that profit foregone in the introductory stage is more than compensated for by profit from repeat sales after the price has been adjusted upwards some time after launch. The object of this approach is to build market share and discourage early competition. This marketing strategy is called *penetration* (see Figure 12.9).

## Target pricing and costing: an integrated strategy

The traditional approach to price setting, which starts by establishing costs and ends with the selling price decision, is turned on its head by this new approach. The first thing to be done in target pricing is to set the selling price in the context of the marketplace and its constraints. This may well involve market research, trial selling in a small geographical area and consideration of the product life cycle. In other words, determine the highest price at which the product will sell the required volume. Next, calculate the desired profit margin and deduct this from the selling price. The resulting figure will be the maximum total cost allowable. The product designers then have to engineer the product so that its cost does not exceed the target cost.

This can be applied to the revamping of existing products as well as new ones. For example, cost savings may be achieved by replacing five components with one larger component, resulting in less labour assembly time even if there is no saving in material purchase costs. Savings may also be made in ordering and storage of components. The effects of production process learning curves are also taken into account when setting the target costs. (This may result in a contract which stipulates a **reduction** in selling price, rather than an increase, after a certain time has elapsed.) Target pricing is thought to have originated in Japan, where it is more commonly used than in other economies. However, its popularity in Europe and North America is gradually increasing.

## Limitations of pricing theory

By now, you will appreciate how important it is to know the market price (i.e. the maximum price at which customers will buy the required number of items). Millions of pounds are spent every year on market research in pursuit of this information. Forecasting the quantities likely to be sold at different prices is an attempt to predict the future. It is as much an art as it is a science and is notoriously difficult to do accurately. So why do businesses spend so much on this each year?

Well, they believe that this forecasting based on current market research gives the best estimate possible. Although the figures are not accurate, they represent the best information available. However, the degree of inaccuracy can be considerable. In other words, prices are very rarely initially set at their optimum level. Businesses adjust their prices according to their experience of the market. If they have set their price too high, they will sell fewer items than desired. When they reduce the price, the opposite may happen. It is a process of trial and error. As the product becomes established, more **actual** market data is gathered and the pricing becomes more effective.

### The manager's point of view (written by Nigel Burton)

Pricing is perhaps the single most crucial area in business management, and yet it is the one which is carried out amid the greatest number of unknowns. Almost every other aspect of the business can be managed from a position of knowledge. Costs, for instance, can be identified and controlled, new products developed and introduced, production processes improved, systems and procedures streamlined. But pricing is a gamble. Market intelligence will act as a guide, but in the end the setting of prices will always be accompanied by a measure of risk. What will the customers' reaction be? Will they be driven to the competition? Will they be driven to adopt different technologies? What will the competition do? These questions are at the heart of every pricing decision, and make the process of running a business so exciting.

There are few rules to apply in the setting of prices. Of course the accountants must ensure that prices are sufficiently high to produce the expected returns, and one of the cost-plus bases (preferably ABC) will enable them to do this. However, in my view, this should be seen simply as a safety net against unacceptably low pricing, and should not play an active part in the price-setting procedure itself. The correct price for a product is the highest price that the market will accept. It is, therefore, primarily a decision for the marketing department. Profits are hard enough to come by at any time, so any pricing of products below their full potential is highly undesirable. Overpricing a product may be a mistake, but it is always much easier to reduce prices at a later stage than to increase them. The use of cost information in the initial formulation of prices may inhibit the imagination of the marketing department!

Pricing is influenced by many factors other than cost. Each business, and most likely each individual product within the business, will have a different set of circumstances affecting its market position. Is there anything about the product which distinguishes it from the competition, and which will allow us to charge a premium price? Perhaps it is easier to look at the situation from the point of view of purchasers. What factors will encourage them to pay the higher price?

Brand identity is clearly one such factor. A BMW and a Ford both have the necessary equipment to get buyers to their destination, but they will pay more for the BMW, either because they perceive that they are buying a higher-quality product, or because it panders to their ego. Whatever their motivation, their perception of the product will have an impact on the market price.

Product quality will usually allow a premium price to be charged. However, the right quality can be defined as that which meets, but does not exceed, the requirements of customers. They will not pay a premium price for a higher level of quality than they need. Also, it is worth remembering that the first priority for a purchasing officer is to ensure that there is material of the right quality available at the right time for use by the production or sales department. This is more important than shaving an extra per cent or two from the price. The loss of production or sales through stock shortages will normally far outweigh any cost-saving advantage.

The quality of the supplier is another key, but often underrated, element. Purchasers need to feel confident that the supplier will always meet their delivery requirements with consistent quality material. They, therefore, may feel more comfortable dealing with a solid, blue-chip company than with a small cut-price outfit which may be here today and gone tomorrow. In the chemicals industry it has been possible for some time to source many raw materials from suppliers in India and China. Although prices are very competitive compared with the European competition, quality has not always been of a consistent standard. Moreover, the extended lead times involved inevitably limit flexibility where quick responsiveness to changing customer needs is paramount. The comfort factor of a local, reliable supplier may be worth paying extra for.

Patented products will clearly command a higher price, and can become significant profit generators if they are in the right market niche. But purchasers are always on the lookout for cheaper, unpatented alternatives, even if it means adopting different technologies or changing production processes. The higher the price, the greater the spur to customers to find cost-saving alternatives.

These are just a few of the many factors which influence the initial establishment of prices, and which will continue to cause price movements, perhaps even on a daily basis. The competition never stands still. It will react to every action taken and, as in a game of chess, the real skill in business is to anticipate the competitor's next move. The marketplace is constantly changing, and prices are being set in the light of the best information available at the time.

There are times when this feels like a leap in the dark. In the chemicals industry, there has recently been a move towards global sourcing. Accordingly, one of our major customers notified us of their intention to source their worldwide requirements for a particular range of products from a single supplier. At the time, this business was split between several suppliers, and everyone was making good profits. We were asked to quote prices for each piece of business in each country. This was a daunting prospect. Business worth millions of dollars was at stake, so, at the end of this process, there were going to be some big losers and one big winner! At what level should we pitch the prices? How much of our existing profit should we give away in order to be sure of picking up the rest of the business? How aggressive would our competitors be as they stood to lose as much as we did? We arrived at a set of prices which we calculated would give us an acceptable return, and submitted them. It was with an enormous sense of relief that we heard we had been successful in picking up the entire contract. But we were nevertheless left with a nagging doubt that perhaps we had pitched the prices too low and given away some profit unnecessarily.

As we basked in the success of this venture, we heard that another major customer was travelling down the same route, another worldwide tender, again with some very profitable business at stake. We went through the same agonizing process, and made our submission. Unfortunately, on this occasion, we had underestimated the aggression of our competitors, who were still smarting from their failure in the previous tender, and we lost the business. Well, you win some, you lose some! Overall, we came out of it just ahead on profit, although at the cost of considerable anxiety.

For both tenders, we had set up a computer model which compared our proposed prices with the underlying costs, enabling us to monitor the overall profitability while we played with different pricing options. As this product range consisted mainly of high-margin-earning products, there was plenty of scope to reduce prices without jeopardizing the minimum returns required. The underlying costs did not play a significant role in the establishment of our quoted prices; for us, the likely action of our competitors was the key factor. In this we were perhaps a good deal more fortunate than many other businesses, where costs are the overriding factor. At this latter end of the scale, I am aware of one company bidding to develop and supply automotive parts for a new range of vehicles due to come to market in five years' time. It quoted a price below today's total cost, on the assumption that advances in technology in the intervening period would generate sufficient cost savings to leave a profit. A high degree of entrepreneurship, as well as courage, is needed to do business on this basis.

You may feel that my comments in this chapter have strayed away from the main management accounting theme of this book. I make no apology for this. I wish to emphasize the point that the setting of prices is primarily a marketing, not an accounting, function. The accounting techniques described in the chapter are, of course, essential as a backdrop against which the marketing people can do their work, and it is the accountants who will monitor whether the pricing proposals will generate the overall returns required by management. But my guess is that, if the pricing of the automotive parts had been left to conservative accountants, the contract would have been lost. And if the worldwide tenders had been left to accountants, the subtle nuances in the marketplace would have been overlooked, and the bid weakened as a result. So, if there is any rule on pricing, it is 'leave it to the marketing people', while keeping a close eye on their decisions within the context of the company's overall financial objectives.

*Summary*

Economic theory helps us to understand the relationships between selling price, unit cost, profit and volume of activity. It tells us that there is an **optimum level of output and profit** rather than a range of continuously improving results. It also makes us aware that the demand for different products is affected by their selling prices to different extents. This is the *price elasticity of demand* concept.

The accounting approach is to establish the cost structure of products and then to increase this by a calculated percentage to give a profit margin. This is the *cost-plus* method with the amount of the 'plus' or mark-up being determined by the organization's required return on capital employed. The full cost is probably used more than any other cost as it establishes a minimum price below which products cannot be sold profitably in the long term.

When finalizing the selling price, it is critically important to consider the **competitive nature of the marketplace**. It is essential to know which products compete directly with yours and what their current prices are. Knowledge of your product's minimum price (equal to its full cost) and an understanding of its elasticity of demand enable you to decide intelligently on its selling price.

Target pricing is a strategy which integrates all three viewpoints discussed in this chapter. It starts by setting the price and then working backwards to establish the desired profit margin and the maximum allowable cost. If this cost cannot be achieved satisfactorily, the product is abandoned (unless there is good reason for its continuation). The result of this is that all the company's products should provide adequate profits, and cross-subsidization of products should be avoided.

There is no getting away from the fact that, ultimately, the price-setting process is **subjective**. The selling price will be based upon the opinions, feelings and intuition of top managers who, hopefully, have their fingers on the pulse of the marketplace.

## *Further reading*

Ahmed, M. N. and Scapens, R. W. (2003) 'The evolution of cost-based pricing rules in Britain: an institutionalist perspective', *Review of Political Economy*, Vol. 15, Issue 2, April.

Atkinson, A., Banker, R., Kaplan, R. and Young, S. (2001) *Management Accounting*, 3rd edition, Prentice Hall, Harlow. See chapter 'Using management accounting information for pricing and product planning'.

Cardinaels, E., Roodhooft, F. and Warlop, L. (2004) 'The value of activity-based costing in competitive pricing decisions', *Journal of Management Accounting Research*, Vol. 16.

Davila, A. (T.) and Wouters, M. (2004) 'Designing cost-competitive technology products through cost management', *Accounting Horizons*, Vol. 18, Issue 1, March.

Horngren, C., Bhimani, A., Datar, S. and Foster, G. (2002) *Management and Cost Accounting*, 2nd edition, Prentice Hall Europe, Harlow. See Chapter 12, 'Pricing decisions and customer profitability analysis'.

Ingenbleek, P., Debruyne, M., Frambach, R. T. and Verhallen, T. M. M. (2003) 'Successful new product pricing practices: a contingency approach', *Marketing Letters*, Vol. 14, Issue 4, December.

Matanovich, T. (2003) 'Pricing services vs. pricing products: don't buy into the duality myth. Focus on value to the customer', *Marketing Management*. Vol. 12, Issue 4, July/August.

Swenson, D., Shahid, A., Bell, J. and Il-Woon Kim (2003) 'Best practices in target costing', *Management Accounting Quarterly*, Vol. 4, Issue 2, Winter.

Upchurch, A. (2003) *Management Accounting, Principles and Practice*, 2nd edition, Financial Times/Prentice Hall, Harlow. See Chapter 8, 'More decisions: price-setting and limiting factors', section 5, 'Price-setting'.

## Answers to self-assessment questions

### S12.1 Profit–volume chart based on economic theory

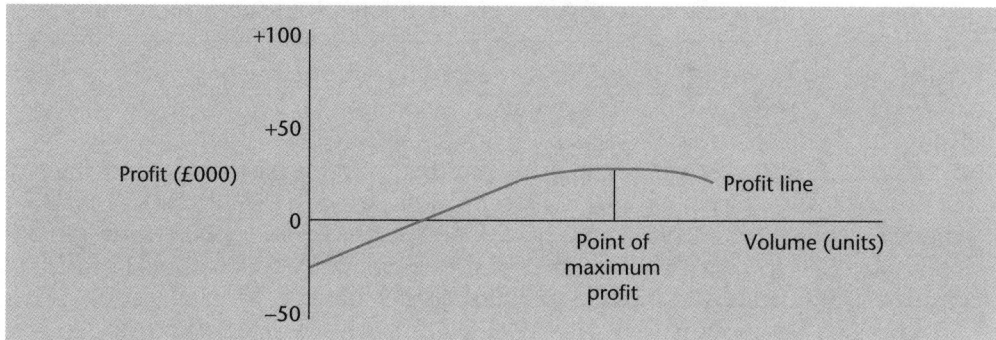

### S12.2 Codex Ltd

|                               | £m  |                    |
|-------------------------------|-----|--------------------|
| Direct materials              | 8   |                    |
| Direct labour                 | 12  |                    |
| **Prime cost**                | 20  |                    |
| Variable production overheads | 1   |                    |
| Fixed production overheads    | 3   |                    |
| **Manufacturing cost**        | 24  |                    |
| Administration overheads      | 2   |                    |
| Marketing overheads           | 4   |                    |
| **Total cost**                | 30  |                    |
| **Required profit**           | 6   | (40% ∞ £15m)       |
| **Total revenue**             | 36  |                    |

a) If it adopted a **prime-cost-plus** approach, the 'plus' margin added would be:

$$\frac{36-20}{20}=\frac{16}{20}=+80\%$$

b) If it adopted a **manufacturing-cost-plus** approach, the 'plus' margin added would be:

$$\frac{36-24}{24}=\frac{12}{24}=+50\%$$

c) If it adopted a **full-cost-plus** approach, the 'plus' margin added would be:

$$\frac{36-30}{30}=\frac{6}{30}=+20\%$$

| CASE STUDY | The Electric Car Company |
|---|---|

Two well-known multinational car manufacturing companies have developed a proto-type small town car fuelled solely by electricity. They intend to market this through a joint venture company called the Electric Car Company (ECC). This vehicle is code-named E1. It will carry a minimum of two passengers and have luggage space adequate for a family shopping trip. The luggage space will be convertible into two child seats, greatly enhancing the flexibility of this urban vehicle. Its maximum speed will be 60 mph/100 kph and it will have a range of approximately 150 miles/240 km from a fully-charged battery. The batteries will be recharged by connecting to a domestic electricity supply and should take no more than four hours to recharge from 'empty'. Harmful emissions from the E1 will be negligible compared with petrol/diesel-engine cars. Based on current energy prices, the E1's fuel cost per mile is about half that of existing equivalent-sized cars.

A comprehensive business plan has been produced to investigate the economic viability of this venture. During negotiations, the joint owners agreed that, due to the risks involved, it was essential that the Return on Capital Employed (ROCE) should be a min-imum of 15% a year. Having completed the business plan they also agreed that, due to the critical nature of forecast sales volumes, independent market research should be commis-sioned to produce a demand forecast at selling prices within £500 of their initial estimate.

## A) Extracts from business plan

The competition has been identified as those petrol/diesel-engine cars which are the smallest in the current ranges of the global car manufacturers. The prices of these to the retail car dealers range from £5,000 to over £10,000 depending on specification. Initially, the E1 will be built to a single basic specification and the prices of the nearest competitors have been identified as follows:

> Car 1 – £5,800
> Car 2 – £5,650
> Car 3 – £5,600
> Car 4 – £5,350
> Car 5 – £5,200

The business plan adopted a selling price of £5,000 for the E1 which gave a profit margin of 20%. It also assumed a level of activity which produced a ROCE of exactly 15%. To enable ECC to produce and market its electric car, capital of £500 million will be needed for buildings, machinery, office equipment, IT systems and other fixed assets. Their best estimate for the production cost of one car is as follows:

|  | £ |
|---|---|
| Direct materials | 1,133 |
| Direct labour | 200 |
| **Prime cost** | **1,333** |
| Variable production overheads | 167 |
| Fixed production overheads | 500 |
| **Manufacturing cost** | **2,000** |

Annual administration overheads are expected to be £15 m, ongoing research and development £45 m and marketing overheads (including advertising) £90 m.

## B) Extract from market research report

### Demand forecast:

| Selling price £ | Annual demand Units |
|---|---|
| 5,500 | 44,880 |
| 5,400 | 53,720 |
| 5,300 | 59,160 |
| 5,200 | 62,560 |
| 5,100 | 64,600 |
| 5,000 | 68,000 |
| 4,900 | 71,400 |
| 4,800 | 74,120 |
| 4,700 | 78,200 |
| 4,600 | 85,000 |
| 4,500 | 94,520 |

*Tasks:*

1 Assuming the market research data to be more reliable than the assumptions made in the business plan, advise ECC on its operating level and selling price. (You are advised to use a computer-based spreadsheet.)

(50 marks)

2 If EEC decided that it needed to spend an extra £10 million on launching the E1, how might it achieve this **without reducing its target profit**?

(20 marks)

3 On no more than two sides of A4 paper, discuss the risks involved in this project. Include a **brief** discussion of the 'price elasticity of demand' and comment on this in relation to the E1.

(30 marks)
(Total 100 marks)

## *Questions*

An asterisk * on a question number indicates that the answer is given at the end of the book. Answers to the other questions are given in the Lecturer's Guide.

## Q12.1* Demarco

Demarco makes miniature mobile generators and has a standard profit margin of 20% for all its products. Its annual budget includes marketing, administration and production overhead allowances of £60,000, £20,000 and £50,000 respectively. It also shows that the company intends to use £18,000 of materials and pay direct wages of £32,000. Marketing and administration overheads are all fixed but 10% of production overheads are considered to be variable. Demarco uses the cost-plus method of setting its selling prices.

*Task:*

Calculate the cost-plus percentage if the base was:

a) variable cost;
b) production cost;
c) full cost.

## Q12.2* Wizkid

WSM Enterprises introduced the Wizkid in 1991 to compete with Action Man. Although the peak demand for these products occurred several years ago, sales have stabilised and WSM sells 15,000 Wizkids a year.

The recommended retail price is £24.99 and the current wholesale price is £10.00. However, the managing director wishes to increase the return on this product and has proposed a 100% mark-up on total variable costs.

WSM has an annual output of 15,000 Wizkids. The fixed costs related to this product are £40,000 and the variable (or marginal) costs are £6.00 per unit.

*Tasks:*

1  What is the breakeven volume of this product if a selling price of £10.00 is charged? What is the profit at this price?
2  What price would the MD like to charge? What would the resulting net profit be if there were no change in demand?
3  The marketing director has forecast a 10% drop in orders if the price is raised as suggested. What would WSM's profit be if this were to happen?
4  Discuss the other factors the MD should take into account when deciding on the selling price of Wizkids.

### Q12.3* Ride-on Lawn Mowers

Ride-on makes and sells a mini-tractor lawn mower called the Luxon. The company is just about to start its new financial year for which the budget (recently approved by its holding company) shows the following:

|                              | £000   |
| ---------------------------- | ------ |
| Total capital employed       | 4,000  |
| Total sales revenue          | 2,800  |
| Total fixed costs            | 1,104  |
| Net profit before tax        | 800    |
| Return on capital employed (ROCE) | 20% |
| Number of Luxons sold        | 1,120  |

Its holding company requires it to achieve a ROCE of at least 20% and Ride-on's directors are awarded annual bonuses if they succeed in this.

Yesterday, Ride-on's main competitor released details of a new product in direct competition to the mower. The Luxon has a selling price of £2,500 but its new rival has been priced approximately £300 below this. After a hastily convened meeting, Ride-on's top managers have decided to reduce the Luxon's price to £2,150 with immediate effect. They also feel that their forecast sales revenue now looks optimistic.

*Tasks:*

Advise them how they might maintain their forecast return on capital employed (ROCE) at 20% now that the Luxon's price has been reduced:

a)  if total sales revenue is maintained at £2.8 million; and
b)  if total sales revenue decreases to £2.5 million.

### Q12.4 Theory questions

a)  What is meant by 'price elasticity of demand'?
b)  Create a numerical example of the 'absorption cost suicide spiral'.
c)  Explain the differences between the accountant's and the economist's approach to pricing.
d)  Why is pricing really a marketing function?
e)  List the stages involved in target pricing.

### Q12.5 Brightwell Shades

Brightwell Shades Ltd has developed a new kind of sunglasses, the Shadewell, whose strength can be manually adjusted. The variable cost of one pair is £50 but the firm is unsure what the selling price should be. During a lengthy board meeting it was decided to commission some market research into the new product's price elasticity of demand. The results of the market research survey have just been received and are summarized as follows:

| Sales price (£) | 60 | 70 | 80 | 90 | 100 |
|---|---|---|---|---|---|
| Sales volume (units) | 16,000 | 13,000 | 10,000 | 7,000 | 4,000 |
| Sales revenue (£) | 960,000 | 910,000 | 800,000 | 630,000 | 400,000 |

It is estimated that when output is equal to, or greater than, 12,000 units the variable cost per unit will reduce to £45. Also, additional fixed costs of £50,000 will be incurred if production exceeds 8,800 units.

*Task:*

Advise the board on the selling price of the Shadewell.

## Review questions

1  Explain the economist's pricing model.
2  Explain the accountant's pricing model.
3  Compare these two models by the use of charts.
4  Discuss the economist's optimum level of output.
5  Explain the concept of price elasticity of demand.
6  Explain cost-plus pricing.
7  Discuss the dangers of cost-plus pricing.
8  Discuss the marketer's view of pricing.
9  Compare the pricing strategies of skimming and penetration.
10  Describe target pricing as an integrating mechanism.
11  Discuss the limitations of pricing theory.

*The answers to all these questions can be found in the text of this chapter.*

CHAPTER

# 14 Budgets and their creation

**Chapter contents**

- Introduction
- Learning objectives
- Budgets and their context
- Functional budgets
- Self-assessment question S14.1
- Self-assessment question S14.2
- Self-assessment question S14.3
- Self-assessment question S14.4
- Self-assessment question S14.5
- Master budgets
- Self-assessment question S14.6
- Types of budget and budgeting methods
- Flexible budgets
- Example 14.1: illustration using the semi-variable cost of water supplies
- Self-assessment question S14.7
- Standards and how they are set
- Limitations of budgets as plans
- The manager's point of view
- Summary
- Further reading
- Answers to self-assessment questions
- Case study: the Omega Document Case Company
- Questions
- Review questions

## Introduction

If you were one of the top managers in an organization, e.g. a director of a company, you would be expected to have a vision of where the organization should be a few years from now. Knowing where you are going is one important aspect of leadership. However, although having a vision is very important, it is not sufficient in itself. You need to know how to go about realizing that vision. First, you need to be able to **make the plans** which will get you to where you want to be. Second, you need to know the best way to **use those plans**. Armed with this knowledge you stand a fair chance of achieving your goals. Without it, you are much less likely to succeed. This chapter is all about how to make those plans, how to create a budget.

**Note**: Although budgets are just as important to service industries as they are to manufacturing industries, their preparation is illustrated in this chapter using examples of manufacturing. Budgets for service organizations are prepared in just the same way but, obviously, without the manufacturing schedules.

**Learning objectives**

**Having worked through this chapter you should be able to:**

- explain what a budget is;
- explain how it fits into the corporate planning context;
- list the positive attributes of budgetary control systems;
- differentiate between fixed and flexible budgets;
- differentiate between incremental and zero-based budgeting;
- create functional budgets;
- create a budgeted profit and loss account, balance sheet and cash flow forecast;
- create flexible budgets;
- define standard cost;
- discuss the issues about the setting of standards;
- discuss the limitations of budgets.

## Budgets and their context

A budget is a predictive model of organizational activity, quantitatively expressed, for a set time period. In plain English, a budget is a plan of operations and activities for the next year (or month etc.), stated in monetary values.

The organization's strategic plan, not the annual budget, is the master plan of the organization. This strategic plan should state the long-term organizational objectives

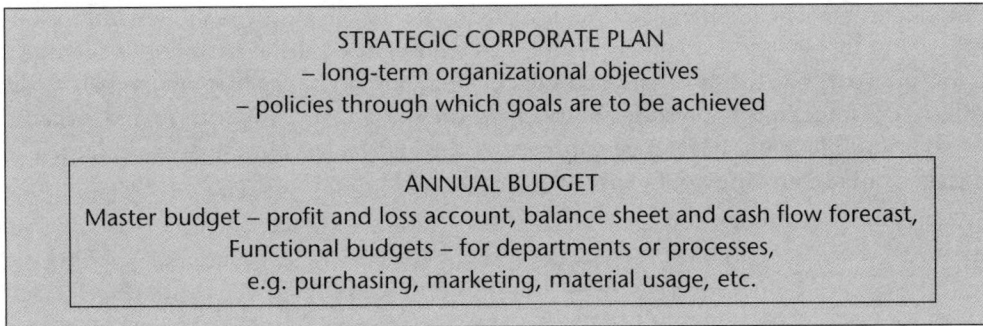

Figure 14.1 **The budget in context**

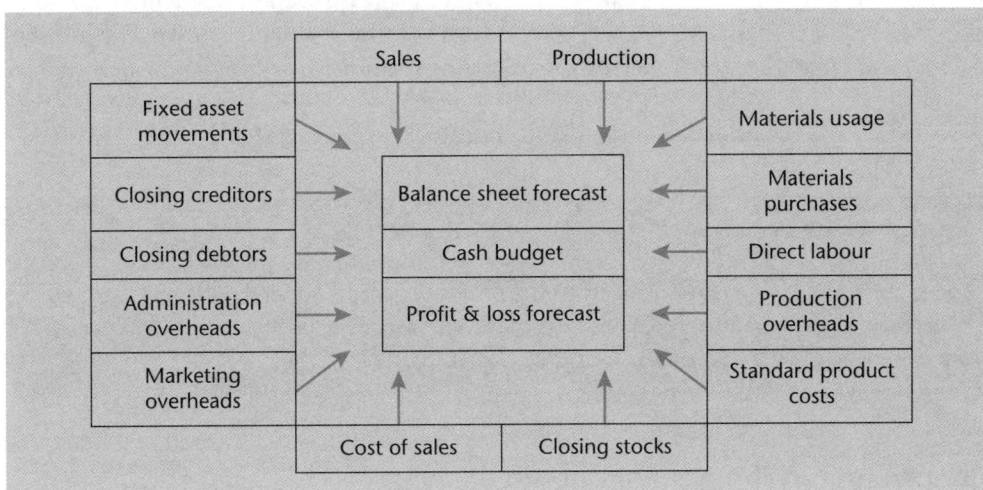

Figure 14.2 **Budget relationships**

and the policies through which these goals are to be achieved. The annual budget is created within the context of the strategic plan (see Figure 14.1).

The relationships between the various constituent budgets are illustrated in Figure 14.2.

# Functional budgets

## The primary budget

Where to start? Does it matter which budget is created first? The answer to this last question is 'yes'. Start with the activity that determines all the other activities. In the vast majority of businesses, this is sales. The amount of goods or services it is realistically considered can be sold in the budget period will influence all the other activities. This primary budget can be thought of as a limiting factor. (However, if titanium components were being manufactured for jet engines and there was a sudden unforeseen shortage of this material, then the limiting factor might be the availability of titanium. In this unusual case, the raw material budget would have to be the first one prepared.)

The sales forecast is the responsibility of the sales and marketing section and, because it is so crucial, it would have to be approved at the highest level in the organization. The management accountant would have little, or no, input into this primary budget.

## The production volume budget

To plan the production volume for a period it is necessary to know the stock levels of finished goods at the beginning and end of that period. These may be determined by a policy such as 'opening stock is to be equal to one-half of the next month's sales'. So, if it is planned to sell 100 items in March and 120 items in April, the stock will be 50 items on 1 March and 60 items on 1 April. As the sales volume is already known, the number of items to be made is determined by the following formula:

**Production = sales + closing stock − opening stock**

| Self-assessment question S14.1 | *Try the following question for yourself (answer at the end of the chapter).* |
|---|---|
| | The sales of Minnow Ltd are planned to be: April 100, May 140, June 120 and July 160 items. Stock levels are planned to be one-quarter of the next month's sales. What are the planned production budgets for April, May and June? |

## The raw material purchasing budget

To calculate this, it is necessary to know how much raw material will be used as well as knowing the policy on raw material stock levels. It may be that, due to the unreliability of supplies, the policy of a particular firm is to have sufficient stock at the start of a month for that month's production. The production volume budget will determine the amount of raw material usage and raw material purchases are therefore calculated as follows:

**Purchases = usage + closing stock − opening stock**

(This formula applies to both quantities and values.)

| Self-assessment question S14.2 | *Try the following question for yourself (answer at the end of the chapter).* |
|---|---|
| | Minnow Ltd plans to spread its production of 1,800 items evenly throughout the year. Each item uses five units of raw material. Minnow expects to start the year with 80 units of raw material in stock but to reduce this by 25% by the end of the year. If each unit of stock costs £6 to buy in, what is the company's raw material purchasing budget for the year? |

## The cost of sales budget

For a manufacturing organization, the cost of sales is calculated by the following formula:

$$\text{Cost of sales} = \text{opening stock} + \text{production cost} - \text{closing stock}$$

(All the items in this equation relate to finished goods only.)

> *Try the following question for yourself (answer at the end of the chapter).*
>
> If Minnow Ltd's stock of finished goods is valued at £30,000 on 1 January and £27,000 at 31 March and the cost of production is £20,000 a month, what is the cost of sales for the quarter?

*Self-assessment question S14.3*

## The cash receipts budget

In order to prepare the cash budget, it is essential to know the amount of money planned to be received in each period. For sales made on 'cash terms' (i.e. transfer of goods and payment for them take place at the same time), the total receipts equal the total sales revenue. For sales made on 'credit terms' (i.e. payment takes place at a later time than the transfer of the goods), the picture is more complicated. The total of receipts in a period depends on the amount of debtors at the start and finish of the period as well as the amount sold on credit terms during that period.

$$\text{Receipts} = \text{opening debtors} + \text{credit sales} - \text{closing debtors}$$

> *Try the following question for yourself (answer at the end of the chapter).*
>
> Minnow Ltd plans to sell 2,400 items for £10 each evenly through the year, half on cash terms and half on credit terms of one month. If its opening debtors were £1,300, what would be the planned total of receipts from all sales during the year?
> (Assume all debtors pay on the due dates.)

*Self-assessment question S14.4*

## The cash payments budget

In order to prepare the cash budget, it is also essential to know the amount of money planned to be paid out in each period. When goods and services are paid for immediately they are received, the total of payments equals the total of purchases. However, when purchases are made on credit terms, the total of purchases must be adjusted by the amount of creditors at the start and finish of the period to give the total amount of payments.

$$\text{Payments} = \text{opening creditors} + \text{credit purchases} - \text{closing creditors}$$

*Try the following question for yourself (answer at the end of the chapter).*

Minnow Ltd buys 1,600 items at £5 each evenly through the year, one-quarter on cash terms and three-quarters on two months' credit. If the company's opening creditors were £750, what would be the total of its payments for the year?
(Assume all creditors are paid on the due dates.)

# Master budgets

## The cash budget or cash flow forecast

This budget is of particular importance to all organizations. If there is insufficient cash to pay all the bills due at a certain time, then the organization may be forced out of business even though it is trading profitably (see Chapter 2).

The summary cash budget for the period is simply

**Opening balance + receipts − payments = closing balance**

However, it is normal to create a detailed cash budget for each month in order to monitor and control the organization's cash resources. It is also useful to know the net result of monthly cash flows. Is more money coming in than going out (i.e. a net inflow) or is more going out than coming in (i.e. a net outflow)? Once this is known, the net cash flow can be combined with the opening balance to give the closing balance.

|       | Cash in         |
|-------|-----------------|
| Less: | Cash out        |
|       | Net cash fow    |
| Add:  | Opening balance |
|       | Closing balance |

It is conventional to give net inflows a positive sign and net outflows a negative sign (shown below by the use of brackets).

The following is an example of a simple cash budget in summary terms:

|       |                 | Jan | Feb  | Mar | Total |
|-------|-----------------|-----|------|-----|-------|
|       | Cash in         | 45  | 49   | 54  | 148   |
| Less: | Cash out        | 37  | 53   | 41  | 131   |
|       | Net cash flow   | 8   | (4)  | 13  | 17    |
| Add:  | Opening balance | 850 | 858  | 854 | 850   |
|       | Closing balance | 858 | 854  | 867 | 867   |

Note that the opening balance for a month must be the same as the closing balance for the previous month. This is only to be expected as exactly the same money is being referred to by each of the two balances.

The illustration below shows these summary figures in bold type together with some of the detailed items that help to make them up.

|  | Jan | Feb | Mar | Quarter |
|---|---|---|---|---|
| Receipts: |  |  |  |  |
| Credit sales | 32 | 37 | 41 | 110 |
| Cash sales | 11 | 12 | 12 | 35 |
| Other | 2 | – | 1 | 3 |
| **Total** | **45** | **49** | **54** | **148** |
| Payments: |  |  |  |  |
| Purchases of materials | 25 | 27 | 25 | 77 |
| Wages | 8 | 8 | 8 | 24 |
| Expenses | 4 | 4 | 5 | 13 |
| Other | – | 14 | 3 | 17 |
| **Total** | **37** | **53** | **41** | **131** |
| **Net in/(out)flow** | **8** | **(4)** | **13** | **17** |
| **Opening bank balance** | **850** | **858** | **854** | *850* |
| **Closing bank balance** | **858** | **854** | **867** | *867* |

Be careful of the two numbers (in italics) at the bottom right-hand corner. They are **not** found by adding across (like all those above them) but by **copying** the opening balance for the quarter (850) and then working down the 'Quarter' column. The resulting number (867) in the extreme bottom right-hand corner should be exactly the same as that on its immediate left. After all, they should both show the balance on 31 March.

The figures above show the months when the cash actually moves, i.e. comes in or goes out. For sales and purchases made on credit terms, this date will always be later than the point of sale or purchase. The cash budget may be dangerously misleading if these timing differences are not taken into account.

Note that the balances on the bottom two lines of the cash budget can be negative as well as positive. This shows that the organisation has a bank overdraft rather than a positive balance, a very common business situation.

When referring to cash budgets, use the terms *net inflow, net outflow, surplus* or *deficit* but **never** *profit* or *loss*.

The cash flow forecast is a very important management tool. It is used to:

- ensure that sufficient cash will be available to carry out planned activities;
- give a warning of the size of overdraft or loan needed;
- plan for investment of surplus cash.

*Try the following question for yourself (answer at the end of the chapter).*

*Self-assessment question S14.6*

Using the pro forma below, create (in pencil?) a cash budget from the following information: Opening balance is £150 *overdrawn*; credit receipts are £100 per month, cash receipts are £30 per month and other receipts are £70 in Feb.; purchases are £100 per month, wages £25 per month, expenses £35 per month and other payments are £15 in Jan.

| Cash budget for quarter ended 31 March | | | | |
|---|---|---|---|---|
| | Jan | Feb | Mar | Quarter |
| Receipts: | | | | |
| Credit sales | | | | |
| Cash sales | | | | |
| Other | | | | |
| Total | | | | |
| Payments: | | | | |
| Purchases of materials | | | | |
| Wages | | | | |
| Expenses | | | | |
| Other | | | | |
| Total | | | | |
| Net in/(out)flow | | | | |
| Opening bank balance | | | | |
| Closing bank balance | | | | |

## The budgeted profit and loss account and balance sheet

These budgets are compiled from information on the functional budgets or provided from elsewhere in the organization. This is best appreciated by working through the case study at the end of this chapter.

# Types of budget and budgeting methods

### Fixed budget

This is a budget based on one predetermined level of activity. Its main function is to act as a master plan for the following year.

### Flexible budget

This is a budget which, by recognizing different cost behaviour patterns, is designed to change as the volume of activity changes. It can be thought of as several fixed budgets, each at a different level of activity, shown side by side.

### Incremental budgeting

This approach to budget creation assumes that there will be little change in activity for next year compared with the current year. So, the numerical amounts (known as *allowances*) are arrived at by taking last year's amount and adding an increment for any known changes and for inflation.

## Zero-based budgeting

This is a method of budgeting which requires each cost element to be specifically justified, as though the activities were being undertaken for the first time. Without approval, the budget allowance is zero.

## Flexible budgets

Shown below is a flexible budget for a firm which expects to sell about 1,400 items a year. However, its market tends to fluctuate year to year and so it also produces budgets for sales of 1,200 and 1,600 items. These are its estimates of the minimum and maximum annual sales.

**Flexible budgeted profit and loss account for y/e 31 December**

| Sales (units) | 1,200 | 1,400 | 1,600 |
|---|---|---|---|
| Sales revenue (£000) | 600 | 700 | 800 |
| Materials | 300 | 350 | 400 |
| Labour | 120 | 140 | 170 |
| Factory overhead | 20 | 21 | 27 |
| Total | 440 | 511 | 597 |
| Gross profit | 160 | 189 | 203 |
| Marketing costs | 16 | 18 | 20 |
| Admin costs | 30 | 30 | 30 |
| Total | 46 | 48 | 50 |
| Net profit | 114 | 141 | 153 |

This shows that net profit does not increase in direct proportion to sales volume. At maximum sales the net profit increases by only £12,000 for the extra 200 units sold over the expected number. But at minimum sales (200 units less than expected) net profit decreases by £27,000. This type of situation arises due to the way in which costs behave (see Chapter 2). Remember that many costs have both fixed and variable elements. For example, the marketing costs above have a fixed component of £4,000 and a variable component of £10 a unit. Sometimes, fixed costs step up. Weekend working had to be introduced to produce the extra 200 items needed for maximum sales. This caused extra labour costs at an overtime premium of 50% and additional factory overheads.

Understanding cost structures is essential for the creation of flexible budgets. If you are asked to create one involving stepped fixed costs you would have to be told both the activity level at which the step happened and the size of the step. But you would probably be expected to calculate the semi-variable costs (such as marketing in the above example) for yourself. One way of going about this is known as the 'high–low method' (also covered in Chapter 1, on cost behaviour).

Example 14.1

# Illustration using the semi-variable cost of water supplies

For the first six months of the year the monthly invoices for the use of water by the business were:

| Month | Usage | Total cost (£) |
|-------|-------|----------------|
| 1 | 520 | 12,080 |
| 2 | 570 | 12,310 |
| 3 | 600 | 12,400 |
| 4 | 510 | 12,040 |
| 5 | 540 | 12,160 |
| 6 | 500 | 12,000 |

Using only the highest- and lowest-usage months, the cost structure can be determined as follows:

| | | |
|--|--|--|
| Highest (month 3) | 600 units | £12,400 |
| Lowest (month 6) | 500 units | £12,000 |
| Difference | 100 units | £400 |

Variable cost per unit produced = £400/100 = £4
Variable cost of 500 units = 500 × £4 = £2,000
Fixed cost (at 500 units) = total cost − variable cost
= £12,000 − £2,000
= £10,000

This can be checked by substituting these values in the other month. In month 3:

|  | £ |
|--|--|
| Variable cost = 600 × £4 = | 2,400 |
| Fixed cost = | 10,000 |
| Total cost = | 12,400 |

When performing this check, be sure to use **only** the other occurrence used in the original calculation (month 3 in this case). Note that many costs do not behave as predictably as water bills.

As this method uses the two extreme values of the variable, it is advisable to check that these are representative of the normal cost behaviour. This can be done by sketching a scattergraph which will show up any 'outliers' or unrepresentative values.

*Try the following question for yourself (answer at the end of the chapter).*

The monthly costs of machine maintenance have been recorded during the past few months as follows. (During July the machine maintenance team were redeployed to assist on emergency repairs to the factory building.)

| Month | Machine Maintenance hours | Total cost |
|---|---|---|
| October | 155 | 2,013 |
| September | 122 | 1,723 |
| August | 135 | 1,902 |
| July | 69 | 280 |
| June | 157 | 2,073 |
| May | 149 | 1,937 |

If the machine maintenance hours for November are planned to be 180, estimate the machine maintenance cost for that month.

## Standards and how they are set

A *standard* is the physical and financial plan for **one unit** of output.

> The standard cost *is the planned unit cost of the products, components or services produced in a period.*
> (CIMA, Management Accounting Official Terminology)

### Example standard cost data for one plastic wheel (type KR2)

| Category | Item | Quantity | Price | Cost |
|---|---|---|---|---|
| Materials: | Plastic beads | 1.2 kg | £2.00/kg | 2.40 |
| Labour: | Type A | 0.25 h | £4.00/h | 1.00 |
| | Type D | 0.10 h | £5.00/h | 0.50 |
| Variable overhead | | 0.35 h | £2.00/h | 0.70 |
| Variable cost | | | | 4.60 |
| Fixed overhead (@ 900 wheels/week) | | 0.35 h | £4.60/h | 1.61 |
| Standard cost | | | | £6.21 |

## Bases for setting standards

There are three common sources for setting standards:

1 Performance levels of a prior period – these are based on recent experience.
2 Estimates of expected performance – these are based on recent experience and knowledge of any imminent changes.

3  Performance levels to meet organizational objectives – these are calculated from set targets; particularly useful if 'target costing' is used.

## Approaches to standard setting

Standards are usually set at either *ideal* or *attainable* levels.

- *Ideal standards* make no allowances for any inefficiencies. They are achievable only under the most favourable conditions and represent the theoretical maximum outcomes. It is not possible for actual performance to exceed ideal standards and their use may demotivate many employees.
- *Attainable standards* are set at high but achievable levels; they represent a challenge. They make allowances for normal working conditions and are achievable by operating efficiently. They are capable of being exceeded and, therefore, can be used to motivate the workforce.

However, it is worth considering who decides what is the attainable level of performance. This decision is normally, at least partially, subjective. Top managers may have a different viewpoint from the budget holders charged with executing the budget.

This potential conflict of interests has led to *participative budgeting* where budget holders are involved in creating their own budgets. Management accounting staff help them to create their budgets, which then have to be agreed at a higher level of management. Two important points arise from this.

First, budget holders gain 'psychological ownership' from being involved in creating their own budget. It becomes 'their' budget rather than someone else's imposed upon them. They have a greater commitment to the success of their budget, which leads to improved performance. Non-involvement leads to a lack of interest in its success.

Second, as budget holders know they will ultimately be held responsible for meeting the budget, they have a natural tendency not to set their own targets too high. The technical term for these 'safety' or 'buffer' factors is *budgetary slack*. This is defined as 'the intentional overestimation of expenses and/or underestimation of revenues in the budgeting process' (CIMA *Management Accounting Official Terminology*).

The final decision on the contents of the budget belongs to senior management. However, this form of centralized control is potentially demotivating. To counteract this, the budget holder is usually given a high degree of responsibility for **how** the budget is achieved. He or she makes the day-to-day operating decisions and decides the tactics for meeting the corporate objectives. This bipartite approach effectively defuses the potential conflict between delegation and centralized control.

## Importance of accurate standards

Badly set standards cause misleading variances whose investigation wastes both time and resources. Variances caused by poor standards are known as *planning variances*. One way to avoid these is by the systematic reviewing and updating of all standards.

Another aspect of accuracy is the question of how the budget allowance is arrived at for discretionary costs. How do you set the budget for items such as advertising or training? This type of cost may vary significantly from year to year. There is no easy answer to this question but managers should be aware of the problems posed by this type of cost.

# Limitations of budgets as plans

In the 1970s, most large UK companies had a planning department employing a significant number of people. The wisdom of that era was that good planning for the next 5 to 10 years would enable the business to operate efficiently by anticipating and being prepared for future changes. Some also had outline plans for the next 15, 20 or 25 years. Many resources were tied up in the planning process. Thirty years later, at the beginning of the twenty-first century, the proportion of resources allocated to this process is far smaller.

The main reason is that the rate of change in the business environment has greatly accelerated during those years and shows no sign of slowing down. To plan in detail for the next 10 years is considered to be a waste of time. The organization may be supplying different products and services in different markets by then. It may have been taken over or it may have acquired other organizations to take it in new directions. The stock markets of the world operate globally and faster than ever before. The amount of uncertainty in the business environment is much greater than it was before. Long-term planning is not seen as an effective use of resources. It is common to produce detailed plans only for the next year, and outline plans for the next three years only.

## The manager's point of view (written by Nigel Burton)

Almost every field of human endeavour can be improved by a little advance planning. This is particularly true of businesses, which are complicated operations consisting of numerous disparate activities and disciplines. Planning is crucial to ensure that all these disciplines are moving forward in the most efficient way for the enterprise as a whole.

In the vast majority of businesses, the most important driving force is the strategic sales plan. The sales department, with its close knowledge of the market in general and of individual customers' needs in particular, is best placed both to determine the growth potential of existing products, and to identify marketing opportunities for new products. Its view of what can be achieved, given the right products and supported by the right infrastructure, will provide the pattern of the company's direction for the foreseeable future.

The activities of all other departments in the company will be directed towards supporting the strategic sales plan. The technical department will develop new products to meet the customer requirements specified by the salesforce. Production will gear themselves up, through new equipment or plant modifications, to meet the sales forecast. Purchasing will identify reliable sources for any new materials required. Even Personnel and Administration will provide an infrastructure designed to support the overall plan.

It is then helpful to pull together the plans of all the departments into a long-range company plan. This should not be a detailed document, but should give an outline of the way the company might look over the next few years. In particular, it should ensure that the timing of any specific initiative is properly co-ordinated. For instance, is the development work for new products being started early enough? How long will it take to get approval for the capacity expansion project? Are we developing our people quickly enough to support the expanding business? All this will also lead to profit and cash forecasts, allowing the viability of the overall plan to be established at an early stage.

This should only be an outline document because the circumstances surrounding it will be constantly changing. Such is the pace of change in all fields now, in production and product technology, in IT and information flow, in increasing competition from all corners of the world, that plans can no longer be rigid. Ideally, they would change as every new circumstance emerged. It may not be practical to keep the company plan regularly updated, but the fact remains that managers must constantly be aware of the impact of external factors on their businesses, in both the short and long term.

The annual budget, however, is quite different. It is a working document, full of important detail, which enables the business to be controlled on a day-to-day basis. In my chemicals company, the establishment of the budget was always the biggest exercise of the year. Although everyone traditionally complained about the amount of time it consumed, there is no doubt that the examination of the detail meant that all managers developed a profound understanding of the dynamics of the business. It was the only time in the year that the elements of the profit and loss account were closely examined, allowing cost/benefit issues to be questioned and cost-saving opportunities to be identified. For the rest of the year, the detailed budget became a yardstick against which actual performance could be confidently and easily measured.

If your company has a relatively stable customer base, it is highly desirable to set up a detailed sales budget by customer and product. A computerized sales reporting system will then be able to highlight with ease the areas where targets are not being met, so that early corrective action can be taken by the sales department. If your business consists of one-off contracts, it is clearly less easy to set up such a monitoring procedure, but it is still important to set up some appropriate measurement to provide an early warning of sales shortfalls.

The same principle applies to both direct costs of production and overheads. The budgeting process provides the opportunity to re-evaluate every aspect of cost. Are the standards used in product costing still accurate? Can we justify the level of expenditure we are proposing for, say, travel or advertising? Are there any new or one-off items we want to budget for in the current year? Or any items incurred last year which we do not expect to be repeated next year? This is why, in my view, zero-based budgeting should be used wherever possible.

In my company, managers were required to justify the whole of their budgeted expenditure each year. Travelling expenses, for instance, were always frighteningly large, as our salesforce used to travel all over the world, but, by breaking this lump sum down into individual trips for each salesperson, it was possible to carry out a realistic review. Is it really necessary to have three trips to the Far East, or will two be enough? The sales manager has to provide a convincing justification. However, not all expense headings lend themselves easily to this type of analysis. Repairs to plant, for instance, was another large sum, which consisted of a mass of generally small items. The problem here is that, despite the use of sophisticated maintenance planning systems, there will always be a large number of unforeseeable repair costs. Moreover, the piece of equipment which incurred costly repairs last year is perhaps unlikely to break down again next year, so there is never an identifiable pattern to repairs. For this type of expense, therefore, we were obliged to adopt the incremental approach, taking average expenditure levels in recent years, and adding or subtracting amounts for known changes. In doing this, however, we accepted that we would be unable to exercise the same level of control as in many other areas of expenditure.

Incremental budgeting is a crude tool which allows inaccuracies and inefficiencies to be built into the system. Take salaries as an example. The actual salaries bill for last year is not the sum of the annual salaries of your employees. Staff turnover will inevitably mean that there are unfilled vacancies at times during the year. Replacement staff may have higher or lower salaries than the previous incumbents. There may have been promotions during the year, with accompanying salary increases. Temporary staff may also have been employed, at a much higher cost than permanent staff. Will overtime patterns be the same next year? As you can see, there are many occurrences which can have an impact on the total salary costs. When you come to budget for the following year, you have two options. You can assume that the same situations will occur again next year, so simply take last year's cost and add on a percentage for inflation. Alternatively, you can construct a detailed budget based on actual salaries and projected overtime levels, perhaps ignoring the impact of staff turnover, as it is impossible to forecast where in the company this will occur. Any savings arising from staff turnover can then be taken as favourable variances next year. My preference would always tend towards the latter option. If the managing director asks you why your department's salaries are over budget, you will be able to give a precise answer if you have a firm, detailed budget. If you have to answer 'Well, I think it's because we were understaffed last year', your credibility will undoubtedly suffer!

A detailed, well-constructed budget will also enable you to understand where there is some slack in the system. This is important for the inevitable moment when you receive an instruction from senior management to find more profit. It is a feature of budgeting that, when the proposals of all the departmental managers are put together, the resulting profit figure is never high enough! You will be asked to find more sales volumes, increase prices, or cut down costs, so it would be an unwise manager who did not leave a little slack in his or her initial numbers. If you work for a large corporation with multiple subsidiaries, the same phenomenon will occur at the higher level, when the budgets of all the businesses are added together. The profit is never high enough to meet the shareholders' expectations, and the instruction will come down to increase your local profit by a further factor. With a detailed budget, you can reflect these amendments by specific changes to your plans, e.g. by deferring the recruitment of new staff till later in the year. With a poorly constructed budget, however, this reiterative process will further distance your numbers from reality, and render the budget even less useful as a yardstick.

*Summary*

- Budgets are medium-term organizational plans expressed in monetary terms.
- They are intended to help the achievement of corporate, strategic long-term goals.
- Detailed functional or departmental budgets are prepared first.
- The summary master budget is prepared last; the process is bottom up.
- Budgets can be fixed or flexible.
- They are usually created incrementally, sometimes by a zero-based approach.
- Standards can be set in different ways and are subjective.
- Their main limitation is that they cannot be easily adjusted for unforeseen changes.

## Further reading

Horngren, C., Bhimani, A., Datar, S. and Foster, G. (2002) *Management and Cost Accounting*, 2nd edition, Prentice Hall Europe, Harlow. See chapter 'Motivation, budgets and responsibility accounting'.

Langford, B. N. (2000) 'Production budgets, simplified', *Folio: The Magazine for Magazine Management*, Vol. 30, Issue 1, 1 January.

Otley, D. (1987) *Accounting Control and Organisational Behaviour*, Heinemann Professional Publishing, Oxford. See Chapter 7, 'Budgetary systems design'.

Upchurch, A. (2003) *Management Accounting, Principles and Practice*, 2nd edition, Financial Times/Prentice Hall, Harlow. See chapter 'Budgetary planning'.

Weetman, P. (2002) *Management Accounting, an Introduction*, 3rd edition, Financial Times/Prentice Hall, Harlow. See chapter 'Preparing a budget'.

## Answers to self-assessment questions

### S14.1

|       |               | April | May | June | July |
|-------|---------------|-------|-----|------|------|
|       | Sales         | 100   | 140 | 120  | 160  |
| Add:  | Closing stock | 35    | 30  | 40   |      |
| Less: | Opening stock | 25    | 35  | 30   | 40   |
|       | **Production**| **110** | **135** | **130** |  |

### S14.2

$$\text{Purchases} = \text{usage} + \text{closing stock} - \text{opening stock}$$
$$= 9{,}000 + 60 - 80$$
$$= \textbf{8,980 units of raw material @ £6}$$
$$= \textbf{£53,880}$$

### S14.3

|       |               | £      |
|-------|---------------|--------|
|       | Opening stock | 30,000 |
| Add:  | Production    | 60,000 |
| Less: | Closing stock | 27,000 |
|       | **Cost of sales** | **63,000** |

S14.4

|  | | £ | |
|---|---|---|---|
| | Opening debtors | 1,300 | |
| Add: | Credit sales | 12,000 | $(2,400 \times 10 \times 0.5)$ |
| Less: | Closing debtors | 1,000 | |
| | | £ | |
| | Receipts from debtors | 12,300 | |
| | Receipts from cash sales | 12,000 | $(2,400 \times 10 \times 0.5)$ |
| | **Total receipts for year** | **24,300** | |

S14.5

|  | | £ | |
|---|---|---|---|
| | Opening creditors | 750 | |
| Add: | Credit purchases | 6,000 | $(1,600 \times 0.75 \times £5)$ |
| Less: | Closing creditors | 1,000 | (200 @ £5) |
| | Payments to creditors | 5,750 | |
| | Payments on cash terms | 2,000 | $(1,600 \times 0.25 \times £5)$ |
| | **Total payments for year** | **7,750** | |

S14.6

**Cash budget for quarter ended 31 March**

| | Jan | Feb | Mar | Total |
|---|---|---|---|---|
| Receipts: | | | | |
| Credit sales | 100 | 100 | 100 | 300 |
| Cash sales | 30 | 30 | 30 | 90 |
| Other | – | 70 | – | 70 |
| Total | 130 | 200 | 130 | 460 |
| Payments: | | | | |
| Purchases of materials | 100 | 100 | 100 | 300 |
| Wages | 25 | 25 | 25 | 75 |
| Expenses | 35 | 35 | 35 | 105 |
| Other | 15 | – | – | 15 |
| Total | 175 | 160 | 160 | 495 |
| Net in/(out)flow | (45) | 40 | (30) | (35) |
| Opening bank balance | (150) | (195) | (155) | (150) |
| Closing bank balance | (195) | (155) | (185) | (185) |

S14.7

It is obvious from the question that July is not a representative month and it should be excluded from your calculations. The scattergraph below confirms this:

|  |  |  |  |
|---|---|---|---|
| High month: | June | 157 | 2,073 |
| Low month: | September | 122 | 1,723 |
|  |  | 35 | 350 |

**Variable cost per hour = 350/35 = £10/hour**

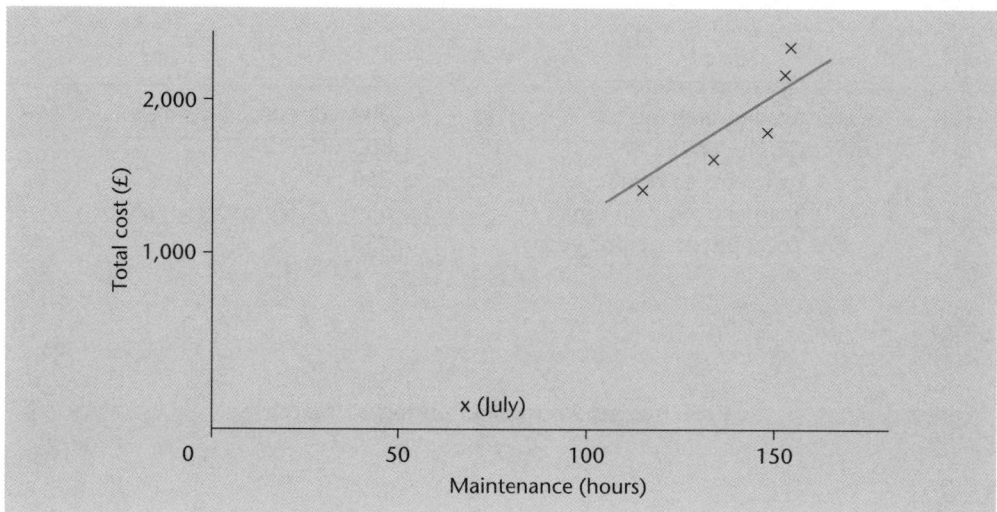

Calculate by using the highest month (June):

|  | £ |
|---|---|
| **Total cost** | = 2,073 |
| **Total variable cost = 157 h × £10/h** | = 1,570 |
| **Total fixed cost** | = 503 |

Check by using the lowest month (September):

$$\text{Total cost} = \text{total fixed cost} + \text{total variable cost}$$
$$= 503 + (122 \times 10)$$
$$= \underline{£1,723}$$

So, the best estimate for maintenance expenditure in November is:

$$\text{Total cost} = \text{total fixed cost} + \text{total variable cost}$$
$$= 503 + (180 \times 10)$$
$$= \underline{£2,303}$$

## CASE STUDY    The Omega Document Case Company

Omega is a long-established firm which used to make many different kinds of leather goods. However, in 2002 it made a loss for the first time in over 20 years. This was due to fierce competition, mainly from the Far East. In response to this, it has slashed its product range to its best-selling and most profitable items. It is hoping to benefit from economies of scale and now plans to make only two types of document case: the Delta and the Alpha.

*Task:*

From the following information, using the pro formas provided, you are required to create a budget for the year ending 31 December 2003.

### Sales forecast

|                        | Delta  | Alpha  |
|------------------------|--------|--------|
| Number of cases sold   | 4,000  | 2,500  |
| Selling price per case | £60    | £55    |

### Standard production data

Omega has only two production departments: Cutting and Stitching.
   Unit costs:

| Direct labour rates | | Raw materials | |
|----------|-----------|------------|--------------|
| **Cutting** | **Stitching** | **Leather** | **Zip fasteners** |
| £6.00/h  | £7.00/h   | £3.00/unit | £1.00/unit   |

### Product content

|                      | Delta    | Alpha     |
|----------------------|----------|-----------|
| Leather              | 2 units  | 4 units   |
| Zips                 | 1 unit   | 2 units   |
| Cutting dept labour  | 2 hours  | 1.5 hours |
| Stitching dept labour| 1 hour   | 0.5 hour  |

## Production overheads

|  | Cutting Department | | Stitching Department | |
|---|---|---|---|---|
|  | Fixed | Variable | Fixed | Variable |
|  | £ | £ | £ | £ |
| Indirect labour | 7,000 | – | 3,000 | – |
| Indirect materials | – | 3,000 | – | 9,000 |
| Maintenance | 2,000 | 1,000 | 500 | 500 |
| Business rates | 6,000 | – | 1,000 | – |
| Depreciation | 8,000 | – | 2,000 | – |
| Electricity | 1,000 | 2,000 | 500 | 1,000 |
|  | 24,000 | 6,000 | 7,000 | 10,500 |

## Marketing overheads

| | £ |
|---|---|
| Salaries | 28,000 |
| Advertising | 24,000 |
| Other | 2,000 |
| | 54,000 |

## Administration overheads

| | £ |
|---|---|
| Salaries | 32,000 |
| Telephone | 5,000 |
| Other | 4,150 |
| | 41,150 |

## Stocks forecast

|  | Raw materials | | Completed cases | |
|---|---|---|---|---|
|  | Leather (units) | Zips (units) | Delta (units) | Alpha (units) |
| Opening stock | 6,000 | 1,000 | 100 | 1,000 |
| Closing stock | 8,000 | 2,000 | 1,100 | 500 |

## Debtors and creditors

Raw materials, labour, all overheads and debenture interest will be paid in full through the bank and cash accounts. Debtors and creditors at 31 December 2002 will pay and be paid during 2003. Debtors and creditors at 31 December 2003 are expected to be £25,000 and £10,000 respectively. One year's interest on the debenture is paid during the year.

## Fixed assets

There are no disposals expected during 2003 but some new equipment will be acquired, on cash terms, for £20,000 just before the end of 2003.

## Expected balance sheet as at 31 December 2002

| Fixed assets | Cost £ | Depreciation provision £ | NBV £ |
|---|---|---|---|
| Buildings | 40,000 | 40,000 | – |
| Machinery | 200,000 | 50,000 | 150,000 |
| | 240,000 | 90,000 | 150,000 |
| **Current assets** | | | |
| Raw material stock | 19,000 | | |
| Finished goods stock | 40,000 | | |
| Total stock | | 59,000 | |
| Debtors | | 15,000 | |
| Bank and cash | | 10,000 | |
| | | 84,000 | |
| **Less: Current liabilities** | | | |
| Creditors | | 8,000 | |
| **Net current assets** | | | 76,000 |
| | | | 226,000 |
| **Less: Long-term liabilities** | | | |
| 10% debenture 2006/08 | | | 120,000 |
| | | | **106,000** |

| *Financed by:* | | | £ |
|---|---|---|---|
| **Shareholders' capital** | | | |
| Ordinary shares | | | 82,000 |
| Retained profit | | | 24,000 |
| | | | **106,000** |

## Pro formas

1 Sales budget y/e 31 December 2003

| | Units | Selling price £ | Revenue £ |
|---|---|---|---|
| Delta | .......... | .......... | .......... |
| Alpha | .......... | .......... | .......... |
| | | Budget revenue | _____ |

2 Production budget y/e 31 December 2003

| | Delta (units) | Alpha (units) |
|---|---|---|
| Planned sales | .......... | .......... |
| Desired closing stock finished goods | .......... | .......... |
| Total required | .......... | .......... |
| Less opening stock finished goods | .......... | .......... |
| Budgeted production | .......... | .......... |

### 3 Direct materials usage budget y/e 31 December 2003

| | Material content (units/case) | Delta Production (cases) | Usage (units) | Material content (units/case) | Alpha Production (cases) | Usage (units) |
|---|---|---|---|---|---|---|
| Leather | ......... | ......... | ......... | ......... | ......... | ......... |
| Zips | ......... | ......... | ......... | ......... | ......... | ......... |

| | Cost/unit £ | Total usage | Cost of materials used £ |
|---|---|---|---|
| Leather | ............ | ............ | ............ |
| Zips | ............ | ............ | ............ |
| | | Budgeted material cost | _____ |

### 4 Direct materials purchases budget y/e 31 December 2003

| | Leather | Zips |
|---|---|---|
| Desired closing stock | ............ units | ............ units |
| Units needed for production | ............ units | ............ units |
| Total required | ............ units | ............ units |
| Less opening stock | ............ units | ............ units |
| Purchases needed | ............ units | ............ units |
| Cost per unit | £............ | £............ |
| Budgeted purchases cost | £............ | £............ |

### 5 Direct labour budget y/e 31 December 2003

| | Labour content in product (hours) | Cases produced | Total labour hours | Rate per hour £ | Total labour cost £ |
|---|---|---|---|---|---|
| Cutting dept | | | | | |
| Delta | .......... | ........... | .......... | .......... | .......... |
| Alpha | .......... | ........... | .......... | .......... | .......... |
| Stitching dept | | | | | |
| Delta | .......... | .......... | .......... | .......... | .......... |
| Alpha | .......... | .......... | .......... | .......... | .......... |
| Budgeted labour hours and cost | | | _____ | | _____ |

**6  Production overheads budget y/e 31 December 2003**

| | Cutting dept (expected 13,000 direct labour hours) | | Stitching dept (expected 6,000 direct labour hours) | |
|---|---|---|---|---|
| | Fixed costs £ | Variable costs £ | Fixed costs £ | Variable costs £ |
| Indirect labour | .......... | .......... | .......... | .......... |
| Indirect materials | .......... | .......... | .......... | .......... |
| Maintenance | .......... | .......... | .......... | .......... |
| Business rates | .......... | .......... | .......... | .......... |
| Depreciation | .......... | .......... | .......... | .......... |
| Electricity | .......... | .......... | .......... | .......... |
| Budgeted overhead costs | _____ | _____ | _____ | _____ |
| Overhead absorption rate per direct labour hour | _____ | _____ | _____ | _____ |

**7  Standard budgeted unit cost of manufacturing y/e 31 December 2003**

| | | Delta | | Alpha | |
|---|---|---|---|---|---|
| | Unit cost £ | Units in product | Cost £ | Units in product | Cost £ |
| Leather | .......... | .......... | .......... | .......... | .......... |
| Zips | .......... | .......... | .......... | .......... | .......... |
| Direct labour: | | | | | |
| Cutting | .......... | .......... | .......... | .......... | .......... |
| Stitching | .......... | .......... | .......... | .......... | .......... |

| | | Delta | | Alpha | |
|---|---|---|---|---|---|
| | Unit cost £ | Units in product | Cost £ | Units in product | Cost £ |
| Production overheads: | | | | | |
| Cutting   – Fixed | .......... | .......... | .......... | .......... | .......... |
| – Variable | .......... | .......... | .......... | .......... | .......... |
| Stitching – Fixed | .......... | .......... | .......... | .......... | .......... |
| – Variable | .......... | .......... | .......... | .......... | .......... |
| Standard cost of product | | | _____ | _____ | _____ |

**8  Closing stock budget at 31 December 2003**

| | Units | Unit cost £ | Total cost £ | £ |
|---|---|---|---|---|
| Direct materials: | | | | |
| Leather | .......... | .......... | .......... | |
| Zips | .......... | .......... | .......... | .......... |
| Finished products | | | | |
| Delta | .......... | .......... | .......... | |
| Alpha | .......... | .......... | .......... | .......... |
| Budgeted closing stock | | | | _____ |

## 9  Cost of sales budget y/e 31 December 2003

|  | £ | £ |
|---|---|---|
| Direct materials usage (3) | ............. | |
| Direct labour (5) | ............. | |
| Production overheads (6) | ............. | |
| Add: Opening stock finished products | | ............. |
| Less: Closing stock finished products | | ............. |
| Budgeted cost of sales | | ............. |

## 10  Marketing and administration expenses budget y/e 31 December 2003

|  | £ | £ |
|---|---|---|
| Marketing expenses: | | |
| Salaries | ............. | |
| Advertising | ............. | |
| Other | ............. | ............. |
| Administrative expenses: | | |
| Salaries | ............. | |
| Telephone | ............. | |
| Other | ............. | ............. |
| Budgeted selling and administrative expenses | | ............. |

## 11  Budgeted profit statement y/e 31 December 2003

|  | £ |
|---|---|
| Sales (1) | ............. |
| Less: Cost of sales (9) | ............. |
| Gross profit | ............. |
| Less: Marketing and admin. expenses (10) | ............. |
| Less: Interest on debenture | ............. |
| Budgeted net profit | _____ |

## 12  Cash budget y/e 31 December 2003 (summary form)

|  | £ | £ |
|---|---|---|
| Opening cash balance | | ............. |
| Add receipts | | ............. |
| Total cash available | | ............. |
| Less payments: | | |
| Purchases | ............. | |
| Direct labour (5) | ............. | |
| Factory overheads less depreciation (6) | ............. | |
| Marketing and admin. expenses (10) | ............. | |
| Debenture interest | ............. | |
| Fixed asset purchases | ............. | ............. |
| Budgeted closing cash balance | | _____ |

13  Budgeted balance sheet of Omega Manufacturing as at 31 December 2003

| | £<br>Cost | £<br>Depn provn | £<br>NBV |
|---|---|---|---|
| **Fixed assets** | | | |
| Buildings | .............. | .............. | .............. |
| Machinery | .............. | .............. | .............. |
| | .............. | .............. | .............. |
| **Current assets** | | | |
| Stocks: | | | |
| Finished goods | .............. | | |
| Raw materials | .............. | .............. | |
| Debtors | | .............. | |
| Bank and cash | | .............. | |
| **Less current liabilities** | | | |
| Creditors | | .............. | |
| **Net current assets** | | | .............. |
| | | | .............. |
| **Less long-term liabilities** | | | |
| 10% Debenture 2006/08 | | | .............. |
| | | | £_____ |
| *Financed by:* | | | |
| **Shareholders' capital** | | | |
| Ordinary shares | | | .............. |
| Retained profits | | | .............. |
| | | | £_____ |

## Questions

An asterisk * on a question number indicates that the answer is given at the end of the book. Answers to the other questions are given in the Lecturer's Guide.

### Q14.1*  Kellaway Ltd

Kellaway Ltd makes aluminium junction boxes for the electrical industry. It makes the boxes in three different sizes: small, medium and large. The following details are taken from next quarter's budget:

|  | Large | Medium | Small |
|---|---|---|---|
| Sales volume (units) | 4,000 | 5,000 | 3,500 |
| *Direct labour:* | | | |
| Fitters and turners (hours/unit) | 1.25 | 0.90 | 0.80 |
| Assemblers and packers (hours/unit) | 0.40 | 0.25 | 0.20 |
| *Direct materials:* | | | |
| Aluminium strips per unit | 2.5 | 1.0 | 0.5 |
| Packaging materials (metres) | 1.25 | 0.75 | 0.5 |
| *Stocks:* | | | |
| Finished goods opening stock (units) | 300 | 400 | 200 |
| Finished goods closing stock (units) | 400 | 300 | 150 |

Rates of pay for fitters/turners and assemblers/packers are £10.00/hour and £6.00/hour respectively. Aluminium strips cost £3 each and packaging is £1/metre. Kellaway plans to have opening material stocks of 220 aluminium strips and 80 metres of packaging. The closing material stocks are 150 aluminium strips and 50 metres of packaging. The quarter's fixed production overheads of £31,700 are attached to product lines on a direct labour hour basis.

*Tasks:*

1  Create the production budget for the quarter.
2  Calculate the unit production cost of each type of junction box.
3  Create the materials usage budget in quantities and value.
4  Create the materials purchases budget in quantities and value.
5  Create the direct labour budget in hours and value.

## Q14.2* Pierce Pommery

Pierce Pommery specializes in the manufacture of dry cider. The 1-litre bottles sell for £3.00 each, with 25% of sales on cash terms and 75% on one month's credit. The budget shows the following sales volumes:

| Month | Litres |
|---|---|
| August | 400,000 |
| September | 340,000 |
| October | 300,000 |
| November | 260,000 |
| December | 320,000 |
| January | 250,000 |

The company's policy is for opening stock of cider to equal one-fifth of each month's sales, but the stock of cider on 1 September was actually 80,000 litres. For stocks of apples, the policy is for opening stock to equal 50% of each month's usage. On 1 September, the stock of apples was actually 2,200 tonnes.

On average, 15 kilograms of apples are needed to produce 1 litre of cider (1 tonne = 1,000 kg). The cost price of apples is £50/tonne in September and October but £150/tonne in November and December as they have to be imported. Direct labour is paid in the month it is incurred and costs £0.20 a litre. Fixed overheads are £30,000 a month (including £5,000 for depreciation). Payment for apples is made two months after purchase but all other expenses are paid for one month after being incurred.

*Tasks:*

1  For the months of September, October, November and for the quarter as a whole, prepare the production budget (in litres) and the purchases budget (in tonnes and £).
2  For November only, prepare the cash budget. (Assume the bank balance on 1 November is £495,900 overdrawn.)

## Q14.3* Norman Ropes

The sales budget for next year for a particular type of rope manufactured by Norman Ropes is as follows:

| Period | Metres | Period | Metres |
|---|---|---|---|
| 1 | 3,000 | 7 | 8,000 |
| 2 | 4,000 | 8 | 7,000 |
| 3 | 5,000 | 9 | 6,000 |
| 4 | 4,000 | 10 | 5,000 |
| 5 | 6,000 | 11 | 4,000 |
| 6 | 6,000 | 12 | 3,000 |

The stock of finished rope at the start of each period is to be equal to 25% of the sales estimate for the period. (Norman Rope's policy concerning finished product stock levels is to have a quantity of rope in stock approximately equal to one week's sales.) Exceptionally, at the beginning of period 1 there will be 1,500 metres of rope in stock. There is no work-in-progress at the end of any period.

This type of rope uses only one material, a nylon cord known as ARN. Many lengths of this cord are twisted together to form the rope. The budget assumes that each metre of rope uses 100 metres of ARN and that each metre of ARN will cost £0.04.

Materials equal to 25% of each period's usage are to be on hand at the start of the period. Exceptionally, the stock at the start of period 1 will be 125,000 metres of ARN. (Norman Rope's policy concerning raw material stock levels is to have a quantity of material in stock approximately equal to one week's usage.)

*Tasks:*

For the first **six** periods, prepare:

a) the production budget (in metres of rope);
b) the materials usage cost budget;
c) the materials purchases cost budget.

## Q14.4 Bishop & Co.

Bishop & Co. manufactures vinyl pond lining for the water-garden industry. The company buys vinyl beads by the tonne and heats and rolls them into large sheets which are then cut to the required sizes. One tonne of beads produces 10,000 square metres of liner. Bishop & Co. is uncertain of demand for next year and decides to produce a flexible budget covering five activity levels from 400,000 square metres to 600,000 square metres in steps of 50,000 square metres.

The vinyl beads cost £800/tonne for purchases of up to and including 50 tonnes per year. Bishop & Co.'s supplier offers it the following bulk-purchase incentive. For annual purchases exceeding 50 tonnes, the cost of every tonne in addition to the first 50 is £750.

The direct labour cost is made up of an annual lump sum of basic pay plus a volume-related bonus operative on all production output.

The present annual capacity of the manufacturing plant is 450,000 square metres. For production above this, a new machine will have to be purchased at a cost of £500,000. (No additional labour will be necessary to operate this highly automated machinery.) Bishop & Co.'s policy on depreciation is to write off machinery in equal instalments over 10 years, assuming a zero residual value.

The cost of insurance cover is a fixed amount up to a production level of 500,000 square metres. Beyond that, there is an additional cost per unit.

Bishop & Co. is currently one of the market leaders (in terms of sales volume) in the vinyl pond liner market although it is very competitive. Bishop & Co. sets its selling price per square metre on a cost-plus basis by adding a 300% mark-up to the total production cost. This covers marketing and administration expenses and leaves a little left over for profit.

*Tasks:*

1  Complete the following production department budget for next year:

| 000 sqm | 400 £ | 450 £ | 500 £ | 550 £ | 600 £ |
|---|---|---|---|---|---|
| Vinyl beads | 32,000 | | | | 47,500 |
| Direct labour | 80,000 | | | | 90,000 |
| Electricity | 8,000 | | | | 10,000 |
| Depreciation | 22,000 | | | | 34,000 |
| Insurance | 11,000 | | | | 11,250 |
| Other production costs | 139,000 | | | | 139,000 |
| **Total** | **292,000** | | | | **331,750** |

2  If demand were to exceed 500,000 square metres and the new machinery was purchased, what effect might this have on Bishop's overall performance? What advice would you give regarding the purchase of the new machinery?

## Q14.5  Chinkin Corporation

The Chinkin Corporation produces surfboards. Its sales have been 300 a month for the last few months but it is about to launch an expansion strategy aimed at increasing sales by 50% over the next four months, April to July. Sales in April are expected to be 300 boards but to increase by 50 units a month until 450 units are sold in July and each subsequent month.

The selling price of the boards is £50 and half the customers pay in the month following purchase. One-quarter take two months to pay and the other quarter pay cash-on-delivery, taking advantage of a 5% cash discount.

Chinkin has planned an advertising campaign for the months of April, May and June, costing a total of £40,000. Half this amount is payable in April and the remainder in two equal instalments in May and June.

To facilitate the increase in production, new plant and equipment costing £18,000 have been ordered for delivery in April, with payment in three equal monthly instalments, commencing in May. The cost of commissioning this machinery is estimated at £2,000 and will be paid to the outside contractors in April.

To lessen the impact of acquiring these fixed assets, Chinkin plans to arrange a three-month loan of £20,000 from its bank and expects to pay interest at the rate of 10% per annum. The interest will be paid in one amount on the same day as the capital sum is repaid. The money is to be transferred into its account on 3 April.

Raw materials cost £20 a unit and are paid for one month after purchase. Chinkin plans to have a monthly opening stock of raw materials equal to each month's production requirements. Similarly, its policy regarding stocks of finished boards is to have a monthly opening stock equal to each month's total sales.

Monthly fixed costs, including depreciation of £600, total £6,200 and are paid for in the month incurred.

The opening bank balance for April is expected to be £11,400 positive. Chinkin's current overdraft limit is £25,000.

*Task:*

Create Chinkin's monthly cash budget for the four-month period April to July and for the four-month period as a whole (work to the nearest £). Advise the corporation accordingly.

## Q14.6  T Ltd

T Ltd is a newly formed company that designs customized computer programs for its clients. The capital needed to fund the company will be provided by a venture capitalist who will invest £150,000 on 1 January 2002 in exchange for shares in T Ltd.

The directors are currently gathering the information needed to help in the preparation of the cash budget for the first three months of 2002. The information that they have is given below.

*Budget details*

The budgeted sales (that is, the value of the contracts signed) for the first quarter of 2002 are expected to be £200,000. However, as the company will only just have commenced trading, it is thought that sales will need time to grow. It is therefore expected that 15% of the first quarter's sales will be achieved in January, 30% in February and the remainder in March. It is expected that sales for the year ending 31 December 2002 will reach £1,000,000.

Clients must pay a deposit of 5% of the value of the computer program when they sign the contract for the program to be designed. Payments of 45% and 50% of the value are then paid one and two months later respectively. No bad debts are anticipated in the first quarter.

There are six people employed by the company, each earning an annual gross salary of £45,000, payable in arrears on the last day of each month.

Computer hardware and software will be purchased for £100,000 in January. A deposit of 25% is payable on placing the order for the computer hardware and software, with the remaining balance being paid in equal amounts in February and March. The capital outlay will be depreciated on a straight-line basis over three years, assuming no residual value.

The company has decided to rent offices that will require an initial deposit of £13,000 and an ongoing cost of £6,500 per month payable in advance. These offices are fully serviced and the rent is inclusive of all fixed overhead costs.

Variable production costs are paid in the month in which they are incurred and are budgeted as follows:

*January  £1,200      February  £4,200      March  £8,000*

A marketing and advertising campaign will be launched in January at a cost of £10,000 with a further campaign in March for £5,000, both amounts being payable as they are incurred.

Administration overhead is budgeted to be £500 each month: 60% to be paid in the month of usage and the balance one month later.

Tax and interest charges can be ignored.

*Required:*

(a) Prepare the cash budget by month and in total for the first quarter of 2002.

*(15 marks)*

(b) Identify and comment on those areas of the cash budget that you wish to draw to the attention of the Directors of T Ltd, and recommend action to improve cash flow.

*(7 marks)*

(c) Briefly explain three advantages for T Ltd of using a spreadsheet when preparing a cash budget.

*(3 marks)*

*(Total = 25 marks)*

CIMA Foundation: Management Accounting Fundamentals, November 2001

## Q14.7  ST plc

ST plc produces three types of processed foods for a leading food retailer. The company has three processing departments (Preparation, Cooking and Packaging). After recognizing that the overheads incurred in these departments varied in relation to the activities performed, the company switched from a traditional absorption costing system to a budgetary control system that is based on activity based costing.

The *foods* are processed in batches. The budgeted output for April was as follows:

|  | **Output** |
|---|---|
| Food A | 100 batches |
| Food B | 30 batches |
| Food C | 200 batches |

The number of activities and processing hours budgeted to process a batch of foods in each of the departments are as follows:

|  | **Food A** Activities per batch | **Food B** Activities per batch | **Food C** Activities per batch |
|---|---|---|---|
| Preparation | 5 | 9 | 12 |
| Cooking | 2 | 1 | 4 |
| Packaging | 15 | 2 | 6 |
| Processing time | 10 hours | 375 hours | 80 hours |

The budgeted departmental overhead costs for April were:

|  | **Overheads** $ |
|---|---|
| Preparation | 100,000 |
| Cooking | 350,000 |
| Packaging | 50,000 |

*Required:*

(a) For food A ONLY, calculate the budgeted overhead cost per batch:
   (i) using traditional absorption costing, based on a factory-wide absorption rate per processing hour; and
   (ii) using activity based costing.

*(6 marks)*

(b) Comment briefly on the advantages of using an activity-based costing approach to determining the cost of each type of processed food compared with traditional absorption costing approaches. You should make reference to your answers to requirement (a) where appropriate.

*(4 marks)*

(c) The actual output for April was:

|  | **Output** |
|---|---|
| Food A | 120 batches |
| Food B | 45 batches |
| Food C | 167 batches |

*Required:*

Prepare a flexed budget for April using an activity based costing approach. Your statement must show the total budgeted overhead for each department and the total budgeted overhead absorbed by each food.

*(10 marks)*

(d) Discuss the advantages that ST plc should see from the activity based control system compared with the traditional absorption costing that it used previously.

*(5 marks)*

*(Total 25 marks)*

CIMA Intermediate: Management Accounting – Performance Management, May 2004

## Review questions

1 Explain what a budget is.
2 Explain how budgets fit into the corporate planning context.
3 List the positive attributes of budgetary control systems.
4 Differentiate between fixed and flexible budgets.
5 Differentiate between incremental and zero-based budgeting.
6 Define standard cost.
7 Discuss the issues about the setting of standards.
8 Discuss the limitations of budgets.

*The answers to all these questions can be found in the text of this chapter.*

# CHAPTER 15

# Using budgets to control operations

## Chapter contents

## Introduction

Having learned how to create a budget, you will have some idea of the complexity of this task. The budget in the case study at the end of the previous chapter comprised 13 schedules; a real organization will probably have many more. Creating a budget uses a great deal of time, effort and money. So it is understandable for the people involved to heave a sigh of relief when the completed budget is accepted by top management. It must be tempting to file it away and get on with some other work. But if the budget is now forgotten about, all the resources that went into it will have been completely wasted!

The creation of the budget means that the plan is now ready to be put into action. This chapter is all about how budgets are **used** to control the activities of organizations, to take them towards their chosen destination.

**Learning objectives**

**Having worked through this chapter you should be able to:**

- explain the basic theory of budgetary control systems;
- state the common formulae for cost variances and sub-variances;
- flex the budget to the actual level of production;
- calculate cost variances and their sub-variances;
- produce a profit reconciliation statement;
- illustrate the relationships between variances;
- discuss the additional benefits of budgetary control systems;
- manage the operating cost of budgetary control systems;
- comment on the problems of 'responsibility accounting';
- discuss the limitations of budgetary control systems;
- list 10 points for good budgetary control.

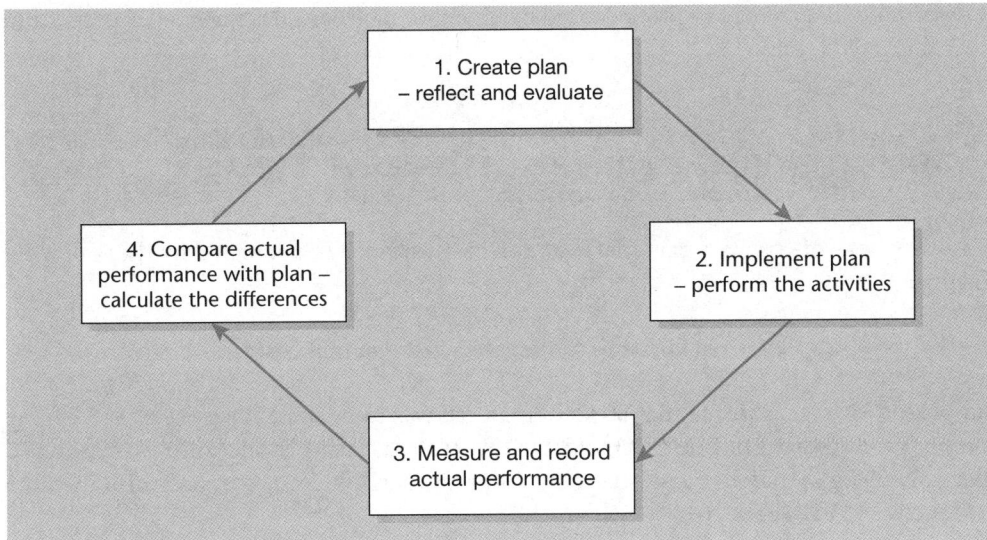

Figure 15.1 **The budgetary control loop**

## The budgetary control system

The basic principle of budgetary control systems is very simple and is best thought of as a cyclical four-step process (see Figure 15.1).

Although the budget is an annual statement, it is usually divided into 12 monthly periods. This is because, if something starts to go wrong, an attempt to put it right needs to be made as soon as possible to minimize the negative effect. For example, if an underground water pipe cracked in month 2, causing the cost of the metered water supply unexpectedly to treble, a comparison of the actual and planned cost at the end of that month would reveal this and corrective action could be taken quickly. If the comparison was not made until the end of the year, the unnecessary extra cost would be much greater. The comparisons need to be made frequently if effective control is to be exercised.

## Variances

Variances are the increases or decreases in profit which occur when things do not go according to plan. Variances are the differences referred to in step 4 of the budgetary control process (see Figure 15.1).

**Profit = sales revenue − total costs**

If sales revenue changes, then the profit will change. If total costs change, then profit will change.

A *variance* is a change in *profit* caused by changes in either sales revenue or costs from their budgeted levels.

## Variance formulae and raw material variances

For every item of cost, e.g. raw material, the cost variance is calculated by the following formula:

**Cost variance = budgeted cost − actual cost**

Suppose the budget showed that 80 kg of material was to be used at a price of £15 per kg: the budgeted cost would be £1,200 (80 × 15). If the actual production record showed that only 65 kg of material had been used and that each kilogram cost only £10, then the actual cost is £650 (65 × 10).

**Cost variance = 1,200 − 650 = +£550 = £550 F**

Note that the answer to this calculation is positive; it is **plus** £550. If the formula had been the other way round, it would have given a negative answer (650 − 1,200 = −550). The formulae are carefully designed so that a positive answer means that the variance will increase profit. This is described as a *favourable* variance and the plus sign is usually replaced by a capital 'F'.

In the above example, it was planned to spend £1,200 on material but only £650 was actually spent. This means that actual profit is £550 more than planned. On the assumption that the more profit the better, this result is 'good' or 'favourable'.

If the answer turns out to be negative, this means that the profit will be less than expected. This type of variance is 'bad' or *adverse* and the minus sign is usually replaced by a capital 'A'. (Sometimes 'U' for 'unfavourable' is used.)

### Sub-variances

It is worth saying at this point that the words 'cost' and 'price' are often used to mean the same thing in colloquial English. However, in variance analysis these words are used in a precise sense to mean two different things. To avoid confusion in the calculation of variances it is a good idea to understand this clearly from the start.

'Price' refers to one item only. 'Cost' refers to the total expenditure for several items. For example, if 10 kilos of flour are bought at a *price* of £2 a kilo, the *cost* of the purchase is £20.

**Cost = price × quantity**

Having got this distinction clear, the cost variance can now be analysed into its two component variances,

**Cost variance = price variance + quantity variance**

This enables us to find out how much of the profit change is due to a change in purchase **price** and how much is due to a change in the **quantity** used. This information may enable us to take corrective action to improve the profit or it may identify areas for further investigation.

## Price variance

$$\text{Price variance} = (\text{budgeted price} - \text{actual price}) \times \text{actual quantity}$$
$$= (BP - AP) \times AQ$$

In the above example,

$$\text{Price variance} = (15 - 10) \times 65 = +325 = 325 \text{ F}$$

It is conventional always to calculate price variances at actual quantities used. This gives the difference in cost **due to price changes only**. (It is not distorted by any change in quantities used.)

## Quantity variance

$$\text{Quantity variance} = (\text{budgeted quantity} - \text{actual quantity}) \times \text{budgeted price}$$
$$= (BQ - AQ) \times BP$$

In the above example,

$$\text{Quantity variance} = (80 - 65) \times 15 = +225 = 225 \text{ F}$$

It is conventional always to calculate quantity variances at budgeted prices. This gives the difference in cost **due to changes in quantity only**. (It is not distorted by any change in price.)

## Reconciliation of variances

|  |  |  |
|---|---|---|
|  | Price variance | 325 F |
| Add: | Quantity variance | 225 F |
|  | Cost variance | 550 F |

These relationships are illustrated by Figure 15.2.

## Terminology

There are two other types of variable cost: direct labour and variable overheads. They can also be analysed into their constituent price and quantity variances. However, these sub-variances are known by different names, as follows:

|  | **Price variance (BP – AP) AQ** | **Quantity variance (BQ – AQ) BP** |
|---|---|---|
| Raw materials | Price variance | Usage variance |
| Direct labour | Rate variance | Efficiency variance |
| Variable overheads | Expenditure variance | Efficiency variance |

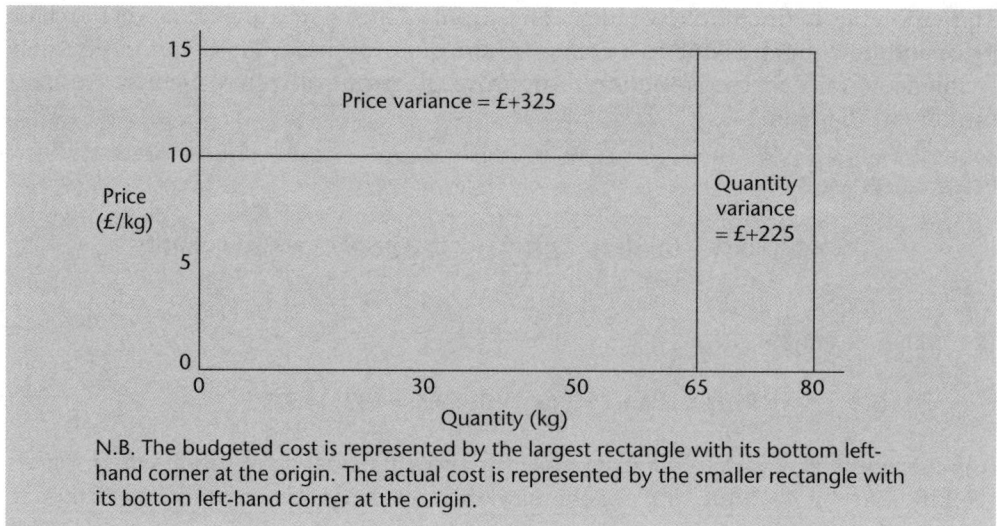

N.B. The budgeted cost is represented by the largest rectangle with its bottom left-hand corner at the origin. The actual cost is represented by the smaller rectangle with its bottom left-hand corner at the origin.

Figure 15.2 **Cost variance analysed into price and quantity elements**

Observe that the same basic formulae are used for each of these cost types. It is possible to calculate all six variances named above if you can remember the two formulae shown at the top of the columns.

**Note:** In this context, the word 'standard' can be used instead of 'budget'.
So,

$$\text{Standard price} = \text{budgeted price}$$

and

$$\text{Standard quantity} = \text{budgeted quantity}$$

| Self-assessment question S15.1 | *Try the following question for yourself (answer at the end of the chapter).*<br><br>Roach Ltd planned to use 100 kg of material at £5 per kg for last week's output. Although its production output was exactly as planned, it used 110 kg of material and paid only £4 per kg for it. Calculate the material cost, price and usage variances. |
|---|---|

## Direct labour variances

The price of labour is the rate at which it is paid, e.g. £9 per hour. The quantity of labour (the number of hours) needed to do a particular job is a measure of the efficiency of the workforce. This is why the sub-variances are known as the *rate variance* and the *efficiency variance*.

Here is an example. SUB Ltd estimates that one particular order will need 30 hours of grade A labour, which is paid at the rate of £10 per hour. After the order has been completed, the records show that only 28 hours were taken, but these were paid at £11 per hour due to a new incentive bonus. What are the direct labour rate, efficiency and cost variances?

$$\begin{aligned}
\text{Rate variance} &= (\text{BP} - \text{AP}) \times \text{AQ} \\
&= (\text{budgeted} - \text{actual rate}) \times \text{actual hours} \\
&= (10 - 11) \times 28 \\
&= -28 \\
&= 28 \text{ A}
\end{aligned}$$

$$\begin{aligned}
\text{Efficiency variance} &= (\text{BQ} - \text{AQ}) \times \text{BP} \\
&= (\text{budgeted hours} - \text{actual hours}) \times \text{budgeted rate} \\
&= (30 - 28) \times 10 \\
&= +20 \\
&= 20 \text{ F}
\end{aligned}$$

$$\begin{aligned}
\text{Cost variance} &= \text{budgeted cost} - \text{actual cost} \\
&= (30 \times 10) - (28 \times 11) \\
&= 300 - 308 \\
&= -8 \\
&= 8 \text{ A}
\end{aligned}$$

> *Try the following question for yourself (answer at the end of the chapter).*
>
> Roach Ltd has a small finishing department employing two people. The budget showed they were expected to work for a total of 4,000 hours during the year just ended. The standard rate of pay used was £6.50 per hour. The payroll shows they actually worked a total of 4,100 hours and were paid a total of £26,650 to produce the budgeted output. Calculate the direct labour cost, rate and efficiency variances.

*Self-assessment question S15.2*

## Idle time variance

Consider the following situation:

$$\text{Budget} = 100 \text{ direct labour hours @ £5/h} = £500 \text{ cost}$$
$$\text{Actual} = 108 \text{ direct labour hours @ £4/h} = £432 \text{ cost}$$

Variance calculations:

$$\begin{aligned}
\text{Labour rate} &= 108(5 - 4) &= 108 \text{ F} \\
\text{Labour efficiency} &= 5(100 - 108) &= (40) \text{ A} \\
\text{Labour cost variance} &= 500 - 432 &= \underline{68} \text{ F}
\end{aligned}$$

Note that the £40 labour efficiency variance is shown in brackets as well as being followed by the capital 'A'. These brackets signify that this is a negative number.

The analysis shows that the workforce were paid less than planned for each hour worked but that the number of hours needed to complete the work was eight more than planned. It indicates that the operatives were inefficient.

But what if the 108 hours included 10 hours that were paid normally but during which no work could be done? Suppose there had been a power cut, preventing operators from using their machines? This 10 hours of idle time means that only 98 hours were actually worked although 108 hours were paid. To get a better analysis of the situation, the variance caused by the idle time needs to be isolated and shown separately.

Amended variance calculations:

| | | |
|---|---|---|
| Labour rate | $= 108(5 - 4)$ | $= 108$ F |
| Labour efficiency | $= 5(100 - 98) =$ | $10$ F |
| Idle time | $= 5(98 - 108) =$ | $(50)$ A |
| Total labour variance | $=$ | $68$ F |

This more detailed analysis shows that, far from being inefficient, the workforce were efficient. They took only 98 hours to complete work estimated to need 100 hours.

Idle time occurs only occasionally, but when it does it is important for its effects to be separated from the other variances. Otherwise the operatives may be unnecessarily demotivated by being identified as inefficient when they are actually efficient. When idle time occurs, the variance formulae are modified as follows:

**Labour efficiency variance = (budgeted hours − actual hours worked) × budgeted rate**
**Idle time variance          = idle hours × budgeted rate**

Note that the idle time variance is always adverse and that the labour rate variance does not change.

| | |
|---|---|
| *Self-assessment question S15.3* | *Try the following question for yourself (answer at the end of the chapter).*<br><br>Roach Ltd has a direct labour budget for June's planned output of 2,000 hours at £10 per hour. Early in July it is found that the planned output for June was achieved but 2,100 hours were paid for at £11 per hour. However, no work could be done for 300 of the hours paid due to a failure in the just-in-time stock control system. Calculate the appropriate variances. |

## Variable overhead variances

Variable overheads are expenses indirectly associated with production activity. Two examples are lubricants for, and maintenance of, the production machinery. The more the machinery is used, the more these items cost. They increase or decrease as activity increases or decreases.

In Chapter 9, we saw that some mechanism is needed to include a 'fair' proportion of these indirect expenses in the product cost. One method often used is to spread these expenses out among products in the same proportion as they use direct labour hours. So, if each product A takes 8 dlh and each product B takes 4 dlh to complete, this means that not only will A have twice the labour cost of B, it will also have twice the variable overhead cost.

Using the example given above of SUB Limited, its variable overhead absorption rate is £3.00 per direct labour hour (dlh). This means that, for the particular order involved, it planned to spend £90 (30 dlh × £3.00/dlh) on variable overheads. The order was actually completed in 28 dlh and the actual cost of the variable overheads was £79.80. Calculate the variable overhead cost, expenditure and efficiency variances.

$$\text{Cost variance} = \text{budgeted cost} - \text{actual cost}$$
$$= 90.00 - 79.80$$
$$= +10.20 = 10.20 \text{ F}$$

$$\text{Expenditure variance} = (\text{budgeted absorption rate} - \text{actual absorption rate})$$
$$\times \text{actual dlh}$$
$$= (\text{budgeted abs. rate} \times \text{actual dlh})$$
$$- (\text{actual abs. rate} \times \text{actual dlh})$$
$$= (£3.00 \times 28) - (£79.80)$$
$$= 84.00 - 79.80$$
$$= +4.20 = 4.20 \text{ F}$$

$$\text{Efficiency variance} = (\text{BQ} - \text{AQ}) \times \text{BP}$$
$$= (\text{budgeted dlh} - \text{actual dlh}) \times \text{budgeted absorption rate}$$
$$= (30 - 28) \times 3.00$$
$$= +6.00 = 6.00 \text{ F}$$

Note that the combination of the expenditure and efficiency variances should give the cost variance.

---

*Try the following question for yourself (answer at the end of the chapter).*

*Self-assessment question S15.4*

Building on the example of Roach Ltd in S15.1–3 above, it was planned to spend £4,400 on variable overheads, giving a budgeted absorption rate of £1.10/dlh. At the end of the year it was found that the actual amount spent on variable overheads was £4,592. Calculate the variable overhead cost, expenditure and efficiency variances.

## Fixed overhead variances

Fixed overheads are those indirect expenses which do **not** vary with output. In this book it is assumed that the organizations looked at operate a variable costing system as opposed to an absorption costing system. (In absorption systems, the analysis of fixed overhead variances is much more complex. This complexity tends to detract from the understanding of budgetary control systems as a whole. Therefore, fixed overhead variances in absorption costing systems will not be covered here. They are not essential for future managers unless you intend to specialise in accountancy.)

We will use a single cost variance (called 'expenditure') for fixed overheads as follows:

$$\text{Fixed overhead expenditure variance} = \text{budgeted fixed overhead}$$
$$- \text{actual fixed overhead}$$

| | | |
|---|---|---|
| For example, | Budgeted fixed overhead | = £300,000 |
| Less: | Actual fixed overhead | = £321,000 |
| | Fixed overhead expenditure variance = | £(21,000) A |

**Self-assessment question S15.5**

*Try the following question for yourself (answer at the end of the chapter).*

Roach Ltd expects its total annual expenditure on fixed overheads to be £180,000 and decides to spread this evenly over its 12 accounting periods. If the amount actually spent on fixed overheads in month 8 is £16,100, what is the fixed overhead expenditure variance for that month?

## The importance of the flexed budget

Suppose you were the manager responsible for a large production facility. For the year just ended, your budget for raw material costs was £9 million but your actual expenditure was only £8 million. Do you deserve a bonus?

It appears you have made a saving of £1 million, but this may not be so. There is not enough information to provide a clear answer. The £9 million budget was to achieve a certain level of production. If that level was achieved, then a bonus is probably deserved. But what if the production output was only half of what was planned? This means that only £4.5 million **should** have been spent on materials, not the £8 million actually spent! In this case, a bonus seems rather inappropriate.

To get meaningful answers when calculating the variances for the variable costs (materials, labour and variable overheads) the actual amounts must be compared with a budget which has been revised to the actual level of output. This revised budget is called the *flexed budget*; it is created **after** the actual figures are known. The effect of using the flexed budget instead of the original budget is that the variances will now show the differences between the actual costs and what those costs **should have been** for the output actually achieved. This is useful information. Variable cost variances based on the original budget will almost certainly be misleading.

Example
15.1

# Illustration with raw materials (manufacturing wheels from raw plastic)

**Original budget:** 10,000 wheels using 5 kg of plastic each @ £2.00/kg
Cost = 10,000 × 5 × 2 = £100,000

**Actual expenditure:** Total cost of plastic used in period was £74,880.
Thus, saving on budget £25,120

Is the production manager to be congratulated on this favourable variance? Yes, congratulations are in order if 10,000 wheels were actually produced.

But what if only 6,000 wheels were actually produced (each using 5.2 kg @ £2.40/kg = £74,880 cost)?

## Flex the budget to the actual level of activity:

Flexed budget: 6,000 wheels using 5 kg plastic @ £2.00 = £60,000 cost
Material price variance = (2.0 − 2.4) × 31,200 = (12,480) A
Material usage variance = (30,000 − 31,200) × 2 = (2,400) A
Actual cost of materials = £74,880

Congratulations are not appropriate in this case.

As you can see from this example, flexed budgets use the same standard amounts as the original budget (1 wheel uses 5 kg of plastic costing £2/kg). The only thing that changes is the level of output or production volume. More often than not, the actual output differs from that planned. **When calculating variances, the first step is to create the flexed budget.**

This does not mean to say that the difference between the original and flexed budget is ignored. This difference is accounted for elsewhere by the sales volume variance (see below).

*Try the following question for yourself (answer at the end of the chapter).*

During week 32, Maykit Ltd planned to produce 50 plastic boxes using two hours of direct labour for each box, paid at the standard rate of £10 per hour, giving a budgeted cost of £1,000. At the end of that week, it was found that 55 boxes had been produced, using 105 hours of labour paid at £10 per hour and costing £1,050. As there is no labour rate variance and the labour cost for the week was £50 greater than planned, is it accurate to say that the labour force must be working inefficiently?

## Sales variances

As sales are concerned with income rather than cost, the sales price variance will differ from cost variances in the following way. If the actual sales price achieved is greater than the budgeted price then the profit will increase, giving a **favourable** variance. So the prices inside the brackets will be the opposite way round (**actual – budget**).

### Sales price variance

Sales price variance = (actual price – budget price) × actual quantity
For example, Sales budget = 20,000 items @ £10; actual = 20,000 items @ £11
Sales price variance = (11 – 10) × 20,000 = 20,000 F

### Sales volume variance

Sales volume variance = flexed budget profit – original budget profit

This is consistent, with the only difference between the original and flexed budgets being the level of activity. The number of items produced is assumed to be the same as the number of items sold and the situation one of making to order and not for stock.

*Try the following question for yourself (answer at the end of the chapter).*

The following data refers to Pike Ltd for the month of May. The original budget showed 400 items sold at £25 each, resulting in a profit of £2,000. The actual performance was 300 items sold at £26 each, resulting in a profit of £1,663. When the budget was flexed, it gave a revised profit of £1,650. Calculate the sales price variance and the sales volume variance.

## The profit reconciliation statement

When the variance analysis exercise is complete, the original budget should be reconciled to the actual results to summarize the findings of the investigation. As the flexed budget is an important part of the analysis, it should be included in the reconciliation. An example of a profit reconciliation statement is shown below.

### Pike Ltd: profit reconciliation statement

| | | £ | £ |
|---|---|---:|---:|
| **Original budget profit** | | | **2,000** |
| Sales volume variance | | | (350) A |
| **Flexed budget profit** | | | **1,650** |
| Sales price variance | | | 300 F |
| Material variances: | Usage | (140) A | |
| | Price | 20 F | |
| | Cost | | (120) A |
| Labour variances: | Efficiency | 75 F | |
| | Rate | (25) A | |
| | Cost | | 50 F |
| Variable overhead variance: | Efficiency | 56 F | |
| | Expenditure | (24) A | |
| | Cost | | 32 F |
| Fixed overhead expenditure variance | | | (249) A |
| **Actual profit** | | | **1,663** |

Note that the adverse variances are shown in brackets. This is not compulsory but the author has found that it helps students to arrive at the correct answers, especially during exams. The capital 'A' or 'F' is compulsory.

---

*Try the following question for yourself (answer at the end of the chapter).*

From the following information (all figures in £000) produce a profit reconciliation statement. Fixed overheads cost 24 less than expected; variable overhead expenditure variance = 5 F and variable overhead efficiency variance = 1 A; labour variances are rate = 14 F and efficiency = 2 A; sales price variance = 18 A; material variances are usage = 39 F and price = 27 A; original budget profit = 400 and flexed budget profit = 431; there is also an idle time variance of 12.

*Self-assessment question S15.8*

---

# Variance relationships

Figures 15.3 and 15.4 illustrate the interrelationships of variances.

# Additional benefits of the budgetary control system

As well as appropriately recording and evaluating performance, budgetary control systems have the following positive effects:

1 They communicate organizational aspirations. The annual organizational plan is distributed to budget holders who are then aware of what is expected of them.

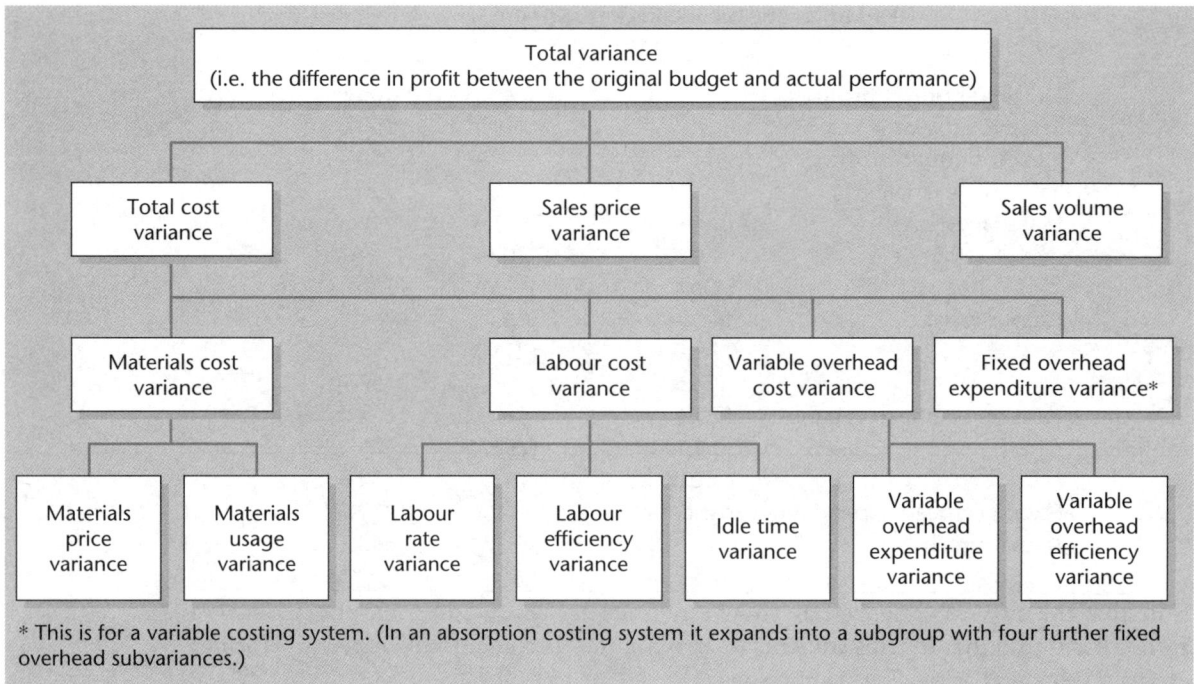

Figure 15.3 **Variance family tree**

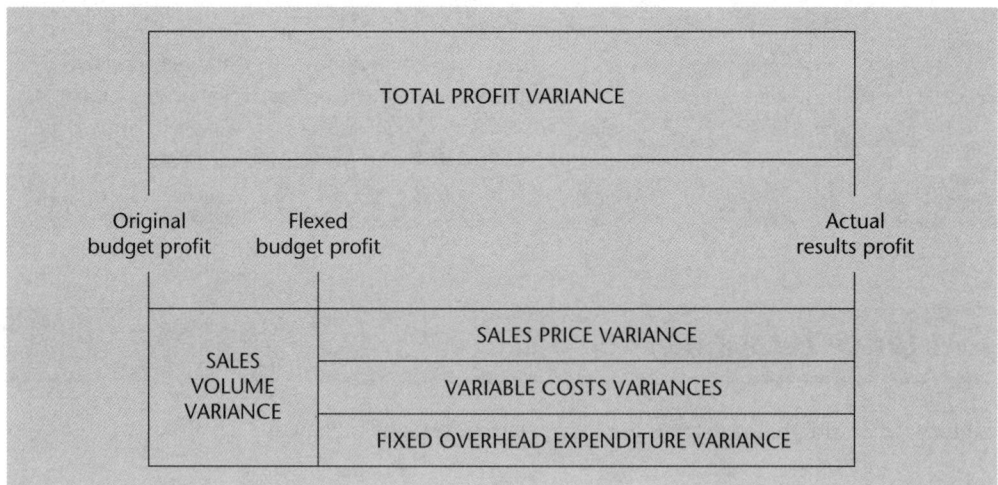

Figure 15.4 **An alternative view**

2 They co-ordinate complex activities. For example, if there is no opening stock of finished goods and the company plans to sell 200,000 items next year, it must budget to produce at least 200,000 items.
3 They authorize budget holders. For example, if the purchasing budget shows that £1 million of materials are to be bought every month, the purchasing manager does

not have to seek permission to spend this amount. The purchasing budget itself authorizes this spending.

4 They motivate budget holders. Budgets can also be used as targets. The performance levels (known as *standards*) in a budget are often set high but attainable in order to encourage improvement.

## Managing the cost of the system

The process of variance investigation is time consuming and has a cost of its own. Organizations need to control this activity. The usual approach is that of 'management by exception'. If operations are going more or less as planned and the variances are small, no follow-up activity takes place. However, where the variances are significant, they are investigated. But how do you know if a variance is significant or not?

This decision is inherently subjective and may vary from business to business. Someone has to decide **in advance** what the significance levels of their organization are going to be. A percentage difference between budget and actual is determined in advance, subject to a minimum amount. For example, a given company may investigate all variances that are at least 5% different from budget provided they are at least £250 in amount. This approach is both relative and absolute. But another company may have a policy of 10% difference with a threshold of £10,000.

## Responsibility accounting

Budgetary control works through people. Functional budgets are delegated to the lowest practical level, where an appropriate person is made the 'budget responsible manager'. For this to work effectively, the lines of authority must be clearly defined. This can be a problem, especially in those organizations operating a matrix approach to their management structure. Where two people are responsible for an item of income or cost, there is always room for dispute as to who should take the credit or accept the blame.

Responsibility accounting usually supports the payment of rewards, such as cash bonuses, to budget responsible officers for meeting their targets. The theory is that the company will benefit from their increased motivation and a 'win–win' situation will occur. For this to happen, the accounting mechanisms must be structured in the same way as the responsibilities. For example, if the regional sales managers are responsible for the value of sales in their areas, the budgets and reporting mechanisms must be analysed over these areas. A single set of aggregated figures for the whole country would not allow the individual responsibilities to be defined or monitored.

This allows companies to achieve their goals through 'management by objective' (MBO) as well as 'management by exception' (MBE). A good example of the latter is the investigation of variances only when they are significant. If actual performance is not very different from budget, things are considered to be going to plan, i.e. no exceptions have occurred.

Another aspect of responsibility accounting is that of **uncontrollable** costs. Not all costs are completely within the control of management. For example, the business rates for the factory may be one item on the production manager's budget. If the cost of these rates is completely outside that person's control, he or she is likely to be demotivated when held responsible for an adverse variance. To avoid this, either the situation should be made very clear in the variance analysis reports or the uncontrollable items should be extracted and isolated in a budget of their own. Unfortunately, problems still arise from some costs that are **partially** controllable. For instance, the cost of running the computerized management information system may be partly based on the manager's ability to retain experienced staff (temporary IT staff are expensive). But it is also based on the rates of pay in the marketplace. The manager may be responsible for the first but not for the second. In this case, it would be up to that manager to justify any adverse variances arising, if he or she can.

## Limitations of the budgetary control process

For many, many years, most organizations have operated a budgetary control system. This management accounting technique has been enormously successful. Yet, during the last few years there have been signs of firms moving away from traditional budgeting. IKEA (furniture), Asea Brown Boveri (engineering), Svenska Handelbanken (banking) and Borealis (petrochemicals), all huge multinational organizations based in Europe, are examples of this trend. They believe that there is more to measuring and controlling business performance than can be expressed by a traditional budget. The main influence on their thinking is the accelerating rate of change in the business environment. Many organizations are finding that their environment is not only constantly changing but changing faster and faster as time moves on.

Budgets tend to reinforce the 'old' way of doing things. Budget managers have many other responsibilities pressing on them when the budget creation deadline is imminent. To reflect changing circumstances, changes may need to be made concerning which data is shown. Consequently, the layout of the form would need to be changed, but this would have to be approved at a high level, which would take considerable time and effort. The normal 'efficient' approach to this situation is to use the same form as last year, meet the deadline and get on with the next task. Over the years, the budget format becomes more and more divorced from reality and less effective in improving performance.

Having said this, budgets are still very effective and necessary instruments of control for the vast majority of organizations. If budgets were removed without something better being put in their place, the organization would almost certainly start to deteriorate.

### The manager's point of view (written by Nigel Burton)

As discussed in the previous chapter, the first major objective of budgeting is to complete a detailed review of the business, and set up a budget framework which ensures that the company is progressing down its designated strategic path. The second objective is to monitor performance against that budget, but with the minimum amount of time and effort.

The main advantage of a detailed budget is that it provides a sound basis for management by exception. Once the budget is agreed, all departmental managers know exactly what is expected of them, in terms of the level of sales to be achieved, or the amount of cost they can incur. Subject to the normal safeguards, they are authorized to spend the amount budgeted in furtherance of their departmental objectives. Moreover, the managing director knows that he or she has nothing to worry about, providing managers are performing within the budgeted parameters. The MD simply reviews the numbers for any significant variances, and then gets on with the job of running the business.

The key to effective management by exception is the IT system. Information must be presented in such a way as to minimize any further analysis work. My company, for instance, used a simple but effective system for monitoring sales. This showed orders due out this month, by volume, sales value and marginal income (contribution), set against the budget for the month. Initially, it summarized these items for the whole company, but there was a feature which allowed the user to 'drill down' through the layers of product group and product line, to individual customer/product level. It took a matter of moments, therefore, on arriving at the office each morning, for me to update myself in detail on the progress of this month's sales. I knew exactly which customers and which products had so far failed to meet expectations. I was so familiar with our performance at all times that the monthly management accounts served merely to confirm what I already knew. Not only did this allow me to spend my time more productively, but also it gave me a detailed knowledge of our current situation from which to answer the regular stream of questions from our head office in the USA.

We had a similar 'drill down' system with which to interrogate previous months' results. By the simple expedient of ranking sales on the basis of variance from budget, an analysis of the causes of shortfalls and overachievements was the work of a few minutes. By presenting the information in the right format, all the traditional, painstaking sales analysis work was completely eliminated. It should be borne in mind that users at different levels in the company, e.g. managing director, sales manager or sales executive, may need the information in a different format, so a cleverly designed system should address the needs of all.

Analysis of manufacturing variances is another case in point. As we have seen above, each production batch will generate at least six variances. In any given month, the factory will produce hundreds of batches, so an enormous amount of variance information is produced. Each batch's variances will tell a slightly different story. In chemicals manufacturing, no two batches are ever the same. The raw materials may have slight differences in specification, the chemical reactions might not work in precisely the same way, and even atmospheric temperatures and humidity might play their part. As a result, processes may need a further input of materials, or perhaps more reaction time or a longer cooling period. Each divergence from the standard generates manufacturing variances. How much time should be spent analysing it all? While a manufacturing process is at the development stage, the production staff will clearly wish to examine all the information in detail, looking for clues which will help them to improve the efficiency of the processing. Once the process has stabilised, however, the production staff will, for the most part, ignore small variations on batches, and look for regular trends which indicate that a process change is required. They will only look at individual batches where there is either a significant variance or a complete batch failure.

Standards may sometimes be set as targets, in order to encourage greater efficiency in the factory. This can be a two-edged sword. The standards are incorporated in the product costs, so, if they are drawn too tightly (showing low costs), there is a risk that the salespeople might be misled into thinking that they can reduce their selling prices. Production's failure to achieve the standards will emerge as adverse manufacturing variances on the profit and loss account, but will be seen as a local production problem, rather than an issue for the whole of the company. Conversely, if the standards are drawn too slackly (showing high costs), production will have a nice, comfortable time. However, the resultant higher costs might discourage sales-people from quoting more competitive prices and generating more business. In my view, standards should always be set at expected performance and not at 'target' levels. However, if there is still a requirement for a target, production can always be asked to produce at a specified level which will result in favourable variances. If they achieve this consistently, it can then be transferred into the product costs, and everyone is happy.

As in many areas of management accounting, the secret of success is to keep it simple but effective. When setting up new systems, there is a natural tendency to over-elaborate. One wants to feel that a thorough and professional job has been done, and perhaps too little thought is directed at the practical aspects of managing the system when it is up and running. I have already described some of the benefits and pitfalls of the activity-based costing system, which my US head office decided to install throughout the organization (see Chapter 10, on activity-based costing). One of the more complex aspects of this system was variance reporting. Normal standard costing principles were used, so the normal manufacturing variances described earlier in this chapter were generated. However, to make the product costs more accurate, and therefore of greater value to the salesforce, the standards were changed every three months. Actual performance was then monitored against the new standards, but, as the original standards were still the basis of the budget, we had another set of variances capturing the difference between the original and revised standards. Somehow, for every batch produced, the number of variances had grown to 16! The monthly variance printout was three-quarters of an inch thick. We were swamped with information and, as a result, gave less attention to this area than we might otherwise have done.

A similar example of overkill occurred with our performance-monitoring reporting. We had developed a simple graphical representation of eight key measurements which we felt reflected our overall performance as a company on a monthly basis. These included the percentage of batches achieving specification without rework, the percentage of orders dispatched on time, and the number of customer complaints received. By combining these eight measurements, we arrived at a single company performance indicator. It was crude, perhaps, but effective, as it helped to focus the minds of employees throughout the company on the need for high-quality performance. Our head office was quite taken with this concept, and decided to adopt it throughout the organization. However, head office increased the number of measurements to 30, some of which were rather dubious as performance monitors. Purchase price variance was one example. Does a favourable PPV reflect a good performance by the purchasing department? Not necessarily. If the market price was coming down, perhaps the variance should have been twice the size. Conversely, a 10% adverse variance could be a fine performance if the market price had actually gone up by 20%. So the selection of performance monitors should be done with a great deal of care. Nevertheless, we duly submitted our data (a time-consuming exercise in itself), and the worldwide results were published in a vast monthly tome. This contained so much information, much of it flawed or inconsistent, that no one ever bothered to look at it, and the motivational impact was completely lost.

A really good information system, whether it is performance monitoring or budgetary control, will tell the users exactly what they need to know, nothing more, nothing less.

And it will do so with the minimal amount of input from the users. Experience will help in deciding the right level, although even experienced managers can fall into the trap of immersing themselves in excessive amounts of data. It is one of the features of this technological age that there is more information available than the human mind can reasonably assimilate, and one of the most important business skills is the ability to specify exactly the information you want and the format in which you want it. Another significant business skill is obtaining the necessary programming time in the IT department, but that is another story!

*Summary*

- The budgetary control process is a continuous closed-loop system.
- It consists of planning, recording, comparing, evaluating and acting.
- The differences between budget and actual are known as variances.
- Cost variances can be analysed into their constituent price and quantity variances.
- The budget should be flexed before the cost variances are calculated.
- Sales volume variance is the difference in the original and flexed budget profits.
- Profit reconciliation statements give a complete summary of the variance analysis.
- Spin-offs include communication, co-ordination, authorization and motivation.
- System operating costs are controlled by a 'management by exception' approach.
- Budget holders can be demotivated if held responsible for non-controllable costs.
- Budgetary control systems do not measure the effect of missed opportunities.
- A few large successful organizations claim to have recently abandoned budgeting.
- The vast majority of organizations still operate budgetary control systems.

*Ten points for good budgetary control*

1 Areas of responsibility are clearly defined.
2 Budgets are held at the lowest practical management level.
3 Non-controllable items are clearly identified.
4 Reporting system is routine/automatic.
5 Reporting periods are short.
6 Reports are produced soon after the period end.
7 Variance significance levels are pre-established.
8 Significant variances are always investigated.
9 Corrective action is taken where possible.
10 Senior management exemplify the importance of the budgetary control system.

## Further reading

Atkinson, A., Banker, R., Kaplan, R. and Young, S. (2001) *Management Accounting*, 3rd edition, Prentice Hall, Harlow. See Chapter 11, 'Using budgets to achieve organisational objectives'.

Budding, G. T. (2004) 'Accountability, environmental uncertainty and government performance: evidence from Dutch municipalities', *Management Accounting Research*, Vol. 15, Issue 3, September.

'FA kicks off new budget control system' (2004) *Computer Weekly*, 30 November.

Horngren, C., Bhimani, A., Datar, S. and Foster, G. (2002) *Management and Cost Accounting*, 2nd edition, Prentice Hall Europe, Harlow. See chapters on 'Flexible budgets, variances and management control 1 & 2'.

Merchant, K. A. (1998) *Modern Management Control Systems: Text and Cases*, Prentice Hall, Englewood Cliffs, NJ.

Otley, D. (1987) *Accounting Control and Organisational Behaviour*, Heinemann Professional Publishing, Oxford. See Chapters 5 and 9, 'Performance appraisal' and 'Accounting for effective control'. (Other chapters concentrate on the 'human' aspects of budgetary control.)

Player, S. (2003) 'Beyond the budget games', *Intelligent Enterprise*, Vol. 6, Issue 16, 10 October Supplement.

Shim, J. and Siegel, J. (2005) *Budgeting Basics and Beyond*, 2nd edition, J. Wiley & Sons, NJ.

Upchurch, A. (2003) *Management Accounting, Principles and Practice*, 2nd edition, Financial Times/Prentice Hall, Harlow. See chapters 'Budgetary control' and 'Analysis of variances'.

Weetman, P. (2002) *Management Accounting, an Introduction*, 3rd edition, Financial Times/ Prentice Hall, Harlow. See chapters 'Standard costs' and 'Performance evaluation and feedback reporting'.

## Answers to self-assessment questions

### S15.1

$$\text{Budget: } 100 \text{ kg @ } £5/\text{kg} = £500 \text{ cost}$$
$$\text{Actual: } 110 \text{ kg @ } £4/\text{kg} = £440 \text{ cost}$$

$$\text{Price variance} = (BP - AP) \times AQ$$
$$= (5 - 4) \times 110 = 110 \text{ F}$$

$$\text{Usage variance} = (BQ - AQ) \times BP$$
$$= (100 - 110) \times 5 = (50) \text{ A}$$

$$\text{Cost variance} = \text{budget cost} - \text{actual cost}$$
$$= 500 - 440 = 60 \text{ F}$$

Note: The combined price and usage variances should equal the cost variance.

**S15.2**

Rate variance = (budgeted rate − actual rate) × actual hours
$$= (BR \times AH) - (AR \times AH)$$
$$= (6.50 \times 4,100) - 26,650$$
$$= 26,650 - 26,650$$
$$= \text{zero (The actual rate paid must also} = £6.50/\text{hour.)}$$

Efficiency variance = (budgeted hours − actual hours) × budgeted rate
$$= (4,000 - 4,100) \times 6.50$$
$$= (-100) \times 6.50$$
$$= -650$$
$$= 650\ A$$

Cost variance = budgeted cost − actual cost
$$= (4,000 \times 6.50) - 26,650$$
$$= 26,000 - 26,650$$
$$= -650$$
$$= 650\ A$$

Note: As the rate does not vary, the efficiency variance should equal the cost variance.

**S15.3**

Rate variance = (budgeted rate − actual rate) × actual hours paid
$$= (10 - 11) \times 2,100$$
$$= -2,100$$
$$= 2,100\ A$$

Efficiency variance = (budgeted hours − actual hours worked) × budgeted rate
$$= (2,000 - 1,800) \times 10$$
$$= +2,000$$
$$= 2,000\ F$$

Idle time variance = idle hours × budgeted rate
$$= 300 \times 10$$
$$= -3,000$$
$$= 3,000\ A$$

Labour cost variance = budgeted cost − actual cost
$$= (2,000 \times 10) - (2,100 \times 11)$$
$$= 20,000 - 23,100$$
$$= -3,100$$
$$= 3,100\ A$$

S15.4

$$\begin{aligned}
\text{Cost variance} &= \text{budgeted cost} - \text{actual cost}\\
&= 4{,}400 - 4{,}592\\
&= -192\\
&= 192\ \text{A}
\end{aligned}$$

$$\begin{aligned}
\text{Expenditure variance} &= (\text{budgeted absorption rate} - \text{actual absorption rate})\\
&\quad \times \text{actual dlh}\\
&= (\text{Budgeted abs. rate} \times \text{actual dlh}) - (\text{actual abs. rate}\\
&\quad \times \text{actual dlh})\\
&= (1.10 \times 4{,}100) - (4{,}592)\\
&= 4{,}510 - 4{,}592\\
&= -82\\
&= 82\ \text{A}
\end{aligned}$$

$$\begin{aligned}
\text{Efficiency variance} &= (\text{BQ} - \text{AQ}) \times \text{BP}\\
&= (\text{budgeted dlh} - \text{actual dlh}) \times \text{budgeted absorption rate}\\
&= (4{,}000 - 4{,}100) \times 1.10\\
&= -110\\
&= 110\ \text{A}
\end{aligned}$$

Note: The combination of the expenditure and efficiency variances should give the cost variance.

S15.5

$$\begin{aligned}
\text{Fixed overhead monthly budget} &= 180{,}000/12 = 15{,}000\\
\text{Less: Actual expenditure in month 8} &= \underline{16{,}100}\\
\text{Fixed overhead expenditure variance} &= -1{,}100\\
&= \ \ 1{,}100\ \text{A}
\end{aligned}$$

S15.6

As the actual output is different from that planned in the original budget, the first step is to **flex the budget** to the activity level of 110 items.

Flexed budget (activity level = 55 items):

$$\text{Cost} = 55\ \text{units} \times 2\ \text{hours/unit} \times £10/\text{hour} = £1{,}100$$

$$\begin{aligned}
\text{Labour cost variance} &= \text{budgeted cost} - \text{actual cost}\\
&= 1{,}100 - 1{,}050\\
&= +50\\
&= 50\ \text{F}
\end{aligned}$$

Labour efficiency variance = (budgeted hours − actual hours) × budgeted rate

$$= (110 - 105) \times 10$$
$$= +50$$
$$= 50 \text{ F}$$

Labour rate variance = (budgeted rate − actual rate) × actual hours

$$= (10 - 10) \times 105$$
$$= 0$$

These results show that the workforce are working **efficiently**; the statement made in the question is not accurate.

## S15.7

Sales price variance = (actual price − budgeted price) × actual quantity sold

$$= (26 - 25) \times 300$$
$$= +300$$
$$= 300 \text{ F}$$

Sales volume variance = flexed budget profit − original budget profit

$$= 1,650 - 2,000$$
$$= -350$$
$$= 350 \text{ A}$$

## S15.8

### Profit reconciliation statement

|  |  | £000 | £000 |
|---|---|---|---|
| **Original budget profit** |  |  | 400 |
| Sales volume variance |  |  | 31 F |
| **Flexed budget profit** |  |  | 431 |
| Sales price variance |  |  | (18) A |
| Material variances: | Usage | 39 F |  |
|  | Price | (27) A |  |
|  | Cost |  | 12 F |
| Labour variances: | Efficiency | (2) A |  |
|  | Idle time | (12) A |  |
|  | Rate | 14 F |  |
|  | Cost |  | 0 |
| Variable overhead variance: | Efficiency | (1) A |  |
|  | Expenditure | 5 F |  |
|  | Cost |  | 4 F |
| Fixed overhead expenditure variance |  |  | 24 F |
| **Actual profit** |  |  | 453 |

# CASE STUDY    Anomira Ltd

Anomira Ltd is a wholly owned subsidiary of an industrial conglomerate. It produces one standard size of sealing compound used in the motor vehicle industry. As the new management accountant of this company, you have been asked to explain why the actual results differed from the budget for the year just ended. You ascertain the following information.

The budget was for a volume of 100,000 units produced and sold, each using 2 kg of material at £3.00 per kg. The total of variable overheads was expected to be £100,000 and the fixed overheads £250,000. Total sales revenue was planned to be £1,500,000 and the 50,000 direct labour hours planned were expected to cost £250,000. The variable overhead absorption rate is £2.00 per direct labour hour.

The actual performance for last year showed production of 90,000 units and no change in stock levels over the year. Sales revenue was £1,440,000 and 196,000 kg of material was used, costing £529,200. Variable overheads were £94,500 and fixed overheads £255,000. The total cost of direct labour was £232,750 for 49,000 hours. However, 1,000 of these hours were completely non-productive due to a breakdown of the heating system during exceptionally bad winter weather causing the factory to be temporarily closed.

*Tasks:*

1  Perform a variance analysis (in as much detail as the information will allow) reconciling the actual profit to the budgeted profit.

(40 marks)

2  On one side of A4 paper, suggest possible explanations for any significant variances you have found.

(20 marks)

3  On no more than two sides of A4 paper, discuss budgetary control and responsibility accounting in organizations. Include comments on any dangers/limitations inherent in this technique.

(40 marks)
(Total 100 marks)

# Questions

An asterisk * on a question number indicates that the answer is given at the end of the book. Answers to the other questions are given in the Lecturer's Guide.

## Q15.1* Welco Ltd

Welco Ltd manufactures one type of hydraulic jack. The labour force, who are all paid at the same rate, assemble and finish two bought-in components. Each jack uses two metal castings and one rubber seal. The jacks are very popular and Welco sells all it can make. It budgets to make a profit of £4,400 each month.

The budget is as follows:

| | Standard (1 item) | £ | Budget (1,100 items) £ |
|---|---|---|---|
| Rubber seals | (1 @ £2) | 2 | 2,200 |
| Metal castings | (2 @ £3) | 6 | 6,600 |
| Direct labour | (10 minutes) | 1 | 1,100 |
| Fixed overhead | | 7 | 7,700 |
| | | 16 | 17,600 |
| Sales revenue | | 20 | 22,000 |
| Profit | | 4 | 4,400 |

The £7 fixed overhead consists of production, marketing and administration overheads. It is based on production and sales of 1,100 jacks (the budgeted activity level for each month).

Last month, the actual results were as follows:

| | |
|---|---|
| Number of jacks made and sold | 1,050 |
| | £ |
| Rubber seals (1,060 @ £1.95) | 2,067 |
| Metal castings (2,108 @ £3.25) | 6,851 |
| Direct labour (190 hours @ £5.90) | 1,121 |
| Fixed overhead incurred | 7,600 |
| | 17,639 |
| Sales revenue (1,050 @ £19) | 19,950 |
| Actual profit | 2,311 |

*Tasks:*

1 Flex the budget to the actual level of activity.
2 Analyse the variances in as much detail as the figures will allow.
3 Create a profit reconciliation statement.

### Q15.2* Stanley & Co.

Stanley & Co. manufactures door frames from a bought-in wooden moulding. The budget for one door frame has costs of £20 for materials and £6 for labour. Each frame has a standard usage of 5 metres of wooden moulding at a standard cost of £4.00 per metre. Each frame has a standard time of 0.50 hours and the standard rate of pay is £12.00 per hour.

The budget for April was for 2,200 frames with a material cost of £44,000 and a labour cost of £13,200.

However, 2,100 frames were actually produced in April, taking 1,000 hours to make at a total labour cost of £13,000. Also, 11,550 metres of wooden moulding were used at a total cost of £43,890.

*Tasks:*

1  Calculate the cost, quantity and price variances for materials and labour in April.
2  Suggest possible reasons for these variances.
3  If 50 of the 1,000 hours paid were during a power cut which prevented work continuing, what changes would you make to your answers to parts 1 and 2?

### Q15.3* Ivanblast computer game

Bigcheque Ltd has created a new computer game called Ivanblast. It knows it will only have a five-week period from launch in order to market this successfully before pirating will reduce its sales to virtually zero. The budget for this period is:

|  |  |  |  | £ |
|---|---|---|---|---|
| Sales: | 25,000 games | @ £50 | = | 1,250,000 |
| Production materials: | 25,000 blank CDs | @ £1.10 | = | 27,500 |
| Variable overheads: | 25,000 games | @ £0.50 | = | 12,500 |
| Fixed overheads: |  |  | = | 800,000 |
| Net profit |  |  | = | 410,000 |

(Note that, like many firms with highly automated production facilities, Bigcheque Ltd considers its production labour to be all fixed in nature. So, **all** labour costs are included in the fixed overheads.)

The actual results for the five-week period are shown below (no stocks of raw materials or finished computer games were left over at the end of the period).

|  |  |  |  | £ |
|---|---|---|---|---|
| Sales: | 30,000 games | @ £45 | = | 1,350,000 |
| Production materials: | 30,250 blank CDs | @ £1.00 | = | 30,250 |
| Variable overheads: |  |  | = | 15,000 |
| Fixed overheads: |  |  | = | 850,000 |
| Net profit |  |  | = | 454,750 |

*Tasks:*

1  Prepare a variance analysis for the period in as much detail as the figures allow.
2  Produce a statement reconciling the budgeted profit with the actual profit.
3  Comment on your findings.

## Q15.4  Fripp Ltd

| Variable costs | Standard costs (1 item) | Original budget (10,000 items) £ | Actual results (11,000 items) |
|---|---|---|---|
| Material A | 5 kg @ £2.00/kg | 100,000 | 66,000 kg @ £1.50/kg |
| Material B | 10 kg @ £4.00/kg | 400,000 | 99,000 kg @ £5.00/kg |
| Labour | 2 hours @ £15.00/h | 300,000 | 20,900 hours @ £16.00/h |
| Variable overhead | 2 hours @ £3.00/h | 60,000 | 20,900 hours @ £3.00/h |

*Task:*

Calculate the variable cost variances of the above in as much detail as possible.

## Q15.5  Elbo Ltd

Elbo Ltd makes roof tiles. It has two production departments: moulding and packing. It makes two different sizes of tile, the Handi and the Jiant. The following table shows the standard costs of labour per pallet of tiles (one pallet contains 144 tiles):

| Department | Labour type | Standard hourly rate £ | Standard production hours per pallet Handi | Jiant |
|---|---|---|---|---|
| Moulding | A | 5.00 | 4 | 6 |
| Moulding | C | 4.00 | 5 | 8 |
| Packing | A | 5.00 | 1 | 2 |
| Packing | B | 4.50 | 2 | 3 |

During October, 400 pallets of Handis and 150 pallets of Jiants were actually produced and the following labour hours and costs were incurred:

| Labour type | Moulding department Actual hours worked | Actual pay (£) | Packing department Actual hours worked | Actual pay (£) |
|---|---|---|---|---|
| A | 2,600 | 12,480 | 695 | 3,336 |
| B | – | – | 1,250 | 5,875 |
| C | 3,180 | 12,720 | – | – |
| Totals | 5,780 | 25,200 | 1,945 | 9,211 |

*Tasks:*

For the month of October:

1  Create the labour budget (hours and £) for (a) Handis and (b) Jiants.
2  Calculate the budgeted direct labour cost of one pallet of Handis and one pallet of Jiants.

3  Calculate the budgeted total labour cost of each department and of the whole factory.
4  Calculate the direct labour cost variance for each department and for the factory.
5  For each department and labour type, analyse the cost variances into their rate and efficiency variances.
6  Comment on your findings.

## Q15.6 JK plc

JK plc operates a chain of fast-food restaurants. The company uses a standard marginal costing system to monitor the costs incurred in its outlets. The standard cost of one of its most popular meals is as follows:

|  |  | £ per meal |
|---|---|---|
| Ingredients | (1.08 units) | 1.18 |
| Labour | (1.5 minutes) | 0.15 |
| Variable conversion costs | (1.5 minutes) | 0.06 |
| The standard price of this meal is |  | 1.99 |

In one of its outlets, which has budgeted sales and production activity level of 50,000 such meals, the number of such meals that were produced and sold during April 2003 was 49,700. The actual cost data was as follows:

|  |  | £ |
|---|---|---|
| Ingredients | (55,000 units) | 58,450 |
| Labour | (1,200 hours) | 6,800 |
| Variable conversion costs | (1,200 hours) | 3,250 |
| The actual revenue from the sale of the meals was |  | 96,480 |

*Required:*

(a)  Calculate
  (i)   the total budgeted contribution for April 2003;
  (ii)  the total actual contribution for April 2003.

*(3 marks)*

(b)  Present a statement that reconciles the budgeted and actual contribution for April 2003. Show all variances to the nearest £1 and in as much detail as possible.

*(17 marks)*

(c)  Explain why a marginal costing approach to variance analysis is more appropriate in environments such as that of JK plc, where there are a number of different items being produced and sold.

*(5 marks)*
*(Total = 25 marks)*

CIMA Intermediate: Management Accounting – Performance Management, May 2003

## Q15.7 TBS

TBS produces two products in a single factory. The following details have been extracted from the standard marginal cost cards of the two products:

| Product | S3 | S5 |
|---|---|---|
| | £/unit | £/unit |
| Selling price | 100 | 135 |
| *Variable costs:* | | |
| Material X (£3 per kg) | 30 | 39 |
| Liquid Z (£4.50 per litre) | 27 | 45 |
| Direct labour (£6 per hour) | 18 | 24 |
| Overheads | 12 | 16 |

TBS uses a standard marginal costing system linked with budgets.

Budgeted data for the month of October included:

| | S3 | S5 |
|---|---|---|
| Sales (units) | 10,000 | 10,000 |
| Production (units) | 12,000 | 13,500 |
| *Fixed costs:* | | |
| Production | | £51,000 |
| Administration | | £34,000 |

Actual data for the month of October was as follows:

| | S3 | S5 |
|---|---|---|
| Sales (units) | 12,200 | 8,350 |
| Production (units) | 13,000 | 9,400 |
| Selling prices per unit | £96 | £145 |
| *Variable costs:* | | |
| Material X | 270,000 kg costing | £786,400 |
| Liquid Z | 150,000 litres costing | £763,200 |
| Direct labour | 73,200 hours costing | £508,350 |
| Overheads | | £347,000 |
| *Fixed costs:* | | |
| Production | | £47,550 |
| Administration | | £36,870 |

*Required:*

a)  Calculate the budgeted profit/loss for October.

*(2 marks)*

b)  Calculate the actual profit/loss for October.

*(3 marks)*

c)  As a management accountant in TBS you will be attending the monthly management team meeting. In preparation for that meeting you are required to:
  (i)  Prepare a statement that reconciles the budgeted and actual profit/loss for October, showing the variances in as much detail as is possible from the data provided.

*(15 marks)*

(ii) State, and then briefly explain, the main issues in your profit reconciliation statement.

*(5 marks)*
*(Total = 25 marks)*

CIMA Intermediate: Management Accounting – Performance Management, November 2004

## Review questions

1  Explain the basic theory and cyclical nature of budgetary control systems.
2  State the common formulae for cost variances and sub-variances.
3  Discuss the importance of flexing the budget to the actual level of production.
4  Describe the purpose of a profit reconciliation statement.
5  Give examples of the possible relationships between variances.
6  Discuss the additional benefits of budgetary control systems.
7  Explain how the operating costs of budgetary control systems can be managed.
8  Comment on the problems of 'responsibility accounting'.
9  Discuss the limitations of budgetary control systems.
10  List 10 points for good budgetary control.

*The answers to all these questions can be found in the text of this chapter.*

# Budgets, behaviour and beyond budgeting

## Introduction

Have you ever thought of starting a business of your own? You may have thought carefully about how you were going to do this; you may even have committed your plans to paper. However, even with the help of meticulously detailed plans, there is no guarantee that you will be able to fulfil your ambitions. Even if you are one of the few who does manage to 'achieve' your idea, it is almost certain that the reality of what you have created will be different, to some extent, from your original idea. It may be better or worse than you expected or just different. To quote John Lennon, 'Life is what happens to you whilst you are making plans!'

The point is that making things happen is not just down to you. Every aspect of the world around you will have an impact on your actions; on many occasions you will have to modify your ideas and intermediate objectives. If you do not, your chances of success will diminish. Business activities do not happen in a vacuum; they are influenced by their many different environments: economic, social, legal, cultural, political, technological, et cetera. Businesses are also affected by the behaviour of their competitors, employees, suppliers, and government. In the modern age, these factors are changing increasingly quickly. Is it possible for a CEO alone to react to these continual changes as they impact the various elements of his business? Or is it more sensible to delegate a measure of control to individuals who have direct responsibility for the affected areas?

In many companies, the instinct of the senior management is to maintain tight controls over the activities of the business. After all, everything that happens in the company is their legal responsibility. In the industrial age, this approach worked because companies dominated their markets (i.e. suppliers not customers were in charge). As a result, *efficiency* was the critical success factor. These conditions led to the development of the command and control management model with functional hierarchies, budgetary control systems and centralized decision making.

This traditional approach is a *deterministic* way of managing. However, in recent years there has been a distinct power shift in the market place. Due to the increased speed and scope of communications, typified by the Internet, the customer is more in charge than the supplier. In the twenty-first century, business needs to replace its traditional deterministic model with a *systemic* one. To succeed on a long-term basis in their complex, highly-competitive markets, they need to satisfy the interests of all of their stakeholders: customers, suppliers, employees, shareholders, government and society.

In the past, budgets were the primary mechanism for command and control. These days, advancing technology and communications provide management with alternative methods of imposing this control. Yet, budgets are still widely used for setting annual targets, and forming the basis for bonus calculations. Employee financial incentive schemes are a form of 'fixed performance contract' consisting of predetermined, unchangeable targets based on budgets, balanced scorecards, etc. Remuneration is offered to employees dependent on the achievement of these targets. These devices are referred to alternatively as 'bonus schemes', 'employee incentive schemes' and 'share option schemes'. Employee targets are based on figures in the original budget *which is fixed*.

They are based on a prediction and used in a deterministic way. Predictions, as Jan Wallander (former CEO and Chairman of Handelsbanken) pointed out, are mainly of two types: *'same weather tomorrow as today'* and *'something really abnormal'*. In coping with the first type, budgets are trite and of limited use, being merely an extension of the historical trend adjusted for minor known changes. However, in the case of the second type they will almost certainly be wrong because the timing and impact of large changes are difficult to predict. If they are followed, for example by building up or reducing stocks or staffing, the probable outcome is that some corporate value will be destroyed. Strengthening the fixed performance contract by tying incentives to the achievement of (likely to be wrong) targets aggravates the problem.

Even without financial inducements, managers have a positive desire to achieve the budget figures, not least because they are partially responsible for creating those figures. The participatory budget creation process is deliberate and designed to give managers psychological ownership of the business plan. If the plan is not achieved, it reflects badly on the manager who consequently 'loses face' in the eyes of his colleagues. There is a lot of pressure on managers to 'make their numbers'.

The trouble with this is that it encourages managers to play budget games (see below). Where people's personal remuneration is concerned, their imaginations become very 'creative', resulting in the manipulation of activities, the distortion of information and an increase in their personal rewards. Due to the prevalence of these activities, a significant body of people now believe that fixed performance contracts have become part of the problem of poor business performance rather than its solution.

This is usually the context in which people first encounter the 'Beyond Budgeting' philosophy. Its title has become synonymous with the abolition of budgets. This is unfortunate as managing without budgets is not Beyond Budgeting's main idea; rather, it is a consequence of it.

Dissatisfaction with traditional budgeting has grown to the extent where opposition to it is mainly co-ordinated under the single umbrella movement of 'Beyond Budgeting'. This international movement operates a Beyond Budgeting Round Table (BBRT) with its own website (www.bbrt.org). The BBRT describes itself as a collaborative that offers shared learning, performance management research and consulting support to its members.

Two of the leading lights of this movement are Jeremy Hope and Robin Fraser. They have written a book entitled *Beyond Budgeting – How Managers Can Break Free from the Annual Performance Trap*, published by Harvard Business School Press in 2003. In their summary at the end of Chapter 4, they conclude that:

> *By removing the budgeting process and fixed performance contract, firms are able to change the attitudes and behaviors of people at every level of the organization. In particular, they are likely to eradicate the undesirable behaviors that result from setting a fixed target that must be met even though the outcome is highly uncertain.*

**Having worked through this chapter you should be able to:**

Learning objectives

- describe the weaknesses of traditional budgetary control systems;
- define and describe the various types of 'budget game';
- explain the exacerbating nature of employee cash incentive schemes;
- describe mechanisms for moving future sales to the present;
- describe mechanisms for moving present sales to the future;
- evaluate the utility of budgetary control systems;
- describe the 'Beyond Budgeting' management model;
- list the six principles of 'devolved leadership';
- list the six adaptive processes recommended to replace budgeting;
- describe the management model used by Svenska Handelsbanken;
- describe the management model used by the Toyota production system;
- explain the difficulties in the adoption of the 'Beyond Budgeting' philosophy;
- state the arguments against the 'Beyond Budgeting' model;
- list some of the findings of the 'Better Budgeting' open forum in 2004.

# The weaknesses of traditional budgeting

The 'tried-and-tested' method of controlling corporate performance is budgeting; it is used by almost every business in existence. (The creation and use of budgets is covered in previous chapters of this book.) In brief, it can be seen as a cyclical four-stage process (see Figure 15.1):

1 Create plan.
2 Implement plan.
3 Measure performance.
4 Compare plan with performance and evaluate differences.
5 Create next plan,
6 etc.

Of course, actual performance rarely, if ever, turns out to be identical to the original budget. Unforeseen events and unplanned internal changes occur at various times throughout the financial year. Managers respond to these deviations from plan as they arise and set new directions/objectives appropriate to the new situation. In this way, the annual performance of the business should at least resemble the last revision of the budget. So why does the traditional budgetary control system often produce disappointing results? What are its weaknesses?

First, unlike the business environment, budgets do not change. The rate of change in the environment is continuously increasing but the budgetary control system was designed almost a century ago when things changed much more slowly. For instance, in the 1920s, if you wanted to hold an important face-to-face meeting with a business associate in the USA, it would take you at least a week to travel there! It is now possible to travel there and back in the space of a day. The modern technological environment allows for vastly increased speeds of communication; examples include video-conferencing and IP communications which allow voice-, video- and data-sharing as well as real time drawing on virtual whiteboards (e.g. Skype and MS Messenger).

Today, speed is a key factor, but this is not just a technological issue. The business world has become so much more competitive, that if companies do not respond fast they really suffer. Today, it is essential that businesses respond fast and change continually. ***The world has changed but the way we manage has not.*** This idea is the main theme of Professor Gary Hamel's 2007 book, *The Future of Management*, in which he exhorts managers to revolutionize their practices to meet the radically changed business environment of the twenty-first century. He says, 'Contrary to popular mythology, the thing that most impedes [management] innovation in large companies is not a lack of risk taking. Big companies take big, and often imprudent, risks every day. The real brake on [management] innovation is the drag of old mental models. Long-serving executives often have a big chunk of their emotional capital invested in the existing strategy' (page 54).

Any single change in a business activity may have repercussions on many other activities and affect many other people. The introduction of a new product by a competitor may cause you to want to change your sales plan. But any such change will impact on purchasing, manufacturing, administration, marketing, etc. These areas are controlled by different budget-responsible officers who will need to agree the changes which will then be referred to senior management for authorization.

Most organizations are bureaucratic because they have functional structures and centralized decision making. They need to be more decentralized and more organized around their processes (i.e. activities that create value for customers) in order to respond faster and do things in a less costly way. The organizational structure and processes need to be continually reassessed. A possible downside of this is that the amount of work may stifle innovation. In extreme cases, in the cause of self-preservation, managers may learn to respond negatively to innovative ideas even though they may be good for the business.

Also, the widely adopted practice of giving cash bonuses to managers based on their actual performance measured against budget is detrimental to many companies. These personal incentive schemes may be expressed in 'narrow' terms which ignore their effects on other parts of the business. Also, the achievement of their individual budget targets can become more important to managers than acting in the best interests of the company **as a whole**. Budget-responsible officers often exhibit what is known as 'gaming behaviour'.

## Budget games: definition and types

The term 'budget games' refers to certain behaviours exhibited by budget-responsible managers. Some games involve their making their budget figures easier to achieve than they actually expect; others involve some form of manipulation and/or misrecording of their actual performance. The object of playing these games is to create some benefit for the employee, *even if the company suffers as a result.*

Managers may appear to act in the best interests of their organization, e.g. reaching or exceeding income targets but not exceeding expenditure allowances. However, in reality, their actions may well result in the organization performing worse than it otherwise would have. Also, an unfortunate side-effect of these games is that misinformation is introduced into the management information systems and future decisions based on this will tend to be less effective than they otherwise would have been.

Managers prefer to be seen by their peers to be in control of their budgets and to be thought of as being 'on top of things' and good at their job. This desired respect from their peers encourages them to play these games. However, their motivation for playing them is greatly increased when their personal remuneration is linked to meeting targets based on budget figures. The fact that annual bonuses are often based on budget targets results in the playing of these games being very common.

There are several different types of budget game but the most common is where managers build 'slack' into their targets. The budget is constructed by negotiation between the budget holder and senior management (possibly with the technical support of a management accountant). The idea is that the budget holder is more likely to achieve his or her 'own' target than one imposed from above. But because the bonus depends on meeting his or her targets, the budget holder will be tempted to make them easier to achieve. So revenues tend to be underestimated and expenses overestimated.

Over the years, most executives have experienced their budget estimates of expenses being cut back in the name of efficiency. However, if they expect their estimates (known as 'allowances') to be cut back, they may well overestimate them in the first instance to avoid any reduction. If they expect an overall (or blanket) cutback of 10% they may inflate their suggested allowances by an appropriate amount and end up with the number they originally wanted.

'Virement' is another game played as the year progresses. This is the recording of an expense under the wrong heading. For example, if the budget allowance for travel has already been reached before the end of a budget period, further travel expenses in that period may be incorrectly classed as training or some other item that has not used up all its allowance. This makes budget holders appear to be better at controlling expenditure than they actually are by hiding their overspending.

If, towards the end of a budget period, it looks as though an expense allowance will be underspent, it is common for the budget holder to go on a 'spending spree', buying items not strictly necessary at that time. These items would not have been bought had the budget expense allowance been lower. Note that this unnecessary spending behaviour may perpetuate the error in future years. In the eyes of the budget holder, it helps to avoid cutbacks in that particular expense budget in the next period; better to have the money available just in case it is needed than not to have the 'buffer' it creates.

Salespeople are often paid partly by commission on the sales they make. If the commission is triggered by sales reaching a certain value and the salespeople think they are not going to reach this threshold, they may attempt to bring forward 'regular' sales from the next period into the current one. Of course, these brought-forward sales will create a problem regarding the commission earned next period, but increased sales to other customers may more than compensate for these brought-forward sales. Most people prefer 'jam today' rather than 'jam tomorrow'.

On the other hand, in a good period, the salespeople may have sold well over estimate and reached the amount where the commission payments are capped at a maximum level (this is normal corporate practice). It may be that the salespeople could sell even more before the end of the period but why should they? They will not earn anything extra for doing so and these 'additional' sales will go towards next period's bonus. The effect of this on the business is that sales **and their resulting cash flow** will be delayed.

**The effect of the budget games identified above is to feed misinformation into the budgetary control system (which is an important part of the management information system). In turn, this will cause poor decisions to be made throughout the organization, resulting in suboptimal performance. As all budget schedules are interdependent, incorrect figures in one area will cause incorrect figures in other areas. Activities throughout the organization will be based on misleading information!**

This offers an insight as to why traditional budgetary control systems are not as successful as they should be. Their theoretical strength is always undermined to some extent by *normal self-centred* human behaviour.

## The effect of employee cash incentive schemes

Before looking at the last two games in more detail, we will look at how these employee incentive schemes operate, particularly those offering cash bonuses. First of all, employees are offered additional pay for reaching targets based on their budgets. However, companies

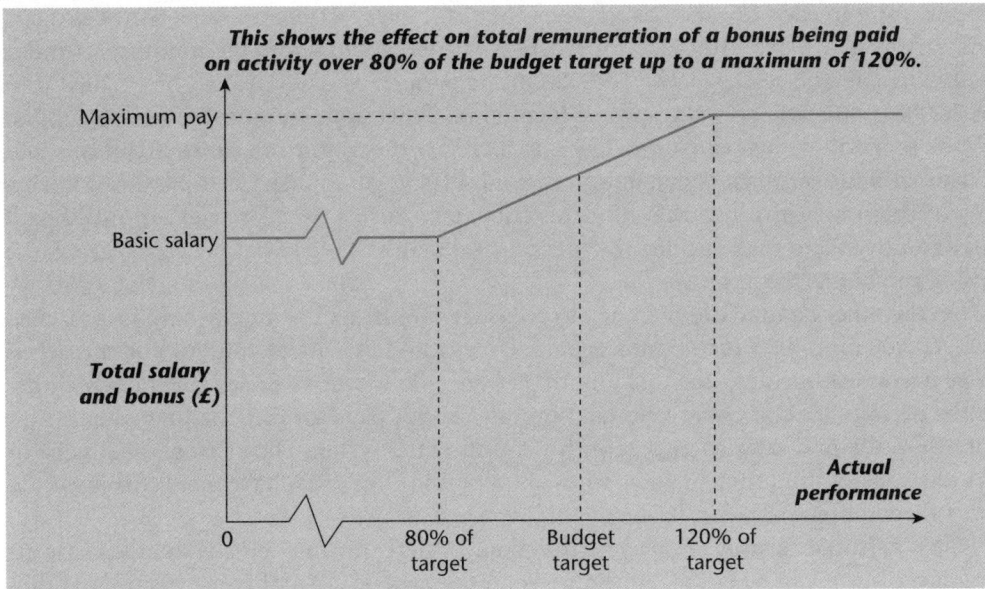

Figure 16.1  **Bonus related behaviour**

acknowledge that the business environment may be better or worse than assumed for the creation of the original budget. To compensate for this, the threshold figure triggering the payment of a bonus is set below the budget allowance, say at 80% of that amount. From the company's point of view, this ensures a significant amount of the target is met before any bonus is paid.

Once the threshold has been reached, the activity will continue and the bonus will increase accordingly. However, companies like to keep their expenditure under control and will normally place an upper limit on the amount of bonus that can be earned in any period. This upper limit may be set at, say, 120% of the budget allowance (see Figure 16.1).

To help understand the above, consider the example of a salesman whose budget states that he is to sell £50,000 of goods every month. He is on a bonus scheme which rewards him with 10% of sales value above £40,000 (80% of budget) subject to a sales cap of £60,000 (120% of budget). If he sells goods worth £40,000 or less in the period he earns zero bonus, if he sells £50,000 he earns £1,000 bonus, if he sells £60,000 he earns £2,000 bonus and if he sells £70,000 he still earns £2,000 bonus.

Imagine you are this salesman; it is approaching the end of the month and you have sold only £28,000 and you estimate that you will not sell more than £35,000. You realize it is most unlikely that you will earn any bonus this month. What effect do you think this will have on your motivation? What attitude will you adopt towards selling between now and the end of the month? Most people will stop making any effort to sell above the minimum and have a 'rest' before next month. After all, any sales that can be pushed forward into next month will help enhance the next bonus. This may lead to an active decision to stop selling this month.

Alternatively, if you have reached the bonus threshold before the month-end, you will be motivated to sell. You will want to take maximum advantage of this month's opportunity to earn as much as you possibly can. Every £1,000 of sales above £40,000 will earn you an extra £100. Suppose there is one week left before the month-end and it looks like you will sell a total of £57,000 in the period. Your bonus will be £1,700 (10% of 57,000 − 40,000). This is good but it could be better; you are missing out on £300 of bonus that will be lost to you for ever. Is there anything you can do to avoid this and maximize your earnings? What about next month's 'regular' sales? Is it possible to bring any of them forward into this month? This may cause a problem next month but it may be possible to make up for the 'missing' sales and at least you will have earned the maximum bonus this month.

On the other hand, with one week to go to the month-end, you may have just reached the £60,000 limit for which bonus is paid. How would this affect you? You have reached your maximum earnings for this month and have no incentive to sell for the remainder of the period. But you could help next month's bonus by recording the final sales of this month as the first sales of next month (assuming the system allows this to happen) or actually postponing further sales to then. Why shouldn't you have a rest for a week – after all, you have earned it, haven't you?

This 'personal earnings/bonus management' behaviour may be advantageous to the employee but it can be counter-productive to the business. An obvious example of this, as mentioned above, is where sales are pushed into the future **together with the related cash inflow**. However, there are more subtle ways in which the company can be damaged. These will become apparent as we look in more detail at specific ways in which sales can be *pulled forward* and *pushed back*.

## Moving future sales to the present

One way of pulling sales forward from next month into the current one is to offer 'abnormal' discounts (assuming you have the authority to do so). These are discounts which are not justifiable from the company's point of view but offer an incentive to the customer to buy now rather than later. For example, offers 'only available for a limited period' could fall under this heading.

When selling to distributors/wholesalers ('intermediaries' in the supply chain) it may be possible to engage in 'channel stuffing'. This is where an excessive amount of goods are delivered to suppliers this month with the expectation that deliveries will be smaller next month or that some goods will be returned.

Alternatively, if customers are told by the salesman that he has heard 'on the grapevine' that a price increase is likely next month, it may encourage them to buy more than their normal amounts this month (and less next month). Of course, when no price increase occurs next month, they can be told the good news that this is due to the supplier's good management and that increases have been held off **for the time being**.

The ingenuity of employees to improve their bonuses can be very great. There is one documented case involving the export sale of a large, expensive machine where the trigger for the payment of the bonus to the sales team was its delivery to the customer. Because the machine was not completed in time for delivery in one month, arrangements were made for it to be shipped in kit form for later assembly. This did the trick as the technicality of the machine not being in workable order was not specified by the incentive system and the bonus was paid for the month of delivery. However, the supplier subsequently had to send an assembly team to the customer's premises involving much extra expenditure that it would not normally incur. This unnecessary cost had an adverse effect on company profits but the sales team got their bonuses earlier than they should have.

Pre-dating orders/invoices is another way of pulling sales forward. For example, if the goods are to be delivered on 1 August (the first day of the next period) but you can arrange for the invoice to be dated 31 July (the last day of the current period) then the associated bonus will be paid one month earlier than it should. However, it must be pointed out that this should not be possible if the company has adequate control systems in place. This is breaking the rules rather than bending them and, if employees are caught, they should be subject to disciplinary measures. Having said that, it has certainly happened in the past and, where company control systems are poor, it could happen in the future.

## Moving present sales to the future

On the other hand, if it is in the employees' personal interest to push sales back into the following period, they may arrange for delivery of the goods to be delayed until then. This may be possible by giving incorrect information to the dispatch office. Alternatively, they may be able to arrange for the invoice to be post-dated to the next period. Again, corporate control systems should not allow this to happen but systems are rarely perfect.

A more subtle approach is for salespeople to voice to their customers the possibility of imminent price cuts. The spurious information is passed on under the guise of the salespeople's 'goodwill' towards their customers! Of course, the price cuts must never be guaranteed. The information is presented in the form of a rumour which may or may not turn out to be true. The 'get-out' clause is there to be used next month when no price decreases occur.

A more dangerous approach is for the salesperson to hint that there may be quality problems with the latest batch of manufactured goods and that it may be advisable for the customer to delay ordering until next month if possible. The customer would be asked to keep this information 'confidential', especially as the problem has now been corrected and the next batch out of the factory will be back to the normal standard of quality.

One further way of pushing sales into the future is for the salesperson to lie to the customer about stock availability. Again, this is a risky short-term ploy as the customer may give its business to a competitor to avoid serious delays.

The service sector is equally prone to these distortions. The 'credit crunch' of 2008 illustrates what can happen when incentives are paid to traders in the financial markets. Their bonuses caused them to follow their personal short-term interests by selling mortgages to 'sub-prime' homeowners to increase sales at the expense of long-term credit risk to their employers. This model is flawed because the trader gets his bonuses in the good years but does not have to repay them in the bad years. So the system works in the favour of the employee but at the expense of the long-term interests of shareholders.

The above examples are not confined to budgetary control systems. The same can happen with *any* targets that are negotiated in advance and used as the basis of the performance contract, not just budgets. For example, *balanced scorecard games* are played wherever this management model is adopted.

## The utility of budgetary control systems

There will also be other ways of moving sales backwards and forwards in time. People are nothing if not ingenious when it comes to increasing their earnings. Bonus schemes based on budget targets are very common and successful motivators of employees. Unfortunately, the resulting employee behaviour is not always in the best interests of the business.

There is a significant consensus of opinion that the way in which traditional budgetary control systems are used is part of the current corporate performance problem rather than its solution. Much of this stems from personal incentive schemes being directly linked to budget targets. The 'gaming' behaviour which this encourages often causes businesses to perform less well than they would otherwise do.

The command and control management model was designed to meet shareholders' interests. Unfortunately, when poorly administered, it may do so at the expense of employee and customer satisfaction. The 'fixed performance contract' at the heart of this model has the potential to cause dysfunctional and unethical behaviour, and destroy corporate value. Moreover, it focuses employees' attention on pleasing their bosses in the hierarchy (by meeting their individual negotiated targets) rather than focusing on what they should really do to satisfy customers (which is necessary to meet the long-term interests of shareholders).

In today's highly competitive conditions, a model is needed that meets the interests of *all* stakeholders, not just shareholders. Only a model that serves the long-term interests of customers, employees, suppliers, shareholders, government and society will create the greatest value in the long term. Companies, like Toyota, which have done this have become leaders in their industries. It took them several decades but they have laid the foundations for sustained success, and it will be hard for their competitors to catch them up unless they too adopt a new leadership model.

## The Beyond Budgeting philosophy

Beyond Budgeting advocates a new leadership model. It involves changes in organizational structure and management processes for long-term success in doing business in the twenty-first century, particularly for knowledge-based organizations. It acknowledges a shift from the production-supplier oriented businesses of the industrial age to the competitive, customer-driven, complex knowledge-based entrepreneurial ones of the innovation age. The emphasis changes from continually improving efficiency to the management of complexity. The main idea of the Beyond Budgeting movement is that the management model should be changed to support, not conflict with, the conditions of the innovation age. It achieves this by adopting a system model (i.e. **'Devolved**

| Industrial Age | Innovation Age | Success factors |
| --- | --- | --- |
| Incremental change | Discontinuous change | Fast response |
| Long life cycles | Short life cycles | Continuous innovation |
| Rising prices | Falling prices | Operational excellence |
| Limited choice of product | Extensive choice of product | Customer intimacy |
| Access to capital | Access to talent | Great place to work |
| Passive shareholders | Intolerant shareholders | Effective governance |
| Manual workers | Knowledge workers | Freedom and trust |

**Figure 16.2 Change and success factors**
*Source*: based on information provided by the BBRT.

**Leadership via Radical Decentralization'**) in place of the traditional deterministic command and control model.

The elimination of budgetary control systems is a consequence of this management model, *not its purpose*. Also, it is worth noting that it does not claim its ideas to be suitable for all business conditions. The main aspects of change and the appropriate success factors for this new model are shown in Figure 16.2. In the Industrial Age of the last century, by far the most important success factor was operational excellence. Now, in the Innovation Age of the current century, several other factors are considered equally important (see right-hand column of Figure 16.2).

A few decades ago, large businesses invested significant amounts of their resources into planning departments which would produce detailed plans for the next 10 or 20 years. They considered this worthwhile as environmental changes seemed to happen at a manageable pace. Today, that belief is seldom held; instead 'unpredictability' and 'constant change' are accepted as the norm. Planning for more than about five years ahead is seen as a waste of time and resources by most commercial organizations.

(However, there are some industries, such as nuclear power, that *need* to plan decades ahead; these are the exception rather than the rule. They attempt to build as much flexibility as possible into their plans but in reality there is little scope for them to do so. Because of unforeseen changes in the environment, this tends to produce solutions which do not provide the best possible results.)

The nature of work is also changing. Peter Drucker said that,

> The knowledge worker . . . *must lead in the information age. This leadership has to be visionary and completely different from traditional ways of leadership and management applied in the command and control model.*

Figure 16.3 summarizes the main differences between manual and knowledge workers.

This new breed of worker needs the freedom to be self-directing in order to be effective. McGregor's Theories X and Y (Douglas McGregor, *The Human Side of Enterprise*, 1960) are particularly appropriate here. These are summarized in Figure 16.4. In the Industrial Age, it was very common to refer to employees as 'hands'; this practice is much less common now as it is more appropriate to think of them as 'brains'!

| Manual workers | Knowledge workers |
| --- | --- |
| Productivity gains | Productivity challenge |
| Replaced by machines | Supported by technology |
| Costs to be reduced | Assets to yield a return |
| They need employers | Employers need them |
| Must be supervised | Must direct themselves |

**Figure 16.3 Manual workers v. knowledge workers**
*Source*: based on information provided by the BBRT.

| Theory X<br>*Typical of command and control* | Theory Y<br>*Typical of devolved leadership* |
| --- | --- |
| **Attitude**<br>People dislike work, find it boring and will avoid it if they can. | **Attitude**<br>People need to work and want to take an interest in it. Under the right conditions, they can enjoy it. |
| **Direction**<br>People must be forced or bribed to make the right effort. | **Direction**<br>People will direct themselves towards a target that they accept. |
| **Responsibility**<br>People would rather be directed than accept responsibility, which they avoid. | **Responsibility**<br>People will seek, and accept responsibility, under the right conditions. |
| **Motivation**<br>People are motivated mainly by money and fears about their job security. | **Motivation**<br>Under the right conditions, people are motivated by the desire to realize their own potential. |
| **Creativity**<br>Most people have little creativity – except when it comes to getting round management rules. | **Creativity**<br>Creativity and ingenuity are widely distributed and grossly underused. |

**Figure 16.4 Assumptions about human nature; McGregor's theories X and Y**
*Source*: based on information provided by the BBRT.

# Devolved leadership: structure and principles

The hierarchical structure adopted by most 'traditional' organizations is unsuitable for innovative knowledge-based companies. Hierarchies do not encourage fast response, continuous innovation or trust; in fact, they tend to act as barriers to these things. Devolved leadership needs a network of 'independent' business units/teams to flourish.

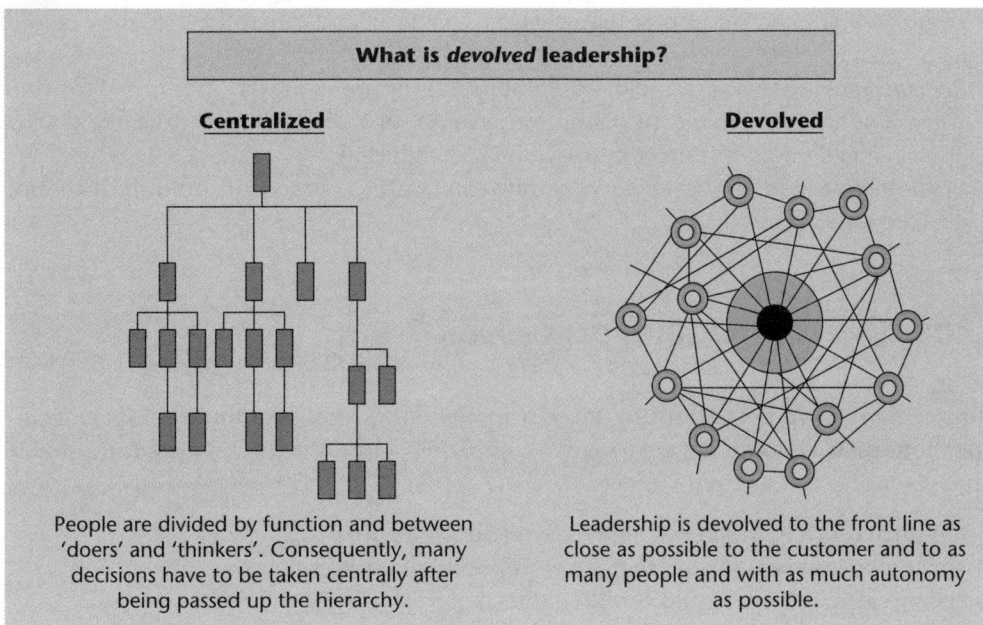

Figure 16.5 **Alternative business structures**
*Source*: reproduced by kind permission of the BBRT.

The more autonomous the units, the more successful the business is likely to be, provided there is at the same time a strong corporate culture. Head offices will still exist but their major role will be that of creating the corporate culture and supporting their 'front-line' business units (see Figure 16.5). In contrast to the old hierarchical systems, the power is devolved to the front line units, and the centralized services become suppliers to them. Thus, the new network organization is driven not through the hierarchy but through its customer–supplier relationships.

In a devolved network, the head office takes a 'hands-off' approach; it sets the direction in which it wants its business units to go then lets them get on with it, taking care not to micromanage them. The individual units not only decide their tactics, they also decide their strategies. A consequence of this is that two units may decide on different strategies in order to realize the direction and objectives set by head office. The justification for this is that their environments and the needs of their customers may not be exactly the same. Moreover, letting each decide what is best for them should lead to greater innovation when best practices are shared. This fundamental delegation of autonomy is described by Beyond Budgeting as 'Radical Decentralization'. This determines the essential structure of Beyond Budgeting organizations.

Devolved leadership operates through the enactment of the following **six basic principles:**

1 *Customer focus:* focus all employees on their customers – not on hierarchical relationships.
2 *Network of teams:* perform business processes via a lean network of accountable teams – not centralized functions.

3 *Empowerment:* autonomous teams given freedom and capability to act – avoid micromanagement.
4 *Responsibility:* create a culture of high responsibility at every level – not just at the top.
5 *Open information:* make information systems open/transparent to enable self-management – do not restrict information hierarchically.
6 *Culture statement:* governance via a few clear values, goals and boundaries – not detailed regulations.

## Adaptive (or flexible) processes

However, organizations adopting these principles almost always find that their traditional budgetary control systems are not compatible with this new management model. The reasons for this are that budgets:

- reinforce centralized, hierarchical 'command and control';
- create a bureaucratic rather than an entrepreneurial culture;
- encourage managers to play budget games;
- are a barrier to flexibility and fast response;
- discourage teamwork by emphasizing individual contributions;
- distort information by combining forecasts and targets;
- use huge amounts of resources, especially managers' time.

This is why Beyond Budgeting recommends the abolition of budgetary control systems and their replacement by the following **six flexible/adaptive processes:**

1 *Relative goals:* corporate goals should be relative (not absolute), aiming for continuous improvement – no fixed performance contracts.
2 *Relative rewards:* reward team (not individual) success using relative (not fixed) targets.
3 *Action planning:* make planning a continuous and inclusive process – not a top-down annual event.
4 *Control:* base controls on relative indicators/trends – not variances against plan.
5 *Resources as needed:* allow teams the freedom to use their resources as they think best – hold them accountable via productivity ratios such as 'cost to income'.
6 *Co-ordination as needed:* co-ordinate interactions dynamically – not via annual planning cycles.

Each of these processes will now be discussed in more detail.

### Relative goals

It is a good idea for corporate goals to be based on external benchmarks and competitor performance. For example, one company might have goals of being in the upper quartile in its industry in terms of profitability or return on equity. It would measure its performance relative to a league table of its competitors' performances ranked from the highest to the lowest, *not* against fixed targets like 20% a year. Using relative measures (if the information can be obtained) is much more effective than absolute measures because it takes into account any changes in business conditions that affect all players.

Budgets are fixed measures based on assumptions decided in advance, whereas relative measures are based on the actual circumstances with the benefit of hindsight. Thus, in bad conditions an organization's good performance may be worse than budget, but it may still beat its competitors, which is the real target.

The performance of work teams (e.g. branches or sales units) may be measured relative to each other. So work teams are empowered to set their own performance targets to improve their position in the league table against their peers. Doing this themselves gives them the psychological 'ownership' to maximize their performance. Instead of creating targets based on plans, scorecards or budgets decided in advance, they strive for relative improvement. It is also important that very few, only high-level measures are used (e.g. profitability), not a host of detailed measures (e.g. the time taken to complete the sales order), because such detailed measures constrain the achievement of maximum overall performance. Senior managers trust managers to work responsibly, but they still hold them accountable for their overall performance. They will challenge them to do better and coach them, but not micromanage them.

## Relative rewards

Under command and control, setting the employee cash bonus threshold at 80% of the budget target is meant to combat a harsh environment such as a level of competition greater than that envisaged by the budget. But if the difficulties faced are such that it is not possible to reach the threshold, no bonus will be earned despite the strenuous efforts made by the employees. On the other hand, if conditions are much more favourable than planned for, employees are able to earn significant bonuses without really trying. The illogicality of this is plain to see, yet this type of bonus incentive scheme is widespread. The effect of operating such schemes is to encourage employees to indulge in the dysfunctional behaviour of 'gaming' as discussed above. They give false and misleading information in order to increase the size of their bonuses. As subsequent business activities are based on this misinformation, it is no wonder that corporate performance suffers. **Financial incentives should *not* be based on predetermined budget targets**.

Hindsight should be used to help decide the amount of bonus payable. Bonuses are paid in arrears so why not take advantage of this and base the rewards more on the efforts made by employees than their achievements? After all, they are not responsible for changes in the business environment so why should they be punished for, or benefit from, them?

Team, rather than individual, bonuses encourage co-ordination of activities which should result in improved performance. For optimal company performance, the bigger the team, the better. The formula for calculating the bonus should be based not on a budget target but on a set of key performance indicators (KPIs). These should be carefully chosen to reflect the appropriate corporate objectives (e.g. profitability, growth, productivity). These objectives can be agreed with each business unit in advance, but without setting specific fixed targets for them. The actual performance of the unit would be determined after the event (e.g. yearly) relative to an agreed set of benchmarks.

Using reward schemes based on group rather than individual performance often raises the question as to whether this is really enough of an incentive. However, in the Beyond Budgeting model, these are not seen as incentives to perform but as rewards for shared success. The incentive to perform is the individual responsibility and the visibility of their results. Making the results of the performance of all units open for all to see is a far greater incentive to individuals to perform, the more so as everyone participates in the same reward pool, which creates peer pressure.

## Action planning

The authority and responsibility to plan their own activities lie with the local teams. All members of the team are encouraged to participate in this. Planning becomes a continuous process, not an annual cycle. Senior management may challenge their teams to perform better, but whatever plans they make are their own. They are judged, not by their plans but by their overall results against a few key measures. Teams are encouraged to concentrate on the continuous creation of value rather than hitting fixed numerical targets.

If they prepare a 'rolling forecast' every quarter for the following five quarters, it is a forecast and not a budget by another name; a forecast is not a commitment. Although it would not contain as much detail as a traditional budget, it would show summary figures of sales, costs, profits and cash flows. It is a realistic estimate of where the unit will be at a future time. Such a forecast helps senior managers to review the financial outlook of the business without being constrained by the corporate financial year or its effect on their own personal remuneration. Based on the position shown by these forecasts, local managers would plan the actions to improve their own performance.

## Control

Actual results should be produced quickly and made available to all interested parties in the organization. This information should include trends and moving averages rather than variance analysis. Patterns and trends can be used to control performance by applying a 'management by exception' approach. Rolling forecasts and benchmarking/league tables should also be used and the actual performance against KPIs reported. Under devolved leadership, such information is produced primarily for local managers to improve their own performance, while keeping senior managers informed.

## Resources as needed

Resources should be provided when required. Resource planning is still essential but it should be done as near as possible to the required date rather than a long time in advance in the original budget.

Local teams use resources as they need them based on their current requirements and up-to-date information rather than an out-of-date budget. Overall control can be exercized by a series of preset limits (for example, a cost to income ratio of no more than, say, 35%). For small projects, more authority to use resources could be devolved to the appropriate teams.

Central services, such as Information Systems or Personnel, should operate on an internal market basis at predetermined prices. This will ensure that they will only be used when necessary; if a service is freely available, it tends to be overused. This should also bring about an increase in the efficiency of central services as they respond to the demands made upon them. (This theory is also embodied in Charles Handy's *Doughnut Principle* of management.)

## Co-ordination as needed

Do not rely on annual budgets: plan more frequently by making periodic service-level agreements with other teams. Manage your short-term capacity in real time by adjusting it according to demand. The whole organization will be more efficient if other teams are seen as internal customers or suppliers. Co-ordination will be improved if teams listen to their customers and respond accordingly. This is different from viewing customer demands as part of your predetermined budget plan. What customers want may not fit in with your budget and you may try to amend their requests to make them fit. How much better it is to respond to customer demands by giving customers what they want, when they want it, instead of being constrained by an out-of-date plan.

*Robin Fraser, one of the co-founders of the Beyond Budgeting movement, has described 'Beyond Budgeting' organizations as those which meet their critical success factors better than their competitors by adopting the devolved leadership management model. Two such companies will now be described.*

---

# Svenska Handelsbanken

Example
16.1

The most frequently quoted example of a Beyond Budgeting organization is the Swedish bank, Svenska Handelsbanken (SHB). At the time of writing, it has about 600 branches (40 of which are in Great Britain, the others being in the Nordic countries, with most being in Sweden) and approximately 10,000 staff. In 2005, its operating profit was £1.2 billion and its assets totalled £130 billion.

One function of its head office in Stockholm is to create new products in response to requests from its branches. However, each branch can decide what price to charge its customers for these products and, if they wish, they can charge different prices to different customers. The responsibility is theirs; each branch must make its own decisions and be assessed on the overall profitability that it achieves relative to its peers.

These pricing decisions are based on the high level of 'customer intimacy' the branch has with each of its customers. It does not adopt a mass-marketing, one-size-fits-all approach, it does not use central advertising and it does not issue product brochures. Each branch advertises locally to the extent it thinks appropriate and produces a branch business plan on a regular basis (primarily for its own use – no one approves it). There are no sales targets or centralized product campaigns.

Branches are responsible for their own customers, with 98% of all credit decisions being made at branch level. Each branch is a profit centre; reporting to head office is restricted to a few profit and efficiency ratios on a monthly basis. Each branch manager has the responsibility for deciding:

- how many staff to employ;
- staff skill profiles;
- how much to pay each employee;
- which customers to approach;
- what products to offer;
- what prices to charge.

This autonomy is reflected in Svenska Handelsbanken's well-used slogan, 'the branch is the bank'. This independence is reinforced by their Internet banking activities. There is not just one Svenska Handelsbanken Internet banking site; each branch has its own website through which existing accounts can be operated if the customer wishes to do so. The service is free of charge and is viewed as a labour-saving benefit by the branch and, therefore, a cost minimization device. They adopt a 'church spire' approach to keeping their customer base local; customers should be physically visible from the top of an imaginary spire adjacent to the branch office. They believe this helps them to achieve a high level of 'customer intimacy', an essential requirement for their way of doing business. One result of this is the very low level of bad debts they incur.

Svenska Handelsbanken has only three management levels: president/CEO, executive vice-president and branch manager. This results in a very flat structure where even the CEO is only two steps away from the customer. It is managed 'bottom-up' and has no annual master plan. Its aim is 'to provide better service at lower cost' (see Figure 16.6).

For more than 30 years, the bank has had only one corporate goal, 'to achieve a higher return on equity than the average of comparable banks in its marketplace'. The direction given to branches is also very simple: each one must aim to be better than average. Of course, this means that half of them will fail! This would be very demotivating and counterproductive *if penalties were consequential*. However, penalties are not imposed and the process is seen as a learning and improvement opportunity. The high level of responsibility that a branch manager has to run his

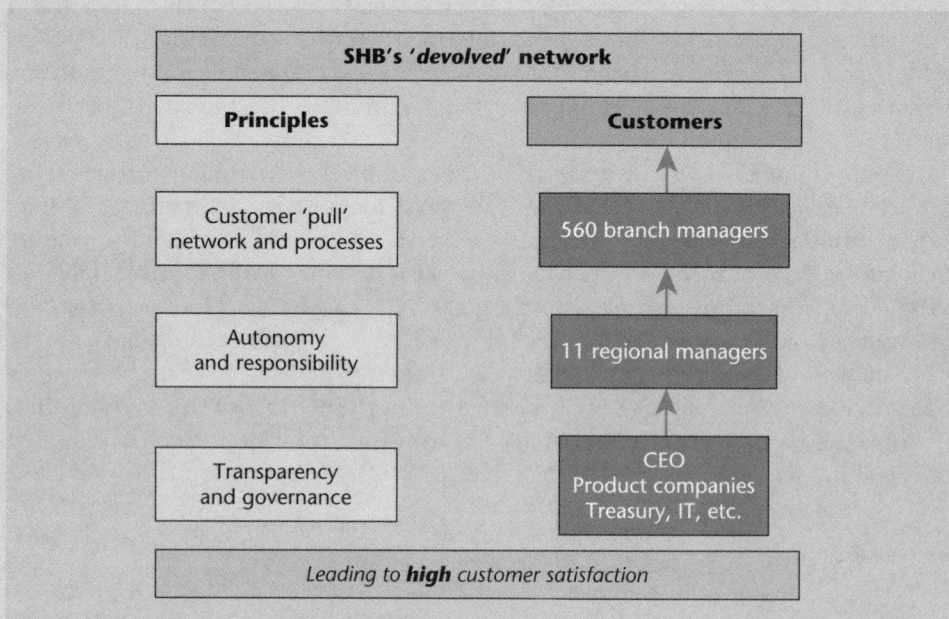

Figure 16.6  **Svenska Handelsbanken's flat structure**
*Source*: reproduced by kind permission of the BBRT.

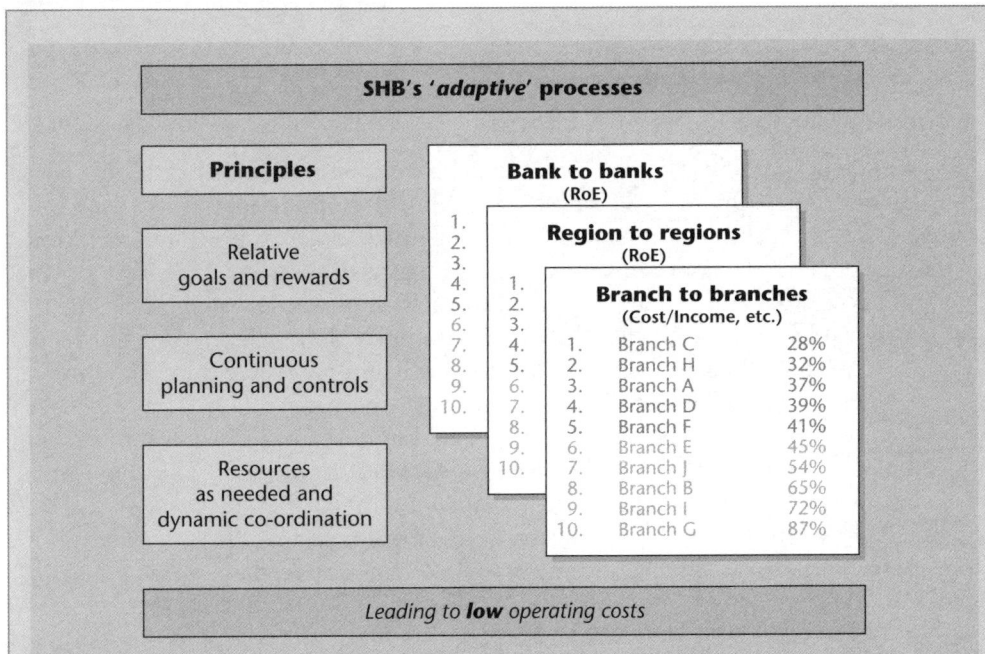

**SHB's 'adaptive' processes**

| **Principles** | **Bank to banks** (RoE) | | |
|---|---|---|---|
| | 1. | | |
| Relative goals and rewards | 2. | **Region to regions** (RoE) | |
| | 3. | | |
| | 4. 5. 6. | 1. 2. 3. | **Branch to branches** (Cost/Income, etc.) |
| Continuous planning and controls | 7. 8. 9. 10. | 4. 5. 6. 7. 8. 9. 10. | 1. Branch C 28%  2. Branch H 32%  3. Branch A 37%  4. Branch D 39%  5. Branch F 41%  6. Branch E 45%  7. Branch J 54%  8. Branch B 65%  9. Branch I 72%  10. Branch G 87% |
| Resources as needed and dynamic co-ordination | | | |

*Leading to **low** operating costs*

Figure 16.7 **SHB's three levels of benchmarking**
*Source*: reproduced by kind permission of the BBRT.

own business and the visibility of his or her branch's performance are the main drivers to improve.

Internal league tables (a form of benchmarking) are created, published and made available to all employees; this information is not restricted to certain special groups but is available to **all** employees. They are created at three levels: bank, region and branch (see Figure 16.7). Branches at the top of the tables have nothing to lose by sharing their 'winning ways' with branches at the bottom, if asked to do so by them. On the contrary, the company as a whole benefits from this knowledge-sharing process and all employees benefit from this in the profit-sharing scheme.

Svenska Handelsbanken's management model is an exemplar of 'devolved leadership'. It considers budgetary control systems to be incompatible with this model and so does not use budgets (and has not done so for the past 35 years). It recognizes that budgets are the result of negotiations and static assumptions, dictating predetermined actions in a world of rapid change. Svenska Handelsbanken believes it is better to know its present position rather than make guesses about the future. It understands that 'better-than-budget' performance may not be good enough in a very competitive world. It prefers to benchmark itself against its competitors – a relative rather than an absolute measure.

It uses the following *adaptive processes* in place of budgets:

- a deeply rooted corporate culture of responsibility and genuine empowerment;
- benchmarking at three levels: company, region and branch;
- internal support-function pricing (sometimes possible to outsource if cheaper);

- ongoing discussions about self-improvement;
- profit-sharing model focuses minds on its overall corporate objective;
- employees are trusted.

Svenska Handelsbanken does not give annual bonuses but it does have a profit sharing scheme which applies to all employees. One-third of annual profits (over and above the average profit of its 'basket' of competitor banks) is put into a deferred retirement income fund and invested for the long term, mostly in the bank's own shares. **The annual amount appropriated to each employee is exactly the same in monetary value.** This means that the clerks at individual branches receive the same value as the head office directors! As this money is not accessible until retirement, 'short-termism' is discouraged in employees. Also, consider the motivating effect of this; each employee, irrespective of their position in the bank, will feel as valued as the Chief Executive Officer. *The size of the team becomes the size of the whole organization and everybody is a shareholder and pulls in the same direction.*

In 2006, Deutsche Bank compared the performance for 2005 of 30 leading European banks using two important ratios, costs as a percentage of income and costs as a percentage of total loans. Svenska Handelsbanken came **top** in both categories (see Figure 16.8). In March 2007, the *Sunday Times* compiled a list of the best UK companies to work for; Svenska Handelsbanken came eleventh out of 650. And for very many years Handelsbanken's customer satisfaction has consistently been above the average of its peers.

Comparison of listed European universal banks with lending > EUR 100 bn and major Nordic banks. Costs including loan losses Jan–Dec 2005.

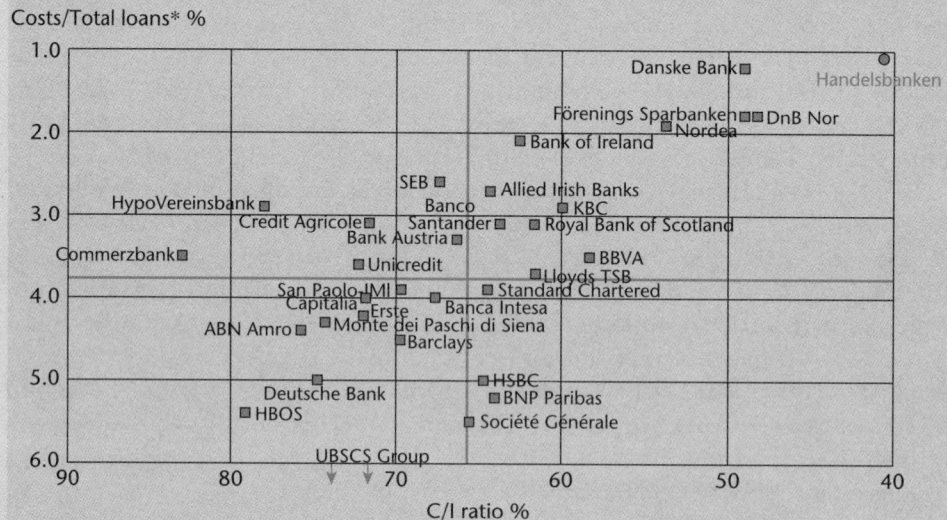

Figure 16.8 **Best cost-to-income ratio**
*Source*: reproduced by kind permission of the BBRT.

Example
16.2

# The Toyota production system

Toyota is one of the biggest and most successful companies in the world. In 2006 it had 286,000 employees, sales of US$160 billion and a net profit margin of 8%. The following paragraphs give an insight into how this success has been achieved. However, it can be categorically stated that budgetary control systems are in no way responsible since the Toyota production system does not use them to drive performance.

Toyota takes customer satisfaction very seriously. This is reflected in the results of a recent J. D. Power Customer Satisfaction Index which put Toyota in first place (followed by Mazda, BMW and Volvo). It operates a 'pull' system, responding to customer orders, rather than trying to sell what it has made. As far as possible, it provides manufacturing resources as they are required through its sophisticated just-in-time system. The Toyota production system does not use budgets; it does make plans but targets are separate from them and are aspirational.

Its employees work in small self-coordinated teams and are encouraged to think of ways of improving the production system. Every single employee is encouraged to challenge the system by suggesting changes. All ideas are treated with respect, even if they only result in very minor changes saving just a few pence per car. This *kaisen* approach of continuous improvement is a fundamental part of their working practices. In just one year in their Kentucky, USA plant, 100,000 suggestions were made, approximately 90,000 of which were implemented!

As well as *kaisen*, Toyota encourages a *genchi genbutsu* ('go and see for yourself') approach which emphasizes the importance of experiencing problems first-hand rather than reading about them in a report. Reports tend to be abstract simplifications of reality and solutions created at a distance can sometimes miss vital aspects of the problem. (This approach is similar to the management accounting techniques discussed in this book; they are abstract models – hopefully useful ones – but can never be as rich as the reality they attempt to represent.)

Genchi genbutsu has been referred to as 'getcha boots on' and go and have a look at the problem yourself. This fits in with the devolved leadership principle of performing business processes via a lean network of accountable teams. Toyota believes that, if the processes are right, the profits will follow, a significantly different approach from keeping expenditure within predetermined budget targets.

But Toyota's aim goes well beyond making good cars. Its unique corporate philosophy is that of:

*Seeking harmony between people, society, the global environment and a sustainable development of society through making things.*

It strives to achieve and maintain mutual trust and respect in its employee relations.

It manages by means (e.g. satisfying customers) rather than ends (e.g. meeting annual targets). It sees itself as a living system, organic rather than rigidly structured; it acknowledges change as a way of life.

Toyota believes in open, transparent information; it communicates ideas to employees using 'A3s', posters on A3-size paper. This means that the information on these has to be concise and clearly expressed, using illustrations where appropriate. These 'bite-sized' chunks of information are much more likely to be read than

'It may only have been a matter of time but the news this week that Toyota has finally overtaken General Motors (GM) to become the world's biggest car maker marks the end of an era. Detroit, once one of the world's industrial capitals, is in irreversible decline, dragged down by its archaic cost structures and working practices. Like in all matters industrial, the power continues to shift east.

Toyota, one of the world's most efficient companies, sold 2.35 m vehicles in the first three months of 2007, beating GM's 2.26 m sales during the quarter. The Japanese car giant's quarterly sales in the US, the critical battleground for the industry, were up 9% year-on-year compared with 3% for GM. The Japanese car maker is widely expected to be the world's top seller for 2006, with global sales of 9.34 m units. GM sold 9.098 m.

Toyota's market share leapt to 15.6% in the quarter, up from 9.3% in 2000; conversely, GM, which commanded 28.1% of the US market seven years ago, saw its share slip to a miserable 23.1%.

GM is cutting North American production by 1 m units and closing 12 North American factories; conversely, Toyota has announced two new factory openings to add to its six North American sites, one in Ontario, Canada; a second in Mississippi, opening in 2010. By next year, the company will have the capacity to make 2 m vehicles a year in North America, up from 1.5 m in 2006.

Toyota's success piles fresh pain on Detroit's Big Three car makers – GM, Ford and Chrysler – which are struggling to adapt to changing consumer tastes while burdened by billions of dollars in pension and healthcare costs. These amount to $18 bn (£8.9 bn, 13 bn euros) in the case of Chrysler alone; the huge legacy costs of Chrysler's retired workers adds $1,000 to the cost of every car rolling off the production line.

American motorists are abandoning gas-guzzlers for more efficient European-style cars and vans. Toyota, having invested millions in factories and a distribution network in the US, is perfectly placed to tap into this shift: the Toyota Camry saloon is America's top-selling car; Toyota's petrol-electric hybrids, led by the Prius and a hybrid version of the Camry, broke through the 500,000 sales mark for the first time in March.

Toyota sold 61,635 hybrids in the year to end-March, a 68% increase on the previous 12 months. Pump prices in the US have risen 33% in the past 11 weeks, according to the US Energy Department.

It is no surprise that Toyota, along with Honda, Nissan and the rest, are stealing a march on Detroit. The US giants have the wrong products and find it hard to adapt. Powerful trade unions have them boxed in.

Small wonder DaimlerChrysler is exploring selling the US side of its business, in a humiliating admission that the German company's great American adventure has failed miserably.'

**Figure 16.9** **'Toyota motors ahead as Detroit's dinosaurs get left further behind'**
*Source*: Ashworth, J. (2007) 'Toyota motors ahead as Detroit dinosaurs get left further behind', *The Business*, 28 April, with permission of the Press Holdings Media Group (The Spectator).

multiple-page instruction manuals. This is one of the tools it uses to build consensus which, in turn, allows it to exercise effective governance.

At the time of writing, Toyota is on the point of becoming the number one car manufacturer in the world! It is one of the most successful companies to have adopted a management model based on the Beyond Budgeting principles. An independent opinion of the magnitude of Toyota's success is provided by Jon Ashworth's article in the 28 April 2007 edition of the magazine *The Business* – see Figure 16.9.

Jeremy Hope, the co-founder of the Beyond Budgeting movement, in a recent IBM survey of CEOs, has stated his opinion that, 'Competitive advantage will increasingly come from the choice of business management model'. Toyota Motor Corporation's Chairman, Fujio Cho, appears to agree with him saying that, 'Toyota views its culture as its most competitive weapon'. The Beyond Budgeting business model seems to be at the heart of Toyota's success even if they do not call it that!

## Membership of the Beyond Budgeting Round Table

Organizations that support or have supported the Beyond Budgeting movement include: A C Neilson, Aldi Supermarkets, American Express, Anheuser Busch, Barclays Bank, BT Group, BG Transco, Boots the Chemists, Cadbury-Schweppes, CIMA, Coors Brewers, Diageo, De Beers, Deutsche Bank, IBM Business Consulting Services, Kingfisher, KPMG Consulting, Mars Confectionery, Port of Tyne Authority, Mastercard, Mencap, Sainsbury Supermarkets, Siemens, Sightsavers International, South West Airlines, Standard Life, Telecom New Zealand, Thames Water, The World Bank, UBS and Unilever. These are just some that I think you may have heard of; there are many more which you may not have. Not all these organizations embrace the Beyond Budgeting philosophy 100% but they all agree that it includes some very interesting ideas worthy of adoption.

## Limitations

The Beyond Budgeting philosophy is to manage in a way that supports, not conflicts with, the organization's critical success factors and the interests of stakeholders. Although this is suitable for *all* organizations, those companies working in Industrial Age conditions might find it hard to make a case for change. For example, a company producing cement powder from raw limestone based in a single location with no competitors and no difficulty in attracting and retaining suitable employees should organize itself to maximize efficiency, almost irrespective of its impact on customer service and employee morale, so that it can achieve the highest returns to shareholders.

Another interesting case is the UK Royal Mail which, until recently, had a monopoly on the delivery of non-business letters, reinforced by law with prices controlled by the national government. When this was so, there would have been no point in instigating the Beyond Budgeting approach. However, the monopoly has now been removed, regulations relaxed and competition encouraged. If the Royal Mail is to survive, it should consider adopting the Beyond Budgeting model of devolved leadership as its structure is already decentralized with many similar branches in existence. Internal competition between branches could transform not only its work practices but also its finances.

If this transformation was attempted, a huge shift in its internal culture would be essential as, at the moment, it is very much a 'command and control' type of organization. Vested interests exist both on the side of management and of the trades union. Both would have to want to achieve the necessary changes but this would entail each of them giving up a significant amount of power. It is encouraging to know that the Royal Mail has shown an interest in these ideas and has been a member of the Beyond Budgeting Round Table for several years.

Without doubt, it is easier to establish Beyond Budgeting practices in brand new organizations than transform established companies which have traditional hierarchical functional structures and have used traditional performance management processes (including budgetary control techniques) for many years. In 1513, the Italian scholar and diplomat Nicholas Machiavelli wrote in his book *The Prince*:

> *there is nothing more difficult to execute, nor more dubious of success, nor more dangerous to administer than to introduce a new order of things; for he who introduces it has all those who profit from the old order as his enemies, and he has only lukewarm allies in all those who might profit from the new.*

This is just as true today as it was 500 years ago. It offers an explanation as to why, if it is such a good idea, Beyond Budgeting has not been more widely adopted. But, although difficult, transformations are possible; at the time of writing, the giant Norwegian oil company, Statoil, is undertaking this huge change process. It will cost many millions in resources but it obviously thinks it worthwhile.

Robin Fraser has said that such transformations stand the greatest chance of success when it is recognized that a major change in leadership is needed, not just a change of accounting systems. He advises that the first step is to assess the 'case for change'. This involves envisaging the whole model (i.e. all 12 principles), understanding the changes required and the costs and benefits of adopting it. If urgency through dissatisfaction with the organization's performance is high enough and the case for change compelling enough, there is a good chance of success. It must be led from the top but in a way that is consistent with devolved leadership. It is not an easy transformation, but judging by the success of pioneers like Handelsbanken and Toyota adopting the model is not a matter of whether, but when!

## The counter point of view

Having read the above summary of the 'Beyond Budgeting' philosophy, you should now consider some of the arguments against abandoning the budget. The following paragraphs present a counter point of view to each of the six 'Beyond Budgeting' adaptive processes stated above. They are the personal opinions of Nigel Burton who has written most of the 'Manager's point of view' sections at the end of each chapter. During his career he has been the accountant, financial director and managing director in an international manufacturing company, and he speaks with the authority of many years' personal experience of these issues. It is fair to say that, although he believes that the practice of budgeting needs to be continually improved, the total abandonment of budgeting would be detrimental to the vast majority of organizations.

### Goals

If you want to be number one in the industry, the first thing to do is to establish the sales and profits of the current leader, and work out a strategy for exceeding them. This will give you a timescale and a required growth rate. You then need to go into the detail, to work out exactly how you are going to generate the increased sales/profits over the coming years, and how much you need to do each year. In other words, you need detailed annual budgets indicating what you need to do to achieve the long-term targets. In this way, budgets can be used as strategic tools rather than mere control mechanisms. At the same time, there is no reason why you cannot benchmark your performance against competitors as you go along, although this will always be a retrospective procedure.

## Rewards

The use of hindsight to determine cash bonuses sounds exemplary but is it possible to separate internal and external business environment factors from the efforts of individuals or discrete teams to produce a monetary formula for the calculation of bonuses? Is it possible to eliminate subjectivity from the bonus calculations? Maybe the bonus should be left entirely to the discretion of the manager, who is best placed to make such a judgement, but do you really want a significant part of your remuneration to be subject to the whim of your superior, whose own bonus might be enhanced if he or she can keep costs pared down to a minimum?

Basing a bonus formula on a small group of KPIs sounds fine at first hearing but it can be difficult to find ones which are objective, quantifiable and relevant. Also, KPIs can be manipulated in just the same way as budget targets by the playing of 'KPI games'.

There is no such thing as a perfectly fair bonus scheme. External factors will always have a bearing on an individual's performance. It is his job to deal with them, and achieve the shareholders' requirements, notwithstanding the difficulties thrown in his way. Effort is all very laudable, but should hardly lead to a bonus if the company has made a loss.

## Planning

A predetermined annual budget does not preclude any thought being given to the way the business is progressing, either long term or short term. For instance, consider an annual production budget containing details of capacity, labour requirements, material costs, etc. This does not prevent the actual monthly production plans being prepared on the basis of actual requirements at the time rather than the original production budget. The existence of a budget does not cause companies to ignore up-to-date information and stick with their original plans no matter what.

## Controls

Trends and moving averages may be useful in some companies, but they can be very misleading, for instance, when a significant past event drops out of the moving average calculation. For other companies, variance analysis is perfectly suitable for assessing performance 'at a glance'.

## Resources

The annual budget acts as a **guide** to future requirements. Companies do not sanction expenditure on capital projects or additional personnel just because it was included in the original budget; all such expenditure needs to be justified at the time. Similarly, management are highly unlikely to turn down a profitable activity simply because it was not included in the budget. If a business thinks there is a good chance of making a profit by doing something outside its budgeted activities, it will find the necessary resources one way or another.

## Co-ordination

Co-ordination is a normal management function. Short-term planning and capacity management are part of the day-to-day functions of management. Listening to internal and external customers' requirements is a TQM idea, and a very good one. It is in no way constrained by the existence of an annual budget. Obviously, managers have to react to the real world. The budget is simply a yardstick against which to assess the impact of their actions.

## Better Budgeting

In 2004 the Chartered Institute of Management Accountants (CIMA) and the Institute of Chartered Accountants in England and Wales (ICAEW) held a joint round table event called 'Better Budgeting'. There were 32 delegates in all including the BBC, GlaxoSmithKline, J Sainsbury plc, Unilever, the Beyond Budgeting Round Table, Atos KPMG Consulting and the University of Bristol.

The idea was to allow top managers from large respected companies and a select few academics and consultants to openly discuss the current state of budgeting and comment on its usefulness or otherwise. The findings of this forum were published in a report entitled 'Better Budgeting'. The text below is a highly summarized account, in bullet point form, of some of the main points arising from the open discussion.

- Budgets suffered a very bad press in recent years based on their high cost, lengthy preparation time and their associated 'gaming' behaviour.
- But most organizations thought budgets were indispensable as they provided a control framework without which management would not be possible.
- However, they admitted that formal budgetary control systems could discourage value-creating, entrepreneurial attitudes; for example, new projects may be abandoned if budgetary resources are exhausted before the year end.
- Resources may be inappropriately concentrated on perfecting budgetary control systems at the expense of competitive awareness and agility, but, when this happens, it can be countered by a culture of openness and flexibility.
- Budgeting has significantly improved over the last 20 years; organizations are adapting, rather than abandoning, budgets. For example, rolling forecasts are now used much more often, particularly where the business environment changes rapidly such as the telecommunications industry.
- It is important to note that 'forecasts' are not the same as 'budgets'; semantics are an important aspect of this discussion. The data in forecasts are much more summarised and 'high-level' than the detailed information in budgets.

- Creating a budget forces managers from different parts of the organization to discuss things with each other; this inter-functional communication and co-ordination is very beneficial and may not otherwise happen in such depth.
- Delegates thought that a culture of trust and empowerment was necessary for modern budgeting to thrive but acknowledged that, often, the prevailing culture of budgetary control systems was one of blame and mistrust.
- Delegates agreed that the common practice of linking personal remuneration systems to budget targets often resulted in dysfunctional behaviour. (Interestingly, only a few of the delegates operated personal remuneration systems that were linked directly to budget targets.)
- Budgets are evolving incrementally rather than changing rapidly.
- The bottom-up participative approach is gaining favour compared with the top-down centralized one.

The 'Better Budgeting' report goes on to give summaries of the forum's three main presentations. The first is in favour of the continuing improvement of budgetary control systems, the second advocates the abolition of budgets and the third presents the results of a survey of attitudes towards budgeting. *Readers are strongly recommended to study the full report for themselves*; it is freely available as a *technical report* from CIMA's website (see 'Further reading').

## The manager's point of view (by Gary Burmiston)

Settling down on a Friday night after another week at work and it's time to have that small glass of Chablis – a fruity little number I've been looking forward to. Bottle at the ready, glass at the ready, now where's that corkscrew? Five minutes of searching through a drawer, which is well overdue for a tidy, and corkscrew is present and correct. Attempting to remove the cork it splits, second attempt is more successful and the cork is removed but, as the wine sloshes into the glass, I notice small pieces of cork in the wine. Never mind, I'll make do and ignore the pieces. However, on sipping the wine it has a strange taste, cork taint if I'm not mistaken. I persevere but it's not what I had in mind. Ten minutes after settling down I start drinking poor quality wine.

Corks are known for being flawed and their flaws are many:

- they are known as being relatively expensive, with variable quality;
- cork dust cannot be avoided;
- cork taint (2-4-6 Tricloroanysole or TCA to be precise) has a negative effect on wine quality.

Surely there must be something better.

There is; it's called a screw cap and yet when I recall my purchasing experience I immediately bypassed the wines with screw caps as not being 'proper' wines, they surely must be somewhat inferior not to have a cork.

And it's this type of logic that's seen constantly with budgets.

Outlined in this chapter are a plethora of problems with traditional budgeting techniques and the issues outlined are not just hypothetical. As someone who has been responsible for producing a range of companies' budgets over the last 15 years, I find the issues highlighted in this chapter to be wholly consistent with my experiences.

Real examples include:

- **Time.** The time taken to produce a budget can be almost as long as the year itself; the maximum that I've experienced is over seven months. Usually this time is extended due to multiple 'sign-offs' required at various stages of the process. The sign-off process alone can sometimes take longer than the actual budget production process. This is particularly apparent when foreign parents are concerned. The budget is first produced and signed off at a departmental level. It's then consolidated and signed off at a business unit level before going on to be consolidated and signed off at a country level before being ultimately consolidated and signed off at a corporate level. Only by starting a budget process in March can it be completed in time for the following January.

- **Relevance.** Although it can take up to seven months to produce a budget the chances of its being useful are diminished because of the knowledge that has been gained in the months that followed and because of what has happened in the external environment. The starting points for many budgets are the sales and price assumptions. Many changes can happen in seven months to the point where in one organization the budget, which had taken many hours, much effort and caused huge debate in all parts of the business, was used only for January reporting and then was totally discarded as being irrelevant. A price decrease of a major product had rendered the assumptions in the budget irrelevant!

- **Game playing.** Human nature is one of self-preservation and nowhere, in an organizational environment, is this more visible than in the budget-setting process. There are many examples that could be used, but to give a flavour consider the purchasing manager who is incentivized on creating a positive purchase cost variance, i.e. how far below the standard cost he can actually procure goods for. Great in theory; which company wouldn't want to challenge the purchasing manager to get better deals? However, it is also the purchasing manager who sets the standard cost for the goods produced! So he sets a high standard cost and when his actual costs come in lower than standard, he gets a good bonus. However, the selling prices are based on the standard cost. The impact of this is that it limits the ability of the salesmen to negotiate lower prices to gain sales. They assume, incorrectly, that they would be selling the product at a loss. Therefore, as a result of the budget process, sales could be lost.

Budgets are truly and absolutely flawed. Budgets are pilloried as being out of touch with the needs of modern business and accused of taking too long, costing too much and encouraging all sorts of perverse behaviour.

And yet, like corks, we're happy to put up with their limitations. Despite people being aware of the problems, companies by and large regard the budget system and the accompanying process as indispensable.

Corks have a positive image and are seen as emotionally appealing. They are part of the wine culture and the opening of a bottle is almost a ceremony – that pop as the cork comes out of the bottle can signify the start of an event. Do budgets also hold this romanticized sense of experience for us?

The budgeting process has its limitations, and techniques such as Beyond Budgeting show, where it's been implemented, improved results. A powerful case for change and yet research claims that as many as 99% of European companies have a budget in place and no intention of abandoning it. So what is it that's stopping organizations from making the move?

Beyond Budgeting does have its limitations as highlighted within this chapter; however, the major obstacle experienced in industry appears to be taking that first step in agreeing that Beyond Budgeting is the way for an organization to move forward. Being involved with a number of organizations which have tried, and to date failed, to introduce an alternative to the budget process I have observed some common themes as to why senior managers appear reluctant to take those major steps which will drive towards a successful outcome.

First there is the issue of leadership. The success of Svenska Handelsbanken was driven initially by the vision and determination of one man, the CEO, Jan Wallender. He knew the organization had to change and it was his vision of a devolved network that permeated throughout all parts of the organization in a way that inspired people enough to change. Nowadays the decision to move to an alternative to budgeting is still taken at the highest level, but as soon as that decision is made it is often passed down to a project team to implement.

As soon as this happens the implementation is increasingly doomed to failure. All too often this top priority can fall down the list as other issues arise. It could be argued that Beyond Budgeting is just an accounting technique that can be copied and replicated in all organizations; doing A and B will result in the outcome C no matter where or who you are. In the same way David Beckham could argue that taking free kicks is just a matter of kicking the ball in the right place at the right speed. Done correctly, anyone should be able to replicate what he achieves. And yet this rarely happens.

Beyond Budgeting is not a change of technique. It is a change of culture, a change that needs to be driven from the highest level. Project teams are not able to do this. Hearts and minds need to be won over as much as, if not more than, logical intuition.

Secondly, another huge hurdle to overcome is the nature of its implementation. To achieve this successfully it is an all or nothing implementation; you cannot run both budgeting and Beyond Budgeting in parallel to test the water. As mentioned above, this is not just a technique; it is a cultural change and an organization needs to commit fully to it to reap its benefits. The analogy used by the Beyond Budgeting Round Table is that if you want to change the UK to driving on the right you wouldn't stage the implementation by saying on Monday morning buses and taxis can drive on the right and then we'll evaluate the success of the implementation before allowing cars and lorries to change from left to right. Implementation does not have a safety net to fall back on – a very scary scenario for many chief executives – highlighting the importance of strong leadership.

Finally, while there is a good case for change, there is also an excuse for no change. One of the first comments senior managers will make when presented with such a change will be, 'Show me where this has been done and the impact it has had'. Current beacons are few and far between. Svenska Handelsbanken is the leader and other organizations such as Toyota are following to a lesser extent. The critical mass of organizations which can demonstrate the benefits they are achieving through replacing the budget process has not yet been achieved. Therefore, each new company will be seen as an early adopter when many just want to be followers. Why upset the apple cart when they have something in place which works? They know it's flawed, they know it doesn't optimize performance; they know it could be better but they also know it meets their needs and are prepared to put up with the issues budgeting causes. It could be argued that no organization has ever failed due to its budget; it is the actuals that count. So why throw away everything people know for something which is unproven on a mass scale?

Of all the management accounting techniques, budgeting is the one that is used by the majority of companies. It is also the one that is most open to the vagaries of human behaviour, and the examples and issues highlighted in the chapter happen continuously in most organizations on a daily basis. The case for change is great but the people still need to be convinced by the alternatives.

Budgeting as a technique is not necessarily poor – it is how people **use** budgeting that is poor. Beyond Budgeting offers a new way of managing your business without budgets. Alternatively, if the Better Budgeting approach is adopted to make businesses work better, it will not be enough to improve the budgeting process; peoples' behaviours will have to improve.

*Summary*

The current disquiet with budgetary control systems is being addressed in many organizations by attempts at its improvement. This is the route that the majority of businesses are taking. However, there now exists an alternative way of overcoming the acknowledged difficulties. There is a new management model called Beyond Budgeting which is particularly suitable for the twenty-first century. This is a *systemic* management model, one which should respond much better than the traditional *deterministic* model in today's highly competitive, fast-changing business environment.

Its main philosophy is Devolved Leadership through radical decentralization, a kind of permanent empowerment to units within a network organization rather than a functional hierarchy. Getting rid of traditional budgetary control systems is a *consequence* of this new model as the tools of command-and-control are incompatible with it. However, if budgets are abolished, something must be put in their place; these are the adaptive processes proposed by Beyond Budgeting. (There are six principles of devolved leadership and six adaptive processes.) In the right context, this new management model should lead to sustainable competitive advantage; Handelsbanken and Toyota are examples of this, demonstrating the value of the model.

It is pertinent that the foreword to Hope and Fraser's book, *Beyond Budgeting*, is written by one of the most distinguished management accountants of the twentieth century, Charles T. Horngren of Stanford University, USA. In his final paragraph he states the following:

> *Most of the solutions generally proposed for management problems involve putting something new into the organization. In this regard, Beyond Budgeting is very different. Perhaps uniquely, it proposes taking something powerful out to make room for something new and even more powerful. We have all the tools and techniques we need. What we lack is the right overall context for them to work effectively.*

## Further reading

'Better Budgeting – a joint report from CIMA and ICAEW' – see the 'technical report' section of the CIMA website, www.cimaglobal.com

Bragdon, J., 'Profit for Life'. How Capitalism Excels, Society for Organizational Learning.

Bishop, J. (2004) 'Beyond budgeting in practice', *Chartered Accountants Journal*, Vol. 83, Issue 11, December.

Bourne, M. and Neely, A. (2002) 'Cause and effect', *Financial Management*, September.

Brignall, S., Fitzgerald, L., Johnson, R. and Silvestro, R. (1991) 'Performance measurement in service businesses', *Management Accounting (UK)*, November.

Cassell, M. (2003) 'Can we budge it?', *Financial Management* (CIMA), November.

Hamel, G. with Breen, B. (2007) *The Future of Management*, Harvard Business School Press, Boston, MA.

Henschen, D. (2005) 'Amex ends budgeting as usual', *Intelligent Enterprise*, Vol. 8, Issue 4, 1 April.

Hope, J. and Fraser, R. (2003) *Beyond Budgeting – How Managers Can Break Free from the Annual Performance Trap*, Harvard Business School Press, Boston, MA.

Hope, J. and Fraser, R. (2003) 'New ways of setting rewards: the Beyond Budgeting model', *California Management Review*, Vol. 45, Issue 4, Summer.

Howard, M. (2004) 'Go figure', *Financial Management* (CIMA), March.

Hyndman, N., Jones, R. and Pendlebury, M. (2003) 'Use it or lose it', *Financial Management* (CIMA), November.

Jensen, M. C. (2001) 'Corporate budgeting is broken – let's fix it', *Harvard Business Review*, November.

Liker, J. (2003) *The Toyota Way – 14 Management Principles from the world's greatest manufacturer*, McGraw Hill, New York.

Lynch, R. and Cross, K. F. (1995) *Measure Up! Yardsticks for Continuous Improvement*, 2nd edition, Basil Blackwell, Oxford.

Marginson, D. and Ogden, S. (2005) 'Budgeting and innovation', *Financial Management* (CIMA), April.

Prickett, R. (2003) 'Beyond budgeting case study 1, the private company', *Financial Management* (CIMA), November.

Saetre, E. and Bogsnes, B. of Statoil, 'Break with the Budget', http://www.the-financedirector.com/contributors/contributor316/

Shim, J. and Siegel, J. (2005) *Budgeting Basics and Beyond*, J. Wiley & Sons, NJ.

Stockdyk, John, 'Budgeting a thing of the past for Statoil', http://www.accountingweb.co.uk/cgi-bin/item.cgi?id=163586&d=526&h=524&f=525

| CASE STUDY | Medibed |
| --- | --- |

## Background

Medibed manufactures hospital beds. These are complicated mobile platforms with several moving parts. It is located on the outskirts of Bromsgrove and has good connections to the motorway system. Bromsgrove is centrally situated in the UK and has a good quality workforce. Medibed has never experienced any difficulty in finding appropriately trained staff during their expansion over the last 12 years.

The business started when George Wright was made redundant from a firm which is now one of their rivals. As a design engineer, George had some ideas about how the hospital beds he was helping to design could be improved. However, before he had the chance to develop these, his previous firm suffered a severe cash crisis and went into administration, emerging as a much smaller operation under new ownership. George invested his £30,000 redundancy pay into his new business, Medibed, and persuaded a local bank to invest a further £70,000 (secured against his domestic residence).

Starting with only three employees, Medibed has grown gradually over the years to become a well-established, medium-sized company specializing in a single product. George is now 57 years old and has decided to step back from the operational side of the business and cut down his input to one or two days a week. Instead of being both Chairman and Managing Director, he has retained the chairmanship but has recently appointed a new Managing Director, Alex Medlev, from outside the business. Alex is 43 years old and was the production manager for six years of a firm producing office furniture.

It has been a difficult year for Medibed with competition becoming much more aggressive than in previous years. These difficulties can be seen from the following extracts from a recent management meeting chaired by the Managing Director:

*Managing Director*
*You all know that the figures show that the labour force is working below standard. But I'm not sure I believe it. I walk round the factory every day and I don't see any slacking, the atmosphere is good and I have not seen any evidence of demotivation among the operatives. I'm not convinced our budgetary control system is telling us the whole truth.*

*Purchasing Manager*
*Well, it has served us well for many years. I'm not sure we can start to ignore it just because it is telling us something we would prefer was not happening.*

### Production Director

*It's all very well for you to say that but I think Alex has a point. I realize we have to keep our costs down to remain competitive but I am not convinced sourcing a significant portion of our material components from eastern Europe was a good idea. I reckon if we had stuck with our original UK suppliers in the first place we would have been better off all round, despite their higher prices. I suggest we reconsider our position on this as soon as possible.*

### Purchasing Manager

*I don't agree. Just look at the figures and you will see how much money we have saved on our material costs. That is what I was asked to do and I've done it.*

### Production Manager

*I admit the figures look good but we've all played budgetary games at some time or other. I think this is an area we really need to tighten up on.*

### Sales Director

*I think we should remember that the bottom line is still positive. It has been difficult since we had that quality crisis in the first quarter of the year and had to cancel our attendance at the London Trade Show. But we have managed to stay in the black. Admittedly, our volume is well below the original budget but it could have been a lot worse; our past reputation has helped greatly but we can't rely on that any longer. I hope we will soon be in a position to increase our advertising spend up to previous levels but we must maintain the quality of our product. It is absolutely vital to our long-term success. I can't stress that enough.*

### Managing Director

*I can't argue with that but I'm not convinced our traditional approach to performance and control is sufficient to help us do that and achieve our objectives in today's turbulent trading conditions. We are already facing a new wave of cheap imports from the Far East. We've got to be more proactive in improving our performance. Some well-known firms are reputed to have given up budgets and seem to be doing alright without them thank you very much. I know it is drastic but I think we have got to be prepared to be radical in our approach in order to survive. With the agreement of our Chairman, I've just commissioned a report about controlling and improving our corporate performance from the management consulting branch of our auditors. I'm expecting to receive it in the near future, just after the end of the financial year.*

## Medibed's current budgetary control system

Medibed operates a traditional budgetary control system on a quarterly rather than a monthly basis. The financial reporting is also done quarterly. A significant part of the remuneration for the budget-responsible officers is dependent on their achieving their budgets.

The budget responsibilities are as follows:

| Operational Area | Budget-responsible officer |
|---|---|
| Sales | Sales Director |
| Materials budget | Purchasing Manager |
| Labour budget | Production Manager |
| Variable overhead budget | Production Manager |
| Fixed overhead budget: | |
| Marketing | Sales Director |
| Production | Production Director |
| Administration | Managing Director |

The current financial year has just ended and the actual results for quarter 4 (Q4) are expected very soon. The results for the previous three quarters have been known since just before the management meeting two months ago.

## Additional information

- All these budgets **have already been flexed** to the actual level of activity.
- The **Original Budget Profit (OBP)** is £7,550,000.
- The budgeted selling price of one bed is £10,000.
- The actual selling price of one bed is £10,500.
- Variable overheads are absorbed on a labour hour basis.
- Labour operatives can earn bonuses dependent on the completion of their tasks in less than the standard times allowed.

## List of attached schedules

1 Summary budget for year and by quarter
2 Materials budget for year and by quarter
3 Labour budget for year and by quarter
4 Variable overheads budget for year and by quarter
5 Marketing fixed overheads budget for year and by quarter
6 Production fixed overheads budget for year and by quarter
7 Administration fixed overheads budget for year and by quarter
8 Sales budget for year and by quarter
9 Summary of actual results
10 Extracts from materials and labour flexed budgets for Q4
11 Extracts from materials and labour actual results for Q4
12 Variance analysis for the first three quarters

### 1. Summary budget for year and by quarter

| Item (£000) | Q1 | Q2 | Q3 | Q4 | Year |
|---|---|---|---|---|---|
| Materials | 3,738 | 3,429 | 2,849 | 3,605 | 13,621 |
| Labour | 2,136 | 1,936 | 1,628 | 2,060 | 7,760 |
| Variable ohds | 534 | 460 | 407 | 515 | 1,916 |
| *Fixed ohds:* | | | | | |
| Marketing | 1,922 | 1,701 | 1,465 | 1,854 | 6,942 |
| Production | 1,602 | 1,453 | 1,221 | 1,545 | 5,821 |
| Administration | 748 | 645 | 570 | 721 | 2,684 |
| Total costs | 10,680 | 9,624 | 8,140 | 10,300 | 38,744 |
| Sales revenue | 11,890 | 10,990 | 9,100 | 11,550 | 43,530 |
| Profit | 1,210 | 1,366 | 960 | 1,250 | 4,786 |

### 2. Materials budget for year and by quarter

| Item (£000) | Q1 | Q2 | Q3 | Q4 | Year |
|---|---|---|---|---|---|
| Frame | 1,495 | 1,372 | 1,140 | 1,442 | 5,449 |
| Mattress | 1,121 | 1,028 | 855 | 1,082 | 4,086 |
| Motors | 523 | 480 | 399 | 504 | 1,906 |
| Accessories | 599 | 549 | 455 | 577 | 2,180 |
| Total | 3,738 | 3,429 | 2,849 | 3,605 | 13,621 |

### 3. Labour budget for year and by quarter

| Item (£000) | Q1 | Q2 | Q3 | Q4 | Year |
|---|---|---|---|---|---|
| Grade A | 1,142 | 904 | 843 | 1,090 | 3,979 |
| Grade B | 608 | 496 | 407 | 580 | 2,091 |
| Grade C | 386 | 536 | 378 | 390 | 1,690 |
| Total | 2,136 | 1,936 | 1,628 | 2,060 | 7,760 |

### 4. Variable overheads budget for year and by quarter

| Item (£000) | Q1 | Q2 | Q3 | Q4 | Year |
|---|---|---|---|---|---|
| Assembly | 232 | 201 | 187 | 235 | 855 |
| Finishing | 302 | 259 | 220 | 280 | 1,061 |
| Total | 534 | 460 | 407 | 515 | 1,916 |

### 5. Marketing fixed overheads budget for year and by quarter

| Item (£000) | Q1 | Q2 | Q3 | Q4 | Year |
|---|---|---|---|---|---|
| Customer relations | 495 | 412 | 340 | 480 | 1,727 |
| Advertising | 210 | 250 | 180 | 240 | 880 |
| Salaries | 910 | 900 | 945 | 920 | 3,675 |
| Trade shows | 307 | 139 | 0 | 214 | 660 |
| Total | 1,922 | 1,701 | 1,465 | 1,854 | 6,942 |

### 6. Production fixed overheads budget for year and by quarter

| Item (£000) | Q1 | Q2 | Q3 | Q4 | Year |
|---|---|---|---|---|---|
| Assembly | 492 | 476 | 405 | 506 | 1,879 |
| Finishing | 309 | 290 | 251 | 327 | 1,177 |
| Materials handling | 451 | 337 | 215 | 362 | 1,365 |
| Salaries | 350 | 350 | 350 | 350 | 1,400 |
| Total | 1,602 | 1,453 | 1,221 | 1,545 | 5,821 |

### 7. Administration fixed overheads budget for year and by quarter

| Item (£000) | Q1 | Q2 | Q3 | Q4 | Year |
|---|---|---|---|---|---|
| Accounting | 148 | 152 | 150 | 148 | 598 |
| Heat & light | 124 | 44 | 44 | 144 | 356 |
| Site security | 75 | 75 | 75 | 75 | 300 |
| Directors' pay | 200 | 200 | 200 | 200 | 800 |
| General office | 48 | 52 | 50 | 48 | 198 |
| Other | 153 | 122 | 51 | 106 | 432 |
| Total | 748 | 645 | 570 | 721 | 2,684 |

### 8. Sales quantity budget for year and by quarter

| | Q1 | Q2 | Q3 | Q4 | Year |
|---|---|---|---|---|---|
| Number of beds | 1,189 | 1,099 | 910 | 1,155 | 4,353 |

### 9. Summary of actual results

| Item (£000) | Q1 + Q2 + Q3 | Q4 | Year |
|---|---|---|---|
| Materials | 9,540 | 3,659 | 13,199 |
| Labour | 6,070 | 2,072 | 8,142 |
| Variable ohds | 1,498 | 512 | 2,010 |
| *Fixed ohds:* | | | |
| Marketing | 4,806 | 1,909 | 6,715 |
| Production | 4,402 | 1,503 | 5,905 |
| Administration | 2,003 | 684 | 2,687 |
| Total costs | 28,319 | 10,339 | 38,658 |
| Sales revenue | 34,075 | 11,632 | 45,707 |
| Profit | 5,756 | 1,293 | 7,049 |

### 10. Extract from materials and labour flexed budgets for Q4

| | | |
|---|---|---|
| Materials: Motors | 2,880 @ £175 each | = £504,000 |
| Labour: Grade C | 43,333 hrs @ £9.00/hr | = £389,997 |

### 11. Extract from materials and labour actual results for Q4

Note: Due to a power failure, no work could be done during 1,155 of the 42,210 hours. The operatives used this time to have a general tidy-up of their workplaces and then had to wait in the canteen until the power was restored.

| | | |
|---|---|---|
| Materials: Motors | 2,520 @ £200 | = £504,000 |
| Labour: Grade C | 42,210 hrs @ £9.50 | = £400,995 |

### 12. Nine Months' (Q1 + Q2 + Q3) variance analysis

| Item (£000) | Budget for Q1 + Q2 + Q3 | Actuals for Q1 + Q2 + Q3 | Cost variances |
|---|---|---|---|
| Materials | 10,016 | 9,540 | 476 F |
| Labour | 5,700 | 6,070 | 370 A |
| Variable ohds | 1,401 | 1,498 | 97 A |
| *Fixed ohds:* | | | |
| Marketing | 5,088 | 4,806 | 282 F |
| Production | 4,276 | 4,402 | 126 A |
| Administration | 1,963 | 2,003 | 40 A |
| Total costs | 28,444 | 28,319 | 125 F |
| Sales revenue | 31,980 | 34,075 | 2,095 F |
| Profit | 3,536 | 5,756 | 2,220 F |

*Tasks:*

1 **Variance analysis**

Using the information provided:

a) Perform a variance analysis on the Materials (Motors) budget extract for Q4.

(*6 marks*)

b) Perform a variance analysis on the Labour (Grade C) budget extract for Q4.

(*8 marks*)

c) Perform a variance analysis of all budget items for Q4 and present them in a table.

(*4 marks*)

d) Perform a variance analysis of all budget items for the year and present them in a table.

(*4 marks*)

e) Calculate the Sales Volume Variance and the Sales Price Variance for the year.

(*4 marks*)

f) Create a Profit Reconciliation statement for the year.

(*4 marks*)

g) Comment on Medibed's performance for the year.

*(20 marks)*

NB: perform the variance analyses in as much detail as the information given will allow.

*(Sub-total 50 marks)*

2  **Budget games**

Define the term 'budget games'; give six examples of these and state four negative effects they have on companies.

*(14 marks)*

3  **Beyond Budgeting**

If Medibed adopted the Beyond Budgeting management model and abolished its budgetary control system, state six measures you would recommend it to take to fill the resulting vacuum.

*(12 marks)*

4  **Balanced Scorecard**

Design a Balanced Scorecard for Medibed utilizing three items for each of the four perspectives.

*(24 marks)*
*(Total 100 marks)*

## Review questions

1  Describe the weaknesses of traditional budgetary control systems.
2  Define what is meant by 'budget game'.
3  Give examples of six types of 'budget game'.
4  Explain the effect of employee cash incentive schemes on budget gaming.
5  Describe the 'Beyond Budgeting' management model.
6  List the six principles of 'devolved leadership'.
7  List the six adaptive processes recommended to replace budgeting.
8  Describe the management model used by Svenska Handelsbanken.
9  Describe the management model used by the Toyota production system.
10  Explain the difficulties in the adoption of the 'Beyond Budgeting' model.
11  State the arguments against the 'Beyond Budgeting' model.
12  List the findings of the 'Better Budgeting' Open Forum in 2004.

*The answers to all these questions can be found in the text of this chapter.*